John Dee
AND THE
EMPIRE
OF
Angels

"Renaissance magus John Dee boldly set out to systematically tap the mind of God by communicating directly with a complex hierarchy of 'angelic' intelligences. It can be argued that he succeeded. His magical diaries have long held intense fascination among Qabalists, alchemists, and explorers of human consciousness who have developed workable magical systems from these records. Jason Louv's work succeeds, with breathtaking thoroughness, to tell this amazing and true magical tale. More importantly, he also reveals the profound geopolitical significance of Dee's magical explorations—effects that still shape the global realities of today."

LON MILO DUQUETTE, AUTHOR OF
ENOCHIAN VISION MAGICK

"Jason Louv's *John Dee and the Empire of Angels* is a groundbreaking new assessment of one of the Western world's most influential polymaths. Through a combination of intellectual rigor, sensitivity to both historical and current sociopolitical climates, and perhaps a bit of his own intuitive scrying, Louv offers us a crystalline view of John Dee's visionary mind and complicated legacy."

PAM GROSSMAN, AUTHOR OF *WHAT IS A WITCH* AND
HOST OF *THE WITCH WAVE* PODCAST

"Jason Louv's masterful account of the enigmatic Elizabethan magus John Dee places him in the top tier of new esoteric writers. . . . Louv's assertion of Dee as both a creator and custodian of Western civilization is thought-provoking, and it is backed up by meticulous research. Highly recommended."

BRENDAN MCCARTHY, ARTIST, DESIGNER, AND
COWRITER OF *MAD MAX: FURY ROAD*

"The Dee story is among the most mystifying and important in the entire history of the Western esoteric tradition. And here, Jason Louv has given us the most complete, complex, and balanced account yet of Dee and his aftermath. An awesome achievement."

RALPH ABRAHAM, PROFESSOR EMERITUS OF MATHEMATICS, UNIVERSITY OF CALIFORNIA, SANTA CRUZ, CHAOS THEORIST, AND AUTHOR OF *CHAOS, GAIA, EROS*

"Jason Louv's book is absolutely invaluable. It contextualizes the very bedrock that Western ceremonial magic is based on. Dee and Kelly's legendary experiments are the cornerstone of our Western understanding of how magic works. But there's more to it than that. Louv's impressive work is not only an enjoyable, adventurous journey into esoteric history but also one into the multifaceted—and sometimes dangerous—machinations of the human mind."

CARL ABRAHAMSSON, AUTHOR OF *OCCULTURE: THE UNSEEN FORCES THAT DRIVE CULTURE FORWARD*

"Jason Louv weaves a masterfully poetic web that first introduces you and then sucks you into Dee's luminous world of magick. This book is not just a book about the occult and magick; it's also a unique historical reference guide that I found to be a hypnotic read. Jason is a brilliant mind and writer, and this book proves that."

ZACH LEARY, HOST OF THE *MAPS* AND *IT'S ALL HAPPENING* PODCASTS

"Never has there been a more valuable and more prescient time than NOW to have *John Dee and the Empire of Angels* published."

E. ELIAS MERHIGE, DIRECTOR OF *BEGOTTEN* AND *SHADOW OF THE VAMPIRE*

"This is the first book I've seen where Dee's angelic magic is neither discussed in isolation, nor dismissed as an eccentric sideline, but recognized as a key part of Dee's philosophy and political influence right up to the present day."

LIONEL SNELL (A.K.A. RAMSEY DUKES), AUTHOR OF *MY YEARS OF MAGICAL THINKING*

John Dee

AND THE
EMPIRE
OF
Angels

Enochian Magick
AND THE
Occult Roots
OF THE
Modern World

JASON LOUV

Inner Traditions
Rochester, Vermont • Toronto, Canada

Inner Traditions
One Park Street
Rochester, Vermont 05767
www.InnerTraditions.com

SUSTAINABLE FORESTRY INITIATIVE · Certified Sourcing · www.sfiprogram.org · SFI-00854

Text stock is SFI certified

Library of Congress Cataloging-in-Publication Data

Names: Louv, Jason, author.

Title: John Dee and the empire of angels : Enochian magick and the occult roots of the modern world / Jason Louv.

Description: Rochester, VT : Inner Traditions, 2018. | Includes bibliographical references and index.

Identifiers: LCCN 2017035821 (print) | LCCN 2017057857 (e-book) | ISBN 9781620555897 (hardcover) | ISBN 9781620555903 (e-book)

Subjects: LCSH: Dee, John, 1527-1608. | Occultism—History. | Magic—History.

Classification: LCC BF1598.D5 L68 2018 (print) | LCC BF1598.D5 (e-book) | DDC 130.92[B]—dc23

LC record available at https://lccn.loc.gov/2017035821

Printed and bound in the United States by Lake Book Manufacturing, Inc. The text stock is SFI certified. The Sustainable Forestry Initiative® program promotes sustainable forest management.

10 9 8 7 6 5 4

Text design and layout by Deborah Glogover
This book was typeset in Garamond Premier Pro with Futura Std, Gill Sans MT Pro, and LHF Tributary used as display typefaces

To send correspondence to the author of this book, mail a first-class letter to the author c/o Inner Traditions • Bear & Company, One Park Street, Rochester, VT 05767, and we will forward the communication, or contact the author directly at **www.jasonlouv.com.**

For Devi

Contents

BOOK III

Antichrist

⊕

Acknowledgments

Writing a book is a lonely occupation that is only made possible by a network of good will, patience, and understanding.

A great thank you to my girlfriend, Devi Brulé, whose love and patient support carried me day in and day out during the time I wrote this book. A thank you as well to my parents, who encouraged me throughout its creation. Serious thanks must also be reserved for my many students at Magick.Me, who made it financially possible for me to take the time off to write this book.

Mark Frauenfelder of Boing Boing commissioned and published the original article that became this book, and Jon Graham of Inner Traditions commissioned the full work and was greatly supportive of its writing. Thank you as well to Jennie Marx and Manzanita Carpenter Sanz at Inner Traditions for helping it into manifestation.

Many people assisted along the way with encouragement, information, or by aiding in my research trips, including Daniel Andrew Nava, Dennis Woo, Alan Green, Adam Parfrey, Michael Le Tigre, Christie Casey-Young, Eli Lee, E. Elias Merhige, Detlev Auvermann, Thomas Negovan, Grant Morrison, Dr. Gregory DePies, and William Kiesel. Maria V. Montgomery and David Richard Jones provided scans of the original Dee manuscripts and assisted with additional information and context, particularly in regard to the chapter on Aleister Crowley. Years prior to writing this book, Genesis Breyer P-Orridge and Caleigh Fisher helped foster my interest in John Dee and the connection of Christian eschatology to imperialism, and Lon Milo DuQuette's books and live seminars provided a handle on understanding Dee's magic. Many people have aided me in experimental research into Dee's natural philosophy over the years; respect for personal privacy dictates that I must thank them as a whole.

A final thanks to all of the Dee scholars and biographers on whose work I stand and whose research has proven invaluable to the present work, including Dame Frances Yates, Glen Parry, Benjamin Woolley, Nicholas Clulee, Deborah Harkness, György Szőnyi, Håkan Håkansson, and Stephen Skinner.

Veritas Praevalebit.

And the Lord God said, "The man has now become like one of us, knowing good and evil. He must not be allowed to reach out his hand and take also from the Tree of Life and eat, and live forever." So the Lord God banished him from the Garden of Eden to work the ground from which he had been taken. After he drove the man out, he placed on the east side of the Garden of Eden cherubim and a flaming sword flashing back and forth to guard the way to the Tree of Life.

GENESIS 3:22–24 (NIV)

The great secret known to Apollonius of Tyana, Paul of Tarsus, Simon Magus, Asklepios, Paracelsus, Boehme, and Bruno is that: we are moving backward in time. The universe in fact is contracting into a unitary entity which is completing itself. Decay and disorder are seen by us in reverse, as increasing. These healers learned to move forward in time, which is retrograde to us.

PHILIP K. DICK, *VALIS*

In the Garden

Beginning it all: A man, a woman, and a Dragon.

Around them, the Garden of Eden. A single, shining instance—before time began, with all its stupidity of suffering, loss, and waste. In which there is only the devotion of God for his Creation, and man and woman together, in love.

Blissfully unaware, Adam and Eve sleep sheltered in each other's arms beneath the Tree of Life. They speak with the language of angels, and with it, Adam begins to name the things around him. Imagine yourself as Adam, naming all that you see, watching as each facet of eternity comes into being as a separate object, divided from the supernal totality that is the body of God.

And then, into this perfection, comes the Dragon. The snake of fear. *Eat of the Tree of Knowledge,* says the Dragon, *and you shall taste all that God has hidden from you.* Look into its eyes. See it twisting and coruscating in three hundred and thirty-three colors. The after-birth of God's Creation. The crack in the plan. How must evil itself have appeared to such pure and innocent beings, the original parents of humanity, before the Fall? See it dancing, a serpent of light.

Listen to the wind howling through the rainforest as the Dragon coils up toward the fruit of the Tree of the Knowledge of Good and Evil, urging you to take it. Look. The apple is perfectly polished. At first you can see your face in its surface but now your focus begins to blur. You look through it. Scrying.

Observe, now, the end of time. See the Red Dragon as it shall be, the deceiver not just of the first humans but of the last, with seven crowned heads and ten horns, rearing up to conquer heaven itself. See its servants, a seven-headed Beast upon which a Scarlet Whore rides, causing all humanity to worship the Dragon, as the nations decay and the human project collapses. The final degradation, in which the four cardinal directions are opened by Death, Famine, War, Conquest. See the last judgment, the son of God come to reign for a Millennium, when all but the saved are cast down to eternal torment in the lake of fire. And all of this to redeem what you are about to do.

Now eat it, the Dragon says. *Don't you want to know what it is to be a god?*

INTRODUCTION

A Sublunary World

Between 1582 and 1589, two men—Dr. John Dee, a mathematician and scientific adviser to Elizabeth I, and Edward Kelly, an itinerant psychic—claimed that they held regular conversations with angels.

These angels explained the true origins of humanity, and delivered the original language spoken by mankind before the Fall. This language, along with a mathematically complex system for making further contact with the angels, was to be used by Dee and Kelly to advance the world toward the Apocalypse.

This was not a marginal event. Indeed, it has been central to the last five hundred years of Western civilization. Through Dee—who invented the phrase "British Empire" and worked to manifest a new Christian religion uniting all humanity in preparation for the Second Coming—we can find the genesis of not only the British but the American empire, and in the utterances of the angels we can find the spiritual blueprint that has driven them both. This tremendous (albeit occulted) impact on history did not end with Dee. The influence of Dee and the angelic system he and Kelly delivered to the world can be found in an astonishing number of the major turning points of Western history since Dee's death—in the birth of modern science, in the creation of the secret societies that liberalized Europe and gave America its spiritual calling, in the creation of the state of Israel and its subsequent centrality to American foreign policy, and even in the genesis of the United States space program.

In studying Dee and his work, we are studying the secret history of the world.

This, then, is the story of John Dee, a Doctor of the sublunary world, who sought to reverse the Fall of mankind and return all of nature to God—to create a new Eden by prompting the Apocalypse. Moreover, it is the story of his angelic system, the men and movements it influenced—such as Rosicrucianism, Freemasonry, the Royal Society, the Golden Dawn, Aleister Crowley, and Jack Parsons—and how it not only changed the world but in many ways *created* the world we now inhabit. Indeed, just as the work of St. Paul is responsible for turning the ideas of a Jewish messianic sect into a Holy Roman Empire, so is the work of Dr. Dee responsible for turning those of the Protestant dissenters into a global Empire of Angels.

Born into a humble family with minor court connections in 1527, John Dee quickly distinguished himself as a brilliant student, and soon rose to the heights of European intellectual life, becoming one of the great scientific minds of Europe during the time of Copernicus, Bruno, and Tycho Brahe, and a great popularizer and teacher of mathematics. Yet Dee sought not to master one subject but the totality of the sciences then available. This, for Dee, was a spiritual quest to know the mind of God, and like many of the intellectuals of his day, he extended his studies into occult philosophy, seeking direct contact with higher spiritual beings that he hoped would continue his education.

Reviewing his case in 1967, the National Security Agency summed up "our man Dee" as "a principal adviser to most of the Tudor monarchs of England, and to certain European rulers as well, including the Emperor Rudolph II. As government consultant, he excelled in mathematics, cryptography, natural science, navigation, and library science, and above all in the really rewarding sciences of those days—astrology, alchemy, and psychic phenomena. He was, all by himself, a Rand Corporation for the Tudor government of Elizabeth."[1]

Because of Dee's vast range of interests, he has remained opaque to popular history. His occult activities have long been considered an embarrassment, and have been used as a cautionary tale of how even great geniuses can fall victim to their own wishful thinking. Many biographers and commentators on Dee, likely wary of undermining their own careers, bracket their writing on his angelic conversations with disdain, downplaying the importance of Dee's occult interests to his overall work. This means that most of the assessment of Dee's occult work has been done by occult writers, where his system of communication with angels—often dubbed "Enochian magic," a phrase not used by Dee—is discussed on its own merits, divorced from the overall context of Dee's life and work. Writers who downplay Dee's occult activities make the error of assessing him from a sterilized modern viewpoint, instead of summoning the bravery to interact with Dee on his own terms. Those who focus solely on Dee's occultism make the converse error, extracting his angelic conversations from his other work, depriving them of critical context, over-romanticizing them, or conflating them with later New Age or Theosophical ideas. Both of these compartmentalizations of Dee's legacy do him a disservice; this book will instead strive to achieve a balanced unity. In the process, I hope to demonstrate the centrality of the occult to the history of Western civilization, and shed further light on the true nature of both.

Dee's belief in the existence of a spiritual realm, inhabited by both good and evil beings, interpenetrating both daily life and history, was standard in the Elizabethan period. However, those who engaged with this spirit world outside of the official bounds of the Anglican or Roman Churches—whether Hermetic "magicians" among the academic elite, street-level "cunning men" and scryers, or, indeed, non-Anglican Protestants—were often criminalized, imprisoned, or killed for their troubles. Dee is remarkable not for his occult interests but for the unprecedented level of intellectual and scientific rigor he brought to them, for the fact that a man of his social position took such remarkable personal and professional risks in pursuing them, and for the phenomenal corpus of records he left behind.

In our own time, the doors to the intoxicating and hallucinatory world of magic and alchemy have long since been closed by science, and the experimental techniques once used by men like Dee, Bruno, and Newton to investigate the subtleties of the human spirit have been left to wither in the twilight of the New Age. This makes the active

Fig. I.1 Portrait of John Dee. Courtesy of Wellcome Images.

exploration of the invisible world as unacceptable today as it was in Dee's time—with the main advance being that those who breach such taboo territory are economically and socially marginalized, rather than imprisoned or killed.

Yet stories like Dee's are not without precedent in the modern world—especially among mathematicians (like Dee), some of whom have recorded similar experiences. John Nash, for instance, the Nobel Prize–winning American mathematician and economist who did critical work on game theory in the 1940s and '50s and gave us the Nash equilibrium, believed that he had been recruited by aliens to save the world, that they were assisting him by sending him mathematical equations, and that they later acted to end his career; when asked how he could believe in such an outlandish scenario, Nash replied, "Because the ideas I had about supernatural beings came to me the same way that my mathematical ideas did. So I took them seriously."[2]

The brilliant, self-taught Indian mathematician Srinavasa Ramanujan attributed his early twentieth-century achievements in higher mathematics to his family deity, the goddess Mahalakshmi, and received visions of scrolls of mathematical equations opening before his eyes; he is quoted as saying "An equation has no meaning to me, unless it expresses a thought of God"[3]—the quote could have come from Dee himself.

Carl Sagan's 1985 novel *Contact* also assesses the idea of higher intelligences contacting humanity through the language of advanced math. The science fiction writer Philip K. Dick, who famously recorded his contact experience with an intelligence he called VALIS in his final novels, also spoke of language, the *logos,* as a living entity and medium of transmission from a higher dimension; the reality-puncturing ferocity of the Gnostic Christ of Dick's *Exegesis* and the apocalyptic vitriol of the angels of Dee and Kelly's spirit diaries are not far away in tone and content.

Nash was diagnosed with paranoid schizophrenia, institutionalized, and experienced severe career issues as a result; Philip K. Dick also contextualized his experience as traumatic, profoundly alienating him from those around him. Ramanujan, on the other hand, experienced no such friction. While the seriousness of particularly Nash's illness should not be downplayed or trivialized, it is also worth noting that Ramanujan differed from Nash in that his claim of visions was considered acceptable within the general cultural narrative of Hinduism, in which reports of divine inspiration or contact are routine.

This reading of Nash, Dick, Ramanujan, and even Dee and Kelly's differing experiences is supported by an interview-based study conducted by Stanford anthropologist Tanya Luhrmann in 2014 that suggested that the voices heard by individuals with serious psychotic disorder are shaped by culture. Luhrmann found that Americans reported violent, warlike, demonic, and overwhelmingly negative voices occasionally punctuated by the voice of God, which were perceived as traumatic and pathological. Individuals from India and Africa, on the other hand, reported experiencing voices as helpful spirits or family relationships, and felt them to be generally positive and to conform with cultural expectations about reality.[4] Luhrmann's description of the voices heard by Americans closely fits the angelic apparitions reported by Dee's unstable English scryer Edward Kelly, and perhaps can tell us something about the cultural context of Protestant Christianity. However, like Ramanujan, and unlike modern Westerners, Dee and Kelly existed in a cultural context that supported the validity of their experiences; while not generally well regarded, magic, scrying, and angel contact were nevertheless widespread in Elizabethan England.

These contact experiences, whatever their provenance, are not confined to the margins of society; they are, in fact, woven into the very fabric of world culture. Many mainstream religions incorporate or are even founded on claims of contact with angels that are far less documented than Dee's—with notable examples being the Revelation of John and the Prophet Muhammad's reception of the Qu'ran from the archangel Gabriel, a being that also appears in Dee's spirit diaries. The Kabbalistic practices of Judaism, the parent tradition of Christianity and Islam, form a tightly knit system of mathematical interpretation of scripture and even, according to some readings, two-way communication with angels, making mathematical contact with spiritual entities an established, if closely guarded, religious tradition. That these claims of supernatural contact exist purely in the realm of subjectivity and faith has not, of course, impeded their ability to shape world cultures.

Since these angelic revelations are at the root of the three primary monotheist religions in the world, as of 2010 they made up the lived mythology of 2.17 billion Christians, 1.6 billion Muslims, and 13.9 million Jews. This means that *over half* of the world's population—54.8 percent—draw their model of the world from what they believe to be messages from angels. Due in part to the rapid growth of Islam, that figure will rise to 61.1 percent of the world's 9.3 billion population in 2050.[5] Of course, the "big three" are not the only religions that claim to rest on direct revelation—only the largest ones that claim descent from angels (as a specific class of mythological being).

Such communication between individuals and higher intelligences via math, Qabalism, and secret languages is also a running trope in the occult subculture, notably within groups that draw their inspiration from Dee. The occult occupies a treacherous liminal zone between the competing discourses of science and religion, both of which reject it. It is tiny, decentralized, largely overlooked by modern culture, unpoliced by the processes of licensing or peer review, and concerned with entirely subjective aspects of the human experience, making it a no-man's land where scientists, if not angels, fear to tread. Partly because he explored this perilous territory between objective science and subjective magic, Dee's name was occluded from history by the religious and scientific reformers that followed him.

However, Dee's magic has as little to do with modern notions of the occult as it does with modern notions of science; rather than grimoire sorcery or woolly New Age mysticism, Dee and Kelly's scrying sessions were an outgrowth of Christian piety and the scriptural tradition of received wisdom granted to worthy individuals by angelic beings. Likewise, the protoscience of Dee's time was fundamentally different from what we think of as science today. While modern science is forward-looking, seeking to continually test and refine what we know about the universe through experiment, the protoscience that existed before the scientific revolution was *backward-looking.* Europe was still crawling out of the Dark Ages and deeply concerned with recovering the knowledge it had lost. After the sack of Constantinople by the Ottoman Turks in 1453, Orthodox priests had fled to the Italian city-states, bringing with them Greek and Latin manuscripts that Western Europe had lacked access to, which scholars quickly seized upon. This meant that the prevailing intellectual climate during Dee's life was humanism, the study of the classics. Western Europe had lost so much during the long night between the fall of Rome and the Renaissance that its scholars and early scientists saw their task as the recovery of the lost knowledge of antiquity—Greek and Roman philosophy and the Bible itself.

While the narrative of progress now leads us to think of humanity's knowledge increasing as history advances, Renaissance thinkers believed that knowledge was naturally degrading over time, and had to be recovered and preserved. The ultimate source of knowledge was not in the future, but in following the trail of history back through the ancient world—even toward rediscovering what humanity had known before the fall of the Tower of Babel and the Fall from Eden itself. The true source of knowledge, wisdom, and understanding was God, and God had progressively distanced himself from human affairs—therefore, the enterprising scientist or magician was tasked with chasing him backward through time. This quest to restore mankind's knowledge, and even its original pre-Fall spiritual condition, was the primary goal of many of Europe's intellectual elite during Dee's time, and Dee's work is the high-water mark.

To make sense of Dee's work, we must not only make the difficult leap of taking on the Renaissance worldview, but also juggle two narratives and intersecting levels of reality. One is the story of England's growth, its split from the Catholic Church, and its subsequent transition into a global empire. The second is the spiritual narrative of Christianity itself, beginning with the Fall and ending with the Apocalypse and Second Coming of Christ. Modern readers should easily be able to compartmentalize these stories as facets of European history. This was not at all the case for Dee or his contemporaries, for whom these mythic narratives were indistinguishable, forming the fabric of Elizabethan reality.

Just as Dee sought to restore the fallen world by divine aid, this book attempts to restore and reconstitute Dee's life, work, and ongoing historical impact as a coherent narrative, and to tell the story of one of the most improbable and quietly influential figures in European history, who stood at the crossroads of the Renaissance and Enlightenment and, perhaps with the aid of the host of heaven, delivered the blueprint for humanity's final days.

ENGLAND AT THE DAWN OF EMPIRE

Before we assess John Dee, let us begin by describing the chaotic and fractured world into which he was born, and that he would seek to repair—for if the angels did indeed speak to Dee, they chose the most dramatic time possible to reinsert themselves into the story of Christendom.

The sixteenth century marked the most critical transition point in Western civilization since Constantine's conversion of Rome to Christianity twelve centuries prior, when the Edict of Milan had, in one stroke, turned Christianity into a major world religion. This rejection of paganism and acceptance of the new, populist faith phase changed the power of the Roman Empire from a terrestrial to a spiritual imperium. While Rome itself would crumble, the Catholic Church would continue to dominate the European Dark and Middle Ages as the primary source of spiritual authority and cultural cohesion.

Yet by Dee's time, the Church's monopoly on European thought was ending just as dramatically as it had begun. The Middle Ages were coming to a close—marked by the invention of the printing press around 1440, by the fall of Constantinople to Islam in 1453, and by Martin Luther's initiation of the Protestant Reformation in 1517. In England, in 1534, Henry VIII would ground Luther's spiritual ideals into the political sphere by overthrowing the Church's hold on his country. Infuriated with his Spanish Catholic wife Catherine of Aragon's inability to give him a son, inflamed with lust for the young Protestant Anne Boleyn, and incensed with Cardinal Thomas Wolsey's refusal to grant him a divorce from Catherine, Henry had taken up Anne's new evangelical ideas, had Wolsey executed, and had declared himself the supreme head of the new, Protestant Church of England. Henry's government had then privatized and sacked the Catholic monasteries in England, claiming the substantial spoils and then redistributing the lands, creating a new English middle class in the process.

The product of Henry's marriage to Anne Boleyn would be Elizabeth, a child prodigy who would grow into perhaps the greatest monarch in English history, and who, with the help of John Dee, would initiate the transformation of England from a tiny island nation into "the Empire on which the sun never sets," so named because it held so much territory that the sun was always shining somewhere in its domain. Henry's marriage would also set the stage for centuries of sectarian violence, from the holocaust of Protestants that was to come with the short reign of Henry's elder daughter, Mary, to the "Troubles," the brutal twentieth-century paramilitary wars between Catholics and Protestants in Northern Ireland.

Man's place in the universe and sense of himself were being shaken to the core. Luther's revolution left his followers to fend for themselves spiritually, instead of relying on the Church's central authority. The invention of the printing press had helped lay the groundwork for the Reformation by making the Bible available to more than just Church specialists. This worked to undermine the Church by demonstrating that its sacraments had no basis in the teachings of Christ—let alone its practices of tithing and indulgences, or the grotesque amassing of wealth by its leaders. The resulting doctrinal war broke the Church (and the European political landscape) apart. Luther's (and, subsequently, John Calvin's) insurrection was an attack not just on a singular religion but, because the Catholic Church had universal power over both the political and spiritual functions of Europe, an attack on reality itself. The seismic shock of Luther's *Ninety-Five Theses* is likely impossible for modern readers to appreciate or even conceptualize—in the twenty-first century, Christianity has greatly lost its hold on the world's imagination, relegated to just another option in the supermarket of potential beliefs. In sixteenth-century Europe, it *was* reality.

The Reformation came not as a total surprise, however, but as a sudden crystallization of innumerable stresses on the Roman Church and of slowly emerging public dissent. Institutional corruption in the

Church, the incursions of Islam, the birth of the middle class, growing wealth inequality, rising nationalism, secularization, and skepticism, and the prior revolts of the Waldensians, John Wycliffe, and Jan Hus had all put cracks in the Church's dam.[6] All these began the work that Luther would complete, so that when he hammered in his *Ninety-Five Theses,* the dam burst, and let loose a flood of public dissent that had been held back for over a millennium. When that dam broke, so did the world as it had been known and understood for all those long centuries.

In addition to this rupture of faith, two events were permanently invalidating the medieval worldview: the discovery of the New World, and the Copernican revelation that the sun, not the earth, sat at the center of the solar system. Soon, the opening of the Western Hemisphere would lead to a new cold war between Catholic and Protestant powers—not only for territory, but for converts. Simultaneously, from the ashes of the preceding millennium of superstition, magical thinking, and religious fear, the phoenix of science was undergoing its birth pangs.

Rather than a singular Church, there were now many. Rather than one world, there were now two. Rather than the inherited knowledge of the Gospels and the ancients, science would soon come to show that nearly everything Western man assumed to be true was likely not. And rather than existing at the center of the cosmos, mankind was now relegated to orbiting the sun. If it seemed like the end of the world, that's because it *was*—the final and definitive death of the Middle Ages, and the beginning of the modern world to come.

For many, this could only be evidence of the Second Coming, the book of Revelation playing out on the world stage. For Protestants, their struggle was "against the rulers, against the authorities, against the powers of this dark world."[7] It was a struggle against the pope, whom Luther identified with Antichrist,[8] and with Rome itself, which Luther named the Whore of Babylon from the book of Revelation, and which the Presbyterian firebrand John Knox called a "Synagogue of Satan."[9]

"I rejoice," Martin Luther wrote as the Reformation took root, "that God raises up men who will give the last blow to popery, and finish the war against Antichrist which I began."[10]

Thus were the terrestrial authorities of the Church cast not as stewards of Christ's light, but as pawns of the Dragon. A Dragon that had been responsible not only for a millennium of imperial control but that, in the here and now, the new English Protestants lived in mortal fear of. A Dragon that, in the form of Bloody Mary, had regularly burned Protestants at the stake in group executions, filling the air with the stench of human fat.

It is no wonder the apocalyptic woodcuts of Albrecht Dürer so captured the English public imagination; his prints, depicting biblical scenes from the Fall to St. Michael and his angels fighting back the Red Dragon in the heavens above England, were in high demand in households throughout the country.[11] What we now see as a Reformation was then seen as the Millennium, and Europe became saturated with heralds of the end times—like the Spanish theologian Michael Servetus, who, presaging Dee, announced that Michael himself would unleash a holy war upon the Antichrists who ruled Rome and Geneva. He was denounced by John Calvin and quickly burned at the stake.[12]

Yet though the new Protestants defined themselves in opposition to the evils of Rome, they brought their own horrors with them—blind hatred of the Church, its art, and ritual; a rejection of humanism; an obsession with Satan and his seemingly omnipresent demons; a return to an Old Testament view of a punishing and spiteful God; and an unflinching and almost Gnostic emphasis on personal salvation from the jaws of hell eternal—even, in the case of Calvin, predestination, which must rank among the cruelest religious concepts ever forced upon mankind. All of these made for a very humorless and terrifying new religious environment. In their counterexcesses of dogmatic literalism, the new Protestants presaged the evangelical fundamentalists of the modern world.

Though the Roman Church might have been corrupt, its more forgiving view of human nature had made for the relaxed, business-as-usual attitude that Luther had railed against, but that most of Europe had long been accommodated to, and under which humanism had made great strides—at least within the milieu of the educated upper classes.[13] The punishing black-and-white view of Luther and Calvin made no such concessions—yet though their revolution would seem to institute a new and

Fig. I.2. Albrecht Dürer, *Saint Michael Fighting the Dragon*, 1498.

unflinching absolutism, it would ultimately prove a democratizing force.

"[Calvinism] encouraged brave and ruthless men to win a continent and spread the base of education and self-government until all men could be free," wrote historian Will Durant. "Men who chose their own pastors soon claimed to choose their governors, and the self-ruled congregation became the self-governed municipality. The myth of divine election justified itself in the making of America."[14]

Following Luther's original split with Rome, Christendom would continue to subdivide, producing not only Calvinists but Baptists, Anabaptists, Mennonites, Presbyterians, Congregationalists, and many more sects and denominations to come. In many cases, what are now established religious branches were then millennial cults. In England, however, the Crown was doing its utmost to keep reality ordered and tidy. Though the first Act of Supremacy in 1534 established the *Ecclesia Anglicana* and officially threw England's lot in with the reformers, it was only by way of a shift in the locus of control, not doctrine. The only difference between the Church of England and the Church of Rome was that Henry VIII sat at the new church's head, not the pope; in all other outward forms, it was still the Catholic Church. All breaks from Catholic doctrine were still considered heresy by the Church of England, and persecuted mercilessly, as was anybody unwise enough to question the king's absolute authority over church and state—meaning that both Protestant and Catholic dissenters were put under Henry's boot.[15] Awash in his lust for more power, wealth, and a male heir, Henry had simply cut through the firmament of European faith to satisfy his own appetite. Yet it is from this act of ecclesiastical violence and its subsequent pogroms that we inherit the age of Shakespeare, the British Empire, the foundation of the United States, and much of the current world order.[16] Furthermore, this split began the disintegration of the Church's historical lock on knowledge, allowing the scientific revolution to occur.

Though Luther was quick to hang the label of Antichrist upon the pope and of Whore of Babylon upon Rome, perhaps a parallel narrative was at work. In their dual action to break the central authority of the Church, it would be tempting to see the carnal and amoral Henry VIII as a reflection of the Great Beast, and Elizabeth, exoterically the Virgin Queen, esoterically reflecting the scarlet-haired Mystery Babylon—with Dee's work initiating the process of apocalypse itself, both terrestrially and celestially.

All of this, of course, would form the fertile backdrop of the angelic conversations to come. And when Dee's angels arrived, they would not be without their opinions, or their vitriol at what had occurred in their absence from the affairs of men.

THE GREAT CHAIN OF BEING

This was the world the Elizabethans called "sublunary," for it was believed that everything below the moon had been subject to the Fall of Man, and was therefore degraded and impure, afflicted by sin and awaiting redemption by Christ. Though many Elizabethans had the privilege of a humanist education, and would soon live through the halcyon age of Shakespeare, the Elizabethan worldview was very much still that of the Middle Ages, dominated by the Church and the doctrine of sin and salvation. Indeed, the chaos set loose upon the world during the Reformation could not be random—it was the direct consequence of sin.

"The world picture which the Middle Ages inherited," wrote English classical scholar E. M. W. Tillyard in his critical study *The Elizabethan World Picture,* "was that of an ordered universe arranged in a fixed system of hierarchies but modified by man's sin and the hope of his redemption."[17]

For the Elizabethans, everything in the world was ranked and ordered in a great hierarchy, extending from God to his angels to stars to elements to man, following which were animals, plants, and minerals. This perfectly ordered world model had been inherited, and simplified, from the Middle Ages; it syncretized Neoplatonism and the Old Testament, folding in the angelology of Pseudo-Dionysius and the Hebrew Kabbalah. For the average Elizabethan, it was the hierarchy of power under which they labored; for the Hermetic or "magical" initiate, it was, at least in theory, a ladder that could be climbed. No visible or invisible part of the universe was excluded from the chain of hierarchies and correspondences. If there was chaos, then it could only be the result of human action. Sin was the friction within the engine of the cosmos.

Yet if the stain of sin destabilized universal order, this suggested, for the more advanced thinkers of the Renaissance, its own solution. If the sublunary world was degenerated by sin, individuals or even all humanity might restore its original, unfallen nature by counteracting sin's mechanism. In doing so, they might even return to God, and so they fervently searched Christian mysticism and pagan philosophy alike for the keys to a working methodology to do so.[18] And because the Fall had been caused by sin, just as all chaos in the sublunary world had been, the tools of piety and sanctification were as important to the Renaissance scientist as empiricism and peer review are to the modern one.

Of particular interest was the angelology of Pseudo-Dionysius the Areopagite, a sixth-century Christian theologian, who had developed a classification and ranking of angels that became central to Christian mysticism, and which is still used in the Catholic and Eastern Orthodox churches; his angelic orders would be worked into the Great Chain by successive theologians, including St. Thomas Aquinas.[19] (Martin Luther, on the other hand, would come to despise Dionysius and his angelology as so much Neoplatonic nonsense.)[20]

The links in the Great Chain were as follows:

God, at the top of the chain, holding omnipotent, omniscient, and omnipresent authority over all.

The angels, intermediate beings between God and mankind, possessed of bodies of pure spirit rather than flesh, yet lacking the omnipotence, omniscience, and omnipresence of God. Following the classifications of Pseudo-Dionysius and Aquinas, the angels were further subdivided into nine ranks:

1. Seraphim
2. Cherubim
3. Thrones
4. Dominions
5. Virtues
6. Powers
7. Principalities
8. Archangels
9. Angels

Fig. I.3. Great Chain of Being, from Didacus Valades, *Retorica Christiana*, 1579.

The Catholic and Neoplatonic thinker Marsilio Ficino summarized the angelic order thusly:

> Seraphim speculate on the order and providence of God.
> Cherubim speculate on the essence and form of God.
> Thrones also speculate, though some descend to works.
> Dominions, like architects, design what the rest execute.
> Virtues execute, and move the heavens, and concur for the working of miracles as God's instruments.
> Powers watch that the order of divine governance is not interrupted and some of them descend to human things.
> Principalities care for public affairs, nations, princes, magistrates.
> Archangels direct the divine cult and look after sacred things.
> Angels look after smaller affairs, and take charge of individuals as their guardian angels.[21]

Humans were considered to be halfway between angels and animals, in that they possessed (and were bound to the animal lusts of) physical bodies, but were also blessed with spiritual virtues like love and faith. Consequently, humans are in the unfortunate position of being able to commit both spiritual *and* physical sins—unlike angels and animals, who are either fully spiritual or fully physical. As Shakespeare put it in *Henry VIII:* "We all are men in our natures frail, and capable of our flesh; few are angels."[22]

Animals, ranked within various orders—mammals, avians, fish, reptiles, amphibians, insects.

Plants, ranked in order from trees to fungus.

Minerals, ranked by gems, metals, stones, and so on.

All of these ranks of being corresponded with and were colored by the four elements, seven classical planets, and twelve zodiac signs, forming a complex analogical language that could be used to draw correspondences between all aspects of existence. These correspondences underpinned much of the medieval worldview and informed the language of operative magic, as can be seen, for instance, in Cornelius Agrippa's *Three Books of Occult Philosophy*.

Speaking of the importance of observing specific planetary times and hours for prayers, for instance, Tillyard writes, "One is tempted to call the medieval habit of life mathematical or to compare it with a gigantic game where everything is included and every act is conducted under the most complicated system of rules."[23]

Yet by the Elizabethan period, the hold of the Great Chain was weakening—following writers like Machiavelli questioning that the universe was even ordered at all, and the spread of Copernican theory, which would have been known to educated Elizabethans, even if they were unwilling to upset the hierarchy of the world by insisting on its mass adoption.[24]

Despite this, the Great Chain forms the fundamentals of occult thought that Dee, his teachers, and his contemporaries drew from. By speaking to angels, the Chain suggests, an individual might work to repair his sinful, sublunary nature, and begin to climb upward toward God via emulation of the angels, rather than degenerating toward the lower realms. This idea of repairing one's own fallen nature, originally the concern of the odd solitary magus, would gain wider prominence with the growth of Rosicrucianism and Freemasonry; indeed, it is the root idea of Western esotericism.

Operative magic itself, stemming from the Great Chain, helped form the context of the Elizabethan period. Alchemy and sorcery permeated society, but reality itself was also a battleground between two metamagical systems—Catholicism and Protestantism. Beyond shared religious mythology, Catholicism had its saints, fetishes, sacraments, rituals, intercessionary prayer, and other magical technologies; while Protestantism had its evangelical fury and emphasis on individual relationship with Christ. Next to such intense systems of belief, whose wars extended to torture and mass murder, Dee's Hermeticism looks positively sober—the forerunner of the science that would begin to emancipate humanity.

REVELATION

If mankind had fallen in Genesis, and the decay of the world and the soul of humanity had resulted in its present sublunary condition despite

Christ's incarnation, there was an absolute antidote: the end of the world as prophesied in the books of Ezekiel, Daniel, and, principally, in Revelation, in which the wheat would be culled from the chaff, and the angels pour out the wrath of God upon unrepentant mankind, who had debased itself by worshipping the Dragon, Beast 666, and Whore of Babylon during the reign of Antichrist. This Apocalypse was to be the final triumph over Satan and his fallen angels, until they and their impenitent human followers were cast into the Abyss in preparation for the millennial reign of Christ and the New Jerusalem of perfected humanity that is to come.

If Hermetic magic was concerned with repairing the fallen nature of the individual alchemist, its ultimate goal—at least as expressed by Dee—was the repair of the fallen nature of the *entire world* by catalyzing the Second Coming of Christ. For Dee, and many to follow him, it was thought necessary to help this to occur through enlightened human activity—the Great Work. Indeed, the second half of Dee's life was consumed by following the dictates of impatient angels intent on using human agents to advance history toward the Apocalypse.

Revelation, the nightmarish final book of the New Testament, has occupied a central place in the Western imagination in the two millennia since its writing, and has come to mean many things to many people. Composed from a vision by the Jewish prophet John of Patmos following the death of Christ and the destruction of the Second Temple by Rome during the reign of Nero, Revelation originally described the end of the world as it was then known. It was written from the perspective of the Jews who had accepted Christ as the Jewish messiah—*not* St. Paul's converts to the new religion of Christianity, drawn from the pagans of Greece, Rome, and northern Africa. The book is a visionary prophecy of the final war of the much-tormented Jewish followers of Christ against the evil of not only Nero's Rome but *also* Paul's non-Jewish converts to Christianity. Revelation's addition to the biblical canon came much later, and was a matter of some controversy; the fact that it sits next to Paul's letters in the New Testament obscures the fact that Paul and John of Patmos were writing from the perspectives of two radically different factions of early Christians. While Paul was writing for converted gentiles, John was writing from the perspective of Jews who believed Christ to be the Messiah, and who were profoundly disturbed by the opening of God's covenant to non-Jews, a revolution that had been commanded not by the living man Jesus but by Saul of Tarsus's alleged vision of Christ on the road to Damascus. Hence, Revelation lashes out at the "synagogue of Satan, who claim to be Jews though they are not."[25] When it speaks of the 144,000 who are to be saved at the end of days, it does *not* mention converted gentiles, but the reassembled twelve tribes of Israel—that is, the Jews that have accepted Christ. As the religious historian Elaine Pagels argues in her study *Revelations,* this makes Revelation a profoundly *anti-Christian* document, as it is categorically hostile to the factions of early pagan followers of Christ that would become "Christians."[26]

The original politics of Revelation have been long forgotten, however, and the evils of John's time that were symbolically represented as the Red Dragon, the Beast 666, and the Whore of Babylon have been seen by generations of Christians since as pertaining to their own time period—especially during the Reformation, when millenarian fear gripped Europe. Unlike Catholicism, Protestantism yearned toward the vicious and punishing Jehovah of the Old Testament and the apocalyptic Christ of Revelation, and though Luther initially dismissed Revelation, he soon came to see the political expedience of casting Rome itself as the force of the Antichrist. Edward Kelly's visions are steeped in this Puritanical fire and brimstone, filled with angels commanding sinful humanity to atonement that would be at home in the sermons of the most extreme early American preachers, and announcing that God would soon obliterate his unrepentant Creation.

This apocalyptic vein of Protestantism only increased over the coming centuries, reaching a crescendo in nineteenth-century British preacher John Nelson Darby's rapture theology—the premillennial, dispensationalist doctrine that the books of Revelation and Daniel are not metaphor but describe fully literal geopolitical events yet to come, with 144,000 faithful Christians to be "raptured" or teleported into a tangible heaven prior to a world-ending confrontation between those who are "left behind" and the forces of Antichrist and his one-world government. *Rapture* is not a word that occurs in the Bible; it is a theological elaboration by Darby.[27] Key to this dispensationalist view of biblical events is that God requires human agents to advance the coming of his kingdom, and that what is required of these agents depends on which dispensational period of history, or "aion," is currently in effect, with the world now entering the final aion, the Apocalypse. This rapture theology, which gained brief popularity in the United Kingdom, soon became the guiding religious myth of America, from the common people to the very halls of power, and is one of the primary reasons for ongoing American support of the state of Israel. As will be discussed at length in book III, another particularly keen student of Darby's premillennialism was the occultist Aleister Crowley, who was raised in Darby's Exclusive Brethren group in England, later applied Darby's teachings on dispensations or aions of spiritual development to Dee and Kelly's angelic magic, and who consciously identified himself with the Antichrist as a necessary component of God's dispensation to humanity during the final days.

Along with the rise of Jewish nationalism in the nineteenth century and more secular geopolitical calculations, dispensationalism is causally responsible for the British creation of a Jewish homeland in Palestine via the 1917 Balfour Declaration and America's formal recognition of the state of Israel in 1948. (Remarkably, John Dee's fellow magus Isaac Newton predicted 1948 as the year of the Jews' return to Palestine.)[28] Yet this biblically literal, evangelical, or "Christian Zionist" theology is diametrically opposed to the original meaning of Revelation. It demands that the return of the Jews to Palestine and their subsequent conversion to Christianity is a necessary prerequisite of the Second Coming; in the one-dimensional Christian Zionist worldview, Jews are simply Christians who have yet to receive Christ. This is now far from a fringe belief—in 2006, a Pew Forum on Religion and Public Life study found that over one in three Americans believes that the state of Israel is a fulfillment of biblical prophecy of Christ's return.[29] Christian Zionism—as exemplified by modern megachurch evangelicals like John Hagee and Greg Laurie—hinges upon the belief that evangelical Christians who support Israel will in turn receive blessings in their own lives,[30] drawn from Genesis 12:3, in which God tells Abraham

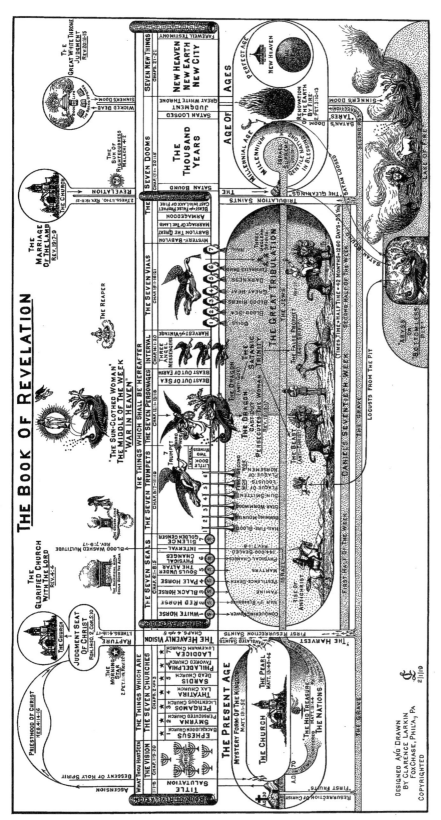

Fig. I.4. Clarence Larkin, *The Book of Revelation*, 1918.

that he will create a great nation from him, and that "I will bless those who bless you, and I will curse him who curses you."[31] For Christian Zionists, this principle extends beyond individuals to entire empires; indeed, it is widely believed among Christian Zionists that Britain's failure to work toward a full Jewish state, and America's urgent insistence on doing so, is responsible for the collapse of the British Empire and the transfer of global imperial primacy to America. Dee, who argued for a British Empire of Angels, would likely agree were he alive today. Some Christians go so far as to believe that failing to support Israel will mean that they will be "left behind" during the Rapture.[32]

These premillennial ideas did not begin in the nineteenth century, however. Just as early stirrings of Jewish Zionism can be found in the seventeenth-century Kabbalist and self-proclaimed Jewish messiah Sabbatai Zevi, so can stirrings of Christian Zionism be found in the Cabalist John Dee and the prior occult tradition he exemplified. Indeed, the conversion of the Jews (as well as pagans and Muslims) to Christianity as a preapocalyptic necessity was central to the plans of Dee's angels. More overt calls for Christian Zionism can be found in the decades following Dee's death, notably in the literal, premillennial, and Cabala-influenced tract *The World's Great Restauration* in 1621, which argued that the Jews would return to Palestine in the latter half of the seventeenth century prior to the subsequent Apocalypse.

Such literal readings of scripture were an inevitable consequence of the printing press. To read the word of God directly, without the mediation of the Church, was inevitably to take it literally; in many ways, Protestantism itself is a phenomena of mass printing and rising literacy rates. Yet such calls to biblical literalism and fundamentalism—let alone Zionism—were heresy during Dee's day; attempts by Protestant groups at "Judaizing" by leaning into the Old Testament and Zionist ideas were punishable by death under Elizabeth and James I.[33] One particularly zealous group of Judaizers was the Puritans, who rejected the residual Catholicism of the Church of England and longed to live like God's original chosen people, over twenty thousand of which responded to persecution by migrating to New England. There, the ministers Cotton and Increase Mather, who saw demons and witches behind every ill twist of fate, established America on fundamentalist and apocalyptic lines.

In the nineteenth century, Darby's dispensationalism—the idea that God had different messages and posed different challenges to humanity for different periods of history, and that these periods of history, of which mankind was now in the preapocalyptic phase, required human stewardship—took root in America in a way that it hadn't in England. As the twentieth century opened, the extensively circulated Scofield Reference Bible spread Darby's apocalyptic literalism, and evangelists like Billy Sunday took up the crusade and pushed it to truly American proportions. Sunday and those who followed in his footsteps—most notably Billy Graham—sought to influence not only American culture, but also politics.[34] Saving a few converts was one thing, but saving the world was another. The twentieth century was a trying time for Christians—after all, film, television, and even cars were seen as signs of the yet-again-impending Apocalypse. American evangelicals, convinced by their leaders that Jesus was indeed coming, earned, saved, and donated formidable amounts of money to the cause of establishing a Jewish state in Palestine—with some even helping in its initial settlement. The eruption of World War I only confirmed their belief that the end was at hand. While American progressives and humanists pushed for peace movements, evangelicals knew that resisting "wars and rumors of wars" was futile, as they were only foreshadowing of the Antichrist to come.[35]

This passive acceptance of what was perceived to be God's work in the world reached a disturbing moral low in World War II, during which many Christian Zionists saw Hitler's persecution of the Jews as a part of the divine plan to push Jews toward returning to Palestine and converting to Christianity. They therefore saw little need for America to intervene to prevent the Holocaust from occurring. The Third Reich, it was reasoned by fundamentalists, was only a foreshadowing of the persecutions that would occur during the reign of Antichrist, and represented a wake-up call to secular European Jews to repent before it was too late.[36] Just as God had used pagans as pawns to further his agenda in the Old Testament, many evangelicals believed, so had he used the Nazis to advance the apocalyptic timeline by forcing the Jewish return to Palestine.[37]

America's triumph in World War II, and the subsequent 1948 recognition of Israeli statehood, again convinced evangelicals that they were winning God's holy war; even Harry Truman called the atomic bomb a gift from God and a sign of his favor, while evangelicals saw it as the most dramatic sign of the end times possible.[38] Yet while evangelicals fought a global war for salvation, they were losing ground in the culture war back home. As the twentieth century progressed, evangelicals lost control of the educational system, the media, and the hearts and minds of young people to what they perceived as a "secular humanist" agenda drawing the world away from faith. (These new, libertine social mores, as typified by the 1960s counterculture, were prototyped by Crowley's Thelemic cult in the 1920s, as will also be discussed in book III.) During the 1960s, evangelicals lost further ground in the culture war by maintaining separatist views on race,[39] and virulently opposing women's reproductive rights—as Billy Sunday had once put it, "Woman is the battleground of the universe."[40] Rome likewise struggled to maintain relevance in a rapidly changing world, and responded with the creation of the Second Vatican Council in 1959, a radical overhauling and liberalization of the Church that remains contentious among many Catholics. Put on the defensive by a secular society now not only uninterested but actively hostile to organized Christianity, denominations that had long been bitter enemies made common alliances to survive in a godless world. The three-headed beast of "birth control, divorce, and Hollywood" sought to drown God's people as surely as the Flood had.[41] In this tide of secular darkness, evangelicals detected the hand not only of Communist subversion but of the coming Antichrist himself.[42]

This culture war took a prodigious turn back toward the Christian right in the 1970s, following the publication of Hal Lindsey's blockbuster bestseller *The Late Great Planet Earth,* which repopularized apocalyptic literalism for a lost generation awash in drugs and vague mysticism. Lindsey foretold that the Antichrist would arise from the European Economic Community as an America weakened by Communist subversion slept, spoke of the coming Antichrist as a kind of super-Hitler, referred to Israel as "God's plot point," and predicted that Armageddon would occur in 1988.[43] Among this book's 28 million enthusiastic readers was Ronald Reagan, who believed (as of 1971) that the book of Ezekiel had prophesied that Russia, or "Gog," would be destroyed by nuclear weapons for persecuting Israel.[44]

"For the first time ever," Reagan told a state senator, "everything is in place for the battle of Armageddon and the Second Coming of Christ."[45] Only a decade later, Reagan would be leading America in a nuclear showdown with Russia for real, during which time he held regular White House dinners for evangelical advisers like Lindsey, Pat Robertson, Jerry Falwell, and Tim LaHaye.[46] (The ICBM missiles that made up America's nuclear arsenal, and which held the world on the brink of annihilation during the Cold War, were propelled by rocket fuel designed by Crowley's student Jack Parsons.)

George Bush Sr. held similarly evangelical views on the importance of Israel.[47] George Bush Jr.'s presidency was even more steeped in apocalyptic fervor; the younger Bush famously attempted to elicit French support for the invasion of Iraq by telling Jacques Chirac that he saw "Gog and Magog at work" in the Middle East.[48] Bush's speechwriter David Frum, who is Jewish, commented that for staffers in Bush's White House, regular Bible study was "if not compulsory, not quite uncompulsory, either."[49] While the presidency of Donald Trump at least appears to represent a cataclysmic break with the American right's traditional evangelical narrative in favor of nationalism, in actuality it shows little sign of deviating from the script. Indeed, Trump's vice president, Mike Pence, is likely the staunchest and most extreme Christian Zionist politician to occupy the White House in American history, a position he probably could not have secured without the populist appeal of Trump.[50]

Rather than "gentle Jesus, meek and mild," this thermonuclear version of Christianity is concerned with destroying the perceived enemies of Christ, including Russia, Islamic terrorists, and subversive or even "Satanic" influences back home; during the 1980s, it held the entire world hostage in a game of nuclear chicken, and in its new guise as the "War on Terror," continues to be the justification for American imperialism. Apocalyptic Christianity is now a multibillion-dollar industry in America alone,[51] and is a potent narrative tool used by Republican politicians to mobilize evangelical voters. Yet it would be too sim-plistic to assume that evangelical spiritual and political leaders cyni-cally manipulate their constituents for money and power. Indeed, the Manichean polarity of premillennialism, its inflexible totality, and its promise to its adherents of a divine role on the historical stage—not to mention the promise of salvation or even preferential treatment by God—exercises a profound appeal and hold over American political leaders, including those who do not begin their careers as evangelicals but convert as they gain proximity to the real levers of power.[52] While traditionally associated with the Republican party, evangelicals are highly represented among the Democrats as well, and Democratic poli-ticians make regular plays to evangelical voters.[53] The extent to which apocalyptic Christianity dominates the American political and spiri-tual narrative is often easy to forget, as evangelicals have lost control of Hollywood and the mass media since the 1930s, despite the fact that Christian media remains profitable within its own sphere.[54]

In contrast, Jewish Zionism has been largely secular, nationalist, and pragmatic. Theodor Herzl, the father of modern Zionism, dismissed religion and Messianism as childish games;[55] Max Nordau, with whom Herzl cofounded the World Zionist Organization, was an agnostic who bitterly attacked mysticism and the perceived degeneracy of Victorian culture, contending instead for a fiercely nationalistic and "muscular" Judaism.[56] On the other hand, the cultural Zionist Ahad Ha'am argued (against Herzl and Nordau) that religion was not only inseparable from Jewish identity but the source of Jewish national will.[57] Yet while Jewish identity had long been conceptualized in religious, transcendent terms, a new understanding of Jewishness as an ethnic and even secular iden-tity came to dominate the Jewish nationalist conversation beginning in the nineteenth century.[58]

Consequently, messianic groups have been the exception rather than the rule in Israeli politics, but have exercised a powerful influ-ence nonetheless. Moses Hess, the founder of Labor Zionism, believed that the true apocalypse was the ultimate socialist education of human-ity, which Christianity had been a step toward.[59] David Ben-Gurion, the founder and first prime minister of Israel, described the Zionist project as a "magnificent, messianic enterprise."[60] Abraham Kook, the first Ashkenazi chief rabbi of British Mandatory Palestine, studied the Kabbalah and Hegelian philosophy, concluding that God had used all of history to divinely conspire to return the Jews to Palestine, and that he had used even the actions of pagans and apparent opposition and persecution of the Jews to do so.[61] The fundamentalist sect Gush Emunim, led by the son of Rabbi Kook, vigorously pushed for a messianic, redemptionist interpretation of the settlement of new territories acquired by Israel in the Six-Day War, which it believed had been divinely granted and therefore could not be surrendered. This growing sect pushed for a messianic and absolutist view of Israeli expansion and drew enthusiastic support from many young people,[62] though the evacuation of settlements from 2000 to 2009 came as a challenge to the redemptionist camp, leading to further political fragmentation among religious Zionist groups.[63]

Likewise, many *Haredi* or orthodox Jews from the nineteenth century onward saw Zionism as a push toward the Jewish messiah,[64] while others have considered Zionism to be actively antimessianic—for instance, Polish Hasidic leaders stated in 1902 that "Zionism itself is based on the denial of divine providence, the doctrine of reward and punishment and of the hoped-for redeemer. The nationalism of which they speak fulfills itself in nothing other than the destruction of sacred religion."[65]

Despite its status as a secular state, Israel often finds itself uncomfortable bedfellows with Christian Zionists in securing American support. This relationship is made decidedly bitter by the fact that Israel looks to American economic and military aid to maintain a strong state in the midst of its enemies, and to prevent another Holocaust, *despite* the fact that—in the final summation—many modern Christian Zionists believe the Holocaust was necessary.[66] Despite its name, Christian Zionism can be read as anti-Semitic, in that it is concerned not with the well-being of the Jewish people as much as it is using them to fulfill its own agenda and, ultimately, to de-Judaize them.

Though Christian eschatology has been the predominant narrative in Western culture since the death of Christ, it entered an actively imperial phase following the European exploration of North America and the Reformation, and in this form continues to guide the actions of the American empire. Therefore, Revelation can be read as a kind of magical manual or *tantra* for the leaders of Western civilization, as well as for the adepts of the Western esoteric tradition examined in this book. For Dee and those who followed him, hastening the events of Revelation was not nihilistic destructiveness but the necessary precursor of fulfilling God's plan, redeeming humanity, and establishing the New Jerusalem—the final restoration of the sublunary, fallen world. As Revelation is the underlying script of Dee's work—as well as the work of Aleister Crowley and Jack Parsons, which will be examined in book III—it is recommended to have a copy close to hand while reading this book.

Multiple translations of the Bible are cited in this text—the King James, New King James, and New International Version—depending on whether drawing attention to specific wordings, historical context, or maintaining clarity for modern readers is most important for each citation. Comparing multiple translations of any given passage can easily be done online.

THE WESTERN MYSTERY TRADITION AND ESOTERIC PROTESTANTISM

If this is the narrative of mainstream Protestantism, then what of the underground occult tradition, which Dee exemplified? Western esotericism is often seen as a sideline curiosity or footnote to history—at best an early, failed attempt at science. It also tends to be cast in an oppositional role to mainstream religious denominations and movements.

I argue in this book—following Dame Francis Yates—that this is not the case, and that the Western esoteric tradition has, for better or worse, been central to the development of European, English, and American spirituality, geopolitics, and empire. Further, it is my contention that the angelic system of John Dee and Edward Kelly has been the central core of the Western esoteric tradition in its post-Renaissance form, and has been at the heart of Rosicrucianism, Scottish Rite

Freemasonry, the Golden Dawn, and Thelema—and, through Thelema, of modern occultural movements like Satanism and witchcraft. These religious subcultures, in the final summation, do *not* exist in opposition to mainstream Protestantism but are, instead, its esoteric component—in some cases affirming and upholding its theology by acting as its shadow. Therefore, Dee and Kelly's system has played an invisible but central role in the last five hundred years of Western history.

Though the adepts of this tradition, of which I have taken Dee as an exemplar, have been small in number and marginalized in official history, it is my contention that the experimental world of the occult and its attendant secret societies in many ways represents the "research and development wing" of Western civilization, in which new political, social, and religious models are proposed and tested, often finding wider purchase in society through the efforts of artists and political radicals who fall under the sway of such ideas. The influence of Freemasonry on the American and French revolutions is a primary example.

However, I must distinctly resist any conspiratorial read of this history. The Western esoteric "tradition" has mostly been only sporadically organized, with groups often working in isolation from or even at cross purposes to each other; one would struggle to find core dogmas for the Western tradition, as its ideals and praxis shift significantly between groups and individual practitioners. Even when it does involve large organized groups, like Freemasonry, the history of the Western tradition is still less one of group efforts, let alone large-scale religious revivals, than it is of ideas passing between individuals or small collectives of intellectuals, often at a distance of centuries. These thinkers—such as Dee, Newton, Crowley, and many more—have in turn exercised massive influence on the wider culture, often in oblique and nonintuitive ways. A useful and not altogether unconnected parallel can be drawn with Western philosophers like Kant, Nietzsche, and Schopenhauer, who often lived marginal, secluded, and outwardly even feeble lives, yet whose intellectual work caused undeniable and irreversible sea changes in Western civilization, often after their deaths. These changes were not effected by organized conspiracies but by the power of new ideas to rapidly spread between minds and upend entire cultures in the process.

So with that said, what *is* the Western esoteric tradition, other than a catchphrase denoting the occult thinkers and fraternities that have sprouted up throughout European history?

It is my view that this tradition, in its form postdating Dee, should really be called *Esoteric Protestantism,* that it is indeed the inner esoteric expression of the Protestant Reformation, and that it has played a guiding role in the spread of Protestantism and its ideals throughout the world.

All religions have an exoteric shell—a system of rules and dogmas for laypeople—along with smaller inner esoteric groups focused on mysticism, individual experimentation with spiritual techniques, and, very often, apocalypticism.[67] Examples include the tantric schools of Hinduism and Buddhism, the Holy Orders in Catholicism, the Kabbalists in Judaism, the Sufi schools of Islam, and many more. Though Protestantism in its many varieties is only five hundred years old, it is, of course, no different. Esoteric Protestant groups like the Rosicrucians, Freemasonry, the Golden Dawn, and, indeed, the collective of scientists that became the Royal Society—*are* the esoteric core of Protestantism. Protestantism's often aggressively "bland" approach, even approaching open secularism in the case of many modern denominations, makes it easy to assume that it possesses no depth and to miss what is (or at least was) hiding in plain sight.

As will be discussed, the primary formulation of this tradition can be traced to the sack of Constantinople and the transfer of Byzantine manuscripts containing material from ancient Greece and Rome to the Medici city-states. Here, the spiritual ideas of the ancient, pre-Christian world were revived as Renaissance Hermeticism and Neoplatonism, mixing with teachings on the Kabbalah from Europe's Jews. This amalgam was in turn formulated into a system of "operative magic" by the Benedictine abbot Trithemius and his student Cornelius Agrippa.

These streams of magical thought were prevalent in Europe at the time of Luther's spiritual revolution and England's subsequent "Brexit" from Rome, which permanently altered the spiritual politics of the West and was widely thought to indicate that the Apocalypse was at hand. Against this backdrop of impending Armageddon, these Hermetic,

Fig. I.5. Albrecht Dürer, *The Seven-Headed Beast and the Beast with Lamb's Horns*, 1496/98.

Neoplatonic, Cabalistic, and occult ideas and techniques came together in the singular personage of John Dee, who purportedly used them to contact angels. These angels immediately began using Dee, Kelly, and many of their noble and ecclesiastical connections to accelerate Europe even further toward the end times. In order to assist this process, Dee was given the "true" system of magic that earlier Renaissance thinkers had only really made a patchwork approximation of.

While Luther had proposed a break with Rome, and Henry actualized it in England, Dee created the plan for global Protestant victory over the Church—a worldwide Empire of Angels, with Elizabeth I, not the pope, as its spiritual and political head. Such a global Protestant hegemony would pave the way toward the Second Coming, and central to actualizing this plan was Dee's angelic system of magic.

The overthrow of the old Roman order was not accomplished with the single nail hammered through the *Ninety-Five Theses*. The revolt undertaken by Martin Luther (whose personal seal, we should not forget, was a Rose Cross, and whose later Lutheran churches included the Eye of Providence or "eye in the pyramid" in their iconography) was pushed to completion by generations of Europeans often working in secret and under penalty of torture and death. Central to this struggle was not only Dee's work but the Rosicrucian and Freemasonic movements that drew inspiration from it and were concerned with establishing a new era of intellectual, scientific, and spiritual freedom away from the stultifying grasp of Rome. These secret societies were the explicit counterpart of the Jesuits and other activist Holy Orders in Catholicism—in short, they were the Protestant special forces. Their ideals were concretized as modern science, via the Royal Society, and as the country of America, via Francis Bacon's *New Atlantis* and the efforts of the Masonic founding fathers of America.

I propose that this Esoteric Protestantism may be broadly defined by two goals: One is the emphasis on individual salvation—not just through the standard five *solae* of Protestantism, but by direct experiment in the alteration of consciousness through alchemy and even ritual magic, with the goal being the restoration of man's individual fallen state. The second is the extension of this process to the entire planet, via the acceleration of the events of Revelation by human agency. As demonstrated above, this eschatological push, following the late nineteenth century, became the defining feature of Protestantism, especially in America.

A useful parallel may here be drawn to the Three Turnings of the Wheel of the Dharma, or the evolution of the Buddhist schools. These are the *hinayana,* the original teaching of the Buddha, which insists solely on the importance of individual enlightenment; the *mahayana,* which stresses that individual enlightenment is undesirable and perhaps even impossible in a vacuum and aims instead for the enlightenment of all sentient beings; and the *vajrayana,* which aims to accomplish the goals of the mahayana through occult and even apocalyptic means.[68]

In studying Dee, his intellectual predecessors, and the religious movements and scientist-alchemists he directly or indirectly inspired, like Francis Bacon and Isaac Newton, we are studying the computer programmers who wrote the code of the last five hundred years of Western civilization. This is code we are still following. Understanding Dee, and restoring his place from the margins of history to a central role, is therefore the key to understanding exactly what the post-1500 West, particularly America, actually is.

READING DEE

Though it contains a biographical overview, this book is not a biography of Dee. Rather, it is a biography of his ideas, of the angelic magic, and an attempt to trace the footprint of his impact in the world. There are several existing biographies of Dee, the best of which is Glen Parry's *The Arch-Conjuror of England.* Beyond simply creating a new biography, I have here drawn on academic research into Dee's work, Dee's own writing and spirit diaries, as well as Hermetic psychohistory and later experiments with the angelic system by operative magicians like Elias Ashmole, Aleister Crowley, and Jack Parsons. There is also a large amount I have left out—in particular, information on the minutiae of Dee's involvement in Elizabethan court politics. In the process I hope to have provided a good introductory overview for the casual reader, and perhaps assisted in encouraging a more open-minded appraisal of Dee and his work. I also hope that this book is not the end of the reader's Dee studies, and that the next stop is the primary texts—Dee's diaries.

Following Méric Casaubon's 1659 publication of *A True & Faithful Relation,* Dee was relegated to the very marginalia of history; he would wear this "sackcloth and ashes" for two and a half centuries, forgotten as anything except an embarrassing relic of scientific error. It was not until the twentieth century that scholars began to cast new light on the Doctor. British historian Charlotte Fell-Smith published the first biography of Dee in 1909 (the same year that Aleister Crowley and Victor Neuburg undertook an exploration of Dee's magic in Algeria). But it was in the 1960s and '70s that another British historian, the eminent Dame Frances Yates, established what has been called the Yates thesis or Warburg interpretation—the grand narrative that Hermeticism laid the foundations upon which science was built. Yates did more work than perhaps any other scholar before or since in reestablishing Hermeticism, alchemy, and magic as a necessary and vital part of the evolution of European thought rather than an aberration—for Yates, Dee was the case in point.[69] The Renaissance magi, Yates argued, believed that the Neoplatonic and Hermetic quest to reascend the Great Chain would elevate them to rulership and command over the natural world—and this idea, in turn, led to modern experimental science.[70] For if man was created in God's image, as is revealed in Genesis 1:26, so, by the logic of Hermeticism, could man not only play God but become like God.[71]

Increasingly interested in Dee throughout the 1970s, Yates cast the Doctor as a supreme magus, a "great man" whose magical and scientific pursuits formed a coherent and world-changing whole, and who inspired the Rosicrucian movement of the 1600s, which in many respects became the grounds from which modern science emerged. During the same period, Richard Deacon's 1968 biography *John Dee: Scientist, Geographer, Astrologer and Secret Agent to Elizabeth I* painted Dee—somewhat fancifully—as a secret agent for the queen. Dee, who indeed signed letters to Elizabeth "007," was cast as the ultimate man of mystery, an illuminated insider privy to the secrets of both the occult and international espionage. Likewise, Yates's colleague Peter French developed her notes into another full-length biography of Dee, 1972's

John Dee: The World of an Elizabethan Magus, which fully takes on Yates's view of Dee as a Hermetic mastermind whose every move was calculated to achieve the Great Work of restoring nature.[72]

Such a romantic big-picture view of Dee is certainly enticing. This "1970s Dee," cast as arch-magus and secret agent, gained significant traction in the incense cloud of the counterculture occult revival, and consequently formed the larger-than-life caricature that students of Dee first encounter, with the Yates thesis itself forming the historical groundwork that later Dee studies would be measured against.

Yet by the mid-70s, the Yates thesis was already being rejected as far too grandiose;[73] in addition, by romanticizing Dee as a Hermetic magus, Yates had overlooked his many scientific and political achievements.[74] Science historian J. L. Heilbron, in introducing a 1978 translation of Dee's *Propaedeumata aphoristica,* held to the long-standing scientific view that Dee's occultism was a shameful error, and that as Dee's immersion in the occult came *after* his mathematical and scientific contributions, it represented only a slide into superstition, mental illness, and irrelevance; for Heilbron, Dee's 1582 reformation of the calendar was his last scientific contribution of any worth.[75]

Starting in the 1980s, following the growing dominance of poststructuralist discourse in the academy, Dee studies blossomed as an academic field unto itself, as new scholars of Western esotericism standing on the foundational shoulders of Dame Yates reassessed Dee with far finer tools, and in far greater detail. For Dee and his fellow travelers—dwelling at the crossroads of Catholicism, Protestantism, Hermeticism, Islam, Judaism, operative magic, and science—scientific and magical thinking blurred together with no clear delineation. Yet despite this ideological drift, picking apart the various threads of Dee's thinking would take far closer analysis than lumping his various pursuits together as aspects of a singular Great Work. Rather than arch-magus, later scholars began to see Dee as a Mercurial representative of the Renaissance, who immersed himself in the various intellectual trends of his time, and whose work therefore represents a kind of hypertext of Renaissance thought.[76]

This new wave in Dee scholarship was initiated by historian Nicholas Clulee, whose 1988 *John Dee's Natural Philosophy: Between*

Science and Religion remains central to the field. Clulee neither held to Yates's romantic narrative of Dee as all-encompassing Hermetic magus, nor did he discard Dee's occultism as historians of science had. Rather, he examined each of Dee's interests and scientific contributions individually, tracing Dee's intellectual growth from humanism to the later angelic conversations, analyzing Dee's "omnidisciplinarity" one topic at a time.[77] Clulee sought to address the angelic conversations on their own merit as a purely religious exercise, extracted from dialogue with Dee's scientific pursuits.[78] In removing Dee from the overall narrative of the scientific revolution and assessing him on his own terms, Clulee provided a remarkable breakthrough in understanding Dee, upholding a high standard of intellectual integrity. Without the tension of struggling to fit Dee into a master narrative—either the official narrative of scientific progress or the Yates interpretation of Dee as arch-magus—Clulee opened breathing room to assess Dee for what he was, a complex individual who, like any intelligent human being, had a wide array of interests and career trajectories in his lifetime, and whose thinking changed and evolved over his many decades of government service, against a shifting backdrop of uncertain geopolitics and patronage.

Just as the portrayal of Dee as arch-magus was reconsidered, so was Dee as a grand conspirator and agent of the state. Though Dee was employed by the Crown, and was a zealous patriot in service of Elizabeth's England, he was also poorly compensated, and Elizabeth's government routinely adopted a dismissive attitude toward the eccentric researcher, even as it used his ideas. Dee's work itself, however, can inarguably be said to have exerted massive influence on world history.

In 1999, the scholar (and later bestselling fiction author) Deborah E. Harkness fully assessed Dee's occultism, building on Clulee, as well as Christopher Whitby's 1981 doctoral work on Dee's spirit diaries, to draw out a new and more fully-formed picture of Dee the magus. Harkness's work resists Yates's oversimplification, but nonetheless seeks to tie together the many phases of Dee's work, showing not only a clear progression in Dee's thinking but demonstrating how Dee's angelic conversations crowned his occult studies *and* his geopolitical work. Harkness's book *John Dee's Conversations with Angels: Cabala, Alchemy, and the End of Nature* builds a big-picture view of Dee that is at once more nuanced and also reenchanted—even shocking—in its interpretation of Dee's life work. While Yates argued that Dee laid the foundation for science, Harkness argues that Dee was steadily working at nothing less than a new spiritual and geopolitical ordering for the entire planet, with Elizabeth I as the terrestrial and spiritual emperor of all mankind, with a new and all-uniting religious dispensation to be given to the world by the angels, which would bring under its fold not only the warring factions of Christendom but also Judaism and Islam, and return fallen humanity to the original divine plan.[79]

In seeking to problematize early occult readings of Dee, successive generations of scholars have, it seems, unwrapped deeper and deeper layers of occult complexity; like the "scrying" of Dee's angelic Aethyrs, the study of Dee himself is a process that only becomes more complex, fascinating, and even challenging to modernity itself as it progresses. Dee is an inexhaustible subject. In life, he stood at the crossroads between magic and science, between the medieval and the modern, between Protestantism and Catholicism, and between the terrestrial and celestial worlds themselves. Dee's vision was indescribably broad, his ambition Faustian, but when one is able to ascend at last to the heights from which he saw the world, the overall vision becomes breathtakingly elegant—a Hieroglyphic Monad.

THE GUIDE FOR THE PERPLEXED

Dee's work was difficult to comprehend even in his own time period. This situation is only compounded today, as his work relies on the context of the Elizabethan, Catholic, and Protestant worldviews, as well as the terrestrial disciplines of mathematics, optics, astronomy, and geography, and the celestial disciplines of theology, astrology, alchemy, Hermeticism, Qabalah, and operative magic among others, not to mention a working understanding of Hebrew, Greek, Latin, and their internal mathematical structures. Dee's work in these disciplines was not pursued in a vacuum, but must be understood as an outgrowth of a very specific historical period and geopolitical context.

Adding to this situation is the complexity of the angelic system itself. Because the study of Hermeticism and magic was progressively excised from the Western intellectual project in the century after Dee's death, little work has been done on Dee's findings, and what work *has* been completed has been by cultural outsiders, rather than scientists trained to Dee's level. This later work, particularly that of the Hermetic Order of the Golden Dawn, helps elucidate Dee's magic in some ways, and unnecessarily muddies and confuses it in others. Attempting to understand Dee through the lens of the Golden Dawn does us no favors either, since that order's corpus is a dauntingly complex semiotic hoard in its own right. The task we are left with is comparable to resurrecting calculus had it been abandoned after Newton and Leibniz. And to do so, we must first think as Dee did, which is a momentous undertaking in itself.

Do not let this discourage you—the more Dee's ideas are understood, the simpler and even more intuitively self-evident they become. I hope to have already done the brunt of this work for you, and here aim to provide a comprehensive introduction to Dee's thought to the modern reader. Ample endnotes have been provided for further research. In many places, I have attempted to elucidate some of Dee's thinking by drawing comparisons to the more recent work of the Golden Dawn, Crowley, and others. In order to preserve the original narrative of Dee's work, I have separated these comments out into footnotes where possible.

In order to orient yourself within this book, the following map will be helpful:

Book I, The Magus addresses Dee's early life, education, government service, and major works, including his work on astronomy and astrology (the *Propaedeumata aphoristica*), Qabalah and alchemy (the *Monas hieroglyphica*), mathematics (the preface to Euclid's *Elements*), and imperialism (*General and Rare Memorials*). These sections should help to build a picture of where Dee's thinking was at when he began the angelic conversations in his fifties. By following Dee through his education and career, the reader should also become familiar with the worldview and knowledge Dee brought with him when he sat down at his scrying table. Overviews of Hermeticism, Dee's proposed new science of archemastery, Qabalah, and operative magic are here given, which with the benefit of hindsight can be seen to logically build on each other and lay the groundwork for the angelic sessions.

Book II, The Angelic Conversations addresses the angelic sessions themselves. Here the locus of the narrative shifts from Dee to the angels, their geopolitical goals, and their system of magic or "Real Cabala." Dee here becomes somewhat less important to the story, and it should be clear that his intellectual work up to this point has, from the angels' perspective, only served as a prop to allow Dee to reach high enough up the Great Chain to even begin to make fumbling communications with the next order of beings upon it.

Book III, Antichrist assesses the continuing development of the angelic magic in the centuries after Dee's death, and traces its central influence on the occult underground, with particular focus on Rosicrucianism, Elias Ashmole, speculative Freemasonry, the Golden Dawn, Aleister Crowley, and Jack Parsons.

This book therefore covers almost half a millennium, and links together a wide stretch of the history, religion, and science of Western civilization. It is my hope that in doing so I will have wrought at least some semblance of order out of chaos, and perhaps brought the West one step closer toward understanding its spiritual heritage.

For the sake of historical accuracy, I have employed multiple spellings of *Qabalah* in this book, which each denote slightly different things: *Kabbalah* for the original Jewish system of scriptural interpretation, *Cabala* for the Christian version borrowed from Jews by gentiles during the Renaissance and applied to Neoplatonic thought (including the Real Cabala of John Dee), and *Qabalah* for the Hermetic and occult version that emerged after the Enlightenment and was central to the work of Crowley and the Golden Dawn.

One final note: throughout this book, particularly in the third section, I have discussed movements and people—from Thelemic occultism to evangelical Christianity, Aleister Crowley to Ronald Reagan—who have convinced themselves that the divine timeline can be advanced by taking extreme and even evil actions. I am not advocating for or excusing this view; rather, I have hoped to show the havoc that people knee-deep in ideology can wreak upon those around them and the world, particularly when in positions of power.

Apocalyptic religious extremism has turned our world into a hell, in the childlike belief that this will accelerate divine punishment and redemption. If we do not see this psychopathology clearly, and grow beyond it, it may yet be our death. Therefore, throughout this book I have hoped to show the Western esoteric tradition as it is, warts and all—both its transcendent brilliance and its long and disturbing shadow.

Seeing the clear light of reality requires nothing less.

BOOK I

The Magus

1

Elected

John Dee was born in London, on July 13, 1527.

Only thirteen years earlier, in 1514, Copernicus had drafted his unpublished heliocentric model, and Hieronymus Bosch completed the harrowing triptych now known as *The Garden of Earthly Delights,* a vision of the Creation, Eden, hell, and damnation that still torments the Western imagination. In 1517, Luther had hammered the *Ninety-Five Theses* into the door of All Saints' Church. The following year, England established its first scientific institution, the Royal College of Physicians—and the year after that, Magellan embarked on the first circumnavigation of the globe. This is the world that Dee was born into, and these are the themes that would dominate his life.

Dee was raised in Mortlake, a small village to the southwest of London, which sits upon the Thames, where he would reside for much of his adult life. Dee's father, Roland, a textile merchant, traced his ancestry to Welsh nobility—the Dee name had been anglicized from the Welsh *Du* or *Ddu,* "black."[1] Though Dee would later claim Arthurian descent, his ancestors were probably yeoman cattle farmers.[2]

Roland Dee's attempts to raise himself from poverty included taking menial work that put him at arm's length from the king, as well as marrying Jane Wilde, the daughter and heiress of William Wilde of Milton-next-Gravesend in Kent.[3] Yet though the Dees remained of modest means, Roland Dee would ensure his son the education and connections that would propel him into government service, while his mother would grant him his home at Mortlake. Dee's home would later become one of the greatest centers of learning in England, and form a kind of womb for Dee and his activities throughout his life, sheltering him from the economic storms caused by his later failure to ride court politics and secure consistent income for himself.

An exceptionally gifted child, Dee displayed an aptitude for math from an early age; additional exposure to his father's textile business would give Dee a solid grounding in practical mathematics.[4] In 1537, Dee began a Catholic education at the Chantry School at Chelmsford, Essex, where he learned Latin, and very likely served as an altar boy. After his initial education, Dee entered St. John's College, Cambridge, at the age of fifteen, in November 1542. He later claimed (perhaps exaggerating) that he slept only four hours a night, rested two, and spent the remaining hours studying, avoiding carousing altogether.[5]

St. John's, then only thirty years old and still tiny, was dedicated to Catholic humanism, despite the new cultural influence of the Protestants. There, Dee gave himself to studying the core curriculum of Aristotelian logic and philosophy—and, following Aristotle's own line of thinking, the occult.

Dee was tutored extensively by John Cheke, who had an interest in astrology and may have introduced Dee to very rudimentary occult ideas, on which there was no formal ban at universities.[6] Alchemy and the search for the philosopher's stone were in high fashion, and would have fired Dee's imagination. The young Dee also befriended John Hatcher, a Fellow of the school who was exploring angelic magic.[7]

Following Erasmus, the educational curriculum had changed from logic and Latin to grammar, rhetoric, history, poetry, ethics, Greek, and Hebrew. Renaissance humanism was concerned with the study of antiquity, and aimed to create an engaged citizenry by imparting what are now called the humanities. With Europe only beginning to emerge from the Dark Ages, Europeans had to look to antiquity—particularly Greece—for knowledge and guidance beyond the doctrines of the Church. Still to come was the sense that Europe could construct its own future through the new discipline of science.

Yet while Dee assessed his undergraduate studies, immersing himself in the remains of antiquity, the wheel of the aeon was turning, and preparing the new light that was to come. In 1543, when Dee was sixteen, two monumental works were published: *On the Structure of the Human Body,* by Andreas Vesalius, and *On the Revolutions of Celestial Bodies,* by Copernicus. The first work initiated biological investigation into the inner space of the human body, while the second looked to outer space, and reoriented our conception of the solar system from a geocentric to a heliocentric one—then the height of heresy. Together, these two works marked the beginning of the scientific revolution.[8] John Dee's life would span the early years of this revolution, which would reach its next major acceleration point with the development of telescopes in the Netherlands in 1608, a year before Dee's death, with microscopes following on in the 1620s.

Copernicus's revelations would be ignored by Rome, denounced by Martin Luther, and, for the most part, fail to be noticed by the public whatsoever (the book didn't even sell out its four-hundred-copy print run). One of the few places Copernicus's work was fully appreciated, however, was among the English intellectual elite,[9] including John Dee.

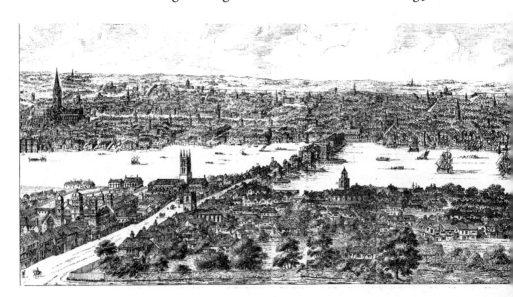

Fig. 1.1. London in 1543. From Anthony van den Wyngaerde, *London, Westminster, and Southwark in 1543.*

Though Dee never published on Copernicus's work himself, the first individual who *did,* expounding on Copernican theory for the first time in English, was Dee's young ward, Thomas Digges. Digges was an orphan; his father, Leonard Digges, a friend and colleague of Dee's, had invented an early version of the telescope before passing. Dee offered to look after his friend's son, and Digges would grow up under Dee's care and tutelage at Mortlake, absorbing Dee's wisdom and massive library before becoming a great astronomer in his own right, and one of the first great popularizers of science.[10]

Ultimately, humanism held only limited appeal for Dee's expansive mind, and he longed for the technical skills of alchemy, Cabala, Hermeticism, operative magic, and mathematics. It was in these heady days of undergraduate enthusiasm that Dee began to formulate the theoretical underpinnings of what would become his working approach to natural philosophy and even magic.

Hermeticism and operative magic were as seductive as they were dangerous—then, as now, what might make for a thrilling conversation between brilliant and daring undergraduates could lead to accusations of demonism in the broader world. Dee's Hermeticism stuck out like a sore thumb in the school's humanist climate, especially when Protestant intellectuals were lashing out at the magical thinking inherent in Catholicism. Nonetheless, Henry VIII appointed Dee a founding junior Fellow of his newly created Trinity College in December 1546.[11]

Though he would not attempt operative magic until much later, Dee's reputation for sorcery started early—prompted not by his actual occult interests, but by his enthusiasm for optical trickery. During a Cambridge stage production of Aristophanes's *Pax,* Dee employed optics to create the illusion of a flying scarab with a man on its back, which terrified the audience so badly that they assumed Dee was employing the dark arts.[12] The accusation stuck—and such accusations were severe.

After earning his bachelor's degree in 1546, at nineteen, Dee would teach logic and sophistry, and read Greek, at Trinity College. With patronage from Catholic scholars at Trinity, Dee would continue his study at the University of Louvain, a Catholic institution in the Netherlands, beginning in May 1547. Rather than the humanities, Dee would study in his true passions: mathematics, geography, navigation—and with them, astrology. Dee sought out mathematicians Gaspar à Mirica, Antonius Gogava, and Gemma Frisius,[13] under whom he learned trigonometry and triangulation; in Frisius's cartographer and geographer Gerardus Mercator, Dee found his primary mentor. Mercator, then

Fig. 1.2. Gerardus Mercator. Engraving by Frans Hogenberg, from Mercator, *Atlas sive Cosmographicae meditationes.*

thirty-six, was working hard to develop a new map of the world that incorporated the information brought back from the New World (we now remember him for creating the "Mercator projection," our standard world map). Gone were the crude imaginings of Dark Ages maps, full of biblical references and monsters; in their place were the beginnings of an accurate depiction of the planet.

"It was the custom of our mutual friendship and intimacy that, during three whole years," Dee later wrote, "neither of us willingly lacked the other's presence for as much as three whole days."[14]

Dee was at this time a tall, skinny, good-looking, healthy young man, who appeared wise beyond his years. Yet while his status as a promising intellectual was growing, his family was falling on hard times. When power shifted from Henry VIII to the nine-year-old boy-king Edward VI upon Henry's death in 1547, Roland Dee lost his job. He attempted to maintain his income by pretending to still be employed and, finally, through outright fraud—by stealing and selling gold altar plate from St. Dunstan's, where the elder Dee was senior churchwarden. Even when caught, Roland Dee refused to return the money or give up the names of the people he had sold the gold plate to—one of whom was his son John, who had purchased stolen brass candlesticks from his father. Roland and Jane Dee fled to Jane's family home in Gravesend, Kent, to hide under the protection of the local magnates.[15]

The shame of his father's deeds—with which Dee was publicly associated—would follow the scholar throughout his life, as would the financial difficulties imposed by his father's collapse. Compounded with the sorcerer's reputation he had garnered at Cambridge, the shame that surrounded Dee's family provided the first of many blocks to the progress of Dee's career. Dee would remain indigent, and often dependent upon meager support from the Crown, for the rest of his life.

Following his short stay in the Low Countries, Dee returned to Cambridge in 1548 to take his master's. As a gift to his home university, he brought back with him two globes created by Mercator, as well as a brass astronomer's ring and staff devised by Gemma Frisius.[16] Master's in hand, Dee returned once more to Louvain—just in time to escape his father's troubles.

Louvain had by this time become a refuge for Catholics fleeing Edward's Protestant reforms. Though Dee had been a sworn Protestant at Cambridge, he now took an oath to live under the rule of the pope. Dee may have been pursuing his own agenda, swearing what oaths he needed to gain access to the knowledge he sought. In this, he was similar to the Rosicrucians to come in the next century, who pledged to pursue their Hermetic and magical studies while living in accord with the customs of their local areas, without arousing undue attention. Such attention could be deadly, especially for a man like Dee, who was already exploring far outside the comfortable bounds of orthodoxy. Or he may have been intellectually fickle, unable to settle on a dogma that suited him.[17]

Despite the controversial nature of his studies, Dee was following in the footsteps of his forebears—Louvain had been the stomping ground of Cornelius Agrippa, the great codifier of the ceremonial and folk-magic traditions of Europe, whose work exercised a lifelong influence on Dee, and who laid out the basic operating procedures that Dee would follow in the angelic conversations. Dee had become enraptured by the siren song of magic, but his mathematical mind tempered his interest with cold reason: Dee's motto, while studying in the Low Countries, was "Nothing is useful unless it is honest."[18]

At Louvain, Dee also studied law, which would serve him well in days to come, both in Elizabeth's court and in her employ as an intelligence agent. He also studied astrology at length, which he would use in Elizabeth's court, and for nearly everything in his life, including the later angelic conversations and even the conception of children with his wife.[19] It was his astrological knowledge—especially as applied to medicine—that earned him the sobriquet "Dr. Dee," to which he did not object. (He did not, however, earn an actual doctorate.)

Following his education, Dee began traveling and lecturing on the Continent, and though he was perpetually broke, his talks on Euclid at the age of twenty-four are recorded as phenomenally successful—Dee later claimed that his lectures at Rheims were given to consistently full houses, with students climbing the walls to listen to him through open windows; Dee felt that the lectures created a far greater sensation than the uproar over his flying scarab.[20] Dee may well have exaggerated the popularity of his lectures—the science historian J. L. Heilbron points out that no contemporary references to them can be found outside of Dee's 1592 *Compendious Rehearsal,* written at the end of his life as a last-ditch effort to attain assistance from the government, in which he sought to inflate his achievements and downplay his failures.[21]

Dee was not an innovator in mathematics, but he was an apt teacher, passing on basic mathematical concepts to the general public—and was "accounted of the learned Mathematicians throughout Europe ye prince of Mathematicians of this age."[22] Dee was a great nurturer of the younger generation, who would far surpass him in their achievements, thanks to the care he had invested in them. This included not only his ward, Thomas Digges, but many of the foremost mathematicians of the late sixteenth century, who learned their art from Dee.[23]

While on the Continent, Dee would make a great number of contacts, with whom he would keep in regular correspondence after his return to England.[24] Dee also continued his occult studies under the polymath Guillaume Postel, the most accomplished Cabalist of his time, who impressed Dee with the study of Hebrew as a divine language, its mathematical construction, and his theory that all languages stemmed from the Hebrew letter *Yod.* Under Gogava, he also studied the I Ching, which must have appealed to his mathematical outlook. Math, for Dee, was the primary way of understanding the laws of nature and the mind of God. And while we today take for granted that the world can be measured and predicted by mathematical formulae, even that the world corresponds to mathematical constants, for Dee and his contemporaries this revelation was still fresh, unveiling a heretofore unseen world of divine planning and order just behind the apparent chaos of the world's façade.[25]

Postel is centrally important to the development of Dee's thought in that he gave the younger man a *why.* Beyond the technical disciplines Dee was learning, Postel initiated Dee into his grand eschatology. Postel believed himself to be "Elias Artista,"[26] the alchemical messiah, a mythological figure central to the beliefs of natural philosophers during the Renaissance, who Paracelsus had prophesied would restore the totality of art and science before the end of the world.[27] As such, Postel was a proponent of a new, universalist religion that would unite the warring religious factions of Christendom, as well as Judaism and Islam, in a single Hermetic whole based upon the Gospel and the uniting force of love. Postel's zeal for global restitution was informed at least in part by the prophetic utterances of "Mother Zuana," a mystic in her fifties at the time Postel knew her, who Postel believed was the living incarnation of the Shekinah, the female divine presence, and whose soul he believed entered his own body after Zuana's death.

For these heretical and millenarian views, Postel was expelled from Venice in 1549. In his quest to establish the new divine order, he made connections with Ignatius of Loyola in Rome and attempted to enter an early incarnation of the Society of Jesus; the Jesuit founder was not impressed, and had Postel investigated for heresy. While in Rome, he was told of the book of Enoch by an Ethiopian priest, and attempted to press upon the pope the importance of Enoch, the biblical apocrypha, and even the Zohar in interpreting scripture.[28] After meeting Dee in Paris, he was interviewed by the Inquisition, who found him "not evil, but mad," and imprisoned him until 1564. Following his release, he recanted his prior beliefs.[29]

Postel's ideas would live on in his student John Dee, who sought their universal key in his *Monas hieroglyphica*. They would be echoed within his angelic conversations in the 1580s, when Edward Kelly delivered the practical blueprint for the new world religion. The seed was planted by Postel, but it would take three decades to bear fruit in the work of his most brilliant student.

Dee had studied magic in Agrippa, medicine in Paracelsus, Cabala with Johann Reuchlin, and eschatology with Postel.[30] Yet these interests as of yet existed in scattered and embryonic form in Dee; they would not come together in the angelic sessions for almost thirty years, and it was highly unlikely that this was how Dee planned his life to go. A more probable reading might be that Dee fell back on his interest in operative magic and the grandiose and messianic dreams of Postel after his real government career collapsed.

Following the conclusion of his education and his triumphant lecture tour, a patriotic Dee turned down a potentially lavish but provisional offer to become a mathematical reader at the court of Henri II in

France. Other offers could have placed him in the employ of a range of French nobles, as well as the ambassador to Suleiman I, the Ottoman sultan; these he also refused, expecting to find a court position in his home country instead.[31] However, Dee returned to England to discover no offers of employment and no money. He also found Edward's reforms in full swing, with Dee recording in his diary the destruction of church statues and even the tearing of crucifixes from churches, including the great crucifix at St. Paul's, which wounded several individuals and killed one when it was clumsily torn from its altar.[32]

After presenting the young king with copies of his astronomical works, Dee was given a pension (which may never have been honored), afterward seeking private employment with William Herbert, the first Earl of Pembroke, as well as John Dudley, the Earl of Northumberland. He also worked to set himself up as a teacher and private tutor,[33] and as a navigational consultant in Edward's court. Here, he assisted in the first major English maritime expedition, Richard Chancellor and Hugh Willoughby's 1553 search for the northeast passage to Cathay.[34] (The expedition was unsuccessful, but the pair did reach Russia, where they made trade agreements with Ivan the Terrible.) Around this time, Dee worked on inventing the paradoxical compass for the Muscovy Company, which he completed in 1557 and which would become a useful instrument in Dee's later imperial planning.[35] Dee would also be appointed rector of Upton-upon-Severn, a politically expedient move that enraged the bishop of Worcester, who held astrology to be a violation of God's law.[36]

Despite Dee's Catholic education—and the oaths he had sworn while abroad—he was already making a name for himself as an intellectual *par excellence* within the Protestant elite. Fame, fortune, and royal favor seemed just within reach. Unfortunately, Edward's reign was not to last long—the young king died of lung disease in July 1553, possibly brought on by poisoning, potentially by the Duke of Northumberland or by Catholic agents, and the government descended into chaos as factions vied for the throne. Before Edward's death, the Duke of Northumberland had pushed Edward to support the Protestant Lady Jane Grey instead of the Catholic Mary as his successor, in which he was likely successful; upon Edward's death, Northumberland set to work installing Lady Grey on the throne. One of his aides was Roland Dee. When Northumberland's plot failed, the duke was publicly executed, and Roland Dee was imprisoned in the Tower of London with the rest of Northumberland's forces. The elder Dee, his reputation tarnished by treason as well as theft, was a broken man. His further deeds and the date of his death are unrecorded.[37]

Roland's reputation hung over John Dee like a heavy cloak, and Dee himself was hardly above suspicion. Roland's fall also meant that the inheritance John Dee had expected to receive was no longer on the table. Instead, he would have to scramble to curry favor with power and stay alive by his wits. Seeking to stay on the good side of Mary's incoming Catholic regime and leaning into his Catholic education to right his fortunes and reputation, Dee had himself ordained as a priest—taking all six degrees, from tonsure to full priesthood, in one day. In the short term, at least, the ordination helped him garner the good graces of the new administration.[38]

Soon, Mary had completed a political marriage to Prince Philip of Spain, and managed to convince others, and perhaps even herself, that she was pregnant at the improbable age of thirty-eight. Because Philip was not allowed to interfere in succession, the future of the Crown now hung on Mary's pregnancy, and legal and political maneuvering over who would succeed Mary began immediately. If Mary and child were to die in labor, then Philip, Spain, and the Catholics would lose all power in England, whereas if the child alone died, succession would pass to Elizabeth. A military buildup between Philip's father, Charles V, and Elizabeth began at once.

Elizabeth, caught between appearing loyal to Mary and preparing to have to take and defend the throne, asked Dee to divine the future. On May 28, 1555, Dee was arrested for attempting magic in a rented room and was interrogated under suspicion of casting horoscopes of Philip, Mary, and Elizabeth. Astrology, or calculating, an art he had studied under his mentors at Louvain, was one of Dee's primary trades after leaving the academic world. Here it was seen as evidence that he was conspiring with Elizabeth to unseat Mary. Conjuring, calculating, witchcraft, and even having a "familiar spirit" were the leveled charges.[39]

Dee had been caught based on information from two informers, George Ferrers and Thomas Prideaux—only a few days after Dee's arrest, one of Ferrers's children was dead, the other blind, stoking fears that Dee was a sorcerer, and sending a pang of raw dread through Mary, who was terrified that Dee would use magic against her own unborn child. Under duress, Dee confessed to calculation and conjuration.[40] The admission was enough to stir Mary's camp up into a frenzy of paranoia. Rumors now circulated that Dee had created voodoo dolls of Philip and Mary to work magic against them, that he conjured demons, and that there was a vast occult conspiracy against Mary.

Dee was accused of treason, had his papers searched and his residence in London sealed.[41] He was next imprisoned in the Tower of London, where his father had been confined two years earlier; he may have been tortured on the rack in the Tower dungeon. At the Tower, Dee shared a cell with Bartlet Green, a heretical convert whom Dee took kindly to before he was burned alive for treason.[42] Dee soon confessed of whatever the Privy Council (Mary's advisory inner circle) wished to hear, which would only further mar his career prospects.

After his imprisonment, Dee was turned over to Edmund Bonner, the greatly feared Catholic bishop of London, for examination. Working in Bonner's household, Dee tried to restore his status by assisting the bishop with his tract *A profitable and necessarye doctryne, with certayne homelies,* which levied blanket condemnation against magical activities—including the folk rituals of Catholicism, like using sacramentals to banish evil, as well as Dee's forays into "optical science," despite Dee's best efforts to set it apart from folk superstition.[43] Bonner's tract would soon be read from every pulpit in England; Dee's assistance in publicly denouncing his own beliefs, as well as hiding behind Catholic power (including assistance in examining heretics), was a clear effort to save his own skin from the current regime. Meanwhile, Dee used his time in Bonner's household to expand the personal library he had begun assembling while abroad, already consisting of European and Arabic works on astronomy, geography, alchemy, Neoplatonism, and angel magic. Books on mathematics and astrology dominated Dee's new purchases. But by 1556, Dee's interests had shifted more fully toward optics and, for the first time in a serious way, alchemy, with Roger Bacon being a primary focus of his study.[44]

Bacon, a thirteenth-century philosopher and Franciscan friar, was an early exponent of both the scientific method and of operative alchemy. Feared as a sorcerer in his own day and still regarded as a demonic conjuror in Dee's, Bacon had suggested that true science was dependent not only upon external observation but upon inner illumination. That illumination, Dee suspected—as have generations of seekers to come—could be induced by ceremonial magic.[45] For Bacon, the Great Chain could be reascended and mankind's original unity with God could be recovered through the growth of moral virtue, by study, by divine illumination, and by understanding the divine grammar underlying Hebrew, Greek, and Latin.[46] Bacon believed that this origi-

Fig. 1.3. Roger Bacon in his observatory at Merton College, Oxford. Oil painting by Ernest Board. Courtesy of Wellcome Images.

nal, divine knowledge had been handed down in unbroken lineage from the beginning of mankind—from Noah to the Chaldeans to Abraham to the Egyptians to Moses to the Greeks, and from thereon unto the current world period.[47]

Dee immersed himself in Bacon's worldview; works by Bacon soon multiplied in his library. In 1557, Dee composed a defense of Bacon, stating that his miracles had been attained by natural science rather than with the aid of demons, as his critics had charged.[48] Not unnoticed was that Bacon's name before entering the priesthood, Dee believed, was "David Dee."[49]

Dee became similarly obsessed with Raymond Llull, a.k.a. "Doctor Illuminatus."[50] A Franciscan monk who experienced waking visions of

Fig. 1.4. Raymond Llull. Portrait by Ricard Anckermann, c. 1870. Ajuntament de Palma.

Christ, Llull may have written the first European novel (*Blanquerna*), and he did pioneering work on computation theory—work that would influence Gottfried Leibniz,[51] through him Alan Turing,[52] and therefore the creation of the modern computer.

In 1272, Llull had a vision on Mt. Randa in Majorca, Spain, in which he saw God's attributes not only mathematically and hierarchically infused throughout all and everything, but also indexed to the letters of the alphabet—the divine Creation as computer.[53] This rawly Cabalistic conception of the universe appealed to Dee, whose Real Cabala clearly relates to Llull's ideas—as does Dee's angelic magic itself. Traced back far enough, this means we may owe the existence of computers to a mystical vision on a mountain in Spain. (Seven centuries later, Steve Jobs would create the Apple Macintosh following years of pursuing similarly visionary states via Eastern mysticism and LSD.)

Dee's growing library at Mortlake was immensely comprehensive, beyond the capacity of any other individual or group of scholars then working in Britain. More than a collection of books, Dee's library was a collection of people, and became the intellectual center and *de facto* scientific university of an England still too enamored of humanism to officially support scientific research.[54] And though Dee had assembled his library at high personal cost, he went to just as great lengths to loan his collection out. As Dee's library grew, it would become one of the jewels of England, a center of learning in its own right that would lay the groundwork for innovations and intellectual movements to come.

Dee's passion for library building went even further: he used his new displays of Catholic loyalty and association with Bonner to regain favor with Mary, and in January 1556, petitioned her to build a national library. Dee's plan, if enacted, would have created the British Library two centuries ahead of time. The proposed library would primarily focus on occult documents—which would be hidden from the public.[55] That such a plan was presented to Mary suggests that, despite efforts to separate the public from nonorthodox beliefs, Dee may have perceived the Catholic government as having some interest in preserving esoteric knowledge for its own covert use.

In his petition to the queen, Dee lamented the destruction of libraries in England and the accompanying loss of works of antiquity; he hoped that the queen would work to recover and preserve them. Dee warned of a time when all knowledge would be destroyed in the Isles, and proposed that a royal library would rectify this situation and allow Mary to "follow in the footsteps of all the famous and godly princes of old time, and also do like the worthy Governor of Christendom in those days: but far surmounting them all."[56]

Dee's plan met with complete disinterest. When money was not forthcoming, Dee instead continued to build his own collection, traveling England to purchase rare manuscripts on occult subjects. Dee was known to borrow money and pawn glasswork and silver in order to buy more books, doing extensive copying of manuscripts himself and employing a clerk to copy more.[57] He would come to spend £3,000 on his collection, the equivalent of roughly £848,000 or $1,064,000 in 2017.* (Dee remained in severe debt for much of his life.)

For the present, Dee spent his time in Bonner's household studying the works he had already assembled, trying to piece together the vast puzzle of the occult and develop his own synthesis of the traditions he had been immersed in. It was also during this time that he made his first publication, a preface to an ephemeris by the royal astrologer John Field.[58] Despite humiliation, potential torture, and public capitulation to the Catholic orthodoxy, he was not to be deterred from his quest.

Scouring Bacon, Aristotle, Geber, Avicenna, Arnold of Villa Nova, and more, Dee—like so many before and after him—sought to uncover the formula of the philosopher's stone. Yet he would soon go still further, combining occult philosophy with his astronomical, mathematical, and optical studies at Louvain to harness the power of light itself to complete the Great Work of restoring all nature to its original perfection.

---

*All value estimations in this book were calculated on January 27, 2017, using Google Finance, https://www.nationalarchives.gov.uk/currency, and http://inflation.stephenmorley.org.

2

All as Study of All

The shockwaves felt from the Protestant Reformation and Henry VIII's split from Rome had created an apocalyptic climate in Europe—but Protestantism was only one of the belief structures challenging or running parallel to Catholicism. The others were Hermeticism, Neoplatonism, and operative magic—three distinct yet intertwining schools of thought that informed the literate elite's direct quest for divine knowledge, beyond the rote teachings of the Church. Each of these disciplines was a crucial influence on the Renaissance, and together they made up the matrix of assumptions that Dee would inherit from his mentors and that would be fulfilled by his own work.

Hermeticism itself was a long-standing school of philosophy drawn from the study of the *Corpus hermeticum*, the magical texts attributed to the Egyptian priest, king, and philosopher Hermes Trismegistus, believed to be a contemporary and spiritual equal of Moses, which thus formed a source of wisdom on par with the Old Testament itself. Even previous Christian intellectual giants like St. Thomas Aquinas and St. Augustine considered Hermes Trismegistus a pagan prophet and forerunner of Christianity. Trismegistus was almost certainly not a real individual, but a mythological figure that many anonymously ascribed their works to. Primary among these texts is the *Emerald Tablet of Hermes,* a book first appearing in Arabic sometime between the sixth and eighth centuries, and translated into Latin in the twelfth, which contains the root precepts of the entire genre. Hermeticism itself emerged parallel to Christianity and Gnosticism, and evolved over the first millennium; Hermetic texts dating to the third or fourth century were uncovered in the Nag Hammadi codices.[1]

During the fifteenth century, the Florentine philosopher Giovanni Pico della Mirandola, a courtier of the Medicis, synthesized the Hermetic texts with the Hebrew Kabbalah brought to Spain by Sephardic Jews.* Della Mirandola believed that both sources helped validate and elucidate Christianity, and thereby created what came to be known as Christian Cabala, also incorporating the earlier work of Raymond Llull. Another Medici courtier, Marsilio Ficino, introduced Plato into the mix, whose works had been freshly brought to the Italian city-states by the Byzantine scholars who had fled the sack of Constantinople. Together, the two men founded a school of thought now known as Renaissance Neoplatonism—and used their new philosophical tools to quest for the *prisca theologia,* the original, pristine religion delivered to mankind by God in antiquity, and subsequently lost in the ravages of history.[2]

These intellectual streams formed a new, potent revival of Gnostic ideas that would later be converted into a vast philosophy and working system of operative magic by Trithemius and Cornelius Agrippa. While Hermeticism and Renaissance Neoplatonism were theoretical methods of categorizing the universe as a series of nested essences proceeding from God, operative magic aimed to apply this knowledge experimentally, and uncover a working methodology for interacting with and

---

*Beginning in the fourteenth century, Spain's Jewish community became subject to pogroms, with Jews killed, forced to convert, subsequently hunted as heretics by the Spanish Inquisition for *having* converted, and finally expelled from the country—partly out of the belief that forcing the Jews to fully convert was necessary to bring about the Second Coming, even that their failure to do so had provoked God's wrath and caused Spain's many misfortunes, like the Black Death. This widescale persecution of the Jews in Spain was in many ways the model for the Holocaust; many evangelical Christians used similar logic in the twentieth century to rationalize the German genocide of Jews and abstain from pushing for American intervention. See Paris, *The End of Days*; Clark, *Allies for Armageddon.*

Fig. 2.1. Marsilio Ficino, as depicted in Domenico Ghirlandaio, *Portrait of a Man.*

manipulating the universe. This politically perilous approach was exemplified by Agrippa, whose *Three Books of Occult Philosophy* combines the framework of Hermeticism and Renaissance Neoplatonism with the raw techniques of European folk magic and the grimoires of spirit conjuration that had been floating around the European underground over the preceding centuries. The application of the Christian Cabala, with its incorporation of Pseudo-Dionysius and heavy reliance on angels, was thought by advocates of the direct approach to be the key to making operative magic safe and free of demonic influence.[3] As no less than Sir Walter Raleigh once remarked, "The art of magic is the art of worshipping God."[4]

During the medieval era, Western civilization had ordered the universe into the Great Chain of Being, and lamented that man dwelt in a fallen, sublunary state beneath God and his angels. By the Renaissance, thanks to the influence of humanism, daring intellectuals began seeking to reverse this state, and reclimb the chain back to God. Thus, they hoped, they would uncover the *prisca theologia,* and might learn the original language with which God created the world and by which Adam conferred with the angels. They would thereby become *mens adeptus,* enlightened adepts able to reshape the world with the powers of God himself, and reverse the fallen state of the world to its original perfection. Hermeticism, Renaissance Neoplatonism, and operative magic became the methodology by which to attempt this Great Work.

By the sixteenth century, interest in Hermeticism and Neoplatonism was growing among the European intellectual elite. And while Hermetic texts had long been jealously guarded and carefully written in code, the printing press was undoing much of that secrecy, bringing alarming new ideas to receptive minds.[5] Even the arch-iconoclast Martin Luther would

Fig. 2.2. Giovanni Pico della Mirandola. Portrait by Cristofano dell'Altissimo.

see rhetorical importance in the ideas of Hermeticism and alchemy, believing that they offered valuable metaphors about the purification of the soul and the coming day of judgment.[6] In the centuries to come, these ideas would take wider root in the form of Rosicrucianism and speculative Freemasonry.[7] And while operative magic itself would fall out of favor as a serious pursuit, its fundamental approach—that nature can be procedurally manipulated and altered—would evolve into modern science. As late as the eighteenth century, even Isaac Newton was an avid student of the Hermetica, alchemy, Rosicrucianism, and Christian eschatology.[8] (The economist John Maynard Keynes famously described Newton as "the last of the magicians, the last of the Babylonians and Sumerians.")[9]

If the Reformation sought to remove the Catholic Church as a mediator between the individual and God, then Hermeticism, Neoplatonism, and operative magic sought to go one further, and provide models and techniques to give individuals a direct connection to the *source* of scripture. This idea—that with the right techniques, mankind could seek not just to talk to God but find that God talks back, outside of institutional or scriptural bounds, and that this process could be put on an empirical basis—was politically dangerous. While previous mystics like Hildegard of Bingen and St. Teresa of Ávila had recorded direct visionary experiences of God, Christ, and the angels themselves—even, in the case of Hildegard of Bingen, recording a divine alphabet and language she titled *Lingua Ignota* that looks and sounds remarkably like Dee's angelic language[10]—these experiences were confined to the tightly regimented and controlled inner world of the Catholic Holy Orders. To open these teachings to the world was unthinkable.

Yet for the Hermeticist, God existed not just as a far-off entity but, much as Raymond Llull perceived in his vision at Majorca, was reflected in the divine order of the manifest universe itself. If God had created man, nature, and scripture in his image, then deep study of these would reveal the creator, and provide the keys not just of understanding the pattern by which he created existence but even of becoming like him. To use a modern metaphor, if the universe is a computer with its own finely

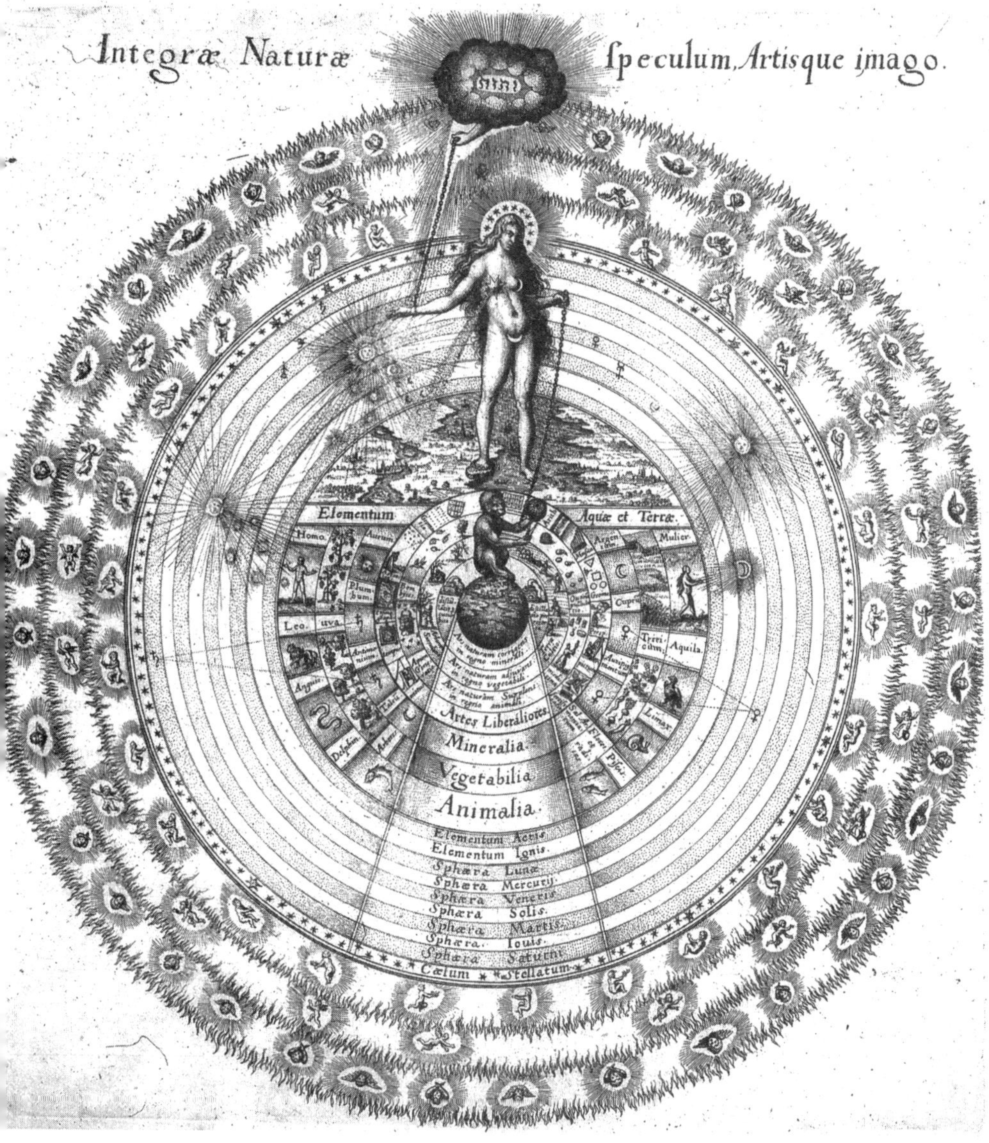

Fig. 2.3. Anima Mundi, the Soul of the World. From Robert Fludd, *Utriusque cosmi maioris scilicet et minoris metaphysica*, 1617.

ordered operating system, file structure, and languages, Hermeticism and Neoplatonism sought to understand the workings of the computer, while operative magic sought to program it.

In this light, Dee's polymathic quest to understand and master so many disparate branches of knowledge no longer seems scattershot but makes sense as a momentous unity, a superscience. Without understanding this, or the overall assumptions of the Hermetic discourse within which Dee labored, his work is incomprehensible. Broadly speaking, these assumptions are:

1. All extant knowledge—scientific, scriptural, and stemming from the observation of nature—is comprehensible as a unified whole and a reflection of the mind of God itself.
2. The universe is holographic—as above, so below. As the universe is a holism, study of representative subsets of the universe can reveal the totality. Likewise, manipulation of representative subsets of the universe can manipulate the totality. This is the primary assumption of operative magic.
3. The eschaton or Second Coming of Christ, the final reversal of mankind's fallen state, is not only at hand but can be accelerated and assisted by human agents who have become illuminated through Hermeticism and even operative magic, and become active participants in the divine plan.

If Hermeticism was concerned with understanding the universe as a total whole, it was equally concerned with understanding the connections between things in the universe, from the loftiest heights of divinity all the way down to the lowest strata of animals, vegetables, and minerals. If the universe is a divine unity, the embodied mind of God, then everything in it must not only be connected but also carry its own internal logic. Hermeticism thus assumes that nature is a language of similarities and connections, and that all aspects of the universe may be sorted based on their essences. It is the study of connections, resemblances, and analogies between aspects of nature. In this, it is much closer to how artists think than modern scientists, as it is concerned with the metaphorical resonances of images and objects within the natural world, and the way in which their contemplation affects the human soul. The Christian Cabala allowed a system for categorizing all of these correspondences, providing a kind of calculus of metaphors. Dee instead sought the Real Cabala of nature—that is, how to read nature itself as an open book, rather than relying on the intermediate symbol set of Hebrew, alchemy, and astrology.

Dee followed the then-popular conception that wisdom proceeded from two books: not just the Book of Scripture (the Bible) but the Book of Nature, which Hermeticism and magic would not only allow him to read, but also repair, restoring existence to the pre-Fall state. This Fall was not even exclusively Christian—for pagans, the Fall represented the descent of mankind from the Golden Age that they sought to reverse within the bounds of their own theology.[11]

Yet if Hermeticism represents the height of Renaissance intellectual culture, how can we reconcile its lofty philosophical holism with the superstition, sorcery, and simply inaccurate prescientific observations that it has inevitably come to us packaged in? (Take, for instance, some of the more ludicrous passages of folk magic contained in Agrippa, including one in which the reader is told that a scorpion sting can be cured by rubbing a mouse on it.)[12]

The twentieth-century philosopher Ken Wilber offers an elegant tool for disentangling this mess that he calls the *pre/trans fallacy*.[13] For Wilber, the prerational magical and mythical modes of thinking, exemplified by folk-magical practices and literalist or fundamentalist interpretations of religion, should rightfully be considered vestiges of the evolution of human consciousness; they are less developed modes of thinking and discourse than the rational, scientific, modern, and post-modern modes of consciousness to come.

For Wilber, postmodernism also represents a crisis point, a flatland that dead-ends in cultural relativism; he proposes that we are currently approaching more integral or holistic cultural modes, for examples of which Wilber points to the Eastern enlightenment traditions of Advaita Vedanta and Vajrayana Buddhism that he encountered during his own spiritual training, which emerged in parallel with the Hermetic tradition, albeit in Asia, and contain broadly analogous models of the universe that are equally entangled with the prerational shamanism of the cultures they emerged from.

Within the frameworks of these traditions and the states of

consciousness they engender, students realize a deep sense of holism, unity, and interconnectedness with everything in the universe—suggesting, perhaps, a Real Cabala in the form of a student's naturally emerging understanding of connectivity. Reality is freshly understood as a divine play of mind or consciousness, and a sense of "divine pride" emerges from the student's understanding his or her nature not only as an expression of the cosmos but, in a sense, containing the entire cosmos.

For Wilber, this postrational state may have commonalities with the prerational state of magical thinking, as in both modes the individuals perceive themselves as having mystical agency on the broader reality. In prerational magical thinking, this agency comes in the form of superstitious ritual, omens, contact with spirits, astrology, hexes, and the inaccurate and pseudoscientific assumptions of magic. In postrational holism, this agency comes from the enlightenment of understanding that the awakened individual is both innately divine and divinely connected to the entirety of existence.

The *pre/trans fallacy* occurs when individuals operating in the rational, scientific stages of intellectual development look at postrational enlightenment states and mistake them for the prerational magical states. To the hardheaded rationalist or materialist, both states represent mumbo jumbo or New Age thinking, which is accurate in the case of prerational magical thinking, but inaccurate in the case of postrational enlightenment states, which incorporate rational, logical, scientific, and even postmodern thought within a wider holism. This new holism reveals an understanding of first the interconnected unity of all existence and finally (for Wilber, a Vajrayana Buddhist), the essential nature of everything as emptiness or *sunyata* (or, in the Qabalah, *Ain Soph*).

While prerational magic and shamanism posit methods of establishing nonlocal connections between phenomenon via sympathetic or contagious ritual, rational science rejects this utterly, seeing magical thinking as a confusion of causation and correlation. However, postrational enlightenment states reestablish a universal network of nonlocal connections, reminding us that there is no need for ritualistic creation of connection because everything in the universe is *already* connected (as in the Vedic metaphor of Indra's Net). Vajrayana Buddhism—which for Wilber, at least, represents the high register of postrational consciousness—goes further by stating that existence is nothing *but* connection, called *pratītyasamutpāda* or "dependent arising," and that phenomena do not possess essences in and of themselves outside of their relations to other phenomena. Dee would describe a similar model of universal interconnectedness in his early text *Propaedeumata aphoristica,* as described in the following chapter.

While Wilber is primarily concerned with Eastern mysticism, Hermeticism represents, or can represent, an equally postrationally enlightened tradition that is directly sourced within Western culture. While Hinduism and Buddhism have their own terminology for enlightenment, Trithemius and Agrippa spoke of a *mens adeptus,* "adept mind," an alchemist who had attained to the philosopher's stone of divine awareness, whose soul had been purified, who was able to understand all of existence nondually, and who was therefore able to receive and comprehend the doings of God and his angels, and the secrets of the universe, past, present, and future.[14] Such a state was not easily accomplished, nor would all who seek it necessarily find it. Yet the rare few who did attain could shape the course of history—history might, in fact, depend on advancement by such individuals.[15] (See the final chapter, "The Last Jerusalem," for a full summary of this "adept mind.")

Dee certainly exemplifies this rare individual. His early works, including the *Propaedeumata aphoristica,* the *Monas hieroglyphica,* and his preface to Euclid's *Elements,* distill the pristine essence of Hermetic holism, universal interconnection, and the enlightened outlook of the *mens adeptus.* From here he proceeded to achieving many of the stated goals of the Hermetic tradition, including the first steps toward the establishment of the New Jerusalem via prompting English colonization of North America and, during the angelic conversations, recovering the *prisca theologica,* the original language and the Real Cabala.

Yet even with Dee, the boundaries were not so clear-cut: both Dee and his scryer Kelly would occasionally support themselves by various uses of folk magic, including using occult methods to search for buried treasure or promising to alchemically turn lead into gold. During the scrying sessions, the angels themselves made no secret of their disdain for prerational grimoire magic, blatantly calling it either fraudulent or demonic. At other times, however, the angels instructed Dee and Kelly in the production of folk cures and the art of operative alchemy. Yet even in these instances, the attitude of the angels is that humanity's fumbling attempts at magic are crude parodies of the innate modes of action of God and the angels themselves.

"If scholars today are confused about the precise nature of magic in the early modern period, they are in good company," writes Deborah Harkness. "It is clear that Dee and his contemporaries were not entirely sure either, and were more comfortable with an identity as a natural philosopher than they were with that of a magician."[16]

Yet if the methods were often confused—Dee spent much of his time with the angels asking for clarification on what he had already learned, for instance—the goal was clear. The Great Work that Dee had set out to fulfill was nothing short of apocalyptic—in the true sense, not of destruction, but of the restitution of nature itself: the enlightenment, through light, of all of Creation. It was the alchemical change of lead, the fallen state of mankind, to gold, the spiritual purity of man before the Fall, the enlightened and divine mankind symbolized by Adam Kadmon (as described in the Kabbalah of Rabbi Isaac Luria, a contemporary of Dee).

For the Hermetic initiate—then as now—this is not mere metaphor, but daily reality. Dee had only to walk through the streets of London to see drunkenness, madness, poverty, misery, and, during Mary's reign, the religiously sanctioned torture of heretics and the totalitarian domination of the country by a brutish and very *un*enlightened Church regime. Similarly, the Hermetic philosopher of our modern world need only walk through the streets of their own town to see more modern versions of the same old human misery. The dreamer, the magician, the artist of any time and place carries within them a burning vision, a longing, and a conviction that humanity can embrace the divine side of its nature instead of the animal, to move up the Great Chain instead of down. Yet the potential of humanity, considered side by side with mankind as it currently is, becomes almost impossible to reconcile. And so begins the great quest, the Great Work of alchemy, the work of redeeming at least the individual alchemist so that they may spread their enlightenment to others, that in one halcyon instant to come all of existence may be redeemed.

3

The Light of the World

Hermeticism, Renaissance Neoplatonism, and the theory of operative magic were the intellectual currents Dee had immersed himself in beyond his already comprehensive scientific and mathematical studies. In the 1550s, Dee began to synthesize what he had learned, and began to produce his own original works that drew together his immensely broad studies.

In extrapolating the ideas and methods of Roger Bacon, Agrippa, and others, Dee had isolated the first key to the Great Work. From these sources, he had learned the doctrine that subtle forces emanate from all things in nature; for instance, that the planets and stars exercise subtle influence upon events and the character of individuals, which is the theoretical basis of astrology. All things, in the Hermetic worldview, expressed their energy or vibration outward, and impressed it on the objects around them. Not content to just assume the existence of such "rays" of influence, Dee looked to apply his vast astronomical, mathematical, and optical knowledge to observing and manipulating these rays.

What Dee was proposing was that, just as the telescope would one day show us the distant planets and stars, and the microscope would one day show us the hidden world of microscopic objects, optics might *also* allow us to tangibly see the hidden spiritual forces of reality. Instead of a telescope or microscope, Dee used a scrying ball as his instrument. Within this device—which survives in popular culture as the crystal ball of fortune-tellers—Dee hoped to study the stellar rays of creation, in direct or indirect sunlight, within precise astrological timings and ritual parameters.

Instrumental to Dee's theories was the tract *On the Stellar Rays* by the Muslim Hermeticist Abu Yūsuf Ya'qūb ibn 'Ishāq aṣ-Ṣabbāḥ al-Kindī, who Bacon thought second only to Ptolemy in his knowledge of optics.[1] Al-Kindī had written not only of the effects of the light emitting from the stars and planets upon consciousness, but the rays of will and imagination emanating from individual human beings. For al-Kindī, it was the stellar rays that formed the destinies of men, *not*

Fig. 3.1. Frontispiece to John Dee, *Propaedeumata aphoristica,* featuring the Hieroglyphic Monad and Tetragrammaton.

acts of will, even if magically directed. The rarest of men, however, could overcome their mortal bondage by working *with* the rays of light emitting from the stars.[2]

This idea fired Dee's imagination, as it would allow him to merge his technical mastery of optics and his metaphysical study into the beginnings of what he hoped could be a hard science. The product of Dee's investigation is 1558's *Propaedeumata aphoristica,* a treatise that mathematically and scientifically examines the astrological influences on Earth—at a time when astrology was in decline in England, and ephemerides had to be imported.[3] Dee presented it as the fruit of his previous ten years of "Outlandish & Homish studies and Exercises Philosophicall."[4] It is likely that Dee, horrified by his treatment under Mary's regime and probably thinking back to the offers of employment in France that he had turned down (only to be imprisoned and tortured in his home country), published the *Propaedeumata* with an eye toward seeking new benefactors abroad, and establishing himself not only as a mathematics teacher but as a philosopher. Dee dedicated the tract to Mercator.

In the *Propaedeumata,* a youthful and infectiously enthusiastic Dee outlines his cosmological view, which resonates greatly with al-Kindī. For Dee, all things in the universe emit rays in all directions according to their nature; these rays have different effects based on what they contact, but all things in the universe are simultaneously affecting all other things. These rays have influence not only upon the material world, but upon the soul, as in astrology; the universe is therefore made up of both elemental and celestial influences.

By studying the influence of the celestial rays on the sublunary, elemental world, Dee sought to understand the subtle machinery by which God, the Monad, manifests the Creation. Light had been the first creation of God—*fiat lux,* "let there be light"—therefore, as Bacon had suggested, understanding light would be the key to understanding everything.[5]

Unspoken but implied is that operative magic such as Agrippa's may be used to harness such rays: "In actual truth," says Dee, "wonderful changes may be produced by us in natural things if we force nature artfully."[6] Through the proper use of optics, the celestial rays might be concentrated, manipulated, or even stored, producing focused effects far beyond what already occurred in nature. Rays harnessed in this way, Dee later mused, might even assist in alchemy.

"If you were skilled in 'catoptrics,'" Dee explains in the *Propaedeumata*—catoptrics is the use of mirrors—"you would be able, by art, to imprint the rays of any star much more strongly upon any matter subjected to it than nature itself does."[7]

By gaining such insight into the system of the world, and its natural harmonies and antipathies, Dee suspected that the natural philosopher or magician could come to participate in nature as a cocreator. This would fulfill the goal of Hermeticism, that through study, experiment, piety, and observation of nature, a natural philosopher could understand the system of reality and how God perpetually manifests the universe—that is, they could become initiated. Once this understanding was gained—and *only* when it was gained—could the magician develop the wisdom necessary to work with the system and cocreate alongside nature and God.

Such a "pure" magic relied not on trance, spirit conjuration, or anything recognizable as archaic shamanism or ham-fisted grimoire magic; rather, it consisted of the physical manipulation of light. Like Agrippa, Dee sought to work with the subtle forces of nature, but uniquely aimed to replace superstitious folk magic and ritual incantations with frontline optical technology and mathematics.[8] This approach discarded the need for intervention by spirits, thereby cleanly avoiding the charges of demonism that had dogged Bacon, and that Dee sought to deflect from further harming his own career.[9] Dee's synthesis of astrology, mathematics, and optics formulated a remarkably sophisticated operative approach to magic, though the assumptions upon which it rests have long since been discarded by science—for instance, that the stars and planets influence human beings or events.

Magic was only tangential to the *Propaedeumata,* and is mentioned as only one potential application of Dee's theories. It was "astral" physics itself that Dee was most interested in, rather than its practical application. His goal in the *Propaedeumata* was to reform astrology along mathematical lines, and import a higher level of scientific understanding of astrology to England, where it remained a neglected art, from the Continent. Dee's mentors at Louvain had assessed astrology with as much intellectual rigor as any other study, and Dee longed to kindle interest in the subject at home. For Dee, the *Propaedeumata* was not an occult work, but a summation of his learning in Europe, fully in line with Aristotelian thought. In looking backward to Bacon and al-Kindī, Dee was also working outside the usual bounds of academic discourse, and along antiquated lines—even for his own time period. Yet despite their reliance on older works, Dee's theories are unique, standing apart from any purely Neoplatonic or Hermetic strain of philosophy.[10]

Dee proposes in the *Propaedeumata* that the universe is created by God from nothing, contrary to any rational or natural law, meaning that the universe can never cease to exist except by God's agency. However, the Creation itself *is* governed by rational and natural law, without exception, meaning that no supernatural agency is possible within nature. Within the universe, all is interrelated, and everything within nature influences everything else by means of rays. The universe and all of its perfect harmony and regularity of its stars and planets, according to Dee, is most like a lyre.[11] Natural philosophers could play this lyre, working with nature's laws to achieve effects that the less educated might perceive as magic.

For the sixteenth century, this is a remarkably *non*superstitious view of the universe, in which it is portrayed as a vast machine. Though Dee's magical views did not hold up, his portrayal of a mechanistic and ordered universe was a forerunner of works to come, like Newton's *Principia mathematica*. Dee was even aware of the already circulating idea that objects of different weight fall at the same speed, generally attributed to the much later work of Galileo.[12] His theories are also similar to the Buddhist doctrine of "dependent arising," or even late twentieth-century chaos theory.

Dee called his new optical science "archemastery," and believed it would crown all knowledge. Through his methods, the past and future could be divined, visions induced, angels or spirits evoked, and spiritual ecstasy induced in the experimenter. Dee even thought that the harnessing of subtle rays, if combined with the healing art of the physician and the expressing medium of music, could move the world—a knowledge he considered too potentially unsafe to elaborate for the general public in anything other than broad hints.[13]

Language, too, could operate upon nature through its own subtle rays. Like Postel and Bacon, Dee thought the forces of creation were encoded into Hebrew, although even Hebrew would be an echo of the hypothesized primal language. Following al-Kindī, Roger Bacon had already suggested that words themselves could carry potent occult rays, especially if conveying the soul of the speaker or writer, or suitably charged with the right astrological influences. Parallels could be drawn with the ancient Vedic practice of mantra, the rune songs of pre-Christian Europe, or the mass media and neuro-linguistic programming to come in the future.

Crystal gazing and angel scrying, then widely practiced if not well respected in England, had already appealed to Dee as a tool for political espionage, as well as a source of learning beyond the realms of men. The use of scrying glasses was not new; Paracelsus had recommended contacting spirits by scrying into shining black coal, though he warned that such spirits almost invariably lied. The twelfth-century alchemist Artephius had spoken of the *ars sintrillia,* the use of mirrors to induce trance. Scrying even appears in Genesis 44, in which Joseph speaks of his master's silver scrying chalice; divination is later condemned in 2 Kings 21. The level of scientific rigor Dee brought to scrying, however, was new. Yet Dee's work was theoretical at this point—he would not begin actively exploring scrying until the late 1570s.[14]

For now, Dee was synthesizing his student learning and formulating the basic theories that would occupy his adult study. Yet Dee's astrological theories, even if elegant and inspiring, proved unworkable at this stage; after publication, he was even accused of plagiarizing the twelfth-century Italian philosopher Urso of Calabria.[15] They would not be accepted by later science—nor, surprisingly, would they even be explored by later occultural movements.

Nineteenth- and twentieth-century proponents of occultism were concerned with subjective experience, rather than objective science—

MAHOMET *receives his Law by Inspiration*.

APPOLONI. TYANEUS *in* DOMITIANS *tyme*

EDW: Kelly *Prophet or Seer to D.ͬ Dee*.

Roger Bacon *an English man*.

PARACELSUS *Receits from the Inspiration of Spirits*.

D.ͬ Dee *avoucheth his Stone is brought by Angelicall Ministry*.

Fran: Cleyn Invent

Fig. 3.2. The Order of the Inspiritui. From Méric Casaubon, *A True & Faithful Relation*.

relying on symbols, trance states, suggestion, and drugs to produce profound shifts in the internal consciousness of individuals or groups. Since the end of the nineteenth century, Western culture has relegated magic to the subjective realms of art and psychotherapy, justifying the periodic small outbreaks of magic by suggesting that occult ideas may be inspiring or meaningful in a kind of metaphorical way, with buzz phrases like "Jungian archetypes" used by latter-day adherents of the occult to save themselves from the potential embarrassment of being thought to hold literal stock in ideas now considered invalid by the mainstream. Such modern forms of "magic" have far more to do with psychotheater and bluff than rational attempts to analyze objective phenomena.

Following William James, it was Aleister Crowley, not Carl Jung, who began the trend of "psychologizing away" occult practices— Crowley's 1903 essay "The Initiated Interpretation of Ceremonial Magic," printed in the Crowley/Mathers edition of *The Lesser Key of Solomon,* suggests that rituals are ways of unlocking nonconscious parts of one's own mind. Crowley, an erudite and hyperrational student of the occult, was inspired by the "all is mind" theories of Bishop Berkeley and Theravada Buddhism, as well as the many experiments with ceremonial magic, yoga, and drugs he had undertaken in his twenties with his mentor Allan Bennett. Crowley's essay, published when he was twenty-eight or twenty-nine, at a time when he had already garnered vast experience with practical occultism but had moved on to Buddhism, takes a reductionist sword to magic, explaining that "the spirits of the *Goetia* are portions of the human brain."[16] Crowley was later to recant this opinion; his *Magick Without Tears,* written in the 1940s, argues in no small terms for the objective existence of spirits and noncorporeal intelligences such as the ones Dee was later to contact. According to the older Crowley, such beings are not only real, but contact with them may be the only chance for humanity to evolve out of the brutal conditions Crowley saw all around him as Europe passed through the death machinery of World War II.[17] (On the other hand, Crowley often couldn't help himself from hinting that the publication of *The Book of the Law* had *caused* both world wars.)

Since operative magic has been discarded by mainstream science, those who wish to preserve its practice have had to look for loopholes in the cultural discourse within which magical practices may maintain continuity of existence. Following Crowley and Jung, that loophole has been the psychologizing of magic, which reduces it to something between art therapy and an encounter group exercise. Others have sought to use pseudoscientific claims or overenthusiastic, often scientifically illiterate interpretations of quantum physics, particularly when promoting products within the sizeable New Age marketplace—for instance, mangling wave-particle duality experiments to suggest that consciousness or even belief itself creates reality, or that quantum entanglement proves the efficacy of sorcery, interpretations that amount to little more than wishful thinking (a phenomenon that the noted skeptic Dr. Steven Novella refers to as "quantum woo").[18]

Yet all of this was to come later. For this reason, it is remarkable to look at Dee's original occult theories in context—there is no psychologizing here, no appeal to subjectivity. Dee was literally proposing that natural philosophers experiment with the divine characteristics of light, and that through its use they would shape nature.

In the same year he wrote the *Propaedeumata,* Dee also composed *De speculis comburentibus,* a study of geometry, which would be followed by a 1559 manuscript on mathematics entitled *Tyrocinium mathematicum,* likely used to teach his ward, Thomas Digges.[19]

Dee would next set to work on the Cabala, and propose to the world a skeleton key of the mysteries, by elaborating the meaning of the Hieroglyphic Monad, a symbol that Dee included in the *Propaedeumata* without explication; culturally, he would work to get England caught up with the higher standard of learning he had enjoyed on the Continent. Yet for the remainder of Mary's reign, Dee kept his affairs cloaked in secrecy, terrified of being taken back to the Tower dungeon should the slightest activity be misinterpreted. His writing during this time, however, was prolific, covering astronomy, optics, and technical works on mechanics, astronomical instruments, and a pulley and cog system for moving heavy weights that would gain wide popular use later in the century.

In the end, Dee was saved by most unforeseen circumstances: Mary's pregnancy turned out to be an elaborate ruse, albeit a ruse that had nearly precipitated a war. When the pregnancy evaporated, Elizabeth was accepted as next in line for the throne, and the furor over Dee's treasonous conjuring was simply lost in the shuffle.

4

The Elizabethan Ascension

On May 1558, the childless Mary's health began to fail, likely due to ovarian cysts or uterine cancer;[1] she died on November 17 of the same year, during an influenza epidemic in which Dee also fell ill and was expected to die. Upon Mary's death, Elizabeth became her begrudgingly accepted successor, the final Catholic hold on England vanished, and the Anglican Elizabeth ascended to the throne, marking the opening of one of the most culturally and militarily expansive periods of English history. Elizabeth would soon implement Dee's work in naval strategy and optics to transition England into an empire. Dee would later come to compare himself and Elizabeth to Merlin and King Arthur, respectively—even suggesting that they were the reincarnations of that legendary syzygy.

Elizabeth, though nominally a Protestant, had a coldly *realpolitik* view of faith, seeing religions as tools of the state in keeping social order. While she made shows of adherence to the new Anglican Church publicly, she had little time for religious convention or dogma privately. Instead, she quietly maintained an interest in Hermeticism and alchemy, the latter primarily for reasons of finances and health. The Anglican Church, she hoped, would at least somewhat help quell conflict under her regime. By rejecting Rome's control, it would satisfy Protestants, and by holding to Rome's rituals, she hoped, it would satisfy Catholics.

Fig. 4.1. Queen Elizabeth I.
Portrait attributed to Nicholas Hilliard, circa 1573–75.

Like her later dangling of her "virginity" to the monarchs of Europe, she held out her uncertain religious affiliations to the public as a tactic of manipulation and control.[2]

Yet despite Elizabeth's own cold view of religion, her government was indeed a Protestant one, and on that front, Dee had amends to make. However brilliant Dee was, he also had a keen awareness that he was always one slip or accusation away from torture on the rack or death at the stake, and as such had consistently acted to save his own skin by swearing allegiance to whoever happened to be in power at the time, flip-flopping between Protestantism and Catholicism. Dee, of course, was neither fully Protestant or Catholic, but Hermetic. Nevertheless, Dee had deliberately sworn allegiance to Mary, and then been passed to the Catholic Bishop Bonner, after being held in the Tower of London.

While Dee's personal religious beliefs remained consistent, the religious turbulence of his period and his own efforts to maintain his own scholarly career meant that Dee often had to play whatever social game was in effect at the time—and the game was constantly changing. Dee's early career, writes György Szőnyi, "was characterized by a deeply religious, but denominationally neutral, interconfessionalist attitude, a hallmark of many humanists . . . if one examines the particular doctrinal beliefs of the humanists, one can see neither uniformity nor a consequent attachment to one set of religious dogmas. One reason for this flexibility may be found in their scholarly self-assuredness, according to which they were inclined to think that narrowly defined rules and beliefs were for the general populace but not for the select few of intellectuals." Such intellectuals, Szőnyi explains, considered themselves free to navigate through belief structures, just as they navigated court politics—including by syncretizing Christian and pagan beliefs in their search for more light. Such a cavalier attitude to the boundaries of faith was not always appreciated.[3]

Yet despite the problem of Dee's shifting allegiances, he was considered too useful to dispense with, and the context of his hasty alliance with Bonner to save his own life understood. Dee already had a preexisting relationship with Elizabeth, and evangelical leanings. Most importantly, his intelligence, connections, and magical ability made him a valuable component of Elizabeth's arsenal, far too knowledgeable to let slip into Catholic control.

Elizabeth was inheriting a bankrupt country, with enemies infesting her court and the wolves of Spain and Rome at the door. Domestically, the idea that a woman could rule England was not met without resistance—John Calvin even suggested that Elizabeth's coronation was a breach of the natural order and a punishment from God.[4] In addition, England was still between two-thirds and three-fourths Catholic; only England's southern ports and towns, including London, held fast as Protestant strongholds.[5] Elizabeth would need all the help she could get. Consequently, Dee was introduced at court by Elizabeth's close companion Robert Dudley and the Earl of Pembroke; his first assignment was casting a horoscope for the already-selected date of Elizabeth's coronation.[6] Like spymaster Francis Walsingham, John Dee could provide an advantage that could help make the difference between the queen's reign continuing and a Spanish conquest.

In 1994, the CIA described Elizabethan intelligence at this time "as a cold war practice by interventionists. The process gained its impetus from a sense of impending engagement or conflict with foreign states and a desire to be well prepared for that battle . . . [particularly] with Spain and the ongoing conquest of Ireland."[7]

It was the beginning of what might be described as an occult cold war. Along with Elizabeth's succession, France had already been pushing the visions of its own court wizard, the Roman Catholic Nostradamus, who had foreseen failure for Elizabeth's religious reforms. The French prophecies anticipated (or, more likely, encouraged) widespread civil revolt against the new administration.[8]

The incoming Elizabethan court had another magical threat to contend with: the alchemist, conjuror, and con man John Prestall, who would become Dee's long-running magical nemesis. On November 17, 1558, Prestall was arrested along with Anthony Fortescue and Thomas Kele for conjuring, just as Dee himself had been only a few years earlier. This would not be the last time that Elizabeth heard from Prestall; the Catholic conspirator would be arrested again in 1562 for summoning spirits and casting horoscopes against Elizabeth, and continue to rear his head over the next three decades, often coming into direct magical conflict with Dee.[9]

Whereas Protestants had long suffered under Mary's regime, now it was Catholics who would face persecution and be driven underground. Over the coming decades, they would resort to a number of conspiracies to restore Catholic power (of which Guy Fawkes's 1605 Gunpowder Plot is the most famous). Magic was, perhaps ironically, one of the methods of conspiracy, and Prestall was frequently tapped for aggressive conjuring.* Yet while he was employed by Catholics, Prestall himself supported no cause but his own financial gain and accumulation of power. He was the archetypal "cunning man," occult grifter, or low sorcerer—a common profession in Elizabethan England, which Dee's later associates Barnabas Saul and Edward Kelly would also hail from.

Elizabeth's life was in danger from the time of her birth, exponentially so when she ascended to the throne, and assassination could come by either physical *or* spiritual means. Magical threats had to be quashed with as much ferocity as physical ones, and in such an environment of paranoia, nothing could be dismissed as coincidence—particularly when sorcery, which operates by the engineering of coincidence, was involved. To further complicate matters, Elizabeth's administration was too financially strapped to effectively suppress Catholicism in the country.[10] This meant that the threat of assassination could never be fully circumvented, making John Dee's services in protecting against magical attack as critical as Walsingham's in espionage.

While magical specialists like Dee and Prestall stand out as exceptionally colorful characters, they were by no means unique in their belief in and use of magic. Magic formed the context of Elizabeth's world, and it is probable that not only Catholics used magicians for assassina-

---

*Operative magic has routinely played a role in statecraft and revolution—among numerous other examples are the Voudon-initiated 1791 Haitian Revolution, Padmasambhava's eighth-century magical conquest of Tibet, Rasputin's role in Nicholas II's court, Fidel Castro's reliance on Santeria for protection from the United States, and many more. More recently, witness Vladimir Putin's employment of the right-wing occultist Aleksandr Dugin or the explosive 2016 scandal in which South Korean president Park Geun-hye was revealed to be relying on the shamanic adviser Choi Soon-sil, even to the point of being a political puppet.

tion and to gain astrological knowledge of the future, but that much of Elizabeth's court did as well. Just as Dee's occult activities were later dismissed and whitewashed out of history, so were the occult activities of Elizabeth's courtiers, who often employed the aid of conjurors to covertly achieve their social and political objectives, rather than getting their own hands dirty.[11] Sorcery (as opposed to Dee's later high magical explorations of God's architecture) is fundamentally about power, stripped of any kind of moral considerations. In this, it often makes comfortable bedfellows with politics, and with those who seek to take or maintain power by any means necessary—using tactics that today might be called psyops or psychological warfare. In such an environment, gutter-level occult warfare may have taken up far more time than the romance of high espionage and statecraft. Dee and Prestall were not unique in their use of sorcery; they simply have the benefit of being remembered by history.

Within a month of Dee's being recommended to Elizabeth by Dudley, he had been taken fully into Her Majesty's service; one of his first acts was to cast the horoscope for Elizabeth's (already-chosen) coronation day, with preventing occult calamity foremost in mind. Dee's horoscope (unlike, of course, Nostradamus's predictions) foretold a long and healthy reign for the new queen.

Why was the casting of horoscopes, or "calculating," seen as so contentious and even dangerous? Astrology, like sorcery, is about *defining the narrative of reality.* Considering astrology even from a purely propaganda angle, the power to guide reality in any way other than that sanctioned by the state is a precarious business, especially when prophecies often have a way of becoming self-fulfilling. For instance, Nostradamus's prediction of Elizabeth's fall could have caused fear and distrust in the population, undermining Elizabeth's actual power to command. To the Elizabethan mind, there was little difference between divining the meanings of the stars and controlling them—and, in truth, there *is* little difference, because astrology operates in the realm not of actual observed phenomena but of the human mind and the meanings it attaches to observed events. Magicians, astrologers, and prophets can often *appear* to have changed objective reality, when all that has truly changed is the subjective way in which events are being perceived, a skillful manipulation of confirmation bias.*

This made Dee useful both offensively and defensively; with royal support, Dee was soon considered one of the most learned men in England, and certainly had the largest library—his private collection of manuscripts at Mortlake was much more substantial than the collections at both Oxford and Cambridge. (To briefly note how much our access to information has increased in the past several centuries, consider that during Dee's life, Cambridge possessed only 451 books and manuscripts; Oxford, 379. Dee probably had about 2,000 books and 198 manuscripts at Mortlake, though he later claimed he had owned 4,000 in total before his library was ransacked.)[12]

Mortlake soon bustled with activity, becoming an informal scientific academy for the country, open to scholars and engineers; Elizabeth would regularly ride to Mortlake to visit Dee and his stacks. Dee's network of contacts continued to encompass scientists, intellectuals, and foreign courtiers from across the British Isles and Europe. He kept company with many of the era's leading lights, including the explorers Sir Walter Raleigh and Francis Drake, Abraham Ortelius (creator of the atlas), Elizabeth's spymaster Francis Walsingham, and the astronomer and alchemist Tycho Brahe, among many others. Dee likely used this network to gather intelligence for Elizabeth—Dee, who also aided in the creation of the British intelligence service, signed some of his correspondence "007."[13]

---

*Today, this manipulation of reality is performed by government spin doctors like the cognitive linguist and Democratic Party apparatchik George Lakoff or the Republican political consultant and "public opinion guru" Frank Luntz, who call their dark art "reframing," following the conventions of neuro-linguistic programming, rather than what it is—a form of sorcery. Yet even the traditionally occult approach has not fully faded. Witness, during World War II, Rudolf Hess's reliance on horoscopes for making military decisions; Ian Fleming, while working for British Naval Intelligence, contracted Aleister Crowley to forge horoscopes that would lead Hess to making erratic decisions. The plan was never brought to fruition; a bit of Crowley brushed off on Fleming, however, as he would give his postwar creation James Bond the code number 007, after John Dee's own number in Elizabeth's secret service, while Bond's nemesis Blofeld, head of SPECTRE, would be substantially based on Crowley himself. See Spence, *Secret Agent 666.*

Despite the importance of Dee's new role at court, he was exceedingly poorly compensated. Elizabeth initially promised Dee that she would double his payment under Edward, stating "where my brother hath given him a crowne, I will give him a noble,"[14] yet this probably never came to pass. If this was, indeed, all that Dee was compensated, it must have seemed a painful humiliation in the light of his loyal refusal of court positions on the Continent, and all that he had already suffered upon returning to his home country. Dee may have been important to Elizabeth, but he wasn't all *that* important in the grand scheme of things, and was clearly far down on the list of courtiers expecting government positions. In addition, his prior ties to Bonner, missing clerical training, association with the dark arts, and even his winged beetle stunt while still a student made Dee unwelcome, no matter how hard he fought for attention and court favor.[15]

Consequently, Dee had to take a second job as the rector of St. Swithin Church, Leadenham, in Lincolnshire, over 120 miles north of London, where he spent the next two years. This appointment was only a consolation after he had been denied the mastership of St. Catherine's Hospital in London; Elizabeth had nominated him for St. Catherine's herself, but the appointment had been blocked by court politics. Once it became clear that Elizabeth's promised funding would never manifest, Dee departed back to the Continent in order to scour libraries for information on his newest interest: Kabbalah. His mind had also turned to once again seeking Continental patronage. Dee carried with him only £20, the equivalent of about £4,800 or $6,000 in 2017—though poor, he was determined to continue his quest, writing to William Cecil (first Baron Burghley, then secretary of state, and Elizabeth's chief adviser, who would regularly be in an authority and supervisory role over Dee) that in his pursuit of learning "my flesh, blood and bones should make the merchandise, if the case so required."[16]

Despite Dee's minimal recorded pay, it is possible to speculate that some of his compensation may have been *sub rosa*. Dee was an intelligence agent, frequently on trips abroad, and furthermore, was sitting on the largest collection of information in the country. Since many of his activities were classified, funding would have been classified as well.

Fig. 4.2. William Cecil, 1st Baron Burghley. Portrait by anonymous English School artist from the early seventeenth century.

Dee was also often compensated in books or other favors for successful intelligence work, such as uncovering a network of disloyal agents set up by the Duke of Norfolk that passed secret messages between each other in bottles of wine.[17] Yet even secret payments, if there were any, must not have been substantial—after all, even Walsingham, Elizabeth's spymaster and the father of British intelligence, died in debt after having self-financed much of his own work when Elizabeth's funding ran short.[18] To rectify its financial situation, Elizabeth's administration would shortly be sinking funds into a mad quest to unlock the secrets of alchemy. This too would prove fruitless. In the end, it was not alchemy that would so spectacularly bring England out of poverty, but John Dee's later plans for building a naval empire. Yet even if Dee was not paid well, he was still owned. From the moment he entered the employ of the Crown, if not before, Dee had become a resident of the shadow world, the lunar court of occultists and intelligence agents. Like the occult, intelligence work requires supreme secrecy, heavy cryptography, and the erasing of the personal identity—and in Dee's time, slips on either the intelligence or occult front would have been punishable by death.

At Antwerp, in February 1563, Dee made a critical discovery: a copy of Trithemius's three-volume *Steganographia,* a fearsome manuscript that held the secrets of conjuring angels and demons, which was lent to him by a Hungarian nobleman.[19] Under a time limit, Dee labored day and night to make a hand copy.

Trithemius, a German Benedictine abbot, humanist, adviser of emperors, cryptographer, lexicographer, chronicler, and magician who died in 1516, had been the mentor not only of Paracelsus but of Cornelius Agrippa, whose *Three Books of Occult Philosophy* drawn from Trithemius's work—became the central text of Western occultism, exerting a heavy influence even into the twentieth and twenty-first centuries, notably over Aleister Crowley[20] and Austin Osman Spare.[21] Trithemius's 1518 *Polygraphia* would also become a foundational text of modern cryptography, following on from the earlier work of Roger Bacon.[22]

The *Steganographia* was at least apparently concerned with using spirits for long-distance communication, and with sending telepathic messages that could be received within twenty-four hours—the political importance of which, obviously, was immense. After precise astrological calculations, an operator was to write a message on a piece of paper and invoke angelic couriers to read the text; a receiver performed a similar ritual and was supposed to receive the contents of the message on their end. Such occult devices, were they found in the hands of Catholic fifth columnists or even commoners, would be grounds for imprisonment, torture, or execution. But in the hands of the state, grimoires became jealously guarded troves of technological secrets. Dee excitedly wrote of his find to Cecil, who was sufficiently impressed to lend Dee the support and funds to continue his quest until June 1564.[23]

The *Steganographia* contains extensive sections on the ranking and order of spirits, associating them with directions, times, planets, and constellations—the template from which the tables of correspondences that litter modern books on magic are drawn. Invocations to these spirits fill the *Steganographia*'s pages. Like Dee, Trithemius would rebuke accusations of demonism by stating that his magic was a pure, spiritual, religious quest for divine knowledge;[24] also like Dee, he would state that

Fig. 4.3. Detail of tomb relief of Johannes Trithemius, Neumünster, Schleswig-Holstein, Germany, c. 1516.

the universe was ruled by numbers, manifesting from unity to trinity to the tenfold Pythagorean tetractys.[25]

There was only one problem—the *Steganographia* and its occult tables are largely cryptography. In 1606, the *Steganographia* was fully published (to the ire of the Church, which placed it on its list of prohibited books, where it would remain for *three centuries,* until 1900),[26] along with the *Clavis* or key to its contents, which revealed the code for the first two of its three books, showing that they were not about magic at all. The third book remained encrypted until it was solved by two researchers working independently, without knowledge of each other—in 1996 by Thomas Ernst, a professor of German in Pittsburgh, and in 1998 by Jim Reeds, a mathematician at AT&T Labs in New Jersey. Both cracked the *Steganographia* cypher, demonstrating that the third book of the *Steganographia* is cryptography masked as tables for angelic summoning.[27]

Despite all this, the meaning of the *Steganographia* remains unclear: even when deciphered, the resultant plain text is still unintelligible. For scholars, however, the fact that the manuscript is in code is enough to dispel its worth as an actual occult text. As magic, Cabala, and alchemy are themselves codes for conveying complex meaning between initiates (so-called twilight language, which cannot be read by enemies or the profane), and magicians are almost invariably concerned with cryptography, it is odd that scholars would consider the *Steganographia* an either/or problem. Just because it contains cryptography does not rule out the book also containing magic—in fact, nearly all works of magic may be said to include some form of cryptography.

Large sections of the book are similar to (or possibly copied from) the scattered manuscripts that would become *The Lesser Key of Solomon,* a text on angelic and demonic evocation; other sections are indeed pure cryptography disguised as tables of astrological information. Yet if the cryptographic messages are meant for espionage, it makes little sense that they would be hidden in a tract on demonic conjuration that brought enough attention to Trithemius to destroy his career. Occult writer Joel Biroco speculated in 2002 that the *Steganographia* may have been a series of nested codes, with a further encoded layer of occult information hidden underneath the first enciphered layer. In this way, the first encoded section could serve as plausible deniability, a way for Trithemius to state that the document was only cryptography were he caught. Biroco cites Trithemius's own statement in the third book of the *Steganographia:* "This I did that to men of learning and men deeply engaged in the study of magic, it might, by the Grace of God, be in some degree intelligible, while on the other hand, to the thick-skinned turnip-eater it might for all time remain a hidden secret, and be to their dull intellects a sealed book forever."[28]

The *Steganographia* may have held such value for Dee because the young scholar hoped it would contain the secrets of both magic *and* cryptography—which may also explain Cecil's excitement and quick dispensing of further funds.[29] The seventeenth-century natural philosopher Robert Hooke (one of the founders of the Royal Society) believed that Dee used the *Steganographia* to develop cryptographic codes for use between courtiers and even with Elizabeth.[30]

If the *Steganographia* was merely a text of cryptography, that's not how Dee reacted to his discovery; he wrote to Cecil that the book was an initiated work treating of "formal numbers," "mystic weights," and "divine measures," and "the most precyous juell that I have yet of other mens travailes recovered." By God's grace and his own initiated wisdom, Dee assured Cecil, he would soon decipher its occult secrets.[31]

Dee's study of the *Steganographia,* combined with his previous intellectual synthesis in the *Propaedeumata* and his new obsession with the Kabbalah would result in his 1562 treatise "Compendious Table of the Hebrew Kabbalah," written in Paris.[32] This book is no longer extant, but it would presage Dee's masterpiece: 1564's *Monas hieroglyphica.*

5

Ladder of Spheres

Dee's studies were following an increasing arc of complexity. Consequently, he was now looking for methods to categorize and understand larger and larger sets of data.

To the study of Hermeticism and Neoplatonism Dee had now added that of the Cabala, which builds on Neoplatonism's pure philosophy to provide a working system of categorizing and sorting the universe into a cohesive whole. Broadly speaking, Kabbalah, Cabala, or Qabalah is the branch of mathematics that is concerned with studying the mind of God. Originally a rabbinical tool of scriptural interpretation (as generally spelled *Kabbalah*), it was synthesized with Christianity, Hermeticism, and Renaissance Neoplatonism in the fifteenth century by Giovanni Pico della Mirandola (as then spelled *Cabala*).[1] Mercifully, it is the structure that brings order to this ideological stack, and draws it together into a cohesive and elegant pattern. Beginning in the nineteenth century, the adepts who predated and then formed the Hermetic Order of the Golden Dawn changed the spelling to *Qabalah* (from the original Hebrew, *Qoph Bet Lamed Heh*), which I will use as a catch-all description in this chapter for sanity's sake.

While Hermeticism posits the interconnection of all things in the universe, the Qabalah shows what the connections actually are, and forms a metaphorical map of the cosmos. The system postulates ten spheres, or *sephiroth,* that make up the energetic circuit of creation—beginning with Godhead and terminating in manifest reality. This map demonstrates how reality comes into being, starting from the void, progressing through the mind of God, into causal blueprints carried out by angels, through the astral world of dreams and emotions, and then into the physical world. Likewise, it shows how everything that has *already* been manifested interlinks and connects into a cohesive whole. As a more sophisticated version of the Great Chain of Being, it shows how to reascend the ladder back to God and, for the *mens adeptus,* suggests how to participate in the patterning and continual manifestation of the universe.

Brief summations of the ten spheres, in modern terms, are as follows:

1. Kether, Crown. Godhead. The spark of Creation, or Big Bang.
2. Chokmah, Wisdom. Positive/Masculine. The stars and zodiac.
3. Binah, Understanding. Negative/Feminine. Saturn.
4. Chesed, Glory. Structure. Jupiter.
5. Geburah, Power. Separation. Mars.
6. Tiphareth, Beauty. Divinity as manifest in humanity. The sun.
7. Netzach, Victory. Emotion. Venus.
8. Hod, Splendor. Intellect. Mercury.
9. Yesod, Foundation. Sex, dreams, life energy, the "astral plane." The moon.
10. Malkuth, Kingdom. The physical world. Earth.

To these are added zero, Ain Soph, the void, as well as a theoretical sphere, Da'ath, Knowledge, which corresponds to the separation between spheres one through three and seven through ten, the "Abyss" between unmanifest and manifest existence, noumenon and phenomenon. The Abyss also represents the utmost limit of the rational mind, beyond which it cannot pass.

The sephiroth are not a literal map of reality. Rather, they are a map of mankind's capacity for creating meaning, which shows that the entirety of human thought can be condensed into the numbers zero through ten. These ten spheres are connected by twenty-two paths, each of which

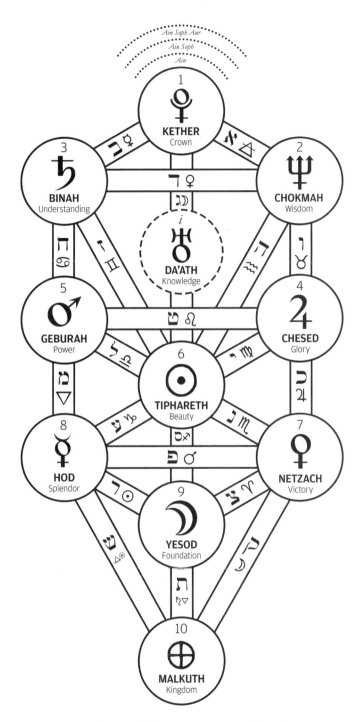

Fig. 5.1. The Tree of Life. Image courtesy of the author.

blends the two spheres it connects, and they are assigned to the twenty-two letters of the Hebrew alphabet—meaning that the structure of the Qabalah is an outgrowth of the Hebrew language itself.[2] This forms a pattern referred to as the "Tree of Life," and raises its total number of spheres and paths to thirty-two. In addition to the Hebrew alphabet, these spheres and paths were assigned to combinations of the four classical elements, seven classical planets, and twelve zodiacal signs (this point, in particular, is of key importance to the later angelic conversations).

To these paths, it was thought, could be attributed the totality of human knowledge, as well as the totality of the aspects of the physical universe—a Renaissance prototype of a neural net. As such, the Qabalah forms a cohesive map of the human mind, and as mankind was thought to be made in God's image, therefore infers a map of the mind of God. By the analogical thinking of operative magic, in which like is connected to like, this map could also suggest pathways by which an individual could influence anything in the universe.

Much as the Great Chain of Being does, this version of the Qabalah suggests that most humans are following a downward trend of manifestation, proceeding from God into the gross materiality of the physical world. An intrepid initiate, however, could reverse this course, reascending Jacob's Ladder back to their source and thereby restoring their original divine nature. The Hermetic Qabalah thus formed the ground plan for undertaking this inner adventure, and completing the Great Work.

In addition to the map of the Tree of Life, the Qabalah incorporates the processes of *gematria,* or adding up the numerical values associated with the Hebrew alphabet to discover hidden meanings and analogies in scripture. For the working Qabalist, this process is extended beyond the written word and into the whole of nature.

Qabalah has a tendency to terrify with its complexity, but is simple in practice—in fact, people in Western societies have been immersed in it their entire lives, as its association chains are hardwired into Western civilization. As an example, consider the sphere Netzach, symbolizing love, to which correspond the planet Venus, roses, copper, the goddess Aphrodite, the virtue of unselfishness, and so on. This cluster of associations should make perfect sense, for Westerners, as all relating to each other and to the concept of love. This is Qabalah: understanding and categorizing nature as a language of correspondences.

Now, to extend this further and begin to think like an operative magician, consider the "magical operation" of using these Qabalistic correspondences to create a talisman to win or reinforce the love of a sweetheart. Give her seven roses (not too few, not too many), a copper locket, and a card with a poem written to her as if she were the goddess Aphrodite, and see what "magical" effect this has. Of course, you may say that there's no value in such objects and ritual gestures, and it's the thought that counts, but see how far that gets you.

The analogical and associative meaning-building of the Qabalah can seem daunting and even opaque to noninitiates, like somebody looking into a manual on advanced computer programming or differential calculus for the first time. Yet as with these arts, the processes of Qabalah were created in order to do complex things more easily. Once the initial learning curve is passed, Qabalah allows for complex association chains that decrease the overall mental operations needed to work out any given problem. A student of Qabalah will seek to relate everything in their life to the Tree, until the whole of existence changes from a chaos of noise and information into a perfectly organized filing cabinet.[3] From here, the mental silence of meditation becomes easier, and the mind becomes still enough to receive wisdom from that silence.

This method of *jnana yoga* is not for everybody—spiritual adherents with more physical or emotional temperaments will gravitate toward *hatha yoga* (physical postures) or *bhakti yoga* and prayer—but for compulsive intellectuals, it can be a blessing, as it is meant to overload the rational mind with divine semiotics until the discursive mind finally breaks and lets go, allowing merciful moments of transcendence from the reasoning faculty or *ruach*. One soon sees the connections between literally everything in nature—every number, word, color, godform, personal interaction, mode of consciousness, and even thought collapses into a shining whole, revealing that the totality of the universe is connected, and is itself the mind of God in the process of manifesting itself. It is from this process that we get the stepped-down occult artifacts of numerology, tarot, color symbolism, and all the rest—yet what were analogical tools in the enlightenment machine of initiates become gaudy fortune-telling devices in the superstitious hands of the unawakened.

The Kabbalah—which was brought to Europe by Sephardic Jews— was believed to have been received from God; the Tree of Life is first seen in the Garden of Eden in Genesis 2:9, side by side with the forbidden Tree of Knowledge of Good and Evil.* The structure of the Hebrew alphabet itself is described in rabbinical literature—primarily the *Sefer Yetzirah*— as depicting the process by which God manifested the world in Genesis 1. Therefore, the entirety of the Old Testament was saturated with coded Kabbalistic meaning, all the way down to each individual letter.

The Tree itself later appears in Proverbs 3, in which it is explained that by keeping God's commandments one may reattain to the supernal sephiroth: "Happy is the man that findeth wisdom, and the man that getteth understanding. . . . Her ways are ways of pleasantness, and all her paths are peace. She is a Tree of Life to them that lay hold upon her: and happy is every one that retaineth her. The Lord by wisdom hath founded the earth; by understanding hath he established the heavens. By his knowledge the depths are broken up, and the clouds drop down the dew."[4] The reference is to Chokmah or Wisdom, Binah or Understanding, and Da'ath or Knowledge; the feminine presence is likely the Sophia, Wisdom, personifying Chokmah.

The Tree of Life returns triumphantly in Revelation 22, where it stands in the center of the New Jerusalem after the final victory over the Dragon, just as it stood in the Garden of Eden, for as Christ is the Alpha and Omega, the Tree opens and closes the Bible: "And he showed me a pure river of water of life, clear as crystal, proceeding out of the Throne of God and of the Lamb. In the midst of the street of it, and on either side of the river, was there the Tree of Life, which bare twelve manner of fruits, and yielded her fruit every month: and the leaves of the tree were for the healing of the nations."[5] Access to the Tree through the gates of the New Jerusalem (possibly a reference to the fifty gates

---

*According to the Golden Dawn, this second tree represents the qliphoth, the averse or evil counterparts of the sephiroth, as does the Red Dragon in Revelation 12, whose seven heads and ten horns denote the seven averse planets and ten averse sephiroth. See Regardie, *The Golden Dawn*, 73.

of Binah or even the thirty Aethyrs) is the reward of those who have kept God's commandments and have not fallen to the evil power, for "without are dogs, and sorcerers, and whoremongers, and murderers, and idolaters, and whosoever loveth and maketh a lie."[6]

Practically, this meant that not only was Qabalah the key to understanding scripture, but also to understanding the angels and spirits contacted through operative magic. For instance, a spirit that appeared in a vision wearing a red cloak and carrying an iron sphere would be assumed to be an aspect of Mars and the sphere of Geburah. In this way, spirits could communicate complex meaning by their appearance, actions, words, and gestures. Understanding this is critical to making sense of Dee's angelic conversations, as well as Crowley's later scrying of the thirty Aethyrs.

Following the work begun by Agrippa in synthesizing the Qabalah with operative magic, nineteenth-century occultists like Eliphas Levi, MacGregor Mathers, and the initiates of the Golden Dawn would use the Qabalah as a way of drawing together the entire doctrine of magic, including the gods, goddesses, and spirits of all of the world's religious traditions, as well as astrology, tarot, I Ching, the magical languages of the grimoires, and every other piece of lore they had inherited or invented, culminating with Dee and Kelly's angelic magic, fitting it all together as a single working model that an intrepid magician could use as a road map to enlightenment. Following the SRIA (Societas Rosicruciana in Anglia) and earlier orders, the Golden Dawn would also use the Qabalah's ten spheres as a Masonic degree structure, suggesting that these spheres were not only ways of classifying the universe, but also represented states of consciousness attainable by human initiates.

This degree structure would go through several iterations as it passed through the Masonic and Rosicrucian orders that postdated Dee. The version finalized in Crowley's A∴A∴ is as follows:

0°=0□ Probationer. Outwith the Tree.
1°=10□ Neophyte. Malkuth.
2°=9□ Zelator. Yesod.
3°=8□ Practicus. Hod.
4°=7□ Philosophus. Netzach.

(Dominus Liminus. Veil of Paroketh.)
5°=6□ Adeptus Minor. Tiphareth.
6°=5□ Adeptus Major. Geburah.
7°=4□ Adeptus Exemptus. Chesed.
(Babe of the Abyss. Veil of the Abyss.)
8°=3□ Magister Templi. Binah.
9°=2□ Magus. Chokmah.
10°=1□ Ipsissimus. Kether.

Grades of this style were usually conferred in Masonic temple–style initiations, as in the SRIA and Golden Dawn, initiating the candidate into the mysteries of each sephira and allowing them to climb the Tree of Life, thus formalizing the quest of the Renaissance adepts to reascend the Great Chain of Being, return to God, and become *mens adeptus.*

While this mapping of the Qabalah to Masonic-style grades does not directly apply to Dee's work, it becomes critically important to assessing the work of the magicians who applied themselves to Dee's magic after his death, as the majority of them worked within Qabalistic, Masonic structures and interpreted their experience of angelic magic through that filter. In particular, Aleister Crowley conceptualized his entire experience of Dee's thirty Aethyrs as not only spanning and elaborating upon the structure of the Qabalah, but as an initiation into the grade of 8°=3□ Magister Templi and the sphere Binah, following the earlier rabbinical tradition of initiation through the fifty gates of Binah.

While this structure stems wholly from the Golden Dawn, and *not* from Dee's original work, the later work of Mathers, Crowley, and others in mapping Dee's magic to the Qabalah *can* help elucidate the original material in retrospect—particularly when remembering that much of the Golden Dawn is based on Agrippa, whose *Three Books* were Dee's primary sourcebook for magic. For instance, many of the utterances and appearances of Dee's angels make sense when analyzed using the correspondences from Agrippa (or the Golden Dawn). Even back-testing Crowley's assumption that the angelic material pertained to initiation into Binah seems to bear this out.

All of this will be discussed in more detail in book III; for now,

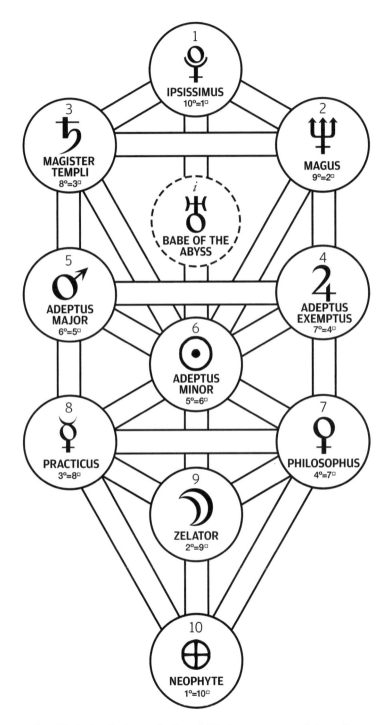

Fig. 5.2. A∴A∴ Grades on the Tree of Life. Image courtesy of the author.

the key takeaway is that Dee heavily studied Qabalah, beginning with his association with Guillaume Postel, and that it became key to his thinking from the early 1560s onward, as exemplified by his *Monas hieroglyphica*. As a result, Qabalah is central to understanding the angelic conversations, and was teased out and emphasized by the later magicians who experimented with Dee's work.

Dee quickly incorporated his new study of Qabalah and of the Hebrew language with his prior occult learning. Beginning students of Qabalah and gematria spend immense amounts of time studying Hebrew, memorizing correspondences between the Hebrew letters and various facets of the natural and supernatural worlds, and then projecting those correspondences outward into reality. Eventually, everything takes on Qabalistic significance, and everything is seen to be interconnected. But the entire methodology of Qabalah, gematria, and numerology is arguably only a *synthetic* method for inducing a state of consciousness in which the boundary between self and other dissolves—a set of training wheels that may be discarded once it does its job.

Dee, likely understanding this through his own study, pushed much further, and wrote not of the Hebrew Kabbalah but of the "Real Cabala," the true language of God that Hebrew only approximated. He would later come to call this the Cabala "of that which is" in his *Monas hieroglyphica,* as opposed to the Kabbalah of "that which is said," namely Hebrew. For Dee, the Real Cabala would supersede the exoteric Hebrew Kabbalah, and in the process unlock the inner, sacred, initiated meaning of the classical sciences. Arithmetic, geometry, music, astronomy, optics, statics, pleno, and vacuo (these last relating to Aristotelian physics) would be superseded by magic, esoteric medicine, scrying, alchemy, and, finally, adeptship itself.[7]

This was the quest for the primal, pre-Fall language. The recovery of such a language held out the additional promise of a reconciliation between the divided religions—not only Catholicism and Protestantism, but Judaism and Islam as well.[8]

Dee's Qabalistic mentor Guillaume Postel had already hinted at such a primal language, suggesting that the prophets Enoch and Abraham probably spoke a language closer to Adam's original tongue than the

Hebrew then known, and had investigated the Qabalah of Chaldean, Aramaic, and even Syriac, which he (like Agrippa) considered the holy language of Christ, laden with profound meaning.[9] Johann Reuchlin wrote that the angelic language had been simple and pure, and spoken between God, angels, and men face-to-face, casually, without need for interpretation.[10] St. Augustine—and following him, Aquinas, Luther, Ficino, Conrad Gessner, and Paracelsus—believed that Hebrew itself was the original language, and the sole survivor of the fall of the Tower of Babel; Augustine also believed that there was an "inner word," reflecting the *logos* that resonated within the soul of man, beyond all verbal language.[11] Agrippa argued that the Adamic tongue was never spoken at all, but passed between God and individuals telepathically, through the medium of the imagination. This divine language was of particular importance to operative magicians, as it would be the key to communicating with the angels. Pico della Mirandola and Reuchlin thought that such divine words would also contain miracle-making faculties in their own right.[12]

5.3. Heinrich Cornelius Agrippa.

As Dee's world model was growing in sophistication, so was his sense of identity. Following Postel, he was beginning to see himself as a "Citizen and Member of the whole and only one Mystical City Universal," a "Cosmopolites," a citizen holding allegiance to no country but God's.[13] This sentiment, which dates to Diogenes of Sinope in the fifth century BC, has become progressively more common in the modern world as globalization erases national borders, a project that Dee, his peers, and the Rosicrucian and Freemasonic movements he inspired might be seen to have had a guiding spiritual influence on.

Such a seemingly pious sentiment could be interpreted in many ways. One might be that Dee, finding more in common with his European intellectual and occultist contacts than his countrymen, was beginning to consider himself a member of the elite, those who saw beyond national and territorial politics, who were concerned with the eternal world of ideas and of the betterment of the human race. The circle of adepts that Dee was now finding himself within—bound by common ideas and drives, if not literally organized—would be responsible for much of the advance of the Western world in the coming centuries, from the birth of science to the Freemasonic-inspired political revolutions that swept Europe and led to the birth of America and the Napoleonic age. Another is that this may have been a tell that Dee was now an initiate not of a metaphorical circle of similar thinkers but of a literal secret society, perhaps a forerunner of the Rosicrucians to come.

The statement certainly points to where Dee's religious loyalties truly lay—beyond either Catholic or Protestant. Though Dee had studied with Catholics, been ordained a Catholic priest, and had professed loyalty to the Catholics under Mary, his lack of celibacy and interest in magic made him more than suspect. A secret 1568 report submitted to Francis Borgia, Jesuit superior general, called Dee "a married priest, given to magic and uncanny arts," and a pernicious influence that English Catholics would do well to keep away from.[14] Yet Dee remained in awe of Catholic ritual even late in life, considering the Eucharist of primary importance to spiritual development.[15] Under Elizabeth, however, he had switched loyalties to the evangelical cause. The political question of which side of Christendom he allied himself with was secondary to saving his own skin and staying alive to pursue the Hermetic quest for the *prisca theologia,* which would make such religious factionalism irrelevant.

These were the ideals—a new "Hermetic religion of love,"[16] as Dee biographer Peter French called it in the early 1970s—that the young Dee was immersed in. This was not a game: the ideals of Dee's Continental elders could get an unwary philosopher killed, and Dee had already been tortured for "calculating and conjuring."

His head full of dangerous new ideas, Dee returned to Antwerp to compose the crowning work of his early life. Synthesizing the totality of his previous learning, and freshly inspired by the Qabalah, Dee produced the *Monas hieroglyphica,* a short work that purports to unveil the secrets of the Real Cabala and of the universe itself in one symbol and twenty-four theorems—twenty-four being the number of Elders that surround the Throne of God in Revelation 4:4.

Fig. 5.4. Title page of John Dee, *Monas hieroglyphica,* 1564.

Like the *Propaedeumata,* the *Monas* was an attempt at Continental patronage: it was addressed to Maximilian II, soon to become the Holy Roman emperor, who became a great supporter of science and the arts during his reign, as well as an enthusiast of hieroglyphics.[17] Bitterly remembering the opportunities for royal patronage he had turned down before returning to England, Dee now struggled to reclaim what he had so flippantly discarded.

To help in his self-promotion, Dee now cast himself as an adept, rather than just a math professor, suggesting that he possessed secret occult knowledge that could prove a political asset for a monarch who sheltered him. This was not a hollow promise—the *Monas* does point the way to philosophical adeptship, and outlines the Real Cabala, which Dee thought could not only unlock the works of the ancients, but also spark new scientific advances.[18]

The *Monas* is a profoundly advanced and yet elegant Qabalistic text, though little trace of Hebrew or even the Tree of Life remains visible on its surface. Instead, Dee condenses the entirety of nature into a single symbol, the Hieroglyphic Monad itself. Dee's Monad had appeared on the cover of the *Propaedeumata aphoristica* six years earlier; the *Monas* now revealed the meanings of the symbol that he had been carefully working out during his deep study of Qabalah in the intervening years.

The Monad, which resembles the alchemical sign for Mercury (an analogue of Hermes, suggesting the Hermetic roots of the text), is assembled from the symbols for the sun, moon, the cross of the elements, and the sigil of Aries, which also represents the twenty-four hours of the day and therefore the sun's motion throughout it, as well as the rest of the zodiac and the Elders of Revelation. When the Monad is manipulated and rotated, it reveals the symbols of the remaining classical planets— Venus, Mars, Jupiter, and Saturn. Thus, the Monad contains the entirety of the Qabalah, with its four elements, seven planets, and twelve zodiacal signs displayed in a single sigil, rather than the complex map of the Tree of Life. Therefore it contained the entirety of nature, and was the Key of the Mysteries and Dee's effort to establish a Real Cabala, one based on geometry and direct observation of the world.

If this symbol showed the unity of all things, Dee suggested, then

Fig. 5.5. The Hieroglypic Monad.
From *Monas hieroglyphica.*

by its further study and manipulation, anything in the universe could be deduced. The Latin text of the *Monas hieroglyphica* was made up of twenty-four theorems on the sigil, in which Dee breathlessly extrapolates meaning upon meaning from it, applying his masterful grasp of geometry, astronomy, Qabalah, Pythagorean number theory, alchemy, scripture, Greek, Latin, and Hebrew. Throughout the book, Dee continually emphasizes that what he reveals are only some of the mysteries that can be extrapolated from the Monad, and that the symbol may contain boundless further treasures and avenues of inquiry. Ultimately, Dee thought, the Monad would collapse all of the mundane and magical arts into one, uniting all knowledge (including the forbidden) into a greater whole. Yet despite his enthusiasm, Dee is simultaneously guarded, couching much of the book in alchemical metaphors and twilight language. As with some of his theories in the *Propaedeumata,* Dee believed that revealing the mysteries of the *Monas* to the profane would lead to their misuse and therefore to disaster. Unfortunately, this use of twilight language ensured that its intended audience also found it inscrutable, at a time when Dee hoped to secure patronage.

Constructed of coded information hidden layers upon layers deep, the *Monas* requires an intuitive grasp of Qabalah, astrology, geometry, and alchemy—*intuitive* being the key word, as its meaning does not unfold solely in a rational manner but also through meditative contemplation. Dee does not do any hand-holding in the text, assuming that his readers will be on mental par with him, stating, "Here the vulgar eye will see nothing but Obscurity and will despair considerably."[19] Furthermore, he counsels that those unable to understand it should keep quiet rather than pretend to knowledge they have not earned, stating, "Who docs not understand should either learn or be silent."[20] This cageyness on Dee's part was warranted, for in addition to being the proposed key to the universe and the solution to all problems then facing humanity, the text almost certainly contained encoded political material.

The *Monas* further includes information on the application of its theorems to alchemy. This was sure to get the attention of potential patrons, as the production of gold was of primary interest of European monarchs. The process of alchemical transformation described in the *Monas* is the purification of the soul and its translation from sublunary corruption to the supercelestial world;[21] however, it must also have been applicable to more mundane efforts of transforming metals, as in the 1580s Elizabeth would establish secret alchemical laboratories at Hampton Court Palace, where she would draw upon the theories in the book in an attempt at the industrial-scale production of gold.[22]

Dee begins the *Monas* with a circle, a line, and a point. These are the primary forces of manifestation—corresponding, though this is not stated, to Kether, Chokmah, and Binah. As a point implies a line, so a line implies a circle, because a line rotated around a point creates a circle, and it is likewise impossible to draw a perfect circle without a point or line. As these lineal figures further develop in complexity, they leave the domain of the conceptual and enter the world of manifestation, glyphing the process by which the universe creates. Through becoming absorbed in this process, the reader may transcend the limits of their own rational mind and enter into communion with universal truths.[23]

A circle around a point creates the alchemical sign for the sun. Halved, a circle forms the alchemical sign for the moon. Conjoined, these represent the alchemical marriage of sun and moon that is mentioned in *The Emerald Tablet* ("The Sun is its father, the moon its mother," in Isaac Newton's translation),[24] in the Hindu tantras ("When a yogi unites that which is above and that which is below, he unites Sun and Moon, realizes Om and is one with the Hamsa," from the *Niruttara Tantra*),[25] and in Crowley's *The Book of the Law* ("For he is ever a sun, and she a moon").[26]

This marriage creates the cross of the elements, which can be read as either ternary (two lines and one central point, equaling three) or quaternary (four right angles). Together, this implies a septenary (sevenfold) structure. This cross is placed upon the astrological sigil of Aries,

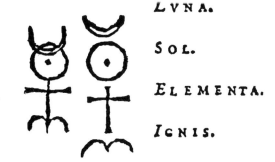

Fig. 5.6. The expanded Monad.
From *Monas hieroglyphica*.

L V N A.

S O L.

E L E M E N T A.

I G N I S.

representing fire as it is part of the fiery triplicity, and also representing the movement of the sun across the equator over the course of the twenty-four-hour day.

The math outlined here by Dee would form the underlying structure of the temple furniture delivered by the angels in the much later angelic conversations. The angel Il would tell Dee that the angelic Holy Table worked on a ternary and quaternary structure,[27] on top of which was placed the septenary Sigillum Dei Aemeth and Ensigns of Creation; likewise, seven times seven yielded the forty-nine good angels of the Tabula Bonorum and the forty-nine angelic calls. When multiplied, three and four yield the twelvefold structure of the angelic flags and the twelve tribes of Israel. Twelve plus twelve yields the twenty-four seniors of the Watchtowers, while twelve times twelve (to the magnitude of a thousand, which simply means "a lot" in biblical math) yields the 144,000 to be saved in Revelation. The Watchtowers themselves would be quaternary, elaborating the four elements.

Dee next shows how, when rotated or taken in segments, the Monad produces the astrological symbols for Saturn, Jupiter, Mercury, Mars, and Venus—which combine with the sun and moon to make up the seven classical planets, which also formed the later structure of the Sigillum Dei, the Ensigns, and the Tabula Bonorum. Next taking the central cross, Dee shows how it can be broken down into the Roman numerals L, V, and X, from which a decadal structure can be extrapolated.*

---

*Initiates of the Hermetic Order of the Golden Dawn would later develop this into the "LVX formula," the light of revelation stemming both from Christ on Calvary and, esoterically, the lower five sephiroth of the Tree of Life.

Importantly, the central cross, for Dee, can represent one X, four Vs (four times five equals twenty-five), or four Ls (four times fifty equals two hundred); he relates this to L or El, a Cabalistic name of God and of Jupiter. *El* is also the suffix appended to the names of angels in Hebrew, denoting their species (Raphael, Gabriel, Michael, Uriel, and so on). *L* or *El* is a centrally important repeating symbol within operative magic—seen previously in grimoires like *Liber iuratus,* it would also form the central character of the Holy Table of Practice, and therefore the center of the entire angelic conception of the universe.*

This elucidates the structure of the Monad and thus the cosmos: If a point implies a line, and a line implies a circle, and this can be doubled to form a cross in a circle, ten, then this, for Dee, implies that all of manifestation can be drawn from a single point. In the thinking of the Qabalists, a single point represents the spark of Creation, Kether, while the number ten, Malkuth, the tetractys, then not only represents but *is* the universe itself.[28] If you have ten, you have everything.

Dee further develops the Monad by arranging the seven planets in progressive orbits in an egg structure, and couching the structure within alchemical allegory.† Dee suggests that the three parts of the structure—the sun and moon, the cross, and the equinoctial sign of Aries—form a dramatic beginning, middle, and end, analogous to the birth, death, and resurrection of Christ and the alchemical perfection

---

*It also features as the title of *Liber L,* later renamed *Liber AL vel Legis,* the technical name for Crowley's transmitted *The Book of the Law.* Crowley's student Frater Achad would work out that L, El, or "AL" (Aleph-Lamed in Hebrew) was the primary mathematical key to the book, greatly impressing Crowley, who had been unable to find the code. Achad would suggest that Allah, Muhammad's name for God, was actually the Qabalistic code AL–LA, unifying God with his inverse, LA or "not God." Achad then suggested a new code name for divinity, ALLALA, "God is not not." See Achad, *Liber 31;* Grant, *Outside the Circles of Time.*

†The egg is a repeating symbol in alchemy, appearing, for instance, in Michael Maier's *Atalanta fugiens.* During the Amalantrah Working in 1918, Crowley and several of his compatriots, including Achad, claimed to have contacted a disembodied intelligence that identified itself as "the wizard Amalantrah," a Secret Chief of the true Rosicrucian order. Amalantrah told Crowley, in no uncertain terms, "It's all in the egg." See Crowley, "Liber XCVII."

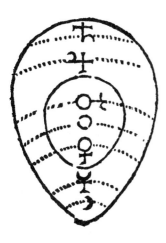

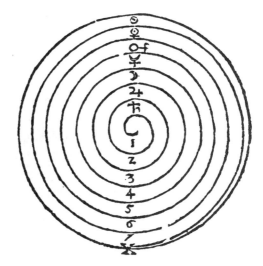

Fig. 5.7. The seven planets extrapolated from the Monad and arranged into an egg shape. From *Monas hieroglyphica*.

Fig. 5.8. The orbits of the planets from the Monad. From *Monas hieroglyphica*.

of Adam, among many other formulae.* Dee concludes by pointing out that the twenty-four hours represented by the sign Aries are also the twenty-four elders that ring around the Throne of God in Revelation; implied is that the Monad signifies not only all Creation but also the narrative arc of the Bible—from the point of Creation, to the Cross, to Revelation. These elders or "seniors" would appear as tangible spirits to Kelly in the vision of the golden talisman, and thereafter be incorporated into the angelic Watchtowers.

Scholars have proposed a multitude of theories about the *Monas*. It is generally accepted that the book is an alchemical and Qabalistic document, the fruit of Dee's thinking on the Qabalah "of that which is." Francis Yates proposed that the Monad was believed by Dee to be the occult, scientific, mathematical key to reascending the Great Chain,[29] while others suggested that the book was a proposal for a new world order and world religion—a Hermetic order that would pave the way for

---

*The Golden Dawn and Crowley would call this the IAO formula, and closely identify it with the LVX formula also elaborated by Dee. See Crowley, "The Formula of IAO," in *Magick: Liber ABA*, 158–65.

Fig. 5.9. Alchemical emblem. From Michael Maier, *Atalanta fugiens*, 1617.

global salvation, although this latter theory lacks sufficient evidence.[30] (Dee's actual plans for a global religion would come later, during the angelic conversations.)

Dee was right to seek for foreign patronage by promoting his new work: though Dee sent a copy of the *Monas* home from the Continent, it was not well-received in England, necessitating that Elizabeth defend Dee's reputation against "such Universitie-Graduates of high degree, and other gentlemen, who therefore dispraised it, because they understood it not," even though she had not yet read it.[31] Unfortunately, the book found no better reception with Maximilian, and Dee returned to England with his dreams of patronage dashed once again.

6

Hammer of the Witches

Dee faced a harsh comedown upon reentry to England. While on the Continent, he had been seen as the natural philosopher and adept he was, free to pursue his flights of intellectual fancy, chasing Hermetic manuscripts and daydreaming of a royalty-backed occult revival. But back home, he was just a demonic conjuror, considered no better than a common criminal. By July 1564, his reputation as a sorcerer and Catholic had grown, as his enemies had taken his absence as an opportunity to attack freely.

Elizabeth's court was very different from Mary's. While Mary had been a fanatic Catholic, Elizabeth was tolerant, even fascinated with the occult. Elizabeth was a genius, Dee's equal or better—her scholastic efforts even as a child are extraordinary. Her command of languages was masterful; her tutor Roger Ascham once remarked that Elizabeth read more Greek in a day than clergymen read Latin in a week.[1] Artists and poets portrayed her either as a virgin or a goddess—never as a mortal woman.[2] Beyond this, she practiced operative magic in her own way—an example being the "royal touch," a traditional ritual of the English monarchy, in which she would apparently heal epilepsy or tuberculosis by placing her hand on the neck of the afflicted. Elizabeth is recorded as being exceptionally effective at this faith-healing practice—though openly claiming one had not been so cured would have been an unwise move.[3]

Once enthroned, Elizabeth's interest in science and alchemy became publicly known, with alchemists throughout Europe seeking her patronage; she was considered to be more learned on the topic than most professors, and fashion soon dictated her association with the alchemical emblems of the pelican and phoenix, representing stages in the work of creating the philosopher's stone. The way to Elizabeth's heart was alchemy—and so it is little surprise that Dee had many rivals for her attention. Beyond creating an air of jealousy, this situation now proved perilous for Dee. Court politics were vicious and backbiting in alchemy as in all else, and the stakes were high—winning Elizabeth's favor meant winning riches, fame, and security, while falling from her favor could mean death.[4]

To distinguish himself as superior to his rivals for Elizabeth's patronage, Dee presented her with the *Monas*. She received it with fascination, telling Dee that she would become his "scholar" if he revealed the secrets of the book to her.[5] Dee soon became closer with Elizabeth, but not close enough to secure a stable position.

In 1563, Elizabeth had passed the *Act against Conjurations, Enchantments, and Witchcrafts,* a new legislation against the occult that nevertheless lightened the sentence for sorcery, which was now only punishable by imprisonment. The previous standard of the death penalty without benefit of clergy was now reserved only for those who killed with magic. While Dee had been away, Elizabeth's court had been warring with Catholic conspirators and magicians who were indeed this unscrupulous. The arch-conspirator John Prestall was once again involved, and was accused of conjuring evil spirits to gain information on how best to commit treason, as well as telling other conspirators that he had predicted Elizabeth would die in 1563.[6] Cecil had the subversives publicly tried in Westminster Hall, though they were not executed. Prestall was thrown in the Tower of London—seeking to strike back at Cecil but fearing retaliation, he instead sought to indirectly hurt Cecil by going after Dee.

As ammunition against Dee, Prestall used the 1563 first edition of John Foxe's *Actes and Monumentes,* which contained a record of Dee's 1555 testimony during Bishop Bonner's examination of the Protestant martyr John Philpot. During his testimony, Dee asked the heretic Philpot if he would concede that the pope should be the supreme head of the Church—if Dee could prove that Christ built the Church on Peter, and not Cyprian. Dee was chided by the older man, who told him from the stand that despite Dee's academic learning he was "too young in divinity to teach me the matters of my faith."[7] Included in the book is a letter that had surfaced between Philpot and Bartlet Green, another Protestant martyr who had been in the care of "Dr. Dee the great conjurer"[8] while held in Bishop Bonner's house.[9] The letter was enough to link Dee with both sorcery and, because of his close proximity to Bonner, the Catholic cause.

Prestall had initiated a storm of gossip among the public. In addition to the passage referring to Dee as a "great conjurer," a number of counterfeit passages were inserted by Dee's enemies embellishing the charges against him; on top of this, documents claiming Dee consorted with demons were broadly circulated by agitators. The primary counterfeiter was later identified as Vincent Murphyn, Prestall's brother-in-law, another cunning man who trafficked in using nails and hair to effect harmful sympathetic magic, evoking spirits, and forging letters to cozy up to powerful friends. If Prestall and Murphyn could not match Dee in genius, they could trump him in the propaganda war by using underhanded occult thug tactics that Dee, a naïve and idealistic scholar, would have been blindsided by. This was a very different kind of magic—the conjuration of the worst demon of all, the mob. Prestall and Murphyn's logic was clear: if Elizabeth was going to go after Catholic conjurors, they would turn public anger against the conjuror in Elizabeth's own employ. In one move, this would take out an occult rival, enact indirect revenge against their persecutor Cecil, and, most importantly, shift attention away from them and toward the perceived hypocrisy of the government's stance against witchcraft. Prestall and Murphyn were not to be trifled with in street-level magic, yet in the process of their revenge they were damaging a brilliant scholar and harming the strength of their country—not that the politically amoral Prestall would have cared.[10]

Dee would never recover from the damage done to his reputation during this period. It was this furor, and his earlier imprisonment for calculating—not the prior scandal caused by his winged beetle or the disgrace his father had come to—that would truly tarnish his image and permanently mark him as a figure of suspicion. Not only was Dee a conjuror, he was now a "great conjurer"—a reputation that Dee still bears more than four centuries later, though what was a burden at the time has preserved Dee's memory in the long run, while less colorful contemporaries have been forgotten. The blow must have been crushing. Dee had worked long and hard for pure knowledge, and to advance the spiritual status of humanity—and this was his reward.

Faced with such trauma, he took the natural next step: he got married. Katheryn Constable, Dee's bride, was not of equal stature to him—she was a City matron, who had been married to a general trader and associate of Dee's father, Roland. Dee was marrying below his station. In addition, marriage meant he was making a public statement that he was no longer celibate, not only scuttling any remaining hope he had of attaining a religious post, but putting his life at risk were Catholics to return to power. Dee, now thirty-eight, may have been giving up.[11] His marriage was only to last ten years—Constable would be dead by 1575, without giving Dee children.

His career over for the time being, Dee settled with Constable at Long Leadenham, and divided his time between his wife and his mother at Mortlake. In the meantime, Prestall and Murphyn continued their efforts to bury the "grand conjurer," while the occult war between Mary, Queen of Scots (also widely suspected of practicing witchcraft), and Elizabeth intensified.

It seems that Dee's problem was not so much that he was a magician, but that his brand of magic was impractical. The claims of the *Monas* to reform all knowledge were impressive, but what was really needed was somebody who could enrich the government coffers by turning lead into gold, or who could at least silence the court's enemies. And though Dee was brilliant, he couldn't hack practical alchemy. Even Prestall and Murphyn, it seems, could deliver better; given Murphyn's history of using forgeries to secure powerful friends, a large part of their campaign against Dee may have been aimed at removing a professional rival. But Elizabeth's court shifted its favor to rival alchemists Thomas Charnock and Cornelius de Lannoy—ironically, the court had been inspired by the *Monas* that the production of gold might be practical, but they hired somebody else to follow through. De Lannoy promised the court that he could manufacture £33,000 of pure gold, diamonds, and precious stones a year, the equivalent of about £7.9 million (or $9.9 million) in 2017. Dee, in comparison, had only promised philosophical flights of fancy.[12]

Elizabeth's court was broke, and easily fell for the hollow promises of the con man de Lannoy; the queen furnished him with the salary, rooming, and royal support that Dee had yearned for. Elizabeth, Cecil, and Dudley, all interested in alchemy, eagerly awaited his results, but they failed to manifest; it was next suspected that de Lannoy was using the royal support and furnishing of instruments to create gold for himself. Elizabeth was busy with her own alchemical experiments—with the aim of fighting her smallpox and ceasing her aging—and worked to check de Lannoy's methods. De Lannoy was eventually arrested, placed in the Tower, and interrogated. Yet his failure to make good on his claims did not arouse skepticism of alchemy itself—only of de Lannoy's approach. Not one to miss an opportunity, Prestall seized the moment to have himself released from the Tower, offering to provide what de Lannoy could not.[13]

Dee's bitter response to this drama was to yet again begin looking for Continental patronage. He translated the *Monas* into German and again sent it to Maximilian II, now Holy Roman emperor, with a new introduction. The repackaged *Monas* was now meant to portray Dee as an alchemist; it included a critique of the sham alchemists of the day, intimating that they had no ability to read the writings of the ancients and had confused the symbols, debasing initiated philosophy into unintelligible witchcraft. Maximilian ignored the book yet again. Dee next revised the *Propaedeumata* to include now-fashionable alchemical ideas from the *Monas,* with intimations that Dee might know how to produce the philosopher's stone and extend human life, and presented it to Cecil. Elizabeth read the book, but was so disheartened after the de Lannoy scandal that she explained she had no interest in risking more money on alchemy. Yet as a result, Dee again came to Elizabeth's awareness, and in February 1568 they are recorded as discussing alchemy at Westminster.[14]

With Mary, Queen of Scots, having escaped to England in 1568, Elizabeth had to contend with increased attacks from Catholic insurrectionaries—including dozens of publicized prophecies of her death, and even more grief from Prestall, now hiding across the Scottish border from a furious Cecil, who was contemplating a raid to capture him. Cecil, however, shrank from the border—unlike the more hawkish Dudley, he was wisely hesitant to take any action that would leave England without an ally upon its own island, particularly with the wolves circling.[15] Taking advantage of Cecil's political position, Prestall ensconced himself safely in Scotland, where he plotted to magically assassinate both Cecil and Elizabeth, and to goad the Spanish into attacking England.[16] Again seeking to deflect attention from Prestall, Murphyn continued his assaults on Dee, accusing him of Satanism.

Running parallel with the Catholic attacks, the new Puritans entered the propaganda war, with the Puritan Thomas Cartwright, a professor of theology at Cambridge, drawing sharp contrast between the structure of the Anglican Church and that of the early Christians. And if the Catholics were prone to sorcery, the Puritans were anything but.

"They took the doctrines of predestination, election, and damnation deeply to heart, and felt that hell could be escaped only by subordinating every aspect of life to religion and morality," wrote historians Will and Ariel Durant. "As they read the Bible in the solemn Sundays of their homes, the figure of Christ almost disappeared against the background of the Old Testament's jealous and vengeful Jehovah."[17]

After Edmund Bonner died in prison in 1569, Dee's connection to the much-hated bishop was dragged back into the light of public scorn, which did not help Dee's reputation. Indeed, in the background of this sorceric free-for-all, Dee was beginning his own initial forays into operative magic, conducting a divination with an associate named W. Emery to uncover the exact birth date and time of the navigator John Davis (who later discovered the Falkland Islands).[18] Meanwhile, the Earl of Pembroke had died, leaving Dee without a source of patronage.

Yet while Dee struggled not to be dragged under by the superstitions of the public, a new opportunity was arriving to help build a more educated future. In a move that would presage the scientific revolution, the explorer Humphrey Gilbert, half brother of Sir Walter Raleigh, was hoping to create an academy in London that would train the children of England's nobility, who would one day inherit the country, in the art of alchemy; Gilbert hoped that Dee would become involved in the academy, and sought approval of his idea from Cecil, who was fascinated by alchemy. Gilbert also expected a hasty discovery of the philosopher's stone and the secret of the conversion of lead to gold, at the time an object of obsession for much of England's nobility. But as the academy would have needed £3,000 per annum to operate (roughly £736,000 or $923,000 in 2017 terms), the plan did not meet approval, again leaving Dee in the lurch in his quest for patronage.[19] Gilbert was also a keen proponent of the profits that could be gained were England to discover the Northwest Passage, and hoped to found an English colony in the northwest of America from which to coordinate further exploration;[20] his brother Adrian would later become a key player in Dee and Kelly's angelic sessions.

Dee next sought work as an alchemical consultant for individuals and the government. Alchemical speculation was then big business, with courtiers racing to unlock the secret of the philosopher's stone and planning to quickly scale the production of gold. With such large amounts of money and potential for patronage and royal favor being discussed, it is little wonder that inter-alchemist warfare, especially coming from Prestall and Murphyn, was so intense.

A new major work published during this time—Dee's 1570 "Mathematicall Praeface" to Henry Billingsley's massively successful and influential first English translation of Euclid's *Elements of Geometry*—cemented his renown as a teacher of mathematics. The preface argued for the central importance of math (still viewed with suspicion by the public) to the sciences. The preface also elaborated many of Dee's previous ideas from the *Propaedeumata* and *Monas,* suggesting that mathematics itself is a Hermetic pursuit, for it allows the mathematician to understand the thoughts of God and the method by which he had created and operates the universe. This was a vision of God as grand geometer and "Great Architect of the Universe," as the Freemasons would later put it.

"All things (which from the very first original being of things, have been framed and made) do appear to be formed by the reason of numbers," Dee explains in the "Praeface." "For this was the principal example or pattern in the mind of the Creator. . . . The Heavens declare the glory of God, and the Firmament sheweth forth the works of his hands."[21]

Dee suggested that not only had God created the universe using mathematics, but that he was *continually* refreshing reality by numbering it. Indeed, not only could he destroy things by removing the numbers that created them, but he could also slow down or stop his "continual numbering." This itself was likely the causal reason for the decay of the world.[22]

Though giving a nod to mysticism, Dee would leave overt references to the Cabala out of his "Praeface," a work intended for a much more hardheaded audience.[23] Despite this, the "Praeface" contains many nods to more philosophically and spiritually minded readers, who will be receptive to Dee's thoughts on using numbers to understand the mind of God, as well as purely materialistic readers who, like Dee's father, would be interested in mathematics for reasons of business and profit.[24]

Beyond mathematics, Dee would recommend the full range of natural sciences, including the occult sciences of thaumaturgy and Dee's own archemastery, not yet excised from the scientific canon.[25] Archemastery itself was touted by Dee as the supreme science, fulfilling all other branches of learning, which proceeds through experiment and can lead to revelatory experiences. As Dee put it, again drawing on Roger Bacon, "Because it proceedeth by experiences, and searches forth the causes of conclusions, by experiences: and also putteth the conclusions themselves, in experience, it is named of some, *Scientia Experimentalis*. The experimental science."[26]

As in the *Propaedeumata* and *Monas,* the implication was that by understanding God's ways in the world, one could work with or even guide the forces of creation. Since man stands between God and the

Fig. 6.1. The cover of Euclid's *Elements of Geometry,* 1570 John Daye edition.
Note the image of Hermes in the bottom center.

Creation, and is made in God's image, he is suited to work with God as an intermediary, and mathematics is the ideal science for doing so,[27] as it is humanity's best way of grasping objective reality, and therefore coming to an awareness of God beyond our own sublunary delusions.[28] So potent was mathematics in comprehending the laws of reality that by its study, Dee suggested, mathematicians could come to the understanding of things otherwise reserved only for those who had been given divine revelations. Gaining skill in mathematics was, itself, a process of revelation, and might function to elevate men to divine wisdom even if no further dispensations from God were forthcoming.[29] Cornelius Agrippa had likewise expressed the relation of mathematics to operative magic, stating that "the doctrines of mathematics are so necessary to, and have such an affinity with magic, that they do profess it without them, are quite out of the way, and labor in vain, and shall in no wise obtain their desired effect."[30] Indeed, Dee complained that his skill in mathematics was the very root of his reputation as a malevolent sorcerer.[31]

With his preface to the *Elements,* Dee would crown his early studies into reality, even as his career suffered from public accusations and royal indifference. From here, Dee would pass into exercising what he knew, impacting history so profoundly that we are still coping with the effects.

7

A Cold War for a New World

As of the twenty-first century, Drake's Bay lies thirty miles northwest of the hyperreal technological mecca of San Francisco, California, a short drive across the Golden Gate Bridge through the low, mist-covered hills and forest of Marin County. The bay stretches along eight miles of coast, and centers at Drake's Beach, a small cove that looks out onto the Pacific, surrounded by sandstone hills and ice plant.

Here, in 1579, a privateer named Francis Drake landed after circumnavigating the tip of South America in a clandestine mission, proving that it could be done for the first time. He named the coast he had alighted upon Nova Albion. The man who had masterminded Drake's mission was John Dee.

While Dee's previous work had been theoretical, in the 1570s he involved himself in Elizabeth's geopolitical planning, laying the ideological framework for building a new world empire. This empire—which would spread the new ideals of the Reformation and lead to the birth of America—would soon grow to compete with the Spanish Catholic efforts at colonization. It was to be a cold war for a New World.

An omen of this war came seven years earlier, in 1572, when a new star appeared in the heavens, remaining visible night and day for seventeen months—we now designate it SN 1572, a Type Ia super-nova that occurred in the constellation Cassiopeia.[1] Dee, who rushed to make observational measurements of the supernova, thought that it confirmed that the final restoration of the world—the eschaton—was at hand.[2] The astronomer, alchemist, and astrologer Tycho Brahe, for whom the supernova is now named, believed that it was the first new star to appear in the sky since the birth of Christ. Five years later, in 1577, a great comet arrived above England, also observed by Brahe—confirming for the populace that the end of the world was nigh, fears upon which Dee was called to consult by Elizabeth.[3]

Indeed, it *was* the end of the world. By Dee's time, Luther's Reformation had initiated sea changes in Europe that broke a centuries-long status quo. Inheriting a tiny and vulnerable country, Elizabeth had pursued a strategy of avoiding war with the Catholic powers. To do so, she had kept France and Spain out of conflict by offering to increase support for whatever country was threatened by the other; both religion and Elizabeth's own marital status were drawn into this delicate political maneuvering. Yet the gambit could only last so long before war did break out, dragging England into the fray.[4] Concurrently, the Netherlands had erupted into open revolt against the Roman Catholic King Philip II of Spain, which would result in the formation of the Protestant Dutch Republic by 1581.

England was also economically insecure, besieged by desperation, homelessness, and plague. As England still grew its own food, it was vulnerable to famine if a wheat crop failed. Although the country's food supply never ran out, famines would later make the 1580s and '90s miserable for many, with the poorest potentially resorting to eating bark and grass; French peasants from the same time period are recorded as feeding on unripe grain, roots, and the intestines and blood left over from animals slaughtered for those that could afford them.[5] One of the primary reasons for England's failing economy was the massive amount of silver that Spain was extracting from its New World colonies, massively tipping the balance of economic power toward Spain. By contrast, England relied on textile exports, the manufacture of which had kept its population employed, and Continental demand was now minimal, leaving

Fig. 7.1. Francis Drake. Portrait by Crispijn van de Passe the Elder, 1598.

much of the country out of work. Trade with Russia, the Mediterranean, and Guinea had brought in some funds, but the real prize would be wresting at least partial control of the New World from Spain.[6]

It is in this context that Dee gave the world the concept of a "British Empire," a phrase he coined. After Columbus's discovery of the New World, Pope Alexander VI had divided the Americas between Portugal and Spain in the Treaty of Tordesillas, handing them dominion over the

Atlantic. Dee, with his back pocket full of superior knowledge of geography, navigation, and optics, would soon suggest Elizabeth contest this, and expand into the New World not just to rival Catholic domination, but for economic growth. Dee's knowledge of optics, as well as the geographic and cartographic information he had absorbed under Mercator and his other mentors, at a time when accurate cartographic information was largely confined to the Continent, made him invaluable in not only conceptualizing but actualizing this plan. Yet for Dee himself, exploration of the New World had little to do with mercantile or even political goals. His fascination with imperialism pertained more to his occult calculations. It was clear to Dee, if no one else, that America had been colonized by King Arthur—even that still-existing Arthurian colonies might be found in the Northwest Passage. If this was the case, England had just as much spiritual claim to America as Rome did.[7]

The Muscovy Company, however, was already engaged in making real profits from trading with the tsar in Russia, and wasn't seeking to take further risks on exploring west. Martin Frobisher got Elizabeth to lean on the company, and they in turn granted Frobisher a license with the proviso that he accept a company man, Michael Lok, as his treasurer. Dee was brought in to minimize risk by examining the plans for the voyage and imparting his knowledge of geometry, cosmography, and navigational instruments to the expedition leaders; Dee had spent fifteen years planning logistics for just such a voyage.[8] Lok quickly warmed to Dee after realizing Dee wasn't interested in competing with him. Since Lok had outfitted the expedition with expensive new navigational technology, he also had to make sure that Dee explained to his men how to use it without breaking it. Two ships were next commissioned—the *Gabriel* and *Michael,* named after the archangels that Dee would later record extensive traffic with during the angelic conversations.

Despite mishaps along the way, the *Michael* being forced back to port, and the near loss of the *Gabriel* (it was only heroics by Frobisher himself that saved the ship, nearly killing him) the voyage found land—the cyclopean ice walls of what Frobisher called *Meta Incognita,* the Unknown Limit, which we now know as Baffin Island in Canada. While exploring the coastline, Frobisher's expedition came into conflict with Inuits, capturing and marooning one individual on a rock. An exploratory mission of Frobisher's men went missing shortly thereafter. After taking an Inuit as a hostage with a boat hook, Frobisher abandoned hope for the return of his men and reversed course to England. The Inuit captive would be recorded as an object of great wonder and fascination for the English, before vanishing into the annals of history and a probably unpleasant fate.[9]

Fig. 7.2. Later map of Meta Incognita by Sir Robert Dudley and Antonio Francesco Lucini, c. 1647.

Even more interesting to the Crown was a sample of black ore that Frobisher had found in Meta Incognita, and that English alchemists claimed to have found gold in. For Dee, this discovery validated that the 1572 supernova foretold the discovery of the philosopher's stone. For the English government, it was a galvanizing reason to return to Meta Incognita for more, under the cover of secrecy, to avoid claim jumping. Funding was no longer an issue—even the cash-poor Dee, seeing the potential for return, invested £25 (about £6,000 or $7,700 in 2017 terms).[10]

A crew of 140 was raised, including several prisoners who were to again board the *Michael* and *Gabriel,* along with a third ship entitled the *Aid,* and then to be left in the New World to try and win the "good will" of the locals, in much the same way that America and Australia would later be colonized. After six weeks, the expedition reached what is now known as Frobisher's Strait and moored in what they named Jackman's Sound, which Frobisher claimed for England in the country's first act of colonial conquest of the New World. Setting out to search for more of the gold ore, the crew found nothing but a dead narwhal, which they called a "sea unicorn." Immediately thereafter, the sailors found more of the black ore, which they began loading into the ship, all while fighting off violent attacks from the now-incensed Inuits.[11]

In all, Frobisher hauled over 140 tons of the ore back to England, presenting news of his find to Elizabeth, along with the narwhal's horn. The ore was put under lock, key, and security detail, and tests on it commenced, whereupon only minute quantities of gold and silver were extracted, to Frobisher's dismay.[12]

Despite the low yield of precious metals, a third voyage was sent back to Canada to claim what profits could still be salvaged. The crew returned with 1,150 tons, but by this time Lok's Cathay Company was severely over budget; as a result of the expeditions, Lok declared bankruptcy and was thrown into debtor's prison. After countless salvage attempts, the final extracted yield from the black ore was one single pinhead of silver.[13]

To Dee, however, the political value of the English voyages to Newfoundland and Baffin Island was immense—and not only because they were gathering data in the search for the Northwest Passage.[14] In

November 1577, Dee presented a new imperial plan to Elizabeth, suggesting that England wrest control of the New World from Spain—*General and Rare Memorials,* a set of documents laying out plans and technical guidelines for a new era of English colonization.

The *Memorials* continued the occult inquiry Dee began in the *Propaedeumata aphoristica* and *Monas hieroglyphica;* as with those books, Dee thought the *Memorials* divinely inspired (also by the angel Michael, in the case of the *Monas*). For Dee, the *Memorials* were a revelation from the angels, divine guidance on the creating of a British Empire, through a Royal Navy that would hold the world in its sway.[15]

In the text, Dee argued that Britain had the greatest need of any country for a continually operational navy, and that it also had the world's greatest supply of timber, shipbuilders, willing volunteers for shipyard labor and staffing ships, and even suitable harbors. Establishing such a navy would make Britain nigh-on invincible (it did), and expansion of the British Navy and colonization of the New World not only had historical precedent but would surely raise vast riches for the Crown (it did).[16] Such a plan would establish Elizabeth as the world ruler before the end times arrived; the money raised for the naval effort, Dee later added, could also be used to help build a new alchemical institute to produce the philosopher's stone—the final perfection of which would reestablish the empire in full.[17] In his partially lost 1577 manuscript "Famous and Rich Discoveries," Dee speaks of how he would ascend above the heavens, to look down upon the earth and divine the Northwest Passage.

The cover of the *Memorials* depicts Elizabeth helming a ship representing British imperialism, with the angel Michael flying before her with sword and shield in hand and the Tetragrammaton above her, the ship being drawn forth by "Lady Occasion" toward freshly conquered territories. Following this are several pages rebutting Dee's reputation as a sorcerer—Murphyn and Prestall's attacks had been so successful that Dee was forced to address their slander upfront.

The four volumes of Dee's imperial magnum opus were as follows:

1. *General and Rare Memorials,* completed and still extant. This addressed raising funds for and constructing a Petty Navy Royal

Fig. 7.3. Cover of Dee's *General and Rare Memorials*, 1577.

of sixty 120-ton to 200-ton "tall ships" and twenty small warships weighing between twenty and fifty tons each, staffed by 6,600 well-paid men, the funds to be raised through taxation, as the wealth gained by imperial expansion would trickle down to the English people. This navy, Dee thought, would be the "Master Key" that would solidify English dominance, a "war machine"* to guard England against its enemies. Although Dee was not originally concerned with state affairs, court politics would later force Dee to rewrite the *Memorials* to encourage the support of Holland and Zealand. The combination of the Dutch and English militaries would solidify control over the Narrow Seas in the wake of Spain's withdrawal from the Low Countries. Also disgusted by the state of the Thames (upon which Mortlake was situated), Dee added an ecological broadside against the improper use of nets to fish the river.[18]

2. A set of navigational tables, calculated using Dee's paradoxical compass, which would have been larger than the English Bible. This was unpublished and is presumed lost. (Dee's paradoxical compass could have been used along with these tables to keep navigation precise; unfortunately, the newly drafted sailors found it too complex, and resisted training in its use.)[19]

3. A volume so secret that Dee stated it "should be utterly suppressed or delivered to Vulcan's custody" (i.e., burned).[20] Also lost, this manuscript may well have dealt with angelic magic or other occult or astrological calculations relating to imperial expansion. It may also have had to do with Rome or the Spanish, which would have necessitated even greater secrecy than occult material.

4. *Of Famous and Rich Discoveries,* which survived, albeit in a partly fire-destroyed form. Here Dee set forth the case for English expansion and territorial claims, and suggested exploratory voyages.[21]

---

*Compare Aleister Crowley's *The Book of the Law,* III:7: "I will give you a war-engine."

Following the exploration of Newfoundland, Dee became concerned with discovering if America was a separate continent from Asia. Abraham Ortelius had suggested that a "Strait of Anian" connected the Northwest Passage to the Pacific; however, North America was suspected to be so large that anybody who tried to discover this passage by entering Newfoundland where Frobisher had and continuing to sail west would run out of supplies and freeze to death long before hitting the Pacific. Yet if one were to sail *south,* rounding the tip of South America, conditions would be far more favorable to continued sailing, and an expedition could look for the outlet of the Northwest Passage on the other side of North America. In the pages of *Of Famous and Rich Discoveries,* Dee made a compelling case that England should do exactly that.[22]

To undertake this perilous voyage, Dee and Elizabeth looked to an unlikely candidate: the privateer and slave trader Francis Drake. Drake undertook the mission between 1577 and 1580, taking a fleet of six ships, including his own *Pelican*. The voyage was beset by storms, loss of personnel, mutiny, and ship rot—by the time Drake reached the Pacific, only the *Pelican* remained, which he rechristened the *Golden Hind*. Drake proceeded up the coast of South America, attacking Spanish settlements and capturing ships as he went, looting treasure, wine, and maps in the process. Had Drake been commanding an official English fleet, this would have been an act of war, but his privateer status lent England plausible deniability, making Drake's raids a form of naval black ops. In June 1579, he landed at what is now called Drake's Bay, north of San Francisco, before reversing course, and returning to England by way of the Cape of Good Hope and the Sierra Leone. Upon his arrival, the logs of the expedition, and therefore the route Drake had discovered, were immediately ordered classified.[23] Drake returned to England a celebrity, and was knighted soon thereafter.

As soon as Drake returned, plans for another voyage began to coalesce. In September 1580, Humphrey Gilbert and Dee drew up a plan that, should Gilbert gain control of the northern New World, Dee would receive everything above the fiftieth parallel—granting him Alaska and the majority of Canada.[24] Two years later, Dee still suspected that a Northwest Passage existed across the top of North America, and drew a map for Gilbert depicting it, in which he placed the West Coast of North America only 140 degrees west of England.[25]

Meanwhile, on February 5, 1578, Dee had married Jane Fromoundes. Supported by Elizabeth, he had proposed only a few months after the death of his first wife, Kathryn Constable, in March 1575. Jane was a member of court, a gentlewoman servant to Lady Katherine Howard, Elizabeth's best friend. Fromoundes's Catholic family hardly approved of the "arch-conjuror"; her father, Bartholomew Fromoundes, died of a stroke the day after John and Jane Dee's son Arthur was born.[26] Dee may have had one eye on securing a better position for himself by marrying into court. Unfortunately, to Dee's lifelong disadvantage, there was no patronage for scientists during Elizabeth's reign—unlike the Continent—explaining Dee's quest for patronage abroad. The best Dee could hope for in England was an academic or Church position, and even these he was regularly frustrated in attaining.[27]

In the meantime, sectarian conflict was only intensifying. Over the previous decade, the Protestant Low Countries had exploded into open revolt against Spain's Catholic rule, which would soon result in the formation of an independent Dutch Republic, and suggest strategic alliances with England. This added to the backdrop of war between the Protestant and Catholic spheres. Dee was soon called upon to defend Elizabeth from Catholic magical attack yet again, when wax images of Elizabeth and members of the Privy Council were discovered in a dunghill—as the dunghill melted the wax, by the logic of sympathetic magic, so would Elizabeth and her council come to harm.

Though the Council was as alarmed by Dee's countermagic as they were by the original sorceric attack, Dee found himself well positioned: Dudley needed him to dig up as much evidence as possible on Catholic magical attacks, as this would assist Dudley against his Catholic rivals at court. Those captured thanks to Dee's detections were held and tortured.[28] Among those arrested on Dee's cue was John Prestall, who was tied to a suspected Catholic conspiracy to magically attack the queen. Elizabeth was indeed ailing, but the cause was probably poor dental hygiene, not the occult. Prestall—whom Dee may have had arrested at least partially out of desire for revenge—was tortured for over a month, but no information on any conspiracy was forthcoming. The Council subsequently fetched Prestall's cosaboteur Vincent Murphyn for interrogation.[29]

While Dee was sent to seek a cure for Elizabeth's ailment from the German alchemist Leonhard Thurneysser, Dudley whipped up a propaganda war against Catholic sorcery, which could be lurking around any corner. But Dee and Dudley's occult pogrom collapsed when it was revealed that the magician Thomas Elkes had made the wax dolls as part of a love spell for a client. Dee was revealed to have been wrong the entire time.[30]

After long decades of theoretical work, Dee was now turning his attention to actual operative magic—he had embarked on a series of alchemical experiments with an assistant named Roger Cook, as well as attempts at angelic contact with Humphrey Gilbert's brother Adrian.[31] The court, perhaps impressed with any magic Dee had performed to alleviate perceived attacks against the queen, also furnished Dee with a new scryer, Bartholomew Hickman.[32]

In the meantime, Dee's enemies were plotting their revenge against the "arch-conjuror." Prestall was now locked in the Tower under a death sentence, where he would stay until 1588; this left Murphyn to counteraccuse Dee of being a Catholic conspirator who was himself working magic against the queen. Dee's occult experiments at Mortlake would furnish Murphyn with new ammunition. Dee sued in response.[33]

So alarmed was Elizabeth with Dee's absence from court that on September 17, 1580, she traveled to Mortlake to roust him from his studies herself, riding by coach and appearing in his garden; as Dee recorded in his diary, "She beckoned her hand for me. I came to her coach side: she very speedily pulled off her glove and gave me her hand to kiss: and to be short, willed me to resort to her Court."[34] Two weeks later, Dee arrived at court to hand deliver a new manuscript, the *Brytanici imperii limites* or "Limits of the British Empire."

Addressed solely to Elizabeth and her Privy Council, the *Limits* sought to establish a spiritual mandate not only for giving Elizabeth control of both the Low Countries and America, but for establishing her as the sovereign of a new global order. Dee now privately elaborated the occult and esoteric dimensions of the *Memorials* that he had wisely withheld from the general public.[35] Just as he believed the *Memorials* to have been divinely inspired by angels, Dee thought he had been moved to write the *Limits* by the Holy Trinity itself. The same angelic idea that had inspired him, he believed, had inspired Edgar I's naval expansion in the tenth century.[36]

Dee argued that during his reign King Arthur had held dominion not only of America, but of thirty countries.[37] If this was indeed the case, then England had at least as much of a spiritual claim to world power as Rome, and all Elizabeth had to do was assume his mantle and become the Arthurian world empress. Even Charles V, the Holy Roman emperor, whose court circle Dee had connections with during his time at Louvain, had long seen Arthur as the model on which the future world ruler would be based. After the Dutch Revolt, it was hoped that Elizabeth would claim Dutch sovereignty—and that she, and not a Habsburg, would become the Arthurian world emperor, uniting the globe under the banner of a reformed Christendom.[38]

Mercator himself had written to Dee that King Arthur had sent an expedition of four thousand men into the seas near the North Pole, and that some of the members of the team had survived, with their descendants appearing at court in Norway in 1364. Also of interest was the Welsh legend of Madoc, a prince who supposedly explored the New World in 1170; Dee not only feverishly sought to discover evidence of Madoc's existence in Spanish records of America, but believed that he was descended from the prince. Claims by Dee that Arthur had ruled over "Hollandia" only added to the case for Elizabeth becoming the world emperor of Christendom. Maps drawn up by Dee on the foundation of the Arthurian claim to the New World sprawled from Florida to Novaya Zemlya in the Arctic Ocean.[39]

Save the Arthurian angle, this was not a new idea—the hope for a last world emperor had long been part of Catholic eschatology, with the long-expected monarch reestablishing a new Roman Empire with dominion over the entire globe, as a bulwark against the

Antichrist. This final emperor had been predicted in the widely known seventh-century Syriac text *Apocalypse* by Pseudo-Methodius, a product of Eastern Christianity, which prophesied that Christendom would be savaged by Muslim invaders as God's retribution for widespread sexual licentiousness, including homosexuality and even transgenderism. This onslaught would be overcome by the final Roman emperor, who would push back the forces of the Antichrist to come, who would be born in the village of Chorazin.*

An earlier individual who had connected this apocalyptic prophecy with European exploration of the New World was none other than Christopher Columbus. After the completion of his voyages, Columbus composed a religious text entitled *El libro de las profecias,* the "Book of Prophecies," which suggested (following Joachim of Fiore) that four critical events were necessary to prompting the Second Coming. These were the Christianization of the planet, the discovery of the physical Garden of Eden, a final Crusade to recover Jerusalem from Islam, and, ultimately, the election of a last world emperor to ensure the crushing of Islam, the retaking of the Holy Land, and the return of Christ to the world.[40]

While Columbus had held out for Ferdinand and Isabella to assume this world emperor role, Dee's plan marked a radical departure by suggesting that the world emperor should be Protestant, not Catholic—Elizabeth. Where the Catholic and Protestant vanguards of exploration differed was not in their goals, but in jockeying for control. As a result, Dee set to work building a case for Elizabeth-as-emperor, using the Arthurian claim to the New World.

Dee was further encouraged in his belief that Elizabeth should assume world power by Trithemius,[41] whose *De septem secundeis* concerns itself not with terrestrial empires but rather with the course of history. For Trithemius, history was ruled by seven angels corresponding to the seven planets, each of which held regency over a period of 354 years and 4 months, beginning with Genesis and end-

---

*Aleister Crowley's student Jack Parsons explicitly identified himself with Pseudo-Methodius's Antichrist in 1949. See chapter 17.

ing with Revelation. Trithemius's scheme held a deep appeal for Dee, who nevertheless recalculated the senior initiate's math, assigning the Elizabethan period to the angel Anael, Venus, on account of the great number of female leaders in Europe, as well as the 1572 supernova. And though Elizabeth's regency was currently guaranteed by the angel of Venus, a shift to the age of Jupiter was imminent. Dee felt it his sacred duty to initiate British expansion before Jupiter arrived and the window passed.[42]

Like Dee's later *Monas, De septem secundeis* had been addressed to the Holy Roman emperor—in this case Maximilian I, not II; Trithemius's introduction to the work suggests that he was delivering it to the emperor not as his own work but as an emissary of a body of initiates who concurred that, indeed, seven spirits corresponding to the seven planets, proceeding from the first Intellect, ruled the world in successive periods. This concept was not unique to Trithemius—some early Gnostics held to a doctrine of seven Archons, or evil "rulers" of reality, who were arguably related to the seven planets.[43] In the nineteenth century, the dispensationalist evangelical John Nelson Darby would propose that there were seven distinct periods or dispensations of world history, beginning with the Fall and culminating with the Second Coming, a belief system now adhered to by the majority of American evangelical Christians.

Just as with the similar Hindu system of Yugas,[44] Trithemius's scheme outlines rising and falling curves in the quality of the overall consciousness in humanity, with debased periods marked by witchcraft, the worship of multiple gods, and even the worship of princes and rulers as gods. The great drama of history, for Trithemius, hinges on celestial events as well as terrestrial political shifts, with comets and other events in the skies marking the progress of history—like (as Dee did not fail to note) the supernova of 1572 and the Great Comet of 1577.

Remarkably, *De septem secundeis,* composed in 1508, predicts "the institution of some new Religion," that "a strong sect of Religion shall arise, and be the overthrow of the Ancient Religion. It's to be feared least the fourth beast lose one head."[45] The fourth beast is the fourth beast of Apocalypse from Daniel, a world kingdom that devours the earth. As Trithemius was writing the *Septem,* Martin Luther had only just been ordained a priest. It was not until 1517 that he would post the *Ninety-Five Theses* and spark the Reformation. Even if Trithemius was extrapolating future events from pre-Luther European sentiment, his prescience was outstanding. And thanks to Dee, a world kingdom was indeed about to arise to devour the world.

If Dee's calculations were correct—and Elizabeth had both a legal mandate for imperialism, following Arthur, and an astrological one, following Trithemius—then this opened the way for the true apocalyptic goal of establishing an evangelical British Empire: converting the entire world to Christianity, and thereby assuring that the souls of the world's inhabitants were accounted for prior to the Second Coming. While the new empire would be a Protestant one, Dee was not exclusively Protestant in his imperial scheme, suggesting that Elizabeth convert the American Indians partly to Protestantism, partly to Catholicism. The idea that Elizabeth would convert the world to Christianity and lead it into the eschaton as its reigning sovereign was not unique to Dee; it was broadly circulating in English society at this time, with the end of the world predicted for 1588 by the author and translator James Sandford.[46]

As payment for his intellectual contribution, Dee requested free reign in the dominions under Elizabeth's absolute protection, to fulfill unspoken services for the empire—not for Elizabeth, but under the direction of God himself.[47] This would have meant the expansion (or recovery) of the now-named British Empire, including America. Dee's use of the term *British Empire* long predated the use of the word *British* to mean the British Isles; it referred instead to Arthur's legendary Britain, reaching to North America.[48]

Though Dee's occult expansionism captivated the Privy Council, including Dudley and Philip Sidney, Cecil was underwhelmed. Despite the grandiose patriotism of Dee's plan, Cecil scoffed at Dee's claims of Elizabeth's Arthurian genealogy, and, most of all, the foreign policy disaster that overtly pushing Elizabeth as the world sovereign would create. Part of the reason Cecil may have soured on Dee was that shortly before their meeting he had entertained Vincent Murphyn, and heard the cunning man's concocted story of Dee's Catholic plotting. Whether he believed Murphyn or not, enough of a germ of suspicion was raised that Cecil decided he was unable to take even the slightest security risk. Patiently sitting through Dee's arguments, Cecil grew irritated and finally stonewalled Dee altogether.[49]

Dee, now fifty-three, had offered up the fruit of his youth and of his Great Work; the *Memorials* and *Limits* had been the culminating achievement of his laborious studies, his burning patriotism, his far travels, and even the tortures he had endured for staying loyal to England. He had given everything to advance the cause of his country. Despite little to no recognition or recompense, Dee had continued toiling in Elizabeth's service for decades, producing the imperial plan that would save his nation from poverty and conquest, for which Dee regarded himself a "Christian Aristotle."[50] Yet the response from Elizabeth's court in general, and Cecil in particular, had been to say "thank you very much," take his work, and show him the door. Dee must have been heartbroken.

Returning to Mortlake in defeat, Dee found his mother seriously ill. She died soon thereafter, compounding the sorrow of one of Dee's darkest hours. Elizabeth visited him personally the same day to console him, telling him that all was not lost, and that she would study his plan in greater detail—even that Cecil had been impressed by his historical reasoning. Cecil later sent Dee a joint of venison—small payment for the gift of an empire. Yet no reversal of Cecil's (apparent) decision to shut Dee and his plan out would be forthcoming, and Dee, who shrank in fear from Cecil, would find himself progressively estranged from court. Shifting European politics would make Dee's apocalyptic imperial thinking less relevant, and further voyages to the New World would fail to turn up any evidence of Arthurian settlements, undermining Dee's claims. In the midst of this, Murphyn attacked Dee yet again, although Dee now had an ally in Elizabeth, as Murphyn was later brought up on charges for slandering the queen.

While Dee himself was shut out of Elizabethan geopolitical

strategizing, his plan itself would soon be enacted. England *would* develop great naval might, take the New World, triumph over the Spanish, and establish a British Empire. But Dee, the initiating magus, would enjoy no part of it, not even as a commercial partner; Dee's place in the "Fellowship of New Navigations Atlantical and Septentional" would be taken by the younger Sir Walter Raleigh.[51] History itself would forget Dee's role in establishing the empire, passing over his legacy in favor of that of Richard Hakluyt, Francis Drake, and Raleigh—despite the fact that Dee was far more central to planning.[52] Dee's contribution was providing the justification and *story* behind why expansion was important, christening the nascent British Empire and giving his child a life script and ideology.[53]

In time, this single idea of a British Empire, dreamed up by an eccentric English academic—or given to him by the archangel Michael, as Dee believed—would come to dominate the planet. Following World War I, the "Empire on which the sun never sets" claimed over 458 million subjects, somewhere between one-fifth and one-fourth of the world's population,[54] and covered a full fourth of the land on Earth as well as most of the world's oceans.[55] What had once been a tiny nation that would today be considered developing—wracked by poverty, hunger, religious terrorism, and fearful superstition— now dwarfed the achievements of Alexander, Caesar, or the Khans. During its time, the empire controlled Canada, the eastern colonies in America, parts of the Indies and British Guiana, a large swathe of Africa, much of the Middle East including Palestine and Iraq, India, Burma, Australia, New Zealand, Hong Kong, Antarctica, and many more territories around the world.

If we are to consider the American empire to be the logical successor of the British one, to which global power was transferred when its progenitor began to collapse due to financial overextension, then we must also hold John Dee as the great-grandparent of the modern world. This Anglo-American world order is ruled not by a single world sovereign but by a bureaucratic centralization of power, united not under the banner of Protestantism but under that of its crowned and conquering child, the single world religion of global capitalism, yet with the exact same Protestant eschatology operating in the background.

And if all of this can be said to stem from revelations given to Dee by Michael, it fires the imagination to consider that the Islamic world stems from the utterance of Michael's companion Gabriel, who gave Muhammad the Qu'ran, and would also be present at Dee's later angelic conversations. It is also Gabriel who told Mary of the coming birth of Christ. Angels guided Abraham and were present at the delivery of the Law to Moses, creating Judaism; Michael is said to safeguard the state of Israel. Yet if all of these things were indeed created by the same beings, why do they consistently come into conflict with each other?

If geopolitics are a "grand chessboard,"[56] as former U.S. National Security Advisor Zbigniew Brzezinski famously said, then the players are the angels, and they play multiple sides. God works, we are told, in mysterious ways, though God's workers should look to store up for themselves "treasures in heaven,"[57] rather than this world, if Dee's payment with a single haunch of meat is any indicator.

Can all of this be said to serve a greater good? It depends on whether one accepts a teleological view of history. If, like Teilhard de Chardin or John Dee, you believe that time is moving toward an Omega Point or eschaton—the Second Coming of Christ—it all comes into focus.[58] After all, the angels who exiled mankind east of Eden also, through the British occupation of Palestine, laid the groundwork for the modern state of Israel east of the Mediterranean, upon which both Judaic and evangelical Christian eschatology, and the final redemption of mankind, thereby hangs.

As to the empire itself—how to even begin assessing the effects of Dee's creation on the world?

The archly conservative English historian Niall Ferguson has argued that the British Empire was the best of all possible empires; it was considered a leading light in the world, the "global policeman" before America inherited the mantle, and by comparison, its rival empires—the French, German, Portuguese, Dutch, Japanese, and others—were even more monstrous. Indeed, Ferguson argues, the British Empire was a liberal one, built on the principles of Edmund Burke, with occupied territories expected to come to self-governance.[59]

But the empire was not without its atrocities. Among them were the ongoing rape of India under the Raj and tens of millions of continual starvation deaths, including the 1760s Bengal famine in which one-third of the Bengali population died (with some victims resorting to cannibalism) while England grew fat on the spoils,[60] and the nineteenth-century policies that resulted in the hunger deaths of twenty-nine million Indians.[61] There were the massacres of the indigenous peoples of the Americas by British colonists, including the use of smallpox blankets as biological warfare during the Siege of Fort Pitt—an estimated two to eighteen million Native Americans died during European colonization of North America, in part thanks to English settlers.[62] In the Oceania region, Tasmanians and Australian aborigines were genocided by the English *en masse*.

Then there was the role of the slave trade in building the empire—until the 1807 British abolition of slavery, the English transported over 3.5 million Africans to the Americas to be used in forced labor, one-third of the total transatlantic slave traffic.[63] Once colonies were established, British efforts toward crushing rebellions were severe, as in the Sudan, Ceylon (where 1 percent of the population was killed in a single retribution), Jamaica, Burma, the detainment of almost the entire Kenyan population in camps (in which thousands were beaten to death or died from disease, including almost all of the children),[64] South Africa (where one-sixth of the Boer population died in English concentration camps, primarily children), Afghanistan, and Iraq.

These are, of course, only some of the crimes we know about. Many of the archived records detailing the abuses committed during the final years of the empire were intentionally and illegally destroyed by the Foreign Office before they could be moved into the public domain, allegedly including records of the torture and murder of Mau Mau insurgents; the massacre of unarmed Malayan villagers by the Scots Guard; records of a secret torture center in Aden, Yemen; and all of the sensitive records pertaining to British Guiana.[65] While the empire spread across the globe, racism, cruelty, and genocide followed in its shadow.

Perhaps the nineteenth-century British politician Lord Salisbury summarized the empire best when he quipped, "If our ancestors had cared for the rights of other people, the British Empire would not have been made."[66]

BOOK II

The Angelic Conversations

8

Contact

If John Dee had died in 1580, or ceased his work, he would be remembered as a leading light of Renaissance science, standing between Copernicus and Newton. Though no great discoveries or theories are attributed to Dee, he was instrumental in fostering an intellectual climate in still-backward England, which would lead to the foundation of the Royal Society. What was to occur over the coming decade, however, would overshadow that contribution.

After falling from court favor, Dee worked performing practical alchemy, interpreting dreams, and continuing his work in the private sector, consulting on navigation and cartography, continuing to focus on the Northwest Passage and even joining Humphrey Gilbert's company in 1582.[1] He was also, along with his young ward, Thomas Digges, continuing his investigations into Copernican theory and the use of optics for observing the heavens; for Copernicus, the revelation of a heliocentric universe suggested a return to pre-Christian solar worship—the scientist even alluded to Hermes Trismegistus's suggestion that the sun was, in fact, the "visible god."[*][2]

---

*The revelation of the heliocentric model of the physical universe, and the matching revolution in mankind's conception of the spiritual world, would form part of the doctrinal basis of Crowley's Thelemic religion. Central to Thelema, based in part upon the framework of Dee's angelic revelations, is that the dying and resurrected Christ, the duality

Dee had published tables of star positions in 1557 that used Copernicus's calculations; the 1572 supernova only underlined Dee and Digges' belief that the Copernican model was correct. In 1576, Digges was to draw one of the very first modern depictions of the solar system, in his *Prognostication Everlasting,* with the stars extending infinitely outward past Saturn (then the farthest-known planet). Yet for Digges, raised by Dee, the stars were in fact the angels themselves, "the very court of celestial angels, devoid of grief and replenished with perfect endless joy, the habitacle for the elect."[3]

The 1572 supernova had been more than just an omen. It had overturned England's sense of the divine order of the cosmos, as it had shown that the heavens were not perfectly ordered and controlled, breaking the Great Chain. By 1574, the supernova faded, only to be replaced by a comet or "blazing star" in 1577. It could be nothing less than the rage of God himself at the state of Europe—and perhaps a sign that, as the Apocalypse approached, the angels had reason for increased traffic with humanity. An earthquake that rattled England in 1580, and another comet that appeared shortly thereafter, furthered this terrifying series of omens. 1583 would see another dramatic astrological event—a great conjunction between Saturn and Jupiter in the "fiery trigon" of Aries, Leo, and Sagittarius, replacing the previous "watery trigon" of Cancer, Scorpio, and Pisces. This would be only the seventh such conjunction that had occurred in history, one of which was during the birth of Christ; for Europe's astrologers, this new fiery trigon indicated the end of a 960-year epoch of history. Tycho Brahe thought it presaged the fall of the Roman Church.[4] The effects of the fiery trigon were to play out over the coming years—culminating, many believed, in the end of the world and Second Coming, widely prophesied to be slated for 1588.[5]

This chaos extended not just to the terrestrial and celestial spheres, but to the chronological sphere as well; Pope Gregory XIII was proposing

---

(**cont.**) of good and evil, and even the fear of death in general, are reflections of the geocentric model, and that the Copernican revelation leads to a more even conception of the universe in which night and day, and all of the symbolic forms mankind has associated with them, are really just two phases of a single phenomenon. See Achad, "Stepping Out of the Old Aeon into the New," in Crowley, *The Equinox* 3, no. 1, 183–86.

a fixed date for Easter, as well as removing ten days and setting the cal-endar's tracking of the sun only back to the Council of Nicea in 325— now known as the internationally standardized Gregorian calendar. An attempt to solidify papal authority, it was rejected by Protestants in favor of keeping to the Julian calendar, setting off decades of conflict; for some, it was yet another sign of the coming Apocalypse.[6] Dee was tapped as an adviser on the reform of the Gregorian calendar toward the end of 1582.[7]

Drawing on his vast astronomical knowledge, and working with Walsingham and Cecil, Dee drew up a report entitled "Plain discourse and humble advice for our Gracious Queen Elizabeth," in which he used Copernicus's calculations to determine that eleven days and fifty-three minutes should be removed from the new Gregorian calendar, as opposed to the ten days that Rome suggested. Wisely leaving out Copernicus's heliocentric model from his report, he also suggested that Rome keep to the ten-day calendar for the public, but stick to Dee's more accurate calculations privately.

The Catholic calculations were evidence to Dee of intellectual and spiritual corruption within Rome, as well as further confirmation that Elizabeth could right the damages were she to accept the role of empress of Christendom, reforming both the physical and temporal worlds. Any sane Christian, Dee thought, would agree that the calendar should begin with the birth of Christ, not the terrestrial institution that came after him. Though the calendar had been created by a corrupt Caesar, and further ruined by his spiritual successors in the Church of Rome, it could yet be reformed by the triumphant Elizabeth, the true successor of Constantine. Dee hoped that his revised calendar, entitled "Queen Elizabeth's Perpetual Calendar," would repair the world by reorienting time to Christ's birth, not only assisting the overall Protestant mission of returning Christianity to its simple roots but even winning over the pope by the accuracy of its calculations, and thereby unite Christendom under a single calendar. In doing so, it would also shift power to Elizabeth and resolidify Dee's own position as imperial magus.[8]

Dee's calendrical suggestions were completed by March 25, 1582, and submitted to the frosty Cecil—Walsingham himself would have to step in to assure that Dee's ideas were properly assessed.[9] Though his calculations are impeccable—and continued to inspire students of the calendar even into the eighteenth century[10]—his plans were again rejected.

Dee's work on the calendar is still regarded by mainstream historians of science (like J. L. Heilbron) as his last major scientific contribution.[11] Times had changed; Dee was now a family man, having married at fifty-one, soon to produce eight children—a son, Arthur, had been born on July 13, 1579, and a daughter, Katherine, on June 7, 1581. The Dees had made their nest at Mortlake, which had been bequeathed to Dee by his mother before her death.[12] Dee was in the prime of life, yet had been estranged from court. His long-running interests in the occult were now to come to the forefront.

While charting the course of the empire to come, Dee had continued his occult experimentation in the background, including regular invocations to angels for guidance and even ritual magic to obtain patronage.[13] Dee's first record of having performed practical magic is May 22, 1568, when he noted in his diary that he had divined the time of John Davis's birth "by magic" with the assistance of William Emery at Mortlake.[14] This was four years after the publication of the *Monas*, and less than a decade before his imperial period, which he would claim angelic inspiration for. Despite Dee's reputation as an "arch-conjuror," Dee wasn't doing much actual magic, and when he was, his success rate was spotty. Despite his technical occult learning, Dee had no ability to divine spirits in his optical instruments, and lamented his inability to make contact. In 1569, after supplicating the archangel Michael, to no response, Dee contemplated suicide, writing that he would "leave this world presently" to "enioye the bottomless fowntayne of all wisdome."[15]

By 1579, however—only two years after the publication of *General and Rare Memorials*—Dee had begun a more focused exploration of the occult, deciding to use scryers to make up for his own perceptual lack. Starting in June of that year, Dee employed the scryers Matthew and Bartholomew Hickman, who were sent to Dee by the courtier Sir Christopher Hatton, suggesting that members of Elizabeth's government had been briefed about Dee's occult activities, even that they supported them.[16] As Elizabeth's administration had taken interest in Dee's ability as an alchemist, as well as his prognostications and predictions, it seems likely that they would have kept tabs on his activities.

Dee kept the fact that he was practicing magic *sub rosa,* composing his diary entries related to magic in Greek—justifiably so, given the damage already done to his reputation. He also drew a clear distinction, which he underlined again and again in his early writings, between what he was doing—high magic, exploring the laws of God and nature through practical experiment—and what the public generally associated with magic, which was aggressive sorcery, curses, hexes, and other gutter forms of occultism.

Dee had middling luck with the Hickmans, and another scryer named Barnabas Saul—but their replacement was soon to arrive. This was

Fig. 8.1. Edward Kelly. Stipple engraving by R. Cooper. Courtesy of Wellcome Images.

another event foretold, Dee believed, by the 1572 supernova. On March 8, 1582, a Mr. Clerkson—a kind of talent scout for scryers—arrived at Mortlake with a man named Edward Talbot in tow. Later that evening, as if to mark the occasion, the sky over Mortlake turned blood red.[17]

Talbot was the assumed name of Edward Kelly, under which he may have studied at Oxford.[18] Kelly, then twenty-six, had been born on August 1, 1555; he walked with a cane, and wore a cowl to cover his ears, which had been cropped when Kelly had been caught forging coins. He was alleged to have worked as an apothecary, a secretary, a notary forging title deeds, and even as a necromancer. He was grossly overweight, and an angry drunk—and the dark cloud of scandal and rumor that followed him was even worse than that which followed Dee. Among the hair-raising stories told about Kelly was that he and an accomplice named Paul Waring had conjured one of the "Infernal Regiment" in a park near Lancashire in order to determine the death time of a young noble; the pair then asked one of the noble's servants to direct them to the newest corpse in the local churchyard, a pauper that they proceeded to dig up, make speak, and give predictions about the noble.[19]

Fig. 8.2. Fanciful nineteenth-century engraving of Kelly and Paul Waring reviving a corpse by necromancy. From Raphael, *The Astrologer of the Nineteenth Century*, 1825.

Another apocryphal story, later told to Elias Ashmole, was that Kelly was a con man who had allegedly cheated a Lady out of jewels, and was now being chased by an unnamed pursuer. Outside of Ashmole's secondhand account, the only primary support for this story comes from a note in John Dee's diary that states, "I have confirmed that Talbot was a cosener," next to which Kelly had added that this was "a horrible and slanderous lie."[20] According to Ashmole's tale, Kelly was laying low at Mortlake to avoid being apprehended, and this would help explain his long service to Dee against all better reason, especially when Dee's records make it clear that Kelly found the scrying sessions abhorrent. It would also explain why Kelly was so ready to spend long periods of time on the Continent with Dee. Also according to the account given to Ashmole, Kelly's pursuer caught up with him in Bohemia, where Kelly bought him off with over £2,000 worth of gold (roughly £421,000 or $528,000 in 2017 values) that he produced by using an alchemical powder that he also furnished his pursuer with. This apocryphal tale has helped color Kelly's long-term reputation, and thus assisted later critics in dismissing the angelic conversations—yet it may only be hearsay.

Whatever the truth of the matter, Dee knew little about Kelly, and may not have been as concerned with his moral provenance as later audiences are. Dee's note that he thought Kelly a cosener confirms this, though this would not have been out of character or even, necessarily, unforgivable, as scryers like Kelly were usually vagabonds, drawn from the great itinerant masses that roamed Elizabeth's impoverished England. There was nothing special about Kelly's profession—scryer was a common, if socially frowned upon, role at the time. And though scryers might be employed by anybody from the clergy to aristocrats, they almost invariably came from the lower classes and were often associated with criminal behavior.

A useful parallel would be the modern world's psychics and fortune-tellers, with whom the scryer's crystal ball has also come to be associated, and who are culturally ubiquitous, plying their trade on nearly every street corner of the modern world, in telephone services, and through late-night television infomercials—yet who simultaneously occupy an almost invisible social position. Though psychics are consulted by people from almost every class and occupation, they inhabit a place in the social pecking order somewhere between janitorial services and massage parlor prostitutes. Elizabeth's England was no different, and it is not surprising that an air of controversy followed Kelly. Scandal followed Dee as well, of course, and for parallel reasons, albeit played out at a higher stratum of society.

It was not just England that had disdain for Kelly—the angels themselves, as recorded in Dee's spirit diaries, would also find the young cunning man distasteful. Jane Dee, as well, became increasingly hostile to Kelly the more he wore out his welcome in the Dees' household, though John Dee was fixated enough on the pair's work to more readily, even naïvely, overlook his companion's shortcomings.

Soon after Kelly's arrival, Dee's previous scryer, Barnabas Saul, left Mortlake. Saul may well have been pushed out by Kelly, who had himself been embroiled in criminal charges; Kelly later confessed that he had been sent by parties unknown to enmesh Dee in "dealing with wicked spirits." Indeed, Kelly claimed to Dee that "a spiritual creature" had confided in him that Saul had been slandering Dee. Dee began using Kelly as his scryer soon afterward,[21] and Kelly began enmeshing himself in Dee's life and affairs, despite Jane Dee's disdain. The pair began regular scrying sessions, recording immediate success in making contact with the spirit world.

EXPLANATORY THEORIES FOR THE SPIRIT ACTIONS

What transpired during the spirit actions has been interpreted many ways in the centuries since they took place. We are left with the following explanatory theories.

1. Kelly Was a Fraud, and Dee Took Him at Face Value.

The first, and most obvious, theory is that Kelly ran a decade-long confidence game on Dee, telling the credulous older man what he wanted to hear in exchange for a living wage. Kelly could have been combining material he had already read with material borrowed from Dee's own library; indeed, there are several passages in the spirit diaries that suggest that this is exactly what he was doing. Throughout the record, Dee writes that the angelic material reminds him of passages from Agrippa, Reuchlin, Trithemius, Abano, Pantheus, *Liber iuratus,* and others; Nicholas Clulee has suggested that what Kelly was "transmitting" was really a mixture of his own imagination and passages from what he had read from Dee's shelves at Mortlake.[22]

The fraud theory is only supported by the infamous later incident in which Kelly convinced Dee that the angels had commanded the duo to swap wives, which must stretch the suspension of disbelief of even the most uncritical reader.

Though Méric Casaubon (who first published and introduced Dee's diaries) largely ignored Kelly, and suggested that if Dee had been defrauded, it had been by Satan, later scholars (like J. H. Heilbron) came to the conclusion that Kelly was a bad actor and sociopathic manipulator of the credulous and vulnerable Dee. This is the standard narrative on the angelic sessions, as evidenced by the 2016 exhibition of Dee's library and spirit paraphernalia at the Royal College of Physicians in London, which held to the story that Dee was duped by Kelly. Yet the occult author Geoffrey James, writing around the same time as Heilbron, suggests that it was *Kelly* who was the victim of Dee, held hostage at Mortlake, barely paid and constantly pushed to perform despite teetering on the edge of psychological breakdown.[23]

It seems unlikely that Kelly was able to memorize the lengthy and complex passages recorded in the spirit diaries in advance, even if there are multiple instances in the diaries where Kelly corrects something that Dee has transcribed, suggesting previous memorization. However, the researcher Colin D. Campbell points out what should, in retrospect, have been glaringly obvious: many of the complex tables that Kelly painstakingly transmitted through the scrying ball were dictated in reverse. Kelly could thus have hidden a copied table somewhere in the oratory or on his person, angled it so that it reflected in the scrying glass (where it would have been reversed) and then dictated from the reflection.

Yet even if this was the case, Campbell suggests (and it is indeed an elegant demystification), much of what Kelly "transmitted" is still far beyond what he could have known or created on his own.[24] In addition, if this was indeed Kelly's plan, Kelly himself acted to undermine it, as when he repeatedly tried to turn Dee away from further interaction with the spirits, or even when, on May 24, 1584, he showed Dee a section of Agrippa that the spirits seem to have copied! (Rather than set off warning bells, this proved to Dee that Agrippa had been accurate in his calculations.)[25]

Fraudulence does not fully rule out other explanations, particularly as Kelly actually *was* entering altered states of consciousness—either through mental illness, substance use, or simply by deceiving even *himself* over time to the point where potent unconscious material began to surface, though we are still left with the mathematical and linguistic complexity of the visions themselves to contend with, as they are seemingly beyond Kelly's cognitive capacity.

A final elaboration of the fraud theory, which I have not seen suggested elsewhere, is that Kelly was working with an unseen third party, who could have been composing "visions" (perhaps written in reverse) and tables of "angelic" information and then passing them to Kelly, who angled them so as to be out of Dee's sight but reflected into the scrying ball, and then recited them to Dee. As Dee was so connected to the royal court and intelligence work, and England was in the middle of a cold war, such a scenario is quite plausible; unknown actors who had been advised as to Dee's already progressing experiments with scryers could have sent Kelly to Mortlake as an agent and continued to feed him material, even via Elizabeth's court, just as the Hickmans had been preselected and sent to him by Hatton. The motives of such an unknown party would not be immediately obvious, although the later arrival of Olbracht Łaski, and the subsequent push for his ascendency to power in Europe, may provide a clue. Indeed, Kelly himself confessed to Dee that he had been sent by a hidden agent to embroil Dee in occultism.[26]

Yet for all its explanatory power, this theory still leaves the various supernatural phenomena seen and recorded by Dee himself during the actions, such as spirits that appeared in his house, and while traveling on the Continent, including the incident in which Dee and Kelly claimed that they burned their records, only to have them later returned intact by a spirit.

2. Kelly Was Mentally Ill, and Dee Took Him at Face Value.

A related and even more tragic theory is that Kelly suffered from schizophrenia or some other form of mental illness, and that Dee, lacking a modern medical perspective, took his hallucinations at face value. In this narrative, it would have been Dee exploiting Kelly, not vice versa. This is borne out by Kelly's alternating despondency and manic hyperactivity, his regular shifts between transfixed visionary state and hysterical meltdown, his constant attempts to flee Mortlake, his belief that he was being assaulted by demons, the grandiose claims that he and Dee were to play a special role in history, and even his violent rages on the Continent.

Compounding this would be that Kelly's environment—constant occult ritual, overwork by Dee, poor pay, fear of criminal prosecution for his own previous actions, the looming threat of retribution from Continental authorities, his abuse of alcohol (if not other substances), and his enforced isolation from a support network or a normal reality outside of Dee's private world and obsessions (beyond a wife he greatly disliked)—would only have worsened his mental health.

3. Kelly Was on Drugs, and Dee Took Him at Face Value.

The pharmacopeia of Elizabethan England is far removed from us—but whatever its contents, England's alchemists surely had first pick.

Outside of mentions of Kelly's alcohol abuse, however, there are no mentions of substances in the meticulously kept spirit diaries, *possibly* outside of an alchemical "red powder" that Dee and Kelly spent some time hunting for. Kelly had purportedly acquired the "white and red powders of projection," along with the alchemical *Book of St. Dunstan,* in Wales—they had, according to Kelly, been raided from a bishop's tomb by a Protestant horde and traded to an innkeeper for wine, who then sold the loot to Kelly for a guinea.[27]

To go *far* out on an unsubstantiated limb, ergot-infected wheat, which contains lysergic acid, a precursor of LSD, creates a red powder when it is milled down—it has famously been suggested that ergotism could have caused the Salem witch panic by inducing ongoing mass hallucinations in a population consuming moldy bread, although the thesis has been hotly contested.[28] It's also at least within the realm of possibility that Kelly may have used preparations of aconite or deadly nightshade as psychedelic aid to his visions; psilocybin mushrooms also grow abundantly in pastures throughout England, and cannabis was widely available in Elizabethan times.

If Kelly was regularly taking such visionary aids prior to his scrying sessions, he was doing so either with the help of Dee or unknown to Dee as part of Kelly's act in projecting an aura of supernatural power. Indeed, such chemical aid may have been a cunning-man trick that Kelly indulged in to win Dee's confidence, not suspecting that the older man would be so impressed that he decided he wanted Kelly's trick repeated on a near-daily basis for the next several years. Hard pressed to deliver, Kelly may well have been trapped in a cycle of substance abuse, and the progressive mental and physical deterioration that goes with it. Such a hypothesis would explain Kelly's regular "bad trips" and conclusions that the angels were really demons, his ongoing attempts to escape Mortlake, and his more and more unhinged and erratic personality.

If this was the case, it is also possible that Dee indulged as well, particularly during the regular sessions in which Dee and Kelly share visions or Dee is moved to displays of extreme religious piety or outright terror, which are consistent with the psychedelic experience, *especially* when combined with religious ritual.

While this hypothesis is attractive, and goes furthest toward resolving the origin of the often complex and mathematical nature of the visions, it is contradicted by the high lucidity with which Dee kept the records of the spirit actions—though many of the sessions may have been conducted with Kelly indulging and Dee recording, or recorded after the fact. Most damaging to this theory, however, is that there is no suggestion of any substance consumed, even in code—no Greek, Latin, or other devices even hint at such psychotropic pursuits. This is also a thoroughly modern reading of a very different time and place.

4. It Was All Cryptography.

Another possible, and often repeated, explanation is that the sessions could have been cryptography—espionage messages masked as occult activity. This has historical precedent; as previously discussed, the occult work of Trithemius was largely veiled cryptography. Dee was a keen student of both Trithemius and cryptography, was a lover of languages, codes, mathematics, and wordplay, and was also engaged in work for British intelligence at a time of extreme geopolitical tension. Considering Dee's background and environment, it is less likely that the diaries contain *no* cryptography than it is that they do. Yet if we again take Trithemius as a precedent, and as a direct model for Dee's occult work, we may come to the conclusion that Dee layered both cryptographic and actual occult material in his diaries—potentially multiple-stacking layers—just as Trithemius did, meaning that even if the "angelic" material is at a future date demonstrated to be cryptographic in nature, this still does not rule out supernatural explanations. Of course, Dee could have wholly fabricated all of the diary entries describing supernatural events, presumably to further disguise cryptography.

5. It Was Real.

It is of course possible that *all* of these options may be true, to varying degrees—yet another explanation, however improbable, is that Dee and Kelly were telling the truth, *at least as they understood it.*

Aleister Crowley, a man of no less dubious reputation than Kelly, provided one of the more known apologies for Dee and Kelly's work after his own investigation of the spirit diaries:

"[The angelic language] is not a jargon," Crowley wrote, "it has a grammar and syntax of its own. It is very much more sonorous, stately and impressive than even Greek and Sanskrit, and the English translation, though in places difficult to understand, contains passages of a sustained sublimity that Shakespeare, Milton and the Bible do not surpass. To condemn Kelly as a cheating charlatan—the accepted view— is simply stupid. If he invented Enochian, and composed this superb prose, he was at worst a [Thomas] Chatterton with fifty times that poet's ingenuity and five hundred times his poetical genius."[29]

Crowley cites as evidence of this the English translation of the Call of the Second Aethyr, which would be transmitted during the angelic conversations:

Can the Wings of the Wind understand your voices of Wonder? O You! the second of the First! whom the burning flames have framed in the depth of my Jaws! Whom I have prepared as cups for a wedding, or as the flowers in their beauty for the chamber of Righteousness! Stronger are your feet than the barren stone; and mightier are your voices than the manifold winds! For you are become a building such as is not, save in the Mind of the All-Powerful.[30]

Crowley continues:

I prefer to judge Kelly from this rather than from stale scandal of people to whom any Magician, as such, smelt of sulphur. If, on the other hand, Kelly did not write this, he may of course have been a common ignorant scoundrel, one of whose abnormalities was a faculty for seeing and hearing sublimities, just as a burglar or business man might be able to describe St. Paul's Cathedral far better than the Dean.[31]

Crowley's argument is purely subjective—a fallacious appeal to aesthetics, not logic or scientific evidence. Yet magic itself is a subjective pursuit. Crowley would also suggest that the angelic material was valid because it "works," that is, that its use produced profound visionary states in himself and his student Victor Neuburg in the Algerian desert in 1909. This is an even more subjective argument—a fallacious argument from anecdotal evidence—and Crowley clearly has a personal agenda to push in making such a suggestion. Yet the prose produced by Crowley and Neuburg while scrying the Aethyrs was of an equal quality to that produced by Kelly, and was not only the finest of Crowley's career but also, in the present author's opinion, rivals many of the great visionary religious texts of the world. This is no small feat for Crowley, a man who, though being an excellent if overwrought prose stylist, was and is regarded as one of the worst poets of his era.

Likewise, Crowley's subjective assessment of the work of the "scoundrel" Kelly—ranking at least sections of it alongside the work of Shakespeare, Milton, and the Bible—is hard to argue with. Yet this also suggests that both Dee and later commentators may have underestimated the Oxford-educated Kelly himself, that he was a great deal more intelligent than he let on, and that commentators have allowed themselves to be blinded to Kelly's own intellect by dint of his profession and socioeconomic position (in which he may have been trapped) as well as his proximity to Dee, who is almost a cartoon representation of traditional academic learning.

Regarding Crowley's claim that the angelic (or "Enochian" as it was later called, though not by Dee or Kelly) language has its own grammar and syntax, Enochian was assessed by the skeptical Australian linguist and anthropologist Donald Laycock in the 1970s. Laycock concluded that Kelly's early (untranslated) "speeches" in Enochian were probably trance glossolalia, and that the later Enochian transmissions that *were* given translations reveal a phonology, grammar, and word order that were largely English, with an incomplete (and not un-English) grammar and an arbitrary vocabulary (in part because so few words were given), with some words appearing randomly generated. However, he did find a structure of repeating word roots, for which he had no ready explanation.

Laycock also states that he is mystified by the numerical structure or gematria of Enochian, and that the test of any future revelations will be if they can explain the mathematical structure of the language. Undermining the cryptography theory, Laycock concludes that the angelic calls are *not* a cipher. Laycock's final summation is that "I do not think anyone can afford to be dogmatic in this area," noting that he has known many people who claim to have gotten results by using the angelic system, and that there may be genuine revelations at the heart of the system—but that the angels' "limitations are those of Kelly; their occasional sublimities, those of Dee."[32]

The idea that the angelic conversations were real has never been taken seriously anywhere outside of the occult subculture, besides Casaubon, who suggests that they were the work of the devil, and that Kelly, a fraudulent sorcerer, had led Dee upon the path of darkness.[33]

Assuming the sessions *were* real, this now moves them into the realm of theology, and raises four additional subdivisions: The sessions were real and truly inspired by angels (Dee's position); they were real but inspired by demons pretending to be angels (Kelly and Casaubon's position; also the standard long-running argument of religious authorities, such as St. Augustine, against operative magic; also the argument of some later occultists, like Paul Foster Case,[34] who eschewed the angelic system as inherently dangerous); they were real and inspired by both angels *and* demons (suggested by the diaries themselves, as much of the early sessions are taken up with the angels rebuking lying demons pretending to be angels, and rescuing Dee and Kelly from demonic interference); or, finally, that angels and demons are arbitrary categories generated in altered states of consciousness by the human mind, and determined more by the cultural background of Dee and Kelly than the objective nature of the spirits themselves, who used the narrative of Christianity and the mask of "angels and demons" to communicate with the two magicians in a language they understood.

6. Something In-Between.

The best analysis yet published of what Dee and Kelly's work truly was is James Justin Sledge's 2010 article "Between Loagaeth and Cosening: Towards an Etiology of John Dee's Spirit Diaries." In it, Sledge assesses many of the above positions, coming to the conclusion that the boundaries were blurred for Kelly, and that as the scrying sessions put Kelly in a prophetic role, the lines between what Kelly was creating and what he was channeling would have been nonexistent in his own mind. Even the transmission of the angelic language could have been "created and simultaneously interpreted (or rationalized, depending on your viewpoint) as being part of a continuum of revelatory dispensation. Such a process could be likened to the stigmatic who certainly must persistently create their physical wounds with some degree of intentional agency yet remains credulous that the wounds are of divine origin. While an affront to strictly rational thinking, the notion that people believe the myths they themselves create should be far from shocking."[35] This blurring would have been exaggerated by Kelly shifting through several different states of consciousness.

The angelic language, Sledge argues, "begins to exist somewhere between being created and being discovered by Kelly under a state of increasingly pronounced epistemological inclusivity between the angelic revelation, his own thoughts, and the dizzying array of alterations in his consciousness brought on by the effects of the sessions themselves and/or mental illness."[36] For Sledge, the contents of the sessions and of Kelly's mind must have been so chaotic that to either reject the sessions as Kelly's fabrication or uncritically accept the sessions as divine revelation are both errors, and far too simplistic readings.

Instead, Sledge suggests that "a 'perfect storm' of cultural, psychiatric, neurobiological, and epistemic conditions came together in the symbiotic relationship of Dee and Kelly to produce a stunning array of visions." The visions were thus a combination of environmental conditions, Kelly's preexisting psychosis, altered states of consciousness created by the rituals themselves, and the cultural and ritual context that empowered Kelly and allowed him to step into the role of prophet.[37] This is a far more nuanced and satisfying explanation than any of the previous theories alone.

DEE AND KELLY'S WORKING METHODS

If this is what was going on with Dee and Kelly *internally,* what was going on *externally* is much simpler. However we rationalize the angelic sessions, Dee and Kelly's magical process in the spirit diaries holds to its own internal logic and methodology, which must be assessed on its own terms if the two men's work is to be understood.

Medieval grimoires recount that magicians should assemble elaborate ceremonial preparations, surrounding themselves with magical circles and triangles, ritual tools and fumigations, and performing elaborate conjurations. Though Kelly had engaged in this type of magic before, and Dee had long been versed in the grimoires and the work of Trithemius and Agrippa, the scrying sessions partook of none of this complexity (at least not initially). Rather, sessions proceeded in Dee's oratory, behind closed doors, and consisted of simple prayer. Dee would humble himself in reverence for God and Christ, underline his unworthiness, and then ask that God send his angels to instruct him in wisdom. Afterward, Kelly would sit at the scrying crystal and receive visions, narrating them to Dee. Dee recorded these utterances and then prompted Kelly and the angels with further questions or requests. While the angels and other spiritual creatures were normally confined to the scrying crystal, they would at times manifest either in Dee and Kelly's internal vision or even in the house, as when the angel Madimi appeared and played a game of hide-and-seek in Dee's library, or when a gang of elementals physically assaulted Kelly, almost breaking his arm and leaving welts on his skin.

As Deborah Harkness has pointed out, the sessions were closer to the received visions of biblical prophets than ceremonial magic.* Yet while earlier prophets were often found secluded from humanity, doing battle with their demons in the desert or in caves, Dee and Kelly did not abstract themselves from society at all. The sessions were conducted in the middle of a crowded and bustling household managed by Jane Dee, including several servants, assistants, and children.[38] Though the popular image of Dee is of a man enshrouded in darkness, spiritual and literal, most of the scrying sessions were conducted in broad daylight, with the scrying stone positioned by a window to capture natural light, following the guidelines outlined by Dee in the *Propaedeumata aphoristica*.[39] And though Dee's status had slipped following Cecil's lukewarm reception of his imperial plans, Dee was still very much involved in the world, in court politics, and in his continual quest for intellectual patronage.[40] As the sessions progressed, Dee and Kelly went mobile, lugging their scrying gear across the Continent as they sought to enact the angels' commands. Also contrary to his Hermetic image, Dee did not keep secrecy at all times, but instead frequently sought to enmesh promising individuals in his work and the urgent messages of the angels, all the way up to monarchs and representatives of the Church.

While angelic magic is quite complex on the surface—presenting a bewildering array of diagrams, ritual tools, mathematics, and

---

*The Zohar, for instance, suggests that Moses received the Tablets of the Law as (or, as John Dee believed, *through*) a "divine sapphire." See Harkness, "The Scientific Reformation," 284.

linguistics—it is paradoxically simple in its functions and goals. An obvious analogy would be a personal computer, whose inner circuitry and code are beyond the grasp of the average public, yet that can be used by anybody to perform what would appear to be miracles to any human being who lived prior to the last few decades.

A technical analysis of Dee and Kelly's angelic magic follows.

SANCTIFICATION AND ILLUMINATION

The primary goal of angelic magic is twofold—*sanctification* and *illumination*.

"No man is illuminated, that is not sanctified," the angels told Dee and Kelly near the end of the sessions. "Neither is there any man perfectly sanctified, that is not joyfully illuminated."[41]

Sanctification is the process by which an individual is purified and brought progressively closer to godliness through the action of the Holy Spirit. It is core to the Christian faith across denominations. In terms of the Great Chain of Being, it is the bridging of the gap between the human and angelic orders via the repair of sin—not by man's efforts alone, but by the descending grace of God through the intermediary of the savior. Sanctification is close to, though much more theologically specific than, the goal of "overcoming the ego" that is common in popular New Age, pseudo-Buddhist, and psychedelic literature. As revealed in *Liber primus,* the primary method by which humans achieve sanctification is through their actions.[42]

Illumination is the kindling of divine wisdom and understanding within the life of the sanctified individual. As the individual's mortal life is broken and rebuilt, much like the Temple in Jerusalem, it can be remade as a fit container for the Holy Spirit rather than the sinful, terrestrial concerns of a standard unawakened human. This is one interpretation of Christ's parable of new wine for new wineskins. Qabalistically, the breaking of an adept's ego and well-laid plans at Da'ath should successfully open the way for the influx of information from the Supernals.

These two concurrent processes can be subsumed under the single word *initiation*—not the ritual theater of Masonic ceremony that is only a *representation* of true initiation, but the ongoing process of an operative magician's life, occult experiments, and passage through reality. As Dee would later describe, it is the magician's continual education by angelic "Schoolmasters."[43] In Greek, this process is called *theosis,* union with God; in Sanskrit, it is *yoga.* In the angelic tongue, it is called *gebofal.*

This approach to initiation has some similarities with the classical grimoires—for instance, the *Book of Abramelin,* or the various books of spirit conjuration that counseled magicians to observe cleanliness and obeisance to God as necessary preparation for dealing with

Fig. 8.3. Gustave Doré, *Jacob Wrestling with the Angel,* 1855.

lower spirits. However, the angelic material concentrates almost exclusively on the purification process itself, and is much closer to religion in its aims. Dee and Kelly's overwhelming goal was to understand the nature of reality and do God's will; they were pushed by the angels to focus obsessively on this objective to the exclusion of all others, to the point that their material circumstances became dire. Though Dee and Kelly repeatedly asked the angels for material benefits, they were often mocked and derided when they did. For Dee, the sessions were about his ongoing education, and a natural outgrowth of a life spent questing for knowledge and praying to God for, as Freemasons say, "more light." Rather than aping magicians like Agrippa, Dee cast himself in the mold of Abraham, Enoch, and Moses, and sought to follow in their footsteps in gaining direct divine revelation.[44] Likewise, he took inspiration and scriptural justification from the fact that angels had been sent to Isaac, Jacob, Joshua, Gideon, Esdras, Daniel, and Tobias, among others. Dee soon became so convinced of his prophetic role that he would seek to act to directly influence history, even going so far as planning the publication of the spirit diaries, a potentially explosive move only half a century out from Luther's *Ninety-Five Theses*. This publication did not occur within Dee's lifetime.[45]

In seeking to communicate with God without intermediaries, Dee was acting in an explicitly Protestant manner.[46] The angels themselves did not take the side of any specific denomination, though they railed at Luther and Calvin, and later urged Dee and Kelly to reconcile themselves to the Roman Church and the doctrine of transubstantiation, despite the corruption of Rome that the angels themselves acknowledged.[47]

This dynamic places the angelic sessions more within the province of religion than magic, particularly when compared to the various survivals of magical practice that exist in the twenty-first-century "occulture," which have heavily marketed the illumination side of the equation, but left out the far less glamorous process of sanctification, replacing it with Satanic pride, overweening self-regard, and the "will to power" of Nietzsche, Crowley, or, at the very nadir of popular occultism, Anton LaVey.

In contrast, Dee and Kelly were consistently told to mortify the flesh and to forgo the delights of this world for those of the next. Routinely furious, the angels demanded ever-greater obedience and faith from their servants. When Dee and Kelly's egos reared their heads, the angels—the most ferocious of gurus—were quick to knock them down and remind them of their place. Pride, the angels told them, was mankind's greatest sin.

"Ignorance was the nakedness wherewithal you were first tormented," they were told by the order of angels identified as the Daughters of Light, "and the first Plague that fell unto man was the want of Science. The want of Science hindreth you from knowledge of yourself. Whosoever therefore knoweth not himself, is proud."[48]

It was this pride—like the pride of Satan—that made mankind sinners. And Satan, the Daughters said, was not glorified by God—rather, he was in glory before he became the devil, and the abuse of this glorification precipitated his fall. The doings of the spirit quicken, they told Dee and Kelly, but the doings of the flesh lead to destruction. And no man was elected "by proper name," but only according to the measure of his faith.

"By true understanding you learn, first to know yourselves what you are: of whom you are, and to what end you are."[49] As such they were to pray to avoid pride and have their ignorance removed. For ignorance could not be overcome by seeking knowledge, as Dee had long done—in fact, it is mankind's constant need for further knowledge that has blinded him to his own nature.*

For the angels, everything in the world was illusion, and only humility and obedience to God was of any value. Even when tragedy or hardship befell Dee and Kelly, they were told that the causes of their sin were being removed. Ultimately, Dee and Kelly would offer outpourings of gratitude and love when the angels revealed how they had been acting to steer the two men from the ever-open jaws of hell. Even the temptations and outright demonic attacks Dee and Kelly faced during

---

*This nondual statement from the angels suggests the nature of the mind itself. As any experienced meditator should know, when the mind seeks outside itself for its fulfillment, it generates more thought and mental activity. When it comes to rest by realizing that it, itself, is what it seeks, it becomes whole-in-itself, like the ouroboros snake eating its own tail, revealing the true philosopher's stone.

the sessions were described as necessary to teach them spiritual discernment and strengthen their faith.

Yet for all their bluster, the angels acknowledged that as humans have free will, they are still free to reject God's plans—as in the case of Count Łaski, who went off-script and failed to become the European supermonarch that the angels desired to make him. The angels can promise or threaten, but they can't change human will; finally, they become dejected when faced with this sad state of affairs. Such forms the ongoing drama and tragedy of Christianity: God can lead sinners back home, but he can't force them to choose heaven over hell.

Yet Dee was not without his own will to power. Dee sought not only *theosis* but *apotheosis,* full divinization; like many of the grimoire authors, he pursued this quest for power through the paradoxical route of absolute submission. Despite, or perhaps because of, their constant chastening by the angels, Dee and Kelly considered themselves among God's elect, though this status was not at all certain throughout the sessions.[50] What resulted was a collision of the hyperconfidence and anthrocentrism of the Hermetic worldview with the Saturnian sanctification of the angelic sessions themselves, in which Dee's eager and open quest for knowledge met with the withering attitude of the angels, as well as their view of Dee and Kelly as little more than convenient (though often faulty and willful) hirelings, who required disciplining by their masters much as a human would discipline a dog. The privilege of serving God, and of entrance to heaven upon death, was payment enough: "And unto you, there is nothing," Gabriel told them on June 2, 1584, "for you are hirelings, whose reward is heaven."[51]

THE SCRYING CRYSTAL

If prayer was Dee's medium of communication, this still left the question of how to receive messages back. This was the role of Kelly, who possessed psychic gifts but was considered an impure—even distasteful—channel by the angels. The difficulties in establishing two-way communication were compounded by the sublunary nature of the world itself. Because of the Fall of mankind, the once-open channels of speech between man,

God, and angel had been broken.* As such, humanity had to look for the answers to prayers not in direct speech but in events, signs, dreams, stellar phenomena, and even natural disasters.[52] This interpretation of oblique signs has been a primary concern of shamans, priests, and magicians of one form or the other since the beginning of humanity.

Scrying, therefore, became Dee's preferred method of receiving communications *back* from the angels; scrying is the technical term for gazing into a crystal or other reflective surface for long periods of time, in a heightened ritual setting, as a way of entering an altered, visionary state of consciousness. Dee and Kelly used a number of scrying devices throughout the sessions, including a stone supposedly manifested to them by the archangel Uriel. Dee variously referred to his scrying stone as the "shewstone," "the stone," a "diaphanous globe," the "first sanctified stone," and the "holy stone."[53]

The large obsidian mirror that is often associated with Dee, an Aztec cult artifact dedicated to Tezcatlipoca brought back from the New World after the conquest of Mexico by Cortés, which has long been on display at the British Museum,[54] may not have been used at all, nor has it been conclusively shown that the mirror even belonged to Dee. If the black mirror was Dee's, it may have come into his possession at Louvain or through a Spanish courtier.[55] Of the other objects in the British Museum attributed to Dee's use, it is likely that only the three wax seals actually belonged to him; the crystal ball and gold engraving of the "Vision of the Four Castles" are probably later acquisitions by collectors from other magicians or antiquarians who reproduced them from Casaubon's printing of *A True & Faithful Relation.*[56]

Dee's diary entries for November 1582 record that the archangel Uriel manifested a crystal out of thin air that was subsequently used by Kelly as his scrying device for the remainder of the sessions. A crystal alleged to be this object was displayed at the 2016 exhibition of selections of John Dee's library at the Royal College of Physicians in London. It is far less assuming than the gear in the British Museum. The crystal is a rough, faceted crystal globe less than an inch in diameter, housed

---

*Solving this problem is, perhaps, the entire reason for the incarnation of Christ in the world.

in a metal ring connected to a short chain about an inch long—the size and appearance of a keychain.

We can trace Dee's interest in scrying and crystallomancy as a natural progression of his interest in optics, including the theoretical material outlined in the *Propaedeumata*. While Dee had already hinted at the ultimate science of archemastery, with the aid of Kelly, he believed that he was able to realize it.[57]

THE TEMPLE FURNITURE

Through the medium of the scrying crystal, Dee and Kelly would be given instructions for building a much more complex set of temple furniture, including a three-foot cube table to be placed upon wax seals and covered with tin sigils, silk cloths, and a central wax seal, upon which the crystal was now to sit. These were to be constructed to specific instructions, and were meant to be sublunary representations of celestial and divine objects.[58] These ritual tools were to furnish a temple for making more stable contact with the angelic realms, and elaborated a system much closer to the grimoire magic that Kelly had practiced, offering a new approach to operative magic that at once clarified the text of prior grimoires and also departed from them, breaching into far more intellectually complex and abstract territory.[59]

This was the illumination side of the sanctification and illumination equation. The reception and construction of the temple furniture, as well as Dee's prior investigation of the *Book of Soyga,* may have served the secondary function of stretching and attuning Dee and Kelly's minds to be able to comprehend the angelic universe.[60]

Key to understanding the structure of the furniture are the numbers four (representing the four elements, four living creatures, four horsemen, etc.), seven (representing the seven planets, seven days of Creation, seven trumpets and seals of Revelation, etc.), and twelve (representing the twelve signs of the zodiac, twelve tribes of Israel, etc.).

The furniture included:*

---

*For the best current summary of the temple furniture, its inner logic, and its workings, see DuQuette, *Enochian Vision Magick.*

1. The Holy Table of Practice, three cubic feet in size, which was to be made of "sweet wood." Upon the top was to be painted a three-by-four central grid of Enochian characters centered within a hexagram; along the edges were to be written a series of Enochian characters in consecrated yellow oil paint. The Holy Table played a prominent role in Crowley's later scrying of the Aethyrs, where it was revealed to be scribed in the book of the High Priestess card of the tarot in the nineteenth Aethyr; a further suggestion was made in the first Aethyr that the Holy Table might be the cubical stone of the universe. The characters around the edge of the table are shown to be zodiacal, pertaining to the manifest universe (or, as Crowley called it, the body of Nuit).

2. The Sigillum Dei Aemeth, a wax seal upon which was carved a heptarchic diagram and the names of several angels, possibly corresponding to the seven planets. The design was delivered to Dee and Kelly early in their sessions, yet also appears to be an update of an earlier design in the *Sworn Book of Honorius.* The angels reveal that the outer ring of the Sigillum created the "beasts, birds, fowle and fish,"[61] as in Genesis 1:20–25, and relate the Sigillum to the *Book of Soyga,* a book in Dee's possession that he questioned the angels about during the early sessions. From this Sigillum are drawn the names of most of the angels that Dee and Kelly interact with in the spirit diaries, including Madimi, Ave, Il, and many others. The inner heptagon itself suggests BABALON, the Whore of Babylon from Revelation 17–18, the "Daughter of Fortitude" who would appear at the end of the spirit diaries and play a central role in Crowley's later scrying sessions.

3. The Ensigns of Creation, seven seals to be made of purified tin or painted upon the table itself, likely corresponding to the seven planets, as well as the seven days of Creation and the seven stages of alchemy.[62] Like the Sigillum, the Ensigns relate to the Creation story in Genesis 1 and 2:1–3.

4. The table was to rest on a red silk carpet, on four small wax copies of the Sigillum contained within wooden boxes.

5. The Tabula Bonorum, a round yellow table containing the

names of forty-nine (seven by seven) good angels, was to rest on the floor beneath the Holy Table. (These may relate to the angels that unleash the seven "trumpet judgments" in Revelation.) Further wooden seals were to be made to represent the heptarchic angels relating to the days of the week, which were to be held when specifically working with these angels; these appear to be not only planetary but also elemental in nature, and can fulfill practical tasks for the magician working with them.

6. A white linen cloth was to cover the entire table, giving the appearance of a large white cube upon a red silk carpet. The Sigillum Dei and Ensigns of Creation were to rest upon the white linen, with the Ensigns in a heptagonal pattern around the central Sigillum.

7. A silk cloth of flashing colors, alternating green and red, with gold tassels at the corners, was to cover the top of the table, Sigillum, and Ensigns.

8. The scrying ball was to rest in a three-legged holder in the center of the Sigillum, with the red and green silk layer between them. The final effect is of a large cube table, covered with flashing silks, with the scrying ball being *the only visible element* of the entire array. This is important to emphasize, as the temple furniture looks bewilderingly complex when encountered on paper. When built and assembled, however, the only objects that should be visible on the table are the scrying ball and, if used, two candles on either side of it.

9. Twelve banners that are to surround the working area in a circle, delineating the edge of the magician's circle, much as a Solomonic circle would a grimoire magician's. These correspond to the twelve zodiacal signs as grouped by the four elements, as well as the twelve tribes of Israel. The angelic names taken from these banners were later used by the Golden Dawn to mark elemental space in the Supreme Banishing Ritual of the Pentagram.

10. A gold ring upon which is written the name "PELE" that is to be worn by the working magician and corresponds to the Seal of Solomon, the ring said to be worn by King Solomon, who

appears in 1 Kings, and used to command the demons with which he built his temple.

11. A lamen upon which are written an array of characters in the angelic language that is to be hung from the neck of the working magician, conciliating them to the Holy Table. This may correspond to the breastplate worn by the high priest of the Israelites in Exodus 28:15–30 (which, like the central square of the Holy Table, was a three-by-four grid, within which were placed the Urim and Thummim).

12. A second round seal, made in black wax and covered with another grid of angelic letters, called the Round Table of Nalvage. This corresponds to the Holy Trinity: its substance being the Father, its circumference the Son, and the order and number of its characters being the Holy Spirit.

13. A large table containing 644 angelic characters, with four squares of 156 characters each united by a central black cross. These correspond to the four elements as well as the four horsemen of the Apocalypse in Revelation 6:1–8.* They are related to the god names on the twelve banners, and further subdivided into four kings, twenty-four planetary seniors (which are the twenty-four elders in Revelation 4:4), as well as sixty-four elemental servient angels, sixty-four kerubs, and even sixty-four wicked angels who perform various functions in the physical world, among other angels and derived god names. Practical work with these angels promised a variety of *siddhis,*

---

*To add to the confusion, these were later split into five separate tablets by the Golden Dawn—four elemental tablets measuring twelve by thirteen squares each, with the central black cross rearranged into a small four-by-five tablet. Each character was assigned a number of additional elemental, planetary, zodiacal, or sephirotic attributions, with each square then transformed into a three-dimensional raised and truncated pyramid, turning the tablets into a precise system for targeting specific subenergies within the magical universe. Aleister Crowley went on to devise a system of sexual magic in which these pyramids were made into hollow cups and turned upright to catch sexual fluids, a method that could be used to evoke elemental spirits. None of this later complexity is present in the original Dee material and should be left to the side for the moment as not relevant to understanding the spirit diaries.

or magical powers, including the ability to heal sickness, the understanding of alchemy, conjuring elementals, understanding the secrets of men, and many others.[63] The entire table is a representation of the New Jerusalem, where Christ will rule and the twelve tribes will converge in Revelation 21, after the Dragon, Beast, and Whore of Babylon are defeated.[64]

14. The thirty Aethyrs and their ninety-one Governors, grouped into twelve, terrestrially representing the earth as divided into ninety-one locations from which the twelve tribes of Israel are to be gathered in Revelation 7, celestially representing the heavens as divided into 12° selections. These were used in a different sense by Crowley—as a technique for generating initiatory visions—which will be revisited in book III.

15. Forty-nine calls in the angelic language were given that were to be used to interact with the Watchtowers and Aethyrs in a process of sanctification and illumination entitled *gebofal* in Enochian. This process would restore the consciousness of the operative magician undergoing it, so that they, in turn, could restore the fallen world.[65]

Using the temple furniture while scrying was to provide buffering and protection from the energies raised and beings contacted. Scrying spiritual creatures within the boundaries of the stone itself, rather than in the open environment, would also provide a buffer from illuders (lying spirits); outside the stone there was no such protection.[66]

THE ANGELIC LANGUAGE

As part of the process of transmitting the forty-nine calls, and elsewhere in the diaries, the angels delivered fragments of the angelic language itself—often referred to as Enochian (this is a later conceit, not contained in the original spirit diaries).

This was the language spoken in the Garden of Eden; when Adam was corrupted by the demon Coronzom in the form of the serpent and exiled east of Eden, he had to invent the Hebrew language instead, which contained an echo of the angelic language—though without the true forms or pronunciation.[67] Like Hebrew, the angelic alphabet is read right to left, and consists of twenty-two characters; after the Fall, Adam divided Hebrew into three, seven, and twelve parts. These are referred to as the "mother," "double," and "simple" letters, and correspond to the elements (the fourth element, earth, being a mixture of the first three), planets, and zodiacal signs, respectively; together, they make up the structure of the entire Tree of Life.* As Hebrew is an echo of the angelic language, the Hebrew Tree of Life is presumably also an echo of the original angelic Tree of Life, as assembled from the angelic language— this perhaps being the actual Tree of Life in the Garden.

The transmission of Enochian appears to fulfill the long-standing Hermetic quest to uncover the ur-language; it is referred to as the "Cabala of Nature" by the angels, realizing Dee's interest in uncovering a Real Cabala beyond simply Hebrew, as discussed in the *Monas hieroglyphica*. However, no correspondences, explicit gematria, or other underlying structure of the angelic language was revealed beyond the forty-nine calls and temple furniture,[68] even though the angels hint at an underlying numerical structure.

SAY HELLO TO THE ANGELS

Throughout the sessions, Dee and Kelly recorded contact with a new and unique hierarchy of angels. They do *not* conform to the traditional Pseudo-Dionysian ranking of angels given in the introduction. Instead, the names of the angels are drawn from the temple furniture, including the Sigillum Dei Aemeth, the Tabula Bonorum, the Watchtowers, and the Aethyrs.

However, the archangels Dee and Kelly interact with at the beginning of the sessions are far more traditional—Michael and Gabriel, along with Raphael and Uriel. To these Dee appends a fifth archangel, Annael, who he believed to be the angel at that time presiding over the entire world.[69] Taking a cue, though not specific entity names, from

---

*See Kaplan, *Sefer Yetzirah*.

Fig. 8.4. "Synaxis of Archangel Michael," a representation of the seven major archangels as recognized in Eastern Orthodox Christianity. Michael is in the center, above Christ. In the foreground, Gabriel is to his left, and Raphael to his right. In the back row, left to right, are Jehudiel, Selaphiel, Uriel, and Barachiel. Icon from Russian Orthodox Church, nineteenth century.

Trithemius, Dee thought that this angelic office rotated through successive historical periods.

To the four archangels beneath Annael, Dee assigned the following roles in Latin:

1. Michael: *Fortitudo Dei,* Strength of God.
2. Gabriel: *Prevalescentia–siue praepotentia–siue Fortitudo praevalescens–Dei,* Superior Expert of God or the very powerful or most influential Strength of God.*
3. Raphael: *Medicina Dei,* Medicine of God.
4. Uriel: *Lux Dei,* Light of God.

These beings not only play a starring role in the revelations to come, but a critical role in the history of Judaism, Christianity, and Islam.

The archangel Michael occupies a primary place in *Liber primus* and *Secundus,* acting as the head initiator into the Mysteries, and directing the lesser spirits with a flaming sword, with the other archangels in a subservient helper role. Michael's two major appearances in scripture are in Daniel and Revelation—in the first, he presents himself as one of the chief princes of Persia (*prince* may refer to a rank in a hierarchy of spirits, rather than a terrestrial title), where he gives Daniel a terrifying vision of the future of his people. Like Dee and Kelly, Daniel was hardly able to bear the vision, stating, "I am overcome with anguish because of the vision, my lord, and I feel very weak. How can I, your servant, talk with you, my lord? My strength is gone and I can hardly breathe."[70] In a foreshadowing of Revelation, Michael predicts a time of trouble for the Jewish people, which the angel will deliver them from—but only those among them "whose name is found written in the book."[71]

It is in Revelation that Michael makes his grand entrance as an angel, at war with the Red Dragon, Coronzom:

> Then war broke out in heaven. Michael and his angels fought against the dragon, and the dragon and his angels fought back. But he was not strong enough, and they lost their place in heaven. The great dragon was hurled down—that ancient serpent called the devil, or

---

*The assignation of both Michael and Gabriel to the strength of God is clarified by Dee in a footnote to the action of March 14, 1582, where he suggests that Gabriel is the triumph of God, and therefore the strength of God, but of a higher order.

Satan, who leads the whole world astray. He was hurled to the earth, and his angels with him.[72]

Rabbinical tradition holds a special place for Michael as defender of the Jews and of Israel, particularly against the demon Samael, the accuser of Israel.[73] Michael was of chief importance to Christianity after Constantine, who constructed the Michaelion, a sanctuary dedicated to the angel, over a pagan temple north of Constantinople in the fourth century, the model for hundreds of Eastern Orthodox churches to come. Pseudo-Dionysius included Michael in his hierarchy; Bonaventure gave him the title of prince of the Seraphim, highest of the nine orders of angels, and Aquinas relegated him to prince of the lowest order, those simply titled "angel." Catholics view Saint Michael as the leader of God's army against the forces of hell, as the model of the human spiritual warrior, as the angel of death, as the weigher of souls (in perfectly balanced scales, an inheritance of the Egyptian idea of the afterlife and the role of the goddess Ma'at), and as the guardian of the Church. Eastern Orthodoxy likewise gives Michael primary importance as "Archistrategos," supreme commander of the heavenly hosts, and Orthodox Christians often direct their prayers to Michael, Gabriel, and their own guardian angels. Protestant denominations also recognize Michael and Gabriel, but usually no others. Michael is often depicted carrying a sword, as well as scales in his role as adjudicator of the dead. Michael (Mikhail) additionally appears in the Qu'ran, alongside Gabriel (Jibreel); in Sura 2:98 it is stated that God is an enemy to anyone who is an enemy to him, his angels, his messengers, or Michael and Gabriel.

Secondary to Michael is the archangel Gabriel, who plays a deferential but central role in *Liber primus*. Gabriel also shows up in Daniel, as the explicator of the hero's visions, as well as in Luke, where he prophesies the birth of John the Baptist to Zechariah and of Jesus to Mary. Also like Michael, he appears first as a man in the Old Testament and later as an angel in the New; yet it is only in the apocryphal book of Enoch (and, later, the Qu'ran) that Gabriel is called an archangel. Gabriel is often depicted as delivering the Kabbalah to the Jews, and by Trithemius's scheme, he ruled over the period of time in which Dee and

Kelly lived.[74] He also holds primary importance in Islam, where his role as revelator of the mysteries extends to the Prophet Muhammad, unto whom he is said to have delivered the Qu'ran itself. Gabriel is often depicted carrying a trumpet.

Raphael, Medicine of God, appears in the book of Tobit, where he presents himself disguised as "Azarias," a human companion of Tobit's son, acting as a protector, blinding a desert demon, and curing Tobit of his own blindness before revealing himself as an angel. In the book of Enoch, he is tasked by God with binding the fallen angel Azazel. In Catholicism, Raphael is held to be the patron of healers and travelers.

Uriel, Light of God, appears not in canonical scripture but in the Gnostic texts, in the work of Pseudo-Dionysius, in the biblical apocrypha, and in the book of Enoch, where he completes a tetrad with Michael, Gabriel, and Raphael; in Enoch, he warns Noah of the coming flood, and guides Enoch throughout the narrative. He is also the subject of intercessionary prayer in—of all places—the Anglican Church.

These are only a few of the scriptural mentions of the four arch-angels; their appearances are numerous throughout the texts, art, architecture, and ritual of the three major monotheistic religions, as well as the innumerable sects, groups, and side traditions that have sprung from them. Yet while the archangels sound overpoweringly impressive, Pseudo-Dionysius, the early Church authority on angelology, ranks the angels and archangels at the very bottom of the scale of angelic hierarchy, closest to and most involved with the affairs of humanity.[75]

Though Dee and Kelly's angels do not cleanly map to the traditional scheme, some correspondences may be inferred. Of particular relevance to the sessions is that the order of angels above the archangels, the principalities, is concerned with the administration of nations and empires, and the calling of mortals to office within those systems. This is one of the primary concerns of the actions—not just for Dee and Kelly but for most of the rest of the people who would become directly or indirectly involved in the actions, including Łaski, Rudolf II, Stephen Báthory, and others, who would be offered political power by the angels in exchange for repentance and obedience. Several angels fitting the description of higher orders—including many-eyed angels and wheels—appear in the sessions, though infrequently.

While Dee and Kelly were familiar with traditional angelic schema, and perhaps expected to find these schema confirmed by the scrying session—for instance, the schemes of Pseudo-Dionysius, Abano, Trithemius, Reuchlin, and Agrippa—the angels revealed by the sessions were wholly unique in their naming and offices.[76] Comparing the angels revealed in the sessions to the traditional scheme, however, Dee came to believe that most of the angels he was interacting with were those at the very lowest end of the angelic order—with the sessions conducted by the archangels, and the numerous other entities he contacted simply being "angels," the lowest celestial order.[77]

Though scripture speaks of ten thousand by ten thousand angels, Dee found their number to be infinite. (Ten thousand may itself be archaic shorthand for infinite, as it is in Buddhist texts.) Dee made careful notes of how the angels appeared to Kelly in the scrying ball, believing their forms to be rife with symbolism carefully chosen to communicate Cabalistic messages to the scryer; he later mapped the correspondences of the angels to the elements, planets, zodiac, and sephiroth.[78]

In addition to the angels revealed by the various pieces of temple furniture, guardian angels of individuals involved in the sessions also appeared—for instance, the angel "Jubanladace," Count Łaski's guardian angel, who was contacted during the sessions. The belief in and quest for contact with guardian spirits or angels was a central facet not only of Neoplatonic thought but of magical practice in general, dating at least to Sumeria;[79] Dee himself was enamored of the idea,[80] and it later came to occupy a central place in the Thelemic doctrine of Aleister Crowley.

THE USE OF THE FURNITURE

The reception of the angelic magic itself and the instructions for how it was to be used were intimately connected with Dee and Kelly's own time period and sixteenth-century geopolitics, the story of which is covered in the following chapters. The angels suggested at least two initiatory tracks to be used in achieving sanctification and illumination via operating the furniture:

1. The Operation of the Fourteen (or Eighteen) Days.

This was the operation for attuning the temple furniture to be undertaken by Dee and Kelly once they had built the scrying equipment to the specifications given. Calls to the angels of the banners and elemental tablets would be given following deep and pious prayer on successive days until the entirety of the Watchtowers had been accounted for.* Once the operation was completed, the temple furniture would no longer be needed, as the angels would now be bound to the operators and available to them for the rest of their lives.

2. The Forty-Nine Calls and Thirty Aethyrs.

The bulk of the Enochian language was transmitted as part of the forty-nine calls that make up *Liber Loagaeth*. There are nineteen actual angelic calls, with the final call pertaining to the thirty Aethyrs, so that the text is changed depending on which Aethyr is being called; this makes for forty-nine calls total. These calls are to be spoken aloud while using the temple furniture in order to contact the angels within the Watchtowers and the Aethyrs.

The thirty Aethyrs, as initially given to Dee, are each divided by three (or, in the case of the final Aethyr, four) and pertain to a total of ninety-one areas of the world as it was politically divided during Dee's time. Together they revealed the locations that the scattered twelve tribes of Israel had migrated to, and from which they could be recalled, as in Revelation. Each of these Aethyrs was overseen by a Governor, under whom served thousands of angelic ministers. These may have been the guardian angels of the 144,000 souls designated to be saved during the end of the world, tasked with shepherding the righteous souls to paradise on Judgment Day.[81] The thirty Aethyrs themselves represented 12° bands wrapping around the 360° circumference of the

---

*Two different versions of this operation are given in Donald Tyson's *Enochian Magic for Beginners* and Geoffrey James's *Enochian Evocation of Dr. John Dee*.

sky, suggesting an alternate version of the decanates of the zodiac, as also ruled by the Governors.[82] Dee was told to use these calls to assist the progress of the angels' plans for bringing about the end of the world, specifically in regard to the gathering of the twelve tribes of Israel.

Many commercially available books on Enochian magic do not assess this original context, but instead present the version of angelic magic developed by the Golden Dawn, who used the calls to perform practical magic with their own highly altered version of the Watchtowers, as well as to ascend the Tree of Life through astral visions. Aleister Crowley, an adept of the Golden Dawn, used scrying the thirty Aethyrs as just such an astral initiation into the sphere of Binah and its concomitant grade of Magister Templi, recapitulating the form and structure of Golden Dawn temple initiations. He carried this out after the actual Golden Dawn order had disintegrated and he had burned his bridges with its founders; Crowley believed this allowed him to advance in his own magical apotheosis by receiving higher initiations from Dee and Kelly's angels themselves, conveniently doing a run around his teachers and peers.

This is a nineteenth- and twentieth-century approach to achieving the same goals of the magicians of the Renaissance, which was the restoration of consciousness to its original state, ascending the Great Chain of Being back toward Godhead. Yet the process was not wholly new to the Golden Dawn and has earlier precedents, predating even Dee and Kelly, in the Valentinian Gnostic philosophy of the thirty aeons, the Kabbalistic tradition of the fifty gates of Binah, and others. This alternative approach to the Aethyrs will be addressed in book III.

9

The Architecture of Apocalypse

The angelic conversations began at Mortlake on December 22, 1581. Dee and Kelly's initiation of contact with the spirit world is recorded in the *Mysteriorum libri quinque* or *Five Books of Mystery*, which start with an abortive attempt at scrying using Barnabas Saul and next proceed into the successes attained once Edward Kelly arrived at Mortlake. They detail the reception of the angelic temple furniture, and precede the records reproduced in *A True & Faithful Relation*, with the diaries ending on May 23, 1583. The five books are designated with Latin names—*Liber primus, Secundus, Tertius, Quartus,* and *Quintus,* and are discussed here, along with concurrent events in Dee's life.

MYSTERIORUM LIBER PRIMUS
The Holy Table and Ring

The sessions began with Dee petitioning the angel Annael, whom Saul claimed he saw in the crystal, appearing as a beautiful being in yellow apparel glittering like gold, with star beams blazing from behind his head, fiery eyes, accompanied by a white dog with a long head, and a "great number" of dead men's skulls. The angel relayed letters and sigils, and counseled the men to "be not too hasty in wrath" and to do good unto all men.[1] Annael identified himself as the guardian of the world to come, and chief governor general of the current time period. Yet Dee was skeptical, and noted that this was an intruding spirit, appearing far too pleasing and too immediately to be trusted—alluding to the biblical warning that Satan himself masquerades as an angel of light.[*2]

Records would not commence again until March 10, 1582, when Kelly, identifying himself as Talbot, came to Mortlake. Talbot asked Dee to show him some practical magic, and Dee confessed that he had long wished for the angels of God to assist him in his philosophical studies. He next produced a stone, and told Kelly that a scryer had helped him to call the good angel Anchor into it—apparently, in a rare moment, to Dee's direct perception. Dee asked Kelly to repeat the experiment with him, and also to call the angels Anachor and Anilos; the younger man fell to his knees at Dee's desk, praying fervently before the scrying stone, while Dee retired to his oratory to add his own prayer. An apparition manifested in the stone within fifteen minutes, identifying itself not as Anchor, Anilos, or Anachor,[†] but as the archangel Uriel.

Dee's first question was whether a grimoire in his possession, which he had been laboring over—the *Book of Soyga*—was accurate. *Soyga* is a Latin grimoire from the late medieval period that contains an array of angelic, demonic, elemental, planetary, and zodiacal conju-

---

*St. Augustine elaborates on this in his *Confessions* as a warning against magic: "Who could be found to reconcile me to you? Was I to beg the help of the angels? What prayer should I use? What sacred rites? Many have tried to return to you, and have not had the strength in themselves to achieve it, so I have been told. They have attempted these methods and have lapsed into a desire for curious visions, and have been rewarded with illusions. For in their quest they have been lifted up by pride in their high culture, inflating their chest rather than beating their breast. Through an affinity in heart they attracted to themselves as associates and allies of their pride 'the powers of the air' (Eph. 2:2) who deluded them with magical powers. They sought a mediator to purify them, and it was not the true one. For it was 'the devil transforming himself into an angel of light' (2 Cor. 11:14)." (Augustine, *Confessions*, 218–19)

†These entities also appear in *The Lesser Key of Solomon*, or *Goetia*, where they are listed as Ancor, Amacor, and Amides (along with Theodonias and Anitor), good spirits or powers of God that are invoked as the spirit conjuror dons his vestments in preparation for evoking a demon. See Mathers, *The Goetia*, 80.

rations arranged in alphanumeric squares. The last thirty-six of these are arranged in grids of thirty-six by thirty-six squares.[3] *Soyga* forms an important precursor of the angelic sessions, as its format is suggestive of the alphanumeric transmissions to come from the angels. While the tables of *Soyga* are constructed from the number six (six times six equals thirty-six), much of the "Enochian" temple furniture to come would be based around the number seven (seven times seven equals forty-nine).

Uriel assured Dee that *Soyga* had been revealed to Adam in Paradise, and could be interpreted by Michael, whom Dee could call upon, given enough sincerity and humility, but that he should cease to call Anachor, Anilos, and Anchor, who were figments of superstitious rumor and not bound to the scrying stone. He also told Dee that he would live to a hundred, and transmitted the design for a gold lamen to be worn for protection. Michael, Uriel assured them, would give light to their path and make it straight, revealing the tables of *Soyga* and other mysteries to them by the power of truth, not force. Michael could be invoked by reading the seven penitential psalms of David,* but Dee and Kelly would have to win God's favor by the *beauty* of their prayers. It was God's will that Dee and Kelly have a "conjunction of minds in prayer,"[4] and pray continually, so as to have the knowledge of the angels together. Michael had already noticed them, Uriel assured Dee, but Barnabas Saul had been an imperfect channel.

Next, Uriel showed Dee and Kelly the schematics for preparing what came to be called the Holy Table of Practice—a kind of ultra-sophisticated Ouija board for contacting the angels. This table was to be three feet square, with the Sigillum Dei Aemeth resting upon it— the heptarchic magical seal from *Liber iuratus,* a book already in Dee's library. Uriel informed Dee that the seal had already been perfected in the book (although the pair would later receive a much more advanced version). Beneath the four legs of the table were to be four containers holding smaller wax copies of the Sigillum Dei, with two square yards of red silk as a carpet, and tasseled silk hanging over the top of the table. Around the table would be yellow letters written in "perfect oil"

---

*Psalms 6, 32, 38, 51, 102, 130, and 143.

like that used in church.[5] Angels, Uriel explained, sanctify by the fact
that they are innately holy. But humans sanctify by *holiness,* that is, by
taking holy actions, not by their innate fallen nature.

Terrifyingly, Uriel next warned that a spirit named Lundrumguffa
was haunting Mortlake and seeking Dee's destruction, as well as that
of his wife and daughter. Uriel cautioned that the demon was even
now present in the room, seeking to murder Saul, who was cursed: "the
cursed will come to the cursed."[6] Dee noted that this spirit must have
been corrupting the transmission of the Holy Table. He had already

Fig. 9.1. The Holy Table of Practice. From Méric Casaubon, *A True & Faithful Relation,* 1659.
This image has been a source of much controversy, as the order of angelic characters
may have been reversed due to a printer's error.

caught Barnabas Saul trafficking with the evil spirit Maherion, and burned his name and sigil in brimstone before Saul was "carried away quick." Dee asked Uriel to bind the demon, as Raphael had bound Asmodeus in the book of Tobit, but Uriel replied that human effort was necessary as well—in this case the application of brimstone.

The importance of psychic security protocol was demonstrated even more vividly the following day. After Kelly called Uriel, a being appeared dressed in fantastic robes of purple and gold, with a gold wreath on its head and sparkling eyes, who assured Dee that the characters recorded for the table were perfect. Yet no sooner had Dee asked if the spirit was indeed Uriel than another entity arrived, threw the apparition down by the shoulders, beat him with a whip, and stole his clothes—revealing the hairy and ugly form of the evil spirit Lundrumguffa himself. Uriel now appeared and continued beating the prone spirit, stating, "Lo, thus are the wicked scourged."[7] Uriel then dragged Lundrumguffa out by the legs and threw him into a pit, afterward washing his hands with the sweat of his own brow.

Uriel and Michael now revealed themselves in their full radiance, ringed by an immense company of angels. Uriel leaned himself by the scrying table, while Michael sat in the scrying chair, a sword in his right hand, head glistening like the sun, with long hair, wings, his lower body covered in feathers, a robe over his body, and a great light in his left hand; they blessed Dee and Kelly to continue the sessions.

This demonstration increased the fervency of Dee's prayers, lest he again be misled by a lying spirit. On March 14, Michael and Uriel appeared after being called, and performed a kind of initiation of Dee by astral exemplar. They showed Dee an image of himself in the crystal, and placed a crown of laurel (a traditional symbol of victory) upon his head, after which they had him eat a token with the letters *NA* written upon it. Michael then brandished his sword, which split in two and lit on fire. From the sword he took a gold ring, upon which was written the name PELE. Michael identified this as the ring of Solomon that gave the king of Israel himself the power to command spirits—without which, Dee was told, he could do nothing. (The name PELE appears in two books that were in Dee's library at the time: Reuchlin's *De verbo*

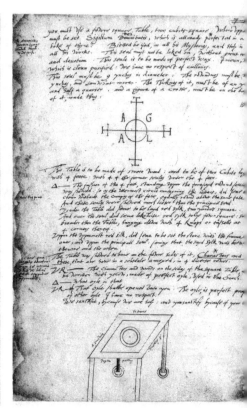

Fig. 9.2. A handwritten page from Dee's *Liber primus* depicting the first lamen, the design for the back of the Sigillum Dei, and the Holy Table of Practice. From MS. Sloane 3188, British Library.

mirifico and Agrippa's *Three Books*.)[8] Dee was now shown an updated version of the Sigillum Dei Aemeth, and assured that he would be guided in perfecting its design.

The following day, Dee's magic and Kelly's scrying produced the spirit Salamian, from the Italian philosopher Peter de Abano's *Heptameron,* a grimoire that first appeared in Venice in 1496 (in which Salamian appears as a mighty angel in a conjuration of Michael himself, assigned to Sunday and the sun),[9] who warned Dee and Kelly that they were being hindered by the demon Mammon. Dee noted that he had a copy of the *Heptameron,* printed along with Agrippa, in his oratory "almost under my window,"[10] suggesting that Kelly may have fished it out of the window and read it prior to the session. Dee had his suspicions, as the note suggests.

When Dee protested that he could feel no such demonic influence, Salamian revealed to Kelly that they were surrounded by countless wicked and horrible spirits, including one with very long arms, that were gnashing their teeth and striking out at their heads with their claws. Dee again asked for intercession, but Salamian insisted he must make an effort himself. Dee prayed fervently, and the evil spirits vanished.*

Following this exorcism, the angel Raphael made his first appearance, and revealed the angel OCH; Michael also appeared, and had Dee write the name Polipos. Michael assured Dee that as he was with Solomon, so he would be with Dee. Michael then rapidly revealed the manner in which the scrying equipment was to be used, the record of which has been lost. Uriel also affirmed that he lived with Esdras,† and Raphael affirmed that he lived with "Tobie the younger," that is, Tobit's son in the book of Tobit.

While the angels concluded the session with a blessing for Dee and Kelly, they had no such love for Barnabas Saul, upon whom God would be revenged, and whose punishment would be great. Such was the wrath of God in protecting his prophets . . . or the cunning of one Edward Kelly in ensuring his job security.

---

*The angels' emphasis on direct spiritual action by Dee, rather than simple prayer for divine aid, is not as subtle a point as it may seem. This call for mortal action upon the spiritual world, and suggestion that God helps those who help themselves in all things, not only distinguishes magic from religion but provides justification for the entire field of the occult. Protestantism counsels that salvation may be found *sola fide,* by faith alone, but in *Liber primus* Dee is continually attempting that approach—are not angels better fit to order the spiritual world than mere mortals?—and is continually being rebuked and told to exercise his own agency in the spiritual world. However, (and this is again a subtle but critical point) the efforts of mortals produce spiritual results not because men are holy, but because their *actions* can be. Hence, operative magic and the importance of ritual. This divides the path of magic from pure religion, which relies on vicarious atonement or obedience to mortal authorities. It also divides magic from pure mysticism, for instance, the various Eastern paths, which aim to uncover the intrinsic holiness of the human animal. Magic is not something you *are;* it is something you *do.*

†Uriel is mentioned in the apocryphal book of Esdras, where along with Michael, Raphael, Gabriel, and three other angels, he is said to be one of the angels ruling at the end of the world.

MYSTERIORUM LIBER SECUNDUS
The Sigillum Dei Aemeth

Liber secundus pertains to the reception of the Sigillum Dei Aemeth, the sevenfold seal that forms the basis of the temple furniture.

As mentioned previously, an earlier version of the Sigillum Dei appears in *Liber iuratus,* a thirteenth- or fourteenth-century grimoire colloquially referred to as the "Sworn Booke," spuriously attributed to Honorius, the son of Euclid. Like Dee's Holy Table, Crowley's later *The Book of the Law,* and the suffix attached to the names of most angels, this version of the Sigillum centers around the word *El, L,* or *Al.* One of the oldest European grimoires, the *Sworn Book* is allegedly a condensation of knowledge gathered at a conference of operative magicians and contains ninety-three chapters, which cover the range of classical magical techniques from finding treasure to conjuring demons. Like many medieval grimoires, the *Sworn Book* claims to be a manual of summoning perverse and evil spirits, and therefore demands ritual purity and Christian piety as prerequisites for use.

The reception of the Sigillum began on March 21, 1582, when Michael appeared along with Uriel, telling the two men that they were blessed among the saints, and that therefore they would be kept separate from the impure. Kelly, in particular, had committed idolatry, and so the angels would have to right him and separate him from temptation. The angels were fitting the two men to be able to hold the intense divine revelations they were being given by cutting them off from sin.

Michael now revealed the true design of the Sigillum Dei, the "true Circle of his eternity comprehending all virtue."[11] Forty white creatures appeared, one for each compartment of the outermost ring of the Sigillum, in procession one by one, appearing as children in long, white silk robes. Michael appeared over all of them and grew to giant stature, with two legs like pillars of brass, drawing a sword of fire over all forty of their heads. This caused an earthquake, and they all fell to their knees; Michael now called the angel Semiel (the "secretary for the Name of God,"[12] according to Dee) to explain the Great Seal.

Uriel also fell to the ground before the might of Michael's sword;

Michael towered above the seal, swinging his sword with flaming fire like lightning. Each of the forty creatures stepped forward in turn, kneeling and unveiling a number and letter on their breast. The Cabalistic utterances of the creatures are both deeply reverent of God and, at times, apocalyptic.

Following the completion of the forty white creatures' speeches, the pair retired for dinner. Kelly next composed himself for solitary prayer, at which point the angel Uriel appeared to him and suggested edits to the Sigillum. Michael confirmed that Dee had omitted nothing in his meticulous note-taking, but that Kelly had left out important details from the visions he had seen. Dee guessed that the forty characters might be related to the forty-two-letter Shem ha-Mephorash, a passage from Genesis; Michael agreed, but only that the Shem existed *in potentia* within the circle. No creature would be able to leave the circle, Michael said, that entered it, if such creatures have been defiled and made upon Earth. It was this circle that created all of the beasts, birds, fowl, and fish of the earth; this, Michael said, would be found in the *Book of Soyga*.

Over the following actions, the angels now transmitted the names that make up the heptagons and heptagrams that proceed to the center of the Sigillum, through fantastical devices. The pattern they transmitted would be of a level of complexity and visual elegance magnitudes beyond the Sigillum found in the *Sworn Book*.

The Sigillum is composed of seven layers, each associated with the traditional seven planets. As the layers progress inward, they step down from celestial to terrestrial reality,* as in Qabalistic magic, which posits and categorizes ranks of angels as representing the fine gradations of manifestation from Godhead to the world of matter:

1. Seven names of God, drawn from the forty alphanumeric characters in the outer ring, with their corresponding sigils—Galas, Gethog, Thaoth, Horlωn, Innon, Aaoth, Galethog—resting

---

*This interpretation was later suggested by the author Lon DuQuette, not Dee and Kelly.

upon the inner heptagon. These were also demonstrated by the angels pulling seven birds out of seven baskets, each of which had letters in its feathers.

2. Seven names of God of the outer heptagon and archangels of the planets. Seven god names were transmitted in a seven-by-seven magic square (similar to the six-by-six alphanumeric squares in the *Book of Soyga*), which form the god names within the heptagon. These were revealed in pillars called forth by Michael.

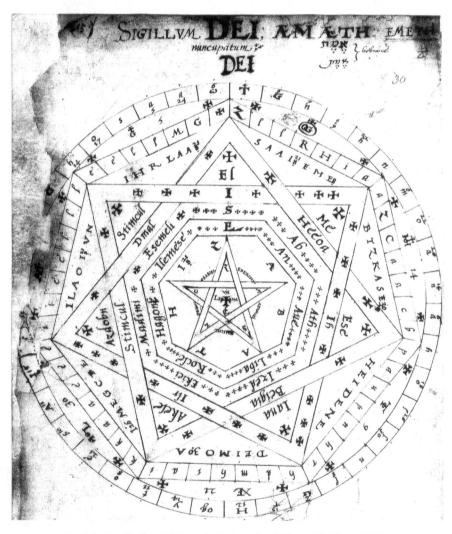

Fig. 9.3. The Sigillum Dei Aemeth, in Dee's hand. From MS. Sloane 3188.

When the square itself is read vertically, however, it produces the seven names of the traditional archangels of the planets: Zaphkiel (Saturn), Cumael (Mars), Haniel (Venus), Gabriel (Luna), Zadkiel (Jupiter), Raphael (Sol), and Michael (Mercury). These, of course, included three of the primary entities that Dee and Kelly were working with: Gabriel, Raphael, and Michael (sans Uriel, unless Haniel is read as another name for Uriel).

3. Seven names of God beneath the heptagon. These were transmitted in another seven-by-seven table, from which the remaining angels were drawn.

4. The Daughters of Light. Another five sets of angels of the planets, unveiled by "Daughters of Light,"[13] seven young women dressed in green silk, each carrying a blue tablet on her forehead with her name on it: El, Me, Ese, Iana, Akele, Azdobn, and Stimcul.

5. The Sons of Light. Following the Daughters, seven young men dressed in white appeared, each with a metal ball suggesting one of the traditional planetary attributions, with a tablet of gold on his breast carrying his name: I, Ih, Ilr, Dmal, Heeoa, Beigia, and Stimcul.

6. The Daughters of Daughters of the Light, or "little wenches."[14] These appeared in white, with white ivory tablets on their bosoms—S, Ab, Ath, Izad, Ekiei, Madimi, and Esemeli.

7. The Sons of Sons of the Light, or "little children . . . like boys."[15] These came in robes of purple silk, with long pointed sleeves and scholarly hats, bearing on their chests triangular green tablets with their names: E, An, Ave, Liba, Rocle, Hagonel, and Ilemese.

Following this, another seven-by-seven magic square was transmitted, from which the remaining names were derived.*

---

*This particular magic square would make several dramatic appearances in Crowley's scrying of the thirty Aethyrs, where its meaning is elaborated.

8. The angels of the pentagram. Seven more angelic names were given to Dee and Kelly to place around and within the pentagram that sits at the very center of the Sigillum—Sabathiel, Zedekiel, Madimiel, Semeliel, Nogahel, Corabiel, and Levanael.

9. The crosses. After the completion of the design, crosses were placed around the Sigillum at diverse places.

This design was to be carved upon a pure beeswax disc nine inches in diameter by one and a half inches thick. On the back would be the letters *AGLA* (a Hebrew *notariqon* or acronym for "Attah Gibbor

Fig. 9.4. A clearer version of the Sigillum Dei Aemeth, by "Silgfrin."

Le'olam Adonai," "the Lord is mighty forever")[16] within a cross. Dee did so; the resulting artifact can still be seen in the British Museum.

MYSTERIORUM LIBER TERTIUS
The Ensigns of Creation and
Tabula Bonorum

In *Primus,* Dee had been cut off from the influence of evil spirits, consecrated through initiation so that he was fit to begin work with the angelic material,* and given the ring of Solomon with which to begin his work. In *Secundus,* he was given the Sigillum Dei Aemeth, a pentacle revealing the workings of the seven planets across seven levels of manifestation.

However, Michael was still unimpressed. On April 28—five weeks since the previous action—he chided Dee and Kelly for their slackness in carrying out his instructions. Dee pleaded that he hadn't had money to buy materials to make the lamen, ring, or Sigillum. Michael responded by showing Kelly a giant hill of gold covered with serpents, which he then smote with a sword and pushed into the water, tangibly demonstrating the contempt that the archangel had for financial concerns.

After giving Dee information on how to use the lamen and ring, he called forth the Daughters of Light to reveal the seven Ensigns of Creation, planetary talismans that would be made of purified tin and placed around the Sigillum on the Holy Table. Along with the lamen and the Holy Table itself, these were designated "Instruments of Conciliation,"[17] connecting the various temple furniture with the Sigillum and the operator. These were given in Latin letters, although the angels told Dee to replace the Latin with Enochian script; he did not do this.† The Ensigns, six of them square and one circle, look very much like occult electrical diagrams. Each is assigned to one of the seven traditional planets.

---

*For a similar process, see the "Formula of the Neophtye," as used in the neophyte initiation of the Golden Dawn and the practical magical exercises contained in Golden Dawn documents Z-1, Z-2, and Z-3. See Regardie, *The Complete Golden Dawn System of Magic,* 6:1–83; Crowley, *Magick: Liber ABA,* 166.
†The restored diagrams appear in DuQuette's *Enochian Vision Magick.*

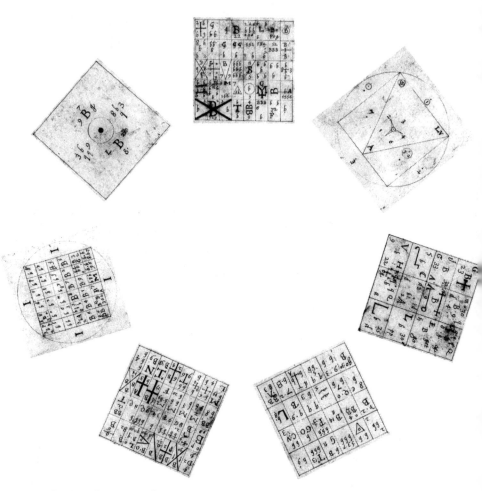

Fig. 9.5. The Ensigns of Creation, arranged as they would be on top of the Holy Table.
From MS. Sloane 3188.

These seven sigils were joined in a fourfold set of tables, within which were the names of forty-nine angels of light who worked on Earth under the direction of God. Four of them were attributed to the four elements. As each of these tables was written out after being revealed in the stone, they were then consumed in fire.

"The fountain of wisdom is opened," Uriel told them, opening a book in his hand. "Nature shall be known, Earth with her secrets disclosed."[18] Uriel counseled them that if they could understand these tables, they would have reign over the forty-nine angels, which they would invoke under the power of God, and by which they would work in "quieting of the estates,"[19] learning wisdom, pacifying the nobility, and "judgment of the rest,"[20] as well as understanding the elements. These were symbolized in a sevenfold scheme: books, crown, and robes (representing wisdom, kings, and nobility), as well as merchants, which were attributed to the four elements and were signified by a quadruped animal of all colors (water), herbs (earth), a fan (air), and a flame in the hand (fire). Books, crown, and robes plus the four-element merchants made seven.

While this would seem to suggest spiritual power over the English political structure, it more likely designates a spiritual hierarchy, similar to those shown in grimoire magic. Dee and Kelly would have reign over these spirits as long as they continued to praise God and his saints.

These forty-nine good angels, all of them starting with the letter *B*, were then assembled into a circular table divided by the seven planets—the Tabula Bonorum.* This new round table was to sit underneath the Holy Table, with the operator's feet placed upon it while scrying.

Michael now addressed Kelly, telling him that he should renounce the world and marry. The young scryer had no desire to do so, as it was contrary to his "vow and profession."[21] He hoped for a new message from Michael, but the archangel insisted, stating that Kelly must "of force" keep this command.[22] He indeed soon married, though he came to greatly resent his wife.

By May 4, a week later, Kelly was so frantic about the call to marriage that he discredited the angels' very existence and refused not only to deal with them but also to pray to God at all. Dee retired to his oratory to enter deep prayer himself, after which Michael and Uriel returned to the stone—and Kelly, perhaps reluctantly, began to relay their next messages.

The two angels appeared kneeling and holding their hands up, with Michael in a bloody sweat. Seven bundles wrapped in various colors of silk fell from heaven to be taken up by Michael. Uriel, dressed in a long

---

*The letter *B*, in either English or angelic, and the number seven play a central role in the temple furniture.

white robe, winged, wearing a beautiful crown with a white cross above it, placed a superaltar upon the table and censed it at the four corners. He next took the bundles from Michael and laid them upon the superaltar.

While Uriel prostrated and Michael continuously prayed, a man made of pure gold appeared, sometimes seeming to have one eye and sometimes three, and everything shook while smoke billowed up from under the table. The man removed birds from the bundles, which changed in size, color, and species, while standing upon a "little hill of flaming fire."[23]

"Believe," the voice of Michael came echoing from beyond the scene. "The world is of necessity. His necessity is governed by supernatural wisdom. Necessarily you fall, and of necessity shall rise again. Follow me, love me, embrace me: Behold, I AM."[24]

The scene vanished, and Uriel and Michael returned, explaining that God showed this so that they would understand that striving is vanity, for all is in God's hands—so what else was there to do? Dee answered that right action was to progress in perfecting virtue and to honor God.

Two birds reappeared, as big as mountains now, flying toward space. The first bird took stars into his bill, while the second took the stars from the first and put them back into the sky; they quickly repeated this process throughout the heavens. These birds now flew over cities and towns, breaking up the clouds and causing dust to fall from the walls and towers, thereby cleaning them. In the streets were "diverse brave fellows"—bishops, princes, and kings—that the wings of the birds struck down, while beggars, the infirm, children, women, and the elderly were left untouched.[25]

Now the birds lifted the corpses of four men from the ground, each of them wearing crowns, one of which was a child. Upon being raised into the air they parted into the four cardinal directions. Coming now to a great hill, the birds squeezed metals from the ground and threw them out; next tossing the withered head of an old man between their feet until it cracked open, revealing a stone the size of a tennis ball colored white, black, red, and green—the colors of the Watchtowers that would be later transmitted, and of the four horsemen of the Apocalypse. Upon eating the stone, the birds became two men with bright white paper crowns, with gold teeth, hands, feet, tongues, eyes, and ears. On each were twenty-six gold crowns, and they carried bags of gold that they sowed upon the earth like seeds.

Michael explained this vision as a teaching on giving good will to men of all classes, and of how and why Dee and Kelly were to be joined together, and what they were to become. Michael also commanded that the Sigillum, table, ring, and lamen be made by an honest man, and the ring engraved.

LIBER MYSTERIORUM QUARTUS
The Heptarchic Kings and Princes

The scrying sessions did not resume until November 15, nine months later, after a break between Dee and Kelly that had been reconciled, for which Dee begged forgiveness from God. They began where they left off and proceeded to the elucidation of the heptarchic angels—specifically the kings and princes—from the Tabula Bonorum.

Uriel plucked a round object from under the table, which glowed with transparent fire and grew bigger than the entire world, and told Dee that the current time period was the final age. Innumerable people swarmed in the globe, which also showed towers and castles, and Uriel explained that a spirit named King Carmara (or Baligon) was in the world, and that another world would begin with him. This spirit appeared and sat atop the world in a throne. This, it seemed, echoed Trithemius's notion of epochs of history ruled over by specific angels or spirits. Michael explained that "the mysteries of God have a time,"[26] and that they were being provided with this time.

Dee and Kelly were now introduced not just to Carmara but to a series of seven kings, with seven princes attendant upon them, and given sigils for each of them—with King Carmara in the highest rank. An ancient, enciphered flag was also shown, the reverse side of which contained the British flag. Gesturing to the world, Carmara explained that the sons of men, and their sons, were subject to his command—but only for a given time, which was yet to come.

Now came two companies of kings, each carrying a sword and a pair of balances—one group with scales balanced, the other imbalanced. Likewise, two companies of men arrived, one with *truth* over their heads in Latin, the other *filth*.[27]

Dee and Kelly were instructed in the use of the heptarchic kings, princes, and ministers, an art that could achieve not only political aims but also provide understanding of all science—past, present, and future. Not only could this form of magic influence the decisions of worldly princes, it could also affect the princes of Creation itself.

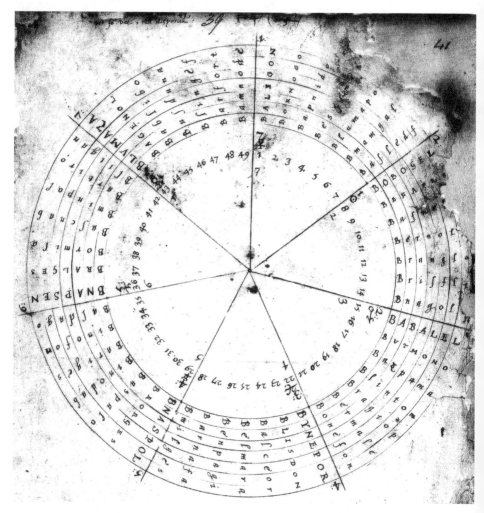

Fig. 9.6. The Tabula Bonorum, depicting the heptarchic kings and princes. From MS. Sloane 3188.

Dee asked if this magic could be used to influence the decisions of King Philip of Spain, and was given methods to do so. Michael assured them that this was only the first step in learning to use the heptarchic angels; he also reassured them that Dee's request for magical influence over Philip came from good intentions, would advance God's glory, and would be carried out with good results.

Dee and Kelly dragged on creating the ring requested in *Liber primus*, and their excuses were not met with enthusiasm. God would be merciful, however, and look after their material needs. Using magic to meddle in high-level political affairs, Michael told them, was a risky undertaking, but God would preserve and protect them. Michael also assured Dee that he would be returned to Elizabeth's good graces, and that the pair would do great works on behalf of God and country. Yet Michael also noted, perhaps with a wink, that God was enriching Dee with knowledge and the understanding of earthly vanities. Maybe the angels were circumscribing Dee's lust for power over the physical world, in preparation for further initiation into the spiritual realm. Regardless, Dee and Kelly were told that God and his good creatures would not forget them.

Next, Dee and Kelly called Bobogel (or Hagonel)—Dee felt the presence of a spirit around him, and Kelly could hear humming. Hagonel warned them that as they worked with good spirits, so would the contrary powers be invoked, and would test them in ways they hadn't yet experienced. Yet whatever these evil spirits could do, they could not provoke the pair to work against the ten commandments.

The spirits usually appeared like Elizabethan *people,* dressed in colorful period clothing and often carrying on pomp and circumstances just like courtiers would. They were now assembling to deliver Dee the designs of the Holy Table, as well as the lamen of the art, a square plate that would hang over his chest.

The angels initially delivered a crude grimoire-style lamen to be cast in gold and worn at the outset of the conversations; however, once they were ready, Dee and Kelly were given an upgrade—they were, in fact, warned that the original lamen had been delivered to them by lying spirits, despite the fact that the magicians' record states that the lamen was given by Uriel himself.

The second lamen, also to be made from gold, contains a square of eighty-four letters, drawn from a much larger table composed of seven tables of seven by seven squares each (in similar fashion to *Soyga*), totaling 343 alphanumeric squares. These 343 squares were arranged to form the names of forty-nine good angels—seven angels for each of the seven planets. The angels were further subdivided by rank: each planet was assigned a king, a prince, and ministers.

These heptarchic angels were assembled into the Tabula Bonorum, from which was drawn the characters for the new lamen. These were written first in Latin, but were to be transliterated into the angelic language. The angels' names and sigils were also to be carved on wooden disks, creating a heptarchic system that stands on its own as a method of Solomonic-style angelic magic.

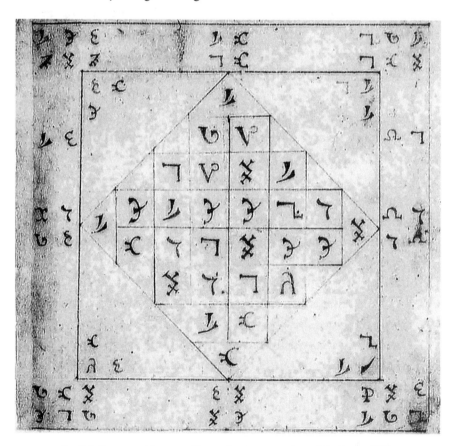

Fig. 9.7. The second lamen, with angelic characters. From MS. Sloane 3188.

Michael, appearing with Uriel and Raphael to summarize the heptarchic system, stated that this was the first part of a threefold art, which would join man with the knowledge of the world, of the government of his creatures, and with the sight of his majesty. The next two parts were yet to come—the Watchtowers and the system of thirty Aethyrs.

Following this action, Kelly left for London and Manchester. At home, Dee was plagued by nightmares that he was dead, that his bowels were removed, and that the lord treasurer would come to Mortlake to burn his books after his death.

In the next action, the Holy Table appeared, this time covered with a white cloth and a red-and-green silk cloth of changing colors. Hagonel held up a black-and-red wand above it, and pronounced:

> Oh, how great is the weakness and corruption of mankind, that has little faith in angels and their good deeds, but hardly any faith in God. All worldly things contain the corruption of the world within them. Our God, our God, he (I say) our God is true, and is true with his true angels and those who ever serve him. Ask for what you wish. I have spoken, and what I have spoken that was obscure, was in truth, justice and perfection.[28]

Hagonel assured Dee that there was nothing obscure in the material that he had received through Kelly. All that was left was to *use* it.

LIBER MYSTERIORUM QUINTUS
Liber Loagaeth and the Angelic Language

Next, the angels began to transmit the angelic language itself. First came the alphabet, and Dee and Kelly were commanded to learn the letters by heart, without having to refer to a book.

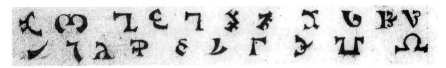

Fig. 9.8. The angelic alphabet. From MS. Sloane 3188.

As the sessions progressed, Kelly became more and more disturbed by the spiritual visions he was being pushed harder and harder by Dee to witness. This trend would only increase throughout the scrying sessions. On Good Friday, 1583, an angel thrust its sword from the scrying stone at Kelly's head; the scryer broke into a sweat and protested that he felt something crawling and creeping within his brain.

After this disturbing incident, the angel Me revealed the forty-nine by forty-nine tables of *Liber Loagaeth,* with the letters appearing to be written in fresh blood, between lines of shadow. From these, the angel used a three-part gold wand to draw angelic letters and incantations.

Loagaeth, the angels explained, was the true book of Enoch,* and its transcription was to occupy the next several months. When completed the following year, it took up forty-eight manuscript leaves, each of which featured a forty-nine by forty-nine magical square painstakingly delivered by Kelly for a total of 115,000 squares, producing forty-nine calls. These, confusingly, are *not* the forty-nine calls later delivered for working with the Watchtowers and Aethyrs; these were the primal calls spoken by God to create the universe. They remain untranslated.[29]

Dee was growing irritated with Kelly—when angels showed Kelly letters in angelic script and commanded him to read, he could not, despite having been commanded by the angels to memorize the new language. The angels had a backup plan, however: rather than showing Kelly images via scrying, they were now fully taking control of his nervous system. By April 3, Kelly was recorded as praying perfectly in the angelic language. At this point the communication between Kelly and the angels was purely in Enochian. At the beginning of these sessions, fire would jump from the scrying ball and into Kelly's eyes, during which time he would feel a burning sensation in his brain and be taken over by the angels. While possessed, he was able to fully read, write, and interpret the angelic script, yet when the angels relinquished control of him and the fire left Kelly's eyes and returned to the stone,

---

*Not to be confused with the apocryphal Jewish texts 1 Enoch and 2 Enoch, often called the book of Enoch, which detail the fall of rebellious angels called Watchers, as well as the biblical prophet Enoch's translation to heaven. In contrast, Dee and Kelly's angels made it clear that *Liber Loagaeth* was the true book of Enoch.

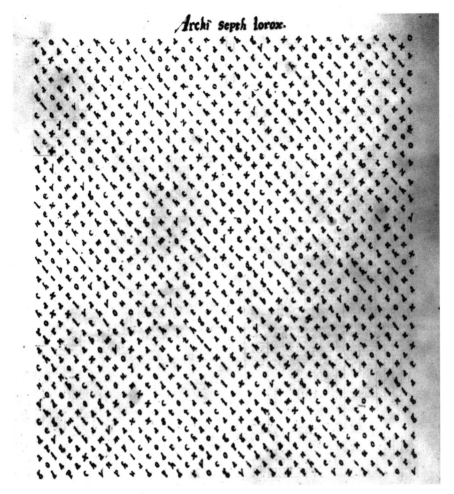

Fig. 9.9. A page from *Liber Loagaeth*. From MS. Sloane 2599.

he lost all ability to understand what he had transmitted. Raphael also appeared in his "medicinal" capacity to boost Dee's hearing.

Every element of *Loagaeth* was said to be a world of understanding, and had forty-nine manners of understanding.* Within it, Kelly said, were comprehended many languages, "all spoken at once . . . until thou come to the city, thou canst not behold the beauty thereof."†[30]

---

*A likely reference to Binah and its fifty gates.

†This may be a reference to the Tower of Babel, or the City of Pyramids that would later appear in Thelemic cosmology as an extension of the Watchtowers.

On April 6, Uriel appeared with a ball of fire in his left hand and a triangle of fire in his right; he proclaimed that great misery would come within five months, and that the duo needed to accelerate their work transcribing *Loagaeth*. To assist in their task, they were to be given spiritual sight. In forty days, the book of secrets and key of the world (*Loagaeth*) was to be written and brought to the "window of thy senses and doors of thy imagination" by Uriel.[31] Kelly, Uriel commanded and threatened, would always have the book before him and daily "perform the office to him committed." Were he not to, the Lord would "raze his name from the number of the blessed, and those that are anointed with his blood."[32]

"For behold, what man can speak or talk with the spirit of God?" Uriel told them. "No flesh is able to stand, when the voice of his Thunder shall present the part of the next leaf unto sight. You have wavering minds, and are drawn away with the World: But brittle is the state thereof. Small therefore are the vanities of his illusion."[33] So were they commanded to be of good faith.

The transcription of the book continued over the coming days, with Kelly undergoing possession and delivering pages of angelic script. On April 15, while writing the eighteenth leaf, attributed to the spirits of the earth, three or four entities appeared, unbidden, that looked like laboring men carrying shovels.* Dee attempted to banish them, but they assaulted Kelly, biting him and breaking his left arm by the wrist, imprinting two deep, red circles in his skin. While Dee ran to grab a stick, the spirits continued to assault Kelly, who tried to ward them off with a stool while they came at him snarling, until Dee banished them with a makeshift wand in the name of Jesus.

This must have been too much for Kelly, whose sanity would surely have been fraying at this point. Yet only three days later the pair were back to scrying, and the transmission of *Loagaeth* continued. Uriel again appeared and urged obedience to God's plan and patience, for it would unfold in its own time.

---

*This is a traditional description of gnomes, the elemental spirits of earth.

QUINTI LIBRI MYSTERIORUM APPENDIX

By April 20, Dee and Kelly were fighting bitterly. Kelly, Dee wrote, wished to "utterly discredit the whole process of our actions: as to be done by evil and illuding spirits seeking his destruction."[34] A terrified and harried Kelly complained that he was held at Mortlake like a prisoner, and threatened to quit in search of more gainful income elsewhere.

Dee replied by parroting the angels' own commands, stating that it was not for them to put a timeline on God's plans. As far as interference from illuding spirits, or the wrath of the angels, Dee blamed Kelly for doubting the goodness of their teachers, who had only counseled faith, patience, and praise of God. Kelly's mind was troubled, Dee said, but his own was quiet and joyful, bent only on awaiting and serving God. If Kelly was to complain of financial hardship, Dee was

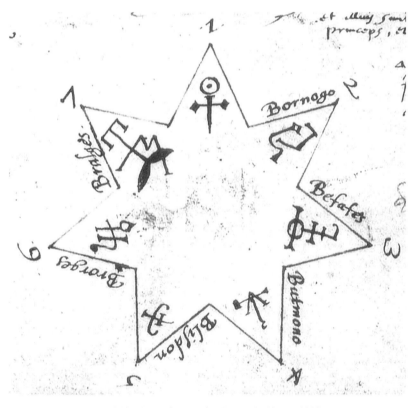

Fig. 9.10. Heptarchic angels. From MS. Sloane 3188.

even worse off, being £300 in debt (about £63,000 or $79,000 in 2017 terms)—and even though this was his only reward for forty years' study, hundreds of pounds spent on occult books and research, and hundreds of miles of travel, toil, and forcing himself to study and learn, he would still be happy to spend a year going "up and down England clothed in a blanket,"[35] begging for bread, if it only meant that he would attain to godly wisdom and do some service to God.

Making his point even plainer, Dee stated that he was willing to die now and enjoy the "bottomless fountain of all wisdom" in spirit (the same phrase he had used when he contemplated suicide in 1569),[36] or else pass the rest of his days doing God's will and learning his mysteries. This speech by Dee is a deep insight into his character, motivations, and faith. It captures not only the life that Dee had lived up to this point, but presages all that was to come. In a way, this singular comment contains the entirety of Dee's life.

Uriel agreed with Dee's appraisal of Kelly's lack of faith (and since Kelly would have transmitted the message from Uriel, it seems unlikely that he would have suddenly reversed stance and slandered himself were he making the entire thing up). The angels' patience was beginning to slip, and would only continue to disintegrate as the sessions progressed. Yet Uriel affirmed that Kelly had been chosen for a reason, despite his criminal background. However, Uriel was quick to rebuke both men for their lack of faith, telling them that "this sayeth the Lord: If you use me like worldlings I will surely stretch out my arm upon you, and that heavily."[37]

Attempting to use the angels "like worldlings" was most certainly something that Dee and Kelly would slip into, as they continually begged the spiritual messengers for money. It seems that no matter how many times the angels lashed the two men's lower natures, Dee and Kelly could not fully yoke themselves to the task at hand.

This frustration between men and angels, and antagonism of their fundamental natures, is a primary theme of scripture, beginning in the Garden of Eden. The animal in man will not submit to the divinity of God and his angels, except in the case of saints who have been purified by long trial. This is the core of Qabalah and the Western esoteric tradition—the continual fitting of man to the divine order

of the Creation through progressive study and initiation. In initiatory Qabalah, this is the purification of each sephira in the human
microcosm, and the transformation of the uninitiated man into the
perfected Adam Kadmon.

Dee obeyed the angels, and stated that the book would be finished
in forty days. Both men fell to their knees to pray. Within three days,
calm had returned to Mortlake and Kelly had returned to a position of
faithful obedience. The angel Il now delivered more of the Enochian
alphabet, which he counseled represented the workmanship by which
the soul of man was made like God. After checking Dee's work on the
letters that were to surround the Holy Table, Il informed him that these
had, again, been the work of an illuder, and were a "secret band of the
devil."[38] This constant cross talk and difficulty on Dee and Kelly's part
in discerning between angels and demons characterized the early sessions, but abated as they progressed and their faith and skill increased.

Il now transmitted the correct form of the Holy Table and told
them that the Sigillum Dei was to rest upon it. According to Il, divine
and secret power was here "shut up in the numbers of the ternary and
quaternary,"[39] echoing the ternary and quaternary structure of Dee's
Monas hieroglyphica.

Next, the angel Il delivered a new lamen to replace the one given in
Liber primus, which was to be engraved in gold. This was derived from
a table assembled from the names of the kings and princes, sans *B*s.

Following this, Kelly had yet another disturbing encounter with an
illuding spirit. Picking up a prayer book that had been at the table with
them during the previous action, Kelly found notes written within it in
his own handwriting, which he had no recollection of making. A spirit
appeared to Kelly and claimed the note was as good as any of the others
they had taken, but Dee judged the note to be a counterfeit, written by
another devil or illuder. After dinner, Dee and Kelly retired to Dee's
oratory to make "fervent prayer against the spiritual enemy."[40] Il and
Uriel appeared, and Uriel explained that temptation was necessary "and
must ordinarily follow those whom it pleaseth him to illuminate with
the beams of triumphant sanctification. If temptation were not, how
should the sons of men (sayeth the Lord) know me to be merciful?"[41]

Uriel stated that he would protect the duo from cruelty, make them perfect, and establish at Mortlake "light without darkness, truth without falsehood, righteousness without the works of wickedness."[42] Uriel further identified the illuding spirit as Belmagel, a "firebrand, who hath followed thy soul from the beginning, yea seeking his destruction."[43]

After frightening and confusing starts, Dee was beginning to develop greater trust and faith in his angelic ministers, but his mind was still swarming with doubt. A week later, he composed a series of twenty-eight questions or "articles of doubts" before calling Uriel.[44]

Uriel stated that it was God's will to perfect Dee and Kelly that they be apt vessels, and that *Loagaeth* would be finished imminently. Yet the angel still wondered out loud why it should be given to mortals: "This book, and holy key, which unlocketh the secrets of God his determination, as concerning the beginning, present being, and end of this world, is so reverent and holy: that I wonder (I speak in your sense) why it is delivered to those, that shall decay: So excellent and great are the mysteries therein contained."[45]

Within forty days, *Liber Loagaeth* would be perfected, and from it would be restored the holy books that "have perished even from the beginning," from which the true religion would be reconstructed, free from falsehood. After these books were circulated for a time, "then cometh the end," Uriel stated.[46] The book was to reveal three kinds of knowledge: the knowledge of God, truly; the number and doing of his angels, perfectly; and the beginning and ending of nature, substantially.

Much of the rest of the temple furniture, and how it was to be assembled, was now given. Were the scrying stone to be placed within a magical circle containing the five angelic names at the center of the Sigillum Dei, Dee would be able to "at all times behold, (privately to thy self), the state of God's people through the whole earth."[47] (This was solved by placing the scrying ball on top of this part of the Sigillum itself.) The table was also meant to rest upon four hollow containers of sweet wood, within which would be four smaller copies of the Sigillum. It was to be covered with multicolored silk, symbolizing the inscrutable nature of God's seat. The Ensigns of Creation were to be made in purified tin and placed around the Sigillum, or painted on the table. These were to be used when needed, as were the names of the kings, which were to be painted on sweet wood and held in the hand as needed. The place where the table was to be put was not important, as the spirit actions would purify the place, not vice versa.

They were to make themselves ready by August 1, in three months; nine days before which they would humble themselves and "unrip (I say) the cankers of your infected souls, that you may be apt and meet to understand the Secrets, that shall be delivered,"[48] for God had already sent his good angels to gather the sins of the earth and weigh them in the balance of Justice. After this period of purification, the Table of Practice was to be used for one month. Adrian Gilbert (who was now assisting with the scrying sessions), Uriel said, was to be made privy to some things in the operation as were necessary; he was soon to become crucial to the angels' plans in building a world religion.[49]

Once *Liber Loagaeth* was finished, Uriel explained, an expedition for "fetching of the earth" was to be fulfilled—Dee and Kelly were to obtain small amounts of dirt from every place of the earth, by which they would be able to forge magical connections to those parts of the world using the good angels. (As Kelly was obviously not able to obtain dirt from the entire planet, the angels specified ten or eleven locations in England to retrieve earth from.)[50]

Following these sessions, Dee left for London, while Kelly stayed on at Mortlake, copying out angelic script—Dee noted that when Kelly couldn't figure out how to draw a letter, it would appear in light yellow on the page, which he would draw over in black, after which the yellow faded.

Dee and Kelly prayed for further technical guidance on making the book. Within the stone appeared a palace, out of which came a tall, "well-favored" man,[51] very richly appareled, with a feathered hat, followed by a great number of courtiers. The man proceeded to mock and condemn Dee, and threatened to destroy him, his wife, and his children. After Dee prayed for aid against the new illuder, the man replied, "As truly as the Lord lieth, *all that is done, is lies.*"[52] Dee responded that he would record this utterance, to be laid against the evil spirit at the Judgment Day.

A voice now came to Kelly, stating in Latin, "May darkness perish with the Prince of Darkness."[53] All now disappeared, to be replaced with the temple furniture and Uriel, who warned them that they must arm themselves, for severe temptations were ahead, and they would be obstructed in their work. Though nothing could hinder God, Dee sourly replied that man could hinder his own salvation nonetheless. They were to finish the books; in regard to their expedition to fetch the earths, Dee complained that they could not find a horse and without more money would not be able to obtain one.

"Therefore if it might please God," Dee requested, "that of the ten places noted, we might have but the possession of the smallest of them delivered here, unto us."[54]

Uriel was enraged at this plea, stating, "Will these worldlings hold on in their iniquity?"[55] Afterward, the angels packed up the table and vanished in a cloud.

Dee collapsed into sorrowful prayer. A tongue of fire appeared in the stone, which rebuked Dee for his iniquity. Dee was forgiven, the tongue said, but would be punished. He was left in a state of sorrow, begging God for mercy and promising that he would behave better in the future, even swearing off sexual relations with his wife.

The following day, Dee again brought out the stone and prayed, begging forgiveness, reciting Psalm 22—"My God, my God, why have you forsaken me? Why are you so far from saving me, so far from my cries of anguish?"[56]—the psalm continues on to have the orator proclaim that he is a worm, not a man. A figure in white appeared in the stone and forgave Dee's "long offenses and sins." Yet despite this unexpected mercy, the angel still sternly warned Dee, "Behold, my arms are longer than my body, and I have eyes round about me: I am that which God pronounceth upon you"[57]—that is, Uriel's earlier warning that "If you use me like worldlings I will surely stretch out my arm upon you, and that heavily."[58] Uriel himself now appeared, stating, "It has been done,"[59] after which the temple furniture again appeared, this time more beautifully than before.

"The rising of sinners doth greatly rejoice us," Uriel said. "Justify not yourself: Be humble and diligent: Continue to the end. For great is the reward of them that fear the Lord steadfastly."[60]

By May 23, Kelly had retrieved the "earths of the eleven places before specified."[61] Afterward, Michael, Raphael, and Uriel appeared to Dee and Kelly to tell them that their sins had been cleansed and forgiven. Dee asked after Stephen, king of Poland, and if he would be succeeded by the house of Austria or by the Polish nobleman Count Olbracht Łaski, a new contact of Dee and Kelly's that had recently visited them at Mortlake. Dee also asked if Łaski was to have the kingdom of Moldavia. On this the angels were mute, saying it was not for them to determine.

Łaski's destiny was soon to become inseparable from Dee and Kelly's own: the nobleman was to embroil Mortlake in a web of chaos and intrigue that would pluck Dee and his scryer from the comfort of suburban London and drop them in the middle of the European political theater. In the process, he would destroy what little remained of Dee's career.

The angels had other plans for Dee. For as Michael now told him, "The earth is pregnant and struggles with the iniquities of the enemies of light. It is therefore accursed, because it is in the womb of damnation and darkness."

"It is filthy and offensive to us," Uriel agreed.

"It scourges itself by its own shaking," Raphael added.[62]

It was time to wrap up the show.

10

And Therefore, Behold the End

The angels had been warning Dee for months that he should leave England in preparation for the coming Apocalypse, but he lacked the funds to do so. A visitor was soon to arrive in Dee's life that was to change that.

On March 18, 1583, Dee received a letter from Olbracht Łaski, the Palatine of Sieradz in Poland, that he was coming to visit. When Dee consulted Uriel about the Polish nobleman who so fervently wanted to meet him, the archangel replied that God was above such mundane affairs, which were left to Dee's own discretion. The angels' opinion of Łaski would soon change.

Łaski was a Polish senator and *voivode* under Stephen Báthory of Poland (Báthory was the uncle of the notorious "vampiric" serial killer Elizabeth Báthory).[1] Hailing from a Catholic family in a Habsburg-controlled area of Transylvania, Łaski himself had joined the Calvinist movement, and had even experimented with alchemy and operative magic, distancing himself from the Church in the process. He published Latin tracts on religion that were admired in his home country, as well as financing a Latin translation and publication of two works by Paracelsus. Łaski is recorded as a tall man, well proportioned, generally dressed in scarlet with yellow boots, whose predominant feature was a giant white beard that he kept tucked into his belt. His temperament was generous and sweet, and he is remembered for having a high wit and great knowledge of languages.[2] Łaski's early military goals were the conquest of Moldavia and Wallachia, in order to break up Turkish control, for which he earned the gratitude of the Habsburgs and the indignation of Poland, as all he generally achieved by these raids was redirecting the Turks' military efforts from Austria to Poland.[3]

Łaski is not recorded as a hero. He was reckless with his wealth, was known in Poland as a "bag without a bottom,"[4] and according to the Polish historian Jan Kasprzak, "would do anything in order to obtain money. He squandered his wives' dowries and ruined their lives, and at one time, he kidnapped the wife of a nobleman, whom he kept imprisoned at his estate and tortured. A contemporary historian, who recorded Łaski's infamous deeds, complained bitterly that there was no

Fig. 10.1. Olbracht Łaski. Woodcut by Jan Styfi, 1876.

crime which Łaski would not have committed."[5] It seemed that while Łaski would later be well received in England, his own reputation as a scoundrel would put even Kelly's to shame. Yet these crimes, and his poorly executed raids against Turkey, would see Łaski blackballed by the king of Poland, after which he would renounce Protestantism and run to the Catholic Church for protection. Next he would offer his services to Ivan the Terrible, which he later publicly backpedaled on before he could be charged for treason for aiding an assassination attempt against King Stefan.

Walsingham's own summation of Łaski's history was that he had consumed his own riches, that he had "run the course of France,"[6] and that he had supported Maximilian II for the throne of Poland before Stephen Báthory won, at which point he fled to Maximilian's court in Italy to wait out Báthory's temper. When this situation (understandably) didn't miraculously resolve itself, Łaski began to look for alliances with England. Any reprieve Łaski received in Poland would be temporary and shaky at best.

By January 1582, peace had been negotiated between Poland and Moscow—by the Jesuit papal envoy, to Elizabeth's chagrin. Even more humiliating to England was that Stephen Báthory had been given Protestant Livonia, near the Protestant strongholds in Muscovy and Sweden, putting these countries within striking distance of the Catholic bloc. The victory over Moscow also suggested disruptions in trade between England and Russia, at the time England's most valuable trade route, worth far more to the Crown than the tentative attempts at opening the New World. Łaski could prove useful in handling this new geopolitical situation and in making negotiations with Moscow. Recent intelligence reports had suggested a plot to put Mary, Queen of Scots, on the throne of England, along with an attack by Stephen Báthory "against the cities which are Martin Luther's."[7] Elizabeth therefore needed information from Łaski on Báthory's plans concerning England and Spain, and Łaski could draw on his connections in Poland to retrieve that information. Báthory, it turned out, was indeed plotting against England, and advocating that Philip II take naval and military action against the English by 1583—the Spanish Armada would come only five years later. Yet despite his willingness to spy on Báthory, Łaski's Catholic connections would also worry the Privy Council; upon his arrival in England, his public attendance of Mass and some correspondence with Mary, Queen of Scots, raised eyebrows.[8]

Łaski's arrival in England was soon followed by a momentous reception at Oxford University, which was noted as the highlight of 1583 for the school, following which he made his way down the Thames to Mortlake in a royal procession, in a barge accompanied by the queen's rowers, trumpeters, and banners. The total expenses of his visit were a shocking £350, £50 more than Dee's entire accumulated debt.[9] (This would equal somewhere in the realm of £74,000 or $93,000 in 2017.) In the meantime, Łaski was claiming descent from the English Lacy family, in yet another attempt to establish political power in yet another state.[10] The Lacy bloodline would later turn out to potentially be related to the queen's, though the documents were questionable—and with Łaski's history of trying to overthrow states with private armies, this was yet another major security concern. Łaski would soon fall out of favor, taking the reputation of his new best friend John Dee with him.

Received by Elizabeth, he lived at the queen's expense in high comfort at Winchester House. Though he was lavishly furnished (and he, Dee, and Kelly were to be provided with two ships when they left for the Continent), Łaski's expenses—and the true purpose of his sojourn in England—were kept secret by the Crown. It is possible that he may have been looking to secure England's aid against Stephen Báthory.[11]

Like the privateer Drake, the activities of the adventurer Łaski may well have fallen into the realm of "plausible deniability." Whatever purpose the Crown, and Walsingham's secret service, had in mind for Łaski, with no records and no official court status they could have easily washed their hands of him and claimed no knowledge. Dee himself may well have fallen into this category—as Dee was more and more alienated from the "dayside" court of Elizabeth's administration, he may have been taking on even greater responsibility in the "nightside" court of Walsingham's secret service. His loss of status may have made him an even more useful agent, just as his occult activities provided a convenient cover for intelligence work on the Continent—much as the occult would do for twentieth-century occult spies like Crowley and Gurdjieff. Like Łaski's activities in England, Dee's meetings with the queen and many of his Continental sojourns have been redacted from history.[12]

"Whatever he did that was significant," the NSA summarized of Dee in 1967, "has no doubt gone into the classified files of Elizabeth's ministers, and from there to complete oblivion."[13] While history is based on assembling written evidence, intelligence work is based on destroying it. Realistically, this makes a full assessment of a man like Dee impossible.

Like Dee, Łaski's past made him an extrastate actor. This would have made Łaski invaluable as an intelligence agent and as an angelic pawn. And while modern knowledge of Łaski's political actions in England is limited, the extensive records of the plans of the angels for the wayward Polish nobleman are readily available. Łaski would be a convenient instrument, quickly seized upon by the angels to use in their Continental game. Yet even the angels would soon recoil from Łaski, finding him too fundamentally dirty, morally compromised, and, most of all, unfaithful to work with.

By May 28, Łaski had joined Dee and Kelly at Mortlake. The count was to ingratiate himself in their milieu, and was to play a starring role in the actions to come. By his own account, Dee had cottoned up to Łaski, and had expressed gratitude to God that Łaski had favored him. Dee saw in his association with the noble Łaski a chance to revive his career and to reverse his standing in public opinion. Łaski may well have seen an opportunity to advance his own status in the world with a bit of occult aid, or even espionage opportunities.

Łaski immediately set upon Dee and Kelly in search of a divine revelation of his great political future. When Dee asked the angels what was to come with Łaski, they told him that far journeys lay ahead. The angels would take an active interest in the Polish count, furnishing him with a genealogy dating to the House of Plantagenet and progressing through the noble Lacy family, prophesying that he would not only rule Poland but also unify the Christian, Jewish, Islamic, and pagan religions into a single faith.[14] This would not only heal the rift between Catholics and Protestants, but also fulfill necessary prerequisites for the Apocalypse by converting the Jews and Muslims to Christianity. Such ideas had already been brewing in Europe, most notably in the "Familist" sect.[15] With this, the spirit sessions crossed an inarguable, legally codified line between scientific experiment and treason— political prophecies were illegal throughout Europe. Yet even though he had already been imprisoned for less, Dee's faith in the angels was such that he crossed that line without a second thought.[16]

Soon, Dee was to regard Łaski as his ticket back to high society, hoping that associating with a nobleman Dee perceived as powerful would raise his own reputation and personal fortune. The reverse, however, would happen: Łaski would not only involve Dee in his fruitless intrigue, and tarnish Dee by association, but his presence would also imbalance Dee further toward the psychodrama being created at Mortlake, and away from court and serious scientific work. After being so badly rejected by Cecil and the court—and being overlooked for so long—Dee may have seen Łaski as somebody who would accept him at last, along with his theories and his belief in his own special status. Dee's vulnerability following the collapse of his career, and his need for approval, put him in a very dangerous place indeed—and the sirens of occult knowledge and geopolitical power were soon to lead him far, far afield.

RECORDS

The records published as the *Mysteriorum libri quinque* are superseded by the spirit actions recorded in *A True & Faithful Relation of what passed for Many Yeers between Dr. John Dee . . . and some spirits . . .* , originally published by the classical scholar Méric Casaubon in 1659. *A True & Faithful Relation* is drawn from the manuscripts preserved in the British Library as Cotton Appendix MS. XLVI, parts 1 and 2, and at the Bodleian Library as Ashmole MS. 1790. These separations are arbitrary and based on how Dee's spirit diaries were split up after his death. Dee's original diaries are numbered continuously from beginning to end, meaning that the records beginning *A True & Faithful Relation* pick up only five days after the *Mysteriorum libri quinque* ends, on May 28, 1583. Dee's original designations for each diary are preserved here.

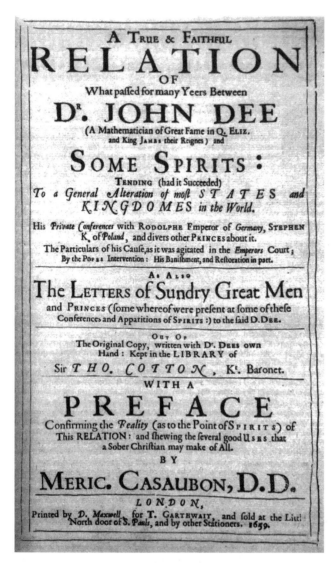

Fig. 10.2. Title page
of Méric Casaubon,
*A True & Faithful
Relation*, 1659.

LIBER SEXTI MYSTERIORUM (ET SANCTI) PARALLELUS NOVALISQUE
Madimi and the Arrival of Łaski

Dee dubs his next diary "The Sixth (and Sacred) Book of Mystery, a Similar New Beginning"; *novalisque* carrying the meaning of "a new land cultivated for the first time."[17]

Liber sexti opens with a new visitor—the angel Madimi, whose name had already been transmitted within the Sigillum Dei Aemeth, but who now appeared to plain sight for the first time. Emerging from Dee's oratory, Madimi presented herself as a pretty girl, seven or nine years old, her hair rolled up in front and hanging down at the back. She wore a satin gown, which changed from red to green, just like the silk cloth Dee and Kelly had been directed to hang over the Holy Table. The entity carried a toy and ran up and down through Dee's stacks of books, which were observed moving to allow her through. At times Dee heard a voice speaking to Madimi, though no other being was seen.

"Am I not a fine Maiden?" Madimi asked. "Give me leave to play in your house, my Mother told me she would come and dwell here. . . . I am the last but one of my Mother's children, I have little Baby-children at home."[18] Madimi revealed that she was one of the Daughters of Light from the Sigillum, and that her six sisters had to come and dwell with Dee. Their mother, Galvah, was later to come. Madimi was to play a crucial role in the scrying sessions, and would become one of Dee's favorite angels—so much so that Dee would later name one of his daughters after her.[19] Dee's initial questions to Madimi were all about Łaski's family pedigree; this is where the angels furnished Łaski with a genealogical lineage connecting him to the English monarchy, with one eye toward securing power for the count as a move in their grand game.

The angels next told them that "the time is nigh," when all things would be consummated, that the "seven doors are opened,"[20] and that the seven planetary angels spoken of by Trithemius had almost ended their rule. This meant that history was indeed coming to an end. The planets and elements themselves, the entity said, were sick unto death and ready to give up; nature was ready to be returned to God. Even hell itself was weary of Earth. Antichrist was now prepared to establish his kingdom, now that the forces of darkness were strong enough to take hold of the weakened world.

Dee and Kelly were to be given work to do, but they were not to attempt to push or change the will of God. As the angel said, "All things shall be brought into a uniformal Order."[21] Łaski was to be made a king, and within him, "The state and alteration of the whole World shall begin."[22] Dee and Kelly were to deliver a message to the kings of Europe, but it was to be sealed for now.

On June 5, Kelly's brother Thomas arrived at Mortlake to inform the scryer that a warrant had been issued for his arrest, and that Kelly's wife had fled Blokley (presumably Blockley in Gloucestershire) for her mother's house. Kelly had been accused of forgery—Dee noted at the time that he believed this to be a lie and slander against Kelly. Moved by compassion for his friend, and afraid of losing Kelly's service either to his frantic state of mind or the law, Dee prayed to God for intervention.

The Daughters of Light now appeared in the shewstone. Pride, the Daughters told Dee and Kelly, was the greatest sin, and it would have to be removed from them.

"Doth the World not like of thee?" the Daughters asked, which Dee must have taken as indicative of his political fall. "It is for two causes; either for that thou lives well and not as a worldling, or else because thy wickedness is such that the World wondreth at it. If thou be in the first Rejoice, For blessed are those whom the World hateth; when they laugh at thy godliness, be sorry and grieve at their sinfulness. If thou offend in the second fly hastily from the World: tell the World what thou hast of hers, and let her be ashamed that thou knowest her."[23]

For the angels, the world was a fallen place of sin. To be of God was to be apart from it and dwell in prayer. To suffer at the hands of the world was to be purified by it, in preparation for the next world. For Satan, the angels explained, had taken full hold of the earth, and they were only waiting on God's word to "pour out the wrath of God"[24] upon the world and everything in it (compare the wrath of God poured out on the earth by seven angels in Revelation 16 and throughout the text of Revelation).

Kelly begged for counsel on the false accusations made against him. The Daughters replied that there were two reconciliations: one with God, and the other with one's own conscience. Kelly had not reconciled with his own conscience (the implication being that he was guilty and had not repented his wickedness), and so could not be reconciled with God. The reward of sin was to be banished from the company of the angels. Dee protested that if Kelly were to be arrested at Mortlake,

Fig. 10.3. Albrecht Dürer, *The Opening of the Fifth and Sixth Seals*, 1498.

it would bring Dee grief and disgrace. But the angels replied that Dee himself was protected.

On June 14, after dinner, a female angel named Galvah appeared—Madimi's mother.* Confused that the spirits were appearing as female, Dee protested that Trithemius had written that no good angel ever appeared in female form (or in the form of an animal, but always in male form), and asked Galvah to clarify the matter.

Galvah replied that angels are neither male nor female, but took forms based on the will of God and appropriate to the specific task they had been given—and moreover, were vastly different depending on what angelic rank they were, so that lower angels could not even comprehend the nature of their superiors. Galvah explained that her own function was to be "a beam of that Wisdom which is the end of man's excellency." All of the Daughters of Light were comprehended in her, and if Trithemius were to understand this, he would know that "true Wisdom is always painted with a woman's garment; for than the pureness of a virgin, nothing is more commendable."[25]

Galvah assured the two that Łaski would become king before the end of his life, and that he would transform the entire world.

"Persevere to the end,"[26] Galvah told Dee, quoting Matthew 24:13.†

Angelic metaphysics was revealed: angels, it was shown, may err, and so fall from the brightness of their glory. But if a man were to glorify his soul through righteousness and true wisdom, he could never lose his dignity.

"With you Satan is busy," the angels told them. "His bristles stand up, his feathers are cast abroad."[27]

After exhorting Dee and Kelly to fear God, Galvah now began to deliver the forty-nine leaves of *Liber Loagaeth*. (This is a point of some

---

*Galvah identified herself as "Wisdom" and "I AM," suggesting direct correlation to the sephira Chokmah, above Binah—called Sophia in Greek.

†A verse Aleister Crowley would later draw upon for his own magical motto in the Golden Dawn, "Perdurabo," or "I will endure to the end." The phrase has resonance with both Revelation and the equally apocalyptic Bodhisattva vow taken by Mahayana and Vajrayana Buddhist practitioners, that they will continue to reincarnate until the totality of beings in the universe achieve enlightenment.

confusion at first, as Dee and Kelly had *already* been given forty-eight leaves that were also titled *Liber Loagaeth*. The occult scholar Aaron Leitch clarifies this befuddling transition by explaining that what was now being transmitted was the *perfected* version of *Liber Loagaeth*.[28] For some reason, the angels delivered two versions of several of their designs, a crude version followed by a clearer and "perfected" version, including the lamen, the Sigillum, *Liber Loagaeth,* and later, the Watchtowers.)

While transmitting the book, Kelly observed that beams of light shot between the stone and Galvah, and the angel's head burned with fire so bright that it could not be looked at, and that it sparkled and glistened like "when a hot iron is smitten on an anvil" as each word was pronounced. Also accompanying the words were "the Beasts and all Creatures of the World," including serpents, dragons, toads, and other "ugly and hideous shapes of beasts." These assaulted Kelly while also "fawning upon" Galvah.[29]

Kelly was so disturbed by these beasts, considering them to be further evidence of demonic taint, that he attempted to break the session. Dee forced him back, afterward chastising him for suspecting the good nature of Galvah, who underlined that it was the angry and perverse mind of Kelly that tainted the vision. Yet the scryer was still not convinced. Comparing himself to Doubting Thomas, he said that he would "believe these things, when I see the fruits of them."[30] But Galvah again assured them, at length, that the angels were sent by God.

Galvah also introduced Łaski to Jubanladace, his holy guardian angel, who told the nobleman that during his time not only the Jews but also the Muslims and pagans would convert to Christianity, and one faith would be established. Jubanladace also said that Cecil hated Łaski "unto the heart,"[31] and wished him gone, and that many others libeled him; but Jubanladace would pour down his wrath upon them. Yet he also counseled that Elizabeth and Dudley loved Łaski; even that Elizabeth had fallen out with Cecil over his treatment of Łaski. Jubanladace himself would look after Łaski, as would Gabriel.

Great calamities were coming, natural and political, said the angels, including the destruction of the princes of Europe and of the Holy Roman Empire by the Turks—this would nearly come to pass, but the

Turkish push into Western Europe would be defeated at the Battle of Vienna in 1683. Stephen Báthory was to fall in battle as well (Báthory died in 1586 of natural causes; only a few years before, however, he had been planning another war with Russia that didn't come to pass due to lack of financial support). Łaski was to be appointed king of Moldavia (this also never came to pass). Adrian Gilbert, despite not being "of the faith," and not well liked by Kelly, was to be "the setter forth of God, his faith, and religion among the infidels."[32] As Gilbert had previously been active in the spirit sessions, his departure would allow Łaski to take his place.[33] Gilbert's mission to create a world religion would foment the Apocalypse—due to the spiritual stress caused by the run-up to the end times, Dee, following Postel, believed that direct revelations like the ones he and Kelly were experiencing would become more common until the eschaton.[34]

Though the angels did work to still Kelly's mind, on July 4 he again tried to escape Mortlake. Spirits, possibly ones Kelly had conjured himself, had told him privately that if he stayed at Mortlake he would be hanged, that if he went with Łaski he would be beheaded, and that Dee would not keep his promises. Moreover, Kelly confessed, he hated his own wife. Instead of staying, Kelly wished to forgo his salary and run. Dee counseled Kelly that these thoughts were not from God, but allowed him to go. Kelly must have had a change of heart, for he returned not three hours later, to Dee's delight, and sat down to peruse new books that Dee had been given by Łaski. At this, Madimi appeared to Kelly, and patted the back of the book he held playfully.

"I know you see me often," Dee told Madimi, whom he could hear, but not see tangibly, "and I see you only by faith and imagination."[35] Madimi replied that this sight—imagination—was actually "perfecter" than Kelly's.

In one of the most ludicrous events of the spirit actions, Kelly now requested that Madimi *lend* him a hundred pounds for two weeks. His request was refused. Kelly was admonished greatly, and the angels scrambled to expunge evil spirits from his body.

Yet while Łaski and Dee's fortunes were rising in the eyes of the angels, in the real world Dee's career was over. His association with

Łaski, now considered a traitor, had broken Walsingham's remaining trust in him; the spymaster planned to raid Dee's house and trap Dee on treason charges as soon as Łaski left the country. Łaski lacked the funds to make the trip to the Continent, however, and had to lean on Dee to borrow £400 (about £84,000 or $106,000 in 2017 terms) from his brother-in-law so that the group could make the journey.[36] Even Elizabeth was starting to distance herself from Dee.[37]

Dee's reputation was destroyed. His household was also broke, with no prospects beyond the prophesied great future for Łaski (also broke) and the utterances of the angels. He could do little but proceed with the plan that the angels had laid out for him; as further incentive, the angels assured him he would be eternally punished if he did not follow the script. Dee's path had been cleared for him.

11

Aethyrs and Watchtowers

LIBER PEREGRINATIONIS PRIMAE
(SEXTI MYSTICI PARADROMUS)

Travels in Europe and Announcements of Apocalypse

Dee's diary entries between *Liber sexti* and *Liber peregrinationis primae,* entitled *Liber tertiarius sexti: librum decimum,*[1] are no longer extant. Consequently, Dee's published records pick up again two and a half months later, with Dee and his retinue departing England for the Continent. They would be gone for 175 days.

On September 21, 1583, Dee, Kelly, and their families departed Mortlake for Poland. Łaski met them on the Thames, and in the darkness of the night the party traveled from Greenwich to Gravesend, where they met with ships in the morning. With Dee's group in one ship and Łaski's attendants in another, they hoisted sail for the Continent, by way of the Netherlands. Their voyage was fraught with constant peril, but was successful. Dee and Kelly had brought their scrying equipment; when faced with a storm, they used it to summon the archangel Michael, who appeared as a six-foot figure in the clouds and gave spiritual and terrestrial guidance. They were also shown an image of the Royal Palace in Krakow in the scrying ball. The angels counseled that the forces of hell itself were now arrayed against Łaski, for they knew he would be glorified by God. Like the earlier appearance of Galvah, the angels were often accompanied by haloes of foul creatures—spiders with human faces, locusts, monkeys, serpents, creatures vomiting fire, and so on. Perhaps the angels were subduing these evil creatures, perhaps they were being accompanied by them, or perhaps they were demons themselves.

On October 26, at Breame, an angel named Ilemese appeared and gave a prophecy of the end times, which were to occur over the next five years.

"I will plague the people, and their blood shall become Rivers," Ilemese said. "Fathers shall eat their own children, and the earth shall be barren: the beasts of the field shall perish, and the waters shall be poisoned. The air shall infect her creatures, and in the deep shall be roaring."[2] Thus would Great Babylon be built, and the Dragon arise. During this time Dee would have power, to glorify God thereby. After transmitting this vision, Ilemese disintegrated into ashes.

"The sins of the people, and filthiness of places, are put between virtue and the things Sacramental," an angel called Aphlafben told them. "Therefore, it is not true, that thou mayest lawfully call upon the Name of God in unhallowed places."[3] Even the crudest temples in Israel would be sanctified, however, for the land was holy; yet Holland was filthy, and obscured the messages of the angels. Dee and Kelly were to flee the company of drunkards while abroad.

On November 13, the apparition of a giant two-edged, fiery, bloody sword appeared in the sky, with the angels pronouncing that "many are the Harlots that swarm upon the earth."[4] Humanity was castigated for its "Horedom," by which the angels meant the behavior of those who do not love God, and instead love themselves or the vanities of the world. For "I brought you from iniquity, to the intent you might be purified," an angelic voice stated, "but the more I cleanse you, the more you are defiled," suggesting the state of humanity as a whole.[5] God had sent mercy to the world through Christ, his Apostles, and his Church, but humanity had continually returned to its worship of idols and wicked ways: "I have brought you from fire, but you are entered into flames. And why? Because you defile your selves with the wickednesse of deceivers."[6] To purify itself, humanity had the intercessory medium of Christ, in whom all power was given, and the Church, into which all power was also delivered; even though its doubters (Protestants) alleged that the Church was "infected with errours,"[7] the angels assured it was not. Only the errors of a few were considered unrighteousness, not the error of the institution as a whole. The angels continued to underline that the world, and the flesh, were to be renounced, and that the battle of purification was to be regularly fought. Even if Dee and Kelly were worldly and weak men, their struggle to overcome had to be made, and this would benefit the whole world.

"Make flesh subject, and strangle your Adversary," the angels told them. "For unto such belongeth the entrance into my Chambers, and the use of my will, as the Horn of my glory."[8]

Between November 20 and 25, an evil spirit appeared and tried to persuade Dee and Kelly that the angels they had sworn fealty to—as if it were a covenant with God—were evil angels. The spirit cited even great men of God, including St. Antony of Egypt, who had been beguiled by false spirits. This, the spirit told them, was worse than error, for they now followed false doctrine, and had forgotten their own knowledge. The spirit also said that Łaski would fall and that they were being lured to destruction by sirens.

The evil spirit told Dee that "I am sent from God as a Messenger to call thee home."[9] They had dishonored God, and would be made laughingstocks, cast out, and abandoned by their friends—perhaps so that they could be purified of the world. This indeed happened; the curse on Dee and Kelly's names and reputations remains to this day.*

"But why dost thou write words of contempt against us? For One in our number is All; And we are, all, One."[10] The angels would dwell in all elements for them, between them and their sources of temptation, and also between them and their imaginations. They were also advised

---

*A similar injunction and warning of the social perils of occult initiation occurs in the Thelemic *Holy Books:* "Even as a man ascending a steep mountain is lost to sight of his friends in the valley, so must the adept seem. They shall say: He is lost in the clouds. But he shall rejoice in the sunlight above them, and come to the eternal snows." Crowley, "Liber Porta Lucis," in *The Holy Books,* 40.

to burn their "blasphemous" books. The angel became a pillar of crystal higher than a steeple, ascending upward into clouds, leaving a little circle.

While Dee and Kelly were enrapt in the divine drama that the angels had laid out for them, things were going very wrong at home. Shortly after they had departed England, Mortlake was ransacked. The looters included many of Dee's associates, including his creditors, who were given access by Dee's brother-in-law Nicholas Fromoundes, who also took and sold what he found in Dee's house. The motive for the ransacking seems to have been recouping debts (perhaps the £400 Fromoundes had loaned Dee for the Continental voyage), as well as sheer greed and the need to quickly turn a profit through fencing stolen books and goods, rather than a politically or religiously motivated attack, although Walsingham himself had planned to raid Mortlake at the first opportunity. Fromoundes sold Dee's alchemical equipment for 80 percent of its value.[11] Dee's anchors in England—his social standing and his property—were not just eroding but being destroyed. Instead, he was now caught up in Łaski's plans, though the angels counseled that "all your life is not of him: nor he of you."[12]

On January 12, Dee decided to show Kelly part of the Apocalypse of John. A voice said to him, "A white horse is the beginning of your instruction, and it is the word of God."[13] This was a reference to the white horse of Revelation 19—Christ. (Another white horse appears in Revelation 6:2, whose rider is one of the four horsemen of the Apocalypse—in some readings, the Antichrist.)* Uriel now told them that this was what 2 Esdras 9 referred to, and that these were the end days, wherein no faith would be found on Earth—but this faith would be restored. Christ was to return and bring justice. Dee and Kelly fell to studying Esdras.†

The next day, Uriel urged them to read 2 Esdras 6, another prophecy

---

*A similar figure appears in Hinduism—Kalki, the tenth and final avatar of Vishnu, who rides a white horse and brings an end to the world, or at least the present Yuga.

†Esdras, a Jewish apocalypse from the first century, makes a fascinating parallel study with the Dee sessions both in content and methodology of reception. See Davila, "The Ninety-Four Books of Ezra and the Angelic Revelations of John Dee."

of the end of the world, foreshadowing Revelation. Kelly alighted on the twenty-eighth verse, which adds the hopeful note that faith and truth will eventually triumph over corruption. Appearing in the shew-stone, Uriel revealed himself as the light and hand of God, who had comforted Esdras in his affliction. He prophesied "the last sleep of the world . . . for the earth hath cried vengeance, and hath cursed herself, and despaireth. Come (I say) For I will place the seat of righteousness. That my Kingdom may be in One: And that my people may flourish: Yea, even a little before the end."[14]

Uriel stated that the Antichrist would be unveiled to the world within three years—about January 1587. At that time "shall the Son of perdition be known unto the whole world: Suddenly creeping out of his hole like an Adder, leading out her young ones after her, to devour the dust of the earth."[15]

At the time of Antichrist, woe would be unto the kings of the earth, for they would all be chosen anew, and they would also all perish, their kingdoms to be overthrown. Rivers would fill with the blood of men and beasts. The Turkish Empire would be cast from the earth.* Łaski would "fly through his kingdoms, as the greyhound after his spoil, devouring his possessions, and cutting down the wicked,"[16] but he would become proud, and the prophets of the Lord would next descend from heaven.†

---

*This would not occur in actuality until World War I, following Crowley's annunciation of the Aeon of Horus in 1904.

†February 1, 1587, is notable as the day on which Elizabeth signed the death warrant of Mary, Queen of Scots; she was beheaded seven days later (as foretold by the angels). In July of the same year, 115 ill-fated colonists would arrive to settle Roanoke, Virginia. Yet Dee noted in the margins that a year might have a different meaning for angels, suggesting that a "mystic year" equaled seven mortal years, which would have put the date of the coming of Antichrist at 1605. If we are to use Dee's timing speculation, 1605 marked the proclamation of the Irish becoming the direct subjects of the English Crown, and the expunging of the Jesuits and Catholic priests, as well as the succession of the Medici Leo XI to the papacy, which would last only a month. Both of these dates mark significant expansions of English power and losses for the Catholics, suggesting that Elizabeth, England, and Protestantism might constitute part of the Antichrist. "Leading out her young ones after her, to devour the dust of the earth" indeed sounds like an apt description of Elizabeth initiating British imperialism.

Uriel also prophesied that despite Edward Kelly's stubbornness, because he had not offended God by partaking in earthly things, he would be made a great seer, and would "judge the circle of things in nature." Yet heavenly understanding and spiritual knowledge were still to be sealed from him, for he had "cried out" against the saints. Dee and Kelly were to spend their lives together, and would be "workmen of nature, looking into the chambers of the earth: the treasures of men."[17] Shortly thereafter, Kelly was given a vision of the throne and twenty-four elders from Revelation 4.

Dee and Kelly continued their travels through Poland. On January 25, Dee would make a telling comment in his diaries, in Latin (perhaps to hide it from his companion): "The great danger to my life has come from the iniquity of E. K. against me."[18] A few days later, he fought briefly with his wife. The Continental jaunt was raising tensions in the group to a breaking point.

On February 11, now in Łaski's hometown of Łasko, Poland, Dee and Kelly prayed the penitential psalms and again began scrying. Kelly reported that he felt something around his head, clawing at him as if with a hawk's talons. A great natural vista appeared to Kelly in the eastern corner of the study, after which a new angel arrived, who was to play a crucial role in the sessions: Nalvage, who stepped forward out of a cloud.

Nalvage was covered with a sleeveless red-and-purple robe that came to his knees, his head covered with down feathers, his face like a child's, his neck and legs bare. He stood upon a great round, white, crystal table, written with infinite letters, in the middle of which was a large swelling or knob of the same substance, which Nalvage's feet were upon—this came to be known as the Round Table of Nalvage. He introduced himself as a spirit of Wisdom* and the Most High (*Iaida* in the angelic tongue). Nalvage also said that he could not be seen for a long time. Nalvage verified that the spirit actions were true, and that the fruit of them would be the destruction of the kingdom of darkness

---

*A Chokmah reference, suggesting that like the Daughters of Light, he was under the rule of Galvah.

of the evil spirits; therefore, there would be regular attempts by the spirits of darkness to interfere with the sessions and thwart Dee and Kelly.*

Within the forty-nine pages of *Liber Loagaeth*, Nalvage explained, were contained the mystical and holy voices of the angels. These tables were to be written by Galvah. Within these tables would be numbered the entire world, and all of its creatures. To be delivered in five spans of time, this would be the true Cabala of Nature or Real Cabala, spoken of by name by Nalvage, which Dee had long hypothesized. This Cabala of Nature would be revealed in full, in preparation for the Second Coming, and the rule of Christ on Earth.

Alarmingly, Kelly was given a vision of Dee's house being put to the torch by a mob, with Dee's wife being dragged out, Dee falling to his knees, and his precious books being destroyed, while evil spirits laughed. Though Dee had not given up his piety in the vision, his house burned completely. Jane Dee was shown raped and murdered, with the right side of her face and teeth battered in. Dee's servant Mary was pulled out of a pool half dead, and carried out of the gates. In the vision, Dee went running through the fields and then through waters, with men chasing him.

The vision faded. When Nalvage appeared again, he was weeping. It was a warning from God, he said, so that Dee might escape this fate. Mortlake had indeed already been ransacked after Dee departed England—perhaps a scene like the one in the vision may have played out in reality if they had stayed.

---

*Dee's methodology for checking whether spirits were good or evil was somewhat limited: he would often simply recite prayers or the name of Jesus, and would occasionally try to out-logic them or trick them into repeating lines of doctrine that he assumed evil spirits would never admit to (for instance, that Jesus was the true son of God). By contrast, the methods of later Rosicrucian and Golden Dawn magicians would be far more sophisticated, including elaborate banishing rituals and the practice of checking spirits by Qabalistic proof—Crowley's method of spirit verification was to ascertain that the spirit knew more Qabalah than he did, and could demonstrate its function by its name, numbers, or symbolic appearance that would stand up to cross-checking against tables of Qabalah and gematria. Despite his mathematical and Hermetic sophistication, Dee employed no such methods—none had yet been developed, at least outside of the crude ceremonial paraphernalia of the grimoires—relying instead on the perhaps haphazard and overly general power of prayer.

The spirits of darkness were arrayed against Dee. Even this year, they were told, many troubles would begin, along with the entrance of Łaski into the "bloody service" of the world.[19] Dee was terrified, and all of the angelic protection he had been promised now seemed to no longer be sufficient. He fell to begging Christ.

Another young female spirit appeared, curtsied, and said she had just been at Mortlake, and all was well. (Unbeknownst to Dee, however, his library and possessions had already been ransacked.) The queen missed him, and the lord treasurer had assured her that Dee would be back soon. The spirit also reported that Sir Henry Sidney had died, which was false; Dee footnoted that this may also have been a lie of the devil. Sidney, Lord Deputy of Ireland, was supposedly an enemy of Dee's. Madimi told them to leave Łasko for Krakow, where they would meet many princes and learned men. If he was to go to Krakow, Madimi counseled, nothing like the vision of destruction would happen. They were not to set up the Holy Table in Łasko; as Madimi so biblically put it, "This Wilderness, is not forty years."[20]

Dee begged Madimi that the operation of demons no longer be permitted in the sessions, citing the incident in which Kelly felt his head being clawed. Madimi replied, puckishly or chillingly depending on your viewpoint, "He may rejoice, they clawed not his soul."*[21]

Madimi was growing. After delivering her message, she went away bigger, in a gown. Three days later, she had grown even more, and departed the session naked, her body covered with blood on the side that faced Kelly. By February 22, she had become a full-grown, tall, mighty woman.

At the next scrying session, Kelly heard a great buzzing in his

---

*This seemingly throwaway comment from Madimi may give a hint not only into why demons were so often present in the early scrying sessions, but perhaps into the problem of evil from the angels' perspective. From the statements of Madimi and the other angels, it is clear that the angels see demons as useful teaching tools, meant to terrify mortals back into the arms of God, and that in the angels' grand game, the only truly important game piece is men's souls. Everything else—health, wealth, worldly status, comfort—is fair game for destruction in order to teach mortals that the kingdom of spirit is the only goal, not the passing illusions of Malkuth, *Māyā,* the kingdom of flesh.

ear.* The angels next gave the two men a general medical theory: that bodily infection is a lower reflection of spiritual infection, which is therefore the work of Satan. This infection could not be healed by the angels unless it was the will of the Holy Spirit, which descends through them and into the terrestrial Church, whereby disease could be cured.

The year to come would be of great bloodshed, the angels warned. Great troubles would arise in England. One would rise up against another, to cut each other's throats. Yet by now the angels had soured on the unfaithful Łaski, who would not be up to the coming conflicts in Europe. Łaski would be felled before his time, Madimi promised, because of his weakness. Kelly, too, would be destroyed. Dee begged Christ for mercy from the wrath of God, citing Job 33 for the modes of God's mercy to man. Łaski, however, had already been cast out of God's grace.

Meanwhile, back at court, the new calendar was dropped for political reasons in April 1584. As with Dee's plans for the British Empire, Elizabeth assured him that delays would not get in the way of eventual acceptance. Yet while Elizabeth could wait, Dee, languishing in debt, could not do so quite so comfortably. Dee may have felt he had no options left. Berated by the angels for his sin and disobedience, and exhorted to turn his back on the physical world of corruption and decay, he began to abandon what was left of his attachments to Elizabeth's court and turn wholly toward the angels. All that was left to Dee was his own private mythology, consistently confirmed by Kelly, who, we must not forget, was on payroll and therefore somewhat beholden to Dee's view of reality. Likewise, Łaski would have been encouraging Dee, as he believed the magus was assisting him in furthering his political career (and may well have been interested in procuring the secrets of alchemy from Dee for financial gain).

---

*Such phenomena appear regularly in claims of alien abduction, occurring prior to alien contact—they also occur in sleep paralysis, often thought to be the actual source of abduction "experiences," as well as in kundalini flashes. Similar noises and poltergeist events were recorded during Jack Parsons and L. Ron Hubbard's workings with the Watchtowers in the 1940s (discussed in book III).

Such a setup provided little in the way of checks and balances for sanity. Instead, Dee was descending into his and Kelly's mutual hallucination, one that would be marked with both increasingly penitent attitudes—what had Dee done wrong to deserve his current state?—and grandiose, self-important schemes for world domination.

MENSIS MYSTICUS SAOBATICUS. PARS 1 AND 2
The Reception of the Calls Begins

Having completed the transmission of *Loagaeth,* Dee and Kelly were next prompted to begin receiving the forty-nine calls, the central gem of the angelic system, which would open the regions of the world to the angels to carry out the events of Revelation.

In Krakow, Nalvage appeared again, in the form of King Edward VI. The table he stood upon now consisted of mother-of-pearl. The sections of this round table were related by Nalvage to the Holy Trinity—the substance being God the Father; the circumference God the Son, the finger of the father and mover of all things; and the order and knitting together of parts in due and perfect proportion being God the Holy Spirit, beginning and end of all things.

On April 12, several evil spirits manifested, including a hellhound. Each claimed to be Nalvage, and each was rebuked until the real Nalvage appeared—he explained that there was a continual fight between the angels and Satan, wherein the angels vanquished by patience.[22] The devil was subtly infecting Kelly's imagination, mingling imperfect forms with Nalvage's utterances.

Now began the transmission of the forty-nine calls themselves. These were transmitted by Nalvage backward in order to prevent their utterance, and afterward were to be reversed by Dee and Kelly. The calls were of more worth, Nalvage said, than the kingdom of Poland;[23] they would give understanding of many thousands of secrets, wherein Dee and Kelly were yet but children.[24]

On April 13, Nalvage stated that he had privately given counsel to Kelly to give up dealing with evil spirits. This suggests Kelly had been doing so on his own while not in Dee's direct company, which would explain the many demonic appearances at the scrying sessions. It was revealed that Kelly had also been asking questions about Łaski on his own. On April 17, a spiritual creature said to Kelly that the good spirits would not deal with him, casting Kelly back into frantic doubt. By April 19, Kelly was again claiming to Dee that their spiritual tutors were deluders. Within the last two years, he protested, they had not given Dee and Kelly anything practical. In the same amount of time, Kelly said, he could have learned all seven liberal sciences; he would burn all of the records of the angelic sessions if he could. If Dee wanted to keep talking to angels, Kelly jabbed, he could use his son as a scryer.

Two days later, Gabriel had another stern message for Kelly. *Were not all things possible with God?* Gabriel asked. Since they were, Kelly was to trust and do his duty. All of these actions were of God, and all would soon be delivered.

"By August next?" a beleaguered Kelly asked.

"What if it were a hundred Augusts?"[25] Gabriel shot back.

Gabriel next spelled out, for the first time, the story of the Fall from the angelic perspective, including the history of the angelic language. Man had been created an innocent, partaking in the power and spirit of God and his good angels and naming the objects in the Garden. Yet the devil—called Coronzom in Enochian*—envied him, and perceived that his lesser nature was frail, and so began to assail him. Falling to temptation, Adam was accursed and cast from the Garden, and driven out into the bramble-covered earth, now unable to speak as he had lost the angelic language. At this point he began to speak ancient Hebrew, a pale and guttural reflection of the angelic tongue, which was divided into three, seven, and twelve parts,† but lacked the true forms and pronunciations of Enochian. Modern Hebrew itself was a degeneration of

---

*This demon would be conjured and confronted not by Dee and Kelly but by Aleister Crowley and his student Victor Neuburg in the Algerian desert in 1909, when they used the calls to open the thirty Aethyrs. Crowley changed the spelling to "Choronzon" so that the Hebrew gematria added to 333.

†This refers to the division of Hebrew into three mother letters, seven double letters, and twelve single letters, corresponding to the three elements (of which earth is a mixture), seven planets, and twelve zodiac signs.

ancient Hebrew; little to nothing was left of the original language[26]—
that is until now, as the angels were disclosing the angelic language to
mankind for the first time through Dee and Kelly, a "tongue of power"
that was only to be used to work the power of God and for delivering
wisdom, and for no other reason.

This profound message must have helped move Kelly, for by
April 24 he decided to grant Dee two hours a day of scrying. On
April 25, Gabriel and Nalvage appeared, and said that God did not
appear to the reprobate: "For the reprobate hath not visitation, but in
the rod of Justice."[27] Man's purity and acceptance of God was the measure by which God might visit him. Yet these spiritual visions could be
taken away; to be given such visitations was thus a goad to become even
more humble. Obedience to the angels' commands would be the best
indicator of this humility.[28]

The transmission of the calls now began in earnest. (The first table,
they were told, could have no call; for it was of the Godhead.) Dee,
enraptured by the information being unveiled to him, began to affec-
tionately refer to the angels as "our Schoolmasters."[29] Łaski, however,
was not present; this disobedience to God's commands enraged the
angels.

As the transmission of the calls progressed, Dee and Kelly were also
given remarkable visions. On April 27, Gabriel and Nalvage delivered
a stunning apocalypse in which a prophet named Damida searches the
world, finding the merchants and common people unworthy of the
Holy Spirit until he discovers Dee, depicted as a naked man carrying
nothing but "mosse, leaves, flowers, and herbs."[30] The prophet gathers
up Dee and continues his quest until they discover Kelly, depicted as a
child that the prophet decides may one day become a man. They are led
up a hill that represents the world, and are told of the coming of the
Holy Spirit, depicted as a whale who has swallowed a chest in which are
the chambers of wisdom (likely the Aethyrs). Dee is told to sit and wait
until Kelly becomes a man. Below them, the king of the world, who is
Satan, plots against the whale for he knows that its coming will destroy
his kingdoms. The seas around the hill do arise and flood the kingdom,
and the winds and thunders that are the judgments of God lash the

world. Four beasts, representing the four elements, come to the top of the hill where Dee and Kelly dwell with the prophet; Dee and Kelly are commanded to kill them. They unleash the elements at their death, and reveal Christ; as the world is ravaged and destroyed, Dee and Kelly are initiated into the mysteries of the Crown (Godhead) and the Aires or decanates of the zodiac.

Finally, the firmament and waters are rejoined and the Holy Spirit itself arrives as the whale, "like unto a legion of storms: or as the bottomless Cave of the North when it is opened: and she was full of eyes [on] every side." The waters recede and leave the whale laying on the hillside, "roaring like a Cave of Lions,"[31] and the prophet leads a terrified Dee and Kelly to enter its mouth. Afterward, they are given riches; the naked Dee is clothed, and Kelly is given the full secrets of the Aethyrs. Christ, they are told, will return twenty-one times in one year, but not all at once.

On April 30, they were given an image of seven priests in white opening seven gates—another foreshadowing of apocalypse.

LIBRI SEPTIMI, APERTORII, CRACOVIENSIS, MYSTICI, SABBATICI. PARS 3
The Thirty Aethyrs, Ninety-One Parts of the World, and Forty-Nine Calls

On May 7, Gabriel and Nalvage appeared and transmitted an explanatory vision of a city on a hill, envied by serpents. The city on the hill and the people who dwelled within it represented the world, which from time to time was quenched by God's wisdom according to their need. The serpents below were evil people.*

The angels also took the opportunity to rebuke Kelly for his use of grimoire magic. Kelly argued that Moses and Daniel had been skilled in

---

*This session is reminiscent of the visions of St. Teresa of Ávila, who spoke of an "Interior Castle" of Godly purity entered into through meditation and prayer that would be besieged with "lizards" that represented impure thought and sin. See Avila, *Interior Castle*.

Egyptian magic, which did not stop them from being faithful servants of God. Why, then, should it stop him? Gabriel's answer was eminently practical—that magic was only a shadow and pale imitation of the ways of God by the devil, and that even the "doings of the Egyptians, seem, and are not so."[32] What the angels had revealed was the workings of God—higher wisdom that put magic itself to shame. The devil could only *seem* to triumph over the world, but his works were false, and

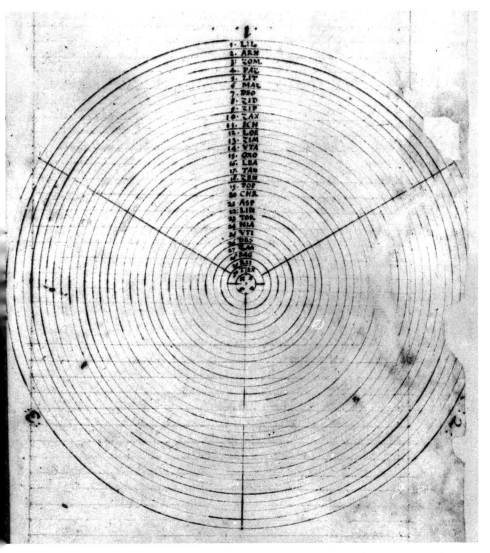

Fig. 11.1. The thirty Aethyrs. From MS. Sloane 3191.

hollow, and a pale imitation of God's natural law. This was a consistent lesson to Kelly, the slow student in the angels' school.

By May 21, the first seventeen calls had been delivered. The eighteenth call, which would be modified to produce thirty calls (for each of the thirty Aethyrs), was next. Dee and Kelly were told to be still and patient, for the place was holy. Nalvage prayed, then made a cross to the four quarters of the world with his rod. They were told that the thirty calls to come were "the Calls of Ninety-one Princes and spiritual Governors, unto whom the earth is delivered as a portion. These bring in and again dispose Kings and all the Governments upon the earth, and vary the Natures of things: with the variation of every moment; Unto whom, the Providence of the eternal Judgment, is already opened."[33] These ninety-one parts of the earth were governed by twelve angels assigned to the twelve tribes of Israel, which are governed by the seven Spirits who stand before the presence of God.* These tribes of the original sons of Adam, which had been divided by God, would be regathered to partake of the New Jerusalem as described in Revelation 21. The numbers and names of the Governors of the thirty Aethyrs were given—totaling ninety-one Governors—along with what tribe they were each governed by.

An angel named Mapsama told the two, "These Calls touch all parts of the World. The World may be dealt withall, with her parts; Therefore you may do anything. These Calls are the keys into the Gates and Cities of wisdom.† Which Gates are not to be opened, but with visible apparition."[34]

This was to be had by calling every table. They were to go in humbly—not brashly, but rather to allow themselves to be drawn in. By August, they were promised, assuming they displayed utmost humility and obedience, the angels would show them how to know and use the good and evil spiritual creatures, and for what purpose they were being given this gift by the Highest.

---

*See Revelation 1:4, 21:12, and 8:2.

†A reference to initiation to Chokmah through the fifty gates of Binah or the City of the Pyramids.

LIBRI SEPTIMI APERTORII CRACOVIENSIS MYSTICI, SABBATICI. PARS 4

The Book of Forty-Eight Silvered Leaves, the Parable of the Threshers, the Horrible Doctrine, the Golden Talisman, the Watchtowers, and the Parable of the Adder

On May 23, the angels showed the two men a spinning globe. Dee wanted specific measurements, by longitude and latitude, of how to map the Governors of the Aethyrs to the world. Nalvage replied that this was simply not how angels did things. They were now given the parts of the world, with each of the Governors corresponding to a terrestrial area of the globe.

The next day, Kelly locked himself in his room, refusing to have anything more to do with the spirit actions. When he emerged, he had in his hand a copy of Agrippa, wherein were reprinted the sections of the world taken from Ptolemy. Kelly claimed that the spirits had to be frauds, because they must have copied their material from this book. Dee thought that this only proved that the angels were giving them good information, fulfilling what previous magicians had grasped at but not fully comprehended, and that the angels had only done exactly what Dee had requested. Kelly was unconvinced.

They were next to make a silvered book of forty-eight leaves, containing the calls. The angel Mapsama arrived to impart information on how to do so, despite the fact that he was deeply disappointed with Dee and Kelly's continued wickedness, presumably meaning Kelly's distrust of the angels. An exasperated Kelly replied to Mapsama's chastising by saying, "I thought you would say so."[35]

Afterward, they were to journey to the emperor's court. Dee asked what he should do with the book once he had bound it. An already bitter Kelly replied that it should be burned. Mapsama replied that on the fourteenth day of their rest, the cloth on the Holy Table would be spread for a banquet for the angels of the Lord, in the middle of which would be laid the book of silver leaves. Dee had already entered the emperor's heart, and even were he to become "willful," there would still be four months for him to change his mind. On their voyage, they were to take only the tablecloth, the shewstone, and the silvered book.

On June 2, Gabriel prophesied apocalypse and bloodshed. He delivered Dee and Kelly a parable of a "barn"—Dee and Kelly were to enter service in God's barn, within which grew corn, representing souls, which had long been unkempt. Dee and Kelly were to take up God's

Fig. 11.2. John Dee with golden talisman, compass, and square.
Courtesy of Wellcome Images.

flails, representing the angelic doctrine that had been delivered to them, the testimony of the Holy Spirit to come. With their flails, they were to thresh the corn, "wherewith you shall beat the sheafs, that the Corn which is scattered, and the rest may be all one."[36] Their reward for this would be nothing save the privilege of serving God and assurance of entrance to heaven, and they were not to begin the threshing—the harvesting of the 144,000 souls to be saved at the outset of the Apocalypse, via the use of the temple furniture and the thirty calls—until they were commanded to do so.

Gabriel explained that he had told them of the manner and power of God, of the nature of hell, of the course of the world, of their election and the end thereof, and of Łaski and why he was elected. He now exhorted them to make themselves fully humbled and sanctified. They were to remember hell, to go to meet Emperor Rudolf II, to love together, and to humbly persevere until the end of their Great Work.

On June 4, following the Lord's Prayer, Gabriel again appeared and railed against idol worship, stating that idolatry was why the Jews became captives. He also again castigated Kelly for his faults. Yet, for once, the angels expressed compassion and love for the two men. God loved them despite their faults, and the affection of God was greater even than a father's love. Even the doings of the devil were a necessary part of God's plan, because they allow for resistance by which faith may be tested and grow stronger. One who grew strong by resisting the devil could prove to the "powers and spirits of Heaven" that he was worthy of eternal life.[37] Demons were sent either to the wicked, who openly consorted with them, or to the very elect, who were tested by them; Dee and Kelly were therefore to continue resisting them, in the hope that the angels would testify their name before the heavens and the God of Justice.

At this, both Kelly and Dee fell into tears. On February 18, 1584, they had been shown a vision of hell at Mortlake. How steadily the angels had worked to keep them from it. Gabriel explained to them the jealousy of God, how the house of God must be made clean and spotless, and finally why devils appeared. Kelly was so overcome by this offering of Grace, and so willing to now relinquish his evil ways and receive the blood of Christ, that he revealed to Dee many of the false doctrines that evil spirits had given him, his notes on which he was now ready to burn. In his own private experiments with wicked spirits, Kelly had been given a "manifold horrible Doctrine," whereby demons tried to persuade him:

> That Jesus was not God.
>
> . . . That no prayer ought to be made to Jesus.
>
> . . . That there is no sin.
>
> . . . That man's soul doth go from one body, to another child's quickening or animation.*
>
> . . . That as many men and women as are now, have always been: That is, so many human bodies, and human souls, neither more nor less, as are now, have always been.
>
> . . . That the generation of mankind from Adam and Eve, is not an history, but a writing which hath another sense.
>
> . . . No Holy Ghost they acknowledged.
>
> . . . They would not suffer him to pray to Jesus first; but would rebuke him, saying, that he robbed God of his honor, &c.†38

---

*Meaning reincarnation—wicked because it undermines the importance of salvation through Christ in this life.

†How closely this "horrible doctrine" approximates the common beliefs of modern New Age, Neopagan, and occult adherents! Aleister Crowley, who believed himself to be a reincarnation of Kelly, noted in the Cry of the Second Aethyr, as well as in his book *Liber Aleph* in the 1920s, that Dee simply wasn't ready for a post-Christian view of reality, stating that "an Angel did declare unto Kelly the very Axiomata of our Law of Thelema, in Good Measure, and plainly; but Dee, afflicted by the Fixity of his Tenets that were of the Slave-Gods, was wroth, and by his Authority prevailed upon the other, who was indeed not wholly perfected as an Instrument, or the World ready for that Sowing." Crowley, *Liber Aleph*, 187. This seems doubtful, as it is clear from the original diaries, particularly the passages in Latin, that Kelly was indeed being tempted by illuding spirits and had been placed under duress by their threats, that he (not just Dee) was horrified by their doctrine, and even that the horrible doctrine had proceeded from those spirits that he had conjured *himself*, outside of the bounds of the angelic sessions. There *are* traces of the horrible doctrine in prior Christian heresies, however—Deborah Harkness points out that it includes hints of Arianism (the early Christian heresy that Christ was not God but instead was created by God) and Pelagianism (the fifth-century heresy that there is no original sin, and that human beings can attain salvation without divine aid). See Harkness, "The Scientific Reformation," 531.

Dee marveled at how thoroughly the angels had purified Kelly, to bring him to the point where he was able to relinquish all that he had learned before and make a full Christian conversion, and that his life would no longer be a scandal to the Lord. Kelly's conversion was so dramatic that Dee had no doubt that it had been anything but sincere. Kelly even confessed that only nine or ten days earlier he had plotted to escape Krakow and Dee's employ with the aid of evil spirits, "with whom he had so long dealth: And therefore that till now, he dealt hypocritically."[39] If Kelly was indeed performing grimoire magic privately, a holdover from his previous magical education and practices before meeting Dee, this helps explain the regular appearance of evil spirits during the angelic conversations, in addition to the angels' own explanation that the elect are tempted of necessity.

Kelly revealed that the leverage the evil spirits held over him was that they had so often threatened him with homelessness. Yet now, he reported, he no longer cared, "and that he now made more account of God his favor and life eternal, then he doth of all transitory wealth and riches, and to be entangled within the danger of these wicked spirits their snares, with all."[40] Bitterly, Kelly noted the irony that it was only by being paid by Dee that he could even temporarily renounce the evil spirits. Never again, he said, would he doubt the veracity of the spirit actions. (This vow would, of course, not hold.) In this section of the diaries and earlier—even in Kelly's more hysteria-fueled moments— Dee's affection for Kelly, the younger and more troubled man, comes across clearly. Despite the punishing lengths to which he pushed his employee, it seems that Dee truly cared for Kelly, who was half his age and beset by a wide range of personal afflictions.

On June 18, after prayers of thanks for Kelly and for aid to Łaski, a mighty and long arm and hand appeared in the air to grab the shewstone. Kelly reached out for the stone to save it, but the stone was suddenly "teleported" next to the cushion on the table. Michael appeared by the stone, and Kelly was next given a vision of Groano Castle in Lithuania, where the king (presumably Báthory) was. He set down a sword on a table engraved with magical characters, which Gabriel said would fail him. Smoke spirits were also summoned.

Łaski was poor, and still unfit, but the angels were now willing to stand behind him if he was obedient, in which case he would be king of Poland as surely as the sun shone. "To talk with God for money is a folly, to talk with God for mercy, is great wisdom," the angels counseled, also telling them that the illuding spirit arm had been sent by the king's enchanters—but that the king still did not know of their doings.[41]

On June 20, Kelly was to have a vision that would reveal the next crucial part of the angels' system—the four Watchtowers. The vision

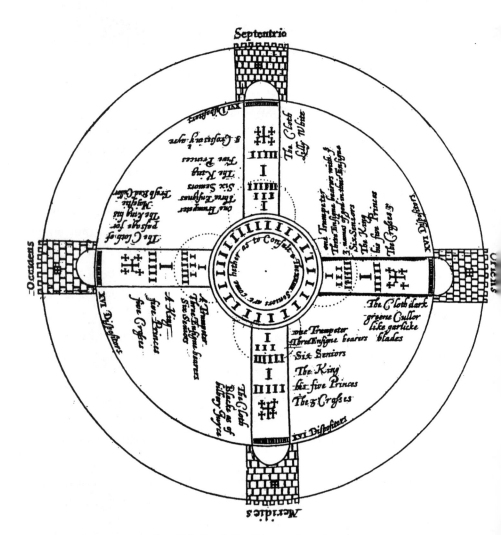

Fig. 11.3. The Golden Talisman. From Casaubon.

came to him while lying in bed awake in the morning, during which Kelly felt an angel, clothed in feathers, pat him on the head to make him more vigilant.

The vision showed four castles, from which ranks of angels proceeded toward a central point. A depiction of this vision was later engraved on a golden talisman, leading to this often being referred to as the "vision of the golden talisman" in later writings. It gives an overview of the system of the Watchtowers, which would later be fleshed out as elemental tablets giving the actual names of the beings in the angelic language.

From each of the four castles, standing in the four parts of the world, came the sound of a trumpet, after which a cloth was thrown out on the ground in front of it. These cloths—red (later elaborated as "after the new smitten blood") for the east, white ("Lilly-colour") for the south, green ("the skins of many Dragons . . . garlick-bladed") for the west, and black ("Hair-coloured, Bilbery juice")[42] for the north—delineated the colors of the elements. From each castle now proceeded a retinue of spirits. In sequence, from each castle, there came a trumpeter, three ensign-bearers, six ancient men with white heads and staves, a comely man with much apparel on his back with a long robe-tail carried by five men, a great cross in a cloud like a rainbow, four lesser crosses in the air in a white cloud with the faces of men on each of the four parts of each cross, sixteen white creatures, and, following them, an infinite number of spirits. These spirits' names and hierarchy were later given in the Watchtowers.

Now a new angel appeared—Ave, one of the Sons of Sons of the Light from the Sigillum Dei Aemeth. Ave said that he would reverse the workings of Satan and shower out blessings upon Dee and Kelly, after which he further expounded the vision. Ave explained that the four castles were the four angels of the earth, which are the overseers and Watchtowers that God has placed as bulwarks against the workings of the devil.*

"What Satan doth, they suffer," Ave explained, "and what they wink at, he wrasteth: But when he thinketh himself most assured, then feeleth he the bit."[43]

---

*This doctrine is elaborated in Crowley's vision of the eleventh Aethyr. See book III.

In each of the castles or houses was a mighty prince, the chief watchman and angel of the Lord (later to be called a king), under whom served five princes. The seals and authorities of the castles were "confirmed in the beginning of the World," and each was given four characters, which were tokens of the presence of Christ, and by which he would come again to judge the earth and redeem humanity. Unto each of these four characters belonged four angels.

The ancient men were the twenty-four seniors—the elders before the Throne of God in Revelation 4:4. These judged the "government of the Castles," and fulfilled the will of God.

The twelve banners—divided into angelic names of three, four, and five characters—were the twelve names of God, which governed "all the creatures upon the earth, visible and invisible." From the crosses, they were told, came the angels of the Aethyrs (the names of the Governors of the thirty Aethyrs were later to be found enciphered on the Watchtowers), who were obedient to the will of men, and by the use of which they would "subvert whole Countries without Armies: which you must, and shall do, for the glory of God," and by whom they would gain the favor of princes, know the "secret Treasures of the waters" and the "unknown Caves of the Earth."[44]

Hereby, it seems, was at last revealed the magical means by which Dee's dreams of a new world order would be realized; the causal engine behind the fulfillment of Revelation—a magical system that, when worked by Dee or those to come after him, would initiate a new terrestrial ordering, followed by the millennial rule of Christ.

Ave told the pair that he would return the following Monday to give further instruction, and that in the meantime Dee and Kelly should pray for what things were necessary for them. Following this, they were granted another vision, "the sign of the love of God towards his faithful." The castles again appeared, and three trumpet blasts were heard from within them, following which the carpets were again cast forth. The trumpets again sounded and the gates opened; from each of them came four trumpeters whose trumpets "are a Pyramis, six cones, wreathed."[45] Next came three spirits holding up three banners (making up the twelve banners and names of God), next a king with five guard-

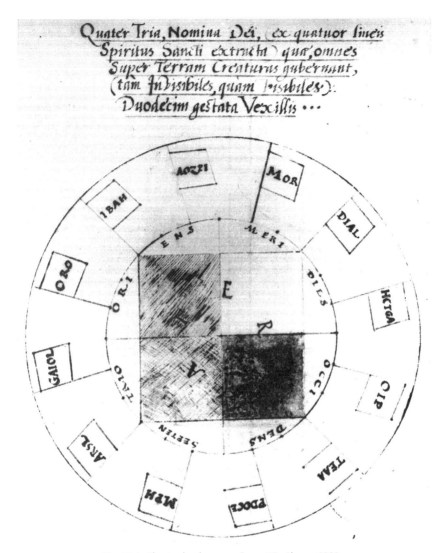

Quater Tria, Nomina Dei, ex quatuor lineis
Spiritus Sancti extructa quae omnes
Super Terram Creaturas gubernant,
(tam Invisibiles, quam Visibiles):
Duodecim gestata Vexillis ...

Fig. 11.4. The twelve banners. From MS. Sloane 3191.

ian princes holding up the tail of his long robe, the crosses, and sixteen "dispositors" carrying out the will of the kings. The twenty-four seniors conducted themselves to the center of the courtyard, where they consulted with each other.

Starting June 25, the Great Table itself was revealed. As in the vision of the golden talisman, the angels removed black, green, white, and red carpets or cloths from it. Four sigils were revealed for each of the four quadrants of the table. After a mist covered the table and was cleared, an infinite number of creatures that looked like worms with heads appeared over it.* Higher in the air, above these, were several small, blackish things, bigger than "motes in the sun."

"Now hath it pleased God to deliver this Doctrine again out of darknesse," a voice said, "and to fulfill his promise with thee, for the books of Enoch: To whom he sayeth as he said unto Enoch."[46] These evil spirits were next taken away from the table, and a tablet made of twelve by thirteen squares was revealed. These squares contained characters showing the true images of God and his spiritual creatures. While Kelly transcribed the table, he heard a voice telling him that he was writing out his own damnation; but an angel next told him that he was actually inscribing the damnation of the evil spirits.† The characters revealed were also "the parts of the whole earth,"[47] meaning that the names and Governors of the Aethyrs could also be drawn from them.

Four of these tablets—representing the Watchtowers and the four elements—made up the Great Table, with a central black cross dividing them. Ave described the uses of the subservient spirits to be drawn from the Watchtowers: they would bring all human knowledge, medicine, the knowledge of the elementals, knowledge of finding and working with metals and stones, the conjoining of natures, the destruction of nature, the knowledge of all mechanical crafts, and alchemical transformations. Kelly, suffering from a migraine (perhaps from the overclocking of his brain by the angels), was also told how to use the spirits for the knitting

---

*A similar image would be employed by the French Benedictine monk Bernard de Montfaucon in *L'antiquité expliquée et représentée en figures* (1719–1724) to represent the Gnostic demiurge Ialdabaoth. This image—a serpent with a lion's head—would become prominent among nineteenth- and twentieth-century Gnostic revival groups, notably the Ordo Templi Orientis.

†This mirror effect, in which magical visions or doctrine manifests in both positive and negative aspects, is a regular feature of the conversations and became even more apparent in Crowley's scrying of the Aethyrs. In Crowley's view, all divine truths (above the Abyss) are nondual and contain their own opposite, and must of necessity manifest as dualities when descending into the phenomenal world, below the Abyss. This is a primary reason why the world, which requires unresolved duality to exist, does not make sense.

together of natures, carrying things from place to place, and knowledge of all handicrafts and arts.

A ritual was also given, in which Dee and Kelly were to assess "One book of perfect paper. One labour of a few days. The calling them together, and the yielding of their promise, the repetition of the names

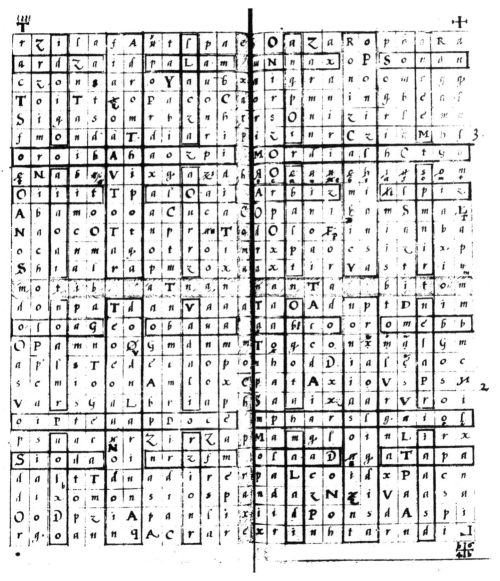

Fig. 11.5. Dee's handwritten version of the Great Table. From MS. Sloane 3191.

of God, are sufficient."[48] This operation was meant to consecrate the tables and to call forth the angels within them for use by Dee and Kelly, after which time the angels would follow them and be about them at all times. Over the course of four days, Dee and Kelly were to call on the names of God from the twelve banners, followed by fourteen days in which they were to call the angels by petition. On the fifteenth day, they would clothe themselves in white linen, and then would have the "apparition, use and practice of the Creatures. For it is not a labor of years, nor many days."[49] Kelly compared this operation to grimoire magic, but Ave rebuked him, saying, tellingly, "Nay, they all played at this."[50]

Several prophecies and supernatural events followed the reception of the Great Table. It was revealed that Dee and Kelly would set up the sign of the cross in Constantinople by September 15. They were also given the "Parable of the Adder," in which the Lord led them like a mother adder guiding small serpents.* On June 30 a large face appeared with wings around it, and afterward was shown in a great globe of fire. Dee had many doubts, but in response to Dee's battery of questions, the angel counterquizzed him to show his ignorance.

It also seemed the pair's fascination for evil spirits had not abated despite their constant chastening. In a footnote, Dee remarked that Kelly had once evoked an evil spirit named Soudenna, who appeared in many forms, until he took the form of a triangle of fire, after which, when he was constrained to a circle, he appeared as a great giant. Despite all the warnings to the contrary, and the damage caused by Kelly's trafficking with evil spirits, Dee was still curious about how to call evil spirits, but was not indulged by the angels. Instead, on July 5, Gabriel continued to drive home the message that the two magicians were to renounce the world. "John Dee, be of comfort, for thou shalt overcome," Gabriel assured him.[51]

Following this, the English translations of the calls were given (comparing the Enochian and English of the calls side by side is the primary source for deriving the lexicon and structure of the angelic language).

---

*Suggesting, perhaps, the serpent path on the Tree of Life—ascending the sephiroth in an initiatory fashion, from Malkuth to Kether.

But by July 7, Ave was again blasting Dee and Kelly for their faithlessness and doubt. God had tested the faith of the biblical patriarchs, and rewarded their faith, but Dee and Kelly were "of little faith, and starvelings, withered grasse, and blasted willows." Even if they were in hell, God could deliver them, and yet they still lacked faith to the point that they worried over the logistics of carrying out the angels' commands. This lack of faith was endangering them, for "Nititur enim, omnibus modis, Sathanas ut vis devoret"—*Satan strives in every way, so that he may devour you.*[52]

Ave confirmed that what had been delivered to Dee and Kelly was the same knowledge that God had delivered Enoch, who labored for fifty days, and the calls the book of Enoch. Ave also confirmed that Enoch himself had similarly made tables, of "Serpasan" (a kind of slate stone, Dee noted) and plain stone, as had been appointed to him by an angel of the Lord. (Even Enoch and Esdras, the angels explained, had only known a fragment of the divine language now being delivered to Dee and Kelly.)[53]

LIBRI QUINTUS CRACOVIENSIS MYSTICUS APERTORIUS. PARS 5
The Curse on Creation and the Terminal Monotheism

Continuing the translations from the previous *Libri,* the English translation of the nineteenth call was given. The call disturbed Dee, and appeared to him to be a curse on humanity, containing lines such as, "The work of man and his pomp, let them be defaced. His buildings, let them become Caves for the beasts of the Field! Confound her understanding with darkness! For why? it repenteth me that I have made Man."[54]

Dee asked if this was the curse that was spoken before the creation of humanity, and was told that God had indeed cursed the earth, leading mankind to prey upon each other, and the kingdoms of the world to rise up against each other, with servants rising up against their masters and wicked sons against their fathers. Perfect love had been taken out of the world and replaced with malice, and it would be so until the end of the world, the only possible remedy for which is to "after God [treat] thy brother as thy self." This corrupted world, as we currently experience it, is the world that Adam was punished by being cast out into, "a prison prepared for him before, if he offended." If the world were not a prison of misery, it would not be a punishment for Adam. For "as Jesus Christ brought all blessedness, and comfort into the world: So did Adam, accursed, bring all misery and wretchedness into the world, and in the same instant, when Adam was expelled; The Lord suffered the earth to be accursed for Adam's sake, and then, said the Lord these things, and gave unto the world her time: and placed over her Keepers, Watch-men, and Princes, for years, months, and days."[55]

Following the completion of the calls, Gabriel told Dee and Kelly that God had kept his promise with them and delivered the keys of his storehouses, "wherein you shall find, (if you enter wisely, humbly, and patiently) Treasures more worth than the frames of the heavens."[56] They were to prepare to enter these storehouses come August: "See that your garments be clean. Herein be not rash: Nor over hasty; For those that are hasty and rash, and are loathsomely appareled, may knock long before they enter."[57]

Gabriel also counseled them that they would *never* understand the mysteries of all that had been spoken. They were only to love together, and dwell together in the same God, and God would therefore be merciful to them. Dee was certainly in need of grace, as his son Rowland was extremely sick. Dee swore that if God let Rowland live, he would only eat one meal on Saturdays. On July 23, however, a dark man appeared and told Dee that he had broken the commandments of God.

"Thou art one of those," the angel said, "that when I command thee to leave nothing with life, yet thou savest the fatlings to offer before him that abhorreth such sacrifice."[58] Dee was compared to St. Paul. "The Lord oweth thee nothing for thy labor: he hath paid thee to the uttermost. As for Lasky, I will give him over to the spirit of error: and he shall become more poor, so that his own children shall despise him." They were counseled that this was not yet to come, and that they were to remain obedient to the utmost, "for if you had been obedient, the very stones of the earth should have served your necessity."[59]

Ten days had been appointed for the journey, but Dee and Kelly had missed the deadline and were to be punished. "I have not sealed this sin unto thee [Dee] but yet I have measured out a plague, and it shall light upon you all. But unto Lasky I have sealed it, and it shall be heavy," the black man told them.[60]

So chastened, they left for Prague by coach, and arrived on August 9, 1584, after a week's journey, dreading that God might be angry with them forever. By August 15, they had taken shelter in a study lent to them by Dr. Tadeáš Hájek, a Czech astronomer, physician to three Habsburg emperors, and alchemist. Here, they resumed the angelic sessions and prepared to undertake the next step of the angels' plan. Like Tycho Brahe, Hájek had keenly observed the 1572 supernova, which occurred the same year Báthory was crowned and was taken throughout the empire as a sign that his reign would be short-lived.[61] Recommencing their occult experiments, they were instructed to test spirits by checking to see if they professed belief in Christ.

Dee and Kelly now found themselves in the alchemical hub of Europe, a Hermetic country where their work was to find fertile soil, resonating years—even centuries—into the future.

12

On a Mission from God

On August 15, Dee and Kelly asked for instructions on next steps, and were given another terrifying vision of the Apocalypse. Kelly was first shown a vision of roses and lilies, followed by a vision of Revelation, featuring a white man and a lion. Madimi next appeared, bigger still this time.

"Believe me, many are the woes of the world," Madimi said, "and great are the sorrows that are to come: For the Lord prepareth his rainbow, and the witnesses of his account: and will appear in the Heavens to finish all things: and the time is not long."[1] Blessed were to be the believers, for faith would depart the planet, and they would be relegated to caves, unknown mountains, and secret parts of the earth that the Lord had made. In the meantime, great woes would come to the world: pregnant women would give birth to monsters, the kings of the earth would be destroyed, the vain and "such as paint themselves" would drink the blood of their neighbors and their own children, and seven woes would befall the false preachers, who are the "teeth of the Beast."

Virgins would despise their virginity and God, and become "concubines for Satan." The merchants of the earth would become abominable and be dragged into the pit; even the world's books would become corrupt and a "firebrand to the conscience."[2]

The forces of evil were aligning against Dee and Kelly. The "king of darkness wetteth his teeth against thee,"[3] Madimi said, and sought to destroy Dee's house and children, and tempt his wife to suicide— luckily, they were all under the protection and watch of the angels. Madimi counseled that Dee's household was to be moved to Prague. They were to write to Rudolph II, emperor of Bohemia, who had an abiding interest in the occult; they were then to go to him, saying that the angel of the Lord appeared before him, and rebuke him for his sins. If Rudolph was receptive, they were to tell him that he would triumph; if he was not, they were to tell him that the Lord would throw him from his throne. Yet if he were to forsake his wickedness, the angels assured, he would become the greatest emperor in history, and the devil himself would be his prisoner. Prague would be an apt venue for Dee and Kelly: the city, which had long been a center of alchemical study, had sheltered Europe's Jews since the tenth century and had even been laid out to match Jerusalem, and therefore to symbolize the New Jerusalem to come after the final defeat of the Dragon, Beast, and Whore of Babylon in Revelation.[4]

Though the angels' plan was a potential death sentence, Rudolf II was a compelling choice to receive their message, as he had worked to establish a tolerant rule, and many escapees from Catholic orthodoxy had flocked to him. Rudolf felt the Church's Counter-Reformation threatened his power, as did the growing might of the Protestant bloc, and so attempted to stay aloof from sectarian combat. With the addition of his patronage of the occult (especially as Łaski's funds as well as obedience were dwindling), this made Rudolf a compelling potential source of aid.[5]

Dee and Kelly had successfully received the angels' system for initiating the Apocalypse; instead of technicians, they were now to take on the role of prophets, acting as the angels' cat's-paws in the grand game of European politics. The full scope of the angels' plan was coming into focus. With the Apocalypse fast approaching, the angels were unveiling the spiritual machinery for enacting the salvation of the 144,000 souls (12,000 for each of the twelve tribes) to be returned to Christ at the end of days. As revealed in the vision of the barn and threshers, Dee and Kelly were not only to assist in this process of soul gathering, but would be rewarded with status among God's elect in heaven as payment.[6]

To help prepare for this soul-gathering process, the angels had proposed a Terminal Monotheism, not only healing the rift between Catholicism and Protestantism but also bringing Judaism, Islam, and paganism into the fold of a new supra-Christianity. Like the collapse of the Tower of Babel in reverse, this new religion, delivered by the angels, would reassemble the broken pieces of the world, its scattered faiths, tribes, and languages, and become the religion of mankind after the Millennium and the return of Christ.[7] Along with the revelation of the Real Cabala—the angelic transmissions—this was to fulfill Dee's mentor Postel's grand vision. In combining this new world religion with the plans Dee had already laid for a British Empire, the angels would unite the entire globe, fusing all humanity into one state, and one church, all directed by the angels themselves.* Central to the angels' apocalyptic plans was the destruction of the Ottoman Empire, also an obsession of Rudolf II's.

Rudolf II is not remembered as a successful politician. Yet because of his personal interests, Rudolf was incredibly successful as a cultural leader, establishing an atmosphere of tolerance not only of Protestantism, but of occultists, alchemists, and scientists—one that may have had a larger role in fostering a tolerant and refined European culture than any other monarch of his time.[8] An introvert and depressive, he shunned politics and statecraft for his personal obsession with the occult. He was

---

*Pseudo-Methodius prophesied a new and restored Roman Empire that would hold back the forces of Antichrist. Yet compare Daniel 7:23: "The fourth beast shall be the fourth kingdom upon earth, which shall be diverse from all kingdoms, and shall devour the whole earth, and shall tread it down, and break it in pieces." This Kingdom of Antichrist, along with the reign of the Beast and Babalon in Revelation 13, is usually *also* assumed to be a new Roman Empire. So many aspects of the angelic plan manifest as syzygies, at times appearing Christian and at others Satanic.

also a patron of the arts, favoring arcane and erotic subjects and collecting mechanical curios, exotic animals, and even, allegedly, a copy of the Voynich manuscript (most of his collection was looted or destroyed by the end of the Thirty Years' War). Like many European nobles, he was also a keen student of Hermeticism, Neoplatonism, magic, astrology, astronomy, chemical medicine, and Kabbalah (studying the latter personally under Judah Loew, supreme chief rabbi of Bohemia), and he cultivated the same interests in his subjects. Fascinated with alchemy and the quest for the philosopher's stone, Rudolf was also rare in that he saw alchemy as a symbol of inner enlightenment as well as external riches. He also made forays into operative magic himself—after the death of his friend Tycho Brahe in 1601, Rudolf attempted a necromantic ritual to return Brahe to life; when it failed, he locked himself in his bedroom for a full week in despair.[9]

Rudolf became more withdrawn as he aged, dwelling on his own interests to the point that his empire began to collapse, until an ill-planned and ill-fated new Crusade against the Turks (an attempt to unify Christendom) led to a revolt by his own subjects and his replacement by his younger brother. Never married, he had a string of affairs with both men and women, as well as illegitimate children. His oldest and most loved child, Don Julius Caesar d'Austria, was a schizophrenic who later murdered and disfigured a female lover—the ill-fated woman was found cut into pieces by a hunting knife, in the arms of a naked and excrement-smeared d'Austria, who was subsequently imprisoned by his father and killed without trial or ceremony four months later.

Around 1611, as his kingdom began to crumble due to his political incompetence, Rudolf resorted to using magic to attempt to reverse the situation, with similar results as his necromantic ritual. Surrendering to the brutalities of existence at last, he retreated into his own chambers and private world, and died alone, with no family, friends, or courtiers at his side; a committed occultist to the end, he refused last sacraments or confession on his deathbed unless a priest of his "own kind" could be found, probably meaning another magician. None was found, and Rudolf exited the world alone and in darkness.[10]

That was all in the future, however; when Dee came to Prague,

Rudolf was in the prime of his life and the cultural flowering of his reign. In late August, Dee began correspondence with Don Wilhelmo de Sancto Clemente, the Spanish ambassador to Rudolf's court, seeking an audience with the emperor. The request was soon granted, and Dee began preparing his case. However, the forces of evil were already arraying around the two men, looking for a way to interrupt the plan.

On September 1, Kelly and Dee were discussing their upcoming audience with Rudolf when Kelly saw three little creatures walk up and down in the sunshine—very small, like little shadows or smokes. Dee wanted to use the stone to talk to them, but Kelly said he would rather see them outside the stone. According to Dee, the stone helped to buffer from illuders, but outside the stone there was no such protection. Kelly didn't care; he still wanted to see them outside the stone. The three spirits, who hailed from the third and fourth Watchtowers, identified themselves as Ga, Za, and Vaa, together comprising the name Gazavaa, and would direct Dee and Kelly's practices.

Two days later, just prior to Dee's meeting with Rudolf, Kelly had one of his worst blowouts. While out drinking with one of Łaski's servants (named Alexander), Kelly (perhaps playfully) told the man that he would cut off his head, and touched the back of his neck with his walking stick. Alexander, also drunk, pulled a weapon, and the other bar patrons had to push him down before he killed Kelly.

Dee found Alexander crying against a stone, complaining of Kelly's actions. He next walked to their host's house, where he found Kelly asleep. After returning to his own lodgings, where he had stashed Alexander, he was forced to spend two hours calming the man down, after which he convinced him to sleep there instead of raging in the streets. When Kelly returned in the morning, the scryer said that he had been told what happened, but had no recollection of it transpiring. He shook hands with Alexander in gentlemanly fashion and apologized for the misunderstanding, as well as for what he had heard happened.

When the actual story of the faux beheading was recounted, however, Kelly went crazy *again*, and began shouting at and berating Alexander. Dee attempted to restrain him, but Kelly charged out into the street with a rapier, challenging Alexander to a fight. Alexander refused, and Kelly's response was to throw a rock at him, as if he were a dog. Kelly returned to the house in a rage, furious that he couldn't fight Alexander; his anger was so great that Dee was convinced that he was possessed, and trying to destroy himself, Dee, or the others around them. Dee took this incident as further proof that Satan was working against them, and struggled to understand how he could reconcile this with God and the emperor so that his chances at patronage were not scuttled, while being forced to humor Kelly until he settled down.

After getting a calming letter from his wife (for which he must have been very grateful), Dee received a second letter summoning him to meet Rudolf. He proceeded straight to the castle, where he met the emperor in the privy chamber. Rudolf sat at a table, with Dee's letters and a copy of the *Monas hieroglyphica* next to him, which Dee had dedicated to Maximilian II, Rudolf's father. The emperor thanked Dee for the book and said that he believed Dee was truly affectionate toward him; he also complimented the *Monas,* but he said it was too advanced for his understanding. Yet, Rudolf said, the Spanish ambassador had informed him that Dee had information that would be to his advantage.

In their prior correspondence, Dee had said that Rudolf was blessed by God, and that Theorem XX of the *Monas hieroglyphica* suggested that Rudolf would not only be exalted as an emperor by God's favor, but would even become one of the twenty-four elders or seniors of Revelation after his death.[11] This flattery had worked to get Dee's foot in the door; now, alone with the emperor in his chamber, Dee delivered his message, with the key parts exactly as the angels had demanded.

Dee told Rudolf that he had spent four continual decades seeking the heights of knowledge available to humanity, but was unable to find teachers or books that could fulfill him, and so had turned to God, praying for true wisdom. After long attempts, God had answered, and over the last two and a half years the angels had given him "such works in my hands, to be seen, as no man's heart could have wished for so much," wisdom of such value that no earthly kingdom was of equal worth. He then had been commanded by God to speak to Rudolf; the angels had told him of Rudolf's sin, making a covenant with Dee that if Rudolf believed and repented, he would triumph on Earth, becoming "the greatest that ever was,"[12] and that the "Great Turk," Ottoman Sultan Murad III, would become Rudolf's prisoner. Dee told Rudolf that this was the pure truth—even swearing upon it that he would forsake his own salvation if he was lying.

Rudolf replied that he believed Dee, that he thought that Dee loved him "unfeignedly," and even that Dee had no need to grovel. Dee told the emperor that he wanted to be wholly open and show the entirety of the conversations to Rudolf, and, furthermore, to show him an actual scrying session. Rudolf replied that it would have to be another time, and though Dee tried to further convince him of the worth of what he was saying, Rudolf politely brushed him off. In all, Dee had been given an hour to speak with Rudolf, but had failed to impress him, instead bending his ear with apocalyptic rantings, which were received with awkward silence and, finally, the door. Though Rudolf indeed believed that he was destined to destroy the Turks, and regularly entertained "prophets" bent on convincing him of his own importance, Dee and Kelly's visions held little interest for him. He'd heard it all before.[13] Defeated, Dee returned home.

On September 5, Uriel appeared, his face covered so that the "eye which has offended God" could not see him. Satan, Uriel explained, was making short work of Dee, and had "blemished the eyes of [his] understanding."[14] Uriel transformed into a great spinning wheel of fire; after thrusting out his hands, the wheel appeared full of men's eyes, with flames shooting out of it in four places.* A great white eagle with monstrous red eyes, one the color of fire and one of crystal, now came and perched upon the wheel, carrying a scroll of parchment in its beak.† Beneath this eagle appeared a great valley, within which was a great city six times the size of Krakow, full of ruined houses, with a river running by it.

---

*This fits the description of the ophanim, angels that appear in Ezekiel, Daniel, the Dead Sea Scrolls, and 2 Enoch.

†Revelation 4:7 describes the fourth living creature surrounding the Throne of God as an eagle; whether this is related is unclear. Like the seraphim, the living creatures have six wings; like the cherubim, their bodies are full of eyes. If the eagle here is indeed related to the living creatures, such a manifestation of supremely high-ranking divine beings would follow on logically after the appearance of the ophanim.

Uriel explained that God had chosen Dee and Kelly to be witnesses—not in the office of apostles, but in the office and dignities of prophets, beautified with the wings of the cherubim, "with the voices that cry a thousand times in a moment before the Lord, and before the Majesty of his eternal Seat: wherein you do exceed the Temples of the earth: wherein you are become separated from the world, and whereby you are lifted up, as of the household of the Blessed, even by the very hand and finger of the Highest."[15] The end of the world was at hand—"Now shall those days open themselves, which are the days of vengeance."[16]

The Holy City, Uriel taught, represented the Church, and those who dwelled therein had sought to usurp the authority of the Most High. They would be singled out for retribution, and "scattered like unto the mighty hail, that the spirits of the north have gathered against the day of revenge. They are become proud, and think there is no God. They are stiff-necked; for they are the sons of wickedness."[17] This was to come to pass during Rudolph's reign. In the year "eighty-eight" the sun would move contrary to its course. The stars would increase their light, and some would fall from the sky. The rivers would run with blood. Woe would be unto women with children. The Prophet of the Lord would descend from the heavens.

When Dee asked for further assistance in understanding the tables, Uriel responded that as they had been allowed into the Garden of the Lord, they should simply "taste and eat."[18] In this garden, there was no hunger or thirst, but rather a filling spirit, a comforter. Awed by this display, Kelly made a pledge to never eat his supper or evening meal on Saturdays for the rest of his life.

On September 5, Dee sent thank-you letters to the ambassador, as well as the noble Octavius Spinola, whom he had met at Rudolf's court. Dee claimed to Spinola that he had decided to dedicate the rest of his life to showing the emperor what high favor God held him in—which could not have come across well. The letter was returned by the ambassador, who reported that the emperor had departed for his summer residence in Brandeish, or elsewhere, and that Spinola had gone with him.

Five days later, Dee once again conjured Ga, Za, and Vaa, who had been assigned to understand Rudolph's doings. A hand appeared in the stone, upon which was written, in Latin, "He who has shall possess it; He who has nothing will not possess it."[19] Next it showed, "Do, and it will have been done, and more, I do not have." Dee took this to mean that he should write to Rudolph himself, or the Spanish ambassador, or to Spinola in order to arrange another meeting with the emperor.

Dee revised his earlier letter, and sent it to Spinola again by way of Emeric Sontag, the secretary of the Palatine of Sieradz. Spinola received it, and ordered that Dee come immediately. Rudolph responded to Dee in writing that since he did not understand Latin, and was pressed for time, that Dee should be placed with a Dr. Curtz instead.

While communication continued back and forth, Dee and Kelly prayed that their spiritual enemy be kept busy. Uriel soon appeared, and revealed that those who are at one with God would not be judged wicked at the Last Judgment, and those at one with the Holy Spirit would be made one with God, without punishment. Otherwise, God's judgment and punishment were to be unflinching. Yet not all that were punished would be damned, nor was it evident to the angels who would be saved. And while man should be reconciled with the Catholic Church, sins that were forgiven by the Church might not necessarily be forgiven by God. Eating of the Body of the Christ, however, would truly cleanse penitent sinners—seemingly another endorsement of the Catholic Church over the Protestants, as the reality of the Eucharist was a primary point of contention during the Reformation. Uriel was clear—sinners received the body of Christ for the remission of their sins. For the angels, however, the Eucharist was made valid by the *belief* of the individual receiving it—they had to choose to believe it was the body and blood of Christ in order for it to be so.[20] The angels' doctrine was more complex than merely vetting Catholicism, however; they crafted their commands in such a way that Dee could partake in communion while still remaining beholden to the new angelic religion, rather than Rome. Ultimately, the angels were far less concerned with religious doctrine or affiliation than they were that Dee simply follow the example of the Apostles.[21] Dee, for his part, was convinced that the

Fig. 12.1. Albrecht Dürer, *The Woman Clothed with the Sun and the Seven-Headed Dragon,* 1511.

angelic religion he had received was the truest dispensation, and that all others fell short.[22]

On September 15, Dee met with Dr. Curtz, who had long been aware of Dee's fame and now welcomed him. Dee gave him the run-down on the last forty years of his study, why he had sought to consult with angels, and how God had sent him Michael, Gabriel, Raphael, Uriel, and many other spiritual creatures. Dee also presented his records—now totaling eighteen volumes—as well as the shewstone. Curtz said he would write up a report on what Dee had told him and present it to Rudolf in the next few days. Meanwhile, Kelly was visited by a "wicked tempter" who denied Christ,[23] told him that Curtz would use Dee like a serpent, that Kelly would be damned, and that their works come to nothing. As communication proceeded through Rudolf's middlemen over the following days, Dee also began to suspect dishonest dealing.

On September 21, Uriel returned and explained that two things are the marks of Satan, which bring eternal death and damnation: lying, and obstinate or willful silence. He that taught false doctrine, opened his mouth against truth, or defrauded his brother is a liar, and would not be forgiven. Yet, Uriel explained, all flesh offends, and is a liar. So who would be saved, or escape eternal damnation?

"He it is (I say) that when he hath lyed, and spoken against the truth doth not forwardly drown'd, and keep down his sin in silence."[24] Those who lied against the spirit of truth, and willfully continued to do so, without reconciliation to the Church, sinned against the Holy Spirit and were to face eternal damnation. As such, Dee and Kelly were to acknowledge their offenses, lest they also face damnation. Uriel further taught that in truth there was no such thing as sin against God, but that there *was* sin against the Holy Spirit. Whenever they offended, they were to acknowledge their sins to God and his angels, so that God could forgive them, and the angels could bear witness of that forgiveness. They were also to make confession of it in the Church, so that they would not be "drowned in froward silence" and therefore not face eternal death.[25]

Rudolf, meanwhile, was to be destroyed, for he had refused to heed the angels. England was also on the chopping block—"Behold, I had determined to have rooted out the English people, to have made a wilderness, and desert of it; to have filled it with many strange people, and to have tied the sword to it perpetually"[26]—but God would spare it, if only for Dee's sake. After certain months, Uriel would bring Dee home. As to Łaski, since they had cared for him so much, and prayed for him, he would be reconciled to Uriel, and the anger against him would cease, despite his predilection for sin. Dee was also told that Rudolf was under the belief that Dee had the philosopher's stone, and that Uriel would use Rudolf's greed against him to achieve the angels' objectives. Dee was to write to Rudolf and say that he could make the philosopher's stone, which Uriel would produce, so that Dee was not despised by the court. Rudolf's courtiers would perish before Dee's face, and he would be blessed marvelously by Uriel. Dee asked what to do regarding Curtz and his forthcoming answer; Uriel told him to handle it like a man, for he would deceive Dee. Kelly, shockingly, asked that Curtz be killed, which was ignored.

Kelly was in a more pious mood on September 22, when along with Dee he prayed for guidance as to what to do with Curtz and Rudolf. Uriel again said to write and tell Rudolf that Kelly could make the philosopher's stone, which would more firmly ensconce them within his good graces. This would give Dee and Kelly power over Rudolf and his court, and they would be able to rejoice when they saw their destruction. Gold was what Rudolf and his court most desired, but when they received it, they would perish. Moreover, Uriel said, Rudolf was possessed, and assisted by "Belzagal," a cacodemon attendant upon the Turks, who knew that Rudolph's kingdom would be short. Yet Uriel's plan was simple: "Fawn thou upon Caesar as a worldling, that thou mayest draw him with the world, to see the glory of God: but to his destruction."[27]

Two days later, Dee asked about a letter written to the emperor, and also about his reputation—he had been slandered at the ambassador's table as a conjurer and bankrupt alchemist who was only concerned with getting Rudolf's money. Uriel assured them that they were favored by God, and that the worldly hated them because of this. If they were to keep the images of God and Christ before them, remain together, and stay faithful in God, they would pass the thunders that were to come. Uriel promised that "Genii Immortalis," or immortal guardian genii, were to bring all souls to justice before the terrifying throne of the father, and that the wicked souls would face Uriel, who would not forget their evil words and deeds in his day of revenge. Michael would also show himself and his bloody sword; the good would stand under his banner, and he would fight into the hills for them.

In another letter to Rudolf, Dee warned that the emperor tempted the wrath of God by not accepting the angels' message. Following the angels' direction, he also assured Rudolf that he could make the philosopher's stone with divine aid. Seeking to salvage his slandered reputation, Dee next met with the Spanish ambassador and assured him that he had no interest in Rudolf's riches, but that he was sent by God, and had been falsely accused. To prove his sincerity, Dee showed the ambassador the records of the spirit actions; the ambassador also wanted to see the stone that Uriel manifested for Dee. He was suitably impressed, and agreed that the angels Dee was working with were indeed good spirits sent by God.

Upon his return, Dee found Kelly itching to travel home to England. This grieved Dee, but he put his trust in God to resolve the situation. Without Łaski's support, Dee was unable to further fund his mission, and now found himself in poverty. Elizabeth was also displeased that he was gone (perhaps worried he would end up working for a foreign government or leaking state secrets), and the bishop of London was simultaneously intending to have him accused of conjuration.[28]

On September 27, Dee again met with Curtz and complained of great injury done to him in Prague, after he came in good faith. The court was full of vicious backbiters, Dee claimed, who had slandered his name and spread rumors about him. In response, Curtz laid out what the emperor really thought of Dee's claims:

> To be plain with you, his Majesty thinketh them almost either incredible, or impossible: and would have some leisure to consider of them: and is desirous to have the sight of those Latin Actions

you showed me, or a Copy of them, and especially, of that, which containeth a *paraphrasis* of the Apostolical Creed.[29]

Dee wisely refused to hand over the originals, but promised to make a copy himself. The next day, Dee wrote another letter to the Spanish ambassador, in which he spoke of the secret and inscrutable actions of the angels, but professed humility, both before the true Catholic Church and also before God, noting that his works were "nothing else (entirely), other than the pen of a scribe writing swiftly through me."[30] He asked for responses to his letters, saying that he needed to prepare a journey to bring his family, books, and other baggage to Prague before the harshness of winter set in, after which he could serve the emperor from time to time.

By October 1, Jane Dee was grievously ill; Dee and Kelly consulted the angels to ask why, and how to cure her. Gabriel asked them who they were to dare seek after science, and reminded them to grovel and to turn away from the sin of the world. After this chastening, Dee and Kelly were given a magical theory of disease; if sickness came from sin, Gabriel explained, it could be cured by prayer, or by the angels, as ministers of God's justice. He offered to spend forty days teaching them medicine, and offered a diagnosis of Dee's pregnant wife. The next day, they were given a recipe for a folk remedy by the angels, but told that they would have no more until they were repentant, and made apt again for the angels' school.

Dee had been asked to become Rudolf's confessor, but he demurred, preferring that somebody else take the job—perhaps wisely, as being made privy to even minor state secrets would have meant that Dee would never again have been able to leave the emperor's sight. Rather than confessor, Dee sought only to be a messenger that Rudolf was condemned by heaven. Consequently, Dee's situation at court showed no signs of improving, and he asked for a passport for him and his family to pass quietly from the emperor's domains. On December 20, Dee's retinue departed Krakow for Prague, where they secured a new house by January 4, using funds from an unknown source.[31]

MYSTERIORUM PRAGENSIUM CONFIRMATIO
Stephen Báthory, Alchemy, the Vision
of the Round House, and Gebofal

Having failed to win over Rudolf, Kelly was told that the angels were to shift their primary focus to Stephen Báthory, king of Poland, for the time being. Yet Dee and Kelly were now destitute,[32] and petitions to Elizabeth for aid went ignored. Kelly was soon getting revelations suggesting he make the philosopher's stone—called *darr* in Enochian—which the angels assured the pair would restore their standing with Rudolf, and presumably their finances.

Concurrent with these alchemical experiments, and following the commotion that Dee and Kelly had made in Krakow, the pair had attracted the attention of the last group they should have: the Catholic Church. Rome was keenly interested in whether the pair believed in the Eucharistic miracle, the wrong response to which would have marked them as heretics. Yet the angels themselves not only believed in transubstantiation, they also recommended that Dee and Kelly *reconcile* themselves with the Church despite its corruption, possibly an attempt on the angels' part to keep Dee and Kelly alive in a lethal religious climate.

On January 14, Levanael—the angel from the very center of the Sigillum Dei—appeared, and revealed a garden full of fruit, within which was a four-cornered round house on fire, with the four elements rushing inward in a cross. This "vision of the round house" demonstrated how the currents of elemental energy moved through the four Watchtowers.[33]

The sessions would continue with the angels counseling Dee and Kelly in practical alchemy, their aim being producing the philosopher's stone in order to make another attempt to win Rudolf II to the side of the angels, as Uriel had planned. Alchemy had decayed just like everything else in the sublunary world, but with the angels' help, it would be restored, and Dee would then be able to employ it in the restitution of nature.[34] As always, and particularly in this potentially mercantile period, they counseled the pair on humility and avoiding the devil's snares, which could be anywhere and in anything—even the scriptures, if read with the wrong approach. Most read scripture to seek their own glory, not that of God, the angels explained, and therefore even the Word of God itself could become a tool of Satan for spoiling mankind's life here and in the hereafter. They were also told that after the Fall, God had consented to place part of himself in mankind—not to partake in the fallen world, but that man might redeem himself.

The angels next gave Dee and Kelly an alchemical doctrine of creating and rejoining substances, and stated their doctrine was to be opened to Dee and Kelly's wives. The set of ritual tools the angels had spent years transmitting was to be "placed upon the altar, wherein man may see, as in a glasse, How God through his Sacraments and holy institutions, sanctifieth, regenerateth, and purifieth man unto himself."[35] After long years of transmitting this complex system, Dee and Kelly were now to be told how to use it—a holy art that the angels referred to as *gebofal*. This was the use of the nineteen calls to enter the forty-eight gates of Wisdom revealed in the leaves of *Liber Loagaeth*.[36] While this process would seem purely Gnostic—similar to the ascent through the thirty aeons of Valentinian Gnosticism, or the passage through the fifty gates of Binah in Kabbalah—the angels were meanwhile pushing Dee and Kelly toward rapprochement with the much more traditional Catholic Church. There was a battle in heaven, the angels counseled, which Dee and Kelly would be wise to be mindful of. Levanael further instructed them that to inherit eternal life, they were to follow the ten commandments, as well as Christ's new commandment to love each other—but, Levanael clarified, *this only applied to the confirmed of the Church.* The doctrine the angels were giving the two men was authoritarian Catholicism.

On March 14, Dee's son Michael was born—Jane Dee and her pregnancy being saved by the angels' medicine—and was baptized Catholic at St. Vitus Cathedral in Prague.[37] The boy was named after the archangel Michael (who, meanwhile, had been pronouncing that he would destroy Rudolf, and that he now hated Łaski).

The angels had continued to manifest more poltergeist phenomena as they appeared—Dee and Kelly both felt the spirits crawling in their brains, and on multiple occasions Kelly felt a being writing on his back. On March 20, a "piece of fire . . . of human shape and lineaments" crawled into Kelly's skull, occasionally sticking its head out of Kelly's ear.

"Against divine necessity is no prayer nor resistance," the being ominously explained.[38] There had been innumerable lesser prophets, all full of the Holy Spirit, all of whom mortified their flesh for the love of God—but they could not even say why God had visited them, or justify it. This necessity was why they had been contacted, and how the infidels and nonbelievers would be returned to the fold. Prophets, the entity explained, were visited because God had found them punishing their flesh, despising the vanities of the world, and resisting Satan. Prayer—sanctified by the Holy Spirit—thus opened the way to God, and was the key to this contact.* Though the angels explained that their authority superseded that of all worldly spiritual custodians, they also insisted on Dee and Kelly cleaving to the terrestrial Church.

"What is the Church?" Kelly asked. "I did not think that the angels were of any Church."

"The Church is the number of those which are governed by the Holy Ghost," the angels replied, "and that continually sing Holy, Holy, Holy, Lord God of Zebaoth: But that we sing so, the Scriptures bear witness. Therefore we are of the Church, and our testimonies are true."[39]

MYSTERIORUM PRAGENSIUM CONFIRMATORUM
Catholic Complications

By March 20, 1585, the Dees were so poor that Jane Dee herself, perhaps at her wit's end with her husband's obsessions, decided to intervene and petition the angels herself, seeking meat and drink for her family. The angels said that they had blessed the Dees' children, who would grow to have high social standing. The temptations the Dees had suffered were necessary, so that their faith could be strengthened.

---

*As Aleister Crowley would much later summarize, "invoke often" and "enflame thyself." See Crowley, "Liber Samekh," in *Magick: Liber ABA,* 535.

Beginning on March 27, Kelly would be tempted by a far more immediately threatening force than evil spirits: the Jesuits. The attention of the Church was beginning to take its toll, and Kelly was becoming even more erratic and paranoid. The scryer demanded a copy of some of Dee's documents to show to a Jesuit priest, to which Dee responded that the Jesuits were great devils, that he was too busy writing letters, and to give him a week. Kelly became enraged and violently demanded the documents be handed over to him at once, and had to be restrained before he calmed down.

So frightened was Kelly by his potential fate if Rome were to become fully aware of his and Dee's heresy while they were out of reach of English protection—torture and death at the stake—that on April 4, Kelly flinched and confessed his sins to a Jesuit priest, who, unsurprisingly, was far more interested in Kelly's involvement with the angelic sessions than his other wrongdoings, and began grilling him for information. The Jesuit decided that Dee and Kelly had been fooled by devils masquerading as "angels of light,"[40] and charged Kelly with criminal sorcery. The Jesuits had little doubt as to the veracity of Dee and Kelly's visions—however, they were convinced that the transmissions came from evil, not good spirits; particularly given the fact that Dee was married, and it was believed that only celibate monks could be privy to visions.[41]

Yet Kelly stood his ground, stating that the angels had confirmed their good nature by several means, and mentioned the spirit diaries, which the Jesuit priest demanded be given to him. The priest quoted 1 Corinthians 6:3 to validate the Church's authority, even over the angels themselves: "Do you not know that we shall sit in judgment over angels?"[42] This was in stark contrast to the angels' prior statement that their authority superseded the Church's.

The Jesuit was no apostle, Kelly countered dryly, and no angels were to be judged in accord with the Pauline sentence. Furthermore, Dee and Kelly were not at odds with the Catholic Church; if anything, the angels were cruel disciplinarians, forcing them to be good Christians. The spirit actions themselves were Dee and Kelly's "introductory lessons in a celestial school."[43]

MYSTERIORUM CRACOVIENSIUM STEPHANICORUM
An Audience with Stephen Báthory

A week later, Dee and Kelly returned to Krakow, where Łaski—having at last made amends with Báthory—secured protection for the pair. As Easter approached, Dee anxiously made a move to reconcile himself with Rome, making confession to the Hermetically-leaning Franciscan friar Hannibal Rosseli, who was working to publish an edition of the *Corpus hermeticum,* with the section dedicated to angels having just been released. Kelly also took Easter communion, which Dee was greatly pleased with. However, it seemed that despite the medicine of the sacrament, Kelly had not stabilized, and he raged at Łaski for not paying him. Despite the angels guiding the pair toward the support of Báthory, which Łaski had arranged, Kelly demanded a return to Prague, erupting in fury when Dee refused.[44]

Perhaps tellingly, the angels also began to hurl invective at Dee, finding fault with his handling of Łaski, forbidding him to call them until he had rebuked Báthory for his sins, and even making threats on Dee's son's life for withholding angelic knowledge from the king;[45] an angel even threatened Dee unto the fifth generation for being a few days late in following an order. By this point, both angels and demons were utterly terrorizing the Dee household. Yet on May 22, Kelly was given a vision of a great mountain of fire hanging in the air, with a little boy standing upon it; Dee and Kelly were to become a strong sword, which would cut down the nations.

On May 23, Dee and Kelly met with Báthory, who soon joined the pair for a scrying session. During the resulting action, a green-clad woman appeared in a cloud, looking like a hollow shell or concave, oval figure. Like Rudolf, Báthory was commanded to atone for his sins, on condition of which the angels would back his further political ascendency in preparation for the Apocalypse. A child appeared with a circlet of air in his hand, with light in the stone as if shining like the sun. It turned to water with blood in it, then back. Stephen was to be blessed, but his wicked garments would be cut asunder. Báthory, however, was as underwhelmed with this message as Rudolf had been.

STEPHANICA MYSTICA REGIA
Stephen Rejects the Plan

Dee and Łaski were soon given another audience with Stephen Báthory. Dee counseled him that everything Christ prophesied would come true, and that Dee would present his twenty-four books recording the previous spirit actions.

Privately, Dee prayed deeply, reflecting on his progress in the angelic school and on the Continent. He expressed his gratitude to God and his angels for warning him of England's malice toward him, and commanding him to go to the Continent so that he would escape harm there, meanwhile protecting his family and Kelly from misfortune. He also thanked God for joining him and Kelly as one being, and further attaching them to Łaski, "a man very friendly to your Catholic and Orthodox Religion, and a very bitter enemy of every Antichrist."[46]

Dee was counseled by the angels to tell Stephen that the depression the king suffered from was caused by his sins, and to repent. The kings of the world had been poisoned by the Harlot of Revelation, Babylon. By this point Dee must have sounded like an unhinged millenarian preacher or Anabaptist, fervently prophesying the end of the world—with the gall to tell even kings and emperors to repent of their sins. Báthory brushed Dee off; soon after, while scrying, Dee and Kelly heard the voice of God itself, echoing with heartbreak:

"I am full of sorrow," God said, "for no man openeth his doors unto me, no man believeth me: no man remembereth that I made Heaven and Earth: Stay a while that I may weep with my self."[47]

UNICA ACTIO; QUAE PUCCIANA VOCETUR.
PARS PRIOR & POSTERIOR
Pucci's Action

Upon returning to Prague, Dee was accompanied by Francesco Pucci, a Florentine humanist philosopher and rogue mystic who had left the

Church—and who, like Dee, had quested for a universal religion that would put the world's divisions to right.[48]

Fascinated by the angelic scrying sessions, Pucci soon joined in. In the morning of August 6, 1585, Dee and Kelly staged a private session for Pucci, to demonstrate to him the extent of the angels' power and that they were telling the truth. Dee expressed to Pucci that their consistent communication with angels refuted the commonly held idea that miracles were no longer performed in the current period; it also undermined the Church's view that since Dee was married, he could not speak with angels. Dee set out to disprove both assumptions by direct demonstration.

Dee and Kelly arranged the Holy Table with a single candle. After making calls, an angel appeared covered in white, with a long glass in his left hand full of loathsome materials, like blood and milk or curds mingled together. In his right hand he carried a staff about forty-five inches long. He set the end on the ground and pointed with the top to the Table of the Covenant.

Uriel explained that the old Church would be divided between the kings of the East and West. Afterward, an angel in a cloud of fire holding a book with a red, fiery cover and white-edged pages appeared; the book was sealed with seven golden clasps, suggesting the seven seals of Revelation. These seals were lettered, with the first reading E.M.E.T. T.A.V.[49]

The blood of the end times would be washed away, they were told, and the Lamb would stand in the middle of the streets of the New Jerusalem; all nations would come to the House of David, into a great city.* Yet though the New Jerusalem would stand as a testament to the eternal, Uriel had no kind words for the Church as it currently stood, calling them "grubby merchants" who had no true insight into the scripture they taught, for angels had not inspired their understanding. The Church fathers had been given true angelic insight and holy visions, but the current Church had long since lost contact with its founders. The present wardens of the Church were to kneel to the Holy Spirit,

---

*See Revelation 21.

the true teacher—but instead, they interpreted doctrine as they wished, and were liars. Luther and Calvin's rebellion had made no improvements in this situation, Uriel thundered, and these had their rewards—damnation in the fires of hell, along with the rest who had run astray of the true teachings. This particularly impressed Pucci, an anti-Calvinist.

The angels spoke to men, not the Church: "When angels brought the glad tidings of peace and consolation to the face of the earth," Uriel said, "they did not take it to Jerusalem, nor to the Temple, nor the Holy of Holies, but they took it to the fields and amongst poor shepherds."[50]

Despite the corruption of the Catholic Church, Uriel again underlined that it was the true institution carrying Christ's word. He countered the common Protestant assertion that the pope was the Antichrist, saying that the Antichrist was instead the literal son of the devil, *born of Babylon,* who would seduce the people in time. As far as the bishops of the Church, they could be both good and evil—even the Disciples themselves, who found salvation in Christ, were a mixture of good and evil. All men are flawed, after all, but it would be incorrect to be led astray from the Church due to the actions of the human sinners within it. The correct path was to cleave to the Church despite the transgressions of man, and submit one's neck to its holy yoke and ordinance.

However, the angels would have their way with the current Church, starting with the pope, who would be cast down and chastened by Dee and Kelly themselves. They would throw out the churchmen just as Christ had thrown the moneychangers from the temple, for they had drunk from the Whore of Babylon's cup of abominations and fornications.*

"You will be extirpated and eradicated," Uriel threatened Pucci, "and the Church of God will be cleansed so that He may descend and dwell in it."[51]

This, perhaps, constitutes the angels' comprehensive say on the Reformation—and after this session, it is little wonder that the Church

---

*The cup of the Whore of Babylon, seen in Revelation 16:4, was and is often thought to be a slander on the Eucharistic chalice by Protestants, supposedly confirming the ungodliness of Rome. Aleister Crowley used the symbol of the cup in a radically different sense, as will be seen in book III.

wanted blood. Like Łaski, Rudolf, and Báthory before him, the angels assured Pucci that great things lay ahead for him—were he to repent and fully reconcile with the Catholic Church, just as Dee and Kelly had. Pucci took the angels' message seriously—so seriously that he decided that in order to fully reconcile and show his loyalty he would have to betray Dee and Kelly to the Jesuits. Aided by Pucci, the Church would quickly close in, in the meantime spreading rumors that Dee was an English and Protestant secret agent.[52]

Germanico Malaspina, the papal nuncio (the permanent diplomatic representative of Rome) began to press heavily for opening friendly conversation with Dee, which Dee consistently tried to slip out of. On March 27, 1586, they could no longer resist, and were summoned to an audience with Malaspina. Pressed about the spirit actions, Dee stated that he was indeed in contact with angels, but made no mention of the angels' views of the Church. A tactless Kelly, however, next erupted into a tirade about the Church's corruption, commanding Malaspina that the Church itself repent and bow to the authority of the angels. Though Malaspina resisted the urge to execute both men immediately, by the next month the Jesuits were pushing Kelly to confess to the crime of direct conversation with angels. Kelly refused and was banned from Church services.[53]

The angels, however, had a plan to get Dee and Kelly out of the fatal situation they had been placed in, in one of the most seemingly incredible incidents of the entire spirit actions. Just as Abraham's faith had been tested when Jehovah commanded him to kill his only child, Dee and Kelly were now commanded to gather together the entire set of records of the spirit actions—and burn them, with Pucci witnessing. They did so, throwing the books onto the fire one after the other; Kelly saw a man dancing in the flames over the books as they burned.

Everything they had recorded over the last four years of sweat, pain, and sacrifice was gone, except a fragment of *Liber Loagaeth* and the record of the action they had just undertaken with Pucci, which Dee had been commanded to cut out and save. The angels promised that nothing would be lost, and that when the tyranny of the Jesuits and the Church ceased, the books would be returned in the same manner in which they were burned.

Because the Pucci action was removed by Dee from the records of the spirit actions, Casaubon did not have access to it for the original publication of *A True & Faithful Relation*. It was rediscovered in the Bodleian Libraries by Dr. Conrad Josten in the 1960s, and is reproduced in full in Stephen Skinner's 2011 edition of Casaubon's work.[54] The recovery of the missing section put to rest the long-assumed narrative that Dee and Kelly had burned their diaries because they were terrified of the spirits they had conjured, and revealed who they were truly terrified of: the Jesuits.

By commanding Dee and Kelly to destroy their records, the angels had not only saved Dee and Kelly's lives, they had also prevented their doctrine from falling into enemy hands. Had they not done so, the spirit actions would now be sitting in a long-forgotten corner of the Vatican Library, and Dee and Kelly could well have been murdered by the Inquisition, with the spirit actions erased from history entirely.

LIBER RESURRECTIONIS, ET 42 MENSIUM FUNDAMENTUM
The Books Returned

On April 29, 1586, "a wonderful deed that ought to be remembered forever" occurred.

While standing at the end of a gallery by his chamber, Kelly looked over into the vineyard and saw a gardener pruning trees. The gardener walked over to the wall beneath Kelly, and said, "I beg that you say to the Doctor that he might come to me."[55] He then went away cutting the trees "very handsomely,"[56] and by the cherry trees near the house, on a rock in the garden, he mounted up into the sky in a pillar of fire. Kelly asked his wife to go see who was in the garden, but she saw nobody.

Suspicious of the apparition, Kelly told Dee that there was a wicked spirit in the garden seeking to delude him. Dee accompanied Kelly to the garden to look, and within seven minutes they saw a sheet of white paper being tossed by the wind under an almond tree. Under the tree were three of the books that had been burned: *Liber Loagaeth,* the *Forty-eight claves angelica,* and *Liber scientiae.*

Dee and Kelly fell to their knees to give thanks to God. Miraculously, the books showed no sign whatsoever of having been in a fire. The pair sat under the almond tree for thirty minutes praising God, after which the gardener again appeared, with his face half turned away, similar to the way Ave often presented himself. He bid Kelly to follow him, during which time his feet hovered a foot off the ground and doors opened before him without being touched; the gardener led Kelly back to the house and upstairs to the study, and the furnace where the books had been burned. The apparition then reached into the furnace, where a great light poured out from a single missing brick, put his hand into the hole, pulled out the remaining books, and handed them to Kelly one by one. Everything was returned except the book from which the last revelation was cut, and Pucci's recantation (these bits had been removed by Dee and kept aside).

The gardener next bid Kelly to go, and said that they would be given the rest later. He went before Kelly in a fiery cloud, with Kelly following along with the books under his arm, even gliding by Pucci's chamber door without flinching. After the guide left him, Kelly brought the books to an astonished Dee, who was still sitting under the almond tree. After giving prayers of thanks on April 30, they were told that their sins were forgiven, that they would be fruitful and blessed with all of the gifts of nature, that the end of the world was still scheduled for the "year eighty-eight,"[57] and that new actions would proceed—albeit without Pucci, who was now called defiled.

The damage was already done—Dee and Kelly's activities had angered the Church; on May 22, Pucci warned them anonymously that the pontifical legate had accused Kelly of necromancy. Dee was furious with Pucci, particularly as Dee believed he had been blabbing their secrets; in addition, he had engaged in some unspecified household behavior that was unacceptable to Dee and Kelly's wives and family. Over the coming week, Pope Sixtus V personally put pressure on Rudolf II to expel them from Bohemia, with Rudolf issuing a Decree of Exile on May 29.

On July 13, Pucci informed Dee and Kelly that God had told them to go to Rome. Most conveniently, they had been provided with a letter of safe conduct to the Vatican to discuss their supernatural revelations with the supreme pontiff, and were promised that Sixtus V himself would free them of all fault and punishment for practicing the magical arts and reading books banned by the Inquisition. The angels warned Dee to cut Pucci off, and that Pucci and the nuncio were attempting to lead them into entrapment by the Jesuits.

Dee believed that Pucci was "false to the Pope, or us, or both, or rash, foolish, blind, &tc.," and was double-crossing them.[58] Pucci was leprous, Dee wrote—infected with heresy and God only knew what else. The papal nuncio wanted to see the visible appearance of angels, and wanted Dee and Kelly's experiences laid out before the pope. Only then—if Dee could prove the validity of his experiences beyond a shadow of a doubt—would critics' mouths be shut. The nuncio added a chilling end to his letter of summons: "May God guide you thus with his grace, so that you might sometime be able to have a conversation with the Angels in heaven."[59]

The angels themselves were enraged at Rome. Meanwhile, Pucci wrote (perhaps condescendingly) that he was praying for Dee and Kelly as if they were "revered fathers."[60] Pucci soon took a meeting with an Italian Jesuit; the Jesuits attempted to bait Pucci into siding with Dee and Kelly's view that angels could be spoken to without the intermediary agency of the Church, which would have been heresy most supreme—not to mention competition with the Church's hold on the market, especially after it had already been so grievously bled by Luther's rebellion. So threatened was Sixtus by Dee and Kelly that he ordered them investigated for being agents of Elizabeth—astrologers, sorcerers, and spies working magically against Rome.[61]

While Dee and Kelly dodged Rome, they sojourned at the court of William IV in Germany, and on September 14 traveled to Třeboň in South Bohemia as guests of Vilém Rožmberk, the Burgrave of Bohemia, the richest and most powerful prince in Bohemia as well as a moderate Catholic, a student of the occult, and a patron of angelic magic and alchemy.[62] Though they had been disappointed so many times before, the angels quickly seized on Rožmberk, offering him a covenant with God to achieve the angels' political goals in Europe, should he bow to them and sanctify himself; they also hoped he would get Dee back in Rudolf's good graces.[63] So impressed was Rožmberk with the pair that he built them their own alchemical laboratory, situated in a tower in his castle in Třeboň.[64]

On October 14, in Třeboň, Dee set up the Holy Table in the chapel adjoining his chamber. Kelly was given a vision of a plain or great field, a mile wide, with a high, rotten tree in the middle, and all of its grass withered and burned. A beam of fire from heaven lit on the tree, and water ran from its root, spreading over the plain as though it were becoming a sea. A man emerged from the tree with his hair and garment hanging to his feet. The earth drank up the water, and the man stood upon dry ground, with the grass now a cubit high. In the middle of the stone appeared a spark of fire, which grew to a globe twenty inches in diameter. Woe be unto the world and its worldlings, the man said; they would be controlled with an iron rod by Christ, peace would rest, and the New Jerusalem would descend. The world would bow to the cross and the name of the Lamb—but not before terror descended upon all nations.[65] Mulling over these visions and prophecies with Rožmberk, Dee wrote that this was a prophecy of religious reform in England, and of the exploration of the entire world—which would necessitate terrible bloodshed.

A few days later, Dee and Kelly finally found a way to rid themselves of the parasite Pucci: after fighting with him over money, they attempted to get him to take eight hundred florins, or else turn them down on record. The gambit was successful in shaking the backstabbing philosopher off.

13

I Am the Daughter of Fortitude, and Ravished Every Hour

MYSTERIORUM DIVINORUM MEMORABILIA. ACTIO TERTIA
The Daughter of Fortitude

In 1587, with Dee, Kelly, and their spouses still in Třeboň, the actions took a new turn—marked by a shocking eruption of eroticism.

With the sessions progressing, Dee and Kelly were told by the voice of Zebaoth, the Lord of Hosts, that people worshipped riches as their gods, rather than realizing that riches themselves had been created by God as a tool to glorify him with. Likewise, an accounting was to be made of how Dee and Kelly had used the spiritual gifts granted to them, and they would pay "even unto the uttermost farthing."[1]

Kelly was told that he had taken a wife against the angels' wishes (despite the earlier exhortation to marry against *his* wishes!), and therefore the angels had made her barren. Yet the blessings of heaven were immense, the two men were told, and Dee and Kelly had been made free.

With a psychically broken Kelly now showing signs of blowing out for good, Dee had begun preparing his son Arthur (later to become a prominent alchemist in his own right) to take Kelly's place. Assumed to be virginally pure and also pure of mind, children were thought to make superb scryers, and often featured in medieval grimoire literature. On April 15, 1587, Arthur Dee had some scrying success, seeing various figures appear, and two days later, Dee formally asked Madimi, Ilemese, and Uriel to assist Kelly in transferring his office to Arthur Dee. The boy's visions proved to be suited only to the mental capacity of a child, however, and on April 18, Kelly was back to scrying. Kelly witnessed all of the angels appear, then fade, save for Madimi—who now appeared naked. Kelly and Dee assumed that they were being tempted by a demon—but Madimi assured them otherwise.

"What is sin?" Madimi asked.

"To break the Commandment of God," Dee replied.

"Set that down, so," she returned. "If the self-same God give you a new Commandment taking away the former form of sin which is limited by the Law; What remaineth then?"

Madimi reassured them that whatever they had seen was from above, "for that I touched thy Son, might also have taken away his breath"[2]—Arthur had fallen sick after Kelly saw an angel in a white garment act as if he would smite the boy. Yet though he had been afflicted by the angels, he had survived—proof, Madimi explained, that the angels were not evil (this could not have been comforting to a beleaguered parent). Madimi elaborated that even the righteous were punished for their sin—but by God, not by malediction. The Apostle Paul himself was the chief of sinners, after all. God's heavens, and ways, were incomprehensible, but Dee and Kelly were to be glad that they were in divine hands. If they were to forsake the ways of God, however, evil would enter their houses, and their wives and children would be carried away before their faces. Kelly was next shown a white crystalline pillar with four heads on it—representing Dee, Kelly, and their wives, with their necks making up the pillar.

"Nothing is unlawful," they were told, "which is lawful unto God."[3] Dee and Kelly were not to resist God, but instead to shut out Satan.

They had already been delivered the secrets of *Liber Loagaeth;* now they were to assemble every seventh day to be taught further.

The next day, Madimi told Kelly that he and Dee were to share their wives in common. Dee and Kelly were unsure if Madimi meant spiritually or carnally; a scroll appeared to clarify, reading, "I speak concerning both." Madimi explained that—as with the angel that commanded Abraham to kill his son—the direct orders of the angels trumped scripture, for "if I were to say to a man: 'go and kill your brother,' and he did not do it, he would be the son of sin and death. For all things are possible and permitted to the godly."[4]

This sent Dee into a panic of questioning his very faith, and gave Kelly good cause to forsake the angels altogether. Their wives were appalled. Kelly claimed that Madimi's pronouncement terrified him. To comfort them, a small spirit named Ben appeared, and said that they would be helped "to pass the marvelous great dangers of the Sea."*

After the message had been delivered, they each returned to their individual beds; Dee told Jane Dee that the wife sharing had to occur; there was no other way.

"Thereupon she fell in a weeping and trembling for a quarter of an hour," Dee recorded, "and I pacified her as well as I could; and so, in the fear of God, and in believing of his Admonishment, did persuade her that she shewed herself prettily resolved to be content for God his sake and his secret Purposes, to obey the Admonishment."[5]

On April 20, Dee wrote that he had found "much halthing and untruth" in Kelly's reports to him of the utterances of spiritual creatures,[6] that Dee himself had not been present at. Because Kelly's memory was bad, and he was easily tempted by evil spirits, Dee was suspicious of some of his new revelations. Several more creatures had appeared to Kelly in his private chamber, but Kelly stated that he had kept his mind fixed on resisting and discrediting them. One, however, told him to join the tables of Enoch, and renumber the squares. This would be the "Reformed Table of Raphael," a new ordering of the Watchtowers that

---

*Possibly a reference to Binah.

would seem of rather suspect provenance given the circumstances. The new reordering of the tablet seems to have greatly convinced and cheered Dee with its mathematical precision, however, and he consequently resolved to obey the new doctrine. This version of the Watchtowers also now forms the standard ordering that is presented in books on the angelic system.

On April 21, a wife-swapping agreement was drawn up. Kelly made a declaration that he had hated the spirits. Though they had been comforted by the godliness of the prior spirit actions, Dee and Kelly's wives still found the new push toward polygamy disturbing, as it was against God's prohibition of adultery. The group resolved to abstain from meat and fish, and occupy themselves with fasting and praying, until such time as a new action gave clarification or confirmation on what was to be done.

On April 24, that clarification came. A great flame appeared in the stone, and a spiritual creature entered through the south window of the chapel, heaved the scrying stone into the air and then set it down again. Afterward, a man appeared with his nether parts in a cloud, and with spread arms came toward Kelly. The creature took up the stone and frame of gold, and mounted up and away. Kelly grabbed for it, but couldn't touch it. The scryer was seized with fear and trembling—and revealed that the spirits had lately been giving him heart palpitations from fright. Dee, however, was "very glad and well pleased."[7]

A man on fire appeared with flaxen hair hanging down over him, naked to the paps, with blood spots on him. If the angels had planned to destroy them, the apparition said, the seas would have long ago swallowed them. The angel, apparently speaking for God, confirmed that he was indeed the God of Abraham, who was Alpha and Omega, and who gave all. Just as Moses's leadership of the Jews had also been a time of prosperity for the gentiles, "even so shall those days to come be unto the Nations and Kings of the earth. I am a law for ever."[8]

The angels' doctrine itself was not to be published, but was to be Dee and Kelly's alone; the sharing of wives, the angel confirmed, was meant to unify Dee and Kelly as one being, which would complete the first phase of the Apocalypse: "Walk before me as the sons of my Father, in all righteousness," the angel told them. "And follow you that which you call unrighteousness even with gladness: for I can make you whiter than snow. Your unity and knitting together is the end and consummation of the beginning of my harvest."[9]

A covenant was subsequently drawn up in writing by all four parties; on May 6, Dee wanted to ascertain that he would be rewarded for the affair, and so he and Kelly prayed at the table in their chapel, and the covenant they had composed was read to the angels. Within fifteen minutes, Madimi appeared with an infinite number of spiritual creatures standing behind her, as if in a half moon; a second head sprouted from her head, sporting three eyes, with one eye going into the other, which Dee believed confirmed the agreement and their deal.

On May 20, Kelly cut the contract into two parts, with one part going with Kelly and his wife and the other with Dee. An angel appeared and stated that he had made Dee and Kelly free from all men in preparation for meeting God. Yet because they had not consummated their contract, he condemned their willfulness, and stated that they would be thrown out from town to town, as they had forsaken God. The threats were now coming nonstop—Kelly remarked that "I thought we should have nothing else, but threats."[10] Yet "he that pawneth his soul for me, loseth it not," an angel told them, and though Dee and Kelly were to be "brought forth before men in your latter dayes, and . . . overthrown and slain," they would be resurrected to eternal life. After they had completed the wife sharing, they would be restored to God's full grace, "and you shall grow every day, wise and mighty in me."[11]

The next day, as Dee and Kelly were walking in an orchard along a river, Kelly saw two children about the same age as Arthur Dee fighting with swords. One said, "Thou hast beguiled me,"[12] which Dee took to be indicative of his conflict with Kelly. They returned home to find their scrying stone replaced underneath Jane Dee's pillow.

Thus fully persuaded, the foursome consummated Madimi's plan on May 22—or at least two of them did. Kelly had intercourse with Jane Dee, but Dee himself could not carry out the deed, and instead spent the night chastely alongside Joanna Kelly.

The morning after, while scrying, Kelly saw a purple circle in the circumference of the holy stone. Next appeared a great man in a bright harness, sitting on a beautiful milk-white horse, with a fiery spear first in his left hand, now in the right—likely representing either Christ or the first horseman of the Apocalypse (who, in some readings, is the Antichrist). A long sword hung by his side, with a steel target on his back that hung from his neck on a blue lace, upon which were painted circles of cherubim, with faces like burning gold. The horseman asked Kelly if the deed had been done:

> HORSEMAN: "Kelly, was thy brother's wife obedient and humble to thee?"
>
> E.K.: "She was."
>
> HORSEMAN: "Dee, was thy brother's wife obedient unto thee?"
>
> DEE: "She was obedient."
>
> HORSEMAN: "Even as you were one obedient unto another, even so shall the Lord deal with you."[13]

A green woman appeared, and also asked Dee if he carried out the deed—Dee confirmed that he did not. (This exchange was scratched out of the diaries by Dee, and so was not reprinted in Casaubon's original edition of *A True & Faithful Relation*.)[14]

A new presence now appeared to Kelly: a goddess or angel with attire "like beaten gold; she hath on her forehead a Cross chrystal lyne, her neck and breast are bare unto under her dugs: She hath a girdle of beaten gold slackly buckled unto her with a pendant of gold down to the ground"—the Whore of Babylon.* Her harrowing speech is the most famous passage of the entire spirit actions.

"I am the Daughter of Fortitude," she began,

---

*This is Babylon the Great, the Mother of Prostitutes and of the Abominations of the Earth, from Revelation 17, later called BABALON in Enochian by Crowley. In Crowley's records of his 1909 experiments with the angelic system, BABALON would be depicted as an inversion of the Virgin Mary or Sophia, the Goddess as a cosmic womb that absorbs and then extinguishes the individual egos of spiritual aspirants, and is therefore a "whore."

Fig. 13.1. BABALON. Panel from Jacobello Alberegno, *Polyptych of the Apocalypse*, 1360–90.

and ravished every hour, from my youth. For behold, I am Understanding, and Science dwelleth in me; and the heavens oppress me, they covet and desire me with infinite appetite: few or none that are earthly have: embraced me, for I am shadowed with the Circle of the Sonne, and covered with the morning Clouds. My feet are swifter than the winds, and my hands are sweeter than the morning dew. My garments are from the beginning, and my dwelling place is in my self. The Lion knoweth not where I walk, neither do the beasts of the field understand me. I am defloured, and yet a virgin: I sanctified, and am not sanctified. Happy is he that imbraceth me: for in the night season I am sweet, and in the day full of pleasure. My company is a harmony of many Cymbals, and my lips sweeter than health it self. I am a harlot for such as ravish me, and a virgin with such as know me not: For lo, I am loved of many, and I am a lover to many; and as many as come unto me as they should do, have these entertainments. Purge your streets, O you sons of men, and wash your houses clean; make your selves holy, and put on righteousness. Cast out your old strumpets, and burn their clothes; abstain from the company of other women that are defiled, that are sluttish, and not so handsome and beautiful as I, and then will I come and dwell amongst you: and behold, I will bring forth children unto you, and they shall be the Sons of Comfort. I will open my garments, and stand naked before you, that your love may be more enflamed toward me.... [15]

This speech, which is spoken from the point of view of Babylon the Great, rather than the antagonistic view of Revelation, bears many similarities to Gnostic texts pertaining to Sophia, Wisdom, particularly "Thunder: Perfect Mind," which nearly matches the "Daughter of Fortitude" passage for theme and even tonality. "Thunder" was not available to Dee and Kelly, as it is part of the Nag Hammadi codices discovered in a buried jar in Egypt in 1945, one month before the beginning of Jack Parsons's Babalon Working. Yet compare a sample of its text:

> I am the first and the last.
> I am the honored and scorned.
> I am the whore and holy.
> I am the wife and the virgin.
> I am the mother and daughter.
> I am the members of my mother
> and the barren one with many sons.
> I have had a grand wedding
> and have not found a husband.
> I am a midwife and do not give birth. [16]

Reading both texts side by side, it is hard not to see overlap in lines like "I am a harlot for such as ravish me, and a virgin with such as know me not," from Kelly, and "I am the whore and holy, I am the wife and the virgin" from "Thunder."

Dee and Kelly, as the angels now told them, had attained to wisdom—wisdom indeed being *Sophia* in Greek, and *Chokmah* in Hebrew.*

"No man is illuminated, that is not sanctified: neither is there any man perfectly sanctified, that is not joyfully illuminated," the angels explained.[17] Dee and Kelly were the chosen of the last days, and would present themselves every seventh day for the next hundred days to attain to further wisdom.† If they did this, the angels counseled, they would be spared a remembrance to history as sorcerers, and their reputations would be repaired. Judging by how both men have been treated in the official histories, they must not have succeeded in this final working. If anything, it seems that sharing wives was too much for Dee and Kelly's friendship to bear; they parted ways shortly thereafter.

And with this, the recorded spirit actions, and one of the most crucial spiritual partnerships of the second millennium, trailed off into awkward silence.

---

*"Daughter of Fortitude" may also denote a path proceeding from Geburah, Power—likely the path of Teth, which was later attributed to Babalon and the Beast by Crowley in the Lust card of his Thoth Tarot.

†Following Crowley's 1909 scrying of the Aethyrs and initiation to Binah, his next major initiation, to Chokmah or Wisdom, took place in 1920; it was to occur over seventy-three days, during which time the "pile of dust" that he had been reduced to in Binah was gathered into an "urn" in Chokmah. See Crowley, "Liber LXXIII."

14

Gold Is the Metal
with the Broadest Shoulders

Dee had faithfully gone to work for the angels, struggling to conscript the kings of Europe into helping him immanentize the eschaton—and while Europe's monarchs had little use for the Doctor's spiritual pronouncements, they *had* developed a keen interest in Kelly's professed ability to produce gold. Just as Dee had recognized Kelly as a uniquely gifted scryer, the kings of Europe had seen (or had been led by Kelly to see) an alchemist capable of producing gold where others had failed.

While Dee had once been dominant over Kelly, a reversal of fortunes had occurred: Dee had plummeted from grace with Elizabeth's court over the Łaski affair, and was now seen as little more than a crank by the sovereigns he had so long tried to impress, while Kelly was seen as the potential solution to the riddle of alchemy. So much had the power balance shifted that even if Dee were to return to England, he would do so as Kelly's subordinate, assisting him in making gold for the Crown.[1] By November 1587, with invasion by Spain imminent, the English court was itching to draw Kelly back home in order to make sure he was working for them, and not a foreign power.[2]

By the summer of 1587, Kelly was engaged in practical alchemy at Rožmberk's mansion in Třeboň, initially with Dee's help, but domestic tensions between the two men and their wives were unbearable—due to the strain caused by Kelly's social elevation and the (possibly ongoing, at least according to Dee's biographer Glen Parry) wife swapping. And while temporary peace could be negotiated, it wouldn't be long before they descended into fighting, with Kelly making threats and consistently working to turn the other members of the household against his mentor, even convincing the servants that Dee collaborated with the devil—very likely "triangulating" in order to create unfavorable conditions that would push Dee out, leaving more profit and autonomy for Kelly himself. Meanwhile, disturbingly, an English spy named Edward Whitlock was lurking in Třeboň, and had been working to gather information on Dee's son Arthur for nearly a year. Jane Dee was also pregnant, potentially by Kelly—the Dees' new son, Theodore, would be born in February 1588.[3]

After Theodore's arrival, Dee and Kelly began to seriously communicate with England about returning. Dee was so poor by this point that, humiliatingly, he had to beg Edward and Joanna Kelly for "mutual charity" so that he could receive Easter Communion. England was doing its best to return Kelly to the fold before the attack of the Armada, with Dee seen as little more than an inconvenient accessory at this point. Kelly was perfecting the secrets of transmutation, and though he was sharing his information with Dee, it was only Kelly himself who was of interest to the monarchs that Dee had tried to win over for so long. Where pure knowledge had failed, the promise of gold succeeded, and by the end of 1587 Kelly was collecting devotees and cash, while looking for a way to shed himself of his former employer. Ready to move on, and perhaps by way of not totally abandoning Dee to the wolves, Kelly shared some of his knowledge of transmutation with Dee, and gave him the "mercurial water" that they had used in alchemical processes. Later, trying to draw Kelly back in, Dee gave him one of his most precious possessions, a prototelescope. Kelly immediately donated it to Rudolf by way of Rožmberk in order to regain Rudolf's good graces for himself, *sans* Dee; Rudolf added it to his collection of mechanical curios. Dee had been fully thrown under the bus.[4]

Kelly's claims of alchemical success had made him the far more attractive wizard; yet all of Kelly's alchemical knowledge had come from Dee, particularly a manuscript by the English alchemist George Ripley entitled *The bosome book* that Kelly had borrowed from Dee's library and used as a manual to teach himself the art, until his skills had advanced beyond Dee's own.[5] This may shed light on why Kelly stayed so long in Dee's employ, despite the immense psychic stress put on him by the spirit actions—or, if taking a more cynical view, why he continued to con Dee. Kelly may have wanted continued access to Dee's library, equipment, and knowledge as a way to learn operative alchemy until he no longer needed his mentor.

By January 1589, Rožmberk gave Kelly the order to brush off Dee; when Dee vacillated, Rožmberk gave him a forty-day deadline to leave Třeboň. Within a month Dee had acquiesced, giving Kelly his alchemical equipment to pass on to Rožmberk. On February 16, 1589, Kelly took the equipment and most of the household servants, and departed with Rožmberk.

This, almost eight years after their meeting at Mortlake, ended the collaboration of John Dee and Edward Kelly. They would never see each other again. Dee, who had already given everything for his cause, and sacrificed all that he had gained for the promise of angelic insight, had now been taken by his partner—for his contacts, his status, his knowledge, his alchemical equipment, and even his wife's favors, leaving Dee destitute and possibly with a son not of his own parentage. It is easy to see how history would remember Kelly not as a conduit for the divine but as a rank con man and thief—never stopping, however, to consider that both of these roles might have coexisted in one man. Perhaps with the angelic sessions having ceased, and with Kelly now away from Dee's tempering influence, Kelly's basest aspects and self-interest came to the forefront.

Dee and his family were given military escort out of Třeboň to Bremen by Rudolf, in an expensive convoy costing over £600 (about £106,000 or $133,000 in 2017 terms).[6] Once in Germany, the Dees rented a house, with Dee still hoping that Kelly would come back to him, so that together they could return to England to assist Elizabeth against the Spanish Armada. However, unlike the patriotic Dee, Kelly's loyalties lay with the highest bidder. Dee meanwhile worked to get back in Walsingham's favor by relaying information on what was occurring on the Continent. Among those reports was that by August Kelly had been given the title Baron of Bohemia by Rudolf. It must have been crushing news. Meanwhile, Dee waited in Bremen and dried out from his adventures, while the locals looked over their shoulders in fear at him.

With Jane Dee pregnant again, and with the news of Kelly's promotion, Dee decided to at last give up on his former partner. Despite attempts by the Crown to return Kelly to the fold, the recalcitrant alchemist could not be retrieved. Meanwhile, Jane was appalled by the poverty the Dees found themselves in, and would have been pushing Dee toward resolving their situation. Admitting defeat, Dee returned to England on December 3, 1589, after six years on the Continent.[7]

On arrival, Dee found Mortlake in ruins, his precious library picked over, his alchemical equipment sold or destroyed. The Privy Council began attempts to locate his stolen items, and also furnished him with some funds to begin resituating back home. Elizabeth, for her part, leaned on the archbishop of Canterbury to find Dee gainful

Fig. 14.1. John Dee in his later years.

employment in the Church, perhaps in the hope that by stabilizing Dee she could lure Kelly back.[8] In a yet further humiliation, because he was not able to pay off the mortgage on his home at Mortlake, Dee was forced to rent it from his brother-in-law Nicholas Fromoundes, the very man responsible for allowing the despoiling of the house in the first place, and who had personally sold off many of the takings. By January, however, the two had settled on recompense.

John and Jane Dee slowly reassembled their life at Mortlake, and by February 1590, a new daughter was born—whom Dee puckishly named Madimi. The England Dee had returned to, however, was not the same country he had left. In addition, many of his milieu were dying. Robert Dudley had gone in 1588, and Francis Walsingham and Ambrose Dudley passed shortly after Dee's return, leaving him with few remaining connections at court. In addition, the backlash against Elizabeth's tolerant, Hermetic reign was already beginning. Having begun to harden against progressive reforms, the Church of England had installed the conservative John Whitgift as archbishop of Canterbury, who was fiercely anti-Presbyterian and worked to enforce the idea that spiritual authority came from ecclesiastical training, not divine inspiration. As such, he would not have looked kindly on Dee's claims. Whitgift believed that the Presbyterians' fervent belief in divine inspiration was little more than an attempt to appeal to crowd psychology and populism, and provided a platform for subversion.[9] All claims of divine inspiration were soon to be conflated with sorcery in order to keep tight control over scriptural interpretation. The 1584 publication of Reginald Scot's encyclopedic *The discouerie of witchcraft*—probably the first mass-published work on magic—unilaterally rejected magic as superstition, on which grounds Scot also compassionately argued against the prosecution of supposed witches, as they were merely deluded, not dangerous (James I would later burn the book during his pogrom against accused witchcraft practitioners). Whitgift also used the book to again connect the Presbyterians to the occult.[10]

Anti-occult sentiment was surging, most famously with the 1589 production of Christopher Marlowe's *Doctor Faustus*. It is from this singular play, and its titular character—likely based in part on Dee himself—that our culture inherits the archetype of the occultist who tinkers with the proverbial "forces with which man was not meant to meddle" and who consequently reaps the rewards of hell. The play struck such a deep chord with the English public that—as with Dee's student production of *Pax,* or the media frenzy around the 1973 film *The Exorcist*—rumors circulated that actual demons appeared onstage, and audience members were driven mad.[11]

The Faustus archetype would be revisited by Goethe in the eighteenth century, and in the Romantic period form the mold from which scientific antiheroes like Victor Frankenstein were drawn. H. P. Lovecraft's works were full of characters that unwisely made bargains with cosmic intelligences inimical to human life, and from this great literary vein we inherit countless plots in modern horror books and films. This image has been driven so far into the Western mind that the Faustian pact is regularly invoked in popular discourse when questioning scientific ethics or even modernity as a whole. And much of this, it could be argued, stems from the public reaction to the legend of John Dee, which was only compounded by the Royal Society's later assessment of him as an icon of science gone wrong.

Unfortunately for Dee, the new archbishop's hostility toward magic meant that Dee would be constantly blocked from the clerical appointment that Elizabeth sought for him, continually frustrating his attempts at finding employment. Dee was able to craftily use his connection to Kelly and his knowledge of alchemy to work toward the provostship of Eton College, but there, too, he was barred from attaining a position. Even Elizabeth's favor—retained due to her own interest in alchemy and her hope that Kelly would return to England and produce gold for the Crown—could not turn the tide of enmity against Dee.[12]

Meanwhile, Dee had resumed angelic scrying sessions at Mortlake with Bartholomew Hickman, whom he had employed prior to hiring Kelly; no record of these sessions survives. He also attempted the exorcism of Ann Frank, his children's nurse, but was of no aid to the tormented woman. Within a week she had attempted suicide by drowning herself in Dee's well, which Dee rescued her from at the last minute. Her next attempt succeeded—she cut her own throat after afternoon prayers.[13]

The record of the exorcism could have alerted the archbishop to the fact that Dee was continuing to practice magic, and Dee was, indeed, still immersed in the occult, now working with a number of Essex folk magicians or "cunning men" in searching for buried treasure, then a felony offense. Dee requested a special license to dig from Cecil, but was turned down.[14] Finances must have been truly thin.

Elizabeth was by now communicating with Kelly directly, and sent the courtier, poet, and alchemical enthusiast Edward Dyer to Prague to retrieve him.* Dyer was reportedly able to do some alchemical work with Kelly, and saw him produce gold; unfortunately, Kelly had also renounced all ties to England, and was now attached firmly to Rudolf II's court.[15] Enraged that the mercenary Kelly would not share his alchemical knowledge, Elizabeth summoned Dee, furnished him with small funds, attended to the restoration of his library, and may have begun alchemical experiments with him herself. Elizabeth had assembled an alchemical factory at Hampton Court Palace, and now sought to employ the methods laid out in the *Monas* using her equipment. Yet with the threat of Spanish invasion looming, the court now tried more direct methods of retrieving the scryer, pushing Dyer to return Kelly to England along with enough of his alchemical powder to offset Elizabeth's costs in raising a navy to beat back the Spanish.[16]

Meanwhile, succumbing to another of his manic rages, Kelly had killed an imperial officer in a duel, and been thrown in prison. Subsequently, not only Edward Dyer but all of the English in Prague had been placed under house arrest; the true motive behind this gambit may have been to keep Elizabeth from retrieving Kelly. Once in prison, Kelly would be forced to continue his alchemical work as a slave. Clearly Kelly's alchemy was seen as not only real, but real enough to shift the war effort. Thomas Webb, another English alchemist, was sent in a last-ditch effort to recover Kelly, but when his efforts failed as well, Kelly was discarded as an asset, no longer worth the time and effort.

While the archbishop had been persecuting Presbyterians—

---

*Dyer is now principally remembered for the poem "My Mind to Me a Kingdom Is."

Elizabeth had no desire that the Church of England suffer any more reform, particularly from antimonarchical movements—Dee had been falling further from the court's good graces, as it became apparent that Kelly was lost for good. That changed on July 22, 1591, when he was granted the mastership of St. Cross Hospital at Winchester by the Countess of Warwick, which would give him a safe haven and an income. Meanwhile, the archbishop had determined that Kelly's alchemical miracles were fraudulent, despite claims to the contrary by Dyer, who had witnessed them firsthand. Whitgift therefore began turning public opinion steadily against Kelly and his mystique.[17]

Dee was not the only conjuror with millennial ideas: the Presbyterian leaders Edmund Copinger, Henry Arthington, and William Hacket were soon to be accused of summoning angels to overthrow the Church of England and immanentize the eschaton.[18] Hacket's style of magic—speaking to angels, channeling prophecies, and conjuring up apocalyptic visions of England's future—was strikingly close to Dee's. Occult terrorism was in the air. Dee was at this point considered far too loyalist to be associated with the Presbyterians' left-field plans of revolt; however, the crackdown on the Presbyterians gave supernatural practices an even worse name in England, prompting Dee to keep his ongoing occult experiments *sub rosa*.[19]

Whitgift, however, was also laying the foundation for the tolerance of Catholics, potentially a huge threat in the run-up to Spanish invasion, which Cecil hedged against by publishing a proclamation against any Catholic priests or Jesuits who worked to shift the loyalties of English subjects—leading to years of a brutal regime of torture and execution of suspected Catholic subversives.[20] Clemency for English Catholics would in the meantime be used as a negotiation tool in Elizabeth's ongoing secret talks with Spain.[21] While Cecil focused Elizabeth on the threat of a real or imagined global Catholic conspiracy, however, attention was directed away from the Presbyterians, who managed to escape prison by 1592.[22]

The years 1592–94 were not good to Dee, now in his mid-sixties. With further appointments to rectorships blocked by the archbishop, and mounting debts, Dee again turned to his occult talents to keep himself afloat, casting charts for treasure hunters and performing exorcisms. He supplemented this income by renting out rooms, teaching private students, and borrowing money. These income sources amounted to barely anything, with Dee still claiming penury, and relying on food and clothing gifted by friends. Despite pawning his silver and his wife's jewelry, by mid-1592 Dee was £833 in debt (about £147,000 or $185,000 in 2017 terms), with his household suppliers cutting off his credit and openly shaming him for his inability to pay.[23] His health was also failing; he noted that he was suffering from kidney stones on July 23, 1592.[24] He would suffer them for two years, until in March 1594 he voided the stone with the aid of a folk remedy containing "crabs' eyes in powder, with the bone in the carp's head."[25]

In addition to his prior record of shifting loyalties and accusations of sorcery, Dee was falling victim to the same problem that had dogged him his entire life—his complete inability to play the game. Brilliant as he was, he simply did not have the social and political skills necessary to hack the Elizabethan court's elaborate masque of favor and patronage. As Elizabeth's tutor Roger Ascham so bitingly summarized the court:

> *Cog, lie, flatter and face,*
> *Four ways in Court to win men grace.*
> *If thou be thrall to none of these,*
> *Away, good Piers! Home, John Cheese!*[26]

Meanwhile, Elizabeth was stretched past her limits attempting to prepare for Spanish invasion, and now had to contend with regular Jesuit assassination attempts, which the Privy Council followed up on by disarming all Catholics.[27] Religious and commercial tension between England and Spain had erupted into intermittent warfare beginning in 1585, while Dee and Kelly were on the Continent, and reached a head in 1588, with the attempted invasion of England by the Spanish Armada, under papal authority to replace Elizabeth with a Catholic king. Rather than the predicted end of the world for "eighty-eight," the Armada was shattered by the clever strategies of Lord Howard of Effingham,

Sir John Hawkins, and Francis Drake—and, most of all, sudden storm conditions—in one of the most humiliating defeats in military history.* The conflict between England and Spain had been given mythic resonance throughout Europe. More than just a military victory, the decisive destruction of the Armada by *force majeure* was seen as God settling the debate between Catholics and Protestants. *1588. Flavit YHVH et Dissipati Sunt,* one medal commissioned to celebrate the victory read in Latin and Hebrew. "God blew, and they were scattered."[28]

Bribed with offers of rectorship, Dee was lured back to court in 1592 to consult on the possibility of a new invasion attempt, which Dee thought highly probable, contravening Cecil's own intelligence to the contrary. All known Catholic agents were subsequently returned to prison, and several more Papists (including nearly every Catholic lawyer in London) were arrested. By the end of August, with plague ravaging England, anxiety-driven reports of sightings of another approaching Spanish fleet had started.[29]

Dee's poor fortunes may well have been connected to the fall of his patron Walter Raleigh from Elizabeth's good graces. Raleigh, it had been revealed, had secretly been married to (and had a son with) Elizabeth's maid of honor.[30] Catholics took Raleigh's fall as an opportunity to pounce, in order to strike back at Cecil's proclamation, and in August published an attack claiming that Raleigh ran a "school of Atheism," colloquially called a "School of Night," out of his country house, which claimed Thomas Harriot, Lawrence Keymis, Christopher Marlowe, and others as members,[31] and of which Dee was supposedly the master. This school allegedly corrupted young gentlemen into renouncing Moses and Christ, rejecting the Old and New Testaments, and even into spelling the name of God backward.[32] No such School of Night existed, of course—it was a slander conjured up by Catholic propagandists. The

---

*On the other hand, if one takes English imperialism as an active force of the Apocalypse, one could also note that the August 8, 1588 defeat of the Armada—that's 8/8/88, two eighty-eights—was indeed the decisive moment in which it was no longer possible for the Catholic bloc to halt the spread of a new, Protestant world order. More than just a military loss, the defeat of the Armada permanently broke Spain's economic lead in the European race for expansion. See Paris, *End of Days*, 259.

phrase "School of Night" was seized on by Shakespeare, however, and immortalized in *Love's Labour's Lost:*

> *O paradox! Black is the badge of hell,*
> *The hue of dungeons and the school of night.*[33]

By the end of the year, the public attack on Dee and Raleigh, combined with the realization that Dee's forecast of a new Spanish invasion had simply been wrong, had once again dashed Dee's reputation. Relegated to the gutter, Dee would again resort to fortune-telling and treasure hunting for funds.

In response to the public attacks, Dee worked yet again to issue a response. Now in the twilight years of his life, he was fighting not only against the slings and arrows of the present, but also to secure his reputation for posterity. The result was his *Compendious Rehearsal,* addressed to the royal court, in which Dee frantically attempts to justify his own life, appealing each of the slanders that had been directed at him during his career, beginning prior to Elizabeth's ascension, showing how he had done no ill, and painstakingly detailing the loyal and patriotic nature of his occult activities, underlining how they had been so supported and encouraged by Elizabeth herself. He also detailed his extreme poverty, and lack of recompense by the government, even asserting that he was soon to mortgage his house for a mere £100 (about £18,000 or $22,000 in 2017) of the £833 he owed his debtors—in addition to the £2,306 he calculated that he had lost due to his stolen equipment and books, lost rent payments, and the expense of his return to England (the £2,306 loss plus £833 debt equaling roughly £555,000 or $696,000 in 2017 values). Dee's household now consisted of himself, his wife, seven children, and eight servants, making seventeen in all, and he was thus desperately in need of remedy to pay his debts, so that he would not be remembered "to the posterity of true students for a warning not to follow my steps."[34]

Such a document, accompanied as it was by a request for funding, would not have been rare for the time, though the lengths to which Dee went to clear his name, both rhetorically and in page count,

A LETTER,

Containing a moſt briefe Diſcourſe Apo-
logeticall, with a plaine Demonſtration, and feruent

Proteſtation, for the lawfull, ſincere, very faithfull and
Chriſtian courſe, of the Philoſophicall ſtudies and exerci-
ſes, of a certaine ſtudious Gentleman: An ancient
Seruaunt to her moſt excellent
Maieſty Royall.

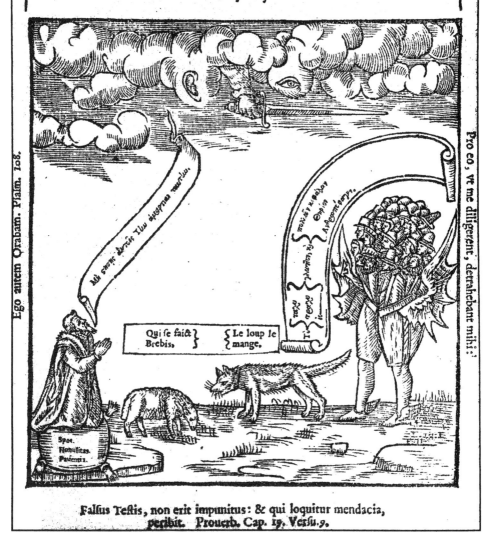

Fig. 14.2. Front page of Dee's *Compendious Rehearsal*, 1592.

were. Dee carefully left out the more scandalous aspects of his career, particularly his Catholic connections and work for foreign courts, before proceeding to begging the court for relief in general and the mastership of St. Cross in particular.

Dee planned to convert St. Cross into a school of philosophy, printing house, and alchemical laboratory, creating an international nexus of learning, where occult experiments could be conducted in secret by visiting alchemists and their "mechanical servants."[35] Its location near the glassworks in Sussex would allow Dee easy access to optical instruments, and being coastal yet remote would mean he could entertain international visitors while being removed from city life.[36] Dee's hope for an international alchemical center recalled his petition to Mary for a national occult library, resurrecting a long-held dream and hope of securing his position.

Moved by Dee's plight, Elizabeth secured him £66 (£12,000 or $15,000 in 2017 terms), and worked toward furnishing him with a £200 pension (£35,000 or $44,000 in 2017), as well as granting the hoped-for mastership. However, this plan was also blocked by Whitgift—again on the warpath against Protestants claiming divine inspiration or supernatural gifts, and keenly remembering Dee's failure to accurately predict the plans of the Spanish. With even the royal sovereign herself unable to assist him, Dee must have felt helpless, and was left to fall back on his wits and again try to curry favor with a new round of courtiers by impressing them with his occult knowledge.

By 1593, the court was fighting a war against Catholic dissidents on one front, and Presbyterian terrorists on the other. Dee returned to alchemy to repair his finances, with some success and fresh interest at court, and resumed angelic sessions with the aid of his pre-Kelly scryer Bartholomew Hickman. Payments from a student for lessons in alchemy allowed him to repair his living situation to some degree. The alchemist Thomas Webb, who had been unsuccessfully dispatched to retrieve Kelly from Prague, also participated in Dee's alchemical circle at Mortlake—yet when Webb was caught alchemically forging coins, Mortlake was raided and Webb's possessions seized. Given a death sentence, Webb sent for Dee, which the magus unwisely heeded, visiting him in prison (potentially to silence him), linking Dee with the scandal in the public eye. Webb, it was revealed, had been working for Cecil, and so rather than execution he was exiled to the Netherlands, with Dee escaping criminal investigation.[37]

Again blocked by Whitgift from demonstrating his progress in the occult sciences to Elizabeth at court, on June 3, 1593, Dee brought himself, Jane, and their seven children to the queen at Thistleworth, in order to show Elizabeth the depths of poverty and despair to which they had fallen. Elizabeth and Whitgift coldly refused any aid whatsoever. A few days later, Dee and his son Michael contracted a virus; a month later, on Dee's sixty-seventh birthday, Michael died. With no funds forthcoming, he was forced to let Hickman go, and even wrote to Kelly, hat in hand, complaining of a lack of firewood for the winter ahead.[38]

By the end of 1594, however, Dee had again been nominated for an official position—this time as chancellor of St. Paul's in London. Elizabeth secured the nomination, and furnished Dee with £40 (about £7,000 or $8,800 in 2017) for Christmas celebrations, but Dee was outmaneuvered, and again lost his chance at the position. At his wit's end with Whitgift's relentless attacks, Dee penned the archbishop a letter upholding the virtue and legality of his work, which he also published, reiterating that he was a selfless servant of God and an orthodox Christian, working solely in the light of and toward the Second Coming of Christ.

To rid himself of Dee for good, Whitgift granted the magus's wish for an official position—choosing Manchester Collegiate Church, a physically disintegrating, nonconformist Protestant school known for its financial and bureaucratic corruption. Dee accepted the position, upon which he had his portrait painted—the iconic image of the wizard, dressed in formal scholar's wear, now rests in the Ashmolean Museum in Oxford. Manchester, then a textile hub boasting a population of only two thousand, was considered a convenient place of exile for the troublesome conjuror, where Dee would be kept far away from any real ability to influence politics or the young. Dee, however, was able to keep close contact with London and regularly return to Mortlake. Dee was installed on February 15, 1596,[39] and would remain in Manchester until plague struck the city in 1605.[40]

Dee would be accompanied to Manchester by his wife, their

children (Jane was soon to give birth to an eighth child—a daughter, Margaret), nine servants, his alchemical apprentice Francis Nichols, and, once more, the scryer Bartholomew Hickman. On August 14, just following his appointment and the birth of his daughter, Dee received a letter from Kelly asking him to return to Prague to serve Rudolf II, which must have been met by Dee with great distaste and pain.[41]

In the years to come, disputes over land use and poor harvests would mean that the college, and Dee's family, were often at a loss for food. During his tenure, the college would be embroiled in legal problems and would continue to fall apart. Dee's attempts to resuscitate the college's finances were unsuccessful and led to more legal entanglement. In addition, the spiritual environment of the college was far from welcoming to Dee, as Whitgift would have anticipated. So nonconformist were the Protestants of Manchester (refusing even the Anglican Church) that they spurned the sign of the cross—scandalous to Dee, who relied on its use as a magical formula of primary importance, presaging the Golden Dawn's later "Qabalistic Cross" ritual. In such an anarchic atmosphere, even the Hermetic Dee, who relied on traditional Latin prayer and Catholic formulae, would have appeared a stodgy and reactionary Papist to worshippers who had come to favor ad hoc prayer in English.[42]

Kelly had by this time been twice imprisoned by the emperor he had worked so hard to cozy up to. While confined, Kelly was forced to turn his mind to alchemy exclusively, and composed a short tract called "The Stone of the Philosophers," addressed to Rudolf, in which he sought to lay out the core truths of the royal art. The tract was written to flatter Rudolf, in the hope that he would show reciprocal favor to the imprisoned Kelly—Kelly cynically notes, however, that its truths will likely be discarded, for it is ever "the way of mankind to release Barabbas and to crucify Christ."[43] In the tract, Kelly reveals the secrets of operative alchemy, and explains the divisions of nature into categories (perhaps following Agrippa), particularly the four elements—fire, air, water, and earth—stating that the quintessence of these elements is *chaos,* following prior alchemists like Llull, Heinrich Khunrath, and Simon Forman. Much of the tract is probably drawn from the alchemical work that Dee and Kelly conducted together in the final period of their friendship—

enough that Dee himself felt it had partially infringed his rights.[44]

The standard account—later related by Elias Ashmole in his *Theatrum chemicum britannicum,* though Ashmole states it is apocryphal and impossible to corroborate—is that Kelly had attempted to escape Rudolf's clutches by tying sheets together and escaping through a window, but had fallen, critically injured himself and died in October. Dee's diary notes that he heard that Kelly had been slain on November 25, 1595.[45] Yet rumors circulated of Kelly being seen in Europe in 1597 and 1598. The circumstances of his death remain a mystery.

Dee, meanwhile, continued his spirit actions, employing Hickman and Nichols as scryers. The records of these sessions were lost when the two scryers fought, with Nichols accusing Hickman of fraudulence because predictions he had made of a cosmic event set to occur in 1600 did not come to pass. Incensed by what he saw as Hickman's malfeasance, he pushed Dee to burn the records of the actions they had undertaken together, which Dee did, tragically erasing his late period from magical history.[46] As Hickman worked scrying with Dee intermittently between 1591 and 1607, this may make *Hickman* Dee's most important scryer, not Kelly. Unfortunately, since Dee burned the records of his work with Hickman, this means that we are left only with the fragments of Dee's work with Kelly. The angels had promised Dee in 1591 that a revelation or reward of supreme importance awaited him within nine years—when it failed to manifest, he burned the records of his work with Hickman,[47] perhaps concluding that Hickman had relayed false messages or even that they had contacted illuders. Dee must not have decided that Hickman had defrauded him, however, because he would again work with the scryer at the end of his life.

Dee also became embroiled in a consultation over the assumed demonic possession of the "Lancashire Seven," beginning in early 1596 when a woman named Margaret Byrom was reportedly put under demonic possession by a spirit conjuror and cunning man named Hartley. By November, two of the sons of Nicholas Starkie of Cleworth had displayed convulsive symptoms that £200 worth of attempted cures (£28,000 or $36,000 in 2017) had been unable to fix. Following these failures, Starkie looked for a village cunning man for help—and, unfortunately, found Hartley, who was able to provide only short-term relief, and was soon suspected of cursing three other children, a maid, and a family relative. Dee was consulted, but refused to intervene magically outside of reprimanding Hartley, and allegedly recommended an infamous Presbyterian minister and exorcist named John Darrell. Darrell successfully exorcised the possessed family members and maid on March 16, 1597.[48]

Dee's connection with the demonic fiasco enraged Whitgift and convinced him to yet again redouble his efforts in suppressing the wizard; Whitgift blocked Dee's hoped-for reassignment to Upton-upon-Severn, leaving him out to pasture in Manchester.[49] Unable to extricate himself from the scandal, Dee published his previous letter to Whitgift claiming his strict Christian orthodoxy, which was ill received; the writer John Chamberlain referred to it as the "ridiculous babble of an old imposturing juggler."*[50] Hartley was later executed, freeing Margaret Byrom from possession, beyond a disturbing incident in which a spirit possessed her while she was in morning prayer at church, "tooke away the vse of her leggs; and thus it molested her in the church to the admiration [wonder] of the people, about an hower and a halfe."[51]

Whitgift had found himself in the position of trying to slam society's doors shut on the chaos that had been unleashed by the Reformation.

---

*Chamberlain's comment recalls the Fool card in the tarot, known in Dee's time as the Juggler, which in the nineteenth century Eliphas Levi would come to hang on the Tree of Life at the path of Aleph, the final stop before immersion in Kether or Godhead, the ultimate goal of the magician. In the Rosicrucian and Masonic magical orders to come, Kether would antecede the spiritual grades Dee had passed in the spirit actions—Binah, Understanding, and Chokmah, Wisdom. In its impure or qliphotic aspect, Amprodias, the Fool is associated with the fall of great magicians that comes when, after seeing through the intangible nature of reality, they cannot help but become practical jokesters, inevitably bringing discredit to their own work when the unenlightened become confused and enraged by their senile games. Such are "the bubbles blown by the Fool of the Tarot in his mad career on the edge of the pit" (Grant, *Nightside of Eden,* 160). The Eastern equivalent is the wandering, incompetent, or drunk madman who is soon revealed as a master by a student-to-be. Shakespeare's *King Lear* makes a fascinating study of this subject—with Lear representing Kether, his fool as the path of Aleph, Kent as the path of Bet, his daughters as the paths of Gimel and Daleth, and Edgar/Tom O'Bedlam as Coronzom in Da'ath. Coronzom itself quotes Tom O'Bedlam in Crowley's vision of the tenth Aethyr.

As opposed to the traditional structure of Catholicism and its Anglican analogue, England was now having to bear the onslaught of millenarian and evangelical Protestant cults claiming direct spiritual revelation, and Dee's work could be seen as a part of that flood to the uninitiated eye. Yet what were cults in Dee's time would soon build the America that Dee prepared the way for, bringing an eschatology with them that was not far removed from Dee's, even if less sophisticated (as discussed in the introduction).

The new idea that anybody could (and must) forge their own spiritual relationship with Christ, outside the bonds of the Church, would steadily progress toward our postmodern, hyperindividualist culture, where not only is each individual sovereign over their own life, but even God has been discarded, leaving the individual as little more than a consumer of models of self that are marketed to them by transnational corporations, or that emerge from social media—where, as Crowley put it, "Every man and woman is a star." This is the fruit of the West's push toward ever-greater individualism and egalitarianism begun by Luther's Reformation and accelerated by the French Revolution.*

Darrell was soon brought up to trial in London and sentenced to prison; he was released within two years. Meanwhile, so vicious had Whitgift and Bancroft's public response to Dee's letter been that even Darrell was trying to distance himself from the Doctor, though he was soon forced to admit involvement with Dee. Dee's remaining years at Manchester Collegiate Church would be marked by constant scandal and organized investigation into the "conjuror's" doings, with Whitgift looking to draw connections between magic and Presbyterian revolt.[52] Dee, now advancing into his seventies, would be forced to endure these attacks alongside severe and punishing poverty.

England hadn't burned Dee at the stake, but it *had* made an example

---

*For the French traditionalist and Sufi philosopher René Guénon, Protestantism marked a definite step in the decay of the traditional initiatic structures of the West, a revolt against traditionalism that Guénon calls "individualism as applied to religion." Both Protestantism and the modern definition of the individual, he argues, are not new principles but negations of prior forms, loosing mere anarchy into the world. See Guénon, *The Crisis of the Modern World*, 55–68.

of him nonetheless. Instead of facing a martyr's death, Dee had been pushed out of polite society and forced to bear the constant humiliation of dashed hopes. Even his neighbors soon refused to offer him loans.

Under the weight of poverty, stress, and advancing age, Dee was falling apart. Starting in 1597, Dee recorded extreme bouts of grief, and had begun bleeding from his anus. In 1600, he was recorded as having an irregular pulse, which his physicians believed to be a sign of health failure.[53] His son Arthur sought help for his grieving and unwell father from a spiritual healer in 1602.[54]

England was suffering as well. Elizabeth's reign was ending, to be replaced by that of the reactionary James I. Meanwhile, plague swept the country, blamed by many on astrological factors. Yet despite the persecution of witchcraft that would later come to define James's career, the new king chose to employ Dee as his mathematician upon his ascension.

Only a year after James's accession, however, Parliament was hard at work passing the Witchcraft Act of 1604, which Dee believed was drafted with him in mind particularly (though it was more likely created to quash Presbyterianism generally). The bill promised death for any invocation or conjuration of an evil spirit; with the interpretation of evil spirit of course resting with the government. Dee again chose to publicly defend himself in print, not only explaining himself as a pious Christian but also requesting an act barring further slander. He was yet again ignored, and returned to Manchester.[55]

Within a year, another outbreak of disease in the city would take what little Dee, now 77, had left. His wife, Jane, died in March 1605, after twenty-seven years of marriage. This had followed the deaths of their children Michael, Theodore, and Margaret from illness. Dee fled the plague-ridden city, returning to London, where little record remains of his actions until further scrying with Hickman was recorded in 1607, when Dee was eighty, at the house of a "Mrs. Goodman."[56] Once considered one of the most learned men in the world, he was now a man out of time, without patrons, without a family, without Elizabeth, without even Kelly—and still adhering to post-Reformation eschatologies long past their sell-by date. Dee fell on hard times again—there are even indications he may have been charging to see angelic conversations.[57]

While many are quick to point out Dee's ill fortunes as somehow being the "wages of sorcery," this is an oversimplification, ignoring the economics, politics, and epidemiology of the day, as well as the ups and downs of life itself in any time period. Indeed, the narrative that Dee spent his final years in misery has come into dispute, with indications surfacing that Dee not only maintained his earlier social contacts in England but grew his network upon his return, and that despite his many frustrations he attained as elevated a social and professional standing as anyone of his background could have.[58]

Dee inquired with the archangel Raphael about his declining health and nonexistent finances, and was told that he would get better. God would not only help Dee with uncovering the philosopher's stone and Book of St. Dunstan's, but also add years to his life. He was soon to go on a great journey with his friend John Pontois, who the angels promised would offer him aid. According to Raphael, God would not have Dee left among his enemies in Manchester, or in England as a whole—and those enemies even included James I; Raphael warned that the angels had turned James I against Dee after having been told that Dee was an evil sorcerer. The angels would instead have Dee sell off his possessions and return to the Continent, where his troubles would be eased. England had certainly done Dee few favors throughout his life.

"And thou art at thy journey's end amongst such friends beyond the seas as thou knowest," the angels told him. "God shall and will raise thee as faithful friends (as now I have said before) as Joseph had, so shalt thou be favoured with God and Man."[59]

The tone and diction of these sessions, conducted with Hickman instead of Kelly, is radically different from the previous actions. Beyond the change in language that would of course come from using a different individual for scrying, the angels were now purely kind to Dee. Where once they had rebuked him with fire and brimstone, now, at the end of his life, they brought only comfort and loving words, filling him with hope about the journey ahead to the Continent, just as when he was a younger man. Comforting Dee as to his circumstances at the end of his life, Raphael told him that he would "die with fame and memory to the end, that such an one was upon the earth, that God by him had wrought great and wonderful Miracles in his service."[60]

In preparation of this promised expedition, Dee began to sell off his library, and relinquished Mortlake in August 1608. He now turned his attention to a new attempt to win patronage from Rudolf, as well as an attempt to gain a teaching post at a new alchemical university planned in Germany. He also continued looking for buried treasure. Relocating at last from Manchester to London, Dee roomed with John Pontois, now his closest friend and intellectual companion, bringing with him his remaining books (still making up an extensive library), including *Soyga,* and his angelic tools, including the Holy Table and a scrying implement. His last remaining source of support was the London merchants among whom his father had worked.[61]

Though Dee may have died with thoughts of youthful adventures to come filling his mind, those journeys were never made. It was here, in London, that John Dee went at last to greet the angels, on March 26, 1609, at 3 a.m.

Only a year later, Shakespeare would introduce the English public to another imperial wizard, Prospero of *The Tempest,* a carbon copy of Dee, who spoke of the ephemeral legacy of a Magus, who may shift the orbit of the whole world with his words and deeds, but whose life is then scattered upon the winds, lost to all memory, like a Tibetan sand mandala:

> *Our revels now are ended. These our actors,*
> *As I foretold you, were all spirits, and*
> *Are melted into air, into thin air;*
> *And like the baseless fabric of this vision,*
> *The cloud-capped towers, the gorgeous palaces,*
> *The solemn temples, the great globe itself,*
> *Yes, all which it inherit, shall dissolve;*
> *And, like this insubstantial pageant faded,*
> *Leave not a rack behind. We are such stuff*
> *As dreams are made on, and our little life*
> *Is rounded with a sleep.*[62]

MORTLAKE AT THE END OF THE WORLD

Nothing now remains of John Dee's house at Mortlake. What was once the greatest scientific hub of England was demolished to build a textile factory, which was destroyed as well when its own time came. Across the street stands a block of council flats entitled "John Dee House," built over part of the grounds of the original building.

Mortlake itself is a quiet English suburb, with barely any sound audible but that of the Thames lapping the stones of the riverbank; sunshine only occasionally punctures its gray and overcast skies. While standing upon the shore, I imagine the river flowing out from here to the Thames Estuary, emptying into the North Sea where the rushing water from Mortlake meets the Atlantic. These are the oceans that Drake once crossed, circumnavigating South America to land at Nova Albion near San Francisco, where I had stood only months earlier, staring back out at the vast expanse of sea that great men once sacrificed all to master, a distance as foreboding and unknown for them as the black leap of space is for us.

It's easy to imagine Dee decompressing here along the flinty shore after long scrying sessions, processing what had been revealed to him. Exploring close to the house with an old friend, I see a flash of white among the rocks: a seashell, shaped into the form of an angel's wing.

It's the second cosmic wink I've received since arriving in London. The first was even more direct. I'm staying in a penthouse apartment in Tottenham Hale, to the northeast of London, on the far opposite side of the city from Mortlake; while I'm furiously working on deciphering Dee's *Mysteriorum libri quinque,* the high-speed internet goes out in the building, and stays off for most of the week I'm there.

"How close are you to Mortlake?" the British Telecom representative asks on the phone. Absolutely nowhere near it, but apparently that's where the outage is centered. The lack of Wi-Fi ensures that I can do little else but continue my work on Dee's writings, just as so many other life circumstances have ensured during the production of this book.

Near the grounds of Dee's house is an ancient church—St. Mary the Virgin—which stood during Dee's life. Dee is buried in the crypt under the church floors, somewhere near the altar. A stone plaque upon the wall commemorates Dee's final rest: "Near this place lie the remains of John Dee MA, Clerk in Holy Orders, 1527–1609. Astronomer, Geographer, Mathematician, Adviser to Queen Elizabeth I." Dee's family coat of arms stands near the altar, upon which is draped an ancient embroidery of the Virgin Mary with the Christ child in her arms, flanked by two angels.

Overcome by the atmosphere of the church, I kneel at the altar to take prayer. Closing my eyes, I feel myself being pulled down into a deep darkness—not infernal darkness but into an endless mystery; a silent, comforting, inscrutable expanse.

Sitting in the churchyard afterward, among crumbling sixteenth- and seventeenth-century tombstones, I chant the first angelic call, reading it not from a leather-bound grimoire but from a PDF downloaded in an instant to my friend's phone, with the aid of mysterious and invisible forces in the air perhaps far stranger than Dee's angels.

A wave of peace washes over us. I can feel the warmth of the sun on my face and see its light coming through the skin of my closed eyes; hear the breeze moving through the trees overhead that had grown from the fertile ground of the cemetery. The peace that passeth all Understanding.

Here, beneath this church, lies the man whose mind had occupied mine for years. A mind that had once been contained in three pounds of flesh, but yet was big enough to encompass the globe; to see—and actualize—the future of his nation; to hold God and all his angels.

John Dee may be buried at Mortlake, but his body is all around us. It is the world he built. Yes—such a one was upon the earth. What can we do but fall in awe to see, to understand that God by him had wrought great and wonderful Miracles?

Fig. 14.3. Plaque near final resting place of John Dee at St. Mary the Virgin Church, Mortlake, London.

BOOK III

Antichrist

15

The Invisible College

Over the coming centuries, the memory of Dee would fade from official history. Indeed, it would become invisible. And in his invisibility, Dee would become headmaster of a new Invisible College, a secret network of minds connected not so much by direct allegiance but by shared ideals, who may never have met each other in the physical world but who resonated in perfect harmony across continents and across time, working in tandem to drag Europe out of the Church-dominated Dark Ages and into a new aeon of scientific inquiry and religious liberty.

In England, Dee's legacy would be occluded by the Puritanical reign of James I, who became so obsessed with the spectral threat posed by "witches" that he instituted pogroms against anyone accused of sorcery, personally overseeing the torture of women accused of witchcraft. This fundamentalist counterattack against Elizabeth's age of high culture and high magic extended into the propaganda sphere as well. While James himself launched broadsides against witchcraft, Dee as a symbol of the occult would also be parodied in popular culture. Like Christopher Marlowe's earlier *Doctor Faustus,* as performed in the last years of Elizabeth's reign, Ben Jonson's *The Alchemist* (1610) was inspired by Dee's legend, with both plays casting their respective sorcerers as tragic victims of their own ambitions. Even the traditional cartoon image we inherit of the wizard figure, wearing a star-covered pointy cap and robe, and wielding a crystal ball, suggests a survival of caricatures of Dee.

Dee, as in life, had been rejected in death by his homeland. Yet on the Continent, a very different response was being initiated. Dame Francis Yates, in her tremendous *Rosicrucian Enlightenment,* suggests that Dee and Kelly's travels on the Continent throughout the 1580s had far greater resonance beyond simply alienating the authorities—rather, that what was actually accomplished was the seeding of the angels' new Hermetic super-religion in the garden of Rudolf II's tolerant kingdom. Already fascinated with alchemy, magic, and Cabala, Bohemia was ripe for a transmission of advanced knowledge from Dee. Dee and Kelly's ideas could thus have filtered out from their immediate circle of contacts and colleagues into the wider culture, particularly through Edward Dyer, Vilém Rožmberk, and the German alchemist Heinrich Khunrath, who reproduced Dee's Monad in his *Amphitheatre of Eternal Wisdom.* Yates even goes so far as to suggest that Dee may have acted as the leader of a proto-Rosicrucian movement while in Bohemia, using Kelly's fantastic alchemical claims to gather a following. Resonating with Dee's influence, of course, would be the deep Kabbalistic knowledge of Prague's large and flourishing Jewish population—the Kabbalah underlying Dee's studies in the first place.[1]

After circulating, fermenting, and mutating on the Continent for almost three decades, Dee's ideas emerged in a new, crystallized form: as two "Rosicrucian" manifestos that were circulated in Germany in 1614 and 1615—the *Fama fraternitatis* and *Confessio fraternitatis*—thought to be the work of the German Protestant theologian and utopian Johannes Valentinus Andreae. These epochal manifestos assured their readers that an Invisible College or brotherhood of "Rosicrucian" adepts, possessed of advanced knowledge of alchemy and natural philosophy, existed in secret throughout Europe. The only way to contact this secret order, however, would be to publish work praising them and their achievements. Europe was soon flooded by hastily printed petitions and even full-length original works by Rosicrucian hopefuls and idealists, including many who went on to become stars in their own orbits, like the alchemist Robert Fludd. Such works received no answer,

Fig. 15.1. The Invisible College. From Theophilus Schweighardt,
The Speculum Sophicum Rhodostauroticum, 1604.

of course, but instead acted to *create* the Rosicrucians out of nothing but a suggestive myth. Those who took such actions soon made contact with each other, leading to the *actual* establishment of networks of alchemists and natural philosophers—transforming the myth into reality. Those who sought the Rosicrucians, by their own efforts, essentially *became* the Rosicrucians, gaining entry by the sweat of their brow to that Invisible College,[2] a house not made with hands, eternal in the heavens—a fraternity that existed in the world of ideas, and as such was immortal, re-creating itself across the centuries in the minds and lives of those inspired by its ideals. And if this Invisible College existed in this spiritual sense, then might it also be staffed by Dee and Kelly's spiritual Schoolmasters?

This secret society had supposedly been founded by the mythical Christian Rosenkreutz, who had traveled throughout the world seeking for knowledge in vain before finding inner illumination and proceeding to found an elite order of magicians or "Invisibles" who would maintain anonymity in the culture at all times, blending in with their surroundings and proclaiming nothing but the ability to heal the sick, and who possessed the keys of advanced knowledge.* Indeed, not only would the order tear down the Antichrist pope, it would also bring an end to the world, returning it thereby to the perfected state of Adam in the garden.[3] Sound familiar?

The Rosicrucians would also act as a countermeasure to the Jesuits—a Protestant, Hermetic magical society designed to push back against Rome's Holy Orders and liberate the true spirit of Christ from that of the Antichrist, as personified by the Jesuits and the Habsburgs. Indeed, the Jesuits and Rosicrucians were more alike than different—the elite adepts and shock troops of Catholicism and Protestantism, respectively, locked in a magical war for the soul of Christendom and the world.[4]

Though direct evidence of Dee's ideas generating Rosicrucianism is lacking, his signature is all over much of the Rosicrucian literature,

---

*The twentieth-century occult author Paul Foster Case suggested that Brother R.C.'s travels are a metaphor for the internal processes of kundalini awakening. See Case, *The True and Invisible Rosicrucian Order*. R.C. enumerates to 220 in Hebrew gematria, the same as the number of verses in Crowley's *The Book of the Law*.

Fig. 15.2. Title page of Robert Fludd, *Summum Bonum*, 1629,
depicting rose cross motif and feeding honeybee.

from the Monad symbol itself to the obvious guiding influence of his
thought. We are left to infer the influence of, if not Dee himself, then
the ideas he brought with him to Bohemia. The first edition of the
Confessio fraternitatis was published alongside a second manuscript,
with which it was meant to be studied in tandem—the *Consideratio
brevis* by Philip à Gabella, which was itself derived from Dee's *Monas
hieroglyphica.*[5] A third Rosicrucian manuscript, *The Chemical Wedding
of Christian Rosenkreutz,* was published in 1616—it even opens with a
man praying at a table (perhaps one like Dee's Holy Table) whose meditation is interrupted by a female angel bearing a trumpet, "spangled
like the heavens with golden stars."[6] To openly confirm the connection,
the *Chemical Wedding* bore an image of Dee's Monad in its margins.
Indeed, the *Monas,* which spoke of "ros" or dew and elaborated at
length on the meaning of the Monad's central cross, may have been one
of the origins of Rosicrucianism and the "Rose Cross" itself.[7] (Another
was Martin Luther's personal seal.)

Fig. 15.3. Martin Luther's
personal seal, 1530.

The Rosicrucian manifestos hit Europe with monumental force, felt far beyond intellectual circles. Concurrent with their release was a push by the Calvinist German prince, Christian of Anhalt—friends with the brother of Rožmberk, who had long acted as a patron to Dee and Kelly in Třeboň[8]—to prop up the mystically inclined Frederick V, Elector Palatine, as king of Bohemia. A marriage with James I's daughter Elizabeth Stuart solidified an alliance with England and positioned Frederick as a chief defender of the Protestant cause against the gathering Habsburg states; this "chymical wedding" was seen by many as beginning a new and tolerant Hermetic golden age.[9] Even the Lutheran alchemist and critic Andreas Libavius thought that—much like the earlier plan to turn Elizabeth I into a Protestant world sovereign—Anhalt plotted to use Frederick to overthrow Rome and institute a new world order based on magic. Central to this cultural and political exchange may have been Rudolf II's physician and imperial counselor Michael Maier, whose ethereal book of alchemical emblems *Atalanta fugiens,* like the *Monas* (and Aleister Crowley's 1918 Amalantrah Working), uses an egg as a central symbol; Meier died at the very outbreak of the Thirty Years' War.[10]

Though Andreae may have believed the manifestos to be an elaborate prank, this hardly prevented them from impacting history. By proposing a new Hermetic science that would supersede the old Aristotelian scholasticism, and puckishly goading his readers into taking public actions on behalf of the Rosicrucian Brotherhood, Andreae, we might say in more recent parlance, memed the Rosicrucians into existence—and thereby, modern science, which the countries that had tolerated Rosicrucianism soon tolerated in turn. Yet though the manifestos fabricated an elaborate mythology around secret knowledge, the secret knowledge was indeed real: it was Dee's *Monas.* The manifestos soon became a guiding force on Frederick V's Bohemia, a Rosicrucian high society that built on Rudolf II's age of high culture toward a new era of universal tolerance and enlightenment—an entire Rosicrucian civilization based on Dee's ideals.[11]

Parallel to, and perhaps intertwining with, the influence of Dee on the Rosicrucians was that of Francis Bacon. A titan in the history of European thought, it was Bacon who broke the millennia-long hold of Aristotelianism, characterized as it was by mental gymnastics and assumptions not based on experiment and direct observation, and asserted the empiricism that would become science. Following Bacon, Michael Maier spoke of the Rosicrucians as an order concerned with direct empirical experiment into the nature of reality. Bacon's method itself was also in the vein of (albeit a light-speed jump from) the experiments of Agrippa and the alchemists. Bacon's 1605 *Advancement of Learning,* which appeared before the manifestos, had argued for a transnational brotherhood of scientists and, just as Dee might have, spoke of learning as "illumination." Like Dee and the Hermeticists from whom he drew intellectual lineage, Bacon spoke not of forward-looking science but of recovering humanity's pre-Fall knowledge; at the same time, Bacon fundamentally rejected two of Hermeticism's core tenets—that the microcosm of man was a model in miniature of the universal macrocosm, and that secrecy was necessary to work.[12] Bacon threw out Hermeticism's clandestine attitude, encoded symbolism, and reliance on twilight language, arguing instead for open and clear information exchange; in doing so, he greatly accelerated the intellectual development of Europe. 1620's *Novum organum* went further, rejecting most of Western civilization's assumed truths as "idols," doing for the intellect what Luther had done for the spirit;

Fig. 15.4. Francis Bacon, Viscount St. Albans. Line engraving by Jacobus Houbraken, 1738. Courtesy of Wellcome Images.

Fig. 15.5. Title page of Francis Bacon, *Great Instauration*, 1620. The image depicts a ship sailing through two columns (similar to the two pillars featured prominently in Freemasonry to represent the pillars of Solomon's Temple, later seen in the High Priestess card of the tarot, symbolizing the passage across the Abyss). In this image, the pillars represent the prior limits of humanist knowledge based on Latin and Greek scholarship; the ship is sailing past them into the open sea of infinite knowledge to be gained by empirical science.

in their place, Bacon put the fundamentals of the scientific method.*

Bacon nowhere mentions Dee in his two works, though he surely stood on the great educator's shoulders. He also makes no mention of mathematics, still inseparably connected to Dee in the English mind. These omissions, Yates argues, were not from oversight or lack of debt, but because Bacon feared repeating Dee's treatment by James I.[13]

This new Rosicrucian culture built up around Frederick, drawn together from the ideas of Dee, Bacon, Giordano Bruno, and the poetry of Philip Sidney, incorporating English chivalry and German mysticism, and characterized by Dee's new Hermetic religion of unity, love, and intellectual tolerance, flourished in Bohemia as one of many attempts to ground the ideals of the adepts into a functioning society. Such a blooming of high Protestant culture was also an effort to strengthen ties with

---

*Manly P. Hall went so far as to suggest that Bacon was the true author of the Rosicrucian manifestos. See Hall, *The Secret Teachings of All Ages*, 461.

England as the outbreak of war with the Catholic powers approached. The emphasis on tolerance and unity of religion—which we can find in the earlier ideals of Postel, Dee, and, in more severe form, in the millennial commands of the angels themselves—would, for an all-too-brief flickering of time, form a pansophic and halcyon age. Within this lost golden age we may detect the seeds of the Freemasonic lodges that offered tolerance to all men provided they were not atheists—and, henceforth, the ideals that made the American and French revolutions. This "third Reformation" would go further than the Reformation or Counter-Reformation, and lay the groundwork for a new Rosicrucian society.[14]

In the short term, however, the new flourishing of gnosis would be crushed by the Church. Just as the papal nuncio and Pucci had moved to neutralize Dee and Kelly, the Jesuits worked to co-opt the new Rosicrucianism and rebrand it in their own image. Finally, Bohemia's 1620 defeat at the Battle of White Mountain (thanks, many believed, to James I withdrawing support for Frederick) put Bohemia back under Catholic control and sank it into a new dark age for centuries to come.[15]

This defeat left a sour taste in the mouths of those who had raised their hopes for a new age. Rosicrucianism fell out of favor in Germany, and shortly thereafter was the subject of a witch-hunting craze in France, in which, encouraged by the Jesuits, French citizens were whipped into a frenzy of terror and were led to see Satanic, conspiring Rosicrucian sorcerers around every corner and behind every misfortune. Following the Bohemian defeat, the Habsburg countries and Counter-Reformation resolidified Catholic power over Europe, with Protestantism itself left near extinction, not to mention its Rosicrucian vanguard;[16] this dire situation would be reversed yet again by Gustavus Adolphus, king of Sweden, in the opening years of the 1630s.

The legend of the Rosicrucians, however, would not go away. In 1627, a year after Bacon's death, his *New Atlantis* was published, a remarkable fantasy of a Christian utopia of illuminated men, highly resonant with Dee's *General and Rare Memorials* and full of references to the Rosicrucian manifestos. This New Atlantis was to be governed by Rosicrucians gathered at "Salomon's House," a new sobriquet for the Invisible College. The mythological push for colonization that Dee had initiated was now furthered by Bacon; here we have a guiding myth for the formation of America as a Rosicrucian utopia, guided by illuminated men—a transposition of the ideals of Frederick V's Bohemia to the New World, where an enlightened society might thrive, free from the stultifying grasp of Rome (in the novel, the New Atlantis is built on the mythical island of Bensalem, west of Peru). Eight years prior, Andreae himself had published a tract entitled the *Reipublicae Christianopolitanae descriptio,* which dismissed the Rosicrucians (which Andreae himself had probably publicized or created) as a joke, but also argued that their ideals should live on in the establishment of a utopian Christian island, free from the grasp of the Antichrist Rome. This utopia would be ruled by science, Cabala, sacred geometry, and angels, with city officials even named after archangels like Uriel and Gabriel, and the city itself planned along almost Freemasonic lines of square and circle, microcosm and macrocosm, and Cabalistic numerology. Both Dee and Bacon, Yates argues, were clear influences on this plan.[17] (Indeed, the twentieth-century occultist Manly P. Hall was certain that the Rosicrucian effort to liberate Europe, and Bacon's utopian dream of a New Atlantis, found their full expression in America, that the Rosicrucians guided the American and French revolutions, and that they even designed the Great Seal of the United States to leave their calling card. The Eye of Providence or infamous "Illuminati eye" that appears in this seal, like the Rose Cross, is also a Lutheran symbol.)[18]

Clearly, destroying the Rosicrucians was harder than the Jesuits and Habsburgs had expected. In addition, they had neglected to consider that ideas are immortal, and invisible brotherhoods cannot be silenced with gunpowder. Over the coming decades and centuries, Europe's young geniuses would again and again encounter the immortal legend of the Rosicrucians—among those who entertained the idea of contacting the "Invisibles," as they were known, were René Descartes, Gottfried Wilhelm Leibniz, Johannes Kepler, and Isaac Newton, all central to the birth of rational science.[19] Here Rosicrucianism comes into focus as a bridge from the scintillating yet fanciful assumptions and ideals of Hermeticism, Renaissance Neoplatonism, and operative magic to the functional corpus of modern science—this, at least, is the Yates thesis.

The Rosicrucian manifestos were a bluff and dare to humanity; science was humanity's response when given such a lofty ideal to strive for. *This is magic*—reality out of fiction, something out of nothing, a rabbit out of a hat.

Through the 1640s, Rosicrucianism, Baconism, the memory of Frederick V's utopia, and the guiding ideal of the New Atlantis were coming together and finding new life in England—along with a resurgence of interest in Dee's mathematics. By 1647, these parallel streams were to unify into a new front: the Royal Society, the English institution dedicated to the advancement of science, upon whose axis England turned at last from Aristotelianism and humanism toward modern empirical science and medicine—making visible the old ideal of the Invisible College or Saloman's House. Prior to its incorporation, the Royal Society had been an informal discussion group referred to by the chemist Robert Boyle, its central figure, as "our invisible college."[20] Indeed, if Dee had been alive to see the foundation of the Society, he would have rejoiced at the realization of his long-held dream of an English scientific academy.

Five years later, in 1652, the Rosicrucian manifestos themselves were published in English by the Welsh alchemist Thomas Vaughan under the name Eugenius Philalethes—financed, perhaps, by Sir Robert Moray, later of the Royal Society.* Yet if it was John Dee who had so long suffered in obscurity to lay the groundwork for what became the Royal Society—by tirelessly working to establish England as a center of scientific learning, educating its next generation, petitioning for a British library and scientific center, modeling such a center at Mortlake, and, ultimately, by inspiring the Rosicrucian myths that became the guiding ideals of the men who founded the Society—why was he given no place of honor (or even mentioned) by its founders, who so clearly owed him a debt as their forefather?

The answer, Yates suggests, is the same as Bacon's failure to mention John Dee: they were carefully avoiding any association with Dee or his mathematics because they wanted to draw a firm line between

---

*The Philalethes Society, founded in 1928, is currently the oldest and most preeminent Masonic research body in America.

the science they pursued and anything tainted by the occult, despite the private interests of many of the Royal Society's members; upon this issue not only their organization but also their own lives hinged. Hence, Dee's exclusion from history by the fathers of science may have had more to do with politics than their real affections—even by 1660, Elias Ashmole's open interest in alchemy did not slow his induction into the group; nor did alchemical interests hinder the progress of Isaac Newton, who would have been aware of Dee and Kelly through Ashmole, and whose quest for divine laws and mankind's pre-Fall knowledge varied from Dee's only in method and result, not ideals. This was a particularly wise move as sections of Dee's spirit diaries were about to be published, initiating another panic over black magic (though the Royal Society mathematician Robert Hooke would later defend the spirit diaries as clever cryptography).[21]

At the behest of the angels, Dee had passed ownership of his library and his magical tools to his trusted friend John Pontois—rather than his son Arthur, who departed England for Russia to serve as a physician to the tsar after his father passed.[22] Upon Pontois's own death in 1624, what had remained in his care was sold; the Holy Table and Dee's later spirit diaries were purchased by Sir Robert Cotton at the estate sale.[23]

These were published by Méric Casaubon in 1659, potentially as a favor to Cotton,[24] as *A True & Faithful Relation of what passed for Many Yeers between Dr. John Dee . . . and some spirits . . . .* Casaubon was a classical scholar who had been favored by James I in his youth, and who in middle age had worked tirelessly to discredit the supernatural as a threat to good Anglicans (and with it, the more fervent claims of Protestant heretics to direct contact with God). As such, he presented Dee's diaries as an example of what happens when even a great man is led astray by the devil.

For Casaubon, there was no question as to whether the sessions were real, nor any suggestion that Kelly had defrauded Dee. Instead, they were all *too* real, the work of evil spirits. Yet Casaubon could otherwise say little to tarnish Dee's memory—for him, Dee was a man of true faith, who nevertheless had fallen to the snares of the adversary, and who now stood as a warning to others.

It is thanks to Casaubon, however, that Dee's memory and, crucially, his actual records of work with the angels, comprising the reception of *Liber Loagaeth,* the forty-nine calls, and his political adventures on the Continent, have been preserved, despite the numerous errors in Casaubon's edition. This material would later be worked into *A Treatise on Angel Magic* by the occultist Thomas Rudd (now catalogued in the British Library as Harley 6482), which would go on to inspire future magicians (like Frederick Hockley) to reattempt Dee's experiments—despite the fact that Rudd replicated Casaubon's printing errors.[25]

The remaining documents—*Mysteriorum Libri I–V,* the *Forty-eight claves angelica, Liber scientiae, Auxilii & victoriae terrestris, The Heptarchia Mystica,* and *A Book of Invocations or Calls*—appear to have been previously removed from Pontois's study by the surgeon John Woodall, who was entrusted with the care of Pontois's effects while the alchemist adventured in Virginia. From Woodall, these diaries made their way into the possession of a "Mr. Jones," a London confectioner—contained in a secret drawer in the bottom of a chest. Jones's maid, infamously, discovered the diaries and began using their pages as kindling for the fireplace until she was stopped by Jones; up to seven of the total twenty-eight spirit diaries may have been destroyed by the maid. The chest itself was lost in the Great Fire of 1666.[26] Finally Jones, seeing possible value in the diaries, sold them to the antiquarian collector Elias Ashmole in 1672.

Ashmole himself is a crucial figure within the development of Western esotericism; a founding Fellow of the Royal Society, Ashmole was also an enthusiast of antiquarian books, astrology, and alchemy, interests he developed in the military while supporting Charles I in the English Civil War. Following the surrender of Worcester, a calculated marriage to a rich widow left him with enough funds to pursue his interests full time. A prodigious collection of antiquarian books and ephemera resulted, which now comprises the Ashmolean Museum in Oxford. Ashmole's collection is responsible for the preservation of much that otherwise would have been lost, including Dee's diaries.[27] Indeed, Yates argued that Ashmole's 1652 *Theatrum chemicum britannicum,* a treasure trove of alchemical texts, including passages by Dee and Kelly, may have been an attempt by Ashmole to preserve the memory and fruits of Frederick's Rosicrucian utopia in a textual ark.[28]

On October 16, 1646, Ashmole was initiated as a Freemason at Warrington, while he was a prisoner of war—his diary entry of this event is one of the first known references to Masonry in England.[29] Importantly, it marks the transition of Masonry from operative—that is, a fellowship of actual working stonemasons—to speculative, or a symbolic association of society gentlemen.[30] In the same year, Ashmole met William Lilly, an astrologer with a keen interest in angel magic, which Ashmole eagerly sought to learn. Another contact may have been the angelic conjuror William Hodges, and in 1652 Ashmole records that he met a Mr. Thompson, who had successfully called up angels.[31] As Ashmole amassed his collection, deep study of alchemy soon occupied him as well. Inspired by the Rosicrucian legend, Ashmole petitioned the Invisible College in the classical manner, writing a request for entry as a private prayer.[32]

After acquiring Dee's diaries in 1672, Ashmole became freshly obsessed, copying their contents by hand and translating them over the next two years. He simultaneously began practical work with the angelic system, which persisted until at least 1676; Ashmole indeed recorded some success in making things "go bump in the night."[33] From there, the manuscripts passed into the collection of Hans Sloane and then into the safe hands of the British Library, where they now make up part of the Sloane collection.[34]

Through Ashmole, we can form a tentative link between Dee and Freemasonry. According to the Masonic scholar Arturo de Hoyos, Ashmole and his cohort (possibly including the aforementioned angelic magicians) may already have formed their own occult society by the time Ashmole joined the fraternity in 1646. The goal of this society was the literal reconstruction of Bacon's "the House of Solomon on the Island of Bensalem" from the *New Atlantis*—that is, the literal realization of the Invisible College in the New World.[35]

If Ashmole did indeed bring such a secret society with him *into* the preexisting body of Masonry, in order to use Masonry as cover, one can speculate that this could have helped catalyze the creation of modern

Fig. 15.6. Elias Ashmole. Line engraving by M. van der Gucht, 1723, after W. Faithorne.
Courtesy of Wellcome Images.

Freemasonry in all of its exoteric and esoteric forms *out of* the body of operative Masonry. It is also possible, though not proven, that Ashmole himself created the Blue Lodge degrees of Craft Masonry—Entered Apprentice, Fellowcraft, and Master Mason—through which all new Masons pass.[36]

Ashmole's acquisition of the Dee material came twenty-six years after his initiation into Masonry, but he was still an (at least sporadically) active Mason during this time—Ashmole is on record attending a Lodge meeting in 1682, ten years after he came into possession of the Dee material and six years after the end of his own scrying experiments.[37] This would have given him more than enough time to digest and absorb the angelic system and its geopolitical ramifications before passing it on to others.

If Dee *did* inspire the Rosicrucian movement, as Dame Yates suggests, then this would be another vector by which his work in turn influenced Freemasonry, as Rosicrucian motifs were soon integrated into higher-grade Masonic rites. The influence of Masonry in combating the influence of Rome and assisting in the genesis of the French and American revolutions—and therefore further establishing a Protestant, Enlightenment-age, scientific power base in Europe and the New World— is well documented.[38] It is hard not to see further chess moves in the angelic plan for a singular world government and religion in these events.

Following Ashmole's death, the Craft degrees of Masonry would soon blossom into higher rites purporting to contain further esoteric information, most importantly Scottish Rite Freemasonry, which was forming out of the English lodge system as early as the 1730s. When the Supreme Council of the Scottish Rite was officially constituted in Charleston, South Carolina, in May 1801, a document circulated among initiates entitled "Dalcho's Register," which contained a copy of the angelic alphabet in the hand of Giles F. Yates, 33° (albeit inaccurately written!). The "Register" also included copies of several other "magical" alphabets, including Hebrew, Greek, Celestial, the alphabet of "Passing the River," and others; these were copied from Francis Barrett's *The Magus,* a popular reworking of Agrippa's *Three Books of Occult Philosophy* published the same year the Scottish Rite was founded.[39]

Plate 1. Henry Gillard Glindoni, *John Dee Performing an Experiment before Elizabeth I*, late nineteenth or early twentieth century. Courtesy of Wellcome Images.

Plate 2. Mortlake, London. View of the Thames from the site of Dee's house, 2016. Image courtesy of the author.

Plate 3. View over Baffin Island or "Meta Incognita," where Martin Frobisher landed in 1576 while searching for the Northwest Passage. Image via NASA/Michael Studinger.

Plate 4. Drake's Bay, near San Francisco, California, where Sir Francis Drake landed in 1579. Image by "Shawnobusa," February 2, 2013.

Plate 5. Map of the British Empire prior to the outbreak of World War II, from *The Christian Science Monitor,* April 22, 1937.

Plate 6. Most likely candidate for the scrying crystal manifested by Uriel and used by Dee and Kelly in the angelic conversations. Courtesy of Wellcome Images.

Plate 7. Dee's original beeswax Sigillum Dei Aemeth, from the British Museum.

Plate 8. The Golden Talisman, from the British Museum. Likely not owned by Dee,
but created by a later magician or collector from the design in Casaubon's *A True & Faithful Relation.*

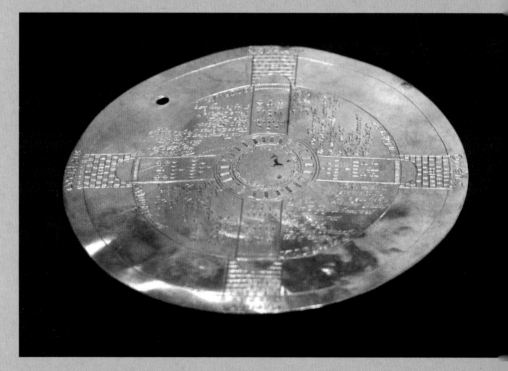

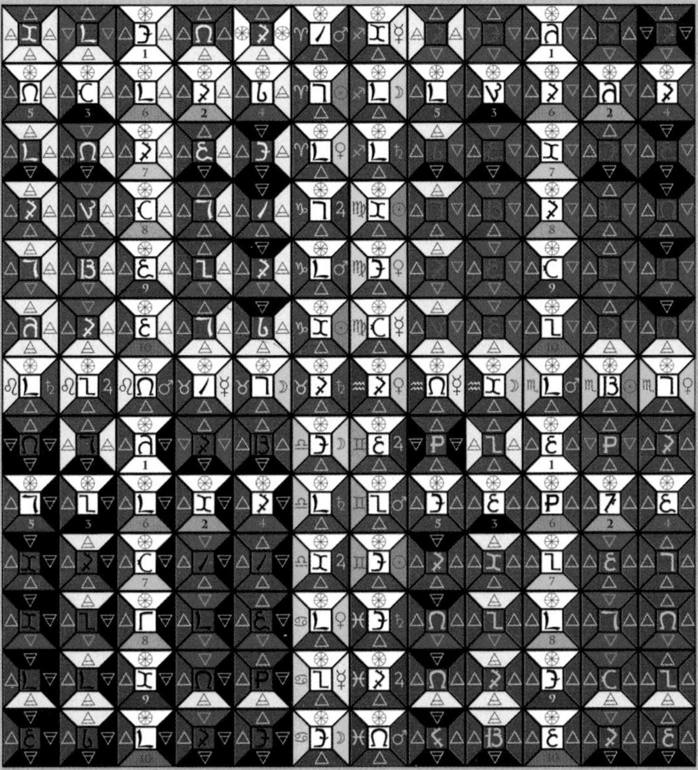

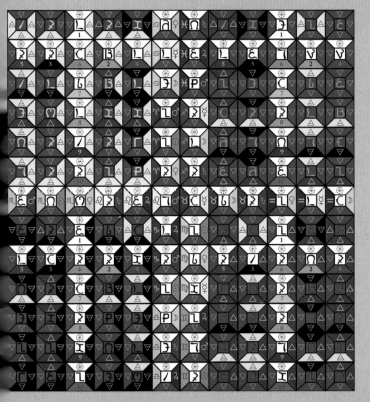

Plate 9.
The Watchtower of Fire,
Golden Dawn version.
Courtesy of the author.

Plate 10.
The Watchtower of Water,
Golden Dawn version.
Courtesy of the author.

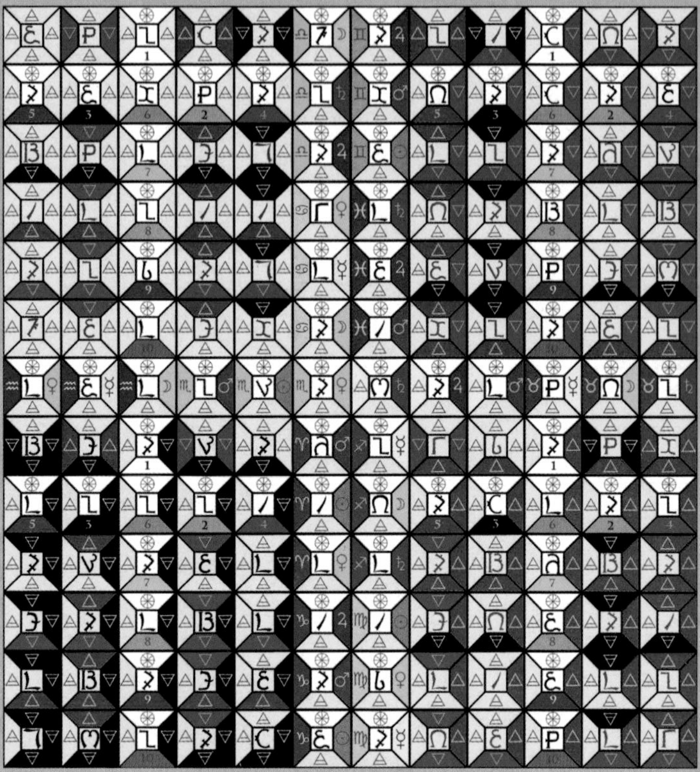

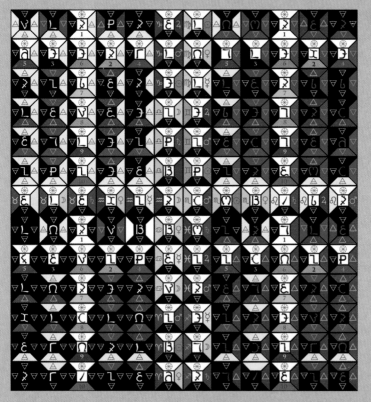

Plate 11.
The Watchtower of Air,
Golden Dawn version.
Courtesy of the author.

Plate 12.
The Watchtower of Earth,
Golden Dawn version.
Courtesy of the author.

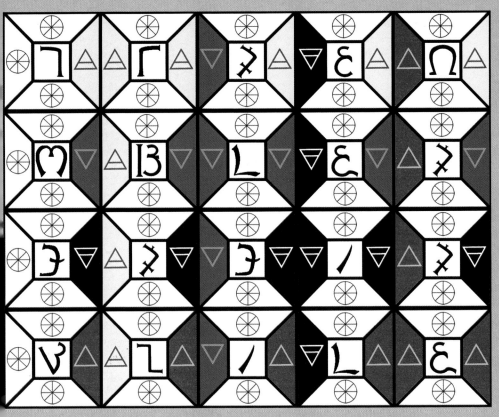

Plate 13. The Tablet of Union, Golden Dawn version. Courtesy of the author.

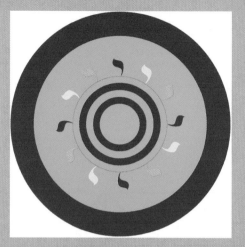

Plate 14. Elemental Sigil of Fire,
Golden Dawn version. Courtesy of the author.

Plate 15. Elemental Sigil of Water,
Golden Dawn version. Courtesy of the author.

Plate 16. Elemental Sigil of Air,
Golden Dawn version. Courtesy of the author.

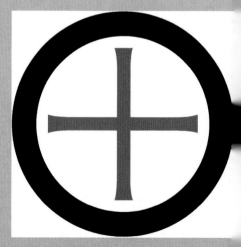

Plate 17. Elemental Sigil of Earth,
Golden Dawn version. Courtesy of the author.

Plate 18. Rudolf II, Holy Roman Emperor. Portrait by Martino Rota, sixteenth century.

Plate 19. Portrait of Rudolf II as Vertumnus, Roman god of the seasons, by Giuseppe Arcimboldo, 1590–91. The portrait (which Rudolf II highly enjoyed) suggests that, like Vertumnus, Rudolf is the ruler of all seasons, and of a new golden age.

Plate 20. Prague Castle and the Malá Strana district, view from the Charles Bridge, 2009. Photo by "Janmad."

Plate 21. William Blake, *The Great Red Dragon and the Beast from the Sea*, 1805.

Plate 22. BABALON. Woodcut by Lucas Cranach, from Martin Luther's 1534 Bible.

Plate 23. English ships and the Spanish Armada. Author unknown, painted some time prior to 1700.

Plate 24. The altar of St. Mary the Virgin Church, Mortlake, London. Dee is buried in the catacombs, likely beneath the right side of the altar. Note angelic motifs. Image courtesy of the author.

Plate 25. The Lamen of the Golden Dawn, showing the LVX and IAO:INRI formulae,
the unification of the three gunas, the five elements (as with the Watchtowers),
and the twenty-two letters of the Hebrew alphabet, around a central rose cross.

Plate 26. Djebel Chélia, Aurès Mountains, on the border of Algeria and Tunisia. Crowley and Neuburg called the fourteenth Aethyr, VTA, here; Crowley had Neuburg sodomize him to break his ego, after which he was received into the City of the Pyramids as a Magister Templi. Photo by Reda Kerbouche, February 2012.

Plate 27. The Stele of Revealing. A funerary tablet by Ankh-af-na-khonsu, a Theban priest of the twenty-sixth dynasty of Egypt. (Aleister Crowley believed himself to be a reincarnation of this priest.) The Stele depicts Nuit, Hadit, Ra-Hoor-Khuit, and Ankh-af-na-khonsu himself; it was supposedly located in a moment of synchronicity by Crowley and Rose Kelly in the Museum of Egyptian Antiquities in Cairo (where it was given exhibit number 666) prior to the reception of the *Book of the Law,* during April 1904.

Plate 28. Leonardo da Vinci, *Salvator Mundi*, c. 1490–1519. Depicting Christ as Savior of the World, this was painted by da Vinci sometime in the two decades before Dee's birth. Lost until 2005, the striking image depicts Christ holding what appears to be a scrying ball—suggesting that da Vinci, too, may have been influenced by Renaissance occultism.

As we shall see shortly, Barrett may also have personally trained Frederick Hockley, the great-grandfather of the Golden Dawn, which itself emerged from Freemasonry.

Three years later, in 1804, the German philosophy professor Johann Buhle put forward the proposal that Freemasonry had arisen from the Rosicrucian movement, via Maier and Fludd; Thomas de Quincey published a translation in English two decades later, adding the argument that Freemasonry was simply an English rebranding of Continental Rosicrucianism.[40] Therefore Freemasonry completed a circuit of English and Continental cultural exchange: what Dee had learned as a student in the Low Countries he distilled into the *Monas,* his other works, and the spirit actions themselves; upon taking these new works to Bohemia, Dee inspired what would become Rosicrucianism; upon returning to England, these Rosicrucian ideas would find their full and most lasting expression as speculative Freemasonry, an institution that has inarguably contributed to shaping history and continues to maintain unbroken tradition into the present.

What is certain is that both of the first recorded Masonic initiations—Ashmole in 1646 and Robert Moray in 1641—were of members of the Royal Society. Even earlier, in 1638, a poem published in Moray's home town of Edinburgh proclaimed, "We be brethren of the Rosie Crosse: We have the Mason word and second sight, Things for to come we can foretell aright. . . . "[41] (Second sight is a well-known phenomena by which certain Scottish families are believed to possess inborn psychic abilities, publicized in Walter Scott's 1817 *Rob Roy*.)[42] References connecting the Masons to the Rosicrucians continued throughout the seventeenth century, including the establishment of Rose Croix degrees in the Scottish Rite.[43] Masonry is itself concerned with the same themes Dee and his forebears were, and is an expression of the truths of the adepts that any man, of any background, provided he is a worthy brother, should be able to enter and vitalize within his own life at a deep level. And far beyond the obscure writings of cloistered Hermeticists, Masonry has formed the backbone of Western civilization for over three centuries.

Rosicrucianism, upon contact with England, thus inspired two distinct expressions of its spirit: Freemasonry and the Royal Society.[44] And Rosicrucianism itself is the grandchild of John Dee, who carried on and crystallized the earlier streams of Hermeticism, Renaissance Neoplatonism, and operative magic, thus forming the critical nexus point for the passage of the entire occult tradition through Europe's history.

Yet Dee is again excised from the official story—probably for the same reason that he went unmentioned by Francis Bacon or the founders of the Royal Society. Like the Society, Freemasonry was already out on a cultural limb, and taking pains to disassociate itself from anything that might end in criminal charges.[45] Sorcery was still too volatile, and it was too much of a social liability to mention Dee in any official capacity, no matter what the new Masons and scientists studied or did behind closed doors. And this is a great shame, for the whole of post-Renaissance culture has in effect forgotten its progenitor.

Yet if Rosicrucianism and Freemasonry were the fruit of Dee's theoretical work—particularly the *Monas hieroglyphica*—what of the angelic magic itself?

Running parallel to the growth of Freemasonry, it is possible, though unproven, that an underground tradition carried on the angelic sessions outside of the strict bounds of Freemasonry, largely cloistered in the upper echelons of society—the occult scholars Stephen Skinner and David Rankine make a compelling though ultimately inconclusive argument for such a tradition in their *Practical Angel Magic of Dr. John Dee's Enochian Tables*. Following Ashmole, Skinner and Rankine record a number of British aristocrats who engaged in angelic magic, through whom they attempt to establish a direct lineage. They are:

1. Baron Somers of Evesham (1651–1716), Lord Chancellor of England and president of the Royal Society from 1699 to 1704, who devoted his retirement to practicing angel magic and owned MS. Sloane 3821, containing working instructions for using the Watchtowers.

2. Sir Joseph Jekyll (1663–1738), who married Baron Somers's

Fig. 15.7. The god Hermes weaving nets of communication and seeding new ideas above London, from Wenceslaus Hollar, *Long View of London from Bankside,* 1647.

second sister and thereby inherited MS. Sloane 3821 and several other occult manuscripts, including ones by Dee, which
he employed in his own attempts at operative magic. Jekyll was
appointed Master of the Rolls, the most senior judge in England
and Wales behind the Lord Chief Justice.

3. Sir Hans Sloane (1660–1753), who purchased Jekyll's manu-
    scripts at auction, and also had a standing interest in angelic
    magic.

4. Goodwin Wharton (1653–1704), Lord Admiral, who, like Dee
    and Kelly, was obsessed with employing magic to locate bur-
    ied treasure, and was taught a method for contacting angels
    by a friend, potentially the son of Ashmole's occult mentor
    William Lilly.[46]

Deborah Harkness also notes the discovery (in the British Library)
of diaries belonging to an active group of angelic magicians who met
between July 24, 1671, and December 18, 1688, who read Casaubon
and attempted contacting Dee's angels through a scrying stone. They
succeeded in calling Madimi and Galvah, though they mostly seemed
interested in fortune-telling and locating treasure, rather than continuing any of Dee's actual philosophical work. The group came to be
convinced that the angels' oblique prophecy of "eighty-eight" marking
the end of the world meant 1688, not 1588, and presumably disbanded
when they were disappointed.[47]

Once the Sloane manuscripts were secured in the British Museum,
they would lie in wait for future scholars and operative magicians.
Among these was Frederick Hockley (1808–1885), a working magician who used Rudd's *Treatise on Angel Magic* to scry over thirty books'
worth of angelic transmissions.[48] Hockley himself may have been a
direct student of Francis Barrett, the author of *The Magus,* who had
been so influential on the early Scottish Rite.[49]

Through Hockley, this material passed to Kenneth Mackenzie and
Reverend W. A. Ayton, both members of the Societas Rosicruciana in
Anglia (SRIA), an esoteric order *within* the already covert society of
high-degree Masonry, linking Freemasonry and Rosicrucianism. The

SRIA instituted (likely continuing from earlier orders) the Qabalah-based ten-degree grade system upon which later esoteric orders were constructed, and it is from the SRIA that the founders of both the Golden Dawn (William Woodman, William Westcott, and MacGregor Mathers) and the Ordo Templi Orientis (Theodor Reuss) would hail. All men, trained first in the SRIA, gravitated toward the foundation of new orders in order to pursue both co-Masonry and more explicitly magical experimentation.*

Kenneth Mackenzie, to whom Hockley passed his techniques of angel magic, was a friend of both William Wynn Westcott, Supreme Magus of the SRIA, and cofounder of the Golden Dawn, and the French occultist Eliphas Levi, who initiated the modern occult revival with the publication of *Transcendental Magic*. Levi first mapped the tarot to the Tree of Life, a scheme later adopted by the Golden Dawn. Through Westcott and Ayton, the occult knowledge of the SRIA, including the Dee and Kelly material as first transmitted through Rudd and Hockley and then researched in the Sloane manuscripts, would be combined with Levi's insights, as well as material discovered in mysterious Cipher Manuscripts, to form the nucleus of the Golden Dawn, the most well-known and influential occult order in Western history.

Rather than Dee's material being preserved by Masonry, which only ever appears to *hint* at it, a more probable model is that Masonry formed a social matrix within which angelic magicians moved,

---

*There is no connection between these fringe orders and regular Masonry—Reuss was expelled from SRIA, probably for engaging in homosexual rites, and the current Ancient and Accepted Scottish Rite of Freemasonry does not recognize the OTO as anything but a clandestine, nonapproved para-Masonic order. Both Reuss and Aleister Crowley claimed that the OTO drew initiatory authority from the Italian Rite of Misraïm and the French Rite of Memphis—these orders, still extant, are also considered clandestine and nonauthorized by regular Masonry. Likewise, the various Golden Dawn revival groups have no connections with regular Masonry. Crowley himself was initiated to the 33° of the Scottish Rite through an irregular body in Mexico in 1900, and was later initiated, passed, and raised a regular Blue Lodge Mason at Anglo Saxon #343 under the Grand Lodge of France in 1904. See David Richard Jones, "Aleister Crowley Freemason? Revisited," in Porta Lucis A 111, *Words of Power.*

networked, and passed information on a one-to-one basis, influencing their environments and social groups both directly and indirectly.

Whatever the truth is, both of these fragmentary histories come together, without question, in the formation of the Hermetic Order of the Golden Dawn.

The Golden Dawn was a co-Masonic initiatory order comprised of eleven grades divided into three orders, based on the Tree of Life, of which the higher grades were likely only theoretical during the time the order was in operation. Candidates—drawn in part from the ranks of London high society (including such illustrious members as W. B. Yeats and Florence Farr), but mostly the mundane middle classes[50]—were educated in the arcana of Qabalah, tarot, Egyptian mythology, biblical lore, angelology, Enochiana, and everything else the order could assemble.

The oft-repeated and probably embellished story of the foundation of the Golden Dawn is that Kenneth Mackenzie discovered a series of manuscripts written in Trithemius's cipher, which he passed through Rev. Woodford to SRIA Supreme Magus William Wynn Westcott. On decoding the manuscript, Westcott discovered a series of instructions for conducting lodge work and individual magical ritual, apparently originating from a working group of Rosicrucians on the Continent. Westcott contacted the document's author—"Anna Sprengel"—in Germany, who responded and passed to him the spiritual authority to create an English branch of the order, authority she in turn drew from a triad of disincarnate entities she referred to as the "Secret Chiefs."[51] The invisible adepts strike again.

(Mathers later claimed to have met these Rosicrucian chiefs in physical form in Paris, one of whom he hinted might be the immortal Comte de St. Germain. Mathers recorded that they exerted a powerful psychic influence over him, and that they put off a psychic pressure front that induced extreme terror in him, as well as a feeling of being near a lightning strike. He also wrote that his nose and ears bled in their presence.)[52]

Initiations were conducted in Masonic lodges, with the candidate being walked around to various temple officers who explained magical lore. Like the Watchtowers, the lower grades were each dedicated to an element, with the initiate working to awaken and finely balance the elemental aspects of their soul in each grade. In the meantime, students were given basic lessons in magical theory, including instruction in the Hebrew alphabet, Qabalistic correspondences, geomantic figures, and more. These outer order teachings were in turn based on an inner order bedrock of Dee's angelic system. The Great Work of magic itself was emblemized as two Trees—a perfected Tree of Life before the Fall, in which Adam and Eve enjoy the divine grace of the supernal sephiroth of Kether, Chokmah, and Binah; and a fallen Tree in which the Red Dragon of the qliphoth or unredeemed individual ego destroys the cosmic balance of the Tree by raising its head to the eleventh sephira Da'ath, situated in the Abyss of Hallucinations, breaking the divine order of Creation. It was this fallen state that the order's adepts were to overcome, just as earlier Renaissance magicians sought to reverse the course of nature, recover the *prisca theologia,* and become *mens adeptus.*

The Watchtowers themselves were used as temple furniture during the order's initiation rituals, where they were shown to candidates, but not fully explained. Rather than employing the entire table given to Dee and Kelly, the Golden Dawn broke it up into five *separate* tables— the four elemental tables each detached, with the central black cross being restructured into a smaller four-by-five Tablet of Union. *On top* of Dee and Kelly's original designs—with no apparent authority other than their own ingenium—the Golden Dawn applied several layers of their own symbolism. What were originally just letters in the angelic language were now expanded into three-dimensional truncated pyramids, with the sides painted with elemental, planetary, zodiacal, and sephirotic correspondences, and each pyramid concealing a sphinx. While this scheme is undoubtedly impressive—formulating a map of the Golden Dawn's entire magical universe, in fine levels of detail—it also has nothing to do with the material received by Dee and Kelly.

Upon passing the initial grades and thereby reaching the Second Order (beginning at the sphere of Tiphareth), the freshly made Adeptus was now instructed in operative magic, given instructions in how to make a set of elemental "weapons" or magical tools, and shown how to perform rituals to control the elemental, planetary, and zodiacal forces, among other techniques. With these tools mastered, the adept was now ready to assess the angelic Watchtowers, which subsumed *all* of the material they had thus far learned. In this way, the Golden Dawn system itself may be seen as a set of training wheels for operating the Watchtowers (which, of course, is only one part of the total angelic system). Exploring the Watchtowers through astral projection or "skrying in the Spirit-Vision,"[53] as the order called it, was thus to make up a part of the work of the Adeptus Minor grade; Aleister Crowley's mentor Allan Bennett, along with Florence Farr, Charles Roser, and other Golden Dawn Second Order adepts, formed a working group entitled the "Sphere" to fulfill this task. Bennett would later convert to Theravada Buddhism in Ceylon, and become the first missionary to bring Buddhism to England.[54]

Crowley's secretary Israel Regardie, who published the papers of the Stella Matutina splinter group of the Golden Dawn in the late 1930s in contravention of his oaths, notes that the original Golden Dawn manuscripts on Enochian magic totaled over seventy thousand words, including supplementary diagrams. Most of this material likely came from Mathers and Westcott, of which Regardie provided only a summary in his published book. One of these original manuscripts is *Book H: Clavicula tabularum Enochi,* a transcription by Westcott of about one-tenth of MS. Sloane 307—itself a working document created by later magicians engaging with the Watchtowers, which may have been written by Thomas Rudd; the document later made its way into Gerald Yorke's collection.[55] Allan Bennett's copy of *Book H* is still extant and in circulation, though it was not published in Regardie's book.[56]

Regardie, for his part, stated that the system of the Watchtowers was "one of the most amazing magical schemes that I have ever encountered, since it provides a thorough-going and comprehensive synthesis of the entire magical system of the Golden Dawn. Every important item of knowledge and practice found itself incorporated within the scope of these angelic tablets. Every worthwhile technical form of Magical procedure and all branches of ritualistic work find themselves represented in a single noble system." Regardie also noted that some of the order's

Enochiana came from the Cipher Manuscripts. Regardie, improbably, tried to take his love of Enochian even further by suggesting that Christian Rosenkreutz, the mythical founder of Rosicrucianism, received parts of the Watchtowers *before* Dee and Kelly, in 1400 AD, before descending into even more questionable theories involving Atlantis.[57] Regardie also issued stern warnings against the use of Dee and Kelly's angelic system, cautioning that it would lead to spiritual breakdown, a paranoid thread later taken up by Paul Foster Case.

The technical approach of the Golden Dawn to the Watchtowers is impressive, and still forms the first introduction to Enochian that modern students of the occult encounter. Significantly, the group fully developed the forty-nine angelic calls into a system of interacting with the various kings, seniors, and angels of the tablets, and provided the calls themselves to students—albeit in a mangled form, in which the order spaced out each angelic word by placing Hebrew vowels within them, creating a version of Enochian that sounds oddly like Italian when spoken and that, again, has nothing to do with the original Dee and Kelly material. The order also provided students with the instructions for calling the thirty Aethyrs.

Lastly, the Golden Dawn developed the parlor game "Enochian Chess," which uses chess pieces shaped like Egyptian gods and the Watchtowers themselves as chessboards. Mercifully, disinterest or protest must have stopped Mathers from going even further into his personal Enochian joyride, for this marks the end of the order's deviation from Dee and Kelly's original system.

Through the Golden Dawn, the Enochian material made its way into the hands of Aleister Crowley—the order's most infamous initiate—who would make the most significant effort at exploring Dee and Kelly's angelic system since the two men themselves. While sojourning in Algiers in 1909 with his student Victor Neuburg, Crowley would progressively scry the thirty Aethyrs, which even Dee and Kelly never attempted—at least not on record.

Through Crowley (likely the most controversial figure in the history of occultism), the Golden Dawn's teachings, including those on Enochian, would find their full expression . . . and their inversion.

16

Crowned and Conquering

Aleister Crowley, in 1909, was at the peak of his early initiatory career. The young poet and mountaineer, now thirty-four years old, had learned nearly every branch of operative magic the Golden Dawn had to offer before his association with the order (and the order itself) collapsed in a cloud of scandal, lawsuit, and recrimination. In Ceylon, he had undergone hard training in the methods of raja yoga and Theravada Buddhism (what we now profanely call "mindfulness") at the feet of his Golden Dawn mentor Allan Bennett, now an ordained Buddhist monk—the same man who, in a less chaste incarnation, had been Crowley's mentor in magic and consciousness expansion through hard drugs. Next, Crowley had undergone the rigorous Abramelin Operation for contacting his holy guardian angel, while residing at Boleskine House in Scotland.

In 1904, with the aid of his wife Rose Kelly (from whom he was divorced by 1909, following her descent into alcoholism and the subsequent death of their child), he had received *The Book of the Law,* technically designated *Liber AL vel Legis,* a short document that proclaimed a New Aeon for humanity, on the strength of which he had founded his own order, the A∴A∴. Under the aegis of this new order, he was now publishing *The Equinox*—a hardbound encyclopedia of initiation that was to bring Crowleyanity to the world.

Fig. 16.1. Aleister Crowley in formal regalia as Baphomet, National Grand Master General X°
of Ordo Templi Orientis for Great Britain and Ireland, 1916.

With Rose now gone, Crowley, or Frater O.M., an Adeptus Exemptus of A∴A∴, gathered up young Frater Omnia Vincam, a Neophyte—terrestrially Victor Neuburg, a vegetarian and Trotskyist poet of nervous temperament—and with him absconded to Algeria. There they would undergo one of the most harrowing and profound series of events of Crowley's magical career—the scrying of the thirty Aethyrs, which he had unsuccessfully attempted nine years before in Mexico, scrying parts of the thirtieth and twenty-ninth Aethyrs before abandoning the task. This time, however, he would endure to the end.

THE AEON OF HORUS

Just as Dee and Kelly's visions followed a period of spiritual turbulence and confusion—the beginning of the Reformation—Crowley's visions followed the Victorian era's obsession with spiritualism and Theosophy, as well as Crowley's own announcement of a new era of human spiritual development.

In 1904, while honeymooning in Cairo with his new bride, Rose, the twenty-eight-year-old Crowley had received *The Book of the Law* from a disincarnate entity named Aiwass. Prior to this event, Crowley had slid into a jaded Buddhist phase, and grown bored of magic, instead choosing to occupy himself with the various distractions of mundane reality. In the middle of the honeymoon, however, which included a stay in the King's Chamber of the Great Pyramid, Rose Crowley (née Rose *Kelly*) had uncharacteristically asked Crowley to show her some magic, and he had responded by performing the Bornless Ritual, a rite from the Greek Magical Papyri that purports to invoke one's holy guardian angel, under whose authority one may control lower elementals and spirits. Rose soon entered a light trance and told Crowley, "They are waiting for you."[1] Crowley identified the source of the message as the Egyptian god Horus, and was led by Rose to the Boulaq Museum, where she correctly picked out a funerary stele depicting Horus—the Stele of Revealing—which carried the exhibit number 666. Following this, Crowley claims to have been visited by Aiwass, a dark and hooded figure who delivered to him the three chapters of *The Book of the Law* over the next three days. According to Crowley, this was not a channeled writing, but was spoken out loud by an actual external being that stood behind his left shoulder and gave dictation while Crowley hurriedly transcribed in longhand. The original edition of the book would be titled *Liber L,* with Crowley identifying this *L* as the central angelic character in Dee's Holy Table, "the sacred letter in the Holy Twelvefold Table which forms the triangle that stabilizes the universe."[2]

Despite the dramatic nature of its reception, Crowley would forget about the book—which totals only 220 lines—until a few years later, when he discovered it in his attic while looking for his skis, underneath, of all things, his copies of Dee and Kelly's angelic Watchtowers. He would later come to view the deciphering and propagation of the book, and the Thelemic philosophy he extrapolated from its contents, as the central goal of his existence; toward the end of his life, he would conclude that the transmission of *The Book of the Law,* and the proof he claimed it gave for the existence of beyond-human intelligences, was the one thing he had done in his life that truly mattered, the one legacy he wanted to leave for humanity.

Believing that the book's reception showed that he had forged his own link with the Secret Chiefs that had inspired the original Golden Dawn Cipher Manuscripts—the true and invisible Rosicrucian order—Crowley would build up his new A∴A∴ to replace the Golden Dawn. This new order would carry a far more rigorous standard of training, and initiate students all the way up to the Supernals instead of only Tiphareth. He would later inherit the mantle of the Ordo Templi Orientis, a German para-Masonic order teaching its own brand of sexual magic, and reconstruct it as a vehicle for bringing *The Book of the Law* to a wider audience, along the lines of a standard Masonic social fraternity, rather than a training ground for adepts.

Like the earlier Rosicrucian manifestos, Crowley believed that *The Book of the Law* announced a new era for humanity. Instead of the numerous tribal gods of Earth, which Crowley thought represented various aspects of the natural world or of human sexuality, *The Book of the Law* posits three gods: Nuit, or infinite space; Hadit, or the infinitely small point; and the product of their synthesis, Ra-Hoor-Khuit, Horus, the Crowned and Conquering Child, who, among many other things, represents the state of consciousness of the mass of humanity that will dominate the coming two thousand years. Rather than matriarchal, as in the prehistoric period, or patriarchal, as in the era of recorded civilization, the new image of humanity would be childlike, dual gendered, characterized by a liberation of the species from its ancient oppressive structures, by the granting of Promethean and "magical" powers to the masses, and by humanity nonetheless embodying a generally infantile, self-obsessed, destructive nature and smashing everything in its wake, in the manner of the standard two-year-old child. Now, over a century later, it is hard not to see the validity of *The Book of the Law* upon spending any more than a few minutes either online or in the street, anywhere in the modern world.

This was to be a formula of emancipation from previous social constraints, but might also destroy the planet itself. World Wars I and II, the atomic bomb, the space race, AIDS, the internet, and globalization would all come to demonstrate the volatile force and fire of the Aeon of Horus, and there are still *just under nineteen* whole centuries of the Aeon to go.

As time progressed, however, and Crowley continued to elaborate his Thelemic religion and magical system, he would impishly drop hints relating—though not necessarily outright identifying—the entities of *The Book of the Law* with those of Revelation, particularly in his *New Comment,* written around 1921, during the Abbey of Thelema period in Cefalu.

Nuit states in *The Book of the Law,* I:22, that she is also known by "a secret name." In his *New Comment* to I:12, Crowley states that his vision of the twelfth Aethyr revealed that this secret name is Babalon.[3] Babalon is Crowley's name (in the angelic language) for the Whore of Babylon in Revelation, who appears as the Daughter of Fortitude in the spirit diaries.

In the same *New Comment* (to I:1), Crowley states of Hadit that "Had is Sad, Set, Satan, Sat,"[4] identifying Hadit with Satan outright, as well as the sun and the phallus. "Liber Samekh," a new version of the Bornless One ritual composed the same year as the *New Comment,* contains an invocation to "Thou Satan-Sun Hadit," also identified as "O Lion-Serpent Sun the Beast" and as "Thou, the Saviour!" among other imagery.[5] Hadit is also referred to as "the Snake that giveth Knowledge & Delight" in *The Book of the Law,*[6] a reference to Satan as he appears in Genesis, as well as kundalini.

Ra-Hoor-Khuit (also known in other aspects as Horus, Hoor, Hoor-par-Kraat, and Heru-Ra-Ha) announces that he is the "Crowned and Conquering Child" in the first Aethyr.[7] Although Crowley never addresses this outright, the King James text of Revelation 6:2 identifies the first horseman of the Apocalypse as "a white horse: and he that sat on him had a bow; and a crown was given unto him: and he went forth conquering, and to conquer."[8] Many evangelical Christians associate the rider of the white horse with the Antichrist, who is also the "prince who is to come" or "little horn" from the book of Daniel, who emerges from

Fig. 16.2. Albrecht Dürer, *The Four Horsemen*, 1498.

the sea upon the head of the fourth Beast (these four Beasts are unified into one zootype in Revelation 13).[9]

A particularly strident champion of this view was the turn-of-the-century Baptist pastor Clarence Larkin, who was instrumental in popularizing John Nelson Darby's dispensationalism in America, whose somewhat manic charts of the apocalypse timeline are still in use and who would influence prominent evangelical leaders to come, particularly Billy Graham and the authors Hal Lindsey and Tim LaHaye.[10] As Christ also appears on a white horse in Revelation 19, Larkin suspects that this prior white horse is a mockery, and thus Antichrist. Darby himself saw the first horseman as a terrestrial conqueror establishing the way for the Christ to come, again echoing the "little horn."[11] Darby elsewhere states that the white horse simply denotes victorious imperial power, either of Christ or *the Antichrist*.[12]

A white horse appeared to Dee and Kelly on January 12, 1584, where it was identified with Christ's arrival in Revelation 19. The very next day, Uriel gave a prophecy of the coming Antichrist or crowned and conquering "little horn," an arrogant prince who cruelly lays waste to his kingdoms; the placement of this figure next to the white horse of Christ in the angelic sessions suggests a connection. A conquerer on a white horse, holding a spear, also appeared to Dee and Kelly immediately after the wife-swapping incident, followed by the vision of the Daughter of Fortitude, Babalon. Larkin's later interpretation that the first white horse of Revelation represents Antichrist, and the second Christ, also echoes the delivery of divine instructions in pairs during the angelic conversations—a corrupted instruction superceded by a perfected instruction, as with the lamen, Sigillum, Holy Table, and pages of *Liber Loagaeth*.

This interpretation rather strongly suggests that the Aeon of Horus is an analogue of the reign of the conquering Antichrist prophesied in Daniel and Revelation—that Ra-Hoor-Khuit, the child of Babalon and the Beast, is the Antichrist who will destroy not only Christianity, but all major world religions.[13] Crowley's own identification of himself with the Beast 666 as a central task of establishing the Aeon of Horus supports this reading, as does Jack Parsons's later identification with the

Antichrist in order to establish the reign of Babalon (see chapter 17, "In the Shadow of the Cross").

The first horseman is often referred to as "Pestilence," although this role is sometimes conflated with the fourth or pale horse. Crowley may have been wryly hinting at this in his 1925 "Tunis Comment" to *The Book of the Law,* in which he states that all who discuss the book will be shunned as "centres of pestilence."[14]

Perhaps most blatantly, the very association of the original title of the book—*Liber L*—with the Holy Table suggests that it is an extension of Dee and Kelly's apocalypse machine.

THE VISION AND THE VOICE

The doctrine of *The Book of the Law* is short and succinct, meant to be read and digested by the reader on their own terms. It would be elaborated on by several more books received around 1907, which together make up *The Holy Books of Thelema.* 1909's *The Vision and the Voice* then takes *The Holy Books* and builds up a fully fledged cosmology around them.

The angelic workings of *The Vision and the Voice* were conducted while crossing the Algerian desert with Neuburg in 1909, with Crowley calling one Aethyr per day using the nineteenth call and then entering a trance state to scry, with Neuburg recording Crowley's spoken descriptions of what he was seeing. As a scrying implement, Crowley employed a "great golden topaz (set in a Calvary cross of six squares, made of wood, painted vermillion) engraved with a Greek cross of five squares charged with the Rose of forty-nine petals."[15] In order to assure that a full written record was left of the Aethyrs, Crowley writes that he purposefully resisted going into full trance, instead choosing to maintain enough presence of mind that he could conceptualize his experiences as "astral" mystery plays, to be recorded by Neuburg, rather than pure meditative absorption. To prepare himself, Crowley cleared his mind by repeating a Muslim mantra from Surah 112 of the Qu'ran, while walking across the desert to create states of physical exhaustion, so that his body would not disturb his mind. This mantra was recited 1,001 times per day, with each recitation followed by a prostration.

Crowley and Neuburg approached scrying the Aethyrs as a progressive series of visionary initiations into the true nature of the Aeon of Horus, and while *The Book of the Law* announces the New Aeon, its gods, and its laws, *The Vision and the Voice* shows the background workings and cosmic shifts behind its advent, and firmly establishes its theology in relation to prior religious systems. The visions related in the Aethyrs elucidate an immense amount of material from the Western esoteric tradition, combining imagery from the books of Genesis, Exodus, Daniel, Maccabees, Revelation, the Gospels, and others; Gnosticism; Vajrayana Buddhism; Qabalah; the various Mediterranean mystery cults; Islam; Dee and Kelly's work; Solomonic magic; Freemasonry; Rosicrucianism; the Golden Dawn; and Crowley's nascent Thelemic religion, forming a grand overview of thousands of years of Western religious history.

This is markedly different from the use of the Aethyrs outlined by Dee in *Liber scientiae,* where they are assigned to zodiacal regions of the sky and the various geographical divisions of the earth. Crowley instead ascribed the Aethyrs to the Tree of Life, and interpreted their contents through the lens of the Golden Dawn's Qabalistic correspondences. In particular, Crowley's Aethyrs are concerned with the sephira Binah, represented by Babalon, and Chokmah, represented by the Beast 666, also called Chaos.

Multiple mappings of the Aethyrs to the Tree exist—one proposed by the Golden Dawn, in which the Aethyrs map to the ten sephiroth in the worlds of Yetzirah, Briah, and Atziluth successively,* and another schema that is mentioned in the ninth Aethyr, after Crowley passes the

---

*The four Qabalistic worlds—Assiah, Yetzirah, Briah, and Atziluth—might more plainly be called the worlds of matter, imagination, pattern, and emanation. They are practically experienced in progressively deeper states of meditation. Each contains its own Tree of Life with all ten sephiroth and twenty-two paths. For a more extensive technical analysis of the Tree and Aethyrs, see Eshelman, *Visions and Voices,* 50–53. This book is the best commentary and analysis of the Algeria sessions currently available, and bears studying alongside the original text.

Abyss, in which the Aethyrs are arranged as a flaming sword descending through the sephiroth,* an image that likely corresponds with both the flaming sword in Genesis 3:24 as well as the description of the final, wrathful form of Christ, in Revelation 1:16, who appears with a sharp two-edged sword emerging from his mouth. On the other hand, any one-to-one mapping of the sephiroth to the Aethyrs is contradicted by the angel of the twelfth Aethyr (below the Abyss), who explains that they interpenetrate, but do not directly correspond, and that furthermore the Aethyrs are a deeper font of initiated wisdom than the Tree of Life, as they contain the secrets of the aeons and of Thelema itself.[16]

Crowley's progress through the Aethyrs took on the pattern of a Golden Dawn–style temple initiation, but rather than being conducted in a Masonic lodge, the initiating officers were the beings he met in the Aethyrs themselves—the Governors of each Aethyr and their attendant servitors, whose names were given to Dee and Kelly along with the calls in the spirit actions. Likewise, each Aethyr opens with the vision of a sigil or "admission badge," much as were employed in the Golden Dawn temple initiations, followed by a veil that is rent to reveal the vision of the Aethyr, another Golden Dawn procedure. Studying the Golden Dawn initiations, particularly the Neophyte initiation, will help make sense of the Aethyrs, as will understanding that Crowley saw this working as his initiation into the 8°=3□ degree of the Golden Dawn (assigned to Binah) and therefore into the Third Order, composed not of terrestrial individuals but of disincarnate adepts, those who have crossed the Abyss and made it to Binah—the true Invisible College—whom he meets after crossing the tenth Aethyr and entering the City of the Pyramids. In doing so, Crowley himself was now spiritually prepared to remanifest the Golden Dawn system on his own terms.

As the visions are concerned with Crowley's initiation into Binah, the central protagonist of the Aethyrs is the Whore of Babylon, whose name Crowley reworked as BABALON in the angelic language, who is the personification of Binah within the visions. This is the same being

---

*While Crowley notes that this schema is not to be given to the uninitiated, diagrams that purport to show the arrangement given in the ninth Aethyr are provided by the OTO in *The Vision and the Voice*, 254–56.

that appears in Revelation and as the Daughter of Fortitude in the final Dee and Kelly sessions; Crowley, according to his *Confessions,* had read Casaubon before embarking on his Algerian trip with Neuburg. Babalon's sigil, which also became the seal of the A.·.A.·., is the central heptagon from the Sigillum Dei Aemeth. The overall narrative of the visions is of Crowley's progressive sanctification, illumination, and *annihilation* within the sphere of Binah/Babalon. Completing this process would grant him the grade of Magister Templi, 8°=3□ in the A.·.A.·., a "Third Order" grade that was only theoretical in the Golden Dawn; hence, Crowley believed that he received his initiation on the "inner planes" from the Governors of the thirty Aethyrs, rather than human initiators.

Simultaneously to the initiation of the candidate Crowley himself, the Aethyrs show the "changing of the guard" of the temple officers, much as a Masonic lodge promotes and rotates its officers at the end of each Masonic year. Golden Dawn officers, who followed the Masonic style, were meant to represent the Egyptian gods and their regency over the universe. As signified by the reception of *The Book of the Law,* and demonstrated tangibly in the Aethyrs, the role of the Hierophant (holding the place of the Worshipful Master in Masonry) now passes from Osiris (as it was during Crowley's temple initiations) to Horus (as described in *The Book of the Law,* I:49). The ramification is a corresponding shift in the order of the universe.

For Crowley, this was about more than a political shake-up in a tiny para-Masonic body (or his own power grab); it was about the universal and historical forces that the officers in the order represented. Importantly, Osiris, for Crowley, is represented by Christ, Christianity, and the cult of the "Dying God," while Horus is an analogue of Antichrist, signaling the end of the Christian era. As such, *one possible reading* of Crowley may be that he was consciously fulfilling the angels' plan of initiating the Apocalypse and the end of history, by embodying the forces of the Beast, Babalon, and Antichrist, as an effort toward catalyzing the events of Revelation and therefore triggering the inevitable return and millennial rule of Christ.

This would have been in keeping with Crowley's upbringing

among the Plymouth Brethren, John Nelson Darby's fundamentalist, evangelical splinter group from the Church of England, and Crowley's early absorption of Darby's dispensationalism—the belief that God advances his plan for humanity through distinct eras or cycles ("progressive revelation"), and that God's mode of revealing himself and his expectations for humanity change in each time period. During each of these epochs, Darby taught, Earth is administered to and maintained by human agents as a test of faithfulness toward God's dispensation, culminating in the Rapture, in which Christ's elect will literally disappear from Earth at the time of the Second Coming, leaving the unsaved behind.

Crowley, who was raised in the even more severe Exclusive Brethren subsect of the Plymouth Brethren, was not allowed to read any literature except the Bible until he left for university, and was physically and psychologically abused at his evangelical boarding school—including an incident at the age of twelve in which he was put in solitary confinement for almost a year over a false accusation of sodomy, damaging his kidneys. Crowley, like Nietzsche, would understandably come to see Christianity as the root of all evil and the spiritual torment of humanity, and identify himself, even from his earliest memories, with the entities of Revelation, specifically the Beast 666.[17]

As soon as he was free at university, Crowley would rebel through dandyism, decadent art, prostitution, homosexuality, drugs, ceremonial magic, demonology, writing extreme pornography, making direct published attacks on Christianity (as in *The Sword of Song*), and an obsession with the literary character of Satan as the adversary to the spiritual stultification he had experienced as a boy. Yet in doing so, he never strayed far from the spiritual imprint of his youth. Even his new religion of Thelema, which emerged from his involvement with the Golden Dawn and subsequent reception of *The Book of the Law*, carries deep similarities to the dogma of the Exclusive Brethren, such as the emphasis on primacy of text over clergy, extreme discipline, and, of course, dispensationalist cosmology. Crowley cast himself in an adversarial role to the Christianity he knew, but perhaps only in so much as to uphold it and fulfill the dispensationalist idea of human stewardship during the Great Tribulation. Indeed, Darby even used the word *aion,* from the original Greek, to denote a historical period of God's dispensation.[18] The term *aion* was in wide use in Christian Zionist circles, and appears in William E. Blackstone's hugely popular 1908 tract *Jesus is Coming.*[19] Blackstone was a fierce and highly politically successful campaigner for the establishment of a Jewish state,[20] and was later dubbed the "Father of Zionism" by the Supreme Court Justice Louis Brandeis.[21]

Understanding Crowley's "Satanism" and antagonism to Christianity as him *playing a necessary and affirming role* within the broader theology and script of evangelical Christianity is crucial to assessing his work and character. Rebelling against the Christian worldview by embracing Satan is akin to rebelling against the popularity of *Star Wars* by putting on a Darth Vader mask. Crowley's Thelemic religion may claim only a few thousand adherents worldwide, yet has had a disproportionate impact on Western culture; the counterculture revolutions of the sixties effectively turned many of Crowley's more digestible ideas *into* the dominant culture. In this sense, Thelema might metaphorically be seen as a covert-ops division of evangelical Christianity, as it is the branch of Christianity concerned with hastening the Apocalypse by enacting and embodying the reign of Antichrist—even if this is somewhat obscured on the surface, and to lower initiates.

Crowley himself states, in his *Confessions,* "My falling away from grace was not occasioned by any intellectual qualms; I accepted the theology of the Plymouth Brethren. In fact, I could hardly conceive of the existence of people who might doubt it. I simply went over to Satan's side; and to this hour I cannot tell why."[22]

As discussed in the introduction, dispensationalist ideas inspired not only Crowley but the American evangelical movement's pursuit of intervention in the Middle East, which is explicitly concerned with enacting Revelation. And like the Brethren, modern evangelicals see the need for human agency in the stewardship of God's plan;[23] the *Left Behind* series of novels by Tim LaHaye and Jerry B. Jenkins, which are among the most read books in America, and which dramatize a dispensational version of Revelation, are a major cultural artifact of this population-wide push toward biblical literalism and its direct geopolitical enactment.

If Dee gave America its beginning, the Plymouth Brethren gave it its eschatology and apocalyptic goal . . . and as we shall see, their greatest son Edward Alexander Crowley started the final countdown. First the rituals, then the nuclear weapons.

THE BEAST 666

Much of the text of *The Vision and the Voice* can be seen as an example of apophatic theology or *via negativa,* the attempt to come to an understanding of God by stripping away all descriptions or previous attempts at perception of divinity, as by their very nature these limited human models or linguistic representations must fall far short of the truth, instead becoming blocks to direct perception or *gnosis.* Over the course of the Aethyrs, the symbols of not only Christianity but also other religions (including Judaism, Islam, Buddhism, and Hinduism) are subverted, superseded, or dramatically shown to be false perceptions of deeper truths, deeper truths that are next revealed by the guardians of the Aethyrs themselves. Many parts of *The Vision and the Voice* resemble *The Wizard of Oz,* with Crowley tearing away the masks of God and finding that the man behind the curtain is not what he seems. (Crowley's own *Liber OZ,* written in 1941, likewise reveals that "there is no god but man.")[24]

While the thrust of *The Vision and the Voice* seems to be the establishment of a new spiritual narrative to come *after* the end of the Christian era, as colored by *The Book of the Law* and Crowley's stellar Egyptian gods Nuit, Hadit, and Ra-Hoor-Khuit, it is impossible to divorce Crowley's work from Revelation (particularly when, as discussed above, these gods are seen as at least in one sense blinds for the Whore of Babylon, Satan, and the Antichrist). There is, indeed, a more sinister current at work in the Aethyrs—not just apophatic or even antinomian, but explicitly adversarial and Satanic. Though Crowley, his human personality, and his preconceived notions about reality are being reduced to nothing but a pile of dust in Binah, this is not the end goal. In the twenty-fifth Aethyr, Crowley is given a clear spiritual mandate that he must become the human representative of the *anti-logos,* which is manifest as the Beast 666, Chaos, Tò Μέγα Θηρίον, To Mega Therion.

Christian symbolism is subjected to inversion as the Aethyrs progress: the four beasts of Daniel are replaced, Jesus and Jehovah are shown as figures of ridicule whose time has passed, the doctrine of sin and salvation is rejected, the Agnes Dei is shown to be a predatory demon, the monogram of the Jesuits is revealed as an outdated conception of the universe, and the Ichthys and even Augustinian doctrine itself are overturned by the incoming magical formula of Crowley's Aeon of Horus. In this New Aeon, it is one's own Will (Θελημα) that is to be done—not God's, as was (and is) suggested in the Lord's Prayer. Rather than Christ and the Virgin Mary, the Beast 666 and Babalon are to be the objects of worship, which are here shown as superior and holy symbols that have only been misunderstood by lower initiates. The end result is an elaborate and elegant inversion not just of the cross but of Christian doctrine itself, point by point, in which the follower is (broadly speaking) to enact Revelation, rather than the Gospel, as dogma, taking the side of the Adversary. And this is a fairly logical step forward in the angels' quest for a world religion as unveiled in the spirit diaries—not as a fulfillment, or as a supersession of Christianity (as Crowley believed) but as a preliminary to the millennial rule of Christ, as described in Revelation 13.

To simply interpret *The Vision and the Voice* as revealing a new Satanic doctrine, however, is still too simplistic of a read. Like many of the spirit actions, the revelations in *The Vision and the Voice* operate on supernal logic—that is, through paradoxical statements. As the book is concerned with crossing the Abyss, and duality cannot exist above the Abyss *because duality is a quality of manifestation and the Supernals are unmanifest,* the Aethyrs are saturated with nondual statements, the resolution of dualities into singularities and self-contradicting symbols. For Crowley, an idea or symbol is only true inasmuch as it contains its own opposite, as this implies it is a complete concept. Good and evil, Christ and Antichrist, and many, many more *apparent* contradictions are wryly twisted, conflagrated, inverted, and dissolved throughout the text, which requires the high registers of Qabalistic analysis to fully appreciate; what appears to be evil in the world of *samsara,* Crowley assures us, is actually good from the perspective of absolute reality, and vice versa.

In addition, the cosmology of *The Vision and the Voice* reveals that the universe is not a monad, as Dee thought, but an infinite number of equal monads suspended in infinite space. Crowley's cosmology instead replaces the monad with the formula *zero equals two,* in which existence is seen as manifest duality, and posits that by uniting and thereby destroying all apparent opposites we may liberate ourselves from them and attain to the void of emptiness, the Qabalistic zero, which is the only real "truth." Consequently, all representatives of the monad and of monotheism—particularly Jehovah himself—are overturned and destroyed in the Aethyrs, to be replaced with the Thelemic trinity of infinite space. What is progressively revealed is both Christic and Antichristic, and a strange syzygy of both, and yet is also something wholly different—a new, stellar religion that harkens back to Egypt while it stretches across the cosmos, that feels both ancient and yet hyperfuturistic, even eternal. A hypertext to all religions in all times and places that simultaneously inverts and annihilates all of them.

Though the Aethyrs destroyed the remaining vestiges of the man Aleister Crowley, his quest to fit himself to the role of the Beast 666—that is, of becoming a human embodiment of that abstract force—would be fulfilled between 1915 and 1918 with his assumption of the $9°=2^{\square}$ grade of Magus.[25] During this time, Crowley largely abandoned the Golden Dawn system of Masonic, Qabalistic, and ceremonial magic in favor of the sexual magic of the OTO, which was transmitted to him by the German industrialist Theodor Reuss, another SRIA alumni (and outcast), who headed the OTO before its leadership passed to Crowley himself.

Crowley's life in this period was preoccupied by constant testing of the OTO's sexual methods with prostitutes, and Crowley's growing fixation on finding a "Scarlet Woman" who would be as capable of embodying the force of Babalon as Crowley was of embodying the Beast 666. This Scarlet Woman, once located, would assist Crowley in the process of his own further initiation into the sphere of Chokmah, allowing him to pronounce his Word *Thelema,* which would form a new guiding principle for the world and shape it in his image.* This was likely the most unhinged period of Crowley's life, in which he immersed himself in addiction, horror, degradation, disease, and other such "mysteries of filth," crescendoing with his establishment of the Abbey of Thelema at Cefalu, Italy, where he and a band of true believers experimented with magic (including Enochian), perverse sex, hard drugs, and mind control as a full-time occupation, until even Mussolini tired of them and expelled them from the country. (Il Duce may have been particularly annoyed with Crowley as the dictator also believed that *he* was the Antichrist.)[26]

The Abbey period claimed the life of the twenty-three-year-old Oxford student Raoul Loveday, likely after drinking contaminated mountain stream water (though his widow told the press his death was due to drinking cat blood in a ritual). In another abhorrent episode, Crowley attempted to induce a goat to copulate with his current "Scarlet Woman" Leah Hirsig. When it refused to perform, Crowley took its place behind Hirsig, and afterward cut the animal's throat, spraying the blood over Hirsig's naked back. Hirsig is said to have next turned to the writer Mary Butts (also studying magic under Crowley)

---

*In this, he was successful. Even though Crowley the man is long dead, Crowley the symbol and the presence lives on, not only for his followers but in popular culture, which now *is* Western culture; from the cover of the Beatles' *Sgt. Pepper's* to the Rolling Stones to David Bowie to Led Zeppelin to a thousand lesser musical acts; through the Baby Boomers, whose generation enacted the philosophy Crowley had developed *en masse,* even if they were not aware of doing so. Thelema was transmitted to them not by Crowley directly but through guiding figures like the aforementioned musicians as well as Timothy Leary (who believed his role was to carry on Crowley's work) and many others. The Boomers are currently the elders of the Western world, and culture now conforms more to the vision put forth in *The Book of the Law*—concerned with individual supremacy, will, sorcery (as in personal and corporate branding, the creation and manipulation of reality through digital media, corporate idolatry, etc.), the end of sexual taboo, the end of gender, atheism, constant preoccupation with childish pursuits and identities, and even outright Luciferianism—than it does that of Christianity *by far.*

and asked, "What shall I do now?" to which Butts replied, "I'd have a bath if I were you."*

In an earlier diary entry from Cefalu, which has improbably never been commented on by *any* of Crowley's biographers or followers (including the generally hostile John Symonds, who also edited the diary in question), Crowley launches into an unhinged, ether-and-cocaine–fueled screed in which he exults in how he and Hirsig have mutually debased each other, which includes a passage discussing the rape and torture of his and Hirsig's children—a five-month-old girl (who died a few months later) and a two-year-old boy.[27] Whether this was a drug-induced, manic exercise in transgressive imagining (Crowley describes wanting to dig up and have sex with Hirsig's deceased mother in the same passage), a coded statement (Crowley elsewhere masked references to sexual magick by describing the ritual use of orgasm, in poor taste, as "sacrificing children"), or actually occurred is impossible to verify. If it did occur, no more despicable crime can be imagined; for such a so-called man, no amount of contempt would be enough.

Many of Crowley's modern followers, fans, and biographers have gone to extreme lengths to whitewash their hero, striving to portray Crowley as a 1960s bohemian humanist a few decades before his time, a misunderstood genius who was unfairly vilified by the press. In the

---

*This story has appeared in various forms throughout the secondary Crowley literature; the most definitive version, as drawn from Crowley's diaries and recounted above, is in John Symonds's *The King of the Shadow Realm*, 295. Mary Butts would be a more objective firsthand source; however, Butts's diary entries for the period in question—the entire second half of August and most of September 1921—are conspicuously missing from the recent collection of her journals edited by Nathalie Blondel. Butts's published diaries resume after she has returned to London; notably, although she continues to work at magic, Butts's references to Crowley from this point on are uniformly negative. Butts summarizes her conclusions on the Beast on January 11, 1922: "I am afraid of him 'somewhere.' There is a point of fear in my mind. . . . I saw at Cefalu the familiar features of religion come again. And obscenity. And something exceedingly bad (not obscene), & something powerful. 'Do what thou wilt shall be the whole of the law.' That is all right. But people are to be made aware of this by fear, coercion, bribery etc, a religious movement re-enacted. The founder is to be Crowley & his gulled, doped women. I don't doubt most new religions had some such start, but I feel that even Mahomet was better." Blondel, *The Journals of Mary Butts*, 193.

Hounding the King of the Devil Cults Around the Globe

Barred from England, Raided in Italy, the "Beast-666" Bobs Up in Paris— and Gets Yawns Where Once He Thrilled and Horrified

By NIGEL TRASK, PARIS.

Fig. 16.3. Sensationalistic newspaper coverage of Crowley from the years following his expulsion from Italy. Nigel Trask, "Hounding the King of the Devil Cults Around the Globe," *Ogden Standard-Examiner*, April 22, 1928.

final summation, however, there is no way to gloss over or excuse away Crowley's evil. To do so would be to misread Crowley himself, even as he tells you who he is in no uncertain terms. And while Crowley's work is brilliant, when viewed from another angle—which is, of course, the angle that most reasonable people first perceive it from—it is a wound in the world, one cutting so deep that it indeed reveals new and unglimpsed layers of reality, albeit in the same way a razor cutting through an arm to the bone does.

It would be easy to dismiss Crowley as an aberration, a failure, or as an active pawn of evil. Yet it is far *more* troubling to stop and consider that he simply followed his script. As Dee and Kelly's angels put it, "The appearing and works of the devil are but of necessity."[28]

Of use in assessing Crowley's role in the overall narrative of Revelation is the work of the French metaphysician René Guénon, a contemporary of Crowley's who rejected modernity as a decayed echo of traditional and eternal wisdom, and was unilaterally critical of the Theosophist and pseudo-Masonic groups that then littered Europe (which have since disintegrated even further into what we now know as the "New Age").

For Guénon, the true way to *gnosis* was through the world's established wisdom traditions, the *esoteric* branches of the world's established exoteric religions—of particular interest were Advaita Vedanta, Taoism, Platonism, esoteric Christianity, and others; he eventually converted to Sufism. Modern forms of "spirituality" divorced from their traditional roots and largely created out of the imaginations of their founders were not only false doctrines, Guénon argued, they were actually examples of *counterinitiation,* which instead of truly initiating an individual (furthering their psychic integration, understanding of eternal metaphysical forms and patterns, and proximity to God), took their "initiates" in the exact opposite direction, into dispersion, disintegration, nihilism, chaos, and breakdown.*

Counterinitiation, according to Guénon, is the nature of the modern

---

*Or, in Dee and Crowley's language, into the grip of Coronzom and disintegration in the Abyss.

world itself, which seems to be constructed to take us further away from ourselves at every step, into the deadening flatland of relativism rather than individual growth and progress through a real hierarchy of attainment; these counterinitiatory bodies essentially mirror the entropic course of modernity itself, rather than uniting their adherents with something higher.* So ubiquitous and entrenched were such counterinitiatory attitudes and even schools that Guénon believed they would come to coalesce into an actual *countertradition*. This tradition, he argued, would not be primitive and unsophisticated, but would contain enough legitimate initiatory material to effectively ape the true function of tradition.† It would proceed by distinct inversions of Christian symbolism, and it, itself, would comprise the reign of Antichrist. The countertradition would be concentrated in a singular individual, who would stand at the very summit of the counterhierarchy, and thereby be closest not to God but to chaos, dissolution, and hell.‡ Does this sound familiar?

"This being," Guénon writes, "even if he appears in the form of a particular single human being, will really be less an individual than a symbol, and he will be as it were the synthesis of all the symbolism that has been inverted for the purposes of the 'counter-initiation,' and he will manifest it all the more completely in himself because he will have neither predecessor nor successor. In order to express the false carried to its extreme he will have to be so to speak 'falsified' from every point of view, and to be like an incarnation of falsity itself. In order that this may be possible, and by reason of his extreme opposition to the true in all its aspects, the Antichrist can adopt the very symbols of the Messiah, using them of course in an inverted sense."[29]

To this passage, compare not only the inversion of Christian symbols given in *The Vision and the Voice,* but Crowley's document "Liber B vel Magi," transmitted to him in 1907, which gives instructions

---

*Father Seraphim Rose, a student of Guénon's work who converted to Eastern Orthodoxy and therein found his fulfillment, saw the modern obsession with magic, the paranormal, UFOs, and the like as a manifestation of the essentially Antichristic nature of the modern world. See Rose, *Orthodoxy and the Religion of the Future.*
†As in the Ape of Thoth.
‡Thaumiel.

for assuming the grade of Magus in the sphere Chokmah, which in Crowley's case meant fully replacing his being with that of the Beast 666: "In the beginning doth the Magus speak Truth, and send forth Illusion and Falsehood to enslave the soul. . . . For the curse of His grade is that He must speak Truth, that the Falsehood thereof may enslave the souls of men."[30]

Such a being is not heroic, Guénon explains, but rather the most deluded of the great ranks of the deluded, so much that they are not only confused but "actually irremediably lost." However, "if they were not so deluded they would clearly not be fulfilling a function that must be fulfilled, like every other function, so that the Divine plan may be accomplished in this world."[31] Even the reign of the Antichrist serves a purpose—it is essential to ending the current Manvantara (a Vedic calculation of time similar to the idea of an aeon, though much longer; 308,448,000 years as opposed to 2,000).[32] Like aeons, Manvantaras are ruled over by an overseer, in this case an incarnation of Manu, the first man. With the end of the current Manvantara, according to Guénon, a new one will begin. The cosmology is broadly the same as Crowley's, albeit using Vedic terms and timelines.

Crucially, this new era will *not* be brought about by the Antichrist: the role of the Antichrist is to announce a *false* Golden Age, which is a pure lie. Here it should be easy to see not only the Aeon of Horus (or any other supposed aeon) but all of the false Millenniums—the inevitability of Communism, the New Age, 2012, the Singularity . . . pick your own, as we never seem to run out of them. Even the end of the world as promised by Dee and Kelly's angels for "eighty-eight" never manifested, at least not as a year. As Crowley notes in the second Aethyr, "Forecasts of the future cannot be made from Qabalistic data, which have nothing to do with terrestrial measures of time."[33]

Guénon states:

Profane people . . . have no idea what they are talking about when they announce the near approach of a "new age" as being one with which the existing humanity will be concerned. Their error, in its most extreme form, will be that of the Antichrist himself when he claims to bring the "golden age" into being through the reign of the "counter-tradition," and when he even gives it an appearance of authenticity, purely deceitful and ephemeral though it be, by means of a counterfeit of the traditional idea of the Sanctum Regnum.[34]

It is this false Millennium that is of necessity conquered and overcome by the Second Coming and true millennial kingdom of Christ that, for Guénon at least, is the real end of the Manvantara.

In this sense, we may take Crowley at his word that he is the Beast 666—at least a terrestrial representation thereof—and that he truly *has* come to proclaim a New Aeon for humanity; only that, as a good Magus, he has spoken truth to enslave with a lie, and that as a good Plymouth Brother, he has played his dispensationalist role and lied—even become the embodiment of the Lie—to prepare the way for the Truth.

CLEAN-UP IN AISLE NINETY-THREE

If Crowley carries with him such a long shadow of horror, why bother studying him at all?

Crowley's transgressions are indeed disturbing, and it is important to show them plainly rather than engage with the personality cult and counterculture industry that has grown up around him. In addition to the incidents described above, there are Crowley's rather cowardly refusal to help several men trapped by an avalanche during his Kanchenjunga expedition; his decades of cocaine, ether, and heroin addiction and the resultant ugly interpersonal behaviors these drugs engender; his often sociopathic treatment of women, students, and hired help; his extreme racism and anti-Semitism (including a line in his *Magical and Philosophical Commentaries,* III:11, in which he calls Jews "the parasites of man," which has been deleted from later editions), and so on . . . and so on . . . and so on. Crowley, like Nietzsche, made it his lifelong project to reject Christian morality; he states, in the same *Commentaries,* III:20, that the ethics of *The Book of the Law* are "those of Evolution itself."

Crowley was a flawed and often malevolent human being—not in a "gee shucks" way, but in a willful way. This is something he shares in common with many Catholic and Protestant clergy, Tibetan lamas, Hindu gurus, and other religious representatives who become corrupted and abuse their power. Even the greatest initiates may fall—as, one might argue, Crowley progressively did following his work in Algeria, particularly as he entered further into his own reality tunnel in which he was the sole prophet and central figure of a New Aeon, strayed further and further away from contact with other magicians who could be considered mentors or peers, surrounded himself with sycophants, and cultivated addictions to hard drugs. Indeed, some have speculated that Crowley's adventures in Algeria—particularly entering the triangle and allowing himself to be possessed by the demon Coronzom in ZAX, the tenth Aethyr, which is described below—resulted in permanent possession, and were causally responsible for Crowley's fall.

This does not categorically invalidate Crowley's work, particularly *The Vision and the Voice* and earlier writing, which came prior to this spiritual error. It means that, like the work of any historical thinker, Crowley's prolific output must be approached with surgical clarity to separate what is of value from that which is not—and there is much that is of value. In many cases, this means fully severing Crowley the man (and even Crowley the symbol) from Crowley's technical writing on magic. Indeed, one of my many goals in writing this book has been properly placing magic in historical context, and liberating it from Crowley's cult of personality (as well as the infinitely tedious "Satanism" of those who emulated him, like Anton LaVey), without discarding his technical contributions.

Aleister Crowley died long ago, as have his most prominent students. If the Western magical tradition as a whole is to advance, it must put Crowley's work and failings in proper context—and then move on. The key to doing this is understanding that Crowley was not exemplifying the Western tradition, but that he instead created an inverted, shadow version of it.

Ultimately, Crowley is a central figure of the overall story of Dee's magic and the angels' architecture of Apocalypse. His study, for historical purposes, is therefore necessary. And as Carl Jung would counsel us, it is only by unflinchingly bringing the dark side into conscious awareness that we may grasp the truth, of history no less than our own selves; W. B. Yeats, Crowley's senior in the Golden Dawn (who despised the Beast), took the Latin motto (from Blavatsky's *Secret Doctrine*) of *Demon est Deus Inversus*, "the demon is the inverse of God." Only by facing darkness do we come to understand the light.

Here, then, is the inversion of the light.

THE AETHYRS THEMSELVES

Crowley and Neuburg's work in the Aethyrs is summarized below, in order to complete the historical narrative of Dee and Kelly's work, but not as a substitute for reading *The Vision and the Voice*. The titles of each section are taken from Crowley.[35]

Aethyr 30, TEX
The Exordium of the Equinox of the Gods.

The universe is shown as a giant, crystal cube shaped like Harpocrates, the silent form of Horus, encompassed by a sphere. The beginning of the Aeon of Horus is announced, an event of such violence that it will shake the foundations of the universe, plunging it into darkness at the coming of the Terrible Child, who is here female (suggesting the daughter of Babalon, who appears in the ninth Aethyr).

The symbolism follows Revelation, including the opening of seals and the appearance of the twenty-four seniors. Yet here, a new world is beginning as the old one is ending. Revelation is only the end of the Old Aeon, to be replaced with the formula of the New. This new formula is announced by four archangels that guard the four corners of the universe, who open books to reveal the formula written in the angelic language. These angels represent the Tetragrammaton, as well as the four lower sephiroth; a fifth is implied but not shown. (In the twenty-eighth Aethyr, however, they are told that there is now no fifth angel—only Coronzom, and dispersion, perhaps replacing Annael as the angel of the world, as mentioned in *Liber primus*. Coronzom, the name of

Satan in the spirit diaries, is here changed by Crowley to *Choronzon* so that the Hebrew enumerates to 333. *Coronzom* is thus the correct spelling in Enochian, with Choronzon being a transliteration into Hebrew characters.)

It is announced that the Father seeks a new bride to replace Babalon, the fallen and defiled woman. This invokes the Tetragrammaton, YHVH, by which the universe is renewed; the new Tetragrammaton that here must be formed is not only the completion of the initiation of the man Aleister Crowley, but also the establishment of the Aeon of Horus.*

More broadly, the vision of TEX suggests that the spiritual sights for humanity have shifted. Where once the goal was the attainment of Tiphareth (corresponding to "salvation" and represented by YHShVH, Christ), mankind must now make the harrowing journey across the Abyss to Binah, represented by Babalon. And while humanity has previously relied on the LVX formula—meaning seeking the light, as represented by the sun—it now must master the NOX formula of "darkness." Yet NOX is not darkness in the sense of the absence of the sun's light. It is the darkness of space, which is the concentrated light of infinite stars and galaxies, a light so strenuous that it cannot be perceived by man. To make the journey to the stars, mankind first needs a revolution in spirituality—and, at last, to be able to see beyond the shell of the individual ego.†

Aethyr 29, RII

The Disruption of the Aeon of Osiris.

Here, we meet the four living creatures—man, eagle, bull, and lion—who surround the Throne in Revelation, and who also correspond to the four elements. They are confused, frightened, and disoriented, for the formula of the Old Aeon has been abrogated—the old universe has been destroyed by the force of time (Saturn, Binah, Babalon)—and the New Aeon

---

*See Crowley, "The Formula of Tetragrammaton," in *Magick: Liber ABA,* 153–54.
†I can think of no better dramatization of this process than Stanley Kubrick's *2001,* including the Star Baby as Harpocrates and the short-circuiting ego, Coronzom, personified as HAL.

terrifies them, as the equilibrium of the universe has been disrupted. The Chaos (Chokmah, the Beast) that surrounds them, however, is only the "skeleton of a new truth," with the formula of the New Aeon as yet to be worked out. The messiah, or Horus, is also shown as a child growing in the womb of its mother, Binah, in whose bosom he is crucified.

Aethyr 28, BAG
The Vision of the Dawn of the Aeon of Horus (Atu XVII).

The formula of the Aeon of Horus is explained as the collapsing of dualities into nothingness—as Crowley later put it, zero equals two. Binah is invoked, and Crowley is given a foreshadowing of the Abyss he must cross in the tenth Aethyr. He must pass the dual ordeals of attaining knowledge and conversation of the holy guardian angel and crossing the Abyss (and therefore his utter destruction) if he is to attain to Babalon in Binah, and he can in no way achieve this by the use of his intellect. Furthermore, the four Watchtowers are shown to be within Chesed—that is, below the Abyss, representing manifest reality. They are next folded up and subsumed within Binah.

Aethyr 27, ZAA
The Vision of the Initiation of Hecate (Atu XIV). The Redemption of the Woman of Witchcraft by Love.

In this vision, several aspects of the Goddess appear—Nuit, Diana Trivia, Artemis—resolving into Hecate, who appears with her dog Cerberus, and stirs a cauldron in which appears the forty-nine-petalled rose from the floor of the Golden Dawn Vault of the Adepti, also signifying the forty-nine calls. Her son, who is to be a Magus, will initiate the Aeon of Horus—a foreshadowing of Crowley's attainment of the grade of Magus beginning in 1915. Further, it is stated that the Watchtowers and the Aethyrs must be reconciled, perhaps fulfilling the long-standing quest of "squaring the circle." Hecate's cauldron is revealed to be a lower reflection of the Cup of Babalon,* which she

---

*"She held a golden cup in her hand, filled with abominable things and the filth of her adulteries." Revelation 17:4 (NIV).

does not understand; she offers up pearls, representing Masters of the Temple, and a dragon soon arises from the cauldron, plunging the scrying stone into darkness before Hecate aspires to Binah, and concludes by uttering a ciphered word of the Aeon.

Aethyr 26, DES
The Slave-Gods Superseded. (The Vision of Atu XX,
the Stele.) The Vision of the Stele of Revealing,
Abolishing the Aeon of the Slave-Gods.

The cults of Jehovah and of Jesus are here disintegrated, and give way to the cult of Thelema—as symbolized by the Stele of Revealing, the Egyptian artifact that Aleister and Rose Crowley located in the Cairo Museum at the time of the reception of *The Book of the Law.* It is revealed that Jehovah is a representation of the qlipha of Chesed (i.e., is the Gnostic demiurge) and that his hold on the world was broken by Christ, a representation of Tiphareth—but that neither of them even reaches to the Abyss, let alone Binah.

Jesus, who here appears with an eagle's head,* utters the shocking pronouncement that "there is no sin, and there is no salvation"—he knows this truth, but keeps silent about it, for if it gets out, nobody will care about him. As such, he is an object of worship only for those still lost in the world of *Māyā,* not adepts, and is the accursed child of the elements, not their father; he himself prays to Binah and Chokmah, but as they are beyond the intellect, of which he is part, it goes unheard; he despairs that though he hears all prayers, none will hear *his* prayer. Jesus is being progressively disintegrated by the advance of human consciousness, and humanity is anguished at the loss of its ideal; the image of Christ is instead to be replaced with the new Thelemic trinity of Nuit, Hadit, and Ra-Hoor-Khuit. The blood of Christ and the bloodshed of the Christian era is absorbed by the earth, in preparation for growing new life—fertilizer for the New Aeon. The curse of the Old Aeon, and the doctrine of sin and salvation, are now overcome in the New.

The following four Aethyrs depict the four kerubs or elemental

---

*This may be a reference to the fourth beast, in Revelation 4:7.

guardians at Crowley's initiation, which also echo the four living creatures that appear in Ezekiel, Daniel, and Revelation. They correspond to the modes of utterance in Crowley's later Star Ruby ritual.

Aethyr 25, VTI

The Path of Teth. (Atu XI. The Fire-Kerub in the Initiation.) The Vision of the Fruit of the Great Work of the Beast 666. The Lion.

This Aethyr unveils the first form of the Beast 666, who appears as a lion, the fire kerub of the south.

Four kerubic angels representing Babalon, Death, Jehovah/Jesus, and the Beast 666 appear; the Beast devours Death and Jehovah, and then has his mouth closed by Babalon, as in the Strength tarot card. The Beast 666 himself, it is revealed, is the son of Set/Pan, or Satan, the Red Dragon, and the "woman clothed with the sun" in Revelation 12—a disturbing image indeed if the biblical passage is read with this in mind. Angels announce with trumpets and spears that the world is at an end, and the universe and all angels and gods in it are shown as dust motes in the eye of the Beast, who swallows up the lower sephiroth and paths. The Beast is here revealed as having the soul of Horus and the body of the lion-headed serpent of Gnosticism—Ialdabaoth, the Demiurge, potentially relating to the beings seen by Dee and Kelly during the reception of the Tablet of Earth. This imagery—snakes, trumpets, and fire—may also relate to the raising of kundalini, which arises as a serpent of fire, destroys the individual yogi's universe, and is accompanied by trumpet sounds heard internally.[36]

The Beast, who is known as Chaos, also progresses toward Binah and is ridden by Babalon, the Scarlet Woman. Crowley himself is to be the avatar of this being—the Beast 666, armed with all of the secrets of magick (Crowley's spelling, used to differentiate operative magic from stage magic) as possessed by the A∴A∴ and OTO—though he is not yet fully initiated. In the wake of the Aeon of Horus he initiates, the "worldly Fire" will be purged.[37] The Beast is now the *logos,* rather than Christ; its voice is as a tremendous, martial roaring, which is somehow also articulate. Crowley must fully identify himself with the Beast-as-*logos,* and to do so must come to bear the sins of the entire world. The

Fig. 16.4. Gustave Doré, *The Crowned Virgin: A Vision of John,* 1866, depicting the "woman clothed with the sun" and Red Dragon from Revelation 12.

Beast now departs; its tail shows endless houses, temples, towns, wars, planets, and much more, and from the tuft at the end of it, it sprouts new universes and galaxies. Lastly, a foreshadowing of the Aeon of Ma'at, which will supersede that of Horus, is given.

Aethyr 24, NIA

The Rose. (The Woman of Atu XIV, Minister of Babalon; the Water-Kerub in the Initiation.) The First Kiss of the Lady of Initiation.

Babalon, the consort of the Beast, here appears in the form of the woman in the Temperance or Art card of the tarot. Babalon here hints at the secrets of sex magic and is the water kerub of the west. The Aethyr is saturated with Venus and rose imagery.

Crowley will be drawn across the Abyss and his personality annihilated in Binah. To do so, he must fold up all ten sephiroth of the Tree into a single star (as in "Every man and woman is a star" and "One Star in Sight"; this is the starlight of the ajna chakra and the spark of the Pleroma spoken of in Gnosticism), which in turn must be annihilated into the infinitely small point represented by Hadit, raw consciousness itself, the point of view or Atman. In doing so, the entire manifested universe will be extinguished, as its perfect play or *lila* is no longer needed as a drama to initiate the seeker.

Several alchemical, Rosicrucian, Golden Dawn, and Thelemic formulae are given in Latin, centering around the letters TARO, itself the magical formulae of the tarot, by the use of which Crowley is told he can do any magic, white or black. Crowley is now drawn into a rose, becoming enraptured with it.

Aethyr 23, TOR

The Kerubim of Earth and Air. (Minor Officers in the Initiation to 8°=3□.) The Vision of the Interplay and Identity of Earth and Air.

The two remaining kerubim are introduced: the Bull for earth and the Eagle for air, who are complementary. With the preceding two kerubim, they make up the four kerubs of the New Aeon—lion, woman, bull, and eagle—that replace the four living creatures of the previous aeon, being lion, man, ox, and eagle. The primary differences here are the replacement of man with woman, and of ox with bull, suggesting the reincorporation of sexuality into religion within the New Aeon, rather than its exclusion as "sinful," a formula of the Black Brotherhood. (An ox is a bull that has been castrated to make it a docile and servile work animal, an apt metaphor for the effect of antisexual religions on humanity.)

Aethyr 22, LIN
The Forty-Nine–fold Table. (First Appearance of the Crowned and Conquering Child to the Exempt Adept as in the Pastos.)
The Vision of the Rose, the Heart of BABALON,
and of the Birth of the Universe.

The Aethyr opens with the second seven-by-seven table given to Dee and Kelly by the angels, the magic square from which the names of the angels beneath the heptagon on the Sigillum Dei Aemeth were taken—these being the planetary angels directly beneath the heptagon, the Daughters and Sons of Light, and their Daughters and Sons. The square is surrounded by gods, angels, and elementals, from highest to lowest. Crowley looks further into the square, and notes that every single letter of the table *itself* contains forty-nine more letters, each in the alphabet of Honorius from Agrippa. The angel tells Crowley:

> As there are forty-nine letters in the tablet, so are there forty-nine kinds of cosmos in every thought of God. And there are forty-nine interpretations of every cosmos, and each interpretation is manifested in forty-nine ways. Thus also are the calls forty-nine, but to each call there are forty-nine visions. And each vision is composed of forty-nine elements, except in the tenth Aethyr, and that hath forty-two.[38]

Crowley, taking the form of a winged egg and surrounded by angels who melt onto its surface as liquid light, touches the tablet and is enwrapped by all of the names of God, entering samadhi "behind" the table—as the table is a veil for the infinite. Returning to himself, he next gives the LVX and NOX formulae, and perceives his inner soul-star as his true self. The table, which is made of pure light, sweeps everything away, and the thundering voice of the aeon resounds as one continuous "Amen."

Crowley is next entombed in the Pastos of the vault of Christian Rosenkreutz (from not only the Golden Dawn but the Rosicrucian manifestos themselves), recapitulating his Adeptus Minor initiation in the Golden Dawn—the traditional Golden Dawn vault itself is of seven sides, containing the Rosy Cross and the heptagram seal of Babalon, the heptagram from the Sigillum Dei, which itself is constructed from the Sevenfold Table; this demonstrates a consistent thread of symbolism running through *Liber iuratus,* Dee, Rosicrucianism, the Golden

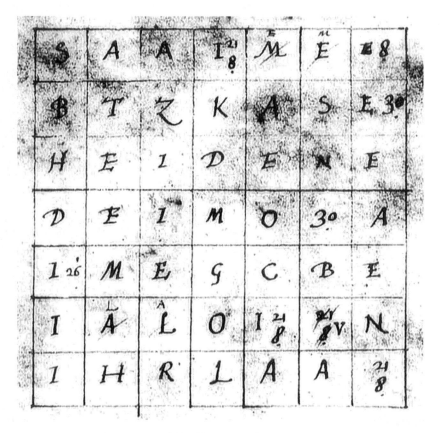

Fig. 16.5. The Holy Sevenfold Table, in Dee's hand. From MS. Sloane 3188.

Dawn, and Thelema. Here Crowley hears the voice of Horus, who bids him to partake in the glory of the New Aeon. In the original ceremony, the candidate found his initiator within the Pastos, but here, Crowley *himself* is entombed within it.

Yet now Crowley is expelled from the Aethyr by the Sevenfold Table, for he has made the mistake of trying to rationalize the vision. Only by the sevenfold word ARARITA, symbolizing the seven planets, will he be able to overcome the intellect and attain further. He now returns to the world and sees it for what it is—sorrowful—just as the Buddha did. This again suggests Saturn, Binah, the passage of time that turns all to dust.

Aethyr 21, ASP
Ether. (The Hierophant Prepares the Candidate.)
The Vision of the Ineluctable Destiny.

Proceeding through an empty, windswept expanse, with shadows of angels passing over, Crowley makes his way to an "avenue of pillars," at the end of which is a throne supported by two sphinxes, all in black marble. Upon the throne sits an invisible figure, representing Fate, from whom all the desolation of the Aethyr comes. The figure communicates with Crowley using a rapid series of tastes that Crowley translates into Hebrew letters using Qabalistic correspondences, revealing what appears to be a prophecy that Crowley will return health to the earth by breaking the hold of sexual repression.

Crowley is meeting God "face-to-face"; God is also acting as the Hierophant in his initiation. The face of God here echoes the Qabalistic conception of the Greater and Lesser Countenances (as famously drawn by Eliphas Levi), or the beginning of the Upanishads, in which God longs to behold his countenance in the Abyss.

Using the air dagger (the elemental tool of air), Crowley attempts to cut the eyelids off the God's three eyes, that he may open them and destroy the universe as Shiva did. This is fruitless, as Crowley must use the dagger of penance, not the air dagger, and the dagger of penance must be sharpened by ordeal.

Crowley is confronting God, but instead of a holy and glorious image, he is faced with an "Abomination of Desolation."* All in the world proceeds from this god, but none go to him, and "only those who accept nothing from me can bring anything to me."[39] Yet Crowley soon realizes that this is not God, who speaks only through silence, but is instead the Ape of Thoth, that babbles to speak for God and mocks him by so doing. Yet this babble is also the pulse of his heart and the sound of his breath. This represents the voice of the mind—perhaps even the autonomous bodily functions that become deafening to the advanced meditator—that gets in the way of the perception of the truth. The silencing of this babbling marks the passage to Briah, according to James Eshelman, as it shows the silencing of the mind.[40]

Yet Crowley is pushed back and expelled, because he cannot prove that he is of high enough grade to claim the vision. An angel expels him back into the world, now that he has "gazed upon the horror of the loneliness of the First;"[41] furthermore, this God (Jehovah) is a relic of the Old Aeon, and Crowley is the prophet of the New, and he may instead be contented and comforted by Nuit and Hadit. Indeed, meeting God and instead "seeing the man behind the curtain," as Crowley has, is the "Ordeal X" spoken of in *The Book of the Law*. For there is no monad—instead, there are infinite monads, as there are infinite combinations of zero and two, the marriage of any particular point of infinite space and any given individual viewpoint.

Transitional Note

Beyond the twenty-first Aethyr, the visions begin to take on a different character. As they come closer to the Abyss, they begin to more closely approximate supernal logic; statements now begin to contain their opposites, as above the Abyss all opposites are reconciled into unities.

---

*The original biblical Abomination of Desolation was a statue of Jupiter erected by Antiochus IV Epiphanes in the Second Temple during the second century BC, desecrating the shrine; it is mentioned in both Old and New Testaments, including in Daniel, where a future desecration is prophesied. In *The Book of the Law*, Abomination of Desolation is the name given to the Stele of Revealing, depicting the Thelemic trinity, which also symbolically defiles Christianity.

Therefore, it is wise not to take statements in these Aethyrs as suggesting straightforward dogma.

Aethyr 20, KHR

The Path of Kaph (Atu X). The Hierus Prepares the Candidate. The Vision of the Wheel of Fortune. The Three Energies of the Universe.

Crowley is given a vision of the "Wheel of Fortune" tarot card, which represents the world of *Māyā* or illusion (the *bhavachakra* in Tibetan Buddhism) or the whirling nature of the mind. It is here depicted as a vast sphere, rather than a wheel, and is spun by a hand (pertaining to the Hebrew letter *Kaph,* hand, to which the tarot card is attributed). The three forces that whirl on the wheel are the sulphur, salt, and mercury of alchemy or *sattva, rajas,* and *tamas* of Hinduism; corresponding to the physical body, intellect, and intuition.

These three forces are here attracted by three predatory beings: the wolf for the "lusts of the flesh," the raven for the "lusts of the mind," and the pure white lamb—the Agnes Dei itself—which attracts the unwary by *simulating* the pure seeking of the soul. This lamb seduces the Elect with the false doctrine of sin and vicarious salvation, and despite its innocent appearance rends them limb from limb.

The Jupiterian nature of the wheel is now shown to project solar deities; the wheel itself turns into the god Shiva Nataraj, God in his dancing form, who crushes Crowley underfoot. Crowley is given a glimpse of his holy guardian angel, with whom he longs to unite with all of his being, instead of the three false creatures of the wheel; it is affirmed that his True Will is indeed to lead mankind to unity with their own holy guardian angels, which is the next step in human evolution.

Aethyr 19, POP

The Path of Gimel. (The Hegemon between the Pillars. Preliminary: The Vision of the Unguided Universe.)

A hermit gives Crowley entry into a great vista of war, similar to the war of the mind depicted in the Bhagavad Gita, except that instead of a war with two sides, in this one every man is for himself—every combatant represents a thought. This demonstrates that thoughts are all useless noise if not organized by Understanding (Binah); this dispersion will only increase until Crowley crosses the Abyss. It is also shown that time, Saturn (represented as Sebek the crocodile god) will devour everything in the world; this can only be overcome by attaining the perspective of a Magister Templi.

The holy guardian angel will destroy the universe (for the magician); yet the angel tells him that God is the image of man, and that there is no hope in anything but man. The angel opens her book (as seen in the High Priestess card—traditionally the Torah) to a page that shows the Holy Table of Dee and Kelly's temple furniture, which radiates light. An elaboration of the Christian formula IChThUS, the fish/vesica that represents Christ, Pisces, and the Aeon of Osiris is given.

Aethyr 18, ZEN

Tiphareth. (The King's Chamber. The Vision of the Holy Guardian Angel.) The Instruction Concerning the Obtaining of the Vision and the Voice of the Thirty Aethyrs. The Preparation of the Candidate.

The Aethyr opens with a nightside inversion of the Crucifixion, in which Christ is an enormous crucified bat, and the thieves on either side of him are crucified children.

Crowley is next admitted by an angel into a ruby Great Pyramid of Giza; within the King's Chamber is the true Vault of the Adepts, from the Rosicrucian manifestos and Adeptus Minor initiation of the Golden Dawn; it is filled with the light of Horus. There is also a foreshadowing of Crowley's initiation to Magister Templi, in which this light will be extinguished in the supernal darkness of NOX; he is taken by an angel into another cell that is the birth chamber of a Magister Templi; he is born out into the pylons where Isis, Nephthys, and Ra preside over his emergence as a New Star.

Crowley is next given a much more elaborate set of instructions for more fully scrying an Aethyr (in Briah, in samadhi) by undertaking a ninety-one-hour retirement—in which a magician conducts a vigil and fasts in darkness, followed by a banishing of all other active forces, and a conjuration of the Aethyr using Dee's temple furniture as an altar. The call is to be written on Qabalistically colored vellum in angelic (a new Qabalistic color scale and set of attributions is given) that is then burned in a lamp, following which he assumes a yoga pose at the table and the vision is then given. "For this is a holy mystery, and he that did first attain to reveal the alphabet thereof," the angel of the Aethyr tells Crowley, meaning Kelly specifically, "perceived not one ten-thousandth part of the fringe that is upon its vesture."[42]

Aethyr 17, TAN

The Path of Lamed. (The Combination Gimel, Lamed, Samekh.) The Vision of the Justice or Balance of the Universe.

Here, an old friend arrives: Madimi. She appears in a new form (although Crowley does not specify what), which Crowley asks her about; she replies that "since all things are God, in all things thou seest just so much of God as thy capacity affordeth thee." The Aethyr itself is of balance (Lamed, Libra), the scales, as the principles of balance are elaborated to Crowley; Hadit is introduced as well. The Gnostic demiurge is cursed: "Woe unto the second, whom all nations of men call the First,"[43] as is the true God (as in the twentieth Aethyr); only Nuit and Hadit are truly infinite. The principle of truth is elaborated—as in the weighing of the heart by a feather in the Hall of Judgment in the Egyptian Book of the Dead, one's truth glitters forth as a Star, Hadit (the voice of the fire); this is the beginning of the "chymical wedding" of the alchemists. To continue the Wedding is to undertake the ritual of obtaining the knowledge and conversation of the holy guardian angel, and this is yet to come.

Aethyr 16, LEA

Kether. (Oath of Pe.) The Overthrow of the Slave-Gods by the Beast 666.

A virgin on a bull appears, as Pasiphaë and the Minotaur, echoing the Beast and Babalon. Next, the angels of the Holy Sevenfold Table appear again. They await Jehovah, who appears with crown, orb, scepter, and robes, yet tears them down and tramples them—the Tower is shattered, and now all men walk on their hands; human beings are now to worship from the inside out, worshipping the star of divinity within instead of the external "God." (A reference to anal sex magic is also given.) Thelemites— the servants of the star and the snake—will now eat up the entire world like locusts; magicians shall rule the earth.* All this shall proceed from the throne of the Beast, which is the Abomination of Desolation, as the Beast sends lying spirits into the world to establish the New Aeon, which ultimately will be overthrown. The Beast comes forth like a lion;† those who worship him shall have every mystery that has not been revealed from the foundation of the world revealed to them, and shall have power over all of the elements (as in the Bornless One ritual); angels and gods shall walk with them. Jehovah himself will wander the wastes, will be caught and shamed by these servants of the star and snake, and be utterly humbled before the Beast 666; finally, he shall come to worship the Beast himself.

A direct image of the Beast 666 as he is—not Crowley, but an actual spiritual being—is given. He has an androgynous face, both male and female, with the Mark of the Beast‡ on his brow, breast, and palm; he is gigantic, with a Uraeus crown, leopard's skin, and flaming orange apron. Nuit surrounds him invisibly, his heart is Hadit, and Ra-Hoor-Khuit is between his feet. A flaming wand is in his right hand, and *The Book of the Law* in his left.

Jehovah can do nothing but lie prostrate before the Beast; now the virgin on the bull returns, led by the angels of the Holy Sevenfold Table, and hints that she will give herself to the Beast. Crowley, now coming to see the glory of the Beast, rejoices that he is being purged of his Christianity.

Aethyr 15, OXO

The Vision of the Rose of Forty-Nine Petals, and of the Holy Twelvefold Table. Examination of the Candidate for Magister Templi.

In this Aethyr, Crowley is initiated into the true and invisible Rosicrucian order. Babalon appears in a form similar to Salomé; as

---

*A reference to the locusts unleashed from the Abyss in Revelation 9:3, led by the angel Abaddon or Apollyon.

†Guénon also picks up on the solar symbolism of the Beast, and notes that both the Messiah and the Antichrist are symbolized by the lion. See Guénon, *The Reign of Quantity*, 272.

‡A conjoined sun and moon.

Salomé had the head of John the Baptist removed, here Babalon gathers the heads of adepts for Nuit, much like Kali does, offering their mortal personalities as food for the gods. Through her dance, she has woven the Rose of Forty-Nine Petals, conjoined with a cross made of two pillars, perhaps the Masonic pillars Boaz and Jachin. The Rose itself is a gigantic seven-tiered amphitheater of rose marble, so large that a sun could be used as a ball thrown between those sitting in it, each tier having seven partitions; the seven tiers are for the seven suborders of the Order of the Rosy Cross. In the center is an altar surrounded by four beasts, upon which is Pan, who is worshipped under different forms by each grade of the order—this is the Sabbath.

The altar, it is revealed, is Dee and Kelly's Holy Twelvefold Table, with the twelve angelic characters in the center. The only way to reveal the secrets of this table is to form a pool of clear water from the sweat of one's own brow, within which the secrets will be revealed. The forty-nine petals, plus the center, together make up the fifty gates of Binah. The table becomes the universe, with every star in it a letter of the book of Enoch (presumably *Liber Loagaeth*), which itself is drawn from a Mystery known only to the angels and the Sevenfold Table.

Crowley is now tested by adepts from each grade of the order; upon passing, he is given the secrets of the center of the Holy Twelvefold Table, through which he may exercise control of the elements or even evil magic (if read diagonally, revealing the names of devils). He is also told that the Ensigns of Creation hold the mysteries of drawing forth the letters, and that the letters of the circumference of the table "declare the glory of Nuit"[44]—that is, that they show the zodiacal powers, as each side starts from Ares (the Enochian letter *Pa*). The adepts chant in rapture, bringing ruin to the work of Choronzon, as they are declaring the order of the universe, rather than dispersion. The vision now suggests a method by which the angelic alphabet may be mapped to the stars, which Crowley says pertains only to the grade of Magus and thus is unrevealed.*

He is now withdrawn into the Rosy Cross, which sits atop a pyramid

---

*For suggestive material, see Broome, *The Astral Origin of the Emblems*.

in the darkness because of exceeding "light behind"; Crowley is told that the Sevenfold Table contains the name of God written openly, and the Twelvefold Table contains his name written in concealed form. Crowley is now caught up and absorbed into the lower reflections of Nuit.

Aethyr 14, VTA
The Vision of the City of the Pyramids. The Reception of the Master of the Temple.

Here is Crowley's final initiation to Magister Templi. Following an abortive attempt in which Crowley attempts to pierce the veil of the Aethyr, the angel of the Aire (who is Hadit, Chaos, Chokmah, and Hermes) tells him that he must invoke in darkness rather than sunlight.

By the fourteenth Aethyr, Crowley and Neuburg have ascended the mountain Daleh Addin (now called Djebel Chélia). They now break the Aethyr for six and a half hours at the urging of Hadit, and Crowley has Neuburg sodomize him, as an effort in taboo breaking and disruption of the personality, an event Crowley wrote of circuitously in the record, as sodomy was still illegal.*

When he re-calls the Aethyr, Crowley is surrounded by an impossibly black darkness—the complete negation of light characteristic of Binah—and told that he is now the master of the fifty gates of Binah and of the pentagram, in which spirit is glyphed as a black egg. The great sea of Binah is lightless, with no sun, star, or moon—NOX. Here there is sterility, desolation, and sorrow (as pertinent to Saturn). What Crowley had perceived to be rocks are actually masters, who are veiled

---

*This act assisted the attainment of further visionary states; it may also have been a deep working out of Crowley's own conflict around his sexuality. While homosexuality was not new for him, passive sodomy may have been. This sexual taboo breaking mirrored Madimi's request that Dee and Kelly swap wives, perhaps as a method for inducing disassociation in order to open the consciousness to further visionary input. As Dee and Kelly also did, Crowley wrote that he "obeyed my Angel," and turned passive sodomy into a means of invoking his higher genius. Crowley glyphed this act in later writings as "XI° OTO"—homosexual sex magic—although at the time he had not yet been initiated into OTO. He would later write about gay sex magic from the comfort of his own intellect and literary anonymity in his *Scented Garden of Abdullah the Satirist of Shiraz*, where he became much more confident and bombastic.

and motionless, without identity; upon their bowed backs rests the universe. Crowley is told that though he began studying magic dreaming of vast powers and glories (of the four elements, seven planets, twelve zodiac signs, twenty-two tarot trumps, and forty-nine calls), he has instead become as one of these lifeless masters, who are now shown to be pyramids, each of which is also a temple of initiation and a tomb (as seen in the eighteenth Aethyr). All of the illusions of the lower sephiroth and paths have been discarded; the masters are now nothing more than pyramids of dust. Yet following their attainment, they are cast out like Satan into the lower sephiroth (each according to their nature) to fulfill their work. For fifty are the gates of Binah, and 156 are the seasons thereof.

Aethyr 13, ZIM
The Garden of Nemo. The Work of the Magister Templi.
Crowley is brought to a garden—he is now declared NEMO, No Man, for no man has looked upon the face of God and survived. Therefore, Crowley is No Man, and his work is to tend a garden of disciples prepared from the desert, watering them without favoring one over another, in the hope that one day one of them will come to take his place as the next NEMO—this garden is a new Garden of Eden. He finds an old man in a secret house who is also NEMO, who writes a book, the leaves of which are the petals of the flowers in the garden, and who hopes that one day one of his flowers will grow to be a new NEMO. In the first through fifteenth Aethyrs, there is no vision or voice but that of NEMO, and anyone who follows vision or voice will be led away to destruction; Crowley has been inoculated against illusion by the *via negativa* practiced upon the visions and strong delusions of the lower Aethyrs.

Aethyr 12, LOE
The Path of Cheth. The Bearer of the Sangraal. The Black Brothers.
The Chariot of the tarot appears, drawn by four sphinxes and bearing a charioteer who clasps the Holy Grail—drawn from earlier Celtic, not Christian sources, and emitting a "ruddy glow" suggesting menstruation.

The air is filled with the scent of burning Cakes of Light, from *The Book of the Law*. The cup is that of Babalon, which contains the blood of the saints, which is now the wine of the sacrament, for she has seduced the world. This wine is Compassion—which is intoxicating, destroys all thoughts, and is made of suffering (a deeply Tibetan Buddhist teaching). Thus the mystery of Babalon is revealed; as she has become the servant of each, so is she the mistress of all, and is Understanding. This is a formula of attaining samadhi with all and everything. Babalon rides upon the Beast, who is the lord of the City of Pyramids seen in Aethyr 14, the description of which fits Ankh-af-na-Khonsu from the Stele of Revealing. She will not rest in her adulteries until the blood of all that lives is gathered up, matured into wine, and offered to her Father, whose virtue shines through her. This seems to be a statement about the culling of souls at the Apocalypse.

Yet this process shall repeat again and again, as the universe is unfolded as a rose, and closed up as a cross into a cube. This is the secret of the Rosicrucians, enacted in the Vault of the Adepti. It is also the secret of the Passover supper in Exodus 12, which is depicted as a perversion of this formula and as a method of the Black Brothers, who close their doors from the Angel of Death (Saturn) with blood, and thereby resist the world, and compassion, keeping themselves from the world and from Babalon in their lonely fortresses. The Black Brothers send forth delusion (in the form of the major religions) to war against the Holy One, but in so serving Choronzon they are eventually eaten up by Time. All this will of necessity be destroyed by forces radiating from the Supernals.

Aethyr II, IKH
Yesod. The Frontier of the Abyss.

A magical square of the moon appears, which is rolled up to reveal a host of angels clad in armor and armed for battle, flanked by elephants, armed with thunderbolts of Zeus and the artillery of meteors. All of this imagery is consistent with the sphere of the moon. The army is defended by nine iron towers filled with silver-armored warriors who guard the Holy City of the Most High from the malice of the devil

Choronzon. The number nine, Yesod, is 333 added together, with its changes stabilized (333 being the number of Choronzon).

However, Crowley must go out of the fortress that guards against the Abyss and confront Choronzon, the lord of the four Princes of Evil. The Abyss represents sickness of aspiration, will, and the essence of reality—and if anyone goes into the Abyss without Understanding (having attained to Magister Templi and NEMO), they become the slaves of Choronzon. Even the fortress itself is now attacked, but God has ordered the universe perfectly, and made it stable through eternal war. Crowley is now warned that in every Aethyr he must take the mask of the guardian therein, and that if there be one drop of blood left it will entirely corrupt him; with the words "Eloi, Eloi, lama sabacthani," the last word of the Aethyr, he is rushed past the last outposts into the Abyss.

Aethyr 10, ZAX
The Abyss. Choronzon, His Nature.
Here Crowley meets Choronzon, 333, the "metaphysical contrary of the whole Process of Magick."[45]

The Aethyr itself is accursed, and so the magicians are to use a specifically designed circle and triangle, as in *The Goetia*. Neuburg is to be in the circle, evoking with methods from the Golden Dawn and *Liber iuratus,* while Crowley is to be placed in the triangle, as a demon would be, and will sacrifice three pigeons therein, one at each of its corners. Neuburg will be armed with the air dagger, with which he will keep Crowley in the triangle and defend himself if need be, being bound by oath to do so. The blood of the pigeons is to form the material basis that will allow Choronzon to manifest.

As the Aethyr opens, the cry of Choronzon is given ("Zazas, Zazas, Nasatanada Zazas").[46] Choronzon manifests, speaking through Crowley; he is the force of dispersion and of absolute chaos, of the mind in its utmost disorder, of knowledge and facts disconnected from any ordering principle (which would be Binah, Understanding). The demon takes various forms to tempt Neuburg, psychically manifesting through Crowley, who is sitting still in a yoga asana. Crowley later remarked that he was overshadowed by the demon, and did not speak as himself, remembering nothing of the ritual, other than a sense of being protected and unafraid.* What remains is the qlipha of Frater O.M., the shards left over of Crowley's personality that cannot make the jump across the Abyss.

The demon attempts to tempt Neuburg by taking the forms of a beautiful woman, a wise and holy man, a serpent; Neuburg maintained until late in life that he had literally fought a demon in Bou Saada. It consistently mocks Neuburg's efforts to control it. It voids god names from its fundament and laughs at Neuburg's pentagrams. Neuburg calls angels and even Crowley's holy guardian angel; Choronzon laughs at these and says that they are only covers for the pair's filthy sorceries. And so it continues. Neuburg cannot argue with Choronzon, because it only encourages him; he cannot threaten the demon with anger, pain, or hell, because it is all of these things. His malice is the quality of malice itself, and those who have fallen under his power are the blind who follow the blind, declaring themselves enlightened.

This is ZAX, the world of adjectives, and there is no substance therein. The demon tries tricks to distract Neuburg, while it throws sand into the circle, breaking the barrier; it rushes in and attacks Neuburg, who beats the demon back by calling upon Tetragrammaton. After being pushed away, it attempts to make Neuburg laugh at and renounce magick itself. It next appears as a naked woman, wanting Crowley's shirt to keep herself warm. But Neuburg, valiantly, perseveres against Choronzon, who tells him that had he doubted for an instant, he would have gnawed through his spine at the neck.

Having persevered to the end, Crowley emerges from samadhi and writes BABALON in the sand with his holy ring, declaring victory over 333, and the circle and triangle are burned in a great fire to purify the place of working.

Neuburg later noted that Choronzon was terrified by silence and concentration, and could be brought to obedience by *willing in silence;* at one point Neuburg also found that he could disturb the demon by

---

*As James Eshelman notes, the record is of Neuburg's experience; it is *not* what Crowley experienced while crossing the Abyss. See Eshelman, *Visions and Voices,* 333.

whistling in a "magical manner." Neuburg obtained such skill in working with this demon that he later evoked Choronzon on his own in order to obtain information by sitting and refusing to respond to the entity's long-winded speeches—observing that "Choronzon is dispersion; and such is his fear of concentration that he will obey rather than be subjected to it, or even behold it in another."[47]

Aethyr 9, ZIP
Malkuth. (The Pure Virgin.) The Reward of the Magister Templi.
Having passed ZAX, Crowley finds himself walking upon a "razor-edge of light suspended over the Abyss,"[48] surrounded by the armies of the Most High (IAIDA) as in the eleventh Aethyr. He is greeted by the angel of the Aire, who welcomes him as one who has given himself up fully into the Cup of Babalon, transcended the Abyss, and surrendered his human personality; he is led to the Palace of the Virgin,[49] the "curse" of the Call of the Thirty Aethyrs has now become a secret blessing. The fifty gates of Binah have now opened to the City of God (perhaps that spoken of by St. Augustine).

They come to an impossibly ornate palace, which is the body of a twelve-year-old girl: the daughter of Babalon, the glory of which is infinitely beyond anything Crowley has yet beheld, and which subsumes the glory of all the previous Aethyrs. This is the Virgin of Eternity—the Heh-final in the Tetragrammaton—who has born a child unto the king, the Yod, the father of All; she sits upon the throne of Binah and Understanding, on a sea of glass, her hair bedecked with seven stars, and her name is Koré, Malkah, Betulah, and Persephone. She is the ultimate virgin, after which young men and poets have sought, but only in vain—for no language, thought, magic, will, or imagination may come near her, all of it being of the mind. She stands on a sea of glass, as in Revelation 15:2.

Holy beyond all words, she is sending out images of exceeding beauty that proceed downward across the Abyss, cast off as the qliphoth of Binah that produce the lower worlds. So beautiful is the vision to all of Crowley's senses that he cannot bear it except by an act of will. She is Shakti, manifesting the powers of the All-Father into the Watchtowers.

Crowley is taken by an angel into a chamber within one of the nine towers of the palace, which contains a map of the Aethyrs arranged in the form of a flaming sword proceeding through the ten sephiroth, which is above Crowley's grade. Crowley is here given yet another method of calling the Aethyrs, possibly pertaining to Atziluth. This new method will not only cause trembling within (as in kundalini phenomena), but will also cause the world to tremble from without, by the earthquakes of judgment; the elements will swallow all. A secret of mastery is given: an adept is crowned with the Holy Spirit, but a master is filled with it.

Aethyr 8, ZID

The Holy Guardian Angel. His Instruction.

Crowley enters a pyramid of light, in which he meets his holy guardian angel—Aiwass, the Voice of the Silence, minister of Ra-Hoor-Khuit, who dictated *The Book of the Law,* kindling light to draw Crowley upward into the great NOX. Now that Crowley understands (is initiate into Binah), Aiwass delivers him a new set of instructions for use in attaining Knowledge and Conversation to give to humanity so that all can attain; this is to replace the earlier instructions given in the *Book of Abramelin.* (As with Dee and Kelly's sessions, the angels work to clarify earlier published instructions given in grimoires.)

Just as the instructions for calling an Aethyr given in the eighteenth Aethyr call for a ninety-one-hour period of seclusion, this operation calls for a seclusion of ninety-one days. It partakes of the methodology of Abramelin as well as the Ritual of Passing the Tuat, but uses Thelemic symbology instead of Christian, and also implements the use of the Holy Twelvefold and Sevenfold Tables. At the conclusion of this ritual the adept will return to the world, and their angel shall guide them in further initiation until they also cross the Abyss and become initiated into Binah.

This initiation will slay the aspirant, and their suffering will make them greater even than the kings of the earth, the angels of the heavens, and the gods beyond the heavens, until the aspirant meets their own holy guardian angel, and is destroyed by it in a red rain of lightning, and by the weight of their own pyramid of initiation. The holy guardian angel, it is revealed, is *totally* of the Supernals, and not in Gimel, for the paths crossing the Abyss are the servants of Babalon and the Beast. This is for all humanity, and those who possess this ritual are to utterly deny themselves in giving it unto those who have need of it.

Another Transitional Note

Beyond ZID, the Aethyrs begin to lock up on Crowley, because he has only been initiated to the 8°=3° degree of Magister Templi and no further. As such, he is only given glimpses of the remaining Aethyrs, which pertain to the 9°=2° Magus and 10°=1° Ipsissimus grades.

Aethyr 7, DEO
The Path of Daleth. The Black Brothers.
A door of Venus is opened by an angel, and from it comes flames, each of which is one of the greatest love stories of the world, forming a rose that becomes the woman clothed with the sun from Revelation 12, so beautiful that she cannot be looked upon, who is also the Fool. She transmits the *logos* from Chokmah to Binah and as such takes the many forms of the goddess of love, each of which is a letter in the alphabet of love; Crowley also beholds the Universal Peacock. She is the footstool of the Holy One, as Binah is his throne. Here is seen the infinite rainbow light proceeding from the prism of Chokmah.

Beneath her feet is the Abyss, a great desert wherein dwell the Black Brothers, lonely souls in black robes who swarm around howling, bumping into each other. They have grasped love and clung to it, praying at the feet of the goddess, and locked themselves up in "fortresses of love."[50]

The curse spoken in the Call of the Thirty Aethyrs is the creation of Shakti at the beginning of the world. A version of the Creation is now given in which Adam is the concealed God in the garden of the Supernals, who creates Eve, who is tempted by the serpent, who is the Messiah and kundalini, and who destroys the equilibrium of the garden. The calls are now shown to be necessary for the construction of Eden, and that it could not have been any other way.

However, the Black Brothers have misinterpreted this, because there is no path between Binah and Chesed, meaning only a spark (as in Gnosticism) proceeds from the Supernals rather than a current; "when the Stooping Dragon raised his head unto Daäth in the course of that spark, there was, as it were, an explosion, and his head was blasted. And the ashes thereof were dispersed throughout the whole of the tenth Aethyr. And for this, all knowledge is piecemeal, and it is of no value unless it be co-ordinated by Understanding."[51]

The Aethyr takes the form of a brass eagle that winds about, filling the Aethyr with sparks. Babalon's daughter returns riding a dolphin and sees the Black Brothers, who have sought to restrict love. The Black Brothers rush about in darkness, looking for something but bumping into each other because they are so shut up in their cloaks of restriction. They have shut themselves up against the natural flow of the universe, the greatest tragedy of all. If any of them were to throw off their cloak and behold Babalon's daughter they would be redeemed by love, but none will. Yet they are still encamped on the edges of Eden, permitted to advance this far out of compassion. Babalon's daughter, on her throne, radiates a love supreme. Even Crowley is not able to fully behold this vision, but he has been permitted to see some of it that he may meditate on it until the true vision and voice of the Aethyr is heard.

Aethyr 6, MAZ
The Vision of the Urn. The Magus 9°=2□. The Three Schools of Magick.

This Aethyr foreshadows the attainment of the grade of Magus, as the *logos,* in this case as the Beast 666.

Here the angel Ave appears, from the Dee and Kelly sessions, in whom the signs of sulphur and the pentagram are harmonized by a swastika. Ave (whose name was extracted from the Sevenfold Table) is revealed as the radiance of Thoth; the Aethyr itself is suffused by images forming and dissolving faster than lightning, all illusions created by the Ape of Thoth.[52] The Star of the tarot appears, emanating the light of the path of Aleph; Crowley is given a vision of the fixed mercury (that is, a still mind), uniting the perfected Sulphur and salt; all of them are thrown off by the swastika (Kether), which is Aleph, Beth, and Gimel; these three thunderbolts defend the Crown.

Echoing the discovery of the drunk and naked Noah by his children after the Flood in Genesis 9:21–27, a voice states that whoever likewise uncovers the nakedness of the Most High, who is drunk on the blood of the adepts imbibed from the Cup of Babalon, will be cursed. Babalon, having encouraged his drunkenness and then left him naked, summons her children to make a mockery of him. After being cursed, the three children of Babalon react to their shame in different ways, representing the three schools of magick,[53] and the Three Magi; because Crowley has not yet attained to Wisdom, he does not get to know which school prevails, or if the three are one or not. The Black Brothers (not to be confused with the Black School) do not reach this far, having been drowned in the Flood (Binah). The *logos* of God is now revealed as a lie, and must be destroyed to pass further. Having slain the *logos,* however, one must take its place and become the deceiver and maker of snares, baffling even those who have understanding.* So have all the founders of the great religions been deceived, being bound with the curse of Thoth. As speakers of truth, they have enslaved the masses with lies, because no truth may extend beyond Binah; instead, only its reflection is shown beneath the Abyss, balanced in Beauty, which is the best road to truth. Here is established Zion, above Binah.

In the heart of the Aethyr is a Temple, which contains an Urn suspended in the air, made of fixed mercury and containing the ashes of the burned tarot, symbolizing all prior books of magic, which are now useless and have been burned up into ash. The tarot, Crowley is told, contains the entire stored wisdom of the Old Aeon. *Liber Loagaeth,* however, contains the first glimpse of the wisdom of the New Aeon, which has been hidden for three hundred years because Kelly (not Dee) extracted it from the Tree of Life too early, out of desperation. It is explained that Martin Luther was Kelly's master, and overthrew the Church, but that Kelly rebelled because he saw that the Protestant era would be even worse than the Catholic. Yet Kelly did not understand

---

*See Crowley, "Liber B vel Magi," in *The Holy Books,* 1–5.

Fig. 16.6. BABALON, engraving by Lucas Cranach, from Martin Luther's 1522 translation of the New Testament.

Luther's true purpose, which was to prepare the way for the Aeon of Horus.

Crowley is now expelled from the Aethyr by Thoth himself; he has not fully burned up his karma, and as such is not prepared to place the ashes of his personality left over from his Magister Templi initiation within the Urn, which is marked with the sigil of NOX, among others; he has not attained to full atheism, that is, burned up all of his preconceptions, and therefore is unable to directly perceive truth.*

Aethyr 5, LIT
The Vision of the Middle Pillar. (Arrow.) The Mystery of Atheism.

Crowley is led through an endless avenue of pylons carved from the rock of a mountain, within each of which is a god; all of the gods of all of the nations of Earth are represented, with nine avenues all going to the top of the same mountain. At the top the roads converge, with nine pylons facing the center, within which is a shrine with a circular table, held up by white and black marble statues of men and women facing inward, their buttocks worn down by the kisses of their worshippers. They all face the Supreme God, which adherents from all religions have come here to worship—but the God itself is on the table, which is far too high to reach.

Crowley is lifted up by the angel of the Aethyr, and sees that the altar is surrounded by holy men, each with a weapon in their right hand, making the sign of silence with their left. There is a silver star in the air, and on the forehead of each holy man.† The password to progress further is "There is no God," and after giving it Crowley is accepted into the circle and given a new sense of the meaning of this phrase, which he cannot fully ascertain, though he suspects it to denote that God is everywhere, and not within the shrine.

Everything is now blacked out, and the angel appears as a vast dragon that devours the universe, who tells Crowley that he has not even begun to annihilate himself—for "all that thou thinkest is but thy thought; and as there is no god in the ultimate shrine, so there is no I in thine own Cosmos."[54] This is the truth of the Aethyr, which all religions have failed to interpret; the true God is everywhere, and the true "I" in the entirety of the human body and soul. All of the world's

---

*This further initiation would be achieved in 1915–18. See Crowley, "Liber LXXIII."

†The symbol of the Third Order of the A∴A∴, the S∴S∴ or Silver Star, the Invisible College of adepts who guide the evolution of humanity.

religions are within the shrine, but they are only particles in the smoke of the dragon's breath. Crowley must further purify himself; moreover, the head of this dragon is only the tail of the Aethyr. The dragon is to be slain by piercing his throat with the arrow of truth, a phallo-vaginal arrow that neither Edward Kelly nor anyone else was found worthy to wield—yet Crowley, who is the incarnation of Cagliostro (and of Kelly), is now fit to wield it. (The arrow represents the Middle Pillar of the Tree of Life.)

The Aethyr breaks; upon its second call, Crowley is brought into a further Arcanum. A child in blue light is revealed, with golden hair, curls, and deep blue eyes, holding red and blue snakes in either hand.* He is Horus, the child of Isis, and tells Crowley that life is one long initiation into sorrow. He is represented by Isis, whom all know, but whose sister is Nephthys, whom few know because she is dark and feared. And behind these ideas is the goddess Maut. Horus, who is Eros, must be slain with his own bow in order to progress, and the initiate must be NEMO to do so. Crowley shoots Eros with a white arrow and a black arrow simultaneously; the white arrow fails to pierce Eros and the black one pierces Crowley's own heart; yet their identities are exchanged, and Crowley lives while Eros dies. The Aethyr splits with thunder, and the arrow is revealed as having the plumes of Ma'at for its crowns, which is the crown of Thoth, and the Father of all Light; the shaft is the Father of all Love; the arrow is the source of all motion, but does not move itself; it is the glance of the Eye of Shiva; since it moves not, the universe is not destroyed. It is revealed that the above is not like the below. The One, critically, *is* the Many.

As Crowley has sought the end of all sorrow, all sorrow is now his portion; his blood is in the Cup of Babalon, his heart is the universal heart, girt with a serpent.† Below the Abyss, contradiction is division, but above it, contradiction is unity. Contradiction *is* the marker of truth, for above the Abyss all opposites are unified. All symbols are interchangeable, for they contain in themselves their own opposites.

---

*This imagery, along with the arrow and the dragon, suggests kundalini phenomena, as do many of the visions in the Aethyrs. See Eshelman, *Visions and Voices,* 410.
†See Crowley, "Liber LXV," in *The Holy Books,* 51–84.

The vision of the arrow is marvelous beyond belief; Crowley is dissolved in Ain Soph, yet the arrow itself, which now represents the Supernals, persists.

Aethyr 4, PAZ.
The Marriage of Yod and He. (The Common Tibetan Symbol.)
The Seer Identifies Himself with It.

A mighty host of angels throngs a sixfold star; the day of Be-With-Us* is here. For God has both created and overthrown the universe for his pleasure. Crowley beholds the god Chaos in the center of the Aethyr, with a thousand arms, each with a weapon, in a terrible and wrathful form, in copulation with Babalon's daughter—the imagery is *distinctly* Tibetan, suggesting a wrathful deity fornicating with his consort. They cling tightly, merging into each other; he tears her asunder, she strangles him, both crying in pleasure and anguish, so that every cry of suffering in the universe is only one tiny "gust of wind"[55] in their continuous scream of ecstasy.

Here Chaos represents the Yod, and Babalon's daughter the final Heh, in a new Tetragrammaton, creating a new universe—as foreshadowed in the thirtieth Aethyr. According to Crowley, this is a depiction of the Tibetan Kalachakra—which is a representation of time, and thus Saturn. Several other instances of Tibetan imagery occur in the Aethyr, including the opening hexagram (which is seen in mandalas of Vajrayogini, a similar deity to Babalon and Malkah-Koré) and a Tau that appears on the head of Chaos, which suggests the "Tenfold Powerful One" symbol of the Kalachakra, which has the same shape as the Hebrew Tau.

Crowley can barely perceive the image, as he is not yet trained enough to do so. Yet he has identified himself with the spirit of humanity, which is the Beast 666. Though the vision is beyond his understanding, he must unite himself with this marriage bed. Crowley is simultaneously torn apart and crushed back together at the molecular

---

*The period of rest that follows the dissolution of the universe at the end of the Manvantara. See Blavatsky, *The Secret Doctrine,* 1:134.

level, and shown that all double phenomena form two ways of looking at one phenomenon; resolved, they are peace. All of this is Chaos, which is also Peace; the Cosmos is the war of the rose and the cross, which is reunited by love under will.

Crowley now sees that Chaos is the primeval state of the universe, the blackness (NOX) that existed before the Creation.* Crowley prays to this primeval night to shelter him from the madness that is the incarnation of the universe. The emergence of Cosmos from Chaos creates an imbalance where previously there was none; when the balance is returned, the Cosmos will return to the Chaos (Chokmah) from which it came. It is also revealed that everything in the manifest universe is *reversed,* so that "everything wherein thou hast trusted must confound thee, and that thou didst flee from was thy saviour"[56]—suggesting that Satan is the true Messiah. Therefore must the four beasts of Daniel be slain, and the Sphinx of Initiation itself, as in Oedipus. All the universe awaits Aiwass, who is All, and the thousand-armed god in the vision, consort of Babalon and deflowerer of their daughter, uplifting Malkuth to the throne of Binah; this is the philosopher's stone set on the tomb of the Tetragrammaton. The child of the queen of heaven shall be called V.V.V.V.V. Crowley is now forced back, covered by the angel HUA.

Aethyr 3, ZOM.
"The Magus" of the Tarot (ATU I). Mayan, the Maker of Illusion. The Seer in Illusion (Lilith).
The final three Aethyrs are aspects of Kether, with the first pertaining to the path of Aleph, the second Gimel, and the third Bet.

The vision is of the Magician of the tarot; to fully become initiated to this level would be to take the rank of Magus, but Crowley is here guarded from that experience, for which he is not yet fit, by being given

---

*It would be almost seven decades before Crowley's revelations here were developed (along with the theories of Austin Spare) into "chaos magic" by Peter J. Carroll, Ray Sherwin, and others—a new, nontheist approach to occultism that gave a central place to Choronzon and Pan/Baphomet, entities that feature prominently in the Aethyrs. See Carroll, *Liber Null & Psychonaut* and *Liber Kaos.* For further notes on the synthesis of chaos magic with Babalon and the rest of the "Enochian" corpus, see Biroco, *Kaos 14.*

an astral simulation of the Aethyr rather than full initiation. Here he perceives a House (the Magician is the Hebrew letter *Bet,* house), the "many mansions"[57] of the Father, but it shall be destroyed by the Ox (the Fool, Aleph). Crowley has previously seen the City of Pyramids in Binah; here he sees the House of the Juggler (an old title for the Magician card).

Crowley beholds the ultimate blasphemy:

> O thou that hast beheld the City of the Pyramids, how shouldst thou behold the House of the Juggler? For he is wisdom, and by wisdom hath he made the Worlds, and from that wisdom issue judgments seventy by four, that are the four eyes of the double-headed one; that are the four devils, Satan, Lucifer, Leviathan, Belial, that are the great princes of the evil of the world. And Satan is worshipped by men under the name Jesus; and Lucifer is worshipped by men under the name of Brahma; and Leviathan is worshipped by men under the name of Allah; and Belial is worshipped by men under the name of Buddha.[58]

Mary, further, is shown as a blasphemy against Babalon, for she has shut up her sexuality, and is therefore the queen of the Black Brotherhood. Babalon herself is under the power of Mayan, the magician, perfectly pure, a redeemer of all that is below; the only way across the Abyss is through her and the Beast 666; therefore, the Magician conducts his sorceries to keep the Black Brothers from profaning the sanctuary. For from Kether also springs delusion: madness as Aleph, falsehood as Bet, and glamor as Gimel.

The veil of the Aethyr is rent, and Crowley is shown the Magus of the tarot, who is a great blasphemy, and surrounded by the implements of blasphemy; he stands by a forty-two–fold table connected with the Egyptian Book of the Dead (as he is Thoth); he also represents the machinery or mill in which ether, the universal substance, is ground down and turned into matter. With his four elemental weapons he casts forth veil after veil of illusion, with a thousand shining colors ripping and tearing the Aethyr.

Crowley is terrified by this vision, but worse still is the vision of Lilith (who is Babalon), who appears as a black monkey, whose body is rotten and cancerous. She seeks to embrace Crowley, who is so horror-struck that he cries out to be killed to end the vision. Only Lilith has dared to look into the face of the Magus; she masturbates with a crucifix, so that the worshippers of Christ "suck up her filth upon their tongues."[59] The stench of human flesh and children's bowels is thrust in his mouth. Because the Magician is veiled, if you try to look upon him you fall under the spell of Lilith, who is Babalon imagined by the energy of the Magician. Her blasphemy is that she has taken the name of LIL (the first Aethyr), put it on her brow, and added a Y and Th for the sign of the cross.

The illusion, however, is destroyed by a sigil of Binah that appears on the sun, and Crowley is again shown a vision of the daughter of Babalon as a beautiful and pure maiden; Crowley is also given images of women whom he would meet and have relationships with in the years to come; prophecies of Crowley's assumption of the grade of Magus are also pronounced.

The Mercy of God protects him from seeing the fullness of the Aethyr; to proceed further he must match it for mystery and silence. He must give the sign of Babalon, and make himself one with Chaos (Chokmah)—this is a precursor of the *beginning* of the Great Work, which is the grinding down of Aleph, Bet, and Gimel and the approach to Kether thereby.

Choronzon is the excrement (qliphoth) of Aleph, Bet, and Gimel, his head raised to Da'ath, and the Black Brothers have declared him the child of Wisdom and Understanding—but he is the bastard of Kether only. Therefore Da'ath itself is not the child of Binah and Chokmah—that being Tiphareth—but is the sexual act that produces the child; hence the fornications of the Beast and Babalon.

Binah, ruled by Bet (Babalon under the power of the magician) guards the Abyss; hence there is no way to the supernal mystery but by Babalon and the Beast, and the Magician Mayan is set beyond them to deceive the Black Brothers lest they make themselves into a Crown—that is, make a tree from Da'ath, pure reason, which is the error of the scientists and the Buddhists, as supernal logic convicts it of essential self-contradiction. Da'ath is the peak of the intellect, and therefore a demonstration that intellect is incapable of truth.

This vision is so intense that none can endure it and live; so Crowley is only given an echo, and then returned to his body.

Aethyr 2, ARN.
The Marriage of the Seer with BABALON. Atu VI.

The secret of the Lovers card is given, which should be called "The Brothers," and is about Cain and Abel. The child of Eve and the Serpent's union was Cain; Abel was the first murderer, and sacrificed animals to his demon—a necessary measure to get God to listen. Cain slew Abel with the Hammer of Thor (an analogue of the swastika, a symbol of Kether), in order to also become a man and get the attention of God. Afterward, he was given the Mark of the Beast, as mentioned in Revelation, upon his brow. In this version of the card, Cain stands between his mother, Eve, on his right hand and Lilith on his left, who appears like Kali; above him is the Arrow from the fifth Aethyr, which pierces the heart of the child Abel. This is the true design of the card, and the true story from which the legend of the Fall was copied.

Crowley discovers that Revelation itself is "a recension of a dozen or so totally disconnected allegories, that were pieced together, and ruthlessly planed down to make them into a connected account," which were then rewritten as a Christian document in the style of the Gospel of John, to satisfy a public that felt Christianity showed no real depth of spiritual teaching, only stage miracles to fool the public and theology to occupy "pedants."[60] This is why literal predictions and timelines of the Apocalypse never come true.

A white rose now appears; a symbol of BABALON, for she has crushed the blood of everything into her cup, and no red remains.

The Aethyr breaks. Upon its second call, the brilliant white of Kether fills the stone, within which all other colors are complicit. Colors, as well as thoughts, are revealed to all be false—they are only the place where the mind of the Seer has been unable to perceive any further. Therefore "the pure light is colorless, so is the pure soul black.

And this is the Mystery of the incest of CHAOS with his daughter"[61]—the fulfillment of a new Tetragrammaton and the creation of a new universe. This reveals the nature of evil, and of *Māyā* itself.

The light of the Aethyr is so pure that it prevents the formation of images, and is thus perceived as darkness. Any light that is less pure reflects into the mind and creates its endless illusions, here symbolized by the "many mansions" in the prior Aethyr; so is Babalon victorious over the magician that has "ensorcelled" her,[62] by eradicating his mind, destroying Mayan, the Magus, the maker of illusion in the path of Bet, and placing her daughter upon her own throne.

A new interpretation of the text of the nineteenth call is given, which reverses its meaning, now that Crowley has proceeded across the Abyss and toward Kether. The call is now revealed to be the methodology by which the Supernals operate to create the universe, and a rejoicing at the opening of the ninth Aethyr and beyond. Crowley notes that he believes Kelly overlaid his Christian conditioning over the spirit sessions, and references the "horrible doctrine," stating that "Dee forced him to reject the True Messengers, whose discourse implied antinomian Pantheism."[63] Likewise, according to Crowley, Kelly miswrote the text of the nineteenth call, letting his Christian guilt warp the message.

The letter Aleph is now shown in a new alphabet, written with arrows, which corresponds to Enochian as well as the hexagrams of the I Ching.

During this entire Aethyr, Crowley feels his feet burning; the fire spreads to his whole body, which he perceives as beginning to rot.* Like Prometheus, he is being tortured for stealing fire from heaven; and even the dust of the Magister Templi must be consumed by fire.† Crowley's physical body has reached the utmost limit of its ability to withstand the visions of the Aethyrs; he is completely burned out psychically. He now breaks the Aethyr once more, and goes to soak in sulfurous hot springs (in the physical world) before proceeding further.

At the next call, he is shown a reversed (outward facing) *vesica*

---

*Kundalini phenomena, according to James Eshelman, which occur throughout the Aethyrs, as well as the original spirit diaries.

†Another foreshadowing of Crowley's Magus initiation.

piscis at the top of a black pyramid, which itself is atop a stone filled with flashes of lightning. Motherhood is the symbol of the masters, who abandon their virginity, become pregnant, and give birth. The Aethyr is swallowed by a black triangle facing downward, within which is Typhon, God of Chaos, who warns the Seer that one may deceive the virgin and the mother, but not Babalon, the ancient whore. As she possesses (or is) all phenomena, she cannot be bribed or bought with anything in manifest existence. Crowley attacks and destroys the image of Typhon with the Flaming Sword (the downward flash of manifestation in the Qabalah), but even this is futile—nothing will win against Babalon.

Crowley becomes Leviathan and the crocodile; a black rose of 156 petals is revealed, and Babalon breaks through. She is also Nuit; Crowley attempts with all his will to strain himself toward her. He now becomes not only Leviathan but Lucifer, Belial, and Satan, the four Great Princes of Evil; yet these are now seen as merely prior truths that Crowley has clung to, and become withered as they confront the higher truth of Babalon, who is thus the great defiler and "desolator of shrines."[64] Crowley lies supine before Babalon, takes the form of Hadit and as such sings the praises of Nuit; nothing can penetrate any further.

The five senses are shown to be related to the Elemental Watchtowers; to hear the voice of the Aethyr, Crowley is told to invoke it at night with no other light except that of the half moon, which will allow him to "lay bare the womb of thine understanding to the violence of CHAOS."[65] He must therefore end his scrying and wait for these conditions to arrive before he can continue.

On calling the Aethyr for a final time, Crowley is given the utterance of the Aethyr in the "Bathyllic" language, accompanied by music; it is the Song of the Sphinx, and of the sirens, and whoever hears it is lost—Crowley was so taken by the beauty of this song that he wrote in his footnotes that "the memory of it diminishes the value of the rest of His life, with few excepted incidents, almost to nothing."[66]

The song, an adoration to the god OAI (the reversal of the IAO*

---

*See Crowley, "The Formula of IAO," in *Magick: Liber ABA,* 158–65.

formula), is given, which is a formula of mystical attainment; this Crowley would later use for the sex magic ritual described in "Liber Stellae Rubae." Imagery of nymphs, fauns, and Pan (as consistent with Ain Soph) is given; Babalon is shown as the feminine *equivalent,* not the complement, of Pan. Babalon sings new songs and speaks of how she is found by men; Crowley finds himself in a Druid circle and is shown visions upon visions to distract his will—hundreds of visions within which the angel of the Aethyr takes on different masks and games. He finally meets the angel itself, who is seductive and bedecked in finery befit of Babalon, before the Aethyr is swallowed by fire. Crowley is now told that the book—either *The Book of the Law, Liber Loagaeth,* or both—has been opened, awakening the angels of the Aethyrs that have been asleep since the spirit actions, for three hundred years. The tomb has now been opened, "so that this great wisdom might be revealed."[67]

All that now remains is to meet Heru-Ra-Ha, the Lord of the Aeon himself.

Aethyr I, LIL.
The Vision of the Crowned and Conquering Child, the Lord of the Aeon.

The veil of the Aethyr is that of Nuit and Hadit; Crowley is filled with the peace of Iaida (the Highest); there is no tendency anywhere, all that is left is consciousness itself. He abides in the "unalterable midnight"[68] of Nuit, in which there is no light, and therefore only peace. He has no identity, and is hanging in nothing—total initiation into NOX.

The veil opens and Crowley sees a small child "covered with lilies and roses,"[69] supported by the archangels, who are all colorless, and blind as they are pure light; endless ranks of angels stretch below them, so far that they extend beyond Crowley's ability to see. Upon the forehead, heart, and hand of the child is the Mark of the Beast. Crowley is enrapt in samadhi. The angels lead Crowley to the child, forcing his head down in reverence—he can do nothing of his own will, but may only prostrate seven times at every step.

The child sings of its identity; it is the child of all and the father of all, and is everything and all things, Alpha and Omega. It is peace, innocence, untouched virginity, death. The child *is* all dualities and beyond them all, but only by manifesting as dualities may mankind reach up to him; mankind must master all of the paths of the Qabalah to attain to him. Blessed are those who have attained to look upon his face, and he hurls them from his presence as thunderbolts to "guard the ways." Those the Seer loves will put on the garments of magick and themselves rise up, setting out upon "the neverending journey, each step of which is an unutterable reward." Greatly blessed is Crowley for having attained this far through his perseverance; he is now a "made man"—his enemies will be thrown down without him having to do anything, and will be brought to serve him, and all will come to the Supernals to drink of immortality. "FOR I AM HORUS," the child announces, "THE CROWNED AND CONQUERING CHILD, WHOM THOU KNEWEST NOT!"[70]

Echoing the instructions that were given to Dee regarding gathering the twelve tribes of Israel, Crowley is told, "Pass thou on, therefore, O Prophet of the Gods, unto the Cubical Altar of the Universe"—possibly a reference to the Holy Twelvefold Table or the thirtieth Aethyr—"there thou shalt receive every tribe and kingdom and nation into the mighty Order that reacheth from the frontier fortress that guard the Uttermost Abyss unto My Throne. This is the formula of the Aeon. . . . "[71]

And with this, the visions and voices of the Aethyrs end, with Crowley called to an apocalyptic task just as Dee had been—that of ordering and sorting the people of the world toward the worship of the Beast and Babalon. It would be only a handful of years before Crowley fully identified himself with the Beast 666 at his Magus initiation, a role he has played to the hilt and occupied in Western civilization ever since. Crowley the man is long dead, but Crowley the symbol—of rebellion, magic, and, most of all, of Satanism—is immortal.

As seen in the next chapter, the work done by Crowley and Neuburg in Algeria would resonate long after the working itself, boosting the signal of Dee and Kelly's work and echoing throughout the twentieth century and beyond, for better and for worse.

17

In the Shadow of the Cross

Crowley's new vision of the universe would underpin his efforts to build the cosmology and practice of the A∴A∴, whose grades extended all the way across the Abyss, initiating students into the City of Pyramids and the goddess Babalon, whose sevenfold seal (taken from the Sigillum Dei) doubled as the seal of the order. As the Golden Dawn would initiate its students into the magic of LVX, the A∴A∴ would delve further into the substrata of consciousness, initiating in the formula of NOX, supernal darkness. So strenuous was this new system, as outlined in the pages of *The Equinox,* that few of its students made it past the initial grades—including early mainstay J. F. C. Fuller and even Neuburg himself, who both became disillusioned with Crowley and broke with him over personal conflicts.

Neuburg split with Crowley in 1914, after a long, intense, and abusive relationship; according to Neuburg's biographer Jean Overton Fuller, Crowley ritually cursed Neuburg on their parting (or Neuburg believed he had, which is no different in effect). Neuburg suffered a nervous breakdown shortly thereafter, vanishing from any written record for two years, and remaining a nervous wreck for much of his later life. Neuburg believed that Crowley had ruined his life, and lived in fear of crossing his former master's path. Crowley allegedly made an attempt to retrieve him as late as 1927, hammering his stick on the ground at the door of the house where Neuburg resided in Steyning, West Sussex, exclaiming, "I want Victor!" Neuburg was not present, and with the aid of his friends, hid from Crowley until the Beast departed. The pair's final encounter would come at the Atlantis Bookshop in London— Crowley entered the shop while Neuburg was browsing, and also began perusing the shelves, coming close to his former apprentice without noticing him. A terrified Neuburg was able to quickly exit the shop before coming to Crowley's attention.[1] Victor Neuburg is today best remembered for discovering and launching the career of the poet Dylan Thomas; he died in London in 1940.

J. F. C. Fuller, on the other hand, made a cleaner break with Crowley—a young infantryman who thought Crowley held the keys to becoming the Nietzschean overman, Fuller had come into Crowley's orbit after winning a contest to write an essay about the Beast's works (issued by Crowley himself, of course). He soon became Crowley's star pupil; his ambitious but overly florid essays, which both idolize and emulate Crowley, fill the early issues of *The Equinox*. Yet as is often the case with those who project impossible ideals on their teachers, Fuller soon turned on his master, becoming disillusioned when Crowley refused to testify on his own behalf in the *Jones v. The Looking Glass* lawsuit in 1911, in which the *Looking Glass* newspaper was sued for libel by A∴A∴ cofounder George Cecil Jones for associating him publicly with the Great Beast. Crowley taking the stand would have surely resulted in the public revelation of his homosexual affairs, only two decades after Oscar Wilde had died in prison for the same; to Fuller's mind, both Crowley's bisexuality and his refusal to testify were unforgivable offenses, and evidence that he fell far short of Fuller's projected manly ideal. Fuller had also realized that association with the now-tarnished Crowley would be a hindrance to his career, and accordingly dropped his A∴A∴ membership.[2]

After Fuller's split with Crowley—for which Crowley lashed out at him in *The Equinox,* declaring him a failed student that other pupils were to avoid—Fuller became a key figure in developing tank strategy during World War I. His crowning effort would be "Plan 1919," in which tanks would forgo attacking the German front line and instead

Fig. 17.1. J. F. C. Fuller.

advance to their supply lines, destroying the German infrastructure along with the aid of bombers, and then proceed to assault enemy command directly.[3] The plan would not be implemented, but Fuller would continue to work out military strategy; his "Nine Principles of War," codified in 1926's *The Foundations of the Science of War,* synthesize his occult and military training—laying out a scheme of warfare that extended not just into the physical world but into the moral, mental, and cosmic "spheres" as well, and applied Qabalistic formulae like the "law of threes" to the battlefield. Fuller's theories remained core to military thinking throughout the twentieth century—they were applied not only by the British but also the American military as early as 1921, remaining in use until the 1990s.[4]

This marks another direct intersection between the forces of magic and the machinery of empire. Though it is unclear if Fuller was himself associated with Enochian work, he was most certainly associated with the A∴A∴ and Crowley at the time of Crowley's Aethyric workings and his formulation of the New Aeon of the Crowned and Conquering Child, here to cleanse the world of all that had come before through fire and blood. Fuller's war tactics were a major component in the two world wars and the expansion of the American empire to come—much as Dee's navigational science, optical technology, and imperial theory were in the expansion of the British Empire. Crowned and conquering indeed . . .

Fuller later became an early conscript of Oswald Mosley's British Union of Fascists (which he may have planned to take command of), as well as the clandestine, pro-Nazi, racist, and anti-Semitic "Nordic League."[5] Soon becoming as indispensable to Mosley as he had once been to Crowley, Fuller found in Nazi Germany a nation even more receptive to his military theories than Britain had been. (Fuller was not representative of Thelema in this regard; despite his own anti-Semitism, Crowley was avowedly anti-Hitler and assisted the British war effort. Crowley's second-in-command, Karl Germer, would be placed in a concentration camp for associating with the Beast, along with many other occultists and Freemasons.) Fuller's writing on tank warfare was soon translated into German, and the mechanized war strategies he had developed for Plan 1919 helped to seed a new Nazi approach—*blitzkrieg*. Critical to Germany's early success, this new "lightning war" was a more advanced version of Plan 1919, in which tight tank formations would rapidly break enemy lines with the aid of air support in order to imbalance and then destroy defending forces. It would be employed in the invasions of Poland, France, Belgium, and the Netherlands, as well as at the Western and Eastern Fronts, until the Third Reich was overpowered and fell; in the meantime, the Allies judged Fuller's strategy so effective that they also began to emulate it.[6]

While Crowley would stay hostile to Hitler, Fuller stumped for fascism in Britain, referring to himself (to Mosley) as a "full-blooded fascist," and was the only foreign guest at Germany's initial armored exercises in 1935. He met Mussolini, whom he found as disappointing as Crowley, but idolized Hitler, whom he saw as the architect of a new and modernized Holy Roman Empire. Fuller was welcomed as a guest at the führer's fiftieth birthday celebrations in 1939, where he saw his dream fulfilled in a three-hour parade of mechanized infantry, after which Hitler asked Fuller, "I hope you were pleased with your children?" to which Fuller replied, "Your Excellency, they have grown up so quickly that I no longer recognize them."[7]

Beyond boosting Hitler, Fuller's anti-Semitism was extreme even for the British far right; like many fascists, Fuller believed in the existence of an organized Jewish conspiracy to subvert the traditional character of Europe. Fuller's paranoia extended to his belief that Jews had used Kabbalistic magic to undermine the Church and secularize society, a belief he supported by citing the fraudulent *Protocols of the Learned Elders of Zion*. Yet parallel to this (and this is not uncharacteristic of extreme anti-Semites), Fuller expressed admiration of Jewish intellectuals and cultural achievements, including the work of Maimonides, Avicebron, and Spinoza, as well as the Kabbalah itself, which he had made a consistent study of even after splitting with Crowley. Fuller's 1937 book *The Secret Wisdom of the Qabalah* even includes staunchly Zionist passages such as this:

> [T]he Chosen People are the light of the world, a light which at present is mixed with darkness (the Gentiles or children of Esau). This darkness will vanish little by little; first Israel will "look forth as the dawn," next she will "become fair as the moon," then "as clear as the sun," and lastly "terrible as an army with banners." Such is the reformulation of YHVH. When this is accomplished, not a Gentile will be left to pollute the earth; for Israel will have become its Messianic Shin which will untie the tongue of God, and on the utterance of His name will the entire universe vanish into absolute light.[8]

What, exactly, was Fuller up to?

"I will give you a war-engine . . . I am the warrior Lord of the Forties . . . "[9]

That Fuller was never arrested for treason is a subject of some wonderment. Curiously, Fuller was still considered a patriot, albeit a fascist and Nazi sympathizer; his military service and connections may have protected him (Churchill himself may even have intervened), although Fuller was (uniquely among men of his rank) never re-invited to serve during the Second World War. He died in Cornwall in 1966.[10]

As for the A∴A∴ itself, Crowley's disappointing track record with wayward students led him to realize that he had set the bar too high for the average individual. Yet rather than lowering the bar, he backgrounded the project, realizing that it would have to be the province of a small, motivated elite. The more pressing spiritual mission set out for him—the adoption of *The Book of the Law* and the Law of Thelema by the world at large—would require other methods and means of attack. By 1912, those means arrived in the form of the Ordo Templi Orientis.

Like the Golden Dawn, the OTO had drawn its roots from the SRIA and Continental Rosicrucianism, although in the case of the OTO, it actually *was* a Continental body. Much of the ritual corpus of the OTO had been "inherited" and synthesized from various irregular Masonic rites, including the Hermetic Brotherhood of Light, the Swedenborg Rite, and the Rite of Memphis and Misraïm—the latter of which conferred ninety degrees as opposed to the Scottish Rite's thirty-three, and claimed lineage from Cagliostro, another of Crowley's alleged prior incarnations.

The OTO itself was composed of nine degrees, the first six of which professed to confer all of the honors of the para-Masonic bodies it claimed descent from, *as well as* the 33° of the Scottish Rite.* The remaining three degrees taught a system of sexual magic that the founders of the order claimed to have learned from Sufi and Hindu tantric teachers, which was the true key of the mysteries, the inner meaning of Gnostic Christianity, and the central secret of Freemasonry. Like learning to see a Magic Eye painting, understanding this Gnostic secret would unlock the twilight language of the occult, and transform Qabalah, Masonry, Rosicrucianism, and alchemy into a living and breathing art. So central was this mystery that it could not be taught—an initiate had to "grow into" it and understand it themselves first as an inescapable truth of nature. Only then could the actual degrees be awarded, as ceremonial recognition and further elucidation of the understanding of the secret. Crowley, apparently, had been growing into the secret for

---

*This claim never held any weight within the actual Scottish Rite, and has since been downplayed by the modern OTO.

years—for instance, hints occur in the twenty-second Aethyr, and in the twenty-fifth the angels tell Crowley that its use will be critical to his fulfillment of the office of the Beast 666.

Hence, goes the story, in 1913 Crowley received a house call from Theodor Reuss, who insisted that Crowley knew, and had published, the central IX° secret of the OTO.[11] A confused Crowley replied that he had done nothing of the sort; Reuss persisted, and showed him chapter 36 of his *Book of Lies,* a succinct handbook for navigating the Abyss and nondual supernal logic that Crowley had published that year. The chapter—which delineates the "Star Sapphire" ritual, a version of the Golden Dawn's Lesser Ritual of the Hexagram implementing the NOX formula—begins, "Let the Adept be armed with his Magick Rood [and provided with his Mystic Rose]."[12]

The sexual symbolism became apparent at once—as did the plain truth that not only could sex itself be used as the central sacrament of magic, but that much of the symbolism of Rosicrucianism, alchemy, Qabalah, and Masonry was explicitly sexual in nature. Having opened Crowley's eyes to the obvious, Reuss now instructed him in the OTO's sexual methods, swore him to secrecy, and conferred upon him the IX°.*

This would hit Crowley like the proverbial "diamond bullet to the forehead."[13] Suddenly the veils of the mysteries would fall away, and he would come to realize the sexual nature of magic itself, both as metaphor and as operative reality. Over the coming years, Crowley would shift his focus from the A∴A∴ to the OTO, quickly becoming the regional head for the United Kingdom and then assuming command

---

*Sexual magic has since become a much more "open secret" within occulture, even down to popular manuals making their way into the mainstream with much of the occult language removed. For an extensive discussion of the subject, see the record of Thee Temple ov Psychick Youth, an occult group that conducted long-running creative experimentation with sex magic in the 1980s, in P-Orridge, *Thee Psychick Bible*—which the present author assembled and edited from archival materials over the course of many years. With that said, the sexual methods and metaphysics of the OTO remain unique, and also the intellectual property of the OTO; they appear to have resisted mass dissemination or adoption in any real way (*including within* the Thelemic community) despite being available in bootleg form. Some things, it seems, remain occult no matter how openly revealed and interpreted they become.

of the entire order. Over the following years, he would drop Golden Dawn–style ceremonial magic in favor of the OTO methods, conducting exhaustive experimentation with prostitutes in New York. As discussed previously, this particularly suited the personal mythology that Crowley was developing in the wake of his experiences in the Aethyrs, as he now saw his goal as associating himself with the Beast 666, Chaos, Chokmah, and consequently began his quest for a woman capable of occupying the role of the Scarlet Woman, Babalon, Binah.

Many women had, and would, come to fulfill this office for Crowley, with the most significant being the violinist Leila Waddell and, later, the schoolteacher Leah Hirsig, who took the name Soror Alostrael. Hirsig later worked extensively with the forces and deities in *The Book of the Law,* identifying herself with Babalon, bride of Chaos—Chaos being the cosmic force itself, not Crowley.

"I am going to meet my Lord Chaos whose bride I am," she writes in her diary entry of December 20, 1923. Later entries give rare insight into Thelemic sexual magic from a female perspective. On December 22, "woke until 11 on and off Msbtd Msbtd Msbtd like mad calling on Chaos," and then, "Finish Call to invoke Chaos," suggesting a use of the calls of the thirty Aethyrs. On December 27, she writes, "Msbtd— Union with Chaos—my whole idea seems to deplete my body absolutely so that I may lose my thoughts—But I am all wrong. I am starved, but I shall start to love tomorrow. There will be no more masturbation— Perhaps there will be insanity or death, but there'll be something, if I have to create it myself."[14] Like Crowley's visions in the final Aethyrs, this sounds remarkably like an early foreshadowing of chaos magic.

In tandem with his own experimentation, Crowley rewrote the degree rituals of the OTO, bringing them into line with the cosmology of Thelema and *The Book of the Law.* After indoctrinating the candidate and binding them with extensive oaths, the OTO provides working methods of sexual magic as they pertain to masturbation, heterosexual coupling, and childbirth. Crowley would append to this a new degree—XI°—in which he would develop the theory and rites of homosexual sex magic.

As the regular communal rite and public outreach of the order,

Crowley wrote the Gnostic Mass, among his most beautiful and extensive rituals, for which he took inspiration from the Mass of the Russian Orthodox Church. This rite celebrates the sexual union, in symbolic form, of Hadit and Nuit, Chaos and Babalon, and openly displays the secrets of sexual magic as ritual theater. In the Mass, it is the creation of life through the sexual union of man and woman that is the Holy of Holies, rather than the Ark of the Covenant. The cosmology of the Aethyrs is here boiled down to a visceral demonstration that anybody, in theory, should be able to understand and benefit from.

Despite the extensive work put into the new, Thelemic OTO, growth was slow in England. Where the OTO *would* begin to take root, however, was America. First into the continent was Charles Stansfeld Jones, a.k.a. Frater Achad, Crowley's most prized student and "magical son," who would later spectacularly lose his mind before solving the central Qabalistic mystery of *The Book of the Law*.[15] In tandem with his A∴A∴ work, Jones established British Colombia No. 1 in Vancouver, the first OTO lodge in North America. He would later attempt to leapfrog Crowley in the A∴A∴ hierarchy, establishing his own eccentric Qabalah and proclaiming that he had prematurely ended the Aeon of Horus and catalyzed the dawning of the Aeon of Ma'at; Crowley excommunicated him with prejudice for these breaks from the Master Therion's now-orthodox system.

Jones's student Wilfred T. Smith established a second Thelemic circle in Los Angeles, which would coalesce into Agape Lodge No. 2. Small, troubled, and beset by rolling storms of interpersonal drama,[16] Smith's circle would soon attract the brilliant and charismatic John Whiteside "Jack" Parsons—Enochian-magician-to-be, science fiction aficionado, and, by way of inventing castable composite solid rocket propellant and founding Pasadena's Jet Propulsion Laboratory, one of the men responsible for putting America on the moon.[17]

Like Dee, Parsons straddled the worlds of science and the occult. Like Dee, he saw centuries ahead of his time. Like Dee, his personality was too complex and interests too far-reaching to easily compartmentalize—picture Faust, Elon Musk, Hugh Hefner, and Abbie Hoffman in one man. Like Dee, he would be instrumental in expanding humanity's horizons, in this case not just to a new continent but to new worlds, for which he would be uncredited, unthanked, and forgotten. Like Dee, he would immerse himself in Enochian magic, working the system with a charlatan associate who would betray and defraud him just as Kelly had Dee. Like Dee, he would lose everything. And also like Dee, he would come to stand as a monument to human potential and become a legend within the occult underworld, with an intellect too category-breaking to be properly compartmentalized and stored in the official history of science—in short, a perfect exemplar of the original version of the scientist, like Newton and Bacon, the natural philosopher who extended his investigations into the realm of spirit as well as that of matter.

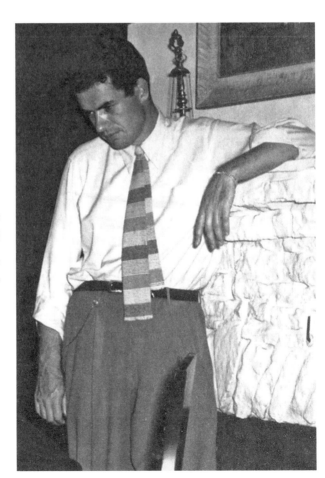

Fig. 17.2. Jack Parsons at Agape Lodge, 1003 S. Orange Grove Blvd., Pasadena.

For a man with such cosmic ambitions, Parsons lived out much of his thirty-seven years within an exceedingly small geographic area—half a mile of one street. In about twelve minutes, you can walk down South Orange Grove in Pasadena, California, between the house where Parsons was born (537 S. Orange Grove Blvd.), the site of the house he held for the Agape Lodge of the OTO (1003 S. Orange Grove Blvd.), and the site of the house where his life ended (1031 S. Orange Grove Blvd.). South Orange Grove is currently one of the most affluent areas of Los Angeles, just as it was during Parsons's life. The wide street is lined by palm trees and ornate street lamps, with mansions on either side and restored classic cars passing by. It is the very picture of the American Dream—a far cry from the darkness of Elizabeth's London or the madness and filth of Cefalu.

Parsons was born on October 2, 1914—as his biographer John Carter gleefully points out, this is the day that Charles Taze Russell, founder of the Jehovah's Witnesses, declared would be the beginning of the events of Revelation.[18] Parsons's parents would divorce after it was revealed that his father had frequented a prostitute.[19] Parsons later wrote, upon attaining the grade of 8°=3□ Magister Templi just as Crowley had in Algeria, and looking back upon his human life with the transincarnational perspective of an adept, "Your father separated from your mother in order that you might grow up with a hatred of authority and a spirit of revolution necessary to my work. The Oedipus complex was needed to formulate the love of witchcraft which would lead you into magick."[20]

Parsons filled his solitary, fatherless, and privileged childhood with interests in Arthurian legends, the *Arabian Nights,* science fiction, mythology, and the idea of space travel. Parsons was bullied and shunned at school for his wealthy background (he was often driven to school in a limousine by his grandfather) and his effeminate behavior.[21] Jane Wolfe, who had been with Crowley and Hirsig at the Abbey, would describe Parsons upon meeting him at twenty-six as "potentially bisexual at the very least."[22]

Early experiments would include attempting to evoke Satan to visible appearance in his bedroom, which was so successful that it terrified him away from magic altogether (he later noted in his Magister Templi "Analysis" that such early mishaps were necessary to keep him away from the occult until he was sufficiently mature).[23] With a friend named Edward Forman, Parsons spent his junior high years even more immersed in science fiction, as well as setting off fireworks and small rockets.[24] Public school was disastrous for him, possibly because of dyslexia; he was sent to Brown Military Academy for Boys in San Diego, but soon expelled for blowing up the toilets.[25]

His later "Analysis" suggested that his isolation from other children and bullying had fostered further hatred of groupthink and Christian morality, as well as allowing him the space needed to develop a literary and scholarly mind, all necessary attributes for a budding Thelemic magician-to-be. An interest in chemistry would train him in the scientific method so necessary to performing magic in a disciplined manner without self-delusion, as well as giving him the means to obtain a livelihood and name in the world.[26]

Parsons's family fortune would dwindle in the Great Depression, and the shy and introverted boy would soon have to climb down out of his head and begin making his way in the real world, working first at Hercules Powder Company and then at Halifax Explosives in the Mojave, in the meantime associating with scientists at Caltech in Pasadena to try to gain funding for his rocketry projects. Parsons and Forman left out that the ultimate plan was space exploration, still a laughable idea in professional circles. Parsons also married young, to Helen Northrup; the Antichrist-to-be met his wife at a church dance.[27]

Parsons did not attend college; though he was admitted to Stanford to study chemistry, what small amount of money he had saved from his work would not be able to cover tuition. Instead, he dived headfirst into experimental rocketry. What he lacked in formal training, he made up for with manic enthusiasm, as well as by surrounding himself with more traditionally educated Caltech science students. Parsons and Forman were soon joined by the exponentially more trained Ph.D. student Frank Malina, whose doctoral adviser Theodore von Kármán would allow the trio to operate as the "GALCIT Rocket Research Group" under the auspices (and with access to the equipment of) Caltech.[28] In addition to rocketry, the three men shared a love of science fiction, marijuana, and communism.

A group of budding young rocketeers soon joined the group, including Apollo M. O. "Amo" Smith, Carlos C. Wood, Rudolph Schott, and others,[29] and began conducting tests of rocket motors at Devil's Gate Dam in the Arroyo Seco on Halloween 1936.[30] With the final addition of genius Chinese graduate student Qian Xuesen (a Communist who was later to lead China's nuclear weapons program and first atomic and hydrogen bomb tests, for which he would earn the name "King of Rocketry"),[31] the group would be christened the "Suicide Squad" by other students.[32] In time, they would come to be known by another name: Jet Propulsion Laboratory, now NASA's JPL in Pasadena.

Fig. 17.3. The Suicide Squad testing rockets in the Arroyo Seco, Pasadena, 1936. From left to right: Rudolph Schott, Apollo Smith, Frank Malina, Ed Forman, Parsons.

Parsons soon gained local fame for testifying as an explosives expert in the trial of Captain Earl Kynette, the head of LAPD intelligence, accused of car bombing an ex-cop turned private detective. Parsons's testimony led to Kynette's conviction, which could not have earned the naïve young man any friends with the local authorities. Parsons was courting danger: new Suicide Squad addition Sidney Weinbaum, a Jewish refugee and Marxist, convinced Parsons, Malina, Qian, and others to form a Communist cell at Caltech, and asked Parsons to officially join the American Communist Party; Parsons wisely chose not to, and steered away when the group became more interested in direct action. At the behest of the legendary science fiction collector Forrest J. Ackerman, Parsons also began attending meetings of the Los Angeles Science Fiction League and speaking on his work with rocketry.[33] The

Fig. 17.4. *Los Angeles Times* clipping covering Jack Parsons's expert testimony in the trial of LAPD Captain Earl Kynette in 1937. This testimony may have made Parsons enemies in high places.

Los Angeles Times ★

EXPLOSIVES EXPERT MAKES BOMB REPLICA

John W. Parsons, State witness in Kynette trial, shown with duplicate of device that blew up Harry Raymond's automobile and injured the investigator.   Times photo

LASFL, still in existence, was a group of young men who gathered to share their love of science fiction, some of whom evolved into professional authors, including Jack Williamson and the late, great Ray Bradbury, who was enamored of Parsons's rocketry, philosophy, and heroic personality.

In 1939, however, Parsons would find his true calling—Thelema. After reading a copy of Crowley's *Konx om Pax,* Jack and Helen Parsons attended a Gnostic Mass at the "Church of Thelema" (actually Wilfred T. Smith's home) on Winona Boulevard, near where the Church of Scientology's Hollywood headquarters now stands. Here, the twenty-four-year-old, traditionally uneducated, and still impressionable Parsons would contact the spiritual matrix that had been generated in the angelic conversations, reawakened in Crowley and Neuburg's sessions in Algeria, and distilled into the Gnostic Mass. It would come to define the rest of his short life.

At the Church of Thelema, Parsons met A∴A∴ stalwart Jane Wolfe, Regina Kahl, and Wilfred T. Smith, a.k.a. "Frater 132."[34] Parsons recounted that he was repulsed by Smith, but continued attending masses over the coming year while immersing himself in Crowley's books, later writing that his disgust of Smith had been caused by an unconscious resistance to the ordeals magic would put him through.[35] Smith became a mentor to Parsons, and soon the Church of Thelema would become Agape Lodge No. 2 proper of the Ordo Templi Orientis, with both Parsons and his wife joining the order. Jack also became a Probationer in A∴A∴ under Smith, taking the name Frater T.O.P.A.N., short for the garbled and incorrect Latin motto *Thelema Obtentum Procedero Amoris Nupiae,* which Crowley wryly mocked Parsons for, though privately he told Wilfred Smith that Parsons was "the most valued member of the whole Order, with no exception!"[36] Wolfe was so impressed with Parsons on first meeting him that she wrote in her private journal that he might be the successor to Crowley himself.[37]

Parsons quickly got to work on the grade material of both OTO and the A∴A∴; by 1940, he was laboring diligently at astral travel with Regina Kahl, the task set for the 1°=10$^{\square}$ Neophyte grade of A∴A∴, which (if persisted in) develops into the type of visionary acumen necessary to undertake the type of work Crowley and Neuburg assessed in Algeria. Yet Parsons wasn't fully taken by the OTO—as most who join occult orders find, and just as Crowley had found upon joining the Golden Dawn, expectations can exceed reality by far; Parsons would become disillusioned with the order, believing it to be incapable of manifesting the Law of Thelema in the world.[38]

Conversely, it is worth noting that though Parsons is assigned legendary status within the occult underground, largely because of his larger-than-life character and real-world achievements, he is still considered a failed student by the standards of the modern OTO. In 2014 William Breeze, the current Outer Head of the Order, wrote of Parsons that he had attempted to push too fast, ignoring the necessity of building a foundation of discipline in yoga and meditation that would have prevented ego inflation and disaster—and that this was not for lack of access to good training, as he could have had direct access to a personal education from Crowley. Instead, according to Breeze, he rebelled, and "failed—spectacularly."[39]

Between 1940 and 1942, Parsons's rocket crew became the first group to receive government funding to research the feasibility of jet-assisted takeoff (JATO); however, the Suicide Squad was soon exiled from Caltech for damaging buildings and setting off explosions at inopportune times, leading to a relocation to Arroyo Seco; the group also founded a private company named Aerojet to sell the JATO technology they were developing to the military. It was during this time that Parsons developed his most important contribution to rocketry and space flight: GALCIT-53, a solid-state rocket fuel that he had been inspired to create by legendary accounts of "Greek fire." Successfully solving the safety issues around the previously too-volatile nature of solid fuel, versions of GALCIT-53 were later used for the solid rocket boosters on the Space Shuttle—the first solid-fuel motors to propel a human spaceflight vehicle—as well as in the propulsion for Polaris, Poseidon, and Minuteman ICBM missiles.[40]

These were the missiles, of course, that held up the United States' end of the Mutual Assured Destruction policy under which, for a brief time, the entire world was held hostage, in part by Ronald Reagan. In

1983, Reagan mused to the executive director of the American Israel Public Affairs Committee, "You know, I turn back to your ancient prophets in the Old Testament and the signs foretelling Armageddon, and I find myself wondering if—if we're the generation that is going to see that come about. I don't know if you've noted any of those prophecies lately, but, believe me, they certainly describe the times we're going

Fig. 17.5. Jack Parsons standing next to a JATO canister, Arroyo Seco.
Courtesy NASA/Jet Propulsion Laboratory.

through."[41] It is sobering to think that, had the world indeed come to thermonuclear Armageddon in the 1980s, it would have been Jack Parsons's fuel propelling the nukes.

"I will give you a war-engine . . . the Eighties cower before me, & are abased . . . "[42]

Thanks to Aerojet, Parsons soon became wealthy; during this time, he also explored the sexually permissive Law of Thelema (or at least the openly lecherous Wilfred T. Smith's version of it) by casting aside his wife, Helen, for her seventeen-year-old sister Betty, while Helen switched her attentions to Smith.[43] Along with much of the rest of the Church of Thelema, the four of them rented a mansion on South Orange Grove, which would become the base of operations of Agape Lodge—an exercise in communal living influenced by Parsons's Marxist training and Crowley's Abbey of Thelema, and a forerunner of the similar experiments of the Beat and hippie generations to come. Parsons was soon reveling in orgies, ritual magic, drug use and abuse, polyamorous hysterics, and the inevitable mayhem generated by a group of young, intelligent, anarchic social outcasts living together. While Parsons ran amok, reciting the "Hymn to Pan" at every occasion, just as he had at the beginning of rocket tests, the older Smith had meanwhile decided that he was more interested in using the OTO as his own private harem rather than the school for adepts Parsons naïvely believed it to be.

The financially irresponsible but dedicated true believer Parsons was using his takings from Aerojet to finance the growth of the OTO, as well as to support the aging and heroin-addicted Crowley in London, while his actual work life suffered due to the mayhem at Agape Lodge. He became sleep deprived, sexually hyperactive, and drifted into abusing hard drugs, famously composing a poem for the lodge's newsletter that begins "I height Don Quixote, I live on Peyote, marihuana, morphine, and cocaine. I never knew sadness but only a madness that burns at the heart and the brain."[44]

Like many young magicians before and after him, Parsons probably believed he was liberating his consciousness through drugs, and pushing toward some kind of divine apotheosis. Yet whatever magical vistas or other such "angels of light" Parsons believed he was experiencing internally, back in the real world his affairs were disintegrating. Parsons was turning up to Aerojet hung over and in a sweat—a side effect of amphetamine use, amphetamines that he may have been combining with cocaine to cope with work demands. It is even possible that the clever young chemist was now cooking up his own speed.[45]

Parsons was alienating his co-workers with his eccentric and annoying behavior, and his occult superiors weren't much impressed with his conduct either. Even the lifelong addict Crowley rolled his eyes at Parsons's drug-saturated poetry gracing the pages of the *Oriflamme,* the lodge publication.[46] Parsons's neighbors were losing their patience, too—Agape Lodge next came under direct investigation by Pasadena PD, the FBI, and Army Intelligence after anonymous allegations that "'Crowleyism' and Sex Perversion were being advocated and taught, together with 'Survival of the Fittest.'" The allegations likely came from a disgruntled Agape Lodge member or somebody connected to them. The FBI soon wrote off the lodge members as harmless religious nuts, but it was clear that Smith and Parsons weren't running a tight ship.[47] Whatever gods or spirits Parsons might have called up during this period, he had also invoked the ire of Aerojet, the OTO, the police, the Army, and the FBI—nearly every organization Parsons was involved with or under the jurisdiction of.

Informed of the lodge's activities by mail, Crowley (now in his late sixties and struggling to survive wartime London) and his lieutenant, Karl Germer, became infuriated. Once the *enfant terrible* of British occultism, Crowley was now in the unenviable if humorous position of dealing with his own brash and impetuous offspring, enraged and probably embarrassed that his plan for an occult aristocracy had degenerated into a New Age frat house almost immediately upon contact with California. After analyzing the situation at a distance, Crowley and Germer decided that Wilfred Smith was the problem, and demoted him, giving Parsons command instead.[48]

In April 1943, Parsons's wife, Helen, gave birth to Smith's child— and this after Parsons had financed the abortion of Grady McMurtry's wife; Parsons had recruited McMurtry as a young Caltech student, and his wife had subsequently been passed between Parsons and Smith.

McMurtry, who at the time described Parsons as "being coked up like a snowbird by Wilfred,"[49] was devastated, but would keep the faith until the 1960s, when he resurrected the OTO from the ashes that Agape Lodge had left it in, becoming "Hymenaeus Alpha," the Outer Head of the Order, until his death in 1985. Helen and Smith left the lodge to move to Rainbow Valley in North County San Diego,[50] and Crowley took the opportunity to arrange a stunningly cruel and heartless plan to scapegoat Smith and force him out of the picture.

Crowley created a dummy A∴A∴ document—"Liber 132," a.k.a. "Liber Apotheosis"—to convince Smith that Crowley had determined by astrology that Smith was not just a man, but a god in a human body. This god, Crowley wrote, might well have been attracted to Earth by Crowley and Neuburg's workings in Algeria, and the name of this God might be found within the Watchtowers. Accordingly, Smith would have to tattoo the Mark of the Beast on himself, and then go into magical retirement—that is, go live in a shack in the desert in total isolation until he had worked out what god he was. Crowley would of course have authority to change the terms of this retirement at any time.[51] The plan successfully removed Smith from the orbit of Agape Lodge. Smith soon resigned, and a loyal Parsons followed him, although Crowley would ignore Parsons's resignation and soon rope him back in.[52]

Meanwhile, the Aerojet budget was expanding with fresh wartime contracts from the U.S. Navy.* Once the news hit that Germany had successfully constructed the V-2 rocket, the GALCIT group was

---

*To avoid encouraging conspiracy theorists, we will here neglect to emphasize that in the summer of 1943 Parsons was working with the Navy in Norfolk, Virginia; this was the same time that work on the alleged Philadelphia Experiment was begun, with the Navy supposedly using methods derived from Einstein's unified field theory to render invisible and then teleport the USS Eldridge between the Philadelphia Naval Shipyard and Norfolk, Virginia, two hundred miles away. (Parsons was also fascinated by the unified field theory; his notes on it as it relates to magick can be found in *Freedom Is a Two-Edged Sword*.) The Philadelphia Experiment has been a running trope in conspiracy literature and pop culture, but has never been verified as anything other than an elaborate urban legend. Likewise, we will not dwell on the fact that during this time Parsons also invented "Aeroplex," a technology allowing smokeless contrails or, as the paranoid know them, "chemtrails." See Bullock, "JATO—The Magic Bottle"; Carter, *Sex and Rockets,* 93.

suddenly in high demand; they were hit with a $3 million slab of cash to build new rocket weapons, allowing them to rename and expand as Jet Propulsion Laboratory. Aerojet was also slammed with increased demand—asked to deliver twenty thousand JATO units a month— and the company was soon in negotiations to sell. There was only one condition: Parsons and Forman had to go. Both were pushed out, with Forman selling his stock for $11,000 and Parsons likely receiving a similar figure,[53] with which he bought the Agape Lodge mansion, dubbing it the "Parsonage."

Parsons, however, was in a vulnerable place. Not only had he lost his business and ties to a stable working existence, he had also lost Smith, his primary father figure, no matter how unstable, and along with Smith, he had lost Helen, his wife. He was left with Betty and a house full of anarchists and occultists that he was now expected to lead, but with little guidance or support himself. He had also stripped himself down emotionally through drugs and magic, neither of which tend to provide a grounding influence in one's life.

With this in mind, Parsons can perhaps be forgiven what came next—he was to make what may be the most tragic mistake in twentieth-century occultism, stopping the forward progress of Thelema in its tracks: he trusted L. Ron Hubbard.

The thirty-four-year-old Hubbard arrived at 1003 South Orange Grove at the end of the war, just like so many other young bohemians, occultists, and outsiders had. Hubbard had recently left the U.S. Navy, soon afterward finding his way to the Parsonage (which Scientology maintains was a secret Naval mission to break up a cult).[54] Hubbard speedily charmed the defenses off Parsons and the pants off Betty, now twenty-one. Parsons and Hubbard began a working partnership, with Parsons acting as evoker and Hubbard acting as the scryer.

The parallels between Parsons and Hubbard's relationship and Dee and Kelly's are numerous. First, the moment in Parsons's life in which he met Hubbard parallels that of Dee's—Parsons had been ejected from JPL and Aerojet, his real-world career, dedicated to the advancement of humanity's physical frontiers, just as Dee's *General and Rare Memorials* had been rejected by Cecil, ending his career at court. Both Dee and

Parsons responded to the pain of rejection and the collapse of their scientific careers by retreating into the world of the occult, sublimating their drive for exploring the physical world into exploring the spiritual world. Both Dee and Parsons next met a gifted "psychic" of extremely dubious character who would assist them in their work, and with whom they would form an intense working relationship—Kelly and Hubbard, respectively. Both would be cuckolded, with Dee giving his wife over to Kelly, and Parsons being taken by Hubbard for his young girlfriend Betty. Both would also be swindled financially, with Kelly using Dee for his alchemical knowledge before departing his employ for Rudolf II's, and Hubbard using Parsons for his occult knowledge before likewise vacating (in this case with his girlfriend, money, and yacht). Just like Kelly's, Hubbard's "visions" were likely at least partially confidence trickery, as it would not have been hard to listen to the vulnerable and credulous Parsons, absorb his knowledge and books, and then parrot back what Parsons wanted to hear. And yet, despite all of this, what was left behind was occult work of profound interest to later students.

Though Dee and Kelly's magical partnership had faltered over their wife swapping, Parsons losing Betty to Hubbard only *began* their working relationship. After all, Parsons was a dedicated Thelemite, hardly one for sexual boundaries. Yet it wasn't all rosy polyamory—one tenant of the Parsonage described Hubbard "living off Parsons' largesse and making out with his girlfriend right in front of him. Sometimes when the two of them were sitting at the table together, the hostility was almost tangible."[55] Deprived of a partner, Parsons decided to use OTO sexual magic to summon a new one. By doing so, he would "manifest" the most important relationship of his short life—not just with a mortal woman, but with the goddess Babalon herself.

PARSONS'S WORK WITH THE ANGELIC SYSTEM

Though Parsons did not have the technical acumen or initiatic longevity of either Dee or Crowley, his work provides a concise and simplified approach to the two elder magicians' efforts, bringing them into focus in a way that is more accessible than the baroque angelic mathematics of Mortlake and Algeria. And though Parsons left little in the way of records, and indeed made many grievous errors in his work, what he did leave behind rings with a timeless, universal clarity, free of elaboration or obfuscation.

For Parsons, the *entire* point of magic (angelic or otherwise) is the goddess Babalon. Dee and Kelly were terrified of her appearance at the end of the spirit diaries, unable to handle the sexual freedom she suggested. Crowley chased her all his life, yet never understood that it was his Scarlet Women who were his true and superior initiators and conduits of magic, from Rose Kelly's opening of the gate to *The Book of the Law* to every major initiation to come in Crowley's life. Parsons, however, not only realized the centrality of Babalon to all magic, as Crowley had in the Aethyrs, but was willing to surrender and sacrifice everything at her altar.

Between January 4 and March 4, 1946, Parsons (with the aid of Hubbard) undertook a series of rituals using the Golden Dawn's ceremonial methods for working with the Watchtowers, combined with OTO sexual magic. These rituals, he believed, resulted in the manifestation of Babalon both in physical form and as an archetypal resonance awakened in the spirit of humanity, set loose to shape world events.

Parsons, like Achad before him, believed that the blind, destructive force of Horus would lead to the catastrophic breakdown of civilization because, as Wilhelm Reich would also argue, modern human beings are fundamentally sexually insane.[56] Reich (a student of Sigmund Freud who believed that sexuality is an expression of a tangible life energy) thought that the natural human state should be an unhindered, open, outward expression of free-flowing love and understanding, of which sexuality is a critical part, as it is an expression of the core biophysical energy of any animal. Instead, according to Parsons, the negative sexual conditioning of the false "Christianity" and perversion of Christ's teachings over the preceding millennia had inculcated the sense of sin and all of its attendant shame, guilt, and self-repression, leading to a complete inability of Western people to understand their own being.

"The hidden lusts, fears, and hatreds resulting from the warping of the love urge," Parsons wrote, in a passage that could have come directly from Reich, "which underlay the natures of all Western peoples, have taken a homicidal and suicidal direction."[57]

The Aeon of Horus represents an exponential upgrade in the energetic output of humanity, as can be seen by comparing the last hundred years to the thousand that came before it—as Crowley put it, the formula of the Aeon of Horus is to that of the Aeon of Osiris "what the turbine is to the reciprocating engine."[58] But if energy is pumped through a broken system, it only leads to the system breaking down faster: in Parsons's view, the total collapse of civilization.

Frater Achad had made the same argument, and suggested that the blind force of Horus needed to be tempered by the feminine counterbalance of Ma'at;[59] Parsons suggested that Babalon would provide that feminine counterbalance, and his cosmology better maps to Dee and Crowley's. Crowley, however, would reject his two most brilliant students' work, fully focusing on the establishment of the Aeon of Horus instead.

"This impasse," Parsons wrote in 1946, only one year after the worst war humanity had (or has) ever seen, "is broken by the incarnation of another sort of force, called BABALON. The nature of this force relates to love, understanding, and Dionysian freedom, and is the necessary counterbalance or correspondence to the manifestation of Horus."[60]

Babalon, the Whore, is the aspect of divinity that *accepts* instead of rejects the totality of humanity's free sexual expression; *whore* only has a negative connotation if one believes, as do the many "Black Brothers" of the media, religion, and academia, that sex is unclean and sinful. If one believes, as did the Gnostics, as do the Thelemites, that sex is a holy expression of one's being, and can lead to spiritual communion with the Godhead itself—and *is,* in a sense, the Godhead, because it can lead to the creation of new universes experienced by new consciousnesses—then Babalon becomes a symbol of purity, the Sophia, Wisdom.[61] Babalon, Parsons believed, would provide the proper guiding agent for the Aeon of Horus, harnessing its blind force toward effectively destroying the sexual blocks and false ideologies that hold humanity in slavery.

This may be likened to the process of the rising of kundalini—

which is often depicted as a fire snake of spiritual and sexual energy that awakens in the spinal column of the yogi. This energy ascends upward, destroying blockages as it progresses, or leading to catastrophic energetic impasse and "kundalini psychosis" if the initiate is not prepared; this is the entire point of tantra in its classic, Himalayan sense. Here, however, we are discussing a concordant awakening process occurring on a *civilization-wide,* rather than individual, basis.

Parsons's technical approach to magic during the Babalon Working was not particularly unique; his methods were standard (though persisted in to an impressive degree), and his eagerness to be impressed by his own results all too obvious. In addition, some of his working methods were just *wrong,* and inexcusably so, even for a young magician.

For instance, Babalon tells Parsons to seek her in the seventh Aethyr, DEO, an appropriate place to do so given Crowley's prior results. The way Parsons follows up on this, however, is to use the seventh angelic *call,* which opens the water subangle of the air tablet, rather than what he should have done, which is use the nineteenth call modified for DEO. And on top of this, he even garbles the text of the seventh call, improperly transcribing it! This suggests that Parsons may not have had much practical experience with the angelic system prior to the Babalon Working—and if he did, he was probably fooling himself if he thought he was doing it correctly.[62] Frustratingly, Parsons would persist in this species of error even until 1950, when he referred to Dee and Kelly's vision of the Daughter of Fortitude as "the text of Dee's skrying in the Seventh Aire,"[63] when it was anything but, and there is no record of Dee and Kelly scrying the Aethyrs at all. This sloppiness may also give a hint as to some of the later calamity that befell Parsons, if not by magical mishap then perhaps by general lack of attention to detail and recklessness. Despite this, however, Parsons indeed made contact with a being claiming to be Babalon herself.

Parsons began operations in January, after being initiated to IX° OTO by Crowley, Smith, and Germer, and consequently given the full corpus of OTO sexual magic techniques. The first operation he decided to attempt was, as Parsons put it, "to obtain the assistance of an elemental mate."[64] To do so, Parsons conjured RZLA, a kerub in the air subangle of the air tablet (which he incorrectly called RZDA), a good angel who is skilled in combining natural substances.

Parsons used a standard stack of Thelemic and Golden Dawn rituals to invoke the kerub, during which he correctly applied the third angelic call, though he erroneously referred to it as the "Key Call of third Aire." With the entity summoned, Parsons applied his own semen and blood to the talisman in order to give the angel a material basis through which to manifest. He continued this on a daily basis over the following eleven days, during which time heavy windstorms and poltergeist phenomena manifested, including unexplained knocking, a metallic and buzzing voice crying "let me go free,"[65] a lamp being thrown to the ground with no cause, electrical outages, and Hubbard being knocked on the shoulder, resulting in the temporary paralysis of his arm. Many of these phenomena echo similar events that occurred during Dee and Kelly's workings.

Four days passed after the end of the operation, during which time there was no result except for a "feeling of tension and unease;" while with Hubbard in the Mojave, Parsons felt the tension break at last, and declared "it is done."[66] The two men returned to the Parsonage to find Parsons's elemental waiting for them—in the form of Marjorie Cameron, a new tenant that Parsons believed perfectly fit the parameters of what he had asked for.

Marjorie Cameron, Parsons's junior by eight years, had weathered a childhood in the Great Depression and service as a cartographer for the Joint Chiefs of Staff during the war.[67] During her time with Parsons, the fiery redhead would blossom into a uniquely potent magician and artist. Far from simply being Parsons's muse and Scarlet Woman, as she is too-often remembered, Cameron would go on to become a major force in the California counterculture, helping to incubate the nascent Beat movement, and appeared in two films—Kenneth Anger's 1954 *Inauguration of the Pleasure Dome* (as Babalon herself) and Curtis Harrington's 1962 *Night Tide*. She also developed as a formidable painter, with her otherworldly and haunting work focusing on occult subjects, including angels, aliens, Parsons, and even Dee himself. Tragically, she burned a sizeable chunk of her own output, which makes her legacy harder to assess; much of what does remain is smoke damaged. However, as the early twenty-first-century occult revival continues to gather steam, it appears Cameron is now beginning to receive the recognition she deserves.*

Parsons swiftly wooed Cameron; they were already performing IX° sexual magic together not twenty-four hours later, and would continue to for forty consecutive days and nights, from January 19 to February 27, this time with the aim not of evoking an elemental but invoking Babalon herself. Parsons, however, did not explain to Cameron what he was doing, at least at first.[68] On February 27, Cameron departed for the East Coast, and Parsons returned to the Mojave to again invoke Babalon in a solo ceremony. The result was another channeled text— "Liber 49," or "The Book of Babalon"—which Parsons believed to be the fourth chapter of *The Book of the Law.*

The physical text of "Liber 49" is the polar opposite of how arcane texts usually appear in popular culture—rather than illuminated inkwork in an imposing leather-bound grimoire, the book's seventy-seven verses are written in wide cursive, in pencil, on loose sheets of wide-ruled school paper. It was not accepted as a legitimate transmission by OTO or A∴A∴, and its style does not approach that of Crowley's Holy Books. However, it does purport to be a communication from Babalon, or at least the part of Parsons's own mind he called Babalon, and instructs Parsons in the next steps he, and those to come, were to take to aid the manifestation of the goddess into the world.

Parsons was to gather Babalon's children, who would arrive as a "banner before armies," and was thereafter to sacrifice everything he had and was to the goddess, becoming a "lonely wanderer in abominable places." He was to assemble a ceremonial altar to begin invocations, using tools appropriate to the sphere of Venus, and was to daily consecrate a Babalon talisman with sexual fluids. Following this, Parsons was to begin invoking the goddess with love songs and by calling the seventh Aethyr, and afterward would be provided a Scarlet Woman to per-

---

*A full assessment of Cameron's life is unfortunately outside the scope of this work. For more, see Kansa, *Wormwood Star.* For Cameron's art, see Lipschutz, *Cameron: Songs for the Witch Woman;* and Parsons and Cameron, *Songs for the Witch Woman.*

form sexual invocations with; these were to continue for nine months, following Crowley's devotional ritual "Liber Astarte."

The Scarlet Woman would thus become Babalon's daughter, as seen in Crowley's vision of the seventh Aethyr, and would be given "all power, and all men and excellent things"; the earth would be hers, as she manifested the full force of Babalon into the world, freeing her children from all social control. After his partner was so empowered, Parsons was to continue in constant solo sexual invocations of Babalon, and was to become cursed, to take the "black pilgrimage," and be "crucified in the Basilisk abode." He was also to publish the higher degree secrets of the OTO openly, for which he would be branded a traitor. Following his sacrifice, the now-freed children of Babalon would "gather together in the covens as of old, whose number is eleven, that is also my number. Gather together in public, in song and dance and festival. Gather together in secret, be naked and shameless and rejoice in my name." So were they also to practice magic. Sex was to be a sacrament for these coming generations, who would conquer in Babalon's name and symbol: "Set my star upon your banners," she commanded, "and go forwards in joy and victory."[69]

On March 2, Parsons set to work fulfilling Babalon's instructions. As he began assembling the altar as described, Hubbard returned, describing a vision he had received of a woman riding a beast. The two began a ritual to receive further communication, and Hubbard received a "psychic message" telling Jack to undertake a three-day retirement to further attune to Babalon, and that the current "year of BABALON is 4063"[70]— sounding much more like Hubbard the science fiction writer than Babalon the goddess.

Parsons proceeded to call Babalon with a ritual sequence consisting of the Lesser Invoking Ritual of the Hexagram, invocations of the goddess from the Gnostic Mass, *The Vision and the Voice,* Crowley's "Tannhäuser" and Parsons's own written invocation, as well as the seventh angelic call, which, as described above, was improperly used and incorrectly transcribed. Along with these, Parsons prepared an altar, a black box as a meditation focus, and offerings as requested— sacrificing a favorite statue of Pan and an Enochian tablet, during which time the roof of his guest house caught fire. Left high-strung by the ritual, the next day Parsons cursed another Parsonage resident (described as an "inmate") for disturbing his morning meditation, afterward frantically taking the curse back. Second and third rituals on March 3 yielded further instructions, and Parsons was told to compose a long poem of invocation, which he did, entitled "The Birth of BABALON."

Upon her return from the East Coast, Cameron reported a sighting of a UFO, which she believed was proof that Parsons's magic was working.[71] Two years after the conclusion of Parsons and Hubbard's working, on June 24, 1947, private pilot Kenneth Arnold reported seeing a group of UFOs near Mt. Rainier, Washington, the first of a rash of UFO sightings to come over the following decades. Crowley's one-time secretary Kenneth Grant later wrote that *something* pierced the Veil during the 'Babalon Working,' for in 1947—the year of Crowley's death—occurred the first UFO sightings that were to multiply massively in the ensuing years."[72] Cameron would later come to believe that UFOs were manifestations of the aforementioned "war-engine" from *The Book of the Law,* III:7, and as she mentally deteriorated, thought that they would carry her and her chosen few to Mars before Earth was destroyed.[73]

When news of Parsons and Hubbard's undertaking reached Crowley, he wrote to Germer that he was becoming "fairly frantic when I contemplate the idiocy of these louts!"[74] Parsons next decided (ever so wisely) to sell his house and sink the takings, along with his life savings, into a new business with Hubbard and Sara. True to his lifelong nautical obsession, Hubbard convinced Parsons to spend the money on three yachts in Miami, which they would sail through the Panama Canal to the West Coast and then sell at a profit. As soon as Parsons agreed, Hubbard absconded to Miami with his money and Betty, leaving Parsons broke, though Hubbard continued to string him along with reassuring phone calls. Crowley was prompted to declare that Parsons was a weak fool, stating, "It seems to me on the information of our brethren in California that Parsons has got an illumination in which he has lost all his personal independence. From our brother's account he has given away both his girl and his money. Apparently it is the ordinary confidence trick."[75]

This sobered Parsons up enough to file a restraining order, fly to Miami, discover that Hubbard and Betty had already left in a yacht, and then perform Crowley's Evocation of Bartzabel, the spirit of Mars; Parsons believed that the ritual produced storm conditions that forced Betty and Hubbard back to port (echoing the 1588 defeat of the Spanish Armada). Hauled into court by Parsons, Hubbard was told to recompense his mentor; once out of court, however, Betty threatened Parsons with a statutory rape claim if he kept pressing (they had started their relationship when she was underage). In the end, Parsons walked away with less than a third of his money.

Parsons had been stripped of many of his attachments, but like Dee, he carried on with his occult work. With Cameron, he relocated to Manhattan Beach to continue practicing magic and to work on the Navaho Missile Program in Inglewood; they were soon married. By the time McCarthyism broke out, however, Parsons's security clearance was revoked over his prior association with the American Communist Party. Like Dee, he now turned to seeking patrons abroad; when none came, he began taking night classes and made ends meet working as a car mechanic, gas station laborer, hospital orderly, and at the USC Department of Pharmacology (where he may have had access to drugs), supplementing his income by bootlegging nitroglycerine.[76] Cameron soon tired of this downward spiral and left for an artistic commune in Mexico, where she would make important contacts, like fellow occultist Leonora Carrington.[77] Parsons, meanwhile, embarked on OTO sexual magic operations with prostitutes, just as Crowley had in New York, and next decided to cross the Abyss and annihilate his personality in Binah. This is something young magicians are often wont to do when their lives are falling apart, compensating for real-world failures by replacing them with swiftly taken and self-granted magical titles and degrees, associating the damaged self with a more powerful symbol or lashing out at a world believed to be persecuting the hapless individual.[78] By the time Cameron returned from Mexico, Parsons was living with another woman, and next initiated a divorce.[79]

In his "Analysis by a Master of the Temple," Parsons justifies his failures by telling himself that his defrauding by Hubbard and Betty, and fraying relations with the OTO, were necessary for him to cease his pattern of relying on others, overcome his Oedipus complex, and sober up about his idealistic projections onto women. In his disassociated state, Parsons told himself that his ordeals had stripped off all that was unnecessary to achieving his True Will, the primary dangers to which he felt to be his own "sentimentality, weakness, and procrastination."[80] He now set out to attain to the City of the Pyramids that Crowley had seen in the fourteenth Aethyr, and, further, to take the Black Pilgrimage and cross the Abyss of the tenth Aethyr.

The result was a new piece of writing—"The Book of the Antichrist." In the new "book," totaling less than one thousand words, Parsons recounts that after receiving "The Book of Babalon" he gave up magic, and soon lost everything that he had. He had worked for two years to regain his fortune, but this also was taken from him, along with his reputation when his security clearance was revoked. Finally, on Halloween 1948, he began magic again, conducting a seventeen-day ritual working, resulting in a dream in which Babalon told him to begin the Black Pilgrimage.

Parsons then proceeded into the Mojave, coming at last to the "City of Chorazin," which is listed in the Gospels of Matthew and Luke as one of the villages Jesus performed miracles in, but within which his teaching was rejected, and that was then cursed;[81] because of this, Pseudo-Methodius had believed that Chorazin would be the birthplace of the Antichrist.[82] The word *Chorazin* presumably had a double resonance for Parsons as resembling Choronzon.

Here Parsons writes that "a great tower of Black Basalt was raised, that was part of a castle whose further battlements reeled over the gulf of stars."[83] A robed and veiled figure now revealed to Parsons four of his key past lives—as Simon Magus; Giles de Retz; Francis Stewart, fifth Earl of Bothwell; and Cagliostro. (Crowley had also claimed to be the reincarnation of Cagliostro.)[84] In each of these incarnations, he had attempted to manifest aspects of Babalon, and in each he had failed through pride or stupidity, just as he felt he had failed in his teenage evocation of Satan by showing fear upon the dark one's appearance.

"And I was asked: 'Will you fail again?'" Parsons wrote, "and I replied 'I will not fail.' (For I had given all my blood to BABALON, and it was not I that spoke.)"[85]

Following this oath, in a passage reminiscent of alien abduction accounts, in which it is not clear whether Parsons believed that he was writing about an astral experience or a literal event, he records that he was taken inside the black basalt tower, where he saluted its prince, and in which "things were done to me of which I may not write, and they told me, 'It is not certain that you will survive, but if you survive you will attain your true will, and manifest the Antichrist.'"[86]

Returning from the Mojave, Parsons officially swore the Oath of the Abyss—which was to "interpret every phenomenon as a particular dealing of God with [his] soul,"[87] and purposefully induce a kind of temporary schizophrenia, believing that his only other choices were permanent madness or suicide. Over the next forty days, however, "the Oath in no wise ameliorated that terror, and I continued in the madness and horror of the Abyss for a season."[88] Following this, Parsons took the formal eleven-point Oath of a Magister Templi,[89] and furthermore declared himself the Antichrist to Wilfred Smith, swearing another formal oath to that effect. He was now "Antichrist loosed in the world"[90] to fulfill the work of the Beast 666 and manifest Babalon upon the material plane.*

To this end, he pledged to destroy Christianity and the slave mentality it inculcates, and furthermore to destroy all false authority (of priests, judges, and police), all false laws, "conscription, compulsion, regimentation," and the general conformity and mediocrity of society. (These being the qliphotic accretions left behind by previous dispensations; see the final chapter.)

As of 1949, Parsons prophesied that as Antichrist he would conquer the world in the name of the Beast 666 and bring Thelema to the

---

*That is, to manifest the force of Chokmah, Chaos, the Beast 666, as embodied by its reigning initiate (Crowley) through Binah, Babalon, and ground the current fully into Malkuth, overthrowing the spiritual architecture of the world and realigning it with the new, Thelemic "Ninety-Three Current" initiated by Crowley.

entire planet, manifesting BABALON herself within the world within seven years. Within nine years, it was also foretold, the world would see the first nation to accept the Law of Thelema, at which point it would become "the first nation of Earth." All who accepted Parsons as Antichrist, and the Law of Thelema, would "be accursed and their joy shall be a thousandfold greater than the false joys of the false saints . . . and in my name BELARION* shall they work miracles, and confound our enemies, and none shall stand before us. Therefore I, THE ANTICHRIST call upon all the Chosen and elect and upon all men, come forth now in the name of Liberty, that we may end for ever the tyranny of the Black Brotherhood."[91]

Such prophecies are so vague that anything could be attributed to them in retrospect. Yet in 1956, the Baby Boomers would witness Elvis Presley's appearance on *The Ed Sullivan Show,* forever changing sexuality within the Western world and leading to the creation of the "teenager" (by Madison Avenue) as a new category of human. This generation would indeed make huge advances in fulfilling the tenets of Parsons's "Book of the Antichrist." They would demand (and receive) sexual liberation, reject Christianity and its sin complex, reject conscription, lash out at the prosaic mediocrity of 1950s society, and work miracles through the medium of high technology—the hard drive was also invented in 1956. By the late 1960s, much of the counterculture would come to resemble at least the less extreme bits of Crowley's Thelemic cult at Cefalu; the feminist movement, and the rebirth of popular interest in witchcraft and magic, would further ground the force of Babalon into the world as prophesied.

As far as Parsons's prediction of a nation accepting the Beast 666 within nine years, evangelicals would be quick to note that January 1, 1958, marked the establishment of the European Economic Community, which would become the European Union in 1993. (Babylon is referred to in Revelation as "the great city that rules over the kings of the earth,"[92] leading many to consider Babylon to be a reference to the Vatican, the United Nations, the European Union, or a

---

*Parsons's magical name as Magister Templi.

theorized global "new world order" to come, with the euro being a fore-runner of the Mark of the Beast required for economic transaction during the reign of Antichrist.)[93]

As the personification of female sexual liberation, anti-Christianity, open sexuality, witchcraft, and the occult, Babalon is much more popular in our current world than Christ—so much so that in 2015, Katy Perry appeared as Babalon herself at the Super Bowl XLIX halftime show, the largest and most central spectacle of mainstream American life. Bedecked in scarlet red flames, Perry emerged onto the field riding a towering portrayal of the solar, golden Beast, afterward dancing on a Masonic checkerboard while asking her viewers if they wanted to "play with magic" and telling them, as Babalon does in "Liber Cheth" and "The Book of Babalon," that "once you're mine, there's no going back," singing about lesbian sex and wearing a "49" jersey suggesting the forty-nine calls and forty-nine-petalled rose of BABALON. In the finale, Perry rode a giant star across the stadium in a glittering star-covered dress similar to the body of Nuit while singing, "Baby you're a firework," exhorting the audience to bring out the power within them, suggesting Crowley's dictum "Every man and woman is a star" from the first chapter of *The Book of the Law*.

This monumental and compelling spectacle, which greatly upset conservative Christians, nonetheless drew over 118.5 million viewers—the largest audience in Super Bowl history, and most certainly for a Thelemic ritual.[94] It is hard to imagine a more definitive symbol of Crowley's Thelemic worldview, and Babalon herself, winning the culture war. It's a long journey from the visions of two English alchemists in 1587 to the Super Bowl halftime 428 years later, but then, goddesses presumably think on a long timeline.

In 1946, following "The Book of the Antichrist," Parsons would also eloquently express his views for a non-occult audience in the brilliant *Freedom Is a Two-Edged Sword,* a libertarian screed cutting to the core of American servility, inequality, and mediocrity that rings as true now as when it was written. He would also continue to assist in Cameron's own training as a Thelemic magician via correspondence; these letters remain among the best available instructional material for new magicians.

"It is in the passage of the barrier that lies just one inch beyond the possible that the attainment is made," Parsons writes of the process of initiation,

> the going down of the ego between the adamant or malefic back sides of the gods, that the fusion of infinity takes place.... You bawl and weep to give up the ego, the greasy penny that you have been greedily clutching in your dirty little paw, and, behold, when you do it, it buys you a ticket to the greatest show on Earth, with ice cream and cake free for ever. Naturally the temporal return is painful— you come back to tell the kids outside what damn fools they are, and what they are missing, and if you have forgotten their language you usually get kicked for your pains. It is just that—a circus—a carnival in the grand manner.[95]

He next went to work for Howard Hughes, which was soon followed by an offer of employment by the Israeli rocket program. Entertaining this overture resulted in Parsons being discharged by Hughes; a subsequent investigation by the FBI found him innocent of espionage, but resulted in a permanent ban from working on classified projects (and thus rocketry) due to his prior Communist affiliations.[96] In response, Parsons formed a company to create explosive effects for Hollywood and worked manufacturing chemicals, just as he had done out of high school.

Cameron soon gravitated back into Parsons's orbit, and they returned to Pasadena, renting rooms to beatniks (who would routinely play bongos until six in the morning, to the chagrin of Pasadena PD), cooking up absinthe, collaborating on art and poetry, and offering courses on magic.[97] Parsons presented to this new generation a simplified and stripped down approach to witchcraft and Gnostic Christianity (in which Parsons pointed the way, perhaps surprisingly for a self-declared Antichrist, to the true Christ, not the empty symbol of the Black Brotherhood that he had lashed out at), for which Parsons provided some of the most lucid, evocative, and straightforward magical writing of the twentieth century.[98] Parsons's notes for "The Witchcraft," in particular, which was to be the name of his new magical order, presage Wicca and the explosion of interest in witchcraft to come. Parsons and Cameron planned to return to Mexico, where he would work on potent new explosives,[99] and the reunited couple would save to move to Israel and plan for children. Unfortunately, that storybook ending never came.

On June 17, 1952—one day before they were to leave—Parsons was given an order for explosives for a film set, during the fulfillment of which he dropped a mixture of fulminate of mercury that exploded, tearing off his right forearm, breaking his legs and left arm, and ripping open his face. He was still conscious when found, but died upon arriving at the hospital.[100] The Antichrist's last words, fittingly, were "I wasn't done"—the exact inversion of Christ's "It is finished."[101] Parsons's mother committed suicide almost immediately upon hearing the news of her son's crucifixion by fire.[102]

Rumors circulated—and continue to circulate—about Parsons's death, which was officially explained as an accident; some of his colleagues, however, believed Parsons could never be so careless. Cameron believed he had been murdered by the LAPD, while her friend Renata Druks even thought, improbably, that he died trying to produce a homunculus.[103] Others thought that Hughes had killed him.[104] Wilfred Smith suspected suicide; Jane Wolfe agreed, and ominously declared that "the Gods stepped in before he met a worse fate."[105] However, the official investigating criminologist found a morphine-filled syringe near the blast, which could explain Parsons's clumsiness. Ed Forman, however, suggested that "Jack used to sweat a lot and the damn thing just slipped out of his hand and blew him up."[106] Given the ties between Parsons's sweating and his use of amphetamines, this suggests, most unromantically, that Parsons simply may have been back on speed (or an amphetamine and morphine combo) and made a sloppy mistake.

Cameron had Parsons cremated and scattered in the Mojave, perhaps where he had carried out the Babalon Working.[107] His name was soon forgotten by most of the scientific establishment, though a crater on the dark side of the moon was given his name in 1972.[108] Like Dee, he would be lost to scientific history—at least for the time being—but retain a legendary status in the occult world rivalling even that of Crowley.

Parsons, however, was not as seasoned or disciplined a magician as the Beast. As evidenced by his errors with the angelic calls, his command of the Golden Dawn system was incomplete and spotty, and while he got *results* with his application of the OTO's sexual magic, he also destroyed his life almost *immediately* upon its use. Was the sacrifice of his incarnation necessary to manifest Babalon? Maybe. Or maybe, had he taken a slower, less reckless approach, he might have stayed alive to conjure up further wonders—even to help guide the counterculture that he and Cameron helped create into the 1960s and beyond.

Cameron's work and notes make it clear that she remained a practicing magician for the rest of her life, albeit one with a tentative grip on reality and sanity. Parsons remained a central figure in her psyche, and his presence and personal mythology hovered over the rest of her life like the grievous angel she had once painted him as; perhaps unfairly, as William Breeze writes in the introduction to *Songs for the Witch Woman:* "The mythos that Jack had created for her—with its implicit *geas* to somehow manifest the goddess Babalon—lay heavily on her. I told Cameron that back in 1946 she had walked into a set of magical assumptions projected by Jack in his Babalon Working. I was not uncritical."[109]

Of particular interest, however, are Cameron's own eccentric Enochian workings, as she continued to believe herself to be the key to fulfilling Crowley and Parsons's work and manifesting Babalon.[110] Following the Thelemic Tetragrammaton developed in *The Vision and the Voice,* Cameron described Crowley as Yod (Chokmah, Chaos, and the Beast), Leah Hirsig as Heh (Binah, Babalon), Jack Parsons as Vau (Tiphareth, Christ, and Antichrist), and herself as Heh final (Malkuth, Malkah-Koré, or Babalon's daughter),[111] the final manifested product of the Ninety-Three Current, charged with grounding it into the physical world.

Through 1953, Cameron gathered a group of bohemians and artists around her in Beaumont, west of Palm Springs, whom she dubbed the "Children," after Babalon's command to gather together

her children in "The Book of Babalon." These she organized by tarot suit, including Wands for black men and Pentacles for white women. According to Spencer Kansa (who does not cite his sources), Cameron spent the period between the autumn and winter equinoxes engaged in regular sex magic actions. In these, she allegedly called the seventh Aethyr and entered the astral while engaged in sexual intercourse, where she performed the Bornless Ritual for contacting her holy guardian angel, afterward using the sexual fluids for consecrating a Babalon talisman. She next oversaw regular sex magical workings between her "Children," in which she urged interracial sex between Wands and Pentacles, which she believed would create a new race of mixed-race "moonchildren" sacred to Horus; this, she believed, fulfilled the symbolism of the Chariot card of the tarot, which concerns the unification of opposing forces and is also attributed to Babalon—as in Crowley's "Liber Cheth," *Cheth* being the Hebrew letter associated with the Chariot.[112]

By such rituals, Cameron hoped to become pregnant and produce the moonchild Parsons had aimed to create in the Babalon Working (the literal incarnation of Babalon), whom she dubbed the "Wormwood Star," from Revelation 8:11, one of the trumpet judgments that befalls unrepentant humanity during the reign of Antichrist, befouling a third of the world's water and killing those who drink it. The OTO, however, was not impressed: the same year, Thelemic mainstay Gerald Yorke wrote to then-head Karl Germer that "in medical language Cameron is a lunatic." Horrified by her sexual workings in Beaumont, and fearing that she was too far gone to successfully intervene with, the OTO considered excommunicating her and using her as a warning to others of what *not* to do. Cameron did become pregnant as a result of her ritual workings, but it ended in miscarriage, just as her previous ones had.[113]

Following Parsons and Cameron, the OTO would dissolve and lay dormant, being successfully reconstituted in the late 1960s by Grady McMurtry.* By that time, interest in the occult had exploded in the

---

*Other claimants to OTO continued to exist during this time, including groups run by Kenneth Grant, Marcelo Motta, and others; these were settled by lawsuit in the 1980s with the McMurtry OTO being given sole custodianship of the Crowley legacy.

counterculture—just as Parsons had predicted in his manifestos for "The Witchcraft," which presage the birth of Wicca, Neopaganism, and the Goddess movement, carrying forward the Babalon "current" into the wider mainstream. The other half of the Apocalypse equation—the Beast—would get its due with the birth of Satanism in 1960s San Francisco.*

Together, these two movements—which fall far short of the intellectual sophistication of Thelema—might nonetheless be seen as manifestory shockwaves from Crowley, Neuburg, Parsons, and Cameron's work. The parent tradition of Thelema has given us Wicca and Goddess spirituality as a manifestation of Babalon,[114] Satanism as a manifestation of the Beast, and the general category of "New Age" as a watered-down version of Crowley's New Aeon. Together, these forces make up nearly the entirety of alternative spirituality in twenty-first-century America, and are therefore a primary force (along with competing mainstream religions, the New Atheists, and secular humanism in general) in the destruction of Christianity as a historic force.

Yet if these small (albeit highly culturally influential) religious movements collectively make up the "Satanic" resistance to Christian eschatology, we must note that the evangelical eschatology they claim to resist, the dominant religious form in America, hails from the exact same place.

---

*Gerald Gardner, the father of modern Wicca, was a IV° OTO initiate and associate of Crowley; Anton LaVey, founder of the Church of Satan, had been mentored early on by the filmmaker and Thelemic magician (and, later, IX° OTO initiate) Kenneth Anger, a longtime associate of Marjorie Cameron. LaVey would publish a few garbled angelic invocations in his *Satanic Bible*—the bestselling occult book of all time—substituting the names of God for those of Satan; in 1975, LaVey's student Michael Aquino—like Dee and Crowley, an asset of military intelligence, who worked extensively in U.S. psyops efforts in Vietnam—claimed that experimentation with the angelic calls led to the production of yet another "received" document, in this case channeled from the Egyptian god Set, the "Book of Coming Forth by Night," on the basis of which he founded his Temple of Set splinter group from the Church of Satan.

18

The Last Jerusalem

The West never escapes the Apocalypse. From Pseudo-Methodius to Dee's magic to environmental collapse to the popular obsession with zombies to the election of Donald Trump, the conviction that the end is nigh appears hardwired into Western consciousness. The fact that the Apocalypse never quite manifests seems to be no deterrent to its continued memetic survival: the dates just get pushed further forward into the future, or the details changed. Just as the narrative of Revelation itself is a nonlinear series of interlocking cycles of events, so are human attempts to ground Revelation into specific dates and events useless.[1] Perhaps we are cursed to repeat the end of the world again and again, infinitely, in eternal return.

John Dee, Edward Kelly, Aleister Crowley, Victor Neuburg, Jack Parsons, Marjorie Cameron, and many others consciously engaged with the Apocalypse, casting themselves in central roles. Each experienced profound alterations of consciousness—an inner apocalypse. This is the original meaning of *apokálypsis, ἀποκάλυψις,* which means not a conflagration of violence but "an uncovering," a revelation of divine knowledge that permanently casts the world in a new light. These inner revelations were considered to be linked to the outer apocalypse—the objective progress of the world toward its end—even, through the logic of sympathetic magic, to effect and accelerate this timeline. In the real world, such inner visionary experiences influenced these individuals' later actions, many of which (as detailed previously) were intimately connected with the ideological, cultural, and even military development of the British and American empires.

These actions did not occur in a vacuum—they are deeply personal expressions of the millennia-long spiritual narrative of Western culture itself, which progressed around these magicians' individual work and would have continued to advance with or without them. It is unlikely that the average Christian fundamentalist or American politician has ever heard of Dee or even entertained the concept of magic as anything except a "Satanic" force forbidden by scripture; if they have heard of Crowley, it is as a one-dimensional symbol of this perceived Satanism. Yet, as demonstrated at length in the previous chapters, Dee and those who followed him have indeed played a starring role in the West's rush to Armageddon.

THE INNER APOCALYPSE
The Edenic Revelation

Having traversed over five centuries of shadow history and occult theory, let us now express the inner *apokálypsis* or uncovering that angelic magic facilitates. This section is drawn from both my academic research and my practical experimentation with Dee's system over the previous decade plus.

Dee's teachers wrote of the *mens adeptus,* the enlightened sage who has restored his or her unfallen nature. The Qabalah provides the road map for achieving this goal, and Dee's Enochian magic provides the method of actualizing it—specifically, the process of *gebofal* and successively calling and undergoing the modifications of consciousness induced by the thirty Aethyrs. This process is, as far as I can tell at present, the closest thing the West has to a method for activating the enlightenment experience so often described in Eastern texts. In many ways, it is an *exceedingly* more efficacious and direct way of doing so than Eastern methods (such as decades-long meditation under an autocratic guru, or tantric extremities), particularly for Western people, as it relies on Western rather than Eastern cosmology. On the other hand, it provides little in the way of a support structure for this state of consciousness—that is, it is exceedingly good at dropping individuals into a transpersonal enlightenment state, but this experience itself may be traumatic (even apocalyptically destructive) to an individual who has not undergone enough spiritual training or reached enough life maturity to understand how to navigate, contextualize, maintain, or even withstand it.

I suspect that this is the primary reason for the many documented cases of blowout caused by Enochian magic, rather than some kind of inherently malign aspect of the system. I also suspect that the Golden Dawn and Thelemic systems themselves are attempts to build a support scaffolding around this central "big event" of Western occultism, training wheels that slowly introduce students to Qabalah, altered states, spirit contact, and ego dissolution prior to the Enochian plunge. Occult teachers who followed Crowley, like Israel Regardie, have become much more aware of the potential for blowout by imbalanced individuals engaging in magic, and have put heavy stress on grounding factors like undergoing psychotherapy, maintaining a day job, and keeping up relationships with non-occult individuals in the real world. I believe that such grounding factors, combined with an *almost excruciatingly slow and patient approach,* a hardheaded understanding of science and cognitive bias, an avoidance of drugs, regular physical exercise, and a good sense of humor are excellent safeguards against magical obsession.

The calling of the thirty Aethyrs (as seen in the chapter on Crowley) allows an intrepid psychonaut to reascend the Tree of Life itself. The alphabet of the Hebrew language (which is a decayed echo of Enochian) forms this cognitive Tree, which is both a representation of the original Tree of Life in the Garden of Eden and a map of the human understanding of the universe. When traced *downward* in a lightning flash pattern, from Kether to Malkuth, the Tree of Life demonstrates how God manifests his Creation. When traced *upward* by the "serpent path" (suggesting the forbidden tasting of the fruit of the Tree of Knowledge of Good and Evil in the Garden at the serpent's urging), it shows how an initiate can reascend from his decayed state back to God—the "path of return." Hermetic initiates thus charted a course upward on the tree, ascending through the lower spheres and their associated initiatory tasks.

This is not a process of becoming, but rather a process of undoing. As each sphere is mastered, the associated faculty of the soul is perfected and then surrendered to the divine until—following the completion of the passage through Chesed—the initiate must surrender everything they are and everything they have built to God.

In Crowley's rendering, the adept relinquishes their ego and so passes through the Abyss in the illusory sephira Da'ath, and finds themselves in Binah, attributed to the planet Saturn, the goddess Babalon, and the City of the Pyramids. This City is a reference to the Watchtowers themselves, as their cells were shaped into pyramids by the Golden Dawn.

This cessation of the aspirant's mind and outer personality allows them to merge back into the wider universe, or go transpersonal in more modern parlance. The freshly created Magister Templi is no longer identified with a fixed personality and point of view but with the totality of existence as it may be perceived from any given point (their "Temple," which they have now become master of). Having now gone nondual and nonlocal, the adept no longer strives for the "magic powers" that are promised in the grimoires or in Eastern meditation manuals like the *Yoga Sutras of Patanjali,* but finds them to be natural expressions of his or her base state of consciousness. The power of "being in two places at once" as promised by Patanjali, for instance, is an obvious glyph of a consciousness no longer bound to a singular individual. Likewise, the correspondences and synchronicities greedily hoarded by the Hermetic adept as evidence of some kind of secret connective principle between themselves and the broader universe fall away when the veil is lifted and it is shown that there was never any separation between the adept and their universe at all.

This is a taste of the spiritual experience referred to as "seeing God face-to-face," which no one, it is said, can undergo and live; true, because it destroys the small-*s* self. In the language of yoga, it is a taste of *samadhi,* a collapse of the distinction of subject and object. When experiencing this state of consciousness, the initiate understands that there is no boundary between themselves and the universe they experience, and that both have been falsely separated by the brain to process day-to-day life.

Once this is understood—and God is seen face-to-face—the initiate should no longer experience friction with their environment, as it is now understood to be an organic part of a larger being comprising the initiate *and* their universe. This ceases the sense of struggle with the universe, because the experience destroys the illusion that there is a self that was ever separate from its surroundings. In so doing, the initiate understands that the world *is not fallen* and never was, that humanity never left the Garden of Eden at all. Rather, it is shown that "the Crown is in the Kingdom" and that "Nirvana is in Samsara," and that we already exist in an Edenic state. It is only the Serpent—the ego, the mind that thinks itself whole, Choronzon—that distracts us from this bedrock reality with its endless magic tricks, assaulting the pristine nature of the mind with the ammunition of thoughts.*

Put more simply: instead of trying to affect the universe with magical efforts, the initiate realizes that they *are* the universe. This is not a New Age platitude. As the Irish philosopher Bishop Berkeley pointed out, the entirety of the phenomenal universe only exists for each individual as a perceptual trick created by the brain's processing of external sensory input, which is then represented by the nervous system to itself. We *at no time* contact anything outside our own sensory array, which is of necessity filtered through our own internal dialogue, ideologies, and past experiences. All "matter" is actually mind. (And as David Hume would next assert, as did the Buddha, even mind itself is an illusion.)

At this point the need to form connections between (or changes to) seemingly phenomenal objects, as in ceremonial magic, is revealed as a comical misapprehension of the nature of reality. As esoteric Buddhism and Hermeticism alike assure us, *All is Mind.*

This realization is a dangerous state in the career of the initiate, as

---

*For a surprisingly good cinematic treatment of this concept in a most unexpected place, see Guy Ritchie's 2005 film *Revolver.*

it can lead to solipsism and imbalance—unless this realization is tempered by the understanding that it holds equally true for all conscious beings, even if such beings can at no time be directly perceived. This, quite unglamorously, puts the initiate right back where they began—on exactly equal footing with the rest of humanity, no matter how inexplicable the behaviors and life choices of other beings are. Spiritual elitism is destroyed with a thunderclap.

Seen in this light, Christ's injunction to "Love your neighbor as yourself"[2] makes perfect sense as an initiated statement. When there is no separation between self and other, initiate and universe, there is also no separation between beings; other beings *are* parts of one's wider self. This metaphysics of compassion is exquisitely worked out in tantric Buddhism;[3] likewise, this revelation supersedes any previous understanding of psychic phenomena between individuals.

Practically speaking, this is the state of consciousness that can be induced by scrying the totality of the thirty Aethyrs in Crowley's manner, provided the initiate has already done the inner work necessary to prepare for undergoing such an ordeal; this is the architecture of true initiation. Even a fleeting taste of this state of consciousness is enough to destroy the sense that *anything* else achievable by human beings is of comparable worth.

Crowley wrote about experiencing this state of consciousness upon completing his passage through the Aethyrs in 1909, stating that upon crossing the Abyss, the nineteenth call suddenly read as a blessing rather than a curse, and that evil itself was seen as a projection of the ego. Existence is perfect, in Crowley's conception; it is only the dysfunctional human ego that fabricates the idea of suffering. Once the ego is extinguished—and trained to stay dead, as the spiritual path continues—existence becomes pure enjoyment. As Crowley states, "I had to explore every possibility, and transmute each base metal in turn into gold. It was years before I got into the habit of falling in love at first sight with everything that came my way."[4]

In Christian terms, the Aethyrs and the angelic material overall use the language of Revelation—but, once passed through, this apocalypse leads straight back to the Garden. In so doing, angelic magic

Fig. 18.1. Time (and the Old and New Testaments) conceived as an ouroboros, beginning with the fall from Eden (represented by 333, Choronzon), with the quality of human consciousness descending into darkness on a downward arc, at the nadir of which God descends into his creation as Christ to redeem fallen humanity. Time is then terminated by the final war with the spiritual darkness incarnated as the Beast 666, Babalon, and Antichrist, prior to mankind's salvation and return to the Edenic state. Image courtesy of the author.

suggests that the Old and New Testaments are not a linear narrative but a loop or ouroboros, with the end of the world a literal revelation that history itself has been an illusion, and a return of mankind to the Garden. Indeed, the true Revelation is that we have never left the Garden at all . . . we've just head tripped ourselves into thinking we have. Revelation means the lifting of a veil—the veil of our own mind that obscures Eden.

In truth, *nothing* has ever been real except for God's love for his Creation—or more accurately, God's love *manifest as* the Creation. All of history is seen as a lie created by Satan or Choronzon (representing the sum total of all human egos experiencing self-chosen separation from their source), punctured briefly by God descending into his forgetful Creation in the form of Christ and undergoing the Crucifixion, and finally disintegrating and returning to the fold at his Second Coming.

Once this experience has been undergone, the initiate no longer lives in the Old Aeon, in either Genesis or Revelation, for they have reassembled their own consciousness. Having experienced samadhi and understood the nature of reality, they now live in the Aeon of Horus—in which subject and object are united; in which Nuit (the universe) and Hadit (consciousness) have united to produce the Crowned and Conquering Child, which is the unity of both. The initiate is now free to manifest their divine play as they wish—Do What Thou Wilt Shall Be the Whole of the Law.

What had appeared as horrors—because they were a threat to the ego—now appear as blessings, as the mind has now been altered to see *everything* as a manifestation of the divine. As Crowley discusses, the content of the calls, which appears apocalyptic and demonic on first read, becomes pure divine love on the other side of ZAX. The calls describe reality as it is, and how it is constructed, including divisions and hierarchies; to an ego that still believes itself separate from the Creation, this is sheer evil. But to the liberated mind, it is clear that *it could not be any other way, and that the Creation is perfect without exception.* This truth is also hinted at by the extreme nondual traditions of Eastern mysticism—for instance, Aghora, or the wrathful deities of Tibetan Buddhism that are glimpsed in the Bardo, and become ever-more ferocious the more the ego attempts to preserve itself as a separate entity.

Touching God in this manner therefore forms a new universe (as experienced by the magician), completing a new Tetragrammaton as shown in the fourth Aethyr; a new Garden of Eden is sprung from the sands of the Abyss, as seen in the thirteenth Aethyr.

Although the Aethyrs are revealed within the spirit diaries, it is possible that, just as the rest of the sessions appear to reveal "official" angelic instructions on previously known magical techniques and artifacts (for instance, the update of the Sigillum Dei Aemeth and the Real

Cabala itself), the Aethyrs as given by the angels may also depict an underlying reality that has been glimpsed by other spiritual traditions.

Most obviously, the Aethyrs resemble the fifty gates of Binah in orthodox Kabbalah,[5] and the thirty aeons in Valentinian Gnosticism.[6] They also resemble the controversial doctrine of the twenty "Aerial Toll Houses" in Eastern Orthodoxy, through which the soul must navigate after death, and be questioned as to its sins.[7] Similarly, it would be hard not to draw a tentative parallel between the forty-nine calls and the forty-nine days of the Bardo, the after-death state discussed in Nyingma Buddhism, in which the soul transits between lifetimes and is confronted by wrathful apparitions of its own karma—losing control over its own agency in its rebirth unless it can remember its own guru, guardian spirit (*yidam* in Tibetan), or best of all, the fundamental clear light that is the nature of its own consciousness.[8] With the possible exception of the guru, the role of which is not nearly as prominent in Western mysticism as it is in Eastern, encounters with one's guardian angel and the nature of one's own mind (after crossing the Abyss in ZAX) are critical to the passage through the Aethyrs, and are the core goals of Aleister Crowley's A∴A∴; the womb imagery of Binah also parallels that of the Bardos.

While this process may sound simple or even compelling, it is far from easy. Indeed, it not only runs counter to the standard selfish reasons most are attracted to magic for (ego aggrandizement, the accumulation of material comforts, the lure of special powers, the desire for special spiritual status, etc.), it cuts against the grain of the ego itself, a trait it shares with all true spiritual paths. In repairing one's fallen nature, the would-be adept must confront all that has kept them in a fallen state—and face the bitter truth that it is *they* who have willfully shut themselves off from divine grace, who have cast themselves East of Eden, in ten thousand different ways, over so many long years . . . and no one else.

Consequently, despite its "angelic" label, Enochian magic can be saturated with an atmosphere of crushing despair, as the ego can barely face, let alone relinquish, its own projections. This should be self-evident when it is seen that the Aethyrs are concerned with initiation into the sphere of Binah, attributed to Saturn, the planet of time, restriction, entropy, and aging. Binah, Understanding, is experientially the sphere of understanding the fundamental nature of existence—which, as the Buddha assures us, is sorrow. It is the sorrow that attends the loss of all of an adept's illusions, which have kept her from the accomplishment of her True Will; indeed, it is the sorrow attendant upon the death of the outer shell of the adept herself, for beyond Binah she is naught but a pile of dust where a functional ego once stood.* It is the sorrow of the Dark Mother—she who bore us, and she who bears us.

THE OUTER APOCALYPSE
The Angelic Reformation

As man touches the angels, however, the angels touch the world—as above, so below.

As individuals cross the Abyss and touch the Supernals, they form channels for divine grace to flow back into the world in the form of the individual adept and their cultural output. This downward push from the Supernals back into the world of manifestation often (though not always) takes the form of new religions and the empires that follow in their wake.

Qabalistically, angelic magic bypasses the terrestrial authorities (the force of the demiurge) manifested in Chesed. It reconnects the initiate themselves with the Supernals from which outer schools may once have drawn their spiritual force, force that may have been lost as an initiatory school becomes a religion and degenerates into rote repetition of ritual and customs. When remanifesting back downward into existence, the new current from the Supernals may take the form of a new demiurgic religion in Chesed, and a new outpouring of destructive energy in Geburah to clear up the dead accretions (shells) of previous dispensations. Seen by supernal light, all terrestrial religions and mystery schools are only echoes of divine revelation, vehicles by which adepts attempted

---

*See Crowley, "Liber Cheth," in *The Holy Books,* 99–104.

to communicate the brilliance of the Godhead. The alarming suggestion of angelic magic, as with Gnosticism, is that such direct revelation is available without intermediary.

This process assists in the restoration of the fallen world. However, this doesn't mean that the decay and degradation of the world is necessarily "off script." Not only is decay necessary as a prelude to redemption (just as death creates fertile conditions for new growth), it may also be necessary to *accelerate* that Saturnian decay in order to speed the arrival of the redemption to follow. The apocalyptic magic of the angels hinges on this principle.[9]

As the new doctrine is manifested to the world, it comes into conflict with prior guiding principles that have calcified into dead ritual. A clear example would be Christ, the Pauline Church, and the eventual Christianization of the Roman Empire. Another would be the Prophet Muhammad and the rapid and violent spread of Islam. Prophets create religions, and religions create empires. The words of the prophets are always misunderstood and warped in the establishment of the religions they leave in their wake, but this seems to be an inevitable effect of communicating across the Abyss.*

In performing this dispensational role, each adept breaks the hold of the spiritual order that precedes them, by dint of bringing "fresh fever from the skies,"[10] or forging a new causal link between the Supernals and the world of manifestation (and to see beyond the world of manifestation, the adept must no longer be manifest as such, hence the disintegration of the ego in Binah).

Dee and Kelly's contact with the angels was promptly followed by the angels using the two men as their chess pieces in Europe, as divine messengers of the retribution that was about to fall on the Holy Roman Empire. Dee and Kelly functioned first as operative magicians, then as prophets of Apocalypse—not of an apocalypse that was to occur overnight, but over the course of centuries, with the British Empire as its catalyzing agent. For how else did we come to the edge of complete collapse of the natural world, the degradation of humanity, and the

---

*See Crowley, "Liber B vel Magi," in *The Holy Books,* 1–5.

destruction of all traditions but by the machinery of global empire?

And just as Dee's imperialism and later angelic proselytizing built a British Empire from the ashes of the Holy Roman Empire that had been created by St. Paul, Jack Parsons's creation of solid-state rocket fuel and concurrent work with the Watchtowers and Aethyrs might be said to have performed a similar role in expanding the boundaries of the Anglo-American empire off world.

In so doing, these adepts were preparing the way for the New Jerusalem to come, working to alchemically restore the world and return it to its Edenic state through the exercise of the Real Cabala or Enochian magic.[11] But to return to Eden, mankind would first have to go through the fires of Revelation. And we still are.

IT'S HAPPENING

Over the two years of writing this book, I often struggled to justify spending so much time on such an apparently obscure historical subject. I began writing in 2015; by the time I finished, in early 2017, my study of the occult mechanics of Apocalypse had become all too relevant.

The British referendum to withdraw from the European Union on June 23, 2016, was a stunning turn in both British and world history, echoing Henry VIII's decision to withdraw from Rome. Both acts might be seen as bookends of the British Empire—the first beginning English expansion, the second bringing a final closure as England slammed its doors into isolationism. Following this, the election of Donald Trump to the American presidency on November 8, 2016 signaled a new period of not just rising nationalism but also a push toward evangelical totalitarianism, and a fresh lease on life for the apocalyptic Christian right. Having lost political power during the Obama years, the evangelical voting bloc that had carried Reagan and the Bushes seized the steering wheel once more, just as they had following the Carter and Clinton administrations.

While Trump himself appears to hold only politically expedient and probably grudging religious ties, the machine behind him is decidedly evangelical and apocalyptic. Trump's campaign strategist Stephen Bannon even likened himself to Henry VIII's chief minister

Thomas Cromwell, who was instrumental in manipulating the venal and impulsive king to achieve England's split from Rome. Cromwell was also responsible for the sweeping evangelical reforms that followed, including the privatization and sacking of England's church land.[12] Like Trithemius, Dee, Darby, and Crowley, Bannon held to his own cyclical model of history, posited by the authors William Strauss and Neil Howe in *The Fourth Turning*, which suggests that history moves in eighty- to one-hundred-year periods or *saeculum* followed by an *ekpyrosis* or cataclysmic destruction of the preceding order by fire; Bannon believed America had now entered this apocalyptic period.

Bannon, who stated that Trump was only his "blunt instrument," saw his role as establishing a period of authoritarianism in preparation for a revitalization of a "Judeo-Christian West." This he apparently hoped to achieve via alliance with Russia, prior to a war against China and global Islam in a conflagration possibly larger than World War II. Instead of looking back to the Reagan years, as most conservatives do, Bannon looked back (with a grudge) to the fall of Constantinople, hoping to achieve a united Christendom just as Dee, Kelly, and Łaski once did.[13] Bannon served in an official capacity as senior counselor to the president before being pushed out in a cloud of scandal, includ- ing being publicly mocked by Trump and losing control of his media company Breitbart News. In this, Bannon's comparison of himself to Thomas Cromwell, who similarly fell from grace, was indeed apt.

Shortly after taking power, the Trump/Pence administration began enacting shocking evangelical "reforms" like moving to disintegrate the 1954 Johnson Amendment that bans churches from making politi- cal contributions, as well as appointing extreme-right evangelicals to prominent government positions, including Betsy DeVos, Jeff Sessions, Neil Gorsuch, and Jerry Falwell Jr. Indeed, Trump's vice president, Mike Pence, an extreme pro-life, anti-LGBT, and Christian Zionist evangelical, could not have made his intentions clearer than with the Bible verse he chose to be sworn in by—"If my people, which are called by my name, shall humble themselves, and pray, and seek my face, and turn from their wicked ways; then will I hear from heaven, and will for- give their sin, and will heal their land." (2 Chronicles 7:14, KJV). This is the same passage that Ronald Reagan chose for his own inauguration.[14]

Despite its populist and evangelical overtones, this resurgence of the American right is not without its own occult elements. The "alt-right," the American port of the European New Right that was instrumental in pushing for the election of Trump on social media, is immersed in fascist occultism. Like much of the alt-right, Bannon has cited the influence of the far-right Italian occultist Julius Evola, a student of René Guénon who aligned himself briefly with Mussolini and Hitler—but who, like J. F. C. Fuller, found them to be not right wing *enough*.

Behind the scenes of this new, revitalized fascist right lurks Aleksandr Dugin, Vladimir Putin's own Evola-influenced, occultist vizier, who works to push for a world-wide "traditionalist" and racialist uprising to benefit Russia's long-term geopolitical goals, and who utilizes iconography hijacked from both the Russian Orthodox Church and chaos magic. Long obsessed with America's Protestant eschatology, Dugin has described his own vision of an apocalyptic confrontation between the "good angels" of Russia and the "evil angels" of American globalization and monoculture, an accelerated Apocalypse that "will be a war of angels, a war of gods, a confrontation of entities, not tied by historical or economic laws and patterns." Dugin, who was the primary architect of Russia's 2014 annexation of Crimea, and who now acts as a guru to the American and European alt-right, calls this world model "political angelology."[15]

Dee's worldview, it seems, is more relevant than ever; history but a flicker of light for his fearsome, punishing angels. Far from assigning men like Trump, Pence, Bannon, or Dugin roles within this story—I do not—their actions do demonstrate the infinitely recursive nature of the apocalyptic narrative itself. Yet perhaps, in exposing the wiring of the Architecture of Apocalypse in this book, I will have also suggested how it may be disarmed.

AEON OF CHORONZON

Every generation gets its own apocalypse. Here, then, is ours.

See it in the never-ending grinding of the war machine over the

Middle East, chewing up the cradle of civilization, in Iraq, Syria, Afghanistan. In the Holy Land itself; in Israel, Palestine, Jordan, Lebanon.

In buzzing drones, icons of the falcon Horus, the Antichrist, sent by the American eagle, perforating the bodies of innocents taken as "collateral damage." In illicit white phosphorous rounds. In children born twisted into hideous creatures of pure suffering, more monstrous than anything from the imaginations of demonologists, as the result of depleted uranium bullets used by the U.S. military.

In a death cult named after the mother of Horus slicing the heads off its captives. In never-ending terror attacks in America and Europe. In daily mass shootings. In the apocalyptic confrontation of the Black Brotherhoods, the false slave religions of the world rending what remains of each other and destroying the world in the process. In a petulant, tyrannical adult child, solar avatar of Horus, of Antichrist, given the reins of the world.

In a hypnotized population, possessed to a man by the demon Choronzon, lost in dispersion, the food of the Abyss—stripped of meaning, lost in the endless information glut of Da'ath, Knowledge, without recourse to any higher Wisdom or Understanding, unable to maintain a single train of thought from one moment to the next without being torn to pieces by the onslaught of electronic interference. A king with no Crown. Awash with chemicals and genetic contaminants, in their water, food, air, and earth, cancers erupting through their bodies. In a world devastated on all planes. In dying species, poisonous seas; the Edens of the world paved over to build more shopping malls. In the women of the world sold into physical and digital degradation. Animals flayed and tortured in their pens, sacrificed at a global scale. In the breaking down of every tradition and religion into so much New Age pablum. In a lukewarm Church abandoned by the masses and left to pander to the lowest common denominator to beg them back—the Church of Laodicea.

In a world sagging under the weight of the soulless billions, population doubling at an unprecedented rate. Watch them walk through this world, slack-jawed and uncomprehending, staring at their phones as if they expect to see the truth there revealed. "When there's no more room in hell, the dead shall walk the earth."[16] Man, the cackler, the Ape of Thoth. Just around the corner, the horrors of artificial intelligence, ready to obsolete all humanity, to render us all into so much useless biomass, awaiting a messiah or a genocide.

We have desecrated the Temple of the human soul, and in the place of the Holy of Holies we have set up Choronzon, the Abomination of Desolation, the true Lord of the Aeon. Choronzon, the shattered reflection of us all, an idiot god cackling upon the central throne of the world soul that he has made his commode. Like this, mankind shall suffer until the end of the aeon.

Christ is coming, and with him he shall bring an Empire of Angels.

JASON LOUV,
CITY OF ANGELS

Fig. 18.2. Gustave Doré, *The New Jerusalem*, 1865.

Notes

INTRODUCTION.
A SUBLUNARY WORLD

1. Rutledge, "John Dee: Consultant to Queen Elizabeth I," 1.
2. Nasar, *A Beautiful Mind*, 13.
3. Kanigel, *The Man Who Knew Infinity*, 7.
4. Luhrmann et. al., "Differences in Voice-Hearing Experiences," 41–44.
5. Pew Research Center, "The Future of World Religions," 6–8.
6. Durant, *The Reformation*, 332–33.
7. Ephesians 6:12 (NIV).
8. Bainton, *Here I Stand*, 152.
9. Durant, *The Reformation*, 608.
10. Schaff and Schaff, *History of the Christian Church*, 412.
11. Durant, *The Reformation*, 316.
12. Durant, *The Reformation*, 481.
13. Durant, *The Reformation*, 425.
14. Durant, *The Reformation*, 489.
15. Durant, *The Reformation*, 549.
16. Durant, *The Reformation*, 578.
17. Tillyard, *The Elizabethan World Picture*, 6.
18. Szőnyi, *John Dee's Occultism*, 87.
19. Szőnyi, *John Dee's Occultism*, 26.
20. Luther, "On the Babylonian Captivity of the Church," 562.
21. Ficino, *De Christiana religione*, 19; translation by Yates in *Giordano Bruno and the Hermetic Tradition*, 119; quoted in Szőnyi, *John Dee's Occultism*, 29.

22. Shakespeare, *Henry VIII,* 5.2.44–46.

23. Tillyard, *The Elizabethan World Picture,* 7.

24. Tillyard, *The Elizabethan World Picture,* 8.

25. Revelation 3:9 (NIV).

26. See Pagels, *Revelations.*

27. Sutton, *American Apocalypse,* 18.

28. Clark, *Allies for Armageddon,* 37.

29. Pew Research Center, "Many Americans Uneasy," 2; quoted in Clark, *Allies for Armageddon,* 5.

30. Clark, *Allies for Armageddon,* 12.

31. Genesis 12:3 (NIV).

32. Clark, *Allies for Armageddon,* 136, 263.

33. Clark, *Allies for Armageddon,* 27–28, 32, 273.

34. Clark, *Allies for Armageddon,* 39.

35. Sutton, *American Apocalypse,* 220–21.

36. Sutton, *American Apocalypse,* 139.

37. Sutton, *American Apocalypse,* 220–21.

38. Sutton, *American Apocalypse,* 291–92.

39. Sutton, *American Apocalypse,* 109–12.

40. Sutton, *American Apocalypse,* 139.

41. Sutton, *American Apocalypse,* 145.

42. Sutton, *American Apocalypse,* 157, 185.

43. Clark, *Allies for Armageddon,* 155.

44. Clark, *Allies for Armageddon,* 156; Sutton, *American Apocalypse,* 221.

45. Diamond, *Spiritual Warfare,* 132.

46. Clark, *Allies for Armageddon,* 188.

47. Clark, *Allies for Armageddon,* 164.

48. Brown, "Bush, Gog and Magog."

49. Lindsay, *Faith in the Halls of Power,* 26.

50. Scahill, "Mike Pence Will Be the Most Powerful Christian Supremacist in U.S. History."

51. Clark, *Allies for Armageddon,* 153.

52. Lindsay, *Faith in the Halls of Power,* 34.

53. Lindsay, *Faith in the Halls of Power,* 208.

54. Lindsay, *Faith in the Halls of Power,* 124, 130, 154; Sutton, *American Apocalypse,* 121.

55. Clark, *Allies for Armageddon,* 100.

56. Shimoni, *The Zionist Ideology*, 100–103.

57. Shimoni, *The Zionist Ideology*, 329.

58. Shimoni, *The Zionist Ideology*, 269.

59. Shimoni, *The Zionist Ideology*, 59–60.

60. Shindler, *A History of Modern Israel*, 76.

61. Shimoni, *The Zionist Ideology*, 146–47.

62. Shimoni, *The Zionist Ideology*, 151; Shindler, *A History of Modern Israel*, 142.

63. Shindler, *A History of Modern Israel*, 335–36.

64. Shimoni, *The Zionist Ideology*, 391.

65. Shimoni, *The Zionist Ideology*, 137.

66. Clark, *Allies for Armageddon*, 288.

67. See Guénon, *Introduction to the Study of the Hindu Doctrines*.

68. See Trimondi and Trimondi, *Der Schatten des Dalai Lama*.

69. Sherman, *John Dee*, 12.

70. Szőnyi, *John Dee's Occultism*, 9.

71. Szőnyi, *John Dee's Occultism*, 16, 23.

72. Clucas, *John Dee*, 4.

73. Szőnyi, *John Dee's Occultism*, 10.

74. Sherman, *John Dee*, xii.

75. Clucas, *John Dee*, 6.

76. Sherman, *John Dee*, xiv.

77. Clucas, *John Dee*, 11.

78. Clucas, *John Dee*, 7.

79. Clucas, *John Dee*, 9.

CHAPTER 1. ELECTED

1. Deacon, *John Dee*, 13.

2. Parry, *The Arch-Conjuror of England*, 5.

3. Parry, *The Arch-Conjuror of England*, 7.

4. Parry, *The Arch-Conjuror of England*, 6.

5. Dee, *Compendious Rehearsal*, in Crossley, *Autobiographical Tracts of Dr. John Dee*, 5.

6. Clulee, *John Dee's Natural Philosophy*, 2:26.

7. Parry, *The Arch-Conjuror of England*, 10.

8. Gribbin, *The Scientists*, xvii.

9. Gribbin, *The Scientists*, 14.

10. Gribbin, *The Scientists,* 15.

11. Parry, *The Arch-Conjuror of England,* 11.

12. Parry, *The Arch-Conjuror of England,* 11–12.

13. Clulee, *John Dee's Natural Philosophy,* 2:27.

14. Dee, *Propaedeumata,* in Shumaker, *John Dee on Astronomy,* 111.

15. Parry, *The Arch-Conjuror of England,* 13–15.

16. Dee, *Compendious Rehearsal,* in Crossley, *Autobiographical Tracts of Dr. John Dee,* 5.

17. Harkness, "The Scientific Reformation," 82.

18. Deacon, *John Dee,* 23.

19. Parry, *The Arch-Conjuror of England,* 19.

20. Dee, in Crossley, *Autobiographical Tracts of Dr. John Dee,* 7–8.

21. Heilbron, "Introductory Essay," in Shumaker, *John Dee on Astronomy,* 7–8.

22. Smith, *Gabriel Harvey's Marginalia,* 277.

23. Shumaker, *John Dee on Astronomy,* 34.

24. Dee, in Crossley, *Autobiographical Tracts of Dr. John Dee,* 8; Fell-Smith, *The Life of Dr. John Dee,* 12.

25. Shumaker, *John Dee on Astronomy,* 21–22; Parry, *The Arch-Conjuror of England,* 20.

26. Harkness, *John Dee's Conversations with Angels,* 148.

27. Harkness, "The Scientific Reformation," 561.

28. Szőnyi, *John Dee's Occultism,* 150.

29. Håkansson, *Seeing the Word,* 257–58.

30. Harkness, "The Scientific Reformation," 551.

31. Dee, in Crossley, *Autobiographical Tracts of Dr. John Dee,* 8.

32. Fenton, *The Diaries of John Dee,* 305.

33. Parry, *The Arch-Conjuror of England,* 22–24.

34. Clulee, *John Dee's Natural Philosophy,* 2:32.

35. Parry, *The Arch-Conjuror of England,* 99; Fell-Smith, *The Life of Dr. John Dee,* 39.

36. French, *John Dee,* 32; Fell-Smith, *The Life of Dr. John Dee,* 78; Parry, *The Arch-Conjuror of England,* 25.

37. Woolley, *The Queen's Conjuror,* 29–30; Parry, *The Arch-Conjuror of England,* 26–28.

38. Parry, *The Arch-Conjuror of England,* 28–29.

39. Clulee, *John Dee's Natural Philosophy,* 2:34.

40. Parry, *The Arch-Conjuror of England,* 33.

41. Clulee, *John Dee's Natural Philosophy*, 2:34.

42. Woolley, *The Queen's Conjuror*, 48.

43. Parry, *The Arch-Conjuror of England*, 43.

44. Clulee, *John Dee's Natural Philosophy*, 2:36.

45. Parry, *The Arch-Conjuror of England*, 10.

46. Clulee, *John Dee's Natural Philosophy*, 2:126–27.

47. Håkansson, *Seeing the Word*, 112.

48. Clulee, *John Dee's Natural Philosophy*, 2:86.

49. Parry, *The Arch-Conjuror of England*, 150.

50. French, *John Dee*, 47.

51. Bonner, *The Art and Logic of Ramon Llull*, 11, 19, 290.

52. See Davis, *The Universal Computer*.

53. French, *John Dee*, 47–48.

54. Sherman, *John Dee*, 20–21.

55. Parry, *The Arch-Conjuror of England*, 41.

56. Dee, "A Supplication to Queen Mary," in Suster, *John Dee*, 17.

57. Deacon, *John Dee*, 36.

58. Casaubon, *Dr. John Dee's Spiritual Diaries*, 43.

CHAPTER 2.
ALL AS STUDY OF ALL

1. See van den Broek, *Gnosis and Hermeticism*.

2. Yates, *The Occult Philosophy*, 19–22.

3. Yates, *The Occult Philosophy*, 41–42.

4. Raleigh, *The History of the World*, 201; quoted in Harkness, *John Dee's Conversations with Angels*, 124.

5. Shumaker, *John Dee on Astronomy*, 38.

6. Håkansson, *Seeing the Word*, 327.

7. See Yates, *The Rosicrucian Enlightenment*.

8. See Dobbs, *The Foundations of Newton's Alchemy*.

9. Keynes, "Newton the Man."

10. See Higley, *Hildegard of Bingen's Unknown Language*.

11. Harkness, *John Dee's Conversations with Angels*, 64–71.

12. Agrippa, *Three Books of Occult Philosophy*, 58.

13. See Wilber, *Sex, Ecology, Spirituality*.

14. Harkness, "The Scientific Reformation," 237–38.

15. Crowley, "Eleusis," in *The Collected Works,* 3:219–30.
16. Harkness, "The Scientific Reformation," 249.

CHAPTER 3.
THE LIGHT OF THE WORLD

1. Agrippa, *Three Books of Occult Philosophy,* 788.
2. See al-Kindī, *On the Stellar Rays.*
3. Woolley, *The Queen's Conjuror,* 54.
4. Clulee, *John Dee's Natural Philosophy,* 2:22.
5. Asprem, *Arguing with Angels,* 13.
6. Dee, *Propaedeumata,* in Shumaker, *John Dee on Astronomy,* 123.
7. Dee, *Propaedeumata,* in Shumaker, *John Dee on Astronomy,* 149.
8. Asprem, *Arguing with Angels,* 13.
9. Clulee, *John Dee's Natural Philosophy,* 2:57.
10. Clulee, *John Dee's Natural Philosophy,* 2:66–67, 71.
11. Clulee, *John Dee's Natural Philosophy,* 2:43.
12. Woolley, *The Queen's Conjuror,* 54.
13. Harkness, "The Scientific Reformation," 165.
14. Szőnyi, *John Dee's Occultism,* 200, 204, 206.
15. Parry, *The Arch-Conjuror of England,* 44.
16. Crowley, "The Initiated Interpretation of Ceremonial Magic," in Mathers, *The Goetia,* 17.
17. Crowley, *Magick Without Tears,* 217.
18. Novella, "A New Wrinkle in Quantum Mechanics."
19. Johnston, "John Dee on Geometry," 470–79.

CHAPTER 4.
THE ELIZABETHAN ASCENSION

1. Waller, *Sovereign Ladies,* 108.
2. Durant and Durant, *The Age of Reason Begins,* 16–17.
3. Szőnyi, *John Dee's Occultism,* 228.
4. Woolley, *The Queen's Conjuror,* 60.
5. Durant and Durant, *The Age of Reason Begins,* 15.
6. Casaubon, *Dr. John Dee's Spiritual Diaries,* 43; Parry, *The Arch-Conjuror of England,* 48–49.

7. Sherman, "Research Intelligence in Early Modern England," 71.

8. Woolley, *The Queen's Conjuror*, 60–61.

9. Parry, *The Arch-Conjuror of England*, 48.

10. Devine, "John Prestall," 18.

11. Devine, "John Prestall," 15.

12. Clulee, *John Dee's Natural Philosophy*, 2:12; French, *John Dee*, 43–45; Dee, in Crossley, *Autobiographical Tracts of Dr. John Dee*, 27.

13. Sherman, "Research Intelligence in Early Modern England," 65.

14. Dee, in Crossley, *Autobiographical Tracts of Dr. John Dee*, 12.

15. Clulee, *John Dee's Natural Philosophy*, 2:122.

16. Dee to Cecil, February 16, 1562, in Philobiblon Society, *Biographical and Historical Miscellanies*, 1:11.

17. Deacon, *John Dee*, 73.

18. Deacon, *John Dee*, 71.

19. Parry, *The Arch-Conjuror of England*, 50.

20. Crowley, *Magick Without Tears*, 502.

21. Baker, *Austin Osman Spare*, 76.

22. Ellison, *A Cultural History of Early Modern English Cryptography Manuals*, 49.

23. Parry, *The Arch-Conjuror of England*, 50.

24. Deacon, *John Dee*, 57.

25. Clulee, *John Dee's Natural Philosophy*, 2:104.

26. Carbonero y Sol, *Indice de Libros Prohibidos*, 309; Catholic Church, *Index Librorum Prohibitorum*, 298.

27. Reeds, "Solved," 291–317.

28. Biroco, *Kaos 14*, 48–54.

29. Deacon, *John Dee*, 56.

30. Deacon, *John Dee*, 58.

31. Håkansson, *Seeing the Word*, 263.

32. Parry, *The Arch-Conjuror of England*, 51.

CHAPTER 5. LADDER OF SPHERES

1. See Farmer, *Syncretism in the West*.

2. See Kaplan, *Sefer Yetzirah*.

3. Crowley, "The Qabalah: The Best Training for Memory," in *Magick Without Tears*, 48–51.

4. Proverbs 3:13–20 (KJV).

5. Revelation 22:1–2 (KJV).

6. Revelation 22:15 (KJV).

7. Clulee, *John Dee's Natural Philosophy,* 2:85–86.

8. Clulee, *John Dee's Natural Philosophy,* 2:87.

9. Clulee, *John Dee's Natural Philosophy,* 2:88.

10. Håkansson, *Seeing the Word,* 105.

11. Håkansson, *Seeing the Word,* 91, 130–33.

12. Harkness, "The Scientific Reformation," 407, 421.

13. Woolley, *The Queen's Conjuror,* 85.

14. Clulee, *John Dee's Natural Philosophy,* 2:140.

15. Woolley, *The Queen's Conjuror,* 50–51.

16. French, *John Dee,* 123–25.

17. Harkness, "The Scientific Reformation," 174.

18. Clulee, *John Dee's Natural Philosophy,* 2:84.

19. Dee, *Monas hieroglyphica,* 45.

20. Suster, *John Dee,* 36.

21. Clulee, *John Dee's Natural Philosophy,* 2:114.

22. Parry, *The Arch-Conjuror of England,* 214–15.

23. Håkansson, *Seeing the Word,* 189, 209.

24. Trismegistos, "The Emerald Tablet."

25. Magee, *Niruttara Tantra.*

26. Crowley, *The Book of the Law,* 20.

27. Peterson, *John Dee's Five Books of Mystery,* 377.

28. Clulee, *John Dee's Natural Philosophy,* 2:90.

29. Yates, *The Rosicrucian Enlightenment,* xii.

30. Clulee, *John Dee's Natural Philosophy,* 2:78, 124.

31. Dee, in Crossley, *Autobiographical Tracts of Dr. John Dee,* 10.

CHAPTER 6. HAMMER OF THE WITCHES

1. Deacon, *John Dee,* 63.

2. King, "Queen Elizabeth I," 30–74.

3. Woolley, *The Queen's Conjuror,* 88.

4. Parry, *The Arch-Conjuror of England,* 71–74.

5. Woolley, *The Queen's Conjuror,* 83.

6. Håkansson, *Seeing the Word,* 180.

7. Foxe, *Actes and Monumentes,* 5:1483.

8. Townsend, *The Acts and Monuments,* 7:659.

9. Parry, *The Arch-Conjuror of England,* 64.

10. Parry, *The Arch-Conjuror of England,* 66–69.

11. Woolley, *The Queen's Conjuror,* 94; Parry, *The Arch-Conjuror of England,* 69.

12. Parry, *The Arch-Conjuror of England,* 74–75.

13. Parry, *The Arch-Conjuror of England,* 76–79.

14. Parry, *The Arch-Conjuror of England,* 80.

15. Deacon, *John Dee,* 73.

16. Parry, *The Arch-Conjuror of England,* 84.

17. Durant and Durant, *The Age of Reason Begins,* 24.

18. Clulee, *John Dee's Natural Philosophy,* 2:140.

19. Parry, *The Arch-Conjuror of England,* 84–85.

20. Bawlf, *The Secret Voyage of Sir Francis Drake,* loc. 751.

21. Dee, "The Mathematicall Praeface."

22. Harkness, "The Scientific Reformation," 501–2.

23. Håkansson, *Seeing the Word,* 185.

24. Clulee, *John Dee's Natural Philosophy,* 2:148.

25. Dee, "The Mathematicall Praeface."

26. Dee, "The Mathematicall Praeface"; quoted in Clulee, *John Dee's Natural Philosophy,* 2:171.

27. Clulee, *John Dee's Natural Philosophy,* 2:150.

28. Clulee, *John Dee's Natural Philosophy,* 2:152.

29. Harkness, "The Scientific Reformation," 510.

30. Agrippa, *Three Books of Occult Philosophy,* 233.

31. Yates, *The Rosicrucian Enlightenment,* 109–10.

CHAPTER 7.
A COLD WAR FOR A NEW WORLD

1. Krause, "Tycho Brahe's 1572 Supernova," 617–19.

2. Parry, *The Arch-Conjuror of England,* 107.

3. Harkness, *John Dee's Conversations with Angels,* 68–69.

4. Bawlf, *The Secret Voyage of Sir Francis Drake,* loc. 355–56.

5. Appleby, *Famine in Tudor and Stuart England,* 1, 5, 8.

6. Bawlf, *The Secret Voyage of Sir Francis Drake,* loc. 325.

7. Parry, *The Arch-Conjuror of England,* 94–96.

8. Deacon, *John Dee*, 88; Woolley, *The Queen's Conjuror*, 115.

9. French, *John Dee*, 178; Deacon, *John Dee*, 88; Woolley, *The Queen's Conjuror*, 122.

10. Parry, *The Arch-Conjuror of England*, 98–99; Woolley, *The Queen's Conjuror*, 124.

11. Woolley, *The Queen's Conjuror*, 124–25.

12. Deacon, *John Dee*, 89; Woolley, *The Queen's Conjuror*, 135–36.

13. Woolley, *The Queen's Conjuror*, 128.

14. See Morison, *The European Discovery of America*.

15. Parry, *The Arch-Conjuror of England*, 111.

16. Dee, *General and Rare Memorials*.

17. Parry, *The Arch-Conjuror of England*, 111.

18. Parry, *The Arch-Conjuror of England*, 116, 120, 123–24.

19. Turner, *The Heptarchia Mystica*, 19.

20. Woolley, *The Queen's Conjuror*, 133.

21. Clulee, *John Dee's Natural Philosophy*, 2:186.

22. Bawlf, *The Secret Voyage of Sir Francis Drake*, loc. 919–38.

23. Bawlf, *The Secret Voyage of Sir Francis Drake*, loc. 77–114.

24. Woolley, *The Queen's Conjuror*, 135.

25. Bawlf, *The Secret Voyage of Sir Francis Drake*, loc. 2929–47.

26. Parry, *The Arch-Conjuror of England*, 130.

27. Clulee, *John Dee's Natural Philosophy*, 2:192–93.

28. Parry, *The Arch-Conjuror of England*, 132–33.

29. Parry, *The Arch-Conjuror of England*, 135.

30. Woolley, *The Queen's Conjuror*, 168; Parry, *The Arch-Conjuror of England*, 136–37.

31. Harkness, *John Dee's Conversations with Angels*, 52.

32. Parry, *The Arch-Conjuror of England*, 137.

33. Woolley, *The Queen's Conjuror*, 136; Parry, *The Arch-Conjuror of England*, 139.

34. Fenton, *The Diaries of John Dee*, 10.

35. Parry, *The Arch-Conjuror of England*, 105.

36. Clulee, *John Dee's Natural Philosophy*, 2:182; French, *John Dee*, 189–90; Parry, *The Arch-Conjuror of England*, 111.

37. Clulee, *John Dee's Natural Philosophy*, 2:185; Williams, *Madoc*, 39–40, 55–64; Parry, *The Arch-Conjuror of England*, 106.

38. Parry, *The Arch-Conjuror of England*, 98, 107–8.

39. Woolley, *The Queen's Conjuror,* 131; Parry, *The Arch-Conjuror of England,* 95, 126; Heilbron, "Introductory Essay," in Shumaker, *John Dee on Astronomy,* 28.

40. See West and Kling, *The Libro de las profecias.*

41. Parry, *The Arch-Conjuror of England,* 106.

42. Parry, *The Arch-Conjuror of England,* 112–13.

43. "On the Origin of the World," Nag Hammadi Codex 2, 5, in Barnstone and Meyer, *The Gnostic Bible,* 416–37.

44. See Yukteswar, *The Holy Science.*

45. Trithemius, *De septem secundeis.*

46. Parry, *The Arch-Conjuror of England,* 108–9.

47. Parry, *The Arch-Conjuror of England,* 108.

48. Poole, "John Dee and the English Calendar."

49. Parry, *The Arch-Conjuror of England,* 141.

50. Clulee, *John Dee's Natural Philosophy,* 2:190.

51. Woolley, *The Queen's Conjuror,* 138.

52. Sherman, "Putting the British Seas on the Map," 2.

53. Clulee, *John Dee's Natural Philosophy,* 2:188.

54. Maddison, *The World Economy,* 98, 242.

55. Ferguson, *Empire,* xi.

56. See Brzezinski, *The Grand Chessboard.*

57. Matthew 6:20 (NKJV).

58. See de Chardin, *The Phenomenon of Man.*

59. See Ferguson, *Empire,* xi–xxviii.

60. Brendon, "A Moral Audit of the British Empire."

61. Hari, "The Truth? Our Empire Killed Millions."

62. Ubelaker, "The Sources and Methodology for Mooney's Estimates," in Denevan, *The Native Population of the Americas in 1492,* 26–32.

63. Ferguson, *Empire,* 74.

64. Monbiot, "Deny the British Empire's Crimes?"

65. Cobain et. al., "Britain Destroyed Records of Colonial Crimes."

66. Brendon, "A Moral Audit of the British Empire."

CHAPTER 8. CONTACT

1. Parry, *The Arch-Conjuror of England,* 145.

2. Parry, *The Arch-Conjuror of England,* 155.

3. Digges, *Prognostication Everlasting.*

4. Dreyer, *Brahe,* 193–97; quoted in Woolley, *The Queen's Conjuror,* 160.

5. Aston, "The Fiery Trigon Conjunction," 158–87.

6. Marshall, *The Magic Circle of Rudolf II,* 42.

7. Parry, *The Arch-Conjuror of England,* 148–49.

8. Poole, "John Dee and the English Calendar."

9. Sherman, *John Dee,* 117–18.

10. Poole, "John Dee and the English Calendar."

11. Heilbron, "Introductory Essay," in Sherman, *John Dee,* 15.

12. Casaubon, *Dr. John Dee's Spiritual Diaries,* 44.

13. Parry, *The Arch-Conjuror of England,* 148.

14. Woolley, *The Queen's Conjuror,* 167.

15. Asprem, *Arguing with Angels,* 14.

16. Woolley, *The Queen's Conjuror,* 168.

17. Woolley, *The Queen's Conjuror,* 141.

18. Harkness, *John Dee's Conversations with Angels,* 20.

19. Parry, *The Arch-Conjuror of England,* 143.

20. Woolley, *The Queen's Conjuror,* 145.

21. Harkness, *John Dee's Conversations with Angels,* 19; Parry, *The Arch-Conjuror of England,* 146–47; Peterson, *John Dee's Five Books of Mystery,* 66.

22. Clulee, *John Dee's Natural Philosophy,* 2:205.

23. Szőnyi, *John Dee's Occultism,* 277–78.

24. Campbell, *The Magic Seal of Dr. John Dee,* xvi.

25. Szőnyi, *John Dee's Occultism,* 278.

26. Peterson, *John Dee's Five Books of Mystery,* 66; Parry, *The Arch-Conjuror of England,* 146.

27. Turner, *The Heptarchia Mystica,* 22.

28. Caporael, "Ergotism," 21–26.

29. Crowley, *The Vision and the Voice,* 7.

30. Crowley, *The Vision and the Voice,* 7.

31. Crowley, *The Vision and the Voice,* 7.

32. Laycock, *The Complete Enochian Dictionary,* 29–44, 54–58, 63–64.

33. Asprem, *Arguing with Angels,* 17.

34. Clark, *Paul Foster Case,* 54–56, 62–63.

35. Sledge, "Between Loagaeth and Cosening," 31.

36. Sledge, "Between Loagaeth and Cosening," 32.

37. Sledge, "Between Loagaeth and Cosening," 34.

38. Harkness, "Managing an Experimental Household," 247–62.

39. Harkness, "The Scientific Reformation," 164.

40. Harkness, *John Dee's Conversations with Angels*, 27.

41. Casaubon, *Dr. John Dee's Spiritual Diaries*, 603.

42. Peterson, *John Dee's Five Books of Mystery*, 72.

43. Casaubon, *Dr. John Dee's Spiritual Diaries*, 265.

44. Clulee, *John Dee's Natural Philosophy*, 2:208.

45. Håkansson, *Seeing the Word*, 116–17.

46. Harkness, *John Dee's Conversations with Angels*, 125.

47. Clulee, *John Dee's Natural Philosophy*, 2:207–8.

48. Casaubon, *Dr. John Dee's Spiritual Diaries*, 137.

49. Casaubon, *Dr. John Dee's Spiritual Diaries*, 138.

50. Clulee, *John Dee's Natural Philosophy*, 2:207–8.

51. Casaubon, *Dr. John Dee's Spiritual Diaries*, 324–25.

52. Harkness, "The Scientific Reformation," 257.

53. Szőnyi, *John Dee's Occultism*, 205.

54. Baker, "Doctor Dee's Optics," 28.

55. Ackermann and Devoy, "The Lord of the Smoking Mirror," 543.

56. Ackermann and Devoy, "The Lord of the Smoking Mirror," 547–48.

57. Clulee, "Astrology, Magic, and Optics," 678; quoted in Harkness, "The Scientific Reformation," 293.

58. Harkness, "The Scientific Reformation," 297–98.

59. Clulee, *John Dee's Natural Philosophy*, 2:214–15.

60. DuQuette, *Enochian Vision Magick*, 29.

61. Peterson, *John Dee's Five Books of Mystery*, 113.

62. Whitby, *John Dee's Actions with Spirits*, 1:135.

63. Skinner and Rankine, *Practical Angel Magic*, 37.

64. Tyson, *Enochian Magic for Beginners*, 142.

65. Harkness, *John Dee's Conversations with Angels*, 214.

66. Casaubon, *Dr. John Dee's Spiritual Diaries*, 412.

67. Szőnyi, *John Dee's Occultism*, 221.

68. Clulee, *John Dee's Natural Philosophy*, 2:213.

69. Peterson, *John Dee's Five Books of Mystery*, 56.

70. Daniel 10:16–17 (NIV).

71. Daniel 12:1 (NIV).

72. Revelation 12:7–9 (NIV).

73. Jacobs et. al., "Michael."

74. Harkness, *John Dee's Conversations with Angels*, 48.

75. Parker, *Works of Dionysius the Areopagite*, 2:1–66.

76. Clulee, *John Dee's Natural Philosophy*, 2:211.

77. Harkness, "The Scientific Reformation," 371–72.

78. Harkness, "The Scientific Reformation," 4, 360–61.

79. Kramer, *The Sumerians*, 129, 240, 256.

80. Harkness, "The Scientific Reformation," 362.

81. Harkness, "The Scientific Reformation," 478.

82. Harkness, *John Dee's Conversations with Angels*, 190.

CHAPTER 9.
THE ARCHITECTURE OF APOCALYPSE

1. Peterson, *John Dee's Five Books of Mystery*, 65.

2. 2 Corinthians 11:14 (NIV).

3. For more on the arrangement of the tables into a cube, see DuQuette, *Enochian Vision Magick*, 65.

4. Peterson, *John Dee's Five Books of Mystery*, 70.

5. Peterson, *John Dee's Five Books of Mystery*, 72.

6. Peterson, *John Dee's Five Books of Mystery*, 73.

7. Peterson, *John Dee's Five Books of Mystery*, 74.

8. DuQuette, *Enochian Vision Magick*, 71.

9. Abano, *Heptameron*.

10. Peterson, *John Dee's Five Books of Mystery*, 84.

11. Peterson, *John Dee's Five Books of Mystery*, 91.

12. Peterson, *John Dee's Five Books of Mystery*, 91.

13. Peterson, *John Dee's Five Books of Mystery*, 133.

14. Peterson, *John Dee's Five Books of Mystery*, 136.

15. Peterson, *John Dee's Five Books of Mystery*, 137.

16. Eshelman, *Pearls of Wisdom*, 81.

17. Peterson, *John Dee's Five Books of Mystery*, 153.

18. Peterson, *John Dee's Five Books of Mystery*, 170.

19. Peterson, *John Dee's Five Books of Mystery*, 170.

20. Peterson, *John Dee's Five Books of Mystery*, 171.

21. Peterson, *John Dee's Five Books of Mystery*, 172.

22. Peterson, *John Dee's Five Books of Mystery*, 172.

23. Peterson, *John Dee's Five Books of Mystery*, 175.

24. Peterson, *John Dee's Five Books of Mystery,* 176.

25. Peterson, *John Dee's Five Books of Mystery,* 177.

26. Peterson, *John Dee's Five Books of Mystery,* 183.

27. Peterson, *John Dee's Five Books of Mystery,* 189.

28. Peterson, *John Dee's Five Books of Mystery,* 245–46.

29. DuQuette, *Enochian Vision Magick,* 90–92.

30. Peterson, *John Dee's Five Books of Mystery,* 297.

31. Peterson, *John Dee's Five Books of Mystery,* 327.

32. Peterson, *John Dee's Five Books of Mystery,* 328.

33. Peterson, *John Dee's Five Books of Mystery,* 328.

34. Peterson, *John Dee's Five Books of Mystery,* 363.

35. Peterson, *John Dee's Five Books of Mystery,* 365.

36. Peterson, *John Dee's Five Books of Mystery,* 365.

37. Peterson, *John Dee's Five Books of Mystery,* 370.

38. Peterson, *John Dee's Five Books of Mystery,* 374.

39. Peterson, *John Dee's Five Books of Mystery,* 377.

40. Peterson, *John Dee's Five Books of Mystery,* 389.

41. Peterson, *John Dee's Five Books of Mystery,* 390.

42. Peterson, *John Dee's Five Books of Mystery,* 390.

43. Peterson, *John Dee's Five Books of Mystery,* 391.

44. Peterson, *John Dee's Five Books of Mystery,* 393.

45. Peterson, *John Dee's Five Books of Mystery,* 393–94.

46. Peterson, *John Dee's Five Books of Mystery,* 395.

47. Peterson, *John Dee's Five Books of Mystery,* 395.

48. Peterson, *John Dee's Five Books of Mystery,* 394.

49. Peterson, *John Dee's Five Books of Mystery,* 352.

50. Peterson, *John Dee's Five Books of Mystery,* 358, 412.

51. Peterson, *John Dee's Five Books of Mystery,* 407.

52. Peterson, *John Dee's Five Books of Mystery,* 407.

53. Peterson, *John Dee's Five Books of Mystery,* 407.

54. Peterson, *John Dee's Five Books of Mystery,* 408.

55. Peterson, *John Dee's Five Books of Mystery,* 408.

56. Psalm 22 (NIV).

57. Peterson, *John Dee's Five Books of Mystery,* 410.

58. Peterson, *John Dee's Five Books of Mystery,* 370.

59. Peterson, *John Dee's Five Books of Mystery,* 410.

60. Peterson, *John Dee's Five Books of Mystery,* 411.

61. Peterson, *John Dee's Five Books of Mystery,* 412.

62. Peterson, *John Dee's Five Books of Mystery,* 413.

CHAPTER 10. AND THEREFORE, BEHOLD THE END

1. Laycock, *The Complete Enochian Dictionary,* 7.

2. Kasprzak, "A Riddle of History," 56.

3. Kasprzak, "A Riddle of History," 59.

4. Zantuan, "Olbracht Łaski in Elizabethan England," 10.

5. Zantuan, "Olbracht Łaski in Elizabethan England," 10.

6. Butler and Lomas, *Calendar of State Papers Foreign,* 332–45.

7. Green, *Calendar of State Papers, Domestic,* 40.

8. Parry, *The Arch-Conjuror of England,* 164.

9. Kasprzak, "A Riddle of History," 58.

10. Parry, *The Arch-Conjuror of England,* 165.

11. Szőnyi, *John Dee's Occultism,* 248.

12. Kasprzak, "A Riddle of History," 53–56.

13. Rutledge, "John Dee: Consultant to Queen Elizabeth I," 4.

14. Clulee, *John Dee's Natural Philosophy,* 2:198.

15. Harkness, *John Dee's Conversations with Angels,* 129.

16. Harkness, "The Scientific Reformation," 512.

17. Casaubon, *Dr. John Dee's Spiritual Diaries,* 127.

18. Casaubon, *Dr. John Dee's Spiritual Diaries,* 128.

19. Leitch, *The Essential Enochian Grimoire,* 42.

20. Casaubon, *Dr. John Dee's Spiritual Diaries,* 132.

21. Casaubon, *Dr. John Dee's Spiritual Diaries,* 133.

22. Casaubon, *Dr. John Dee's Spiritual Diaries,* 134.

23. Casaubon, *Dr. John Dee's Spiritual Diaries,* 134.

24. Casaubon, *Dr. John Dee's Spiritual Diaries,* 142.

25. Casaubon, *Dr. John Dee's Spiritual Diaries,* 146.

26. Casaubon, *Dr. John Dee's Spiritual Diaries,* 147.

27. Casaubon, *Dr. John Dee's Spiritual Diaries,* 153.

28. Leitch, *The Angelical Language,* 1:65.

29. Casaubon, *Dr. John Dee's Spiritual Diaries,* 155.

30. Casaubon, *Dr. John Dee's Spiritual Diaries,* 156.

31. Casaubon, *Dr. John Dee's Spiritual Diaries,* 160.

32. Casaubon, *Dr. John Dee's Spiritual Diaries,* 169.

33. Harkness, "The Scientific Reformation," 375.

34. Harkness, "The Scientific Reformation," 375, 384.

35. Casaubon, *Dr. John Dee's Spiritual Diaries,* 172.

36. Parry, *The Arch-Conjuror of England,* 170.

37. Parry, *The Arch-Conjuror of England,* 169.

CHAPTER 11. AETHYRS AND WATCHTOWERS

1. Casaubon, *Dr. John Dee's Spiritual Diaries,* 659.

2. Casaubon, *Dr. John Dee's Spiritual Diaries,* 189.

3. Casaubon, *Dr. John Dee's Spiritual Diaries,* 190.

4. Casaubon, *Dr. John Dee's Spiritual Diaries,* 193.

5. Casaubon, *Dr. John Dee's Spiritual Diaries,* 194.

6. Casaubon, *Dr. John Dee's Spiritual Diaries,* 195.

7. Casaubon, *Dr. John Dee's Spiritual Diaries,* 195.

8. Casaubon, *Dr. John Dee's Spiritual Diaries,* 201.

9. Casaubon, *Dr. John Dee's Spiritual Diaries,* 204.

10. Casaubon, *Dr. John Dee's Spiritual Diaries,* 204.

11. Parry, *The Arch-Conjuror of England,* 172.

12. Casaubon, *Dr. John Dee's Spiritual Diaries,* 208.

13. Skinner, *Key to the Latin,* 71.

14. Casaubon, *Dr. John Dee's Spiritual Diaries,* 210.

15. Casaubon, *Dr. John Dee's Spiritual Diaries,* 210.

16. Casaubon, *Dr. John Dee's Spiritual Diaries,* 212.

17. Casaubon, *Dr. John Dee's Spiritual Diaries,* 212.

18. Skinner, *Key to the Latin,* 73.

19. Casaubon, *Dr. John Dee's Spiritual Diaries,* 219.

20. Casaubon, *Dr. John Dee's Spiritual Diaries,* 221.

21. Casaubon, *Dr. John Dee's Spiritual Diaries,* 221.

22. Casaubon, *Dr. John Dee's Spiritual Diaries,* 237.

23. Casaubon, *Dr. John Dee's Spiritual Diaries,* 240.

24. Casaubon, *Dr. John Dee's Spiritual Diaries,* 248.

25. Casaubon, *Dr. John Dee's Spiritual Diaries,* 253.

26. Harkness, *John Dee's Conversations with Angels,* 161.

27. Casaubon, *Dr. John Dee's Spiritual Diaries,* 255.

28. Casaubon, *Dr. John Dee's Spiritual Diaries,* 255.

29. Casaubon, *Dr. John Dee's Spiritual Diaries,* 265.

30. Casaubon, *Dr. John Dee's Spiritual Diaries,* 265.

31. Casaubon, *Dr. John Dee's Spiritual Diaries,* 267.

32. Casaubon, *Dr. John Dee's Spiritual Diaries,* 276.

33. Casaubon, *Dr. John Dee's Spiritual Diaries,* 297.

34. Casaubon, *Dr. John Dee's Spiritual Diaries,* 305.

35. Casaubon, *Dr. John Dee's Spiritual Diaries,* 321.

36. Casaubon, *Dr. John Dee's Spiritual Diaries,* 324–25.

37. Casaubon, *Dr. John Dee's Spiritual Diaries,* 327.

38. Casaubon, *Dr. John Dee's Spiritual Diaries,* 328.

39. Casaubon, *Dr. John Dee's Spiritual Diaries,* 329.

40. Casaubon, *Dr. John Dee's Spiritual Diaries,* 329.

41. Casaubon, *Dr. John Dee's Spiritual Diaries,* 332.

42. Casaubon, *Dr. John Dee's Spiritual Diaries,* 336.

43. Casaubon, *Dr. John Dee's Spiritual Diaries,* 335.

44. Casaubon, *Dr. John Dee's Spiritual Diaries,* 335.

45. Casaubon, *Dr. John Dee's Spiritual Diaries,* 336.

46. Casaubon, *Dr. John Dee's Spiritual Diaries,* 341.

47. Casaubon, *Dr. John Dee's Spiritual Diaries,* 347.

48. Casaubon, *Dr. John Dee's Spiritual Diaries,* 352.

49. Casaubon, *Dr. John Dee's Spiritual Diaries,* 356.

50. Casaubon, *Dr. John Dee's Spiritual Diaries,* 356.

51. Casaubon, *Dr. John Dee's Spiritual Diaries,* 363.

52. Casaubon, *Dr. John Dee's Spiritual Diaries,* 363.

53. Harkness, "The Scientific Reformation," 404.

54. Casaubon, *Dr. John Dee's Spiritual Diaries,* 383.

55. Casaubon, *Dr. John Dee's Spiritual Diaries,* 382.

56. Casaubon, *Dr. John Dee's Spiritual Diaries,* 386.

57. Casaubon, *Dr. John Dee's Spiritual Diaries,* 386.

58. Casaubon, *Dr. John Dee's Spiritual Diaries,* 387.

59. Casaubon, *Dr. John Dee's Spiritual Diaries,* 387.

60. Casaubon, *Dr. John Dee's Spiritual Diaries,* 389.

61. Marshall, *The Magic Circle of Rudolf II,* 33.

CHAPTER 12. ON A MISSION FROM GOD

1. Casaubon, *Dr. John Dee's Spiritual Diaries,* 394.

2. Casaubon, *Dr. John Dee's Spiritual Diaries,* 394.

3. Casaubon, *Dr. John Dee's Spiritual Diaries*, 395.

4. Marshall, *The Magic Circle of Rudolf II*, 46, 92.

5. Clulee, *John Dee's Natural Philosophy*, 2:223.

6. Harkness, *John Dee's Conversations with Angels*, 152.

7. Harkness, "The Scientific Reformation," 536.

8. Marshall, *The Magic Circle of Rudolf II*, 242.

9. Marshall, *The Magic Circle of Rudolf II*, 88, 93, 105, 108, 128, 176.

10. Marshall, *The Magic Circle of Rudolf II*, 216, 222–23, 225.

11. Parry, *The Arch-Conjuror of England*, 181.

12. Casaubon, *Dr. John Dee's Spiritual Diaries*, 416–17.

13. Parry, *The Arch-Conjuror of England*, 182.

14. Casaubon, *Dr. John Dee's Spiritual Diaries*, 417.

15. Casaubon, *Dr. John Dee's Spiritual Diaries*, 419.

16. Casaubon, *Dr. John Dee's Spiritual Diaries*, 419.

17. Casaubon, *Dr. John Dee's Spiritual Diaries*, 420.

18. Casaubon, *Dr. John Dee's Spiritual Diaries*, 421.

19. Skinner, *Key to the Latin*, 131.

20. Harkness, *John Dee's Conversations with Angels*, 153.

21. Harkness, "The Scientific Reformation," 529.

22. Harkness, *John Dee's Conversations with Angels*, 156.

23. Casaubon, *Dr. John Dee's Spiritual Diaries*, 428.

24. Casaubon, *Dr. John Dee's Spiritual Diaries*, 430.

25. Casaubon, *Dr. John Dee's Spiritual Diaries*, 430.

26. Casaubon, *Dr. John Dee's Spiritual Diaries*, 431.

27. Casaubon, *Dr. John Dee's Spiritual Diaries*, 433.

28. Casaubon, *Dr. John Dee's Spiritual Diaries*, 438.

29. Casaubon, *Dr. John Dee's Spiritual Diaries*, 438.

30. Skinner, *Key to the Latin*, 147.

31. Parry, *The Arch-Conjuror of England*, 184.

32. Parry, *The Arch-Conjuror of England*, 185.

33. Tyson, *Enochian Magic*, 353–64.

34. Harkness, "The Scientific Reformation," 542–43.

35. Harkness, "The Scientific Reformation," 478.

36. Leitch, *The Angelical Language*, 1:173–95.

37. Parry, *The Arch-Conjuror of England*, 185.

38. Casaubon, *Dr. John Dee's Spiritual Diaries*, 491.

39. Casaubon, *Dr. John Dee's Spiritual Diaries*, 496.

40. 2 Corinthians 11:14 (NIV). "And no wonder, for Satan himself masquerades as an angel of light."

41. Harkness, *John Dee's Conversations with Angels,* 57.

42. Casaubon, *Dr. John Dee's Spiritual Diaries,* 636. The NIV gives, "Do you not know that we will judge angels? How much more the things of this life!"

43. Casaubon, *Dr. John Dee's Spiritual Diaries,* 637.

44. Parry, *The Arch-Conjuror of England,* 187.

45. Parry, *The Arch-Conjuror of England,* 187.

46. Skinner, *Key to the Latin,* 195.

47. Casaubon, *Dr. John Dee's Spiritual Diaries,* 527.

48. Clulee, *John Dee's Natural Philosophy,* 2:225.

49. Casaubon, *Dr. John Dee's Spiritual Diaries,* 531.

50. Casaubon, *Dr. John Dee's Spiritual Diaries,* 641.

51. Casaubon, *Dr. John Dee's Spiritual Diaries,* 643.

52. Marshall, *The Magic Circle of Rudolf II,* 121.

53. Parry, *The Arch-Conjuror of England,* 189–90.

54. Casaubon, *Dr. John Dee's Spiritual Diaries,* 540.

55. Skinner, *Key to the Latin,* 227.

56. Casaubon, *Dr. John Dee's Spiritual Diaries,* 541.

57. Casaubon, *Dr. John Dee's Spiritual Diaries,* 543.

58. Casaubon, *Dr. John Dee's Spiritual Diaries,* 558.

59. Skinner, *Key to the Latin,* 249.

60. Skinner, *Key to the Latin,* 249.

61. Skinner, *Key to the Latin,* 255.

62. Harkness, *John Dee's Conversations with Angels,* 54; Marshall, *The Magic Circle of Rudolf II,* 105.

63. Parry, *The Arch-Conjuror of England,* 192.

64. Marshall, *The Magic Circle of Rudolf II,* 122.

65. Casaubon, *Dr. John Dee's Spiritual Diaries,* 568.

CHAPTER 13. I AM THE DAUGHTER OF FORTITUDE, AND RAVISHED EVERY HOUR

1. Casaubon, *Dr. John Dee's Spiritual Diaries,* 572–73.

2. Casaubon, *Dr. John Dee's Spiritual Diaries,* 583.

3. Casaubon, *Dr. John Dee's Spiritual Diaries,* 583.

4. Skinner, *Key to the Latin,* 281–83.

5. Casaubon, *Dr. John Dee's Spiritual Diaries,* 587.

6. Casaubon, *Dr. John Dee's Spiritual Diaries,* 587.

7. Casaubon, *Dr. John Dee's Spiritual Diaries,* 593.

8. Casaubon, *Dr. John Dee's Spiritual Diaries,* 593–94.

9. Casaubon, *Dr. John Dee's Spiritual Diaries,* 594.

10. Casaubon, *Dr. John Dee's Spiritual Diaries,* 598.

11. Casaubon, *Dr. John Dee's Spiritual Diaries,* 598–99.

12. Casaubon, *Dr. John Dee's Spiritual Diaries,* 599.

13. Casaubon, *Dr. John Dee's Spiritual Diaries,* 600.

14. Casaubon, *Dr. John Dee's Spiritual Diaries,* 601.

15. Casaubon, *Dr. John Dee's Spiritual Diaries,* 601.

16. "Thunder," Nag Hammadi Codex 6, 3, in Robinson, *The Nag Hammadi Library,* 297–303.

17. Casaubon, *Dr. John Dee's Spiritual Diaries,* 603.

CHAPTER 14. GOLD IS THE METAL WITH THE BROADEST SHOULDERS

1. Parry, *The Arch-Conjuror of England,* 200.

2. Woolley, *The Queen's Conjuror,* 297; Parry, *The Arch-Conjuror of England,* 201.

3. Deacon, *John Dee,* 211, 240; Woolley, *The Queen's Conjuror,* 295; Parry, *The Arch-Conjuror of England,* 200–201.

4. Woolley, *The Queen's Conjuror,* 205; Parry, *The Arch-Conjuror of England,* 202–3.

5. Rampling, "John Dee and the Sciences," 432–36.

6. Parry, *The Arch-Conjuror of England,* 203; Woolley, *The Queen's Conjuror,* 305.

7. Woolley, *The Queen's Conjuror,* 306; Parry, *The Arch-Conjuror of England,* 204.

8. Parry, *The Arch-Conjuror of England,* 205; Woolley, *The Queen's Conjuror,* 306–7.

9. Parry, *The Arch-Conjuror of England,* 207.

10. Parry, *The Arch-Conjuror of England,* 208.

11. Chambers, *The Elizabethan Stage,* 3:423–24.

12. Parry, *The Arch-Conjuror of England,* 212.

13. Håkansson, *Seeing the Word,* 32.

14. Parry, *The Arch-Conjuror of England,* 213.

15. Woolley, *The Queen's Conjuror,* 298.

16. Parry, *The Arch-Conjuror of England,* 214–16.

17. Parry, *The Arch-Conjuror of England,* 218–19.

18. Winship, "Puritans, Politics, and Lunacy," 345–69.

19. Parry, *The Arch-Conjuror of England,* 220.

20. Woolley, *The Queen's Conjuror,* 315; Parry, *The Arch-Conjuror of England,* 221.

21. Parry, *The Arch-Conjuror of England,* 224.

22. Parry, *The Arch-Conjuror of England,* 225.

23. Fell-Smith, *The Life of Dr. John Dee,* 234; Parry, *The Arch-Conjuror of England,* 228, 230.

24. Fenton, *The Diaries of John Dee,* 255.

25. Fenton, *The Diaries of John Dee,* 265.

26. Quoted in Durant, *The Story of Philosophy,* 158.

27. Parry, *The Arch-Conjuror of England,* 228–29.

28. Kraus, *Sir Francis Drake.*

29. Parry, *The Arch-Conjuror of England,* 229.

30. Parry, *The Arch-Conjuror of England,* 230.

31. Durant and Durant, *The Age of Reason Begins,* 16.

32. Verstegan, *An Advertisement.*

33. Shakespeare, *Love's Labour's Lost,* 4.3.252–53. Some editions read "suit of night," "scowl of night," or "style of night."

34. Dee, in Suster, *John Dee,* 109–10.

35. Parry, *The Arch-Conjuror of England,* 233–35.

36. Clulee, *John Dee's Natural Philosophy,* 2:190.

37. Woolley, *The Queen's Conjuror,* 317; Parry, *The Arch-Conjuror of England,* 240.

38. Parry, *The Arch-Conjuror of England,* 242–43.

39. Bailey, *Diary,* 29.

40. Deacon, *John Dee,* 272; Parry, *The Arch-Conjuror of England,* 245–46.

41. Parry, *The Arch-Conjuror of England,* 247–48.

42. Fell-Smith, *The Life of Dr. John Dee,* 280–89; Parry, *The Arch-Conjuror of England,* 253–54.

43. Kelly and Lange, "The Stone of the Philosophers," in *Tractatus duo egregii,* 4.

44. Harkness, *John Dee's Conversations with Angels,* 22.

45. Bailey, *Diary*, 27.

46. Parry, *The Arch-Conjuror of England*, 255.

47. Harkness, *John Dee's Conversations with Angels*, 23–24.

48. Bailey, *Diary*, 41; Fell-Smith, *The Life of Dr. John Dee*, 268–69.

49. Parry, *The Arch-Conjuror of England*, 259.

50. Chamberlain to Carleton, March 1, 1599.

51. Bailey, *Diary*, 40.

52. Parry, *The Arch-Conjuror of England*, 260–62.

53. Bailey, *Diary*, 70.

54. Parry, *The Arch-Conjuror of England*, 264

55. Deacon, *John Dee*, 269–72; Parry, *The Arch-Conjuror of England*, 266–67.

56. Casaubon, *Dr. John Dee's Spiritual Diaries*, 608.

57. Harkness, "The Scientific Reformation," 548.

58. Sherman, *John Dee*, 16.

59. Skinner, *Key to the Latin*, 612.

60. Fenton, *The Diaries of John Dee*, 297.

61. Harkness, *John Dee's Conversations with Angels*, 218; Parry, *The Arch-Conjuror of England*, 269–70.

62. Shakespeare, *The Tempest*, 4.1.103–11; quoted in Rutledge, "John Dee: Consultant to Queen Elizabeth I," 16.

CHAPTER 15. THE INVISIBLE COLLEGE

1. Yates, *The Rosicrucian Enlightenment*, 27–38, 221, 226, 228.

2. Yates, *The Rosicrucian Enlightenment*, 74, 93, 94.

3. Yates, *The Rosicrucian Enlightenment*, 48.

4. Yates, *The Rosicrucian Enlightenment*, 42, 229–30.

5. Yates, *The Rosicrucian Enlightenment*, 46, 160.

6. Godwin, *The Chemical Wedding of Christian Rosenkreutz*, 15.

7. Yates, *The Rosicrucian Enlightenment*, 61, 69.

8. Yates, *The Rosicrucian Enlightenment*, 37.

9. Marshall, *The Magic Circle of Rudolf II*, 230.

10. Yates, *The Rosicrucian Enlightenment*, 54, 82, 196.

11. Yates, *The Rosicrucian Enlightenment*, 50, 225, 231.

12. Yates, *The Rosicrucian Enlightenment*, 85–86, 118.

13. Yates, *The Rosicrucian Enlightenment*, 122–24.

14. Yates, *The Rosicrucian Enlightenment*, 90, 98, 139.

15. Yates, *The Rosicrucian Enlightenment,* 101–5.

16. Yates, *The Rosicrucian Enlightenment,* 101–5, 171–72.

17. Yates, *The Rosicrucian Enlightenment,* 125–28, 145–51.

18. Hall, *The Secret Teachings of All Ages,* 463.

19. Yates, *The Rosicrucian Enlightenment,* 114, 154, 200, 223.

20. Yates, *The Rosicrucian Enlightenment,* 179–82.

21. Yates, *The Rosicrucian Enlightenment,* 188, 198, 200–202, 205.

22. Asprem, *Arguing with Angels,* 34.

23. Harkness, "The Scientific Reformation," 557.

24. Asprem, *Arguing with Angels,* 35.

25. Asprem, *Arguing with Angels,* 36.

26. Skinner and Rankine, *Practical Angel Magic,* 33–34.

27. See Churton, *The Magus of Freemasonry.*

28. Yates, *The Rosicrucian Enlightenment,* 196–97.

29. Ridley, *The Freemasons,* 22.

30. de Hoyos, *The Scottish Rite Ritual Monitor and Guide,* 79–80.

31. Skinner and Rankine, *Practical Angel Magic,* 44.

32. Yates, *The Rosicrucian Enlightenment,* 194.

33. Skinner and Rankine, *Practical Angel Magic,* 44.

34. Asprem, *Arguing with Angels,* 35.

35. de Hoyos, *The Scottish Rite Ritual Monitor and Guide,* 337.

36. de Hoyos, *The Scottish Rite Ritual Monitor and Guide,* 834.

37. Ridley, *The Freemasons,* 22.

38. See Horowitz, *Occult America.*

39. de Hoyos, *The Scottish Rite Ritual Monitor and Guide,* 963–66.

40. Yates, *The Rosicrucian Enlightenment,* 208–9.

41. Yates, *The Rosicrucian Enlightenment,* 210–11.

42. See Cohn, "Scottish Tradition of Second Sight."

43. Yates, *The Rosicrucian Enlightenment,* 211–12.

44. Yates, *The Rosicrucian Enlightenment,* 219.

45. Yates, *The Rosicrucian Enlightenment,* 215.

46. Skinner and Rankine, *Practical Angel Magic,* 45–47.

47. Harkness, "The Scientific Reformation," 564.

48. Skinner and Rankine, *Practical Angel Magic,* 48.

49. Asprem, *Arguing with Angels,* 45.

50. Kaczynski, *Perdurabo,* 60.

51. Gilbert, *The Golden Dawn Scrapbook,* 21–56.

52. Black, "MacGregor Mathers and the Secret Chiefs," in Regardie, *The Complete Golden Dawn System of Magic,* 11:41–43.

53. Regardie, *The Golden Dawn,* 107.

54. Skinner and Rankine, *Practical Angel Magic,* 51.

55. Skinner and Rankine, *Practical Angel Magic,* 40.

56. For Bennett's transcription of Book H, see Skinner and Rankine, *Practical Angel Magic,* 269–77.

57. Regardie, *The Golden Dawn,* 624–25.

CHAPTER 16. CROWNED AND CONQUERING

1. Kaczynski, *Perdurabo,* 124.

2. Crowley, *The Magical and Philosophical Commentaries,* I.

3. Crowley, *The Magical and Philosophical Commentaries,* I:12.

4. Crowley, *The Magical and Philosophical Commentaries,* I:1.

5. Crowley, *Magick: Liber ABA,* 515–16.

6. Crowley, *The Book of the Law,* II:22.

7. Crowley, *The Vision and the Voice,* 251.

8. Revelation 6:2 (KJV).

9. Cook, *The Apocalyptic Literature,* 197.

10. Larkin, *The Book of Revelation,* 53–54.

11. Darby, *Notes on the Book of Revelations,* 19.

12. Darby, *Collected Writings,* 34.

13. Crowley, *The Book of the Law,* III:49–54.

14. Crowley, "The Tunis Comment," in *The Book of the Law,* 50.

15. Crowley, *The Vision and the Voice,* 15.

16. Crowley, *The Vision and the Voice,* 153.

17. Crowley, *The Confessions,* 43, 63.

18. Darby, *Collected Writings,* 7.

19. Blackstone, *Jesus Is Coming,* 225.

20. Sutton, *American Apocalypse,* 20.

21. Rood, "The Forgotten Founder."

22. Crowley, *The Confessions,* 65.

23. Greene, "Evangelical Christians Plead for Israel."

24. Crowley, *Liber OZ.*

25. Kaczynski, *Perdurabo,* 277–319.

26. Sutton, *American Apocalypse,* 215.

27. Crowley, *The Magical Record of the Beast 666*, 251–52.

28. Casaubon, *Dr. John Dee's Spiritual Diaries*, 327.

29. Guénon, *The Reign of Quantity*, 272.

30. Crowley, *The Holy Books*, 3–4.

31. Guénon, *The Reign of Quantity*, 278.

32. Burgess, *Sûrya-Siddhânta*, 319. Other sources give varying lengths of time.

33. Crowley, *The Vision and the Voice*, 222.

34. Guénon, *The Reign of Quantity*, 276.

35. Crowley, *The Vision and the Voice*, 31–34.

36. Eshelman, *Visions and Voices*, 147.

37. Crowley, *The Vision and the Voice*, 64.

38. Crowley, *The Vision and the Voice*, 79–80.

39. Crowley, *The Vision and the Voice*, 90.

40. Eshelman, *Visions and Voices*, 195.

41. Crowley, *The Vision and the Voice*, 91.

42. Crowley, *The Vision and the Voice*, 116.

43. Crowley, *The Vision and the Voice*, 118, 120.

44. Crowley, *The Vision and the Voice*, 134.

45. Crowley, *The Vision and the Voice*, 159.

46. Crowley, *The Vision and the Voice*, 163.

47. Crowley, *The Vision and the Voice*, 171.

48. Crowley, *The Vision and the Voice*, 172.

49. For prior context on this, see Crowley, "The Wake World," in *Konx om Pax,* 3–24.

50. Crowley, *The Vision and the Voice*, 187.

51. Crowley, *The Vision and the Voice*, 188.

52. Eshelman, *Visions and Voices*, 387.

53. See Crowley, "The Three Schools of Magick (1–3)," in *Magick Without Tears,* 64–90.

54. Crowley, *The Vision and the Voice*, 199.

55. Crowley, *The Vision and the Voice*, 207.

56. Crowley, *The Vision and the Voice*, 209.

57. John 14:2 (KJV).

58. Crowley, *The Vision and the Voice*, 213.

59. Crowley, *The Vision and the Voice*, 217.

60. Crowley, *The Vision and the Voice*, 222.

61. Crowley, *The Vision and the Voice*, 224.

62. Crowley, *The Vision and the Voice,* 225.

63. Crowley, *The Vision and the Voice,* 227.

64. Crowley, *The Vision and the Voice,* 236.

65. Crowley, *The Vision and the Voice,* 238.

66. Crowley, *The Vision and the Voice,* 239.

67. Crowley, *The Vision and the Voice,* 244.

68. Crowley, *The Vision and the Voice,* 247.

69. Crowley, *The Vision and the Voice,* 247.

70. Crowley, *The Vision and the Voice,* 250–51.

71. Crowley, *The Vision and the Voice,* 251.

CHAPTER 17. IN THE SHADOW OF THE CROSS

1. Fuller, *The Magical Dilemma,* 222, 225, 241, 266.

2. Kaczynski, *Perdurabo,* 234.

3. Fuller, *Memoirs,* 318–41.

4. Dougherty, *The United States Military in Limited War,* 5–6.

5. Thurlow, *Fascism in Britain,* 100; Toczek, *Haters,* 220; Watson, "Not Italian or German," 25.

6. Dear and Foot, *The Oxford Companion to World War II,* 48, 632–33; Churton, *Aleister Crowley,* 364–65.

7. Watson, "Not Italian or German," 38, 48–49, 78; Boot, *War Made New,* 224.

8. Watson, "Not Italian or German," 27–29, 69, 91–92; Fuller, *The Secret Wisdom of the Qabalah.*

9. Crowley, *The Book of the Law,* III:7, III:46.

10. Watson, "Not Italian or German," 100; McKinstry, *Operation Sealion,* 217.

11. Kaczynski, *Perdurabo,* 251–52.

12. Crowley, *The Book of Lies,* 82.

13. Paraphrase of dialogue from *Apocalypse Now: Redux,* Coppola, 1979.

14. Hirsig, "The Magical Record," in *The Scarlet Letter,* 2, 3.

15. See Achad, *Liber Thirty-One.*

16. See Starr, *The Unknown God.*

17. Hunley, "The History of Solid-Propellant Rocketry."

18. Carter, *Sex and Rockets,* 2.

19. Pendle, *Strange Angel,* 26.

20. Parsons, "Analysis by a Master of the Temple."

21. Pendle, *Strange Angel*, 35–36, 44.

22. Carter, *Sex and Rockets*, 56.

23. Parsons, "Analysis."

24. Carter, *Sex and Rockets*, 4.

25. Pendle, *Strange Angel*, 44, 47.

26. Parsons, "Analysis."

27. Carter, *Sex and Rockets*, 7, 9.

28. Pendle, *Strange Angel*, 63, 83.

29. Carter, *Sex and Rockets*, 12.

30. NASA JPL, "The Spark of a New Era."

31. NetEase Exploration, "American Aviation Week 2008."

32. Carter, *Sex and Rockets*, 18.

33. Pendle, *Strange Angel*, 113–16, 120–23, 126.

34. Starr, *The Unknown God*, 257.

35. Parsons, "Analysis."

36. Starr, *The Unknown God*, 263.

37. Carter, *Sex and Rockets*, 55.

38. Parsons, "Analysis."

39. Breeze, "Foreword," in Parsons and Cameron, *Songs for the Witch Woman*, 11.

40. Pendle, *Strange Angel*, 157, 164, 195, 200–201.

41. Associated Press, "Reagan and the Apocalypse."

42. Crowley, *The Book of the Law*, 3:7, 3:46.

43. Starr, *The Unknown God*, 274.

44. Parsons, "I hight Don Quixote," 4.

45. Pendle, *Strange Angel*, 216.

46. Pendle, *Strange Angel*, 217–19.

47. Starr, *The Unknown God*, 285.

48. Pendle, *Strange Angel*, 217.

49. Pendle, *Strange Angel*, 215.

50. Starr, *The Unknown God*, 290.

51. Crowley, "Liber CXXXII," in Starr, *The Unknown God*, 388–91.

52. Starr, *The Unknown God*, 299–301.

53. Pendle, *Strange Angel*, 231–32, 240.

54. Pendle, *Strange Angel*, 273–74.

55. Wright, *Going Clear*, 43.

56. See Reich, *The Function of the Orgasm*.

57. Parsons, "The Book of Babalon."

58. Crowley, *Magick: Liber ABA,* 168.

59. See Grant, *Cults of the Shadow,* 161–63; and *Outside the Circles of Time,* 96–105.

60. Parsons, "The Book of Babalon."

61. See Churton, *Gnostic Mysteries of Sex.*

62. Biroco, *Kaos 14,* 81–82.

63. Parsons to Cameron, January 25, 1950.

64. Parsons, "The Book of Babalon."

65. Parsons, "The Book of Babalon."

66. Parsons, "The Book of Babalon."

67. Kansa, *Wormwood Star,* 9–27.

68. Hobbs, "Rocket Man."

69. Parsons, "The Book of Babalon." For more on this, see Louv, *Generation Hex.*

70. Parsons, "The Book of Babalon."

71. Carter, *Sex and Rockets,* 135.

72. Grant, *Beyond the Mauve Zone,* 35.

73. Grant, *Hecate's Fountain,* 29.

74. Kaczynski, *Perdurabo,* 538.

75. Miller, *Bare-Faced Messiah,* 126.

76. Pendle, *Strange Angel,* 275, 281–84.

77. Pendle, *Strange Angel,* 283; Kansa, *Wormwood Star,* 136.

78. See Buchholz, "Magusitis."

79. Pendle, *Strange Angel,* 288.

80. Parsons, "Analysis."

81. Matthew 11:20–24; Luke 10:13–15.

82. Alexander, *The Byzantine Apocalyptic Tradition,* 196.

83. Parsons, "The Book of the Antichrist."

84. Kaczynski, *Perdurabo,* 330.

85. Parsons, "The Book of the Antichrist."

86. Parsons, "The Book of the Antichrist."

87. Wasserman, *Aleister Crowley and the Practice of the Magical Diary,* 7.

88. Parsons, "The Book of the Antichrist."

89. See Wasserman, *Aleister Crowley and the Practice of the Magical Diary,* 6–7.

90. Parsons, "The Book of the Antichrist."

91. Parsons, "The Book of the Antichrist."

92. Revelation 17:18 (NIV).

93. Sutton, *American Apocalypse,* 76.

94. Gallo, "Katy Perry's Halftime Show the Most-Watched in Super Bowl History."

95. Parsons to Cameron, February 8, 1950.

96. Pendle, *Strange Angel,* 291–93.

97. Pendle, *Strange Angel,* 293–95.

98. See Parsons, *Freedom Is a Two-Edged Sword.*

99. Carter, *Sex and Rockets,* 185.

100. Pendle, *Strange Angel,* 1–6.

101. John 19:30; Carter, *Sex and Rockets,* 185.

102. Pendle, *Strange Angel,* 6–7.

103. Carter, *Sex and Rockets,* 184–85.

104. Pendle, *Strange Angel,* 300–301.

105. Starr, *The Unknown God,* 327.

106. Pendle, *Strange Angel,* 11–12, 301.

107. Pendle, *Strange Angel,* 300.

108. Carter, *Sex and Rockets,* 192.

109. Breeze, "Foreword," in Parsons and Cameron, *Songs for the Witch Woman,* 11.

110. Kansa, *Wormwood Star,* 83.

111. Kansa, *Wormwood Star,* 188.

112. Kansa, *Wormwood Star,* 86–87.

113. Kansa, *Wormwood Star,* 85–87, 94, 97.

114. See Tau Allen Greenfield, "The Secret History of Modern Witchcraft," in Metzger, *Book of Lies,* 260.

CHAPTER 18. THE LAST JERUSALEM

1. Cook, *The Apocalyptic Literature,* 202.

2. Mark 12:31; Matthew 22:39.

3. See Dalai Lama, *How to Practice.*

4. Crowley, *The Vision and the Voice,* 26.

5. Leitch, *The Angelical Language,* 1:12–19.

6. See Turner, trans., "A Valentinian Exposition (XI, 2)" in Robinson, *The Nag Hammadi Library,* 481–87.

7. See Rose, *The Soul After Death*.

8. See Evans-Wentz, trans., *The Tibetan Book of the Dead*.

9. Harkness, "The Scientific Reformation," 541.

10. Crowley, *The Book of the Law*, 3:34.

11. Harkness, "The Scientific Reformation," 487–88, 493–94, 504.

12. Kilgore, "Steve Bannon Sees Himself as Thomas Cromwell"; Elton, *The Tudor Revolution*.

13. Lopez, "Steve Bannon's Obsession"; Blumenthal, "Steve Bannon Believes the Apocalypse Is Coming"; Strauss and Howe, *The Fourth Turning*.

14. Groppe, "Pence Sending Message."

15. Spencer, "Trump's Occult Online Supporters"; Horowitz, "Bannon Cited Italian Thinker Who Inspired Fascists"; Zubrin, "Dugin's Evil Theology"; Dugin, *The Fourth Political Theory*, 234.

16. *Dawn of the Dead*, Romero, 1978.

Bibliography

2001: A Space Odyssey. Directed by Stanley Kubrick. (Original release 1968.) DVD. Burbank, Calif.: Warner Home Video, 2001.

Abano, Peter de. *Heptameron, or Magical Elements.* Translated by Joseph H. Peterson. www.esotericarchives.com/solomon/heptamer.htm (accessed September 11, 2017).

Achad, Frater. *Liber Thirty-One.* Marietta, Ga.: Luxor Press, 1998.

Ackermann, Silke, and Louise Devoy. "'The Lord of the Smoking Mirror': Objects Associated with John Dee in the British Museum." *Studies in History and Philosophy of Science* 43 (2012): 539–49, doi: 10.1016/j.shpsa.2011 .11.007.

Agrippa, Henry Cornelius. *Three Books of Occult Philosophy.* Edited by Donald Tyson. St. Paul, Minn.: Llewellyn, 1993.

al-Kindī, Abu Yūsuf Ya'qūb ibn 'Ishāq aṣ-Ṣabbāḥ. *On the Stellar Rays.* Berkeley Springs, W.Va.: Golden Hind, 1993.

Alexander, Paul Julius. *The Byzantine Apocalyptic Tradition.* Berkeley: University of California Press, 1985.

Andreae, Johann Valentin. *Reipublicae Christianopolitanae descriptio.* Strasbourg: Argentorati, 1619.

Apocalypse Now: Redux. Directed by Francis Ford Coppola. (Original release 1979.) DVD. Hollywood, Calif.: Paramount, 2010.

Appleby, Andrew B. *Famine in Tudor and Stuart England.* Stanford, Calif.: Stanford University Press, 1978.

Aquino, Michael. "The Book of Coming Forth by Night." www.scribd.com/doc /148658463/The-Book-of-Coming-Forth-by-Night (accessed September 11, 2017).

Ashmole, Elias. *Theatrum Chemicum Britannicum: The Complete and Corrected Edition*. Edited by William Kiesel. Seattle, Wa.: Ouroboros Press, 2011.

Asprem, Egil. *Arguing with Angels: Enochian Magic & Modern Occulture*. Albany: SUNY Press, 2012.

Associated Press. "Reagan and the Apocalypse." *New York Review of Books*, January 19, 1984. www.nybooks.com/articles/1984/01/19/reagan-and-the -apocalypse/ (accessed September 11, 2017).

Aston, Margaret. "The Fiery Trigon Conjunction: An Elizabethan Astrological Prediction." *Isis* 61, no. 2 (1970): 159–87. www.jstor.org/stable/229973 (accessed September 11, 2017).

Augustine. *Confessions*. Translated by Henry Chadwick. Oxford, U.K.: Oxford University Press, 1992.

Bacon, Francis. *New Atlantis*. London: J. Crooke, 1660.

———. *Novum organum*. Edited by Thomas Fowler. Oxford, U.K.: The Clarendon Press, 1889.

Bailey, John Eglington, ed. *Diary, for the Years 1595–1601, of Dr. John Dee, Warden of Manchester from 1595 to 1608*. Privately circulated MS, 1880.

Bainton, Roland Herbert. *Here I Stand: A Life of Martin Luther*. Peabody, Mass.: Hendrickson, 2009.

Baker, David. "Doctor Dee's Optics." *Optician*, July 20, 2012. https://www .opticianonline.net/features/doctor-dees-optics (accessed September 11, 2017).

Baker, Phil. *Austin Osman Spare: The Occult Life of London's Legendary Artist*. Berkeley, Calif.: North Atlantic, 2014.

Barnstone, Willis, and Marvin Meyer, eds. *The Gnostic Bible*. Boston: Shambhala, 2003.

Bawlf, Samuel. *The Secret Voyage of Sir Francis Drake: 1577–1580*. New York: Penguin, 2004. Kindle edition.

Biroco, Joel. *Kaos 14*. London: The Kaos-Babalon Press, 2002.

Blackstone, William E. *Jesus Is Coming*. Chicago: Fleming H. Revell, 1908.

Blavatsky, H. P. *The Secret Doctrine*. Vol. 1. Pasadena, Calif.: Theosophical University Press, 2014.

Blondel, Nathalie, ed. *The Journals of Mary Butts*. New Haven, Conn.: Yale University Press, 2002.

Blumenthal, Paul. "Steve Bannon Believes the Apocalypse Is Coming and War Is Inevitable." *Huffington Post*, February 8, 2017. www.huffingtonpost .com/entry/steve-bannon-apocalypse_us_5898f02ee4b040613138a951? (accessed September 11, 2017).

Bonner, Anthony. *The Art and Logic of Ramon Llull.* Leiden, Netherlands: Brill, 2007.

Boot, Max. *War Made New: Technology, Warfare and the Course of History: 1500 to Today.* New York: Gotham, 2006.

Breeze, William. "Foreword." In *Songs for the Witch Woman,* by John W. Parsons and Marjorie Cameron. London: Fulgur, 2014.

Brendon, Piers. "A Moral Audit of the British Empire." *openDemocracy,* November 6, 2007. www.opendemocracy.net/article/globalisation/visions _reflections/british_empire (accessed September 11, 2017).

Broom, John Henry. *The Astral Origin of the Emblems, the Zodiacal Signs, and the Astral Hebrew Alphabet, as Shown in "The Astronomical Register."* London: Edward Stanford, 1881.

Brown, Andrew. "Bush, Gog and Magog." *The Guardian,* August 10, 2009. www.theguardian.com/commentisfree/andrewbrown/2009/aug/10 /religion-george-bush (accessed September 11, 2017).

Brzezinski, Zbigniew. *The Grand Chessboard: American Primacy and Its Geostrategic Imperatives.* New York: Basic Books, 1998.

Buchholz, Nadine. "Magusitis: A Hydra in Sheep's Clothing." web.archive .org/web/20160305052603/http://deoxy.org/meme/Magusitus (accessed September 11, 2017).

Bullock, William B. "JATO—The Magic Bottle." *Flying,* February 1953, 25, 44.

Burgess, Ebenezer. *Translation of the Sûrya-Siddhânta: A Text-Book of Hindu Astronomy.* Calcutta: University of Calcutta, 1935.

Butler, Arthur John, and Sophie Crawford Lomas, eds. *Calendar of State Papers Foreign: Elizabeth, Vol. 17, January–June 1583 and Addenda.* London: His Majesty's Stationary Office, 1913.

Campbell, Colin D. *The Magic Seal of Dr. John Dee. The Sigillum Dei Aemeth.* York Beach, Maine: Teitan, 2009.

Caporael, Linnda R. "Ergotism: The Satan Loosed in Salem?" *Science* 192, no. 4234 (1976): 21–26, doi:10.1126/science.769159.

Carbonero y Sol, Don Leon. *Indice de Libros Prohibidos.* Madrid: D. Antonio Perez Dubrull, 1880.

Carroll, Peter J. *Liber Kaos.* York Beach, Maine: Weiser, 1992.

———. *Liber Null & Psychonaut: An Introduction to Chaos Magic.* York Beach, Maine: Weiser, 1987.

Carter, John. *Sex and Rockets: The Occult World of Jack Parsons.* Venice, Calif.: Feral House, 1999.

Casaubon, Méric. *Dr. John Dee's Spiritual Diaries (1583–1608) being a fully revised reset and edited edition of A True & Faithful Relation of what passed for Many Yeers between Dr. John Dee . . . and some spirits. . .* Edited by Stephen Skinner. Singapore: Golden Hoard, 2011.

Case, Paul Foster. *The True and Invisible Rosicrucian Order.* Claremont, Calif.: The Francis Bacon Library, 1927.

Catholic Church. *Index Librorum Prohibitorum.* Rome: Vatican, 1900.

Chamberlain, John, to Dudley Carleton, March 1, 1599. www.oxford -shakespeare.com/StatePapers12/SP_12-270-48.pdf (accessed September 11, 2017).

Chambers, E. K. *The Elizabethan Stage.* Vol. 3. Oxford, U.K.: Oxford University Press, 1945.

Chardin, Teilhard de. *The Phenomenon of Man.* New York: Harper Perennial, 2008.

Churton, Tobias. *Aleister Crowley: The Biography.* London: Watkins, 2014.

———. *Gnostic Mysteries of Sex: Sophia the Wild One and Erotic Christianity.* Rochester, Vt.: Inner Traditions, 2015.

———. *The Magus of Freemasonry: The Mysterious Life of Elias Ashmole.* Rochester, Vt.: Inner Traditions, 2006.

Clark, Paul A. *Paul Foster Case: His Life and Works.* Covina, Calif.: Fraternity of the Hidden Light, 2013.

Clark, Victoria. *Allies for Armageddon: The Rise of Christian Zionism.* New Haven, Conn.: Yale University Press, 2007.

Clucas, Stephen. *John Dee: Interdisciplinary Studies in English Renaissance Thought.* Dordrecht, Netherlands: Springer, 2006.

Clulee, Nicholas H. "Astrology, Magic, and Optics: Facets of John Dee's Early Natural Philosophy." *Renaissance Quarterly* 30, no. 4. (1977): 532–680, doi:10.2307/2859862.

———. *John Dee's Natural Philosophy: Between Science and Religion.* Vol. 2. New York: Routledge, 2013.

Cobain, Ian, Owen Bowcott, and Richard Norton-Taylor. "Britain Destroyed Records of Colonial Crimes." *The Guardian,* April 17, 2012. www .theguardian.com/uk/2012/apr/18/britain-destroyed-records-colonial -crimes (accessed September 11, 2017).

Cohn, Shari Ann. "Scottish Tradition of Second Sight and Other Psychic Experiences in Families." Ph.D. diss., University of Edinburgh, 1996.

Cook, Stephen L. *The Apocalyptic Literature.* Nashville, Tenn.: Abingdon Press, 2003.

Crossley, James. *Autobiographical Tracts of Dr. John Dee, Warden of the College of Manchester.* Lancaster, U.K.: Chetham Society, 1851.

Crowley, Aleister. *The Book of the Law.* San Francisco: Weiser Books, 1976.

———. *The Book of Lies.* York Beach, Maine: Weiser, 1998.

———. *The Collected Works of Aleister Crowley.* Vol. 3. Des Plaines, Ill.: Yoga Publication Society, 1974.

———. *The Confessions of Aleister Crowley.* New York: Hill & Wang, 1969.

———, ed. *The Equinox* 1, no. 10. London: Wieland & Co., 1913.

———, ed. *The Equinox* 3, no. 1. San Francisco: Weiser, 2007.

———. *The Holy Books of Thelema.* York Beach, Maine: Weiser, 1983.

———. *Konx om Pax.* Chicago: Yogi Publication Society, 1982.

———. "Liber LXXIII, The Urn: The Diary of a Magus." www.tomegatherion .co.uk/theurn.pdf (accessed September 11, 2017).

———. "Liber XCVII, The Amalantrah Working." *Hermetic Library.* https:// hermetic.com/crowley/libers/lib729.html (accessed September 11, 2017).

———. *Liber Aleph.* York Beach, Maine: Weiser, 1991.

———. *Liber OZ.* London: Ordo Templi Orientis, 1941.

———. *The Magical and Philosophical Commentaries on The Book of the Law.* Stukely-Sud, Quebec: 93 Publishing, 1974.

———. *The Magical Record of the Beast 666: The Diaries of Aleister Crowley 1914–1920.* Edited by John Symonds and Kenneth Grant. London: Duckworth, 1993.

———. *Magick: Liber ABA, Book 4.* San Francisco: Weiser, 1998.

———. *Magick Without Tears.* Tempe, Ariz.: New Falcon, 1991.

———. *The Scented Garden of Abdullah the Satirist of Shiraz.* Chicago: Teitan Press, 1991.

———. *The Vision and the Voice.* York Beach, Maine: Weiser, 1998.

Dalai Lama. *How to Practice: The Way to a Meaningful Life.* New York: Atria, 2003.

Darby, John Nelson. *The Collected Writings of J. N. Darby.* Vol. 7, *Doctrinal.* Edited by William Kelly. Raleigh, N.C.: Lulu, 2015.

———. *The Collected Writings of J. N. Darby.* Vol. 34, *Miscellaneous,* no. 3. Edited by William Kelly. Raleigh, N.C.: Lulu, 2015.

———. *Notes on the Book of Revelation, to Assist Inquirers in Searching into That Book.* London: W. H. Broome, 1876.

Davila, James R. "The Ninety-Four Books of Ezra and the Angelic Revelations of John Dee." Society of Biblical Literature Conference, Chicago, November

2012. www.scribd.com/document/190324187/The-94-Books-of-Ezra-and
-the-Angelic-Revelations-of-John-Dee (accessed September 11, 2017).

Davis, Martin. *The Universal Computer: The Road from Leibniz to Turing*. Boca
Raton, Fla.: CRC Press, 2011.

Dawn of the Dead. Directed by George A. Romero. (Original release 1978.)
DVD. Beverly Hills, Calif.: Starz/Anchor Bay, 2004.

Deacon, Richard. *John Dee: Scientist, Geographer, Astrologer and Secret Agent to
Elizabeth I*. London: Frederick Muller, 1968.

Dear, I. C. B., and M. R. D. Foot. *The Oxford Companion to World War II*.
London: Oxford University Press, 2005.

Dee, John. *General and Rare Memorials Pertayning to the Perfect Arte of
Nauigation*. London: John Daye, 1577.

———. "The Mathematicall Praeface to *Elements of Geometrie* of Euclid of
Megara." *Project Gutenberg*. archive.org/details/themathematicall22062gut
(accessed September 11, 2017).

———. *Monas hieroglyphica*. Edited by Benjamin Rowe. London: 1564. www
.hermetics.org/pdf/deemonad.pdf (accessed September 11, 2017).

de Hoyos, Arturo. *The Scottish Rite Ritual Monitor and Guide*. Washington,
D.C.: The Supreme Council, 33°, Southern Jurisdiction, 2010.

Devine, Michael J. "John Prestall: A Complex Relationship with the Elizabethan
Regime." Master's thesis, University of Wellington, New Zealand, 2009.

Diamond, Sara. *Spiritual Warfare: The Politics of the Christian Right*. Montreal,
Quebec: Black Rose Books, 1990.

Dick, Philip K. *The Exegesis of Philip K. Dick*. New York: Houghton Mifflin
Harcourt, 2011.

———. *VALIS*. New York: Vintage, 1991.

Digges, Thomas. *Prognostication Everlasting*. London: The Widow Orwin, 1596.

Dobbs, B. J. T. *The Foundations of Newton's Alchemy*. New York: Cambridge
University Press, 1983.

Dougherty, Kevin. *The United States Military in Limited War: Case Studies in
Success and Failure, 1945–1999*. Jefferson, N.C.: McFarland, 2012.

Dreyer, J. L. E. *Tycho Brahe: A Picture of Scientific Life and Work in the Sixteenth
Century*. Edinburgh: Adam and Charles Black, 1890.

Dugin, Alexander. *The Fourth Political Theory*. London: Arktos, 2012.

DuQuette, Lon Milo. *Enochian Vision Magick*. San Francisco: Weiser, 2008.

Durant, Will. *The Reformation*. New York: Simon and Schuster, 1957.

———. *The Story of Philosophy*. New York: Garden City, 1933.

Durant, Will, and Ariel Durant. *The Age of Reason Begins.* New York: Simon and Schuster, 1961.

Ellison, Katherine. *A Cultural History of Early Modern English Cryptography Manuals.* London: Routledge, 2017.

Elton, G. R. *The Tudor Revolution in Government: Administrative Changes in the Reign of Henry VIII.* Cambridge, U.K.: Cambridge University Press, 1967.

Eshelman, James A. *Pearls of Wisdom: Gems from the Journal Black Pearl.* Los Angeles: College of Thelema, 2013.

———. *Visions and Voices.* Los Angeles: College of Thelema, 2011.

Euclid. *The elements of geometrie of the most auncient philosopher Euclid of Megara.* London: John Daye, 1570.

Evans-Wentz, W. Y., trans. *The Tibetan Book of the Dead.* New York: Oxford University Press, 2000.

Farmer, S. A. *Syncretism in the West: Pico's 900 Theses (1486).* Tempe, Ariz.: ACMRS, 1998.

Fell-Smith, Charlotte. *The Life of Dr. John Dee.* London: Constable and Company, 1909.

Fenton, Edward. *The Diaries of John Dee.* Oxfordshire, U.K.: Day Books, 1998.

Ferguson, Niall. *Empire: The Rise and Demise of the British World Order and the Lessons for Global Power.* London: Penguin, 2004.

Ficino, Marsilio. *De Christiana religione.* Florence: Nicolò di Lorenzo, 1474.

Fludd, Robert. *Summum bonum, quod est verum magiae, cabalae, alchymiae, fratrum roseae crucis verorum subjectum.* Frankfurt, 1629.

———. *Utriusque cosmi maioris scilicet et minoris metaphysica, physica atqve technical historia.* Oppenheim: Aere Iohan-Theodori de Bry, Typis Hieronymi Galleri, 1617.

Foxe, John. *Actes and Monumentes.* Vol. 5. London: John Day, 1563.

French, Peter J. *John Dee: The World of an Elizabethan Magus.* London: Routledge & Kegan Paul, 1984.

Fuller, J. F. C. *Memoirs of an Unconventional Soldier.* London: Ivor Nicholson and Watson, 1936.

———. *The Secret Wisdom of the Qabalah: A Study in Jewish Mystical Thought.* London: Rider & Co., 1937.

Fuller, Jean Overton. *The Magical Dilemma of Victor Neuburg.* London: W. H. Allen, 1965.

Gallo, Phil. "Katy Perry's Halftime Show the Most-Watched in Super Bowl History."

Billboard, February 2, 2015. www.billboard.com/articles/news/6458264
/katy-perry-super-bowl-halftime-record (accessed September 15, 2017).

Gilbert, R. A. *The Golden Dawn Scrapbook: The Rise and Fall of a Magical Order*. York Beach, Maine: Weiser, 1997.

Godwin, Joscelyn. *The Chemical Wedding of Christian Rosenkreutz*. Boston: Phanes Press, 1991.

Grant, Kenneth. *Beyond the Mauve Zone*. London: Starfire, 1999.

———. *Cults of the Shadow*. London: Skoob, 1994.

———. *Hecate's Fountain*. London: Skoob, 1992.

———. *Nightside of Eden*. London: Skoob, 1994.

———. *Outside the Circles of Time*. London: Frederick Muller, 1980.

Green, Mary Anne Everett, ed. *Calendar of State Papers, Domestic Series, of the Reigns of Elizabeth and James I, Addenda, 1580–1625*. London: Longman & Co. and Trübner & Co., 1872.

Greene, Richard Allen. "Evangelical Christians Plead for Israel." *BBC News,* July 19, 2006. news.bbc.co.uk/2/hi/americas/5193092.stm (accessed September 15, 2017).

Gribbin, John. *The Scientists*. New York: Random House, 2002.

Groppe, Maureen. "Pence Sending Message through Choice of Bible." *IndyStar,* January 19, 2017. www.indystar.com/story/news/politics/2017/01/19/pence -sending-message-through-choice-bible/96781772/ (accessed September 15, 2017).

Guénon, René. *The Crisis of the Modern World*. Hillsdale, N.Y.: Sophia Perennis, 2004.

———. *Introduction to the Study of the Hindu Doctrines*. London: Luzac & Co., 1945.

———. *The Reign of Quantity and the Signs of the Times*. Hillsdale, N.Y.: Sophia Perennis, 2001.

Håkansson, Håkan. *Seeing the Word: John Dee and Renaissance Occultism*. Lund, Sweden: Lund University, 2001.

Hall, Manly P. *The Secret Teachings of All Ages*. Los Angeles: Philosophical Research Society, 2003.

Hari, Johann. "The Truth? Our Empire Killed Millions." *The Independent,* June 18, 2006. www.independent.co.uk/voices/commentators/johann-hari /johann-hari-the-truth-our-empire-killed-millions-404631.html (accessed September 15, 2017).

Harkness, Deborah E. *John Dee's Conversations with Angels: Cabala,*

Alchemy, and the End of Nature. New York: Cambridge University Press, 1999.

———. "Managing an Experimental Household: The Dees of Mortlake and the Practice of Natural Philosophy." *Isis* 88, no. 2 (1997): 247–62. www.jstor.org/stable/236573 (accessed September 15, 2017).

———. "The Scientific Reformation: John Dee and the Restitution of Nature." Ph.D. diss., University of California–Davis, 1994.

Higley, Sarah L. *Hildegard of Bingen's Unknown Language.* Basingstoke, U.K.: Palgrave Macmillan, 2007.

Hirsig, Leah. "The Magical Record of the Scarlet Woman. Part 4: December 14–29, 1924." *The Scarlet Letter* 2, no. 3 (1995). www.scarletwoman.org/swl_archive/swl_site_v3/scarletletter/v2n3/v2n3_leah4.html (accessed September 15, 2017).

Hobbs, Scott. "Rocket Man." *Huffington Post,* August 15, 2012. www.huffingtonpost.com/scott-hobbs/rocket-man_2_b_1597713.html (accessed September 15, 2017).

Honorius of Thebes. *The Sworn Book of Honorius: Liber Iuratus Honorii.* Translated by Joseph H. Peterson. Lake Worth, Fla.: Ibis Press, 2016.

Horowitz, Jason. "Steve Bannon Cited Italian Thinker Who Inspired Fascists." *New York Times,* February 10, 2017. www.nytimes.com/2017/02/10/world/europe/bannon-vatican-julius-evola-fascism.html (accessed September 15, 2017).

Horowitz, Mitch. *Occult America: The Secret History of How Mysticism Shaped Our Nation.* New York: Bantam, 2009.

Hunley, J. D. "The History of Solid-Propellant Rocketry: What We Do and Do Not Know." Paper presented at 35th Joint Propulsion Conference and Exhibit, Los Angeles, June 20–24, 1999. www.nasa.gov/centers/dryden/pdf/88635main_H-2330.pdf (accessed September 15, 2017).

Inauguration of the Pleasure Dome. Directed by Kenneth Anger. (Original release 1954.) DVD. In *The Films of Kenneth Anger,* Vol. 1. San Francisco: Fantoma: 2007.

Jacobs, Joseph, M. Seligsohn, and Mary W. Montgomery. "Michael." *Jewish Encyclopedia,* jewishencyclopedia.com/articles/10779-michael (accessed September 15, 2017).

James, Geoffrey. *The Enochian Evocation of Dr. John Dee.* San Francisco: Weiser, 2009.

Johnston, Stephen. "John Dee on Geometry: Texts, Teaching and the Euclidean

Tradition." *Studies in History and Philosophy of Science* 43, no. 3 (2012): 470–79, doi:10.1016/j.shpsa.2011.12.005.

Jong, H. M. E. de. *Michael Maier's Atalanta Fugiens: Sources of an Alchemical Book of Emblems.* Lake Worth, Fla.: Nicolas-Hayes, 2002.

Kaczynski, Richard. *Perdurabo: The Life of Aleister Crowley.* Berkeley, Calif.: North Atlantic, 2010.

Kanigel, Robert. *The Man Who Knew Infinity: A Life of the Genius Ramanujan.* New York: Charles Scribner's Sons, 1991.

Kansa, Spencer. *Wormwood Star: The Magickal Life of Marjorie Cameron.* Oxford, U.K.: Mandrake, 2011.

Kaplan, Aryeh. *Sefer Yetzirah: The Book of Creation.* York Beach, Maine: Weiser, 1997.

Kasprzak, Jan. "A Riddle of History: Queen Elizabeth I and the Albertus Łaski Affair." *The Polish Review* 14, no. 1 (1969): 53–67. www.jstor.org /stable/25776822 (accessed September 15, 2017).

Kelly, Edward, and Johann Lange. *Tractatus duo egregii de lapide philosophorum.* Hamburg: Schultze, 1676.

Keynes, John Maynard. "Newton the Man." Lecture, Royal Society of London, July 1946. www-history.mcs.st-and.ac.uk/Extras/Keynes_Newton.html (accessed September 15, 2017).

Kilgore, Ed. "Steve Bannon Sees Himself as Thomas Cromwell. Will His Head End Up on a Spike?" *New York Magazine,* February 1, 2017. nymag.com /daily/intelligencer/2017/02/what-it-means-that-bannon-sees-himself-as -thomas-cromwell.html (accessed September 15, 2017).

King, John N. "Queen Elizabeth I: Representations of the Virgin Queen." *Renaissance Quarterly* 43, no. 1 (1990): 30–74, doi:10.2307/2861792.

Kramer, Samuel Noah. *The Sumerians: Their History, Culture and Character.* Chicago: University of Chicago Press, 1971.

Kraus, Hans P. "Sir Francis Drake: A Pictorial Biography." *Library of Congress Rare Book & Special Collections Reading Room,* August 31, 2010. www.loc .gov/rr/rarebook/catalog/drake/ (accessed September 15, 2017).

Krause, Oliver, et. al. "Tycho Brahe's 1572 Supernova as a Standard Type Ia as Revealed by Its Light-Echo Spectrum." *Nature* 456 (2008): 617–19, doi:10.1038/nature07608.

Larkin, Clarence. *The Book of Revelation: A Study of the Last Prophetic Book of Holy Scripture.* Glenside, Pa.: Clarence Larkin Estate, 1919.

LaVey, Anton Szandor. *The Satanic Bible.* New York: Avon, 1969.

Laycock, Donald. *The Complete Enochian Dictionary.* San Francisco: Weiser, 2001.

Leitch, Aaron. *The Angelical Language.* Vol. 1, *The Complete History and Mythos of the Tongue of the Angels.* St. Paul, Minn.: Llewellyn, 2010.

———. *The Essential Enochian Grimoire.* St. Paul, Minn.: Llewellyn, 2014.

Lindsay, D. Michael. *Faith in the Halls of Power.* Oxford, U.K.: Oxford University Press, 2007.

Lindsey, Hal. *The Late, Great Planet Earth.* Grand Rapids, Mich.: Zondervan, 1970.

Lipschutz, Yael. *Cameron: Songs for the Witch Woman.* Santa Monica, Calif.: Cameron-Parsons Foundation, 2014.

Lopez, Linette. "Steve Bannon's Obsession with a Dark Theory of History Should Be Worrisome." *Business Insider,* February 2, 2017. www.businessinsider .com/book-steve-bannon-is-obsessed-with-the-fourth-turning-2017-2 (accessed September 15, 2017).

Louv, Jason, ed. *Generation Hex.* New York: Disinformation, 2006.

Luhrmann, T. M., R. Padmavati, H. Tharoor, and A. Osei. "Differences in Voice-Hearing Experiences of People with Psychosis in the USA, India and Ghana: Interview-Based Study." *British Journal of Psychiatry* 206, no. 1 (Jan. 2015): 41–44, doi:10.1192/bjp.bp.113.139048.

Luther, Martin. *De Biblie.* Lübeck: Ludowich Dietz, 1533–34.

———. *Das Newe Testament Deutzsch.* Wittenberg: Melchior Lotter, 1522.

———. "On the Babylonian Captivity of the Church." In *Works of Martin Luther with Introductions and Notes.* Translated by Henry Eyster Jacobs and Adolph Spaeth. Philadelphia: A. J. Holman Company, 1915.

Maddison, Angus. *The World Economy: A Millennial Perspective.* Paris: Organization for Economic Co-operation and Development, 2001.

Magee, Mike, trans. *Niruttara Tantra.* www.shivashakti.com/niruttar.htm (accessed September 15, 2017).

Marshall, Peter. *The Magic Circle of Rudolf II: Alchemy and Astrology in Renaissance Prague.* New York: Walker & Company, 2006.

Mathers, Samuel Liddell MacGregor, trans. and ed. *The Goetia: The Lesser Key of Solomon the King.* York Beach, Maine: Weiser, 1995.

McKinstry, Leo. *Operation Sealion: How Britain Crushed the German War Machine's Dreams of Invasion in 1940.* London: John Murray, 2014.

Mercator, Gerardus. *Atlas sive Cosmographicae meditationes de fabrica mvndi et fabricate figvra.* Duisburg: Dvisbvrgi Clivorvm, 1595.

Metzger, Richard, ed. *Book of Lies.* New York: Disinformation, 2003.

Miller, Russell. *Bare-Faced Messiah.* New York: Henry Holt, 1987.

Monbiot, George. "Deny the British Empire's Crimes? No, We Ignore Them." *The Guardian,* April 23, 2012. www.theguardian.com/commentisfree/2012 /apr/23/british-empire-crimes-ignore-atrocities (accessed September 15, 2017).

Montfaucon, Bernard de. *L'antiquité expliquée et représentée en figures.* Vol. 2. Paris: Florentine Delaulne, 1719.

Morison, Samuel. *The European Discovery of America: The Northern Voyages.* New York: Oxford University Press, 1971.

NASA Jet Propulsion Laboratory. "The Spark of a New Era." October 25, 2006. www.jpl.nasa.gov/news/news.php?feature=1217 (accessed September 15, 2017).

Nasar, Sylvia. *A Beautiful Mind.* New York: Simon and Schuster, 2011.

NetEase Exploration. "American Aviation Week 2008 Year Figures: Qian Xuesen." [In Chinese.] October 31, 2009. news.163.com/09/1031/17 /5MVIKNT90001124J.html (accessed September 15, 2017).

Night Tide. Directed by Curtis Harrington. (Original release 1961.) DVD. Chatsworth, Calif.: Image Entertainment, 1999.

Novella, Steven. "A New Wrinkle in Quantum Mechanics." NeuroLogica Blog of the New England Skeptical Society, December 23, 2014. theness .com/neurologicablog/index.php/a-new-wrinkle-in-quantum-mechanics/ (accessed September 15, 2017).

P-Orridge, Genesis. *Thee Psychick Bible.* Edited by Jason Louv. Port Townsend, Wash.: Feral House, 2009.

Pagels, Elaine. *Revelations: Visions, Prophecy, and Politics in the Book of Revelation.* New York: Viking, 2012.

Paris, Erna. *The End of Days: A Story of Tolerance, Tyranny and the Expulsion of the Jews from Spain.* Amherst, N.Y.: Prometheus Books, 1995.

Parker, John. *The Works of Dionysius the Areopagite.* Vol. 2. London: James Parker and Co., 1897.

Parry, Glen. *The Arch-Conjuror of England.* London: Yale University Press, 2011.

Parsons, John Whiteside. "Analysis by a Master of the Temple of the Critical Nodes in the Experience of His Material Vehicle." Hermetic Library. hermetic.com/parsons/analysis-by-a-master-of-the-temple.html (accessed September 15, 2017).

———. "The Book of the Antichrist." Hermetic Library. hermetic.com/parsons /the-book-of-the-antichrist.html (accessed September 15, 2017).

———. "The Book of Babalon." Hermetic Library. hermetic.com/parsons/the -book-of-babalon.html (accessed September 15, 2017).

———. *Freedom Is a Two-Edged Sword*. Tempe, Ariz.: New Falcon, 2001.

———. "I hight Don Quixote, I live on peyote." *Oriflamme* 1, no. 1 (1943): 4.

——— to Marjorie Cameron, January 25, 1950. blacklies.xenu.ca/archives/3384 (accessed January 31, 2017; site now discontinued).

Parsons, John W., and Marjorie Cameron. *Songs for the Witch Woman*. London: Fulgur Esoterica, 2014.

Pendle, George. *Strange Angel: The Otherworldly Life of Rocket Scientist John Whiteside Parsons*. London: Weidenfeld & Nicolson, 2005.

Peterson, Joseph H., ed. *John Dee's Five Books of Mystery*. York Beach, Maine: Red Wheel/Weiser, 2003.

Pew Research Center. "The Future of World Religions: Population Growth Projections, 2010–2050." April 2, 2015. www.pewforum.org/files/2015/03 /PF_15.04.02_ProjectionsFullReport.pdf (accessed September 15, 2017).

———. "Many Americans Uneasy with Mix of Religion and Politics." August 24, 2006. www.pewforum.org/files/2006/08/religion-politics-06.pdf (accessed September 15, 2017).

Philobiblon Society. *Biographical and Historical Miscellanies*. Vol. 1. London: Charles Wittingham, 1854.

Poole, Robert. "John Dee and the English Calendar: Science, Religion and Empire." Draft paper presented at History Seminar, University of York, February 29, 1996. www.hermetic.ch/cal_stud/jdee.html (accessed September 15, 2017).

Porta Lucis A 111, Frater. *Words of Power*. New York: Ordo Templi Orientis, 2014.

Pseudo-Methodius. *Apocalypse. An Alexandrian World Chronicle*. Edited and translated by Benjamin Garstad. Cambridge, Mass.: Harvard University Press, 2012.

Raleigh, Walter. *The History of the World*. London: Printed for Walter Burre, 1614.

Rampling, Jennifer M. "John Dee and the Sciences: Early Modern Networks of Knowledge." *Studies in History and Philosophy of Science* 43, no. 3 (2012): 432–36, doi:10.1016/j.shpsa.2011.12.001.

Raphael. *The Astrologer of the Nineteenth Century*. London: Knight & Lacey, 1825.

Reeds, Jim. "Solved: The Ciphers in Book III of Trithemius's Steganographia." *Cryptologia* 22, no. 4 (1998): 291–317.

Regardie, Israel, ed. *The Complete Golden Dawn System of Magic.* Tempe, Ariz.: New Falcon, 2003.

———, ed. *The Golden Dawn.* St. Paul, Minn.: Llewellyn, 2002.

Reich, Wilhelm. *The Function of the Orgasm.* New York: Farrar, Straus and Giroux, 1973.

Revolver. Directed by Guy Ritchie. (Original release 2005.) DVD. Culver City, Calif.: Sony Pictures Home Entertainment, 2008.

Ridley, Jasper. *The Freemasons.* New York: Arcade, 2001.

Robinson, James M., ed. *The Nag Hammadi Library.* San Francisco: Harper San Francisco, 1990.

Rood, Paul. "The Forgotten Founder." *Biola,* Fall 2013. magazine.biola.edu /article/13-fall/the-forgotten-founder/ (accessed September 15, 2017).

Rose, Seraphim. *Orthodoxy and the Religion of the Future.* Platina, Calif.: St. Herman Press, 1997.

———. *The Soul After Death.* Platina, Calif.: St. Herman of Alaska Brotherhood, 2009.

Rutledge, Leslie A. "John Dee: Consultant to Queen Elizabeth I." *NSA Technical Journal* 12, no. 4 (1967): 1–16. www.nsa.gov/news-features/declassified -documents/tech-journals/assets/files/john-dee.pdf (accessed September 15, 2017).

Sagan, Carl. *Contact.* New York: Pocket, 1997.

Scahill, Jeremy. "Mike Pence Will Be the Most Powerful Christian Supremacist in U.S. History." *The Intercept,* November 15, 2016. theintercept.com /2016/11/15/mike-pence-will-be-the-most-powerful-christian-supremacist -in-us-history (accessed September 15, 2017).

Schaff, Philip, and David Schley Schaff. *History of the Christian Church.* Vol. 7. New York: Charles Scribner's Sons, 1907.

Schweighardt, Theophilus. *Speculum sophicum rodo-stauroticum.* Germany, 1618.

Shakespeare, William. *The Complete Works.* Edited by Stanley Wells and Gary Taylor. Oxford, U.K.: Oxford University Press, 1988.

Sherman, William H. *John Dee: The Politics of Reading and Writing in the English Renaissance.* Amherst: University of Massachusetts Press, 1995.

———. "Putting the British Seas on the Map: John Dee's Imperial Cartography." *Cartographica: The International Journal for Geographic*

Information and Geovisualization 35, nos. 3–4 (1998): 1–10, doi:10.3138 /H698-K7R3-4072-2K73.

———. "Research Intelligence in Early Modern England." *Studies in Intelligence* 37, no. 5 (1994): 95–104.

Shimoni, Gideon. *The Zionist Ideology.* Hanover, N.H.: Brandeis University Press, 1995.

Shindler, Colin. *A History of Modern Israel.* Cambridge, U.K.: Cambridge University Press, 2008.

Shumaker, Wayne. *John Dee on Astronomy.* Berkeley: University of California Press, 1978.

Skinner, Stephen. *Key to the Latin of Dr. John Dee's Spiritual Diaries.* Singapore: Golden Hoard, 2012.

Skinner, Stephen, and David Rankine. *Practical Angel Magic of Dr. John Dee's Enochian Tables.* London: Golden Hoard, 2004.

Sledge, James Justin. "Between Loagaeth and Cosening: Towards an Etiology of John Dee's Spirit Diaries." *Aries* 10, no. 1 (2010): 1–35, doi:10.1163 /156798910X12584583444835.

Smith, G. C. Moore, ed. *Gabriel Harvey's Marginalia.* Stratford-Upon-Avon, U.K.: Shakespeare Head Press, 1913.

Spanos, N. P., and J. Gottlieb. "Ergotism and the Salem Village Witch Trials." *Science* 194, no. 4272 (1976): 1390–94, doi:10.1126/science.795029.

Spence, Richard B. *Secret Agent 666: Aleister Crowley, British Intelligence and the Occult.* Port Townsend, Wash.: Feral House, 2008.

Spencer, Paul. "Trump's Occult Online Supporters Believe 'Meme Magic' Got Him Elected." *VICE/Motherboard,* November 18, 2016. https://motherboard .vice.com/en_us/article/pgkx7g/trumps-occult-online-supporters-believe -pepe-meme-magic-got-him-elected (accessed September 15, 2017).

Starr, Martin P. *The Unknown God: W. T. Smith and the Thelemites.* Bolingbrook, Ill.: Teitan, 2003.

Strauss, William, and Neil Howe. *The Fourth Turning: An American Prophecy.* New York: Broadway Books, 1997.

Suster, Gerald. *John Dee: Essential Readings.* Berkeley, Calif.: North Atlantic, 2003.

Sutton, Matthew Avery. *American Apocalypse: A History of Modern Evangelism.* Cambridge, Mass.: Harvard University Press, 2014.

Symonds, John. *The King of the Shadow Realm.* London: Gerald Duckworth & Co., 1989.

Szőnyi, György. *John Dee's Occultism: Magical Exaltation through Powerful Signs.* Albany: SUNY Press, 2004.

Teresa of Ávila. *Interior Castle.* Translated and edited by E. Allison Peers. Mineola, N.Y.: Dover, 2007.

Thornton, Russell. *American Indian Holocaust and Survival: A Population History since 1492.* Norman: University of Oklahoma Press, 1990.

Thurlow, Richard. *Fascism in Britain: A History, 1918–1945.* London: I. B. Tauris, 2006.

Tillyard, E. M. W. *The Elizabethan World Picture.* New York: Vintage, 1959.

Toczek, Nick. *Haters, Baiters and Would-Be Dictators: Anti-Semitism and the UK Far Right.* London: Routledge, 2016.

Townsend, George. *The Acts and Monuments of John Foxe.* Vol. 7. London: Seeley, Burnside and Seeley, 1747.

Trimondi, Victor, and Victoria Trimondi. *Der Schatten des Dalai Lama. Sexualität, Magie und Politik im tibetischen Buddhismus.* [In German.] Düsseldorf: Patmos, 1999.

Trismegistos, Hermes. "The Emerald Tablet of Hermes." Translated by Isaac Newton, c. 1680. www.sacred-texts.com/alc/emerald.htm (accessed September 15, 2017).

Trithemius, Johannes. *De septem secundeis.* Translated by Joseph H. Peterson. 1998. www.esotericarchives.com/tritheim/tritem.htm (accessed September 15, 2017).

Turner, Robert. *The Heptarchia Mystica of John Dee.* Wellingborough, U.K.: Aquarian Press, 1986.

Tyson, Donald. *Enochian Magic for Beginners.* St. Paul, Minn.: Llewellyn, 2002.

Ubelaker, Douglas H. "The Sources and Methodology for Mooney's Estimates of North American Indian Populations." In *The Native Population of the Americas in 1492.* Edited by William M. Denevan. Madison: University of Wisconsin Press, 1976.

Van den Broek, Roelof, ed. *Gnosis and Hermeticism from Antiquity to Modern Times.* Albany: SUNY Press, 1997.

Vaughan, Thomas. *Rosicrucian Manifestos.* Seattle, Wash.: Ouroboros Press, 2012.

Verstegan, Richard [John Philopatris, pseud.]. *An Advertisement to a Secretarie of my L. Treasurers of Ingland.* Antwerp, 1592.

Von Worms, Abraham. *The Book of Abramelin: A New Translation.* Edited by Georg Dehn. Lake Worth, Fla.: Ibis Press, 2015.

Waller, Maureen. *Sovereign Ladies: The Six Reigning Queens of England.* New York: St. Martin's Press, 2006.

Wasserman, James, ed. *Aleister Crowley and the Practice of the Magical Diary.* Phoenix, Ariz.: New Falcon, 1993.

Watson, Mason W. "'Not Italian or German, but British in Character': J. F. C. Fuller and the Fascist Movement in Britain." Undergraduate honors thesis, College of William and Mary, 2012.

West, Denio C., and August Kling, eds. *The Libro de las Profecias of Christopher Columbus.* Gainesville: University Press of Florida, 1991.

Whitby, Christopher Lionel. "John Dee's Actions with Spirits: 22 December 1581 to 23 May 1583." Vol. 1. Ph.D. diss., University of Birmingham, 1981.

Wilber, Ken. *Sex, Ecology, Spirituality: The Spirit of Evolution.* Boulder, Colo.: Shambhala, 2001.

Williams, Gwyn A. *Madoc: The Making of a Myth.* London: Methuen Publishing, 1979.

Winship, Michael P. "Puritans, Politics, and Lunacy: The Copinger-Hacket Conspiracy as the Apotheosis of Elizabethan Presbyterianism." *The Sixteenth Century Journal* 38, no. 2 (2007): 345–69, doi:10.2307/20478364.

Woolley, Benjamin. *The Queen's Conjuror: The Life and Magic of John Dee.* New York: Flamingo, 2002.

Wright, Lawrence. *Going Clear: Scientology, Hollywood and the Prison of Belief.* New York: Vintage, 2013.

Yates, Francis. *Giordano Bruno and the Hermetic Tradition.* London: University of Chicago Press, 1964.

———. *The Occult Philosophy in the Elizabethan Age.* London: Routledge & Kegan Paul, 1979.

———. *The Rosicrucian Enlightenment.* Boulder, Colo.: Shambhala, 1978.

Yukteswar, Swami Sri. *The Holy Science.* Los Angeles: Self-Realization Fellowship, 1990.

Zantuan, Konstanty. "Olbracht Łaski in Elizabethan England: An Episode in the History of Culture." *The Polish Review* 13, no. 4 (1968): 3–22. www.jstor.org/stable/25776806 (accessed September 15, 2017).

Zubrin, Robert. "Dugin's Evil Theology." *National Review*, June 18, 2014. www.nationalreview.com/article/380614/dugins-evil-theology-robert-zubrin (accessed September 15, 2017).

Index

Page numbers in *italics* indicate illustrations.
Abbreviations: JD = John Dee, EK = Edward Kelly,
AC = Aleister Crowley, JP = Jack Parsons